DECEPTION

By the same authors

The Stone of Heaven
The Amber Room

Adrian Levy &
Catherine Scott-Clark

DECEPTION

PAKISTAN, THE UNITED STATES, AND THE SECRET TRADE IN NUCLEAR WEAPONS

Walker & Company
New York

Published by Walker Publishing Company, Inc., New York
Distributed to the trade by Holtzbrinck Publishers

All papers used by Walker & Company are natural, recyclable products made from wood
grown in well-managed forests. The manufacturing processes conform to the
environmental regulations of the country of origin.

LIBRARY OF CONGRESS CATALOGING-IN-PUBLICATION DATA HAS BEEN APPLIED FOR.

ISBN-10: 0-8027-1554-0
ISBN-13: 978-0-8027-1554-8

All maps copyright © 2007 by Jeff Edwards
Visit Walker & Company's Web site at www.walkerbooks.com

First U.S. edition 2007

1 3 5 7 9 10 8 6 4 2

Typeset by Westchester Book Group
Printed in the United States of America by Quebecor World Fairfield

For DEL
16 November 1940—31 December 2005

CONTENTS

CONTENTS

MAPS

ILLUSTRATIONS

Following page 234

Ronald Reagan with Zia ul-Haq
Ghulam Ishaq Khan with A. Q. Khan
Peter Griffin in front of A. Q. Khan's house
Anna Griffin with Henny Khan
Peter Griffin with Dr. Shafiq ur-Rehman
Peter Griffin with Qazi Rashid, Khalil Rashid and Hank Slebos
A. Q. Khan and family
Richard Barlow in Washington
B. S. A. Tahir in Paris
Agha Shahi
Mirza Aslam Beg with A. Q. Khan
A. Q. Khan with Nawaz Sharif
Benazir Bhutto with George H. W. Bush, Barbara Bush and Adif Zardari
Javid Nasir
Maulana Masood Azhar in Kashmir
A. Q. Khan at a press conference with Benazir Bhutto
Satellite image of A. Q. Khan's centrifuge plant
A. Q. Khan giving a lesson on bomb-making
A. Q. Khan in the test tunnels
Cross-section of a Pakistani uranium enrichment centrifuge
A. Q. Khan and colleagues at the Pakistan nuclear test site
The logo of the laboratories
A commercial uranium enrichment plant

A. Q. Khan sporting his medal
Pervez Musharraf with Mahmood Ahmed
George W. Bush inspecting a centrifuge component
Pervez Musharraf with George W. Bush
A neo-Taliban cadre in Miram Shah
Suleiman Abu Gheith
Abu Khabab al-Masri
Abu Musab al-Zarqawi
Abu Musab al-Suri
Al-Qaeda bomb-making manuals
Mohammed Aziz
A. Q. Khan supporters

ACKNOWLEDGMENTS

Deception was pieced together with the help of a trove of official documents—restricted government memorandums, embassy cables, company telexes and classified reports, written by ambassadors, cabinet members, policy makers and civil servants—many of them released under the US Freedom of Information Act (FOIA) thanks to the endeavors of the National Security Archive at George Washington University, Washington. Others were obtained from contacts in India, Pakistan, London, the US, Israel and elsewhere.

However, *Deception* is also a jigsaw of hundreds of interviews with contacts many of whom we first met when we were starting out as foreign correspondents for the *Sunday Times* in Asia more than a decade ago. They too were just starting to rise in their political or military careers, and a large number—still in service today with governments or armies—asked not to be named, fearing the repercussions, especially in Pakistan, where speaking out nowadays gets people ostracized and even killed. Many had in recent years helped us on projects for the *Guardian*, too.

Of those we can name, thanks to Chaudhary Nisar Ali Khan, parliamentary leader of the Pakistan Muslim League (Nawaz), and—in exile—to Benazir Bhutto, Nawaz Sharif and Shahbaz Sharif, who were extremely generous with their time and memories. We also are grateful to Wajid Shamsul Hasan for the laborious job of finding answers to our questions in London, and to Farhatullah Babar for the doing the same in Islamabad. Thanks to Pervez Hoodbhoy for relating his experiences with A. Q. Khan and placing a context on nuclear Pakistan, and to Samina Ahmed, project director for the ICG in Islamabad, for her work on madrasahs and the military. Thanks to Humayun Gauhar, the editor of Pakistan's *Blue Chip* magazine, for his insightful recollections of how

President Pervez Musharraf dealt with the Khan crisis, though of course we have different views on the nature of the real crisis. We are grateful too for the time Brigadier General Mohammed Youssaf spent relating his view on the Inter Services Intelligence agency and Afghanistan as well as to generals Hamid Gul, Mirza Aslam Beg, Asad Durrani, and Khalid Mahmud Arif (who will all vehemently disagree with our conclusions). Farukh Leghari was also patient, as was Qazi Hussain Ahmad. Thanks to V. K. Jaffri and to Iqbal Akhund. Agha Shahi, Pakistan's former foreign minister, with a lifetime of service under his belt, was endlessly energetic, with a sharp recollection for color and detail. He died on 6 September 2006. In particular we want to thank the Karachi-born researcher, fixer and capable journalist who has worked with us since 1996.

In India, too, there are scores of officials, analysts, strategists and politicians who asked not to be named. We thank them. Our appreciation in name goes to only a handful. Thanks to K. Subrahmanyam and Commodore Uday Bhaskar, to Navtej Sarna and Raminder Singh Jassel, as well as to Naresh Chandra, Girish Saxena, Brajesh Mishra and Jaswant Singh. Thanks also to Dilip Sinha and to Kuldip Nayar, as well as to Indra Kumar Gujral and B. Raman.

In the US we would also like to thank those now out of service who contributed considerable expertise and acted as sounding boards. They include Robert Gallucci, now the dean of the Edmund A. Walsh School of Foreign Service, Georgetown University, Washington, and Howard Schaffer, deputy director and director of studies at Georgetown's Institute for the Study of Diplomacy. Thanks too to Robert Einhorn, who provided insight into the North Korean nexus, China–US relations and the tracking of A. Q. Khan, famously beginning every session with the time in which he intended to leave it. Others in Washington who gave up time to place policy in context included Morton Ambramowitz, who took issue with our evaluation of the benefits of the Afghan war and how non-proliferation was offset against it, and Stephen P. Cohen at the Brookings Institution, whose memories of the Reagan administration were helpful, as were those of Dr. Geoff Kemp at the Nixon Center.

Husain Haqqani, now director of the Center for International Relations at Boston University, shared many recollections and insights on Pakistan in the 1980s and 1990s. Thanks also to Michael Krepon of the Stimpson Center, although we hold different views about A. Q. Khan and the Pakistan military.

ACKNOWLEDGMENTS

Thanks too to Leonard Spector, Paul Leventhal, David Albright, Corey Hinderstein, John Isaacs and Henry Sokolski. Dr. Len Weiss was energetic in his recollections of working with Senator John Glenn. We are grateful too to Peter Galbraith, Lee Hamilton, Stephen Solarz and Robert Hathaway. Thanks also go to Ray Close, Robert Baer, Mike Scheuer, Dan Coleman, Dick Kerr, George Shultz, James Lilley, and Robert Oakley. We are also grateful to Richard Barlow for trawling through his archive more times than anyone should be asked, as well as to Steve Coll for his groundbreaking work on the Afghan war and Pakistan; equally to Lawrence Wright for his introduction to the translated world of electronic jihad and to James Mann for his analysis of the Vulcans. Thanks to Dennis Kux for his exhaustive *The United States and Pakistan 1947–2000*, an invaluable reference tool. A special thanks to Mark Siegel for giving us his affable spin and a helping hand, to Moshe Ya'alon, and to Norman Wulf for taking considerable time to give us his invaluable overview of the State Department as well as recollections on North Korea.

Many still in government in the US helped us too, although they voiced considerable fears about talking openly about the closing episodes in *Deception*, claiming that a culture of fear had inculcated federal agencies and departments, where towing the line and political support for the White House were becoming prerequisites for career advancement. In the UK there are many former and serving civil servants who also asked not to be named, although none claimed to have been intimidated. Outside government we would especially like to thank Frank Barnaby and Garry Dillon. Thanks also to Peter and Anna Griffin in France.

We are lucky to be working again with our editor in the US, George Gibson, whose energy and attention to detail have helped us enormously. Thanks go to him and the Bloomsbury/Walker team in New York. In London, we are especially grateful, once again, to Toby Mundy, who has seen the book germinate from a paper-thin idea into a tome, and to all his team at Atlantic, especially Sarah Castleton.

Pakistan, India and neighboring countries

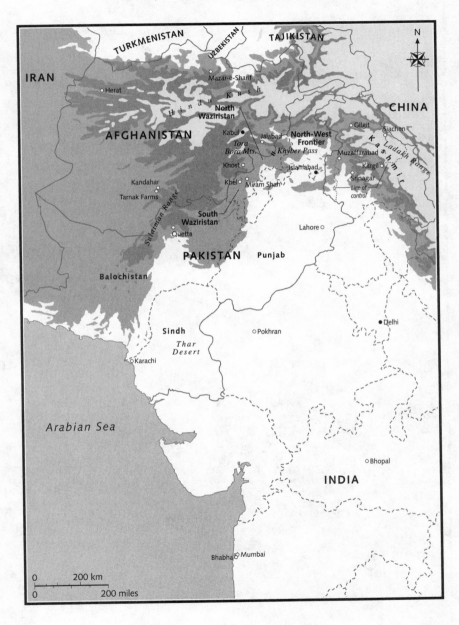

Africa and the Middle East

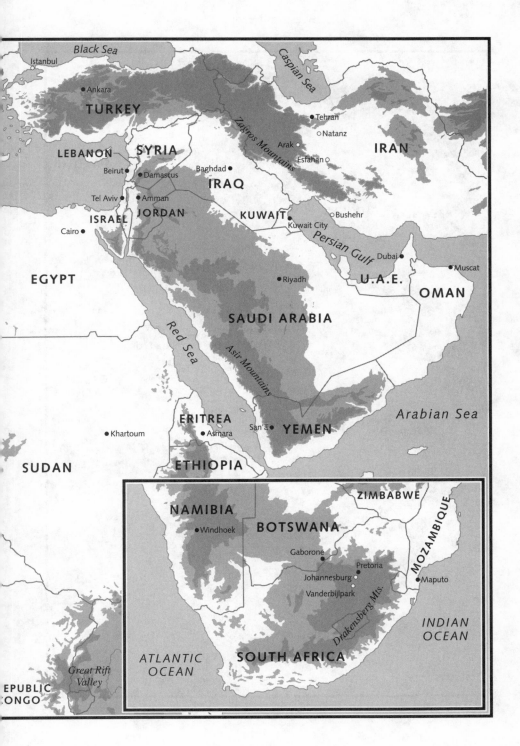

Western Europe

Pakistan and its nuclear facilities

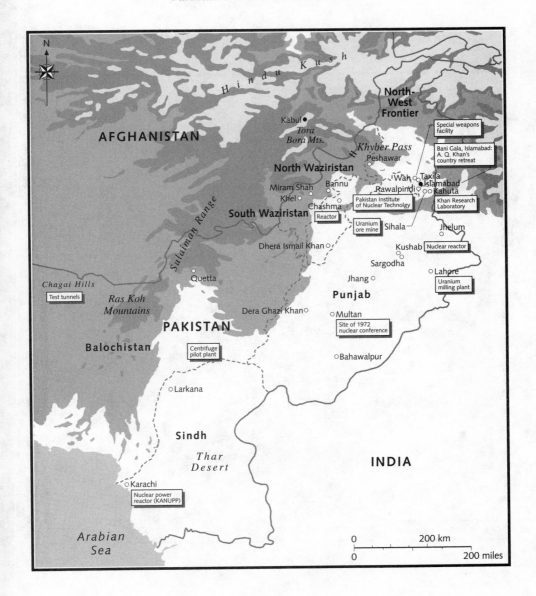

Iran and its nuclear facilities

Kalaye Electric; Atomic Energy Organization of Iran

Suspected nuclear research centre

Heavy water nuclear reactor

Enrichment facility

Uranium mine

Nuclear research facilities

Uranium milling plant

Light water nuclear reactor

INTRODUCTION: THE CORE

This is a story of how our elected representatives have conjured a grand deception, the terrible consequences of which may not become clear for decades to come. It is a chronicle of moral lapses, abysmal judgments, failures of oversight, careless and frequently lazy analyses of the changing world around us which have served to further destabilize it and to empower those bent on global jihad.

The deception was first glimpsed in 2004 when the government of Pakistan announced that its most revered scientist, Dr. Abdul Qadeer Khan, was to make a confession live on Pakistan TV. Dr. Khan, a figure normally cloaked in intrigue, having been associated with Pakistan's covert nuclear program for three decades, appeared on 4 February, speaking in English for the benefit of the wider world, rather than in Urdu for a home audience that would normally cling to his every word.

"My dear brothers and sisters," Khan began, before admitting to what he described as "unauthorized proliferation activities." Khan signed off: "May Allah keep Pakistan safe and secure. Long live Pakistan!" To ensure that what he had done was fully understood in the West, the Pakistan military conducted explanatory briefings in which Khan was said to have run, pretty much on his own, a black market in nuclear weapons technology for client states that President George W. Bush had identified as the "Axis of Evil"—Iran, Libya and North Korea.

The ramifications were appalling. There was heated conjecture around the world about why Khan, caricatured as the Typhoid Mary of nuclear proliferation, had done it—out of political and religious conviction, or for self-aggrandizement? Editorials speculated for whom Khan had done it—the rogue regimes themselves, jihadis in Afghanistan, Osama bin Laden, or perhaps terrorist cells hoping to let off a nuclear device in Europe or America.

President George W. Bush subscribed to the deceit, announcing several days later: "Khan has confessed his crimes and his top associates are out of business." Khan and a small band were guilty of shocking offenses, but there was no need to put them on trial. Bush explained: "President Musharraf has promised to share all the information he learns about the Khan network, and has assured us that his country will never again be a source of proliferation." Pakistan was so on top of the situation that there would be no need to extradite the scientists to the West.

In reality, Khan's confession was a ruse. It takes more than one person to make a mess of this proportion. Khan was the fall guy and his performance papered over the true nature of what many now believe was the nuclear crime of all our lifetimes and undoubtedly the source of our future wars. The nuclear bazaar Khan claimed to have orchestrated certainly existed, but where the public and private stories diverged was that the covert trade in doomsday technology was not the work of one man, but the foreign policy of a nation, plotted and supervised by Pakistan's ruling military clique, supposedly a key ally in America's war on terror. The true scandal was how the trade and the Pakistan military's role in it had been discovered by high-ranking US and European officials, many years before, but rather than interdict it they had worked hard to cover it up.

For three decades, consecutive US administrations, Republican and Democrat, as well as the governments in Britain and other European countries, had allowed Pakistan to acquire highly restricted nuclear technology. In a disastrous epoch, key state assets were then misdirected and countermanded in order to disguise how Pakistan had sold it on. Intelligence gathering in the US was blunted while federal agencies, including the Departments of State and Defense, were corralled into backing the White House agenda and forced to sidestep Congress and break federal laws. Officials who tried to stop the charade were rough-housed, smeared or purged, inflicting terrible damage on America and Europe's ability to see sharply. The US Congress played along too, by folding beneath White House pressure during a period in which political debate that dared level hard questions was portrayed as unpatriotic or even seditious.

The question all of this begged was why anyone would want to place the survival of a military regime in Pakistan above the long-term safety of the world.

Perhaps the only truthful statement on 4 February 2004 was one made inadvertently. Richard Boucher, the US State Department spokesman, characterized the Khan affair as having been a tough call for Pakistan's dictator-president, General Pervez Musharraf. Khan was a national hero and mention of his name in Pakistan was sufficient to make citizens bristle with pride. Having furnished a nation "incapable of manufacturing sharp sewing needles," as Khan liked to put it, with a cutting-edge production line for nuclear weapons able to strike almost every city in India, Pakistan's habitual enemy, Khan had become popularly known as the "Father of the Bomb."

Few people in Pakistan knew that he had become involved in the covert program by accident. While working as a technical translator in Holland in 1972, Khan had read highly classified blueprints for a radical new technique being trialled by a consortium of British, Dutch and German scientists, a breakthrough that would enable them to create fissile material by spinning a derivative of uranium at extraordinary speeds in a centrifuge that resembled a large, upturned cigar case. A savvy Khan had immediately appreciated that the true value of this secret technology lay in a paradox. While the process was classified and revolutionary, its components were commonplace and could be imported by Islamabad "under the wire," with little chance of anyone tipping off the International Atomic Energy Agency (IAEA), the global nuclear police, based in Vienna, Austria.

In 1975 Khan returned to Islamabad with three suitcases crammed full of stolen information. The following year, Pakistan's agents began shopping in Europe and North America for the equipment the country needed, a process coordinated by Khan, who oozed charm and eased their path, having cemented friendships with leading European theoretical nuclear physicists, industrialists, engineers and metallurgists—who also happened to be familiar with clandestine bomb programs run by Western governments.

Intelligence analysts in the US and UK spotted this activity from the start. In their first reports Khan was characterized as a state employee working on a civilian project run by Pakistan's then prime minister, Zulfikar Ali Bhutto. When Bhutto was overthrown in a coup in 1977, the CIA warned that Khan and the nuclear project would become a military prerogative under the authority of Pakistan's new dictator, General Zia ul-Haq. Khan's agents, on purchasing missions around the world, came under the orders of Pakistan's generals and its intelligence establishment, the Inter Services Intelligence agency (ISI).

However, too much knowledge about the Pakistan bomb program rapidly became a bad thing. In 1979, President Jimmy Carter, who had come to power in 1977 pledging to reduce the number of nuclear weapons on the planet, was lobbied by Zbigniew Brzezinski, his national security adviser, to change tack. The Soviets were interfering in Pakistan's neighbor Afghanistan and it looked as if they might reach into Iran too, where the shah, a prime US ally, had recently fallen. Pakistan was a necessary buffer against Communism, Carter was advised, and needed to be wooed. In return for resisting Soviet advances, Washington was willing to turn a blind eye to General Zia's nuclear aspirations.

As the Soviet presence in Afghanistan blossomed into a full-scale invasion, with the Red Army occupying Kabul on Christmas Eve 1980, Carter was replaced by Ronald Reagan, who buried non-proliferation completely, dismantling the US Arms Control and Disarmament Agency, created by John F. Kennedy, and hijacking other independent channels along which intelligence (especially on nuclear trafficking) flowed. The National Security Council and the office of the national security adviser were both downgraded, while the CIA, under director William Casey, became pre-eminent, using intelligence as a political tool to support the Reaganite agenda, rather than to inform it.

Reagan and Casey believed that Afghanistan was a scenario where the US might just win a war without fighting, fuelling instead an arm's-length insurgency, fought by the Pakistan-backed mujahideen, to bog down the Red Army, just as the Soviets had connived to bloody US troops in Vietnam a decade before. US officials converged on Islamabad carrying cash and the message that America would ignore Pakistan's growing nuclear program. However, in the US, Reagan deceitfully insisted that non-proliferation remained a primary policy.

As Pakistan's bomb program burgeoned, it became increasingly difficult to keep a lid on it. What started as pragmatism (a go-getting kind of deal-making, steeped in the optimism Reagan brought to a depressed post-Carter Washington) rapidly bloomed into a complex conspiracy, with State Department officials actively obstructing other arms of government which could not help but fall over intelligence about Pakistan's nuclear trade. Evidence was destroyed, criminal files were diverted, Congress was repeatedly lied to, and in several cases, in 1986 and 1987, presidential appointees even tipped off the Pakistan government so as to prevent its agents from getting caught in US Customs Service stings that aimed to catch them buying nuclear components in America.

If those involved had been outed they would have faced enormous consequences, like the officials felled by the Iran–Contra affair which blew open at the same time, claiming national security adviser Admiral John Poindexter and the National Security Council's Colonel Oliver North after it was revealed that they had been involved in a black operation in which Congress was lied to and federal laws evaded in order to sell arms to Iran and free US hostages. But the Pakistan cover-up was maintained. The deception continued.

The obfuscation concealed from the world Pakistan's cold-testing of a nuclear bomb in 1983 and the devastating intelligence that Pakistan had hot-tested as well, in 1984, with the help of China. The Pakistan–China nuclear relationship was also buried by Reagan's officials, including Beijing's gift to Islamabad of bomb blueprints, radioactive isotopes and technical assistance without bounds. In return, US companies won deals worth hundreds of millions of dollars from Chinese nuclear power contractors.

Reagan's presidency came to an end in 1989, with Pakistan in possession of a deployable and tested nuclear device, much of the program even funded using US aid, hundreds of millions of dollars of which had been diverted by the Pakistan military. The Islamic Republic had a nuclear bomb that could be mated to a missile or dropped from American-supplied F-16 fighter jets, also given by Reagan in the mid-1980s, and its nuclear weapons program had become a shop window for the world's most unstable powers.

At first, the George H. W. Bush administration continued the deception. Pentagon officials became Pakistan's guardians, rewriting intelligence estimates to downgrade the Islamic Republic's nuclear capabilities even while Islamabad and New Delhi were within a hair's breadth of a nuclear showdown. However, when the war in Afghanistan ended, Bush cut Pakistan adrift, terminating aid in 1990, marking the last significant contact between the US and a nuclear-ready Pakistan until cruise missiles slammed into Osama bin Laden's training camps in Afghanistan in 1998. No one was looking at the Islamic Republic, even as intelligence began backing up in Europe, India and Israel to show that its military nuclear network had reacted to the aid cut-off by escalating the black-market deals in nuclear technology, eyeing markets hostile to the West.

By the time President Bill Clinton took office in 1993, and throughout his two terms, an ever more detailed picture was pieced together of Pakistan's dangerous liaisons: Iran in 1987, Iraq in 1990, North Korea in 1993, and by 1997 Libya, too. And in 1998 the septic nuclear crisis in South Asia burst open, with India and Pakistan both testing their nuclear bombs and facing each other down in a knife-edge—and now fissile—confrontation.

The following year, Pakistan once again succumbed to a military coup as General Pervez Musharraf took control. By then, A. Q. Khan was firmly fixed in the collective imagination of his country as the reason for their nuclear prowess, his likeness cut out of cardboard and molded from papier-mâché strapped to telegraph poles and mounted on roofs throughout Pakistan. In a country where there were few role models who strode the international stage (apart from cricketers), Khan was, as a friend observed, "one of the few extremely valuable Pakistanis." Period.

Things would get worse. By the time George W. Bush secured the presidency in 2001, a mountain of incredibly precise intelligence portrayed Pakistan as the epicenter of global instability: a host and patron for Islamist terrorism, ruled by a military clique that was raising capital and political influence by selling weapons of mass destruction (WMD).

Something had to be done and initially it looked as if President Bush might be the man to take the initiative. Shortly before 11 September 2001, CIA director George Tenet gathered a small team of senior officials, with secretary of state Colin Powell, his deputy Richard Armitage, deputy national security adviser Stephen Hadley, deputy CIA director John McLaughlin and Robert Joseph, non-proliferation director at the National Security Council, for a crisis summit.

Even the hawks appeared ready for a change of policy on Pakistan. During Paul Wolfowitz's nomination hearing as deputy secretary of defense, in February 2001, he reflected on the way in which the George H. W. Bush administration had dealt with Pakistan, at a time when he had served in the Pentagon. Wolfowitz conceded: "People thought we could somehow construct a policy on a house of cards. That the Congress wouldn't know what the Pakistanis were doing. I've always thought that policies based on withholding information from Congress are going to fail in the long run. And that there was a clear legal obligation to keep Congress informed."

However, in the days and months that followed September 11, Wolfowitz and others set about building a new house of cards. Pakistan's President Musharraf pledged to round up al-Qaeda and to assist in mopping up the Taliban, giving up their leaders and busting their sanctuaries in the inhospitable border region with Afghanistan. Musharraf became integral to American plans, lending the Pentagon airspace, passing intelligence and mounting operations in regions where no Western soldier could ever hope to go. The Bush administration weighed his value as a potential ally against the harm Pakistan's nuclear program could do, just as Carter and Reagan had done before. Despite overwhelming evidence of a building nuclear crisis, in which a state leaking nuclear technology was also concealing terrorists who were seeking it, the White House decided to do nothing.

More critically, a new narrative was emerging in Washington about WMD, steered by neoconservatives including Wolfowitz, Dick Cheney and Donald Rumsfeld. Since 1998 they had highlighted Iraq, Iran and North Korea as the countries that the US should gun for. Now they lobbied Bush to accede to the first of these, prioritizing "unfinished business" in Iraq. The first Gulf War had failed to follow through and eliminate Saddam Hussein, a leader they portrayed as a rogue proliferator, a state sponsor of terror and, even more bizarrely, as the secular patron of the pious al-Qaeda. For the neoconservatives, Iraq was the next logical step in the war on terror. Pakistan could not be allowed to eclipse this script.

American troops mustered in the Gulf. Colin Powell raised a vial of white powder before the United Nations Security Council, warning of the dangers of overlooking WMD that were concealed in Iraq, while the US sat on intelligence that characterized Pakistan as the most dangerous proliferator. A kind of institutional blindness came upon the White House which prevented anything other than the neoconservative agenda being seen clearly. By 1 May 2003 it was "mission accomplished" in Iraq, and investigators from the newly formed Iraq Survey Group, led by David Kay, set off looking for WMD there. However, the intelligence amassing at the IAEA showed that Pakistan was still the source of it all, as the US had known all along. The IAEA protested, as did Israel, frightened by the prospect of an Islamic bomb up for sale. But Bush continued to stand beside Musharraf, describing him as a good friend, pushing through a $3 billion military and economic assistance package, while the White House began refashioning the Pakistan military's proliferation into an act by a small group of renegade scientists.

In October 2003, Richard Armitage flew to Islamabad to meet Musharraf. The White House agenda was to keep the general onside. A drama was conceived that drew from Musharraf a promise to shut down Pakistan's nuclear black market in return for winning US support for his unelected regime. It was agreed that A. Q. Khan would be arrested, along with a dozen of his fellow scientists, but Pakistan would keep hold of them, allowing the West to pose limitless questions via ISI interrogators but leaving the country's military elite in the clear.

In January 2004, David Kay resigned, telling Congress that there had been no WMD stockpiled in Iraq, and one week later A. Q. Khan was paraded on Pakistan TV. The Islamic Republic was not a proliferator. The coalition in the war on terror was intact and Bush's neoconservative team moved on to the next item on the agenda: war against another nuclear rebel, Iran. However, South Asian experts warned the White House that Pakistan remained the major problem and that something had to be done. Teresita Schaffer, a former US assistant secretary of state for South Asia, the pre-eminent expert on the region, warned: "Without a sustained US effort, we are likely to face a much darker future. The troubles that afflict today's Pakistan are likely to intensify. The government is likely to continue its contradictory policies towards Islamic militancy and the army will strengthen its links with the extremists and the militant movement. The risk of nuclear leakage could recur."

The Bush administration still did nothing, however much Schaffer was proved right. As White House calls for regime change in Iran rose to a clamor in 2006, Pakistan's President Musharraf turned off the intelligence tap, shutting down all investigations into Khan. Then Musharraf's contribution to the war on terror began to fall apart at the seams. Militants arrested in the post-9/11 heat were released and allowed to re-form their jihadi groups under new names. A neo-Taliban flourished in Pakistan's tribal border areas, from where they struck fatally at Afghan, British and American forces. Most worrying, al-Qaeda began merging with Pakistan's home-grown terrorists, spawning new camps, new graduates and new missions abroad. By 2007, Pakistan's nuclear sales network was flourishing again. The Islamic Republic had learned to manufacture the restricted components and materials, electronic equipment and super-strong metals needed for a ready-made nuclear weapons facility which they were selling to anyone who could come up with the cash. Pakistan's arsenal, developed at Washington's grace and favor, was sliding out of control as terrorists gained new footholds in Islamabad.

How long would it be before the rising tide of extremism in Pakistan and the fast-flowing current of illegal nuclear exports would find common cause and realize an apocalyptic intent? Islamabad harbored a regime that had no hard and fast rules, no unambiguous goals or laws, and no line that could not be bent or reshaped. There were plenty of ideologues and Islamic strategists with Armageddon on their minds, like Suleiman Abu Gheith, a spokesman for Osama bin Laden, who declared on a website affiliated to al-Qaeda: "We have the right to kill four million Americans—two million of them children. And to exile twice as many and wound and cripple hundreds of thousands."

Today, as the world battles to deal with a new generation of global terrorism, the quagmire in Iraq, a showdown with Iran and a stand-off with North Korea, *Deception* reveals how all of these nuclear-tinged crises emanated from the mismanagement of one wellspring: Pakistan.

But at a time when action is called for, the world is impotent. The gravest consequence of the Pakistan deception was that in the name of political pragmatism the whole architecture of non-proliferation, the robust scaffolding that was erected in the 1950s by President Dwight D. Eisenhower to prevent nuclear secrets from getting into the wrong hands, has been brought crashing down.

And it all began with an ambitious young man who could not get a job.

1

THE ANGRY YOUNG MAN

The letter came from a private address: 71 Amstelle Street, Zwanenburg, a not-so-smart suburb of Amsterdam, blighted by the constant drone of aircraft hovering over the nearby Schiphol airport. By the time it arrived at the prime minister's secretariat in Pakistan, in July 1974, it had, according to the cabinet minister who saw it first, been creased and burnished by scores of inquisitive fingertips, having been forwarded via the Islamic Republic's embassy in Brussels, vetted by spies from the ISI and scrutinized by the prime minister's security staff.[1]

Initially, aides thought twice about showing it to Pakistan's prime minister, Zulfikar Ali Bhutto. The correspondent, Abdul Qadeer Khan, began by ranting about his failure to secure a job in Pakistan, a familiar refrain from those who were wealthy enough to study abroad and found nothing to do on their return. However, on closer reading this letter had a promising ring to it. Khan claimed to be a physicist who was working for a European nuclear consortium. He had managed to get close to highly classified blueprints concerning a revolutionary new process. It provided a key to unpicking a conundrum upon which Pakistan had foundered for many years: how to build a nuclear bomb.

The letter could not have arrived at a more urgent time. Two months earlier, on 18 May 1974, India had conducted an unauthorized nuclear test deep below the western deserts of Rajasthan.[2] It had done so by betraying the trust of its sponsors in the West and the East. New Delhi had secretly designed and armed its bomb using technologies sold it by the world's established nuclear powers (the United States, United Kingdom, France, China and the Soviet Union) on condition that this knowledge was shared only to meet India's energy needs.

Pakistan felt as if it been duped, as well as eclipsed, outwitted and shamed, by an action that seemed to prime minister Bhutto to confirm India's claim to regional supremacy. Islamabad had to reply. But the science was far beyond Pakistan's capabilities and the trade in the components required to put a nuclear program together would now be policed with extra vigilance by the four nuclear states that were signatories to the 1968 Nuclear Non-Proliferation Treaty (the US, UK, France and the USSR), which forbade the sale of nuclear weapons technology. Anticipating a nuclear arms race in South Asia, the United Nations' nuclear watchdog, the International Atomic Energy Agency (IAEA), based in Vienna, would redouble its efforts, making Pakistan's task that much harder.

Having second thoughts, Bhutto sought a diplomatic solution, sending Sahabzada Yaqub Khan, Pakistan's ambassador in Washington, to lobby for a nuclear umbrella—reassurances from the US that it would act as Pakistan's security guarantor against attack.[3] But Bhutto did not hold out much hope. In the 1960s Pakistan had regarded itself as Washington's "most allied ally" as a result of a trick of geography.[4] It had forged numerous military pacts with a US that feared Soviet expansion in the Middle East and Asia. Those deals had enabled the Islamic Republic to develop its armed forces and maintain its ongoing conflict with India. However, in recent years the US–Pakistan relationship had become strained. Washington had grown to doubt Islamabad's sincerity. A classified memo written for the director of the CIA had catalogued a list of complaints. "Over the past several years the government of Pakistan has taken a long series of actions that have been counter to US interest," it bemoaned.[5] Islamabad had failed to honor America's request to send troops into Laos in 1962 and also had declined to "give good publicity to US military exercises" in 1963. The US also suspected Pakistan of making "secret understandings" with the Chinese premier, Chou En-lai, in 1963 and 1964.[6]

As predicted, secretary of state Henry Kissinger was cold to Bhutto's request. Kissinger argued that if the US gathered up Pakistan in its nuclear folds, it would have had to do the same for other countries in the region, some of whom were far less desirable allies, such as North Korea. Kissinger told Yaqub Khan that India's bomb test was "a fait accompli and that Pakistan would have to learn to live with it." Yaqub Khan came away empty-handed. Bhutto was embittered.

*

It had been only three years before that Pakistan had lost a disastrous war with India, the latest episode in a long-running and bloody feud between the two countries which had begun in 1947 when the Indian subcontinent was partitioned after almost a century of British colonial rule. One country sliced in two: the divvying up of everything from its territory and citizens to its armed forces and munitions supplies. Almost as soon as it came into being as a fully fledged country, Pakistan felt that it was the loser in the deal.

At partition, millions of Muslims had fled their ancestral homes in the central plains and former princely Muslim states of India as stories spread of a nation being formed that would welcome only Hindus. Families were torn apart, villages destroyed and hundreds of thousands were massacred as Hindu turned against Muslim and vice versa, former neighbors and friends killing and mutilating one another, sending hundreds of trains speeding east and west carrying a tide of people to an uncertain future in a new Islamic Republic which was to be formed of two halves: West Pakistan, the land mass west of India that is the Pakistan of today, and East Pakistan, the region east of India that is now Bangladesh. Within a year, Pakistan had lost its founding father, Muhammad Ali Jinnah, to lung cancer, and the country was thrown into political chaos as incompetent and corrupt politicians bent on retribution against India took hold. In its hurry to leave the subcontinent, Britain had left such messy and indeterminate border lines that the two new countries had begun to fight over territory even before the last colonial lieutenant had pulled out. Most contested were East Pakistan (where a sizable proportion wanted independence) and the Himalayan state of Jammu and Kashmir, whose Hindu ruler sided with India against the wishes of his Muslim subjects. India and Pakistan would fight many times over these disputed territories, the most serious conflagration being the war of December 1971, when Indian prime minister Indira Gandhi ordered an assault on East Pakistan which ended after barely two weeks with the Pakistan army forced to offer a humiliating surrender at Dacca racecourse.[7]

Pakistan was not even a quarter of a century old and it had already been wrenched in two. With India's support East Pakistan became Bangladesh, and the Islamic Republic reached its nadir, something that it partly blamed on the US, which had refused to come to its assistance despite urgent requests. The US had imposed sanctions on Pakistan in 1965 after it had used American-supplied weapons against India in a war over the disputed territory of Kashmir.[8] The Islamic Republic would have to rely on its own ingenuity to maintain a credible defense, concluded Bhutto, who had come to power in January 1972 as a result of the East Pakistan debacle. When the US rejected Pakistan for a second time, refusing to take on India over its nuclear test of 1974, Bhutto determined to seek out new strategic relationships beyond the US and to develop Pakistan's own nuclear weapon in order to "save the nation."[9]

Time and time again, Islamabad would wield Kissinger's rejection as a justification for pressing ahead with its nuclear program. Agha Shahi, who in 1974 was Bhutto's foreign secretary, recalled: "If negotiations had gone better and the US had come to Pakistan's aid, you would never have heard of A. Q. Khan." In the gloom of his careworn, modernist villa in Islamabad, in April 2006 the veteran diplomat, who had been involved in Pakistan's secret nuclear weapons program from its inception, felt the need to "give an invaluable lesson." It would be Shahi's last tutorial, for the eighty-six-year-old died that August. He said: "Instead of aiding Pakistan, no sanctions were imposed on India or the countries that had sold the technology to build the bomb: the US, Canada and France."[10] They continued to help New Delhi with its supposedly peaceful nuclear plans: Canada and France supplying power reactors and reprocessing facilities, while the US continued to sell fuel for India's power plants. Shahi said: "I suggested that Pakistan should exploit this logic and strive for a bomb with the reasonable expectation of having no sanctions imposed either." In private, Kissinger was aware of how hollow the US position had been, telling an aide: "It is a little rough on the Pakistanis to require them to do what the Indians don't have to do."[11]

Shahi recalled how Bhutto struck back: "After the Indian tests he called in the scientists and asked for their honest opinions. Could they build a bomb? 'Yes,' they said. 'We are trying to develop the thing, the bomb.' However, it was taking an age and costing a fortune."

German physicist Otto Hahn had discovered in 1938 that by splitting atoms of plutonium or uranium in a chain reaction, known as fission, a vast amount of energy could be released in a very short space of time. If harnessed to a weapon, that energy could be used to produce a nuclear explosion so much more powerful than the largest conventional explosives that a single device could knock out an entire city. Fearing that Germany or Japan might do just this, during the Second World War America had made a massive effort to get there first, in a program led by Robert Oppenheimer at the secret Los Alamos laboratory in New Mexico. Oppenheimer's clandestine Manhattan Project succeeded on 16 July 1945 when the US test-fired the world's first nuclear device in the New Mexico desert. Less than three weeks later, America dropped two nuclear weapons on Hiroshima and Nagasaki, killing 250,000 people. The bombings signalled the end of the war but started an arms race which was quickly joined by the Soviet Union (which tested its first device in September 1949), the UK (October 1952), France (October 1960) and China (October 1964).[12] Others pursued nuclear weapons programs too, but failed to declare them, including Israel, South Africa, Argentina and Brazil. After India joined the nuclear club in 1974, Pakistan set out to get hold of enough fissionable material to support a self-sustaining chain reaction, something known as critical mass.

However, the Islamic Republic's nuclear program was ramshackle. The country had a nuclear reactor, known as the Karachi Nuclear Power Plant (KANUPP), supplied by Canada in a deal negotiated in 1965 by Bhutto when he was foreign minister.[13] KANUPP had fired up on 1 August 1971 and was an ideal facility to exploit for a weapons program. It produced in its used, or irradiated, fuel rods large quantities of plutonium-239, the material that Hahn had used in his early experiments and that the US had used to fuel the Fat Man bomb it dropped on Nagasaki. However, in order to use this plutonium in a bomb Pakistan needed a reprocessing plant to extract it from the rods, something that only a declared nuclear power could supply. So far, only France had offered to do so, for $300 million. The cost was prohibitive and complaints from the other nuclear powers had caused the deal to stall. Then the fortuitous letter arrived from an irate young Pakistani scientist who was confident he could win access to a completely different route, using uranium enriched by a groundbreaking new centrifugal process being pioneered in Europe.

Pakistan's information minister, Kauser Niazi, was with Bhutto when he read the letter and said the contents "electrified the thinking of the Prime Minister."[14] Foreign secretary Agha Shahi, who was also called in to see it, remembered: "Bhutto said to me, 'There's a man called Abdul Qadeer Khan who claims that centrifuges are being used in Europe to produce fissile material.' I told him that all I knew about centrifuges was what I had heard from a stockbroker who I'd sat next to at a dinner party several years earlier in New York. He told me that Americans used them to separate cream in a dairy. I was skeptical but advised Bhutto, 'Give [A. Q. Khan] a chance.' We had nothing to lose."

Information minister Niazi recalled that Khan was keen to offer his services as he had been rejected by other sections of the Pakistani establishment. Khan had written that "a man of his special talents was being ignored." Having been awarded a doctorate in metallurgy (then a rare qualification for a student from Pakistan), he had applied for a job at the People's Steel Mill in Karachi, the first such plant in the country, only to be ignored. Niazi wrote: "This patriot Pakistani also informed [Bhutto] that apart from writing innumerable research papers, he had written an internationally known book. In spite of all of this, the incompetent officials of the People's Steel Mill were unable to make use of his services."

Niazi took charge of Khan's case. "We immediately put the secret services on the job." The ISI reported back.[15] Whether he had got there by determination or chance, Khan had won unique access to information on enriched uranium, the fissile material that the US had used in the Little Boy bomb dropped on Hiroshima in 1945. Khan was worth a punt, the ISI said. They should take a long, hard look at him.

Khan's proposal revolved around the heaviest element on earth, almost twice as heavy as lead. Uranium had been discovered in 1789 by German chemist H. M. Klaproth and was an alternative fissile material to plutonium.[16] "Uranium is more difficult but safe. Very few countries have this technology," Khan had written to Bhutto.[17] Because it was so heavy and dense, only a small amount—about the size of a bag of sugar—was needed to fuel a nuclear bomb. The problem was that although uranium was widely available, mined in Australia, Canada, Niger, Russia, South Africa and the US, in its natural state its potency was so low that it was virtually useless. To convert it into fissile material involved a complicated and experimental process. Raw uranium ore had to be crushed, mixed with water and put through a chemical process to purify it into uranium oxide, a substance better known as yellowcake because of its distinct, vivid hue and claggy texture. But for every 1,000 atoms of yellowcake, only seven would be uranium-235, the fissionable isotope needed to arm an atomic bomb, the remaining 993 being uranium-238, a heavier and superfluous element. For weapons use, the concentration of uranium-235 had to be enhanced from 0.07 percent to in excess of 93 percent, in a complex and inordinately expensive process called enrichment, which most countries were still struggling to master.

Khan told Bhutto that in the early 1950s the British, German and Dutch governments had come together to establish the URENCO consortium, which had opened three test laboratories to develop a method of enriching uranium that was cheap and simple enough to warrant a commercial plant. This would enable Europe's nuclear power industry to become independent of the US, which was one of the few countries to have mastered enrichment, giving it a monopoly over supplies. Scientists at three URENCO labs—Capenhurst in Cheshire, Almelo in eastern Holland and Gronau in West Germany—were experimenting with something called vertical separation, using centrifugal force to split apart the atoms of uranium-235 from uranium-238. To do this they had constructed large centrifuge machines, six-foot-tall aluminum tubes resembling giant upturned cigar cases. Into them was injected a gas refined from yellowcake called uranium hexafluoride (UF_6), which was then spun by rotors fast enough to separate its isotopes. The heavier uranium-238 was thrown outwards and slid down the sides of the centrifuge's drum to the waste pipe below, while the lighter and fissionable uranium-235 concentrated at the central axis to be sucked out through an exit pipe. The machines had to spin at an incredible 70,000 rpm and, as the scientists learned to their cost, a single fingerprint on any of the components could introduce an imperfection that would throw the entire process out of kilter, shattering the centrifuge and everything around it.[18]

Khan's linguistic ability—he spoke English, Dutch and German—as well as his technical background—his degree and doctorate in metallurgy—had led to him being employed as a technical translator for the multinational URENCO consortium, a job that had brought him into close proximity to research for the Dutch prototype, known as the CNOR.[19] Bhutto wrote in the margin of Khan's letter: "He seems to be talking sense."[20] The prime minister's mood lifted. He now toyed with the idea of transforming the Pakistani correspondent from Holland into a super-spy.

Zulfikar Ali Bhutto, the British-educated son of a key aide to Muhammad Ali Jinnah, had harbored a conviction that Pakistan had to go nuclear since October 1958. That year Bhutto had become minister for fuel, electricity and natural resources, and was surprised to learn that Pakistan, just over a decade old, already had a civil nuclear program.[21] It had come into being in 1956 as a result of a US-sponsored program, Atoms for Peace, in which countries that already had the bomb agreed to contribute some of their nuclear knowledge to the developing world. It was the brainchild of US president Dwight D. Eisenhower, whose intent was to head off an arms race by offering nuclear energy in exchange for a commitment not to pursue the bomb.[22]

Pakistan's nuclear project consisted of the grand-sounding Pakistan Atomic Energy Commission (PAEC) and was run by Dr. Nazir Ahmed, a scientist who had previously worked in the country's cotton industry. However, it took Bhutto some time to locate Ahmed, whose operation was in reality nothing more than a small office on the top floor of the main post office in downtown Karachi. By 1958, the only thing PAEC had achieved was to open a high-energy physics lab at Karachi's West Wharf, where ten scientists conducted random experiments the purpose and results of which remained obscure. It was "no more than a signboard on an office. It was only a name," Bhutto moaned.[23]

He began transforming PAEC, "with granite determination," sending hundreds of Pakistani scientists to the US for training under an Atoms for Peace exchange.[24] He also brought into the program Dr. Ishrat Usmani, an atomic physicist who, together with Bhutto, set out to buy all that America had to offer, using US aid money to fund the purchases—a plan that would be mirrored many times over in the years to come.

By 1961, PAEC had a nuclear research center, in Lahore. Two years later it assembled a 5 MW research reactor at Nilore, near Islamabad. After India and Pakistan went to war over Kashmir in 1965, Bhutto had railed: "If India builds the bomb, we will eat grass or leaves, even go hungry, but we will get one of our own. We have no alternative ... atom bomb for atom bomb." Four years later he predicted the conflagration to come: "All wars of our age have become total wars ... it would be dangerous to plan for less and our plans should, therefore, include the nuclear deterrent."[25]

On 20 January 1972, several weeks after Pakistan's humiliating defeat at the hands of the Indian army in Dacca, Bhutto called together his most eminent scientists. They convened in Multan, a city of shrines and saints in the southern Punjab, and sat shaded from the winter sun by a *shamiana*, a multicolored canvas awning, in the gardens of the home of Nawab Sadiq Hussain Qureshi, a wealthy landowner close to Bhutto.[26] Agha Shahi, who was then Pakistan's ambassador to China, recalled: "The meeting was shrouded in secrecy. Of course it was. Which country ever carried out a nuclear weapons program publicly?

And yet in the future we would be accused of sneaking around by countries that had done just the same a few decades earlier."

One of those invited to attend was Samar Mubarakmand, a junior scientist who would go on to play a crucial role in Pakistan's nuclear test twenty-six years later. He remembered being held rapt by the prime minister, who vowed to restore Pakistan's pride.[27] Bhutto told them that fate had placed him in a position where he could make decisions that would lead the country into the nuclear arms race. "Can you give it to me?" he asked, referring to the bomb. Mubarakmand recalled the shocked silence: "We were absolutely dumbfounded." According to most estimates Pakistan was at least twenty years behind India, and Dr. Ishrat Usmani, the PAEC chairman, remembered inserting a note of caution: "Pakistan just didn't have the infrastructure for that kind of program. I'm not talking about the ability to get 10 kg of plutonium. I'm talking about the real infrastructure. Pakistan totally lacked a metallurgy industry. But if you're playing political poker and have no cards, you have to go on betting."[28]

Bhutto scowled, Mubarakmand recalled. He looked to the junior scientists before him for a more positive response. Among them was Munir Ahmed Khan. He had spent five months training at a US lab and had just returned home after several years working for the IAEA in Vienna.[29] Munir Khan would soon replace Usmani at the helm of PAEC, bringing a unique perspective from within the global policing regime for Pakistan to exploit. An arch-bureaucrat, Munir Khan's technical expertise was, however, questionable.

Bhutto repeated his question: "Can you give it to me?" Some of the younger scientists jumped to their feet, tired of the ponderousness of their older colleagues. "Yes, it would be possible," one of them, Sultan Bashiruddin Mahmood, shouted. He would go on to dedicate his career to working on Pakistan's nuclear weapons program with a zealotry that would eventually bring him close to Osama bin Laden and into collision with the US.[30] Bhutto fired back: "But how long will it take to build a bomb?" When Bashiruddin mumbled, "Maybe five years," Bhutto thrust three fingers into the air. "Three years," he said. "I want it in three."

Others tried to introduce a note of caution. "It isn't like making firecrackers, you know," one scientist piped up. "We don't know how long it will take. It's all nonsense. It cannot be done that way." But the younger and more idealistic in the gathering joined in a chorus of "Anybody can make a bomb." One of those leading the clamor for a nuclear device was Sulfikar Ahmed Butt, who within a few years would become procurement manager in Europe for the as yet unknown A. Q. Khan.[31] Butt shouted out: "It can be done in three years."

Bhutto smiled. "Well, much as I admire your enthusiasm, this is a very serious political decision, which Pakistan must make, and perhaps all Third World countries must make one day, because it is coming. So can you do it?" Everybody present agreed to agree that Pakistan could do it, given sufficient resources and facilities. Mubarakmand remembered: "At that conference we really swore to make nuclear weapons. We knew it would be a great odyssey as at the time of partition from India there were hardly any scientists or engineers in our country ... At that time we lived under embargoes. No one would give us literature, hardware, components, technology. For everything we had to struggle. We had to work under adverse circumstances and we took it up as a challenge. We thought, 'OK, you cannot do it for us, we shall show you how to do it.' "

Bhutto brought the meeting to a close. Just hours later, he left on a whirlwind tour of Islamic countries that Pakistan intended to ally itself with, including Iran, Saudi Arabia and Libya.[32] Bhutto was keen to create some distance from the "super-power *shikaris*" (big-game hunters), as he described Pakistan's backers in the West.[33] On tour, with his hat out for cash, he landed in Tripoli where he met Colonel Muammar Gaddafi. What struck Bhutto, after all the cold political maneuvering of the Americans, was the spontaneity of the greeting from the Libyan leader, who planted a kiss on both his cheeks as they stood on the tarmac. Gaddafi promised to give Bhutto whatever he needed to develop the bomb, before Pakistan's prime minister carried on to tour the Middle East, where yet more sponsors were procured. At the end of the trip he called on Chairman Mao in Beijing, whom he had been wooing since the early 1960s. The friendships forged on this tour would be critical in rewriting Pakistan's strategic partnerships, and from these alliances would emerge sponsors in the nuclear weapons field and also, in time, a ready market.[34]

However, more than two years on, nothing had been achieved on the nuclear front. A team at PAEC had pursued the plutonium route and got nowhere with it, and was still arguing with the international community over terms for the purchase of a French reprocessing plant.[35]

*

In August 1974, Bhutto sent for Abdul Qadeer Khan.[36] The message was delivered personally to 71 Amstelle Street, Zwanenburg, by Mr. J. G. Kharas, Pakistan's ambassador to Holland. And while Khan made plans, the ISI dug into his background.[37]

Khan had been in Europe for thirteen years and apparently missed Pakistan desperately. He was an inveterate letter writer, sending dozens of missives back home, copies of which the ISI collated. He wrote to government officials, former teachers, potential employers and the prime minister's secretariat, repeatedly offering to "gift my services to my country." He missed the convivial dinners, his extended family, the gossip and political small talk into the early hours, the endless circular debates about the "Hindu bastards" over the border who had ransacked their old homes in 1947 and how the new Islamic Republic would one day cast a shadow over India.[38] But, the ISI wrote in its notes, there were plenty of Pakistani patriots living around the world. Did this one have anything special to offer the nation?

The trouble with Khan was that he told too many people too many stories that were of dubious provenance. One was of how he was descended from a "General Malik" who commanded the army of Sultan Ghauri, a twelfth-century Afghan king whose army crushed the Hindu forces led by Prithvi Raj Chohan, an illustrious antecedence that was also improbable, the ISI thought.[39] The Khan family's supposed regal associations continued up to his own birth, on 27 April 1936, in Bhopal, then a princely Muslim state in British India. His mother was said to have been called to bring her newborn to a fortune-teller, who, as Khan had told anyone who would listen, had advised her: "The child is very lucky. He is going to do very important and useful work for his nation and will earn immense respect."[40] The ISI suspected that the reality was that as the youngest son of seven children, whose mother and father were in their forties when he arrived, Khan had been mollycoddled and had never grown up.[41]

His hatred of India was real enough. After partition on 15 August 1947, Muslims from the Hindu-dominated states surrounding Bhopal began pouring into the city. Khan's two eldest brothers migrated to Karachi that autumn and, after the nawab of Bhopal was forced to abdicate three years later, Khan's third brother and elder sister fled too.[42] Khan got his chance in August 1952. "After packing a few books and some clothes in a tin trunk, I commenced my journey through Ajmer, Loni, Chittor, Barmeer and finally Mona Bao," Khan wrote.[43] The Indian police and railway authorities stole everything from fleeing Muslim passengers, even his pen. "If anybody protested he was kicked and hit with fists and sticks." Later in life, Khan commissioned an oil painting depicting the last train out of India to hang in Pakistan's Senate Hall.[44]

At the border, Khan cut a lonely figure. He recalled: "I crossed this stretch barefoot on the burning sand with my box on my head and shoes in my hand. When I entered Pakistan I felt like a caged bird just set free." He was brought back down to reality when he joined his brothers and sister in a cramped apartment in Karachi. But he was determined to work his way up.

Just months after US president Eisenhower made his Atoms for Peace speech to the United Nations, Khan enrolled in a physics course at D. J. Sindh Government Science College.[45] The nearest thing he had to a hobby was a small black notebook that he kept in his pocket, in which he would inscribe his favorite poems or verses from the Koran.[46] His only other leisure activity was learning German in preparation for a planned study tour of Europe. But it came to nothing.

The ISI scrutinized Khan's CV. He said he had obtained a science degree from Karachi University in 1960. Digging deeper, the ISI learned that in this period Khan had in reality held a succession of low-paid jobs. They culminated in a post with the inspector of weights and measures for the Karachi post office in which he was paid so little that he gained a reputation for charging *bakshish* to every minor official.

Finally, in 1961, Khan found something that interested him. He took the train to Lahore and visited a public exhibition about Eisenhower's Atoms for Peace vision. There, he learned that metallurgy was a crucial aspect of any nuclear program. He liked the sound of the specialism. But since Pakistan had no metallurgy industry, Khan would have to renew his attempts at getting into a European university. He borrowed money from a brother in Karachi for a one-way ticket to Düsseldorf, where a distant cousin lived. Before leaving, Khan consulted a palmist, something he would continue to do throughout his life. "The initial period of your studies will be tough and hard, but ultimately you will be able to fulfil your desire," he claimed he was told. "You will marry a foreign girl. After completing your education, you will be staying there for some time doing technical work and then you will come back to Pakistan." Then came the resounding conclusion. "People in Pakistan will have great respect for you. Their hearts will be full of love."[47]

But Europe's universities were not so enamored. For months Khan camped on his cousin's floor as rejection letters arrived in the post. In December 1961 he travelled to Holland, ending up in The Hague, where he paced the streets by day and sat on the floor in his hostel, scribbling postcards home, at night. One morning in January 1962, while queueing in a post office his eyes met those of a dowdy young South African girl, Hendrina Donkers. She recalled: "My future husband was enquiring about the charges for sending a postcard to Pakistan, which by chance I knew. He was very homesick and was happy to talk to somebody who knew something about Pakistan."[48] Although both her parents were Dutch, Henny was also an outsider, her family having migrated during the Second World War to South Africa, where she was born. Henny had spent most of her childhood in Zambia and had only recently returned to Europe to study psychology. In Khan she saw "another lost soul." The two promised to exchange letters. "To tell you the truth I never thought that this would lead to anything serious," she remembered. But a few months later Khan wrote, inviting Henny to Düsseldorf, where he was going out of his mind. "We agreed that we wanted to get to know each other better," she said, striking the dull tone of caution familiar to all those who came to know her.

In September 1962, Khan finally received an offer, from West Berlin Technische Universität, to attend a series of introductory lectures in metallurgy. Henny agreed to join him. It was a radical move for a twenty-year-old Protestant woman with few life experiences, and even more unorthodox for a Muslim living thousands of miles from home. And yet beyond their divergent cultures and ethnicity they had much in common: a quiet conservatism and a determination to better themselves against everyone's expectations. "When two people of different cultures are concerned, it requires extra efforts to understand and accept each other," Henny prosaically explained many years later. "We were lucky. My parents were quite broad-minded. This does not mean there were no misunderstandings but we resolved them quite amicably. My parents, however, stressed that I should be very careful."

In September 1963, Khan and Henny moved to Holland to be nearer her parents. He transferred to a course at Delft Technological University. "After spending a few months together ... we agreed that we liked each other and there was a feeling of mutual respect," said Henny. "Like" was a word that she used often, shunning anything stronger. Khan formally asked Henny's parents for permission to marry her and in early 1964, Hendrina Donkers, aged twenty-one, and Abdul Qadeer Khan, twenty-seven, were married at the

Pakistan embassy in The Hague, in a ceremony conducted by first secretary Jamiluddin Hassan and witnessed by the ambassador, Qudratullah Shahab. Although Henny said that her new in-laws were happy with the match, none came to the wedding. "I still feel sorry about that. Even one of his closest friends who was in London in those days, could not come. The only person who participated from his side was one of his Dutch class-fellows," she recalled.[49]

He was Henk Slebos, who today lives in a super-energy-efficient house in Sint Pancras, near the Dutch coast, having made his fortune over three decades as Khan's primary business partner in Europe, sourcing components for Pakistan's nuclear program. Khan and Slebos had met in 1964 in the coffee room of Delft University's metallurgy department. They discovered that they were renting digs in the same suburb, Rijswijk, and decided to make the daily commute together. Slebos recalled Khan as "a serious guy. He did not go very often to student clubs. He was not what one would call a bon vivant." But he was a loyal friend.[50]

The Khans' home life was also dull. "As far as he was concerned, his only hobby was his work," Henny remarked, recalling her husband's student habit of spending each evening deep in thought on the lounge floor surrounded by his books. A photograph from those days shows a prematurely middle-aged and distinctly graying Khan, a clipped mustache and a pen slipped inside his breast pocket. His arm is proprietorially lodged behind his wife's shoulders, her plain features obscured behind a pair of thick-rimmed spectacles, her only adornment a pair of red plastic ear studs.[51] In letters to Western friends, Khan would call her his "honey."[52]

In 1965, Khan scored his first lucky break when Delft accepted him for a master's program in metallurgy. Professor Dr. W. G. Burgers, an internationally respected theoretical nuclear physicist, was assigned as Khan's tutor. With his patronage, Khan mounted a series of small research projects, every one of them later documented by the ISI in search of the real Khan.[53] He did not shine. But he did not fail. Above everything else, Khan was thoroughly charming.

He also took it upon himself to defend Pakistan. The ISI found scores of letters written by him to European newspapers and magazines that he felt had misrepresented the Islamic Republic.[54] In reality he was desperate to go home, and in September 1965 he returned to look for work at the newly opened People's Steel Mill in Karachi. Henny was left with her in-laws, even though she did not speak a word of Urdu. "I am sure that everything was not translated for me," she recalled. "It is difficult, therefore, to say what my mother-in-law's opinion about me was. I was told that she said she was glad to see a foreign girl as her daughter-in-law."[55]

Khan's applications were rejected. The couple returned to Europe and in 1968 he won a research scholarship to the Catholic University of Leuven in Flanders, Dutch-speaking northern Belgium.[56] Founded in 1425, the university was steeped in history and counted among its alumni many famous scientists, including the humanist Desiderius Erasmus and the cartographer Gerardus Mercator. Khan had found his niche. Soon Henny was pregnant and when the doctors at Leuven maternity hospital invited Khan into the delivery room, Henny recalled: "He said: 'I don't know whether I will be able to stay during the whole birth as I don't have any experience.'" But Khan did stay and watched the birth of his first daughter Dina, and he was there again, two years later, when her sister Ayesha arrived.

In these years at Delft and Leuven, Khan made the most important contacts in his life, with fellow students and teachers who would go on to play crucial roles helping him to procure the knowledge and components to build a bomb, and later in assisting Pakistan to export that know-how. The names Henk Slebos, Gotthard Lerch, Heinz Mebus, Albrecht Migule, Friedrich Tinner and Gunes Cire were entered into Khan's address book around now. But they would only come to mean something to the wider world much later. Slebos would be convicted in 2005 of illegally exporting controlled items, intended for Khan, to Pakistan, and was sentenced to twelve months in jail with a $120,000 fine, although he maintained his innocence and launched an appeal. Lerch was put on trial in Germany in March 2006, charged with participating in Libya's nuclear weapons program and violating German trade and weapons laws, allegedly receiving $20 million in payment, although he refuted all the allegations.[57] Heinz Mebus would help Pakistan build two nuclear-related plants in the late 1970s and was arrested in 1984 in Amsterdam while attempting to export equipment for Khan's nuclear program.[58] Albrecht Migule was convicted at the Freiburg Municipal Court in West Germany in March 1985 for trading with A. Q. Khan and sentenced to eight months in prison and a small fine.[59] Friedrich Tinner would be arrested in October 2004 by the German authorities and extradited to Switzerland, where he was charged with producing centrifuge parts in Malaysia and Switzerland for Khan and his clients.[60] Gunes Cire supplied numerous components to Khan and would later be arrested by the Turkish authorities, who accused him of supplying the same to Libya.[61]

Professor Martin Brabers, Khan's mentor at Leuven, sensed that despite his acquired Western appearance, Khan's real loyalties remained with Pakistan.[62] Brabers remembered Khan being particularly disturbed by the 1971 war over East Pakistan, which he followed obsessively on television news. However, despite making many applications, Khan still found that no work was forthcoming from Pakistan.

His luck changed in March 1972 when FDO, a Dutch engineering firm based in Amsterdam, contacted Professor Brabers, looking for a metallurgist-cum-technical translator.[63] Leuven's metallurgy department was well hooked into the European scientific community and Brabers was frequently called upon to match promising young graduates to specialist jobs. This time he thought of Khan. A job that required superficial scientific knowledge but a linguist's brilliance played to Khan's strengths, and Henny pressed her husband to take it.[64] In fact, FDO supplied parts and expertise to Ultra Centrifuge Nederland (UCN), the Dutch partner in the URENCO uranium-enrichment consortium. UCN's plant in Almelo, an unprepossessing town on the Dutch–German border, was running one of the most secretive projects in Europe.[65]

First, Khan had to get through the security screening. An expatriate Muslim from a South Asian country known to be in pursuit of a bomb, Khan should have stuck out like a sore thumb. However, the BVD, the Dutch security service, was bombarded with positive testimonies.[66] Professor Brabers praised his student. The head of FDO's metallurgy department, who had studied with Khan at Delft, provided a glowing reference which noted Khan had been in the West for eleven years, had two young children and planned to settle permanently in Holland with his Dutch wife.[67] According to extracts from the BVD report, the original of which vanished in 2006, Khan's former student colleagues telephoned FDO officials to assure them that he was intent on becoming a naturalized citizen.[68]

Even though the BVD ran a background check, it failed to discover that Henny, whose Dutch nationality was used to back Khan's naturalization claim, was not Dutch at all. She was a Dutch-speaking South African with a British passport, which should have disqualified her as his referee. After FDO assured the BVD that Khan would be working only in low-security departments at their Amsterdam headquarters and not at the top-secret centrifuge project in Almelo, the intelligence service approved limited clearance, rubber-stamped by the Dutch ministry of internal affairs. The Khan family moved into a house at Badhoevedorp, in Amsterdam's southwestern suburbs, in May 1972.[69]

However, within one week of starting work, FDO disregarded the clearance levels awarded Khan and sent him on a two-day visit to the Almelo plant to "familiarize himself with general procedures." Khan later told friends he found the scientists there operated in a decidedly "free atmosphere."[70] The centrifuge hall was housed in the same building as the staff toilets and the coffee shop. As Khan chatted with scientists on 8 and 9 May 1972 he learned exactly what they were doing.

Only four countries, China, Russia, France and the US, were then able to enrich uranium. They did it through diffusion, an expensive and complicated process involving highly corrosive substances and a sophisticated facility, where all the pipes and pumps had to be manufactured from nickel and aluminum alloys, and the entire installation kept free from grease and oil, so as to avoid undesirable chemical reactions.[71] However, at Almelo, scientists had invented the first working prototype for gravitational or centrifuge separation of uranium isotopes. Known as the CNOR, this centrifuge had achieved enrichment levels of 3 percent, enough to fuel a commercial nuclear power plant. This was the same level as was produced by diffusion, but for a fraction of the cost. Although URENCO scientists had never tried it, they calculated that if enriched uranium-235 from the first centrifuge was fed into another, and then into a third, moving on through an entire cascade of interconnected centrifuges, it would eventually be possible to enrich it to the critical mass needed for a bomb.

Khan could barely believe what he was hearing. Returning to FDO's offices in Amsterdam, he began corresponding with Almelo's scientists on a weekly basis—chatty, friendly letters that sought, and found, common ground. Within months, they were telling him of their problems with the CNOR's rotors. The metal arms bent backwards as the centrifuges picked up speed, puncturing the skin of the centrifuge casing, sending shards of metal flying, destroying all around it. Khan suggested that research he had conducted at Leuven into the stresses absorbed by hardened steels was exactly the kind of expertise they needed.[72] He made himself appear invaluable and soon found himself conducting metallurgical research on the Dutch prototype (even though he was barely qualified). The Almelo scientists sent Khan classified design plans and lists of the specialist firms supplying the components. Khan had eased his way into one of Europe's most closely guarded secrets.[73]

He tried to tip off the Pakistan government. Late in 1972 he approached two Pakistani scientists who were visiting FDO, ostensibly to buy a wind tunnel.[74] They exchanged a few pleasantries but Khan was unable to get them alone. Unbeknown to Khan, the two men were on a mission of their own which involved them having to steer clear of all other Pakistani nationals: shopping on behalf of the Multan project, sourcing parts for a plutonium bomb. Uranium was not on the agenda as far as they or Bhutto was concerned. Khan would have to think again.

He bided his time and mined more information. Then, eighteen months later, in May 1974, he saw footage of the Indian nuclear tests on television. Incensed by the West's reluctance to come to Pakistan's aid, Khan immediately wrote his fateful letter to the prime minister, and to his surprise received word back in September that Bhutto wanted his help.[75] Despite being called home, a canny Khan suppressed his excitement and insisted on allaying suspicion by staying put until Christmas, when all of FDO's staff took annual leave.

Over the next three months he used his time wisely. Khan learned that a new project was under way that had so thrilled the URENCO directors that all available personnel had been diverted to work on it. German scientists had made a major breakthrough with a prototype centrifuge, the G-2. It was far more sophisticated than the CNOR, could spin faster and for longer, and the blueprints and technical data had been sent over to Almelo for assessment. Such were the expectations for this new centrifuge that the CNOR prototype which had caused so many problems had been ditched altogether. Khan was determined to get his hands on the G-2 material.

To steal blueprints for such a sensitive scientific breakthrough should have required an audacious act of industrial espionage—if it were possible at all. But it turned out to be easier than Khan expected. The G-2 data had arrived written in German and most of the Almelo scientists could only read Dutch and English. As a technical translator with fluent German, Dutch and English, Khan volunteered his services. Anticipating espionage, the Germans had separated the G-2 report into twelve sections, with instructions that they be distributed to staff on a need-to-know basis and in pieces so that no one person saw everything. Khan was given the two least sensitive sections to translate, the "G-2 working instructions."[76]

Khan managed to persuade his colleagues that he should transfer to Almelo so that he could query anything he did not understand. Space was tight, but in October 1974 Khan was given a desk in Almelo's final planning and design work section, a temporary building set aside from the centrifuge facility. Among UCN scientists the section was known as the "brain-box" and everyone working there assumed that everyone else had top-secret clearances. "A number of security measures were of course in operation, such as the locking of doors and desks and the need-to-know principle, but among staff members concerned there was an open atmosphere, since the problems on which they were working were all interrelated," a subsequent inquiry concluded.[77] Khan shared an office with someone who was translating the pages of the classified G-2 report that preceded his own. This man later admitted to investigators that he was away from his desk for long periods of time, giving anyone in the room ample time to read the material he had left on his desk.[78]

Over the course of three weeks, Khan scribbled away in a small black note-book, copying down secrets.[79] He need not have bothered, because eventually he was able to read the whole report. He learned that it was being sent to FDO's offices in Amsterdam for typing, since "there was only one typist available to the staff of the brain-box" and she did not have the time to do the job.[80] Khan, who had already charmed the FDO typists by regularly bringing them boxes of sweets and cakes, returned to Amsterdam, talked them into handing it over, and copied it all down.

In December 1974, Dr. Abdul Qadeer Khan, Henny and their two children left for Karachi—as he had advised the Pakistani government he would. To their friends and colleagues in Holland they were simply off on a Christmas break. As soon as they landed, Brigadier Imtiaz Ahmed, Bhutto's military secretary, escorted Khan to Islamabad.

Khan was where he had only dreamed of being. He patiently explained to Bhutto how centrifuge technology could be developed at twice the speed of the existing plutonium program being run by PAEC. It was also much cheaper.

India's nuclear budget in 1974 was $130 million, and to date New Delhi had spent $1 billion on its plutonium program.[81] Khan presented a back-of-the-envelope calculation. Using the CNOR or G-2 prototype, the blueprints for both of which he had managed to copy, 180 kg of natural uranium was needed to produce 1 kg of uranium-235 enriched to more than 90 percent. URENCO scientists were feeding UF_6 through the centrifuges twelve to fifteen times in order to achieve 3 percent enrichment. Khan estimated that if the same UF_6 were to be reintroduced into the centrifuges sixty-five or seventy times it would be possible to reach 90 percent enrichment in fifteen days. Each nuclear weapon typically contained about 15 kg of highly enriched uranium, which meant that at a market price of $22 per kg for raw uranium it would cost Pakistan only $60,000 to manufacture enough fissile material for a bomb.

Bhutto was staggered. But the real beauty of Khan's plan was that Pakistan would not even need to source raw uranium oxide on the open market, since Khalid Aslam, a geologist at PAEC, had discovered a vein in the foothills of Pakistan's Suleiman mountain range in 1963 and the country had an enormous stockpile.[82]

Bhutto was sold on the plan but also asked his chief scientific advisers to check out Khan's claims. Bhutto had read the ISI report and could see that Khan was a man capable of credible fabrication. He instructed PAEC chairman Munir Ahmed Khan to interview A. Q. Khan, who informed him about the correct method of procuring nuclear technology. The meeting went badly. Munir Ahmed Khan was not accustomed to being lectured by anyone, especially a forty-year-old expatriate with scant scientific qualifications. According to friends and colleagues, this first discussion set the tone for a rivalry that would span both their careers. And when A. Q. Khan was called back for a second meeting with his prime minister he did his best to undermine the PAEC program.[83]

The plutonium route might take more than two decades, A. Q. Khan told Bhutto, describing the PAEC project as a "white elephant."[84] Bhutto was already aware of how difficult and costly it had been for Pakistan to negotiate the purchase of a reprocessing plant from France (that was still ongoing). Playing on these fears, Khan warned that even if they got the plant, it would be snarled up in IAEA inspections. Centrifuges, however, could be constructed, unobserved, with components available on the open market. No one outside Pakistan need know. Khan piled on the pressure and he did it in a ruthless fashion. He told his prime minister: "Munir and his people are liars and cheats. They have no love for the country. They are not even faithful to you. They have told you a pack of lies."

Bhutto could deal with Khan's ambition and his aggression, he thought. The prime minister concluded after this second meeting: "Khan is the only man who can fulfil my dream of making Pakistan an atomic power."[85] Khan was instructed to take his family back to Holland and keep his head down. He was told to gather all he could about the German breakthrough in centrifuge design, while Munir Ahmed Khan was asked to begin researching the building of a uranium enrichment plant.

2

OPERATION BUTTER FACTORY

In Amstelle Street the Khan family got on with their lives. Abdul Qadeer maintained a well-tended garden of roses and tulips, while Henny gathered a menagerie of lost dogs, cats and injured birds. The only notable facet of Khan's ordinariness was his "special style" of street volleyball. "He smashed the ball from all parts of the court," a neighbor recalled. "He was determined to win and his shot was so dangerous."[1]

Neighbors also noticed that cars with diplomatic plates from Belgium and France had begun showing up after dusk, bringing visitors who would often stay until the early hours. Nobody thought anything of it, even though behind closed doors these diplomats and ISI agents were guiding Khan in what to steal and from whom. When they demanded more information about the centrifuges, Khan began cultivating Frits Veerman, a young FDO machinist and staff photographer, with whom he shared an office.

Veerman was a loner, a genuine geek who revelled in the tiniest new snippet of information about the Almelo labs. He was inquisitive and short of friends. He became a regular dinner guest at Amstelle Street, where he found Henny polite but overshadowed by "Abdul." Khan served up barbecued chicken while they discussed Pakistan, a place utterly foreign to the poorly travelled Veerman. He was fascinated, and Henny suggested places to see while "Abdul" provided telephone numbers for friends and relatives. Sometimes other Pakistanis were there too, but Veerman recalled that they were only introduced on a first name basis. Everything was relaxed and convivial, as the ISI liked to play it, even down to the living-room curtains, which were left open all evening in typical Dutch fashion.[2]

Then one day Khan asked Veerman to photograph centrifuges in the lab.

Being a junior, he agreed, but his suspicion was pricked. When Khan also asked him to photograph documents at his home, Veerman panicked, as strict rules forbade the taking of documents out of the office. Confused, his loyalty divided, Veerman did nothing at first. It was only after Khan offered to pay for him to fly to Pakistan that "suddenly a light lit up in my mind."[3] He went to a public phone box and tried to call his bosses, too frightened to use the one at home. Veerman babbled to his manager about a nuclear spy working in the lab. He mentioned the dinners at Amstelle Street and the Pakistani visitors arriving in cars with diplomatic plates. He recounted how he had seen classified FDO documents lying in Khan's front room. The manager accused him of stirring up trouble.

But then in August 1975, Sulfikar Ahmed Butt, an official at the Pakistan embassy in Brussels—the same Butt who had attended Bhutto's Multan conference—tried to purchase from a Dutch company high-frequency inverters, sophisticated devices that regulate electric current and could be used to control the spinning of centrifuges. As the ones Butt requested were of the same specification as those used in URENCO's G-2 prototype, a leak had clearly occurred from the "brain-box."[4]

Rather than confront Khan, in October 1975 FDO just shifted him to another section. Sensing what had happened, in December, he, Henny and the girls flew to Karachi with three large suitcases. According to Kauser Niazi, Bhutto's information minister, they were stuffed with "Dr. Qadeer's notes."[5]

Khan had brought to Pakistan designs, instruction manuals and lists of suppliers for both the CNOR and G-2 prototypes. Leaving his wife and children with his family, he went straight to Islamabad, only to find the prime minister out of town and Munir Ahmed Khan in charge of the uranium enrichment project. The PAEC chairman had deliberately let things drift, as A. Q. Khan's project directly competed with his own plutonium scheme. A. Q. Khan's team had been put up in a block of former Royal Air Force workshops near the old runway at Islamabad international airport and "the place was full of bats, scorpions and snakes."[6] There were twenty staff members, including eight from the army, all of whom shared "one old pickup and a worn-out wagon" and none of whom had any knowledge of uranium enrichment. Niazi said: "Dr. Qadeer was very disappointed."

On the verge of leaving Pakistan, Khan called on the prime minister on his return. He told Bhutto that "he found himself helpless to do anything in the face of bureaucratic delays."[7] Bhutto sent for Niazi, who urged the prime minister that in order to make use of Khan's capabilities he should let him set up an independent organization. Most scientists working at PAEC could never have dreamed of running their own department, let alone one that answered directly to the prime minister. But Bhutto agreed with Niazi and told Khan that his organization would be free from "checks." He could select the staff. Khan replied that he would like to consult his wife, and Bhutto gave him one hour. Khan reflected later: "You know Napoleon had said that behind the success of every man, there is a woman. I owe all my achievements to my wife. She has always supported me and encouraged me."[8] Henny recommended that her husband accept the post and Bhutto, when he received Khan's acceptance call, banged the table, shouting: "I will see the Hindu bastards now."[9]

Khan asked Henny to write to his FDO superiors, claiming that he was ill with yellow fever. Unaware or unperturbed by the fact that Veerman had turned him in, Khan wrote to him, saying he was stuck in Pakistan: "Dear Frits, it is now almost a month since we left the Netherlands, and I am gradually beginning to miss the delicious chicken." Khan assured Veerman that he planned to return to Amsterdam soon. But the Dutchman was horrified at the thought, believing he had seen the last of the Pakistani spy.[10]

Henny returned to Holland to tidy up their Dutch lives. Friends and neighbors said later that they were not surprised when she told them they were relocating to Pakistan. Even at FDO, no one suspected, one colleague recalling: "I had insisted already for several years that he should return to Pakistan because I saw his future more there than in Holland."[11] Veerman's allegations seemed to have been buried and it would be another three years before the Dutch government admitted that it knew what had been inside Khan's over-stuffed suitcases.

In Islamabad, A. Q. Khan and Munir Ahmed Khan were at each other's throats. Khan had discovered that he still required the PAEC chairman's authority to order parts and appoint staff, requests that piled up on the latter's desk. He turned to his wife in the crisis. While he was eaten up by emotion and anger, Henny was cool and rational. She urged him to make a decision: "My husband realized he was not getting anywhere. Only two options were available. Either call it a day and forget about the project or take the government into confidence and strive for results."[12]

Khan sought out the prime minister once again, who called a high-powered meeting with two men who would come to play pivotal roles in the uranium project: foreign secretary Agha Shahi and secretary general of defense Ghulam Ishaq Khan.[13] On 31 July 1976 they gave A. Q. Khan the authorization to construct his own enrichment facility, the Engineering Research Laboratories. They also gave it a codename: Project 706.

Khan set himself a seven-year deadline to build a bomb. To meet it, he sought out the brightest technicians, physicists and engineers in Pakistan and ripped apart the scientific establishment to get them, offering unheard-of salaries, perks, pensions and government bungalows. "Some of the heads of the organizations made such a hue and cry [about losing their employees] that it seemed as if the heavens would fall in," he wrote.[14] Among those he employed were Dr. Farooq Hashmi, a metallurgist trained at Southampton University, who became his deputy director, Dr. Alam, a British-educated computer programmer and mathematician, and Brigadier General Anis Ali Syed, on secondment from the Pakistan army, who became the head of the Special Works Organization, a military unit created to procure equipment for Project 706. Khan often used his hotline to the prime minister to ensure he got the last word, and by the autumn of 1976 the message had got through: Khan was not to be tangled with.

Searching for a site for the enrichment plant, Khan found Kahuta, a small village with a river running through it, in the hills forty miles southeast of Islamabad, a secluded picnic spot that was popular with foreign diplomats. It was surprisingly close to disputed Kashmir and Indian jets could reach it in less than four minutes. But Khan was more concerned with his proximity to the political whirl of Islamabad and the prime minister. Once the fences went up and the military cordon was laid down, the former picnic spot became out of bounds to all—except those working on Project 706.[15]

In the autumn of 1976 an army corps led by Brigadier Sajawal Khan Malik, one of the Pakistan army's premier civil engineers, was ordered by Bhutto to help Khan raise a nuclear facility at the isolated Kahuta site. Brigadier Sajawal would remain a key aide until Khan retired in 2001, and three years later he was arrested with Khan by the ISI and questioned about his role in the proliferation of nuclear weapons. Today, Brigadier Sajawal is still being held under house arrest at an undisclosed location, but his son, Dr. Muhammad Shafiq ur-Rehman, a bullfrog of a man who had spent most of his life at Kahuta and ran a business with one of Khan's sons-in-law, agreed to talk.[16]

Dr. Shafiq had been eight years old when Bhutto ordered his father to build Kahuta and he had tagged along to the dust bowl of a site from the very beginning. "The night before our first visit, my dad said I would have to go to bed early as he would leave at 5 a.m.," Dr. Shafiq recalled. As the sun rose, they drove out from Islamabad down the road towards Jhelum, turning left just past the international airport and up into the hills. "It was a god-forsaken place," said Dr. Shafiq. "There was nothing except a small little hut, inside which was a small little room and outside, a small little tree beneath which we parked our small little car."

Brigadier Sajawal was part of a top-secret project and elevated by it to the upper echelons of society. He moved with his family to a smart new compound in Rawalpindi, built specially for Khan's key staff.[17] But since the brigadier's arrest in 2004, his son had lived a closely monitored life. Outside his home, a car filled with men smoking cigarettes and muttering into their mobile phones was parked ostentatiously. The ISI spies were everywhere. Down the lane in the pitch black it was possible to pick out the LED glow of yet more mobile phones.

"My dad said that we were involved in something of national importance," recalled Dr. Shafiq. "It was exciting and gradually I learned that Dr. Khan was working on getting Pakistan the bomb." Khan's colleagues became Dr. Shafiq's childhood friends. "Javed Mirza, who was in charge of developing electronic circuitry for Khan, used to fix the video cameras at our family weddings. He'd always joke that he knew his way around missile guidance systems but was incapable of focusing a camera lens." Soon Dr. Shafiq accompanied his father on a regular basis. The first time he met Khan, he was so excited he could barely breathe. "He'd arrived with a lot of fanfare and senior army officers. We were convinced our savior had arrived."

All elements of Project 706 started simultaneously: the building of the main plant at Kahuta, the procurement of essential equipment and materials from Europe, the manufacture of the first prototypes, the establishment of a pilot plant in which to test them, even a weapons design center. Khan had calculated he would need at least ten thousand centrifuges to supply a viable bomb program. He had plumped for the CNOR prototype as it was simpler to build, and since it had been abandoned by URENCO in favor of the G-2 there were dozens of suppliers with vast stockpiles of unwanted components they were desperate to sell. But the CNOR had a design flaw that URENCO had never completely resolved: its bottom bearing, a tiny ball stuck onto a needle and attached to the base plate of the machine's rotor. The needle supported the weight of the rotor as it spun at up to 70,000 rpm, and to counter the friction a spiral groove, virtually invisible to the human eye, was etched on to the underside of the bearing, which sat in a tiny cup of lubricant.[18] High-definition computer-driven lathes had to etch this groove onto the underside of the bearing, and even a minute irregularity would cause the rotor to tilt and the machine to crash. The exact dimensions of the bearing and its spiral groove had been among the most highly classified secrets at the Almelo plant, and it was clear from letters that Khan now sent to former colleagues at URENCO that he had been unable to obtain these specifications.[19]

Khan pressed on. It was just another problem on a long list of challenges to surmount. "It was an uphill task with every step being marred by a new set of intricate problems ... A country which could not make sewing needles, good bicycles or even durable metalled roads was embarking on one of the latest and most difficult technologies," he wrote.[20] The barren mountainside would have to be transformed into a flawless sterile environment. Khan told Brigadier Sajawal that the large centrifuge hall would have to be airtight and needed a ten-foot-deep concrete floor to provide some protection against earthquakes, for which the region was famed. However, so basic was the engineering experience of the brigadier's team that these earthquake precautions would turn out to be woefully inadequate.[21]

The large hall was built into the bedrock and equipped with a sophisticated air-conditioning system as the centrifuges generated enormous heat. The uranium hexafluoride gas (UF_6) that was fed into them would be continuously poured from one centrifuge to the next by a "feed-and-withdrawal system": pipes, valves and compressors that guided the gas on its journey to enrichment. The enriched material (uranium-235) would then be taken to another on-site facility, the "gasification and solidification plant," where it would be stored in two-meter-tall canisters for the designers who Khan hoped to employ at the on-site nuclear weapons workshop to turn it into metal and shape it into small spheres.

A small power station was also constructed to make Kahuta independent of Pakistan's grid, which was so unstable and overdrawn that during the summer large sections of Rawalpindi and Islamabad were plunged into darkness. Khan also insisted that Project 706 aim to become self-sufficient in manufacturing components, and Brigadier Sajawal was ordered to build machine-tool workshops, ready to house state-of-the-art European equipment capable of reverse-engineering centrifuge parts. Aside from the technical sections, Kahuta also needed guard towers, alarm systems, a paved road wide enough for trucks, communications, staff facilities, guest houses for visiting scientists. Brigadier Sajawal estimated that the basic infrastructure alone would take three years to finish. So, while his men bulldozed, Khan and his small team of scientists worked on designing a Pakistani prototype centrifuge (which they called the P-1) from a small laboratory located in the nearby village of Sihala.

Inevitably, news about the intense activity percolated back to diplomats in Islamabad, most of whom were initially more concerned about losing their favorite picnic spot. The CIA station reported to its regional headquarters in Tehran, the Iranian capital: "Something strange is happening at Kahuta. Construction work is going on at a pace quite uncharacteristic of Pakistan. One can see day-to-day progress."[22] Khan later joked: "Yes, the progress could be seen from hour to hour. The Army Corps of Engineers were doing an excellent job."[23]

While Khan was happy to leave the infrastructure to Brigadier Sajawal, the design and assembly of the centrifuges was something he intended to supervise personally. In the autumn of 1976 he began making short trips to Holland, the UK, Germany, Switzerland, Belgium and France, working his personal contacts, looking for everything he needed to build the P-1. At this point, he found an unlikely soulmate in Peter Griffin, a Welsh miner's son and trained production engineer, who, like Khan, could spend hours happily discussing what a sophisticated, precision-made machine tool could do to a simple piece of metal.

Griffin, who would become inseparable from Khan, supplying machines, parts and tools to him for two decades, recounted how, in the summer of 1976, when he was a young sales manager at a Swansea-based machine-tool supplier called Scimitar, he received a phone call that would change his life. For Abdus Salam, the Pakistani-born businessman on the other end of the line, it was a misdial. He had been looking for the British office of US machine-tool giant Rockwell International, which helped make NASA's space shuttle, but instead got the UK agent of its power-tool division in Wales. Nevertheless, the conversation that followed led to an introduction to Khan. Griffin said: "Salam wanted £1 million in Rockwell power tools. Top-of-the-range, US-made equipment. One million pounds of it. Of course I could do the deal even though I was not Rockwell. We agreed to meet in London."[24]

There, Salam revealed that the equipment was for a "brilliant young Pakistani scientist" called Abdul Qadeer Khan, who was "trying to help his country industrialize and enter the modern age." Salam's contact with Khan had come through his local mosque in Colindale, north London, where he prayed alongside an expat Indian Muslim, who one day revealed that an old school friend had contacted him, looking for help importing engineering equipment to Pakistan.[25] When Salam said there was a lot more business beyond the lucrative Rockwell contract, Griffin was initially reluctant to get involved, unsure what the Pakistanis were up to.

However, after his company in Swansea overlooked him for a bonus, Griffin resigned from his job to go after the money, setting up Weargate Ltd from his garage, while Salam processed orders for Khan through Salam Radio Colindale, a down-on-its-luck electrical shop which proved a terrific cover for such a discreet business. After Griffin became a director of Salam's company the following year, they kept the innocuous shopfront but swapped the name to one that better fitted the big-bucks game they had entered in Pakistan: SR International. The firm would become one of dozens run by expat Pakistanis, from similarly unassuming corner stores, supplying components to Khan.[26] To spread the orders around, Salam created other companies, and in August 1977 he introduced Griffin to Khan.

The meeting took place at the Kundan Restaurant in central London. "Round the table was Khan, Brigadier Sajawal, Dr. Farooq Hashmi, his deputy, Dr. Alam, his computer expert, and Brigadier General Anis Nawab," said Griffin. "General Anis was introduced as running a project to industrialize Pakistan, which seemed like a good idea to me. I presumed he was the boss as he was a general but when I said, 'So you're the boss?' he said, 'No, he's the boss,' pointing to Khan, who hadn't said a word. Khan was a great chap in those early days, friendly, clever and generous. As we got to know each other, he'd call me up every week in the UK just for a chat."

Soon Pakistani scientists began to fly in to London looking for components, with Colonel Rashid Ali Qazi, the head of Khan's production machine shop, emerging as Griffin's main contact.[27] Occasionally, Khan would come to supervise the largest orders. There were often loyalties at play beyond Griffin's comprehension. Once, when he tried to convince Khan to stop buying laser rangefinders from China which were actually manufactured by Israel and would have been far cheaper sourced directly from there, Khan had refused. "No, we import them from the Chinese," he said. "The Chinese are our friends."[28]

There was a protocol to all of these trips. After Colonel Qazi returned home, Griffin would receive a telex from Khan listing the components he had decided to order. "I wasn't interested in what the Pakistanis were doing with them," Griffin said. "Just as if I sold a car to someone I would not ask if they were going to use it in a bank robbery. I sold machine tools. I'd box them up and if they didn't contravene export controls send them off to Brigadier General Anis at the Special Works Organization and forget all about it." Later, the names changed. "At one stage it was the Civil Works Organization, then Engineering Research Laboratories, then Kahuta Research Labs, and finally Khan Research Labs."

The trade escalated and Griffin was invited to visit Pakistan. He was only too pleased to go as Khan's outfit were terrible payers and he always had to chase down his invoices. "I loved Islamabad and the way that Pakistanis gossiped so badly," Griffin said. "The minute you stepped out of a room they'd be bitching about you." On his first few trips Griffin stayed with Khan at his Islamabad home. "Ayesha, Khan's youngest, used to come running out whenever I arrived and give me a big hug. She called me *chacha*, uncle. I introduced her to *Wind in the Willows*," Griffin said.[29]

As Khan's procurement network expanded and as even more foreigners began passing through, he opened a guest house next door to his home. After dinner, while Khan wrote his diary, Griffin would sit on the sofa. "Khan was very particular and wanted to be word-perfect in English so he used to ask me how to say things, how to spell words. He kept that diary always, writing almost two hours every night."

Khan's procurement network was blossoming. But he had still been unable to crack the P-1's bottom bearing problem and in August 1976 he risked all by writing to Frits Veerman, telling him he was coming back to Holland. Veerman was terrified. He claimed not to be around. But in September 1976, Khan came anyway and boldly approached an FDO sales manager whom he persuaded to come back with him to Pakistan and sell him discontinued components from the CNOR stockpile. However, Khan would not leave Veerman alone, writing to his former colleague, nakedly exploiting their old friendship. "Very confidentially, I request you to help us," Khan wrote before listing requests for critical and secret technical information. "These ... things are very small, and I hope you will not disappoint me."[30]

When Veerman failed to respond, a determined Khan wrote again. This time he asked Veerman to contact Franz Frencken, another FDO employee: "Ask him if he would be interested in paying me a visit. I would have some technical work for him and a lot of photographic work for you. Why don't you both spend a vacation [in Pakistan] and earn some money at the same time?"[31] Hearing nothing back, Khan began contacting URENCO suppliers directly, including Gotthard Lerch, the sales manager at Leybold Heraeus, a leading West German engineering firm in Hanau that had supplied vacuum pumps, gas purification systems and valves for the CNOR and G-2. Khan was worried that Leybold might go straight to the authorities. He need not have been. Lerch was eager to do some deals on the side and began selling surreptitiously to Pakistan.[32]

Next on Khan's list was the wherewithal to manufacture UF_6, the feedstuff for the centrifuges. Pakistan had a ready supply of the two basic ingredients for manufacturing UF_6: yellowcake from its mines in the Suleiman mountains, and deposits of fluorite crystals. But Khan was missing two industrial processes: first, the fluorite crystals had to be converted into fluorine, which then had to be mixed with the yellowcake at a uranium conversion plant.

Khan contacted Heinz Mebus, an old acquaintance from West Berlin Technische Universität, the school he had flunked to go after Henny.[33] Mebus was installing X-ray machines in West German hospitals when Khan got back in touch, and while he agreed to fit out the uranium conversion plant and the fluorine factory he put Khan on to someone else to supply the necessary equipment. Albrecht Migule, an engineer from Freiburg in West Germany, had been doing business in Pakistan since 1967, when he had built a butter and margarine factory for the son of Pakistan's dictator of the time, General Ayub Khan. After the 1967 deal Migule's company, CES Kalthof GmbH, had won an export contract mining Pakistani fluorite crystals for European customers who used them for everything from manufacturing margarine to toothpaste. He agreed to help Khan.

On 13 November 1976, Albrecht Migule flew to Karachi to sign a $1 million contract to build a fluorine factory with Messrs Arshad, Amjad and Abid Ltd, a textile firm in Karachi that had been opened as a cover for Project 706. The following January, Migule returned to sign a second contract to build a uranium conversion plant on the outskirts of Multan.[34]

In March 1977 the Pakistani government paid for Migule, Heinz Mebus and a third German, Erwin Veldung, a chemist from Munich, to be flown first class to Pakistan to discuss designs for the two plants. On 9 March, at a government guest house on the outskirts of the city, they met the directors of Messrs Arshad, Amjad and Abid Ltd, who were in reality Mohammed Farooq, Khan's head of foreign procurement, Javid Mirza, his weapons specialist, and a third Kahuta employee.[35] After Migule signed a guarantee that his plants would produce 99 percent pure UF_6 in solid bars, Farooq stood up and declared: "Gentlemen, this is a significant hour for us and for our country."[36] According to the contract, the plants would be manufactured as ready-made units in Germany and correspond to the most modern standards of German nuclear technology. They would be shipped in containers to Pakistan and assembled on site.[37]

Such was Khan's haste, and the apparent indifference of the authorities, that he began to take foolish risks, sending Irshad Akhatar, supposedly an engineer with Messrs Arshad, Amjad and Abid Ltd, to Frankfurt with a suitcase filled with yellowcake samples which he wanted to test-run through the German plants. German Customs insisted that the Pakistani engineer open his bag. However, Migule, who had come to meet Akhatar at the airport, managed to talk his way out of it, convincing the official that the yellowcake was "a harmless fluorspar."[38] German Customs were not trained to detect a uranium conversion racket.

Migule's and Mebus's association with Khan's Project 706 would extend even further. Once Khan had found someone he could trust, he would go back time and again, tapping into a network of contacts. Mebus would provide Khan with an opening to the German engineering corporation Siemens, where he recruited a distinctive, blond-haired Turkish engineer, Gunes Cire. Khan also reached out to his old college contact, Henk Slebos, the only friend to have come to his wedding in 1964.

In January 1977, Slebos was unemployed and readily agreed to help Khan obtain centrifuge parts. Slebos knew all of the Almelo suppliers and could provide a European face to ease the passage of more demanding deals. Khan later explained: "You are not willing to sell it to me, but you are willing to sell it to Tom. So Tom buys from you, he takes 10 percent or 15 percent, and he sells it to me. This is purely a business deal!"[39]

Slebos worked hard and collaborated with other Khan agents, including Gunes Cire, with whom he sourced for Pakistan electromagnetic motors, dynamos and aluminum castings.[40] He also did business with Peter Griffin, who recalled first meeting him at Khan's Islamabad guest house.[41]

Unlike Griffin, who insisted he did not know Khan's real intentions, Slebos claimed that Khan was upfront about building a bomb from the very start. "If you allow one half of the globe to have the bomb and exclude the other half because they are considered too stupid or for whatever other reasons, then you are really stepping on my toes," he said.[42] Particularly irksome was the Nuclear Non-Proliferation Treaty that France, the US, UK and USSR had drawn up in 1968 to prevent non-nuclear states from obtaining nuclear weapons. In Slebos's and Khan's eyes, the treaty had simply legitimized the rights of those four countries to hold on to their nuclear weapons and exempted them from any IAEA intrusion. And in controlling the market, the big four had also become the world's top arms exporters. It was a display of the kind of political muscle that nuclear weapons could provide—and that Pakistan wanted.[43]

For Slebos, the Pakistan trade became so normal that he lost sight of how others were outraged by it. Soon after Khan first established contact, he made the mistake of trying to get his old boss, Nico Zondag, involved in the deals. Zondag refused and contacted URENCO's Dutch partner, UCN, warning that Slebos was carrying round a "little suitcase" filled with information about their G-2 prototype. Zondag also tipped off the Dutch intelligence service, telling them exactly what Slebos intended to do, including his planned departure dates to Pakistan. "The only answer I received was: 'If you see him again, grab hold of his suitcase.' I got the impression I was fighting windmills," said Zondag.[44]

By 1977, Khan had procurement operations running across Europe, overseen by ISI field agents operating under the cover of diplomatic postings. Among them was Sulfikar Ahmed Butt, who had been at Bhutto's Multan conference and later baby-sat Khan when he was sent back to FDO to steal more data. Now based at the Pakistan embassy in Brussels, where his official post was as head of the science and technology department, Butt was paymaster to Slebos, Griffin and many more.[45]

Another prolific operation ran out of a residential apartment in Watchberg-Pech, an affluent commuter town outside Bonn in West Germany, from where Ikram ul-Haq Khan, an agent for A. Q. Khan's Special Works Organization, placed orders through Team Industries, an engineering firm near Stuttgart.[46] The front man in the deals was Team's director, Ernst Piffl, who, with ul-Haq, ordered more than $11 million of components in 1977: inverters from Emerson Industrial Controls of Swindon in the UK; rolled rods from Aluminum Walzwerker GmbH of Singen in West Germany; tubes made from specially hardened steel from Van Doorne Transmissie of Tilburg, Holland; and vacuum equipment for gas purification from Gotthard Lerch at Leybold Heraeus in Hanau.[47]

The Pakistanis sometimes referred to their burgeoning network as "Operation Butter Factory," a name that harked back to the 1960s when Albrecht Migule had built a margarine factory for the son of General Ayub Khan. Khan, Butt, ul-Haq and other ISI agents mentioned this in-joke in their correspondence, describing enriched uranium as "cake," "sweets" or "biscuits," the end product produced from the "butter" or UF_6 that Migule had helpfully provided by building the fluorine and uranium conversion plants.[48] But on the ground, Khan's men made very little attempt to cover their tracks, preparing contracts that stipulated delivery directly to the Director General, Special Works Organization, Rawalpindi, and handing out checks from government accounts held at the National Bank of Pakistan.[49]

One reason for this openness was that Khan knew that Europe had no idea what he was up to. Because centrifuge technology was so new and poorly understood, the checks and balances that should have been triggered by the trade failed. Most of the components Khan requested were not on any IAEA list of nuclear-sensitive equipment and were not subject to any European export controls. Even though some of the components were vast, among them a complete gasification and solidification unit (to feed UF_6 gas into the centrifuges and then transform it back into a solid form) which required three Hercules C-130 transport planes to get it to Pakistan, most sales were vetted and approved by Europe's governments. "We were told [by the Swiss government] this [sale] would not touch any restrictions," said Rudolf Walti, head of the Swiss company CORA Engineering, which supplied the gasification unit.[50]

Professor Brabers, Khan's old tutor from Leuven, who was invited to visit Pakistan to see the construction at Kahuta, said: "He had a good set-up, a good organization. Also in buying equipment, he knew all the companies; he knew so many languages, and he is so charming [that] he managed to buy many things that other Pakistanis would not manage to buy."[51]

Greed, lax custom inspections, an overly bureaucratic IAEA, governments' pursuit of their national interests, and antiquated legislation were all being exploited ruthlessly, and clearly Western governments and suppliers under-estimated Pakistan. Dr. Shafiq, whose father was busy building centrifuge halls as components came flooding in, reflected: "Everything came from the UK, Germany and France and was openly transacted. The companies would tell their governments, 'These silly buggers in Pakistan want to spend billions' and their governments would say, 'If these silly buggers have got the cash then let them have it.' We would say vacuum pumps; we need them for oil and gas, etc. But it was all going to Kahuta."[52]

Later, when he had all he needed, Khan openly agreed: "The Western world was sure that an underdeveloped country like Pakistan could never master this technology ... [But] the Western world never talked about their hectic and persistent efforts to sell everything to us. We received many letters and telexes and people chased us with figures and details of equipment they had sold to Almelo, Gronau and Capenhurst. They literally begged us to buy their equipment."[53]

In Pakistan, things appeared to be going so well that in 1976 prime minister Bhutto ordered test tunnels to be constructed at two locations in western Balochistan, five in the Ras Koh range on the Balochistan plateau, and one beneath the sands of the Kharan Desert, a hundred miles to the west.[54] Brigadier Muhammed Sarfaraz, chief of staff at 5 Corps, oversaw the building work along with Brigadier Sajawal. At Kharan, they constructed a vertical shaft 300 foot deep with a 700-foot horizontal tunnel leading off the bottom. In Ras Koh, five horizontal tunnels were bored directly into the side of a mountain. The tunnels were designed in the shape of a double "S" so that if a bomb was detonated, the explosion would move the mountain outwards and the tunnel would collapse inwards. Each one was capable of withstand-ing a 20-kiloton explosion, the same magnitude as the bomb dropped on Nagasaki. Completed in 1980, the tunnels would be sealed until Pakistan was ready.[55]

*

Despite all the activity at Kahuta and Ras Koh, the international community was oblivious to Pakistan's uranium enrichment plans, going all out, instead, to block its ongoing deal with France on the reprocessing plant, which it viewed as a prelude to the production of a plutonium bomb. Straining to see what Pakistan was up to, the State Department put Robert Gallucci, a young official in the Bureau of Non-Proliferation, on to the case. He rummaged around in all the classified material he had access to and concluded that "Pakistan's nuclear industry is not particularly worrisome now" as the Islamic Republic was "at the beginning of its nuclear development." The desire was certainly there since the Indian nuclear tests, Gallucci said, but Pakistan was many years from attaining nuclear weapons status as it was stuck on the plutonium route. As long as the IAEA monitored every move it made on that front, the West need not be unduly worried.[56]

US secretary of state Henry Kissinger had tried to head Bhutto's nuclear ambitions off course during a meeting in New York in 1976, offering him a strange deal.[57] Bhutto was to terminate his reprocessing project in favor of a US-supplied facility that would be located in Iran and be made available to all countries in the region. Dick Cheney, then chief of staff to President Gerald Ford, and Donald Rumsfeld, the defense secretary, had devised the scheme, arguing that Iran needed a nuclear program to meet its future energy needs—even though the country was awash with oil and gas reserves. It was the first proposed US nuclear deal with Iran and would have been extremely lucrative for US corporations like Westinghouse and General Electric, which stood to earn $6.4 billion from the project.[58]

But Bhutto rejected the offer and, fearing that Pakistan was about to proceed to the next stage of plutonium production, the US Senate proposed an amendment to the 1961 Foreign Assistance Act to block economic and military aid, threatening to cut off Pakistan's annual $162 million US aid package.[59] Bhutto was not rattled. The noise from the US Congress suited him fine, as he had no intention of going ahead with the costly reprocessing plant and was concentrating his energies on Project 706. "Bhutto himself was of the view that the work at Kahuta laboratories should be kept concealed from the world by focusing attention on the purchase of the reprocessing plant," recalled Kauser Niazi, his information minister.[60] Always on the lookout for cost efficiencies, Bhutto also hoped that if Pakistan was seen to abandon its reprocessing plans under American pressure it would not have to compensate the French when it finally pulled out of the deal.[61]

*

Ultimately, Bhutto was felled by his own sophistry. In January 1977, Jimmy Carter had been sworn in as US president, advocating a tough non-proliferation stance and more restrictive arms transfers with a greater emphasis placed by Washington on human rights, none of which helped Pakistan. To strengthen his domestic position and to head off the inevitable clash with the US, Bhutto called an early general election that March.[62] His Pakistan People's Party (PPP) had won the 1970 elections on a huge wave of support from the poor and, convinced that his emotional hold over them held firm, Bhutto was sure he would win again easily. But he had not sensed that his high-handedness and increasingly authoritarian personal style, combined with a shift to conservative economic policies and growing collaboration with Pakistan's feudal landlords, had alienated many traditional supporters. Many were instead drawn to a coalition of opposition parties led by Jamaat-e-Islami, an Islamic group headed by Maulana Maududi, a conservative cleric who advocated a pious alternative to the mainstream and sectarian PPP.[63] To date, Maududi's rhetorical call for Pakistan to become a strict religious state had mainly drawn support from students and trade unions, but now, as Jamaat aimed its message at middle-class professionals and the rural poor, Bhutto's predicted landslide victory looked increasingly unlikely.

From the start the campaign took on a religious tone, the *Economist* labelling it an election that would be fought on "whisky, war and Islam."[64] When Maududi charged that Bhutto drank heavily and indulged in "Bacchanalian orgies," his response was that "he drank wine, not people's blood," referring to the murderous sectarian nature of Maududi's supporters who controlled village life in Pakistan's border regions. By election night on 7 March 1977, Bhutto was worried. He invited his friend, US ambassador Henry Byroade, to watch the results on television. Byroade recalled: "[Bhutto] was losing in Karachi. He was losing in Peshawar. Then the Punjab numbers started coming in and guys who were absolute thugs won by 99 percent ... [Bhutto] started drinking heavily, calling Lahore and he said, 'What are you guys doing?' ... I saw Bhutto the next morning ... he hadn't had any sleep, obviously drinking."[65]

However, Bhutto's PPP manipulated its apparent demise and when the results were declared had won 155 out of 200 National Assembly seats, leading to claims that the poll had been rigged and sending rioters into the streets. Maududi called for a general strike and, with the violence heightening, he again attacked Bhutto as a drunk and an atheist. Bhutto was forced to impose martial law in Karachi, Lahore and Hyderabad, and more than two hundred were killed in clashes between demonstrators and the Pakistan army, among whose ranks were many Maududi supporters who resented being used in what they saw as a political dogfight. In the midst of the battle, lines became crossed when a rumor sprung up that Bhutto had been arrested by the military at a reception in Karachi. However, within hours it was revealed to be untrue and the US consul there phoned Howard Schaffer, the US political consul in Islamabad. "The party is over," said a relieved Robert Moore in Karachi, using a clumsy code to infer that Bhutto had not been arrested after all. However, the call was tapped and a different message filtered back to Bhutto.[66]

As the unrest showed no sign of abating, Bhutto attempted to divert attention by claiming that the US was interfering in Pakistan's domestic political situation in order to thwart the country's nuclear ambitions. During an emotional address to the National Assembly, he charged Washington with financing a "vast, colossal, huge international conspiracy" to oust him.[67] "The bloodhounds are after my blood," he railed, adding that foreign dollars were flooding into Pakistan to pay for the rising agitation. Bhutto claimed that Henry Kissinger had personally threatened him during a state visit to Pakistan the previous August, leaning over the plates during an official dinner in Lahore to warn that if he failed to fall in line over the nuclear issue "we will make a horrible example of you."[68] To bang the point home, the prime minister revealed how US diplomats had been intercepted plotting his downfall on the phone. Referring to the Moore–Schaffer call, Bhutto mimicked: "'The party's over, the party's over. He's gone.' Well, gentlemen, the party is not over."

In May 1977, Bhutto ramped up the pressure, ordering his foreign minister to pass a dossier of evidence about alleged CIA plotting to shut down Pakistan's nuclear program to Cyrus Vance, the new American secretary of state. While Vance declined to get involved, Bhutto flew off on a hastily convened tour of six Islamic nations to garner regional support, telling the Saudi monarch, King Khalid, that he had "ample proof" that President Carter was trying to skewer him over the nuclear issue.[69]

But Bhutto failed to sense the uneasiness within Pakistan's military or that Maududi's Islamist messages had hit the mark.[70] Among those who were most unhappy was Bhutto's recently appointed chief of army staff, General Mohammed Zia ul-Haq, who already harbored a secret hatred of the prime minister after he had ridiculed him in public as the "monkey general" who had only been appointed because he was docile.[71] Zia also faced intense criticism from the ranks, who believed that he had leapfrogged more senior and able officers to get the COAS job. To squash dissent inside and outside the military, General Zia began readying a contingency plan, Operation Fair Play, the downfall of Bhutto in a military coup.

Kauser Niazi, the information minister, recalled: "Bhutto was fighting a four-sided battle. On one side he was provoking Carter to put pressure on France. On a second front he was trying to keep the Kahuta plant concealed from the West. On the third front he was fighting with the agitation in the country. And on the fourth front, he was keeping a check on the generals by meeting them every other day. During this period he was casting a net across the world ... for the purchase of necessary parts for the Kahuta Research Laboratory. This was not an ordinary thing. A single man fighting on so many fronts."[72]

In the early hours of 5 July, after both of them had attended an American Independence Day party thrown by US ambassador Art Hummel at his Islamabad residence on Ataturk Avenue, General Zia had Bhutto arrested, the third time the military had assumed power since Pakistan gained independence. From the outside, the coup appeared to have been orchestrated by the US.[73] But in reality the US was far removed from it, panicking over what an unknown general like Zia would do with Pakistan's nascent nuclear program.

Two weeks later, the pressure was pricked. Bhutto was released and General Zia promised to hold fresh elections. But days later he changed his mind. Fearing what his aides described as Bhutto's "vindictive nature," the general rearrested the PPP leader in Karachi on 3 September 1977.[74] Bhutto's eldest child, his daughter Benazir, took up her father's fight. Educated at Harvard and Oxford, the twenty-five-year-old had returned to Pakistan in the middle of the post-election riots and now she flitted between her father's jail cell in Lahore and the public stage, whipping up support as Zia's allies counselled the general to execute the prime minister.[75] "The five rivers will flow with blood if Mr. Bhutto is hanged," she told a rally at Okara, in the Punjab, on 29 September.[76]

Instead of releasing Bhutto, General Zia framed him, laying tenuous charges that he had assassinated the father of a political opponent, reviving an old case from 1975 in which the man had been shot at point-blank range in his car.[77] Eighteen days before the new elections were due to be held, General Zia went on national television to announce the indefinite postponement of the poll, telling the Pakistani people: "I want to make it absolutely clear that I neither have any political ambitions nor does the army want to be taken away from its profession of soldiering."[78]

Incarcerated at Kot Lakhpat jail in Lahore, facing charges of murder and other "high crimes," when his trial began at the Lahore high court on 11 October, Zulfikar Ali Bhutto attempted again to raise the specter of US interference in Pakistan's nuclear program, but the chief justice was unmoved. The family of the man who had been gunned down in 1975 and whose murder had been stuck on Bhutto claimed that the prime minister had masterminded the hit, an allegation that he described in court as "a tissue of lies—a bad novel—a concocted story."[79]

During her father's trial, Benazir Bhutto was held along with her mother, Nusrat, in the jail at Sihala army camp, close to the temporary research lab where Abdul Qadeer Khan was developing his prototype centrifuge. Occasionally she was allowed out to visit her father, as were other friends and colleagues, among them Munir Ahmed Khan from PAEC, who regularly updated Bhutto about the nuclear program. "My father remained in touch with him throughout his detention," remembered Benazir Bhutto. "He would visit on the pretense he was delivering oranges and vitamins. Munir always wanted to talk about plutonium and ongoing negotiations over the French reprocessing plant but all my father wanted to hear about was progress at Kahuta."[80]

Another visitor was Dr. Zafar Niazi. Although he shared the same family name as Bhutto's information minister he was no relative but the prime minister's dentist, a family friend and adviser. Dr. Niazi was also close to A. Q. Khan, and on the pretense of visiting Bhutto to examine his teeth he passed on progress updates from Kahuta.[81] Somehow, the exasperating CNOR centrifuge whose exacting design had made it so difficult to reconstruct in Pakistan was now up and running at the Sihala pilot plant.[82] Khan was even preparing to introduce UF_6 gas into the centrifuge chamber and to attempt, for the very first time, to enrich uranium. It was remarkably rapid progress for a man who just two years before had been a translator at the FDO lab in Amsterdam, and a solace for Bhutto as he awaited his fate.

3

INTO THE VALLEY OF DEATH

On 18 March 1978 the Lahore high court sentenced Bhutto to death. His lawyers filed an appeal, while Benazir wrote to her brother Murtaza in England: "Don't tell the other children, but the supreme court will most probably rubber stamp [the] judgment and they will try to carry it out immediately ... Therefore, all our efforts have to be made now ... TIME IS OF THE ESSENCE."[1] Murtaza was to go immediately to Washington and contact Peter Galbraith, an old friend from Benazir's student days at Harvard University. He now worked in Congress as an adviser to the Senate foreign relations committee and could help contact "the Kennedys, Kissinger, Nelson Rockefeller, George Bush"—and the president. She added a word of advice: "Please be very quiet about these activities ... Try not to get photographed." Murtaza worked hard and appeals for clemency flooded into Islamabad, but Zia was unmoved, saying: "Nobody is indispensable ... or above the law. The higher you go the harder you fall."[2]

In Sihala, A. Q. Khan barely had time to mourn. On 4 April 1978, he revealed to Henny over dinner that he had something extraordinary to share with her. A world-class secret in fact. He had fed a sample of UF_6 through his P-1 centrifuge and produced enriched uranium. "I can say with complete confidence that I was among the very first who knew that Pakistan had broken the monopoly of the Western world," Henny remembered.[3] The following day, Khan sent an official memo to his patrons, Ghulam Ishaq Khan, by now the finance minister, and Agha Shahi, the foreign minister.[4] But by the time they received this news, Zia had usurped their authority over the nuclear program, appointing a general to run it.

Zulfikar Ali Bhutto had always been wary of the military getting their hands

on the nuclear trigger. No military officers were invited to the Multan conference of 1972, and the military's only connection to Kahuta was organizing its
building and security while the ISI prowled Europe for components. But within
weeks of Bhutto's conviction, Zia disbanded the civilian committee, and placed
General Khalid Mahmud Arif, his chief of staff, in charge. Everything that Khan
would do from now on came under the military's purview.

In his first speech as chief martial law administrator in July 1977, Zia had
described himself as a "Soldier of Islam."[5] It was a purposeful image that aimed
to demonstrate both his militarism and his faith. General Zia's family had
come to Pakistan from Jalandhar, in the Indian Punjab, and he was influenced
by the Deobandi sect, a severe and literal branch of Islam closely connected to
the Wahhabis in Saudi Arabia. Believing in a strict adherence to the Sunnah, the
tradition of the Prophet Muhammad, Zia, a general with a maulvi's (preacher's)
sensibilities, immediately set out elevating sharia law, the rules of the Koran,
above the penal codes of Pakistan, whose antecedence lay in British criminal
law. Faith, and a bomb just in case—this was Zia's plan. He also instructed
General Arif to make certain that the enrichment program was successful not
just for Pakistan but for the Muslim *ummah*. Khan's bomb, if ever he got that
far, was to be shared with the entire Islamic world.[6]

For ten years General Arif would be the second most powerful man in
Pakistan, serving as Zia's chief of staff and the deputy chairman of the Nuclear
Command Authority which ran Kahuta. Today he lives in comfortable
retirement in a bungalow in Rawalpindi, his garden filled with cages of canaries.
He recalled that he was not a stranger to Khan when he took over his program,
having met him two years earlier when Khan had come to army headquarters
to get help with the construction of the plant in Kahuta.[7] Now Arif, too, was
informed of Khan's enrichment news and "complimented Dr. Khan on the job
and described the day as the most important day for Pakistan."[8] Bhutto learned
of Khan's breakthrough in his prison cell from Munir Ahmed Khan, one of the
last times they would meet, as in March 1978 Bhutto was transferred to
Rawalpindi district jail as death-row prisoner number 3183.[9]

Khan moved on, seamlessly transferring his loyalties to Generals Zia and
Arif. He plunged himself into the program and, as an inveterate letter writer,
found solace in an old friend, Aziz Khan, an electrical engineer who had
emigrated to Montreal, Canada. Initially, A. Q. Khan tried to entice Aziz to
return to Pakistan and work at Kahuta. But that became the pretext for an

intense and literary friendship, always expressed in handwritten Urdu script, the most sensitive thoughts of the man behind one of the world's most clandestine program, wafting through the unsecured mail for anyone to intercept.[10]

The first letter arrived in Montreal on 13 June 1978. "Received your two letters and lots of literature, I am so thankful," A. Q. Khan wrote. "I am writing this letter to you in Urdu so it would be more intimate."[11] He needed help with understanding the application of new pieces of equipment that he had ordered that spring, with the assistance of Ernst Piffl in Germany. Piffl had negotiated with Emerson Industrial Controls, the British subsidiary of American electrical giant Emerson Electric, to buy high-frequency inverters, described in the technical literature forwarded from Canada. Emerson had supplied the same inverters to the centrifuge plant run by British Nuclear Fuels Ltd at Capenhurst, in Cheshire, as part of the URENCO consortium. But in the UK nobody thought to raise the alarm.

Khan wrote excitedly about his prototype centrifuge. "June 4 was a historical day for us," he told Aziz. "On that day we put the 'Air' in the machine and the first time we got the right product and its efficiency was the same as the theoretical." Khan's "air" was UF_6 and the product was enriched uranium. "We had to see our big bosses so that we could get some money for the budget," Khan wrote. "When this news was given to them they were quite happy and congratulated us. The big bosses said they had full confidence in me despite the objection from a few people." This was a sideways swipe at Munir Ahmed Khan, technically still his superior.[12]

Work at the main Kahuta plant was also in full swing, and Khan revealed to Aziz that two foreign groups were involved. One was from Japan and the second was from Siemens in Germany and included Gunes Cire, the fair-haired Turkish engineer. The gasification and solidification plant from CORA Engineering in Switzerland had just been delivered aboard three C-130 transport aircraft. Khan also revealed that he had sent team member Javid Mirza to the US, where he "had gone to get the training for the control room of the air conditioner plant."[13] Referring to the Kahuta buildings by a numbering system devised by Brigadier Sajawal, Khan continued: "Now he will finish the control room of '54.'"[14]

Again, Khan asked Aziz to come back to Pakistan, but Aziz could not be prised from Montreal, and so many others proved intransigent that Khan asked General Zia to sanction a series of advertisements to lure them back. Carried in newspapers around the world, they promised large salaries and new homes in Islamabad. Applicants were told to contact their local Pakistan embassy and say they were applying for work at the Institute of Industrial Automation (IIA) in Islamabad, the same address used by Khan for component deliveries.[15] "Mention that this is a government department and this is to encourage the industrial progress," Khan advised prospective employees.[16] In his letters to Aziz he asked him to recommend other expatriate Pakistanis, and Aziz duly sent back lists of delegates from conferences he had attended in the US and Canada. Peter Griffin recalled Khan's staffing crisis. "He could only ever offer a meager government salary, but he'd tempt people by saying we'll build you a house that will be yours forever, a pension and travel all paid.[17] Khan fought a continual battle against mediocrity, even among his most senior aides."[18]

But Khan would soon face a more pressing problem. On 8 October 1978 he wrote to Aziz: "Perhaps you must have read in some newspapers that the English government is objecting about the inverters. Work is progressing but the frustration is increasing. It is just like a man who has waited 30 years but cannot wait for a few hours after the marriage ceremony." The British government had finally tripped over Khan's network, but not through diligence. It was envy that exposed the Pakistan connection. Having sent a shipment of twenty inverters to Pakistan, Ernst Piffl had lost the contract after A. Q. Khan suspected he was being cheated on the price. The contract went to Peter Griffin in Swansea, and Piffl blew the whistle, tipping off Frank Allaun, Labor MP for Salford East in northwest England, claiming that the components were being exported to Pakistan's nuclear weapons industry.[19] When Allaun, who was also a renowned peace campaigner, began asking questions in the House of Commons in July 1978, Tony Benn, the minister for energy, announced an inquiry. He froze all further shipments to Pakistan, trapping Khan's inverters in the UK.[20]

The House of Commons inquiry found that the previous December, Piffl had ordered twenty inverters from Emerson Industrial Controls which had been shipped from its factory in Swindon to the Special Works Organization in Rawalpindi. A former Emerson engineer told the inquiry that everyone at the Swindon plant had suspected the inverters were for uranium enrichment but nobody had bothered to stop the shipment as "they were convinced that the Pakistanis would never know how to operate such sophisticated equipment, and that the inverters would all sit in their packing cases until they rusted away."[21] Only after the first boxes reached Kahuta in August 1978 and Khan's technicians sent a telex requesting sophisticated modifications did Emerson realize it had underestimated its customers.

Khan's worries about the hold-up would soon be aggravated. Although the Benn inquiry concluded that Piffl's shipment was legal, as inverters were not on the UK's export control list, in November 1979 high-frequency inverters were added to the UK list of products requiring export licenses, Tony Benn conceding: "We acted in a way that was right and proper. But I have a sort of feeling it wasn't effective, and that what President [sic] Bhutto began and President Zia continued is going to be, if it isn't already, a nuclear weapon in Pakistan."[22]

The export control amendments would make it far harder for anyone to trade with Khan from the UK. Peter Griffin, who had made inquiries with Emerson about two more shipments of inverters after he won the contract off Piffl, was refused an export license under the new legislation. "It was now impossible to do business without being hassled," Griffin recalled. "I would get my usual telex from Khan and the next day a telex from UK Customs with lists of all the new things going onto the export control list, which co-incidentally were all the things Khan had just asked for. Customs started causing me endless headaches. I told the tax and customs people that I was never curious and never asked questions. I did everything within export control legislation. I was a businessman. I never sold a bullet, never sold anything that would kill anyone. When the Brits tried to appeal to my better nature and said, 'This is nuclear stuff that you're contributing to,' I said, 'As far as I am concerned A. Q. Khan's work is for peaceful purposes only and I believe that all countries have an unalienable right to pursue nuclear technology for peaceful purposes. I'll stop just as soon as you stop selling small arms, handcuffs and torture equipment to African countries.'" From now on this would be Griffin's justification for all the work he would do for Khan.

The authorities were unimpressed and Griffin was a marked man. "I had my banking facilities curtailed, the taxman constantly reassessed me, the police stopped me, trying to do me for speeding and drink-driving." Griffin claimed that when he refused to cooperate, the security service MI5 offered him a payment of £50,000. He told them his "integrity was not for sale."[23] But while Griffin declined to play along, others readily agreed. "One of Khan's computer guys was turned when he was negotiating with a British mainframe computer supplier," Griffin recalled. "I'd introduced Khan to the company that was run by an Irishman and his business partner from Essex, who had a Bentley and a private plane. Khan sent over his computer guy to do the business and one day this man was admiring the Bentley when the Essex businessman said, 'You can have one just like it if you agree to work for the British.'" Khan heard the same story too. In 1980 he sacked the "computer guy."

Things were so hot in Britain that Griffin and Abdus Salam decided to move, not just out of their old neighborhoods, but out of Europe. "Salam said to me, let's go to Dubai, a free-trade zone," remembered Griffin. "UK exports to Dubai were not so heavily watched and from there could go anywhere. Salam said he would do it only if he could go to Dubai first, leaving me in the UK to arrange stuff."

Pakistan was not a happy place to be. It was jittery and cantankerous, jangled nerves heightened by the appearance before the supreme court in December 1978 of a haunted-looking Zulfikar Ali Bhutto.[24] Even the stony-faced General Arif was moved and recalled: "The trial of the former PM on the charge of murder was a shameful stigma. The image of the country was at stake."[25] Bhutto used his court appearances once again to accuse the US of interference, but even then he made no mention of Khan or the secret enrichment program. His patriotism would not save him.

On 2 February 1979 the supreme court rejected Bhutto's appeal, despite a request for clemency from President Jimmy Carter. That day Khan wrote to Aziz, in Canada, the only letter in which he referred to his former patron: "[I] have heard that soon there will be a decision of Mr. Bhutto's case. There is some mistrust and apprehension in the air. May God have mercy on this country." Then Khan revealed another sensational breakthrough: he was attempting to link several centrifuges together for the first time, creating a mini-cascade, a gateway to increasing the enrichment of uranium towards weapons grade.[26] Work on the big plant was also speeding up, with the main laboratory buildings, centrifuge hall B-1 and administration block almost finished. "We hope by April many groups [of centrifuges] would be transferred there," he wrote, if he could get more staff. "It is the bad luck of this country that people do not want to stay here. When one leaves he does not want to come back."[27]

By the end of March, his centrifuge cascades up and running, Khan was desperate for a regular supply of UF_6. Referring to the German uranium conversion plant that would guarantee this, but still had not arrived, Khan wrote, using his unsubtle "Operation Butter Factory" code: "By the end of the year the factory should start working, and should start providing 'cake and bread.' Here there is a shortage of 'food' and we need these things very badly." On 28 March 1979, Khan enjoyed the last day of his life that he would spend in relative obscurity. That night Zweites Deutsches Fernsehen (ZDF), a West German television channel, broadcast a documentary unmasking Abdul Qadeer Khan as the head of Pakistan's nuclear weapons program, which was being built using centrifuge blueprints stolen from a Dutch plant at Almelo. The story exploded in Europe and North America, forcing the Dutch government to launch an investigation.

Facing the prospect of having to flail itself in public for having ignored every stage of Khan's infiltration and thefts, the Dutch government decided instead on a cover-up. A confidential Ministry of Economic Affairs memo warned: "It is of the highest priority [to claim] that from the Netherlands, there is not a single contribution to the Pakistani effort."[28] In private, every responsible party passed the buck. URENCO blamed FDO for hiring Khan. FDO blamed UCN for giving him access to a plant that should have been off-limits. It also blamed the Ministry of Economic Affairs for approving his security clearance and lashed out at Khan's former colleagues and tutors for writing him references. But even as the Dutch inquiry got under way, an FDO sales manager was in Islamabad as a guest of Khan.[29]

No one was surprised when an interim report concluded in May 1979 that Khan had had access only to "non-essential aspects of [URENCO's] centrifuge technology and research."[30] Those who attempted to describe whatever Khan had done as a scandal were pummelled. Frits Veerman was taken into custody, interrogated by the Dutch secret police (BVD) and warned: "You may not talk about this any more. It is not your problem. It is dangerous for Holland."[31] However, a second, classified inquiry into the Khan affair reported a starkly different damage assessment. The BVD informed ministers that Khan had been stealing data for months before he left Holland in December 1975 and had probably obtained all the designs for both the CNOR and the G-2 centrifuges. This inquiry also revealed one more disaster, which until then had not been known by anyone outside the consortium: that URENCO scientists had been working on a successor to the sophisticated G-2, a super-centrifuge known as the 4-M, and that its blueprint was also likely to be in Pakistan.[32]

Britain and Germany, Holland's partners in the URENCO consortium, were livid. Both wanted to know why The Hague had not alerted them in 1975 when suspicions had first been raised by Frits Veerman, or in 1976 when Khan had written to FDO staff for technical information, or in 1977 when FDO contractors in Holland were known to have sold Khan components for the discontinued CNOR. Israel, too, demanded answers. It had most to fear from an Islamic bomb. Prime minister Menachim Begin had already sent his Dutch counterpart a letter in January 1979 setting out the consequences for Israel of a nuclear Pakistan, Iran and even possibly Libya, asking for a full account of the scandal, but all he had received back was a vague promise of more information soon.[33] In Washington, the White House distrusted everything connected to the BVD. President Carter junked the Dutch inquiry papers he had been sent and ordered the CIA to carry out its own assessment of how and when, but mostly what had been stolen by Khan.

In Islamabad the furor had done little to slow down Kahuta's progress. In late March 1979, Khan was called to brief Zia and brought with him a ten-page letter in which he argued that Zia should commute Bhutto's death sentence. He had stayed up half the previous night preparing it.[34]

Zia discarded it. Having seen to it that Bhutto was convicted for a crime he almost certainly did not commit, Zia knew that if he let the wily ex-prime minister live, he would find some way to exact his retribution. Days later General Arif began coordinating the execution, scheduled for the early hours of 3 April.[35] Only the weather intervened. A forecast indicated that high winds would prevent the military from flying Bhutto's body from Rawalpindi jail to the family burial plot at Larkana, in Sindh, and he was given one more day to live. On the morning of 3 April, Benazir and her mother Nusrat were brought to Rawalpindi for a final meeting. "Mr. Bhutto put up a brave face," said Arif. "Begum Nusrat Bhutto remained tense but calm. Miss Benazir broke down. She sobbed and wept. Benazir Bhutto recalled that her father beseeched her to leave the country. She reached through the prison bars: "I remember grasping his hands and saying, 'No, papa, I will continue the struggle that you began for democracy.' "[36]

On the evening of 3 April the prison superintendent went to the cell. He found Bhutto sitting on the floor. He asked for a pen and paper and for a shaving kit. "Apparently he said he did not want to die like a bearded mullah," Arif said. "He kept scribbling on a piece of paper between 8.15 p.m. and 9.40 p.m. He appeared mentally preoccupied and disturbed. He started arranging and rearranging his things on the table. At 9.55 p.m. he brushed his teeth. At 10 p.m. he started sweeping his cell." But shortly after 11 p.m. Bhutto lay on his bed. At 1.45 a.m. on the morning of 4 April 1979 he was carried from his bed to the jail "hang-house." A noose was placed around his neck and a hood over his head. General Arif said: "As the clock struck two, the lever was pulled. A few minutes later the doctor on duty pronounced Mr. Bhutto dead. May God bless his soul."[37]

When an expatriate Indian working at a printing press in London in April 1979 began reading material he was typesetting he became intrigued. It appeared to have been written by Zulfikar Ali Bhutto in his death cell and yet, according to the London newspapers, Bhutto had been hanged only days before. The wad of handwritten papers, 300 pages long, must have been smuggled out of Pakistan in a hurry and the Indian typesetter contacted a friend, who sought out another, who informed the Indian high commission in London, which passed the information to its intelligence branch, known as RAW, the Research and Analysis Wing, equivalent to Britain's MI6. RAW's London station immediately arranged for a copy of the manuscript to be forwarded to New Delhi, where it landed on the desk of Giresh Saxena, then a high-ranking RAW analyst.[38] "Sometimes a nugget of gold just falls into your lap," Saxena recalled, with a wry smile, about the discovery that the London typesetter's document was a secret jailhouse testimony titled "If I Am Assassinated" penned by Bhutto, in English, "with the paper resting on my knees."[39]

Before Zia hanged Bhutto, the general had published a series of "White Papers" that denounced the former prime minister's public record and contained dubious evidence concerning the murder charges against him—a kind of public relations exercise that also convinced the supreme court to set aside Bhutto's appeal against his death sentence. Until the manuscript reached Saxena, no one knew that Bhutto had replied to the charges in such detail. Smuggled out of Rawalpindi district jail the manuscript began: "I am confined in a death cell and have no access to the material needed for effectively refuting the false and scandalous allegations in the White Papers. But nevertheless, with all my limitations, I have attempted a reply to the same in the following paragraphs to keep the record straight."

Saxena skimmed over Bhutto's response until he reached an account of the legacy for which Bhutto believed he would always be remembered. The former prime minister wrote: "We were on the threshold of full nuclear capability when I left the government to come to this death cell. We know that Israel and South Africa have full nuclear capability. The Christian, Jewish and Hindu civilizations have this capability. The Communist powers also possess it. Only the Islamic civilization was without it, but that position was about to change ... What difference does my life make now when I can imagine eighty million of my countrymen standing under the nuclear cloud of a defenseless sky."[40]

The Indians already knew that Pakistan was nuclear-bound but Saxena came across a more oblique reference that intrigued him. Bhutto wrote: "My single most important achievement which I believe will dominate the portrait of my public life is an agreement which I arrived at after an assiduous and tenacious endeavor spanning over eleven years of negotiations. In the present context, the agreement of mine, concluded in June 1976, will perhaps be my greatest achievement and contribution to the survival of our people and our nation."

Saxena and analysts at RAW and in the Indian defense and foreign ministries debated what Bhutto could have meant. Given that in his manuscript Bhutto had underscored the significance of Pakistan's nuclear program, he was, the Indians thought, undoubtedly referring to an agreement with a country that had backed it. India had puzzled over Pakistan's enrichment project. Saxena recalled: "We knew the technology had come from Europe and had been watching Khan since 1976, but who on earth would feed Pakistan the know-how to build the bomb, the designs, the missile technology? Who would assist with the major and complex Kahuta infrastructure? Remember they had nothing. They could not do it alone." India was certain that money had come only from the Gulf states and that the Soviets were not involved. "The Soviets were arming us," said Saxena. Initially they considered Bhutto was talking about France and the deal over the reprocessing plant. But that agreement had been signed on 17 March 1976, so Bhutto was clearly referring to something else.

Bhutto's "eleven years of negotiations" meant these mysterious talks had begun around 1965. This was the year of the first Indo-Pakistan war and the moment when India had been caught removing spent fuel rods from its unauthorized plutonium reprocessing facility at Trombay, near Bombay, an event that prompted the international community to suspect that it was building a plutonium bomb. It was also the year in which Pakistan had its US military aid suspended and Bhutto declared his people would be willing to "eat grass" if that would enable them to get a nuclear bomb of their own. Also that year, Pakistan and China had signed their first trade agreement and China had supported Pakistan in its war with India over Kashmir. "Suddenly the penny dropped," said Saxena. "Bhutto's 'single most important achievement' was convincing China to help Pakistan build the bomb."

The man who had negotiated Pakistan's special relationship with China was diplomat Agha Shahi. He confirmed that Saxena's deduction was correct: "1965 was critical for us," he recalled.[41] "We made a pact with Beijing that ushered in decades of assistance we could not have got elsewhere."[42] In 1971, Pakistan and China became even closer when Shahi led calls for the People's Republic to win a seat at the UN Security Council, where Chiang Kai-shek was the US-backed sitting representative of the Chinese people even though he had been exiled to Taiwan. Shahi, then Pakistan's ambassador to the United Nations, said: "We formed a steering committee of thirteen countries. On the eve of the debate George H. W. Bush, who was US ambassador to the UN, came to me and said, 'Agha, don't kick out Chiang Kai-shek.' I sent a cable to our ambassador in Beijing, saying, 'Look, it's touch and go, some people are recognizing the People's Republic, some are sticking with Taiwan. Tell the Beijing delegates to step up the diplomatic lobby.'" The following day Shahi's side won the vote and the People's Republic of China joined the UN for the first time.[43]

When Pakistan went to war with India later that year over East Pakistan, China came out in support of Islamabad, massing troops on India's border at Sikkim, only stepping back when New Delhi threatened to bomb China's nuclear weapons facility at Lop Nor. The following year, Bhutto came to power and immediately signed a series of assistance agreements that made China the principal source of military equipment for Pakistan, a deal that was augmented in May 1976 when Bhutto, accompanied by high-level scientific and military delegations, visited Beijing.

Shahi recalled how the two countries talked about nuclear cooperation. First,

China offered to take over the care of the KANUPP nuclear reactor in Karachi which the Canadians had built in the 1960s but were refusing to maintain due to US pressure. By 1976, the reactor was barely functioning and US intelligence spotted Chinese technicians arriving at the plant soon after Bhutto returned from Beijing. But it did not stop there. Around this time China also agreed to supply UF_6.[44] Back then, Pakistan did not have its own UF_6 production facility and Khan's progress had been hindered in June 1977 when the US, which supplied the UF_6, had threatened to cut off Islamabad. If China had not stepped in, the whole project would have stalled. It was the beginning of a close working relationship with one of the few countries in the world that also had a uranium enrichment program.[45] Shahi revealed that the Chinese also provided tritium, an isotope that could substantially boost the power of a nuclear device, to Pakistan, as well as designs for the device itself and for a nuclear-capable missile. Shahi concluded: "China's support of Pakistan was a deliberate act of sabotage, undermining the value of the Nuclear Non-Proliferation Treaty (that Beijing declined to sign)." The other declared nuclear powers agreed.[46]

General K. M. Arif also recalled the special relationship.[47] "Outwardly we are very different. They are a godless society with no free market or elections. But I cannot think of a single incident over the last fifty years where China interfered in the internal politics of Pakistan or vice versa. China gave freely with no strings. No money was paid for this assistance until President Zia went to China in 1977 and said, 'We are grateful but we should be charged.' China said, 'No, Mr. President, we cannot forget the assistance you gave us when we were out of the UN. We were alone and you helped us.' "[48]

Around the world Kahuta was infamous. On 25 April 1979, Khan's friend in Montreal wrote to say he was avidly reading about Project 706 in the Canadian newspapers. "There is lots of commotion over here, and all the reporters are making lots of propaganda," said Aziz, adding that much of it was so fanciful it read like "the adventures of Sinbad." Aziz enclosed material he had obtained about electrical components available from Motorola, Westinghouse and Union Carbide and, in a reference to Khan's soon-to-arrive German-supplied UF_6 plant, he signed off: "Hopefully the 'butter factory' will start soon."

In his reply, on 4 June 1979, A. Q. Khan seemed overwhelmed by media interest. "My God there is no limit to their tremendous distortion. The whole world is after us ... but at least we have one satisfaction, that from one end of the world to the other we have made people sleepless and have made their lives miserable," he wrote. However, the publicity was now affecting his ability to work. British and American suppliers had cancelled contracts and the US Congress had reimposed sanctions on Pakistan two days after Bhutto was hanged, finally triggering the Symington amendment which barred aid to countries illicitly enriching uranium.[49] "We are sorry because we needed only six more months," wrote Khan, feeling the pinch.

But Khan had a plan B. Sensing a time when foreign parts would dry up altogether, he had been ingenious, fitting out machine shops at Kahuta to reverse-engineer centrifuge components based on the ones he had already bought in Europe, using design molds provided by his European contractors. Although China could help with raw materials, bomb and missile designs, its uranium enrichment program was based on diffusion, completely different from centrifuge technology, in which it had no expertise. Khan was already on the road to self-sufficiency with a state-of-the-art centrifuge production line and looking forward to the time when Pakistan could even become a supplier. "Afterwards we will sell these things to [North America] and will also obtain your services and will earn the foreign exchange because our price will be half the price from your side," he wrote to Aziz.

Aziz wrote back three weeks later, joking that Khan and his team were now so well known that he half expected to see them featured in *Playboy*. "You are famous all over the world." He reported that Khan's project was being debated in the US Senate. "Up until now these people had no idea that [talented] people live in Pakistan. Anyhow they will realise it very shortly. The Assistant Secretary [Thomas] Pickering was ... being televised [speaking at the US Senate]. During the questioning he seemed quite disappointed [about Pakistan's progress], and said, 'We can't stop it ... it is no use crying over spilt milk.' "

In reality, the Carter administration was juggling a crisis in the Middle East and South Asia that made slowing down Pakistan's nuclear capability all the more difficult. A Moscow-backed coup had brought a Communist government to power in Afghanistan in August 1978, with the Soviets emerging as influential and ambitious in a region in which they already counted India as a key Kremlin ally. Pakistan urged the US to intervene, but although President

Carter approved a modest propaganda offensive, and saw to it that money was released for psychological operations—also authorizing the CIA to aid the local mujahideen, warlike Pashtun tribesmen on the Afghan–Pakistan border, who were to be better trained and armed in order to make hit-and-run strikes against the Soviet-backed government—Washington was reluctant to wade into a fully fledged war so soon after extricating itself from Vietnam.[50]

The US was also distracted by events unfolding in neighboring Iran, where revolution had just been declared and Shah Mohammad Reza Pahlavi forced into exile and replaced by a Shi'ite fundamentalist cleric, Ayatollah Khomeini, in February 1979.[51] The revolution seriously panicked Islamabad too. Although the Pakistanis had had no love for the shah, despising his imperial pretensions, and little respect for his US-trained and equipped military, General Zia knew that what had replaced him was far worse. Khomeini disliked and distrusted Zia and had been particularly shocked by his execution of Zulfikar Ali Bhutto, Pakistan's prime minister, whose wife was a Shia. As worrying for Zia was the prospect of Pakistan's Shias, who made up a fifth of the population and were emboldened by Khomeini's rise to power, refusing to abide by a whole host of military-sponsored Sunni laws and regulations recently introduced to pave the way for the "Islamization" of Pakistan.[52]

Pakistan and the US found common cause when, as one of his first acts, Khomeini closed down two US listening stations in northern Iran, knocking out Washington's most important intelligence collection points for the entire region.[53] Blind and threatened, the US began discussing with Pakistan its taking a more active role in Afghanistan, and Pakistan agreed to become America's new eyes and ears in the region.

To balance the equation and plot a course to get Pakistan to roll back its nuclear program, President Carter brought out of retirement Gerard C. Smith, a Yale-educated intellectual heavyweight who had been Eisenhower's director of policy planning and Nixon's non-proliferation chief. In 1969 he had headed the US delegation at the US–Soviet Strategic Arms Limitation Talks in Helsinki, which had led to the Anti-Ballistic Missile Treaty signed by Nixon and Brezhnev in May 1972. With a reputation for finding ways out of sticky situations, Smith was charged with leading a low-key operation to investigate the activities of Khan, while not unsettling Zia. Robert Gallucci at the State Department would assist him.

Gallucci, who had already been tracking Pakistan's nuclear ambitions for three years, set to work gathering every piece of intelligence on the enrichment program, ready to brief IAEA director Sigvard Eklund at the next board meeting, in Vienna in June 1979. His report would also form the basis of an intelligence estimate that would help the White House decide how to deal with Kahuta—if it was forced to go it alone. The results of Gallucci's initial trawl were shocking and confirmed the need for sensitivity and speed. Gallucci discovered what Khan had been describing in private correspondence to Aziz in Montreal. By working in the margins of the IAEA trigger-list, taking advantage of the world's ignorance about centrifuge technology and slack export controls in Europe and North America, Khan had been able to import virtually every piece of kit Pakistan needed for a fully functioning uranium enrichment plant, even down to manufacturing its own spare parts.

"Khan had done it so quickly that everyone was trying to catch up," remembered Gallucci.[54] "I first heard of Pakistan enrichment in January 1978 when I became a division chief at the State Department's Bureau of Intelligence and Research. By the time I moved down the corridor to policy planning the following year, Khan was virtually self-sufficient." Gallucci was asked to put together a color-coded diagram showing what a Pakistani centrifuge looked like and where each part had come from. "The levels of collusion and professed ignorance among European companies was staggering. Some even had staff based at Kahuta." Even while the Dutch inter-ministerial inquiry had been under way, the Pakistanis had continued placing orders for Dutch components, including steel tubing from Van Doorne Transmissie, which attempted to export the shipment in July 1979.[55]

Acting as Carter's junkyard dog, Smith flew to Vienna and delivered a blunt message to Sigvard Eklund, a sanitized account of which "emphasized the extreme sensitivity of the information."[56] A few weeks previously, Gallucci had flown to Islamabad, borrowed a car from the US embassy pound and attempted to drive to Kahuta. When challenged by Pakistani security officials, Gallucci revived the old picnic spot story. The officials were not amused and Gallucci was sent packing, but not before he had taken a few photographs, which he showed to Eklund. The IAEA director said he was deeply shocked to learn of such extensive facilities already built, although he admitted having received several warning signals, including a recent approach from a Dutch URENCO engineer who had shown the IAEA a photocopy of a large Pakistani order for maraging steel, an alloy so strong and expensive that it was used almost always for jet plane engines and centrifuges.[57] Inexplicably, the IAEA had ignored it.

Perhaps the shame of publicity would halt Pakistan, Eklund now argued.[58] The Americans balked. Relations with Pakistan were tense and Smith wanted everything kept under wraps while they decided how to confront General Zia. When Eklund asked Smith if he could discuss the evidence with anyone else, Smith said no. When they met again to discuss Pakistan two days later, Smith persuaded the IAEA to keep quiet with assurances that Pakistan was still years off configuring a nuclear device.[59] Smith was performing a high-wire act: containing Pakistan's program in such a way that other arms of government back home could still continue to woo the Pakistani military.

Within weeks, Kahuta was front-page news anyway, after two Western diplomats were beaten up for straying too close to the enrichment plant. Pol le Gourrierec, the French ambassador, and Jean Forlot, his first secretary, had decided to follow Gallucci's lead and take a look for themselves. This time the Pakistani security guards had not reacted so politely.[60] For twenty-four hours General Zia said nothing, before contacting the French government and wryly advising them that "the incident might not have taken place had the ambassador been flying the French flag from the bonnet of the car." Exasperated, the French responded pettily by refusing to invite Zia to a forthcoming Bastille Day celebration, and as a sign of solidarity the Yugoslav ambassador protested "by taking his official car—flying the flag—up the Kahuta road and driving extremely slowly past the wall protecting the large construction site."[61] The score-settling theatricals belied the scale of the unfolding crisis.

All imports now ceased. "They are even stopping nails and screws," wrote a frustrated Khan to Aziz.[62] But thanks to Khan's ingenuity, it did not matter much as "we are making the inverters and transformers ourselves." Having been identified as the ringmaster in Pakistan's nuclear operation, Khan also resumed his habit of writing angry letters to European newspapers and magazines. "I want to question the bloody holier-than-thou attitudes of the Americans and the British," he railed in one. "These bastards are God-appointed guardians of the world to stockpile hundreds of thousands of nuclear warheads and have the God-given authority of carrying out explosions every month. But if we start a modest program, we are the Satans, the devils."[63]

But Washington saw nothing modest in Kahuta. The president's General Advisory Committee on Arms Control and Disarmament, a high-level body of former officials, scientific experts and military officials appointed to come up with non-proliferation initiatives, began considering a tough stance on Pakistan. Charles van Doren, its assistant director, warned: "We see the makings, and quite a bit more than the makings, of another Indian [nuclear test] disaster coming up. This is a railroad train that is going down the track very fast, and I am not sure anything will turn it off."[64] Although the US had tightened up export controls and slammed suppliers for selling to Pakistan, van Doren concluded: "We may be a little late."

General Brent Scowcroft, who had served as national security adviser to President Gerald Ford, raised a controversial proposal. Although his words were redacted from the declassified file, some of those at the meeting recalled that Scowcroft recommended a military strike on Kahuta. Gerard Smith had suggested as much before he flew to Vienna, and the CIA had learned that a similar assault was also being considered by Israel.

Although no decision was taken, when the *New York Times* quoted a White House official as saying that sabotage or a commando raid were being considered as options to prevent Pakistan from exploding a bomb, Pakistan air force MiG-19 and Mirage fighters were scrambled over Islamabad, while Kahuta was ringed with French-supplied Crotale missiles and anti-aircraft guns.[65] Days later, on 14 August, Aziz wrote to Khan from Montreal to report another debacle. Pakistani scientists living in the US and Canada had been accused of supplying materials to Khan and were under investigation.[66] Khan replied immediately. He was furious. "The way they are after us, it looks as if we have killed their mother." The pressure was getting to him.

In October 1979, Gerard Smith called for one last diplomatic offensive. Pakistan's foreign minister, Agha Shahi, and General K. M. Arif had been invited to Washington and Smith proposed to sandbag them. Agha Shahi was expecting a warm welcome, convinced that the Afghan coup and the fall of the shah had increased Pakistan's leverage. But as soon as he and Arif arrived, he realized that all the Americans wanted to talk about was Pakistan's nuclear program.

Shahi met first with President Carter and then with Carter's hard-nosed national security adviser, Zbigniew Brzezinski. "I said to him, you are so against proliferation and India has blown up the bomb, so why not give a guarantee to non-nuclear states that they would be subject to a Security Council nuclear umbrella?" Shahi recalled.[67] It was the same request Kissinger had refused point-blank in 1974, and Shahi fared no better. "So, then we had the big meeting," Shahi said. "On one side of the table there was me, General Arif, Sahabzada Yaqub Khan, our Washington ambassador, and General Jilani, our secretary general for defense. On the US side was Cyrus Vance, the secretary of state, Warren Christopher, his deputy, and more than ten CIA people. I turned to Yaqub Khan and said, 'They must think we are the Soviet Union.' "

Christopher did most of the talking, Shahi recalled. "He told me he wanted Pakistan to sign the NPT [Nuclear Non-Proliferation Treaty]. I said we would sign gladly if India signed. He said, 'You must sign anyway.' I said, 'No. India poses a nuclear and conventional threat to us.' Christopher said, 'We want you to give a commitment that you will not transfer this technology to another country.' I said, 'We can give this guarantee.' He said, 'You must commit not to carry out a nuclear explosion.' I said, 'To be frank we have not reached that state of capability but if and when we do, we will consider the pros and cons.' "

Cyrus Vance stood and led Shahi into a side room, where he was introduced to Gerard Smith. "I was totally shocked. He was the most formidable US negotiator. Smith said to me, 'You think you are improving your security but you have no idea how far ahead the Indians are. They can utterly destroy you. Do you know you are entering the valley of death?' I was taken aback. I said, 'Mr. Smith, I am at a great disadvantage talking to you, as you are the foremost expert on nuclear weapons. But it seems to me you don't have to be a nuclear weapons expert to understand the strategic importance of having one. The value lies in its possession, sir, and not in its use.' " A terrible silence descended upon the room.

Within days all thoughts of containing the nuclear crisis in Pakistan were eclipsed. Iranian students had stormed the gates of the US embassy in Tehran and taken sixty-six Americans hostage.[68] The initial plan had been to occupy it for three days and issue a series of communiqués that would explain Iran's grievances against America.[69] But after a week, the hostages were paraded at the gate, blindfolded and shackled. Despite the release of thirteen female and African-American hostages on 19 and 20 November, the crisis looked set in. Then, after false rumors spread around the Islamic world that Israel and the US had seized the Grand Mosque in Mecca, America was attacked again, this time in Pakistan. On 21 November, supporters of the Islamic group Jamaat-e-Islami besieged the US embassy compound in Islamabad. A mob burned it to the ground, with the loss of four lives. Similar attempts were made to break into the US consulate in Karachi. Weeks later, the US embassy in Tripoli was also raided, but this time US Marines forced the attackers back.

Although the US embassy incident left relations severely bruised, Pakistan was virtually the only ally the US had left in the region. Agha Shahi un-expectedly received a call from Kurt Waldheim, UN secretary general, asking for Pakistan's help in resolving the hostage crisis. Shahi had already met Khomeini in March, a month after his return, and agreed to make a second trip. Alone in Tehran, Shahi reminded the ayatollah that Pakistan was the first country to recognize the Iranian revolution, "but all your friends think the hostage taking is against the law. Khomeini said, 'You say the US prisoners are hostages and diplomats but let me tell you they are all spies.' I pleaded, 'Please meet Mr. Waldheim.' Khomeini said, 'You should see the graves of our martyrs.' "

That night Shahi's negotiations were interrupted when Hashemi Rafsanjani, the new leader of the Iranian legislature, came to see him at the Royal Tehran Hilton and gave him a Reuters report stating the Soviets were mounting an invasion of Afghanistan. "I was shocked. I said to him, 'A Muslim country is being swallowed by the Iron Curtain.' " A KGB team dressed in Afghan army uniforms had attacked the presidential palace and shot prime minister Hafizullah Amin and his mistress in a bar on the top floor.[70] Shahi had been scheduled to be in Kabul at a meeting with Amin but a snowstorm had forced a postponement and the phone call from Waldheim had sent him to Tehran instead. Now he caught the first plane back to Islamabad as 85,000 Soviet soldiers converged on Kabul.[71]

Washington considered its options. Sitting back and letting Zia deal with the Afghan situation was no longer one of them. The Soviet expansionism that had engulfed Afghanistan might now gobble up its neighbors in South Asia and the Middle East. The CIA had picked up rumors that Iran was next. Brzezinski argued that Moscow had to be stopped. But as the American people would not support a US-led ground invasion post-Vietnam, he recommended fighting a proxy war through the Afghan rebels.

Properly to arm a guerrilla war out of sight of the Soviet Union (lest it become enraged and invade Pakistan too) would require Islamabad's cooperation in order to establish a secure corridor for US munitions to pass from the Persian Gulf, up through Pakistan to the Northwest Frontier Province and into the Khyber Pass. It would necessitate the full support of Pakistan's ISI, which reigned along the porous Afghan border, where the distinction between Afghan and Pakistani tribesmen blurred, so as to get the munitions to the mujahideen fighters. Most importantly, it would also require a vast injection of US funding.

But there was a serious problem. Brzezinski spelled it out in a classified memo to the president. "To make the above possible we must both reassure Pakistan and encourage it to help the rebels. This will require a review of our policy toward Pakistan, more guarantees to it, more arms aid, and, alas, a decision that our security policy toward Pakistan cannot be dictated by our non-proliferation policy."[72] It was a radical recommendation. Brzezinski was advocating that Carter drop his commitment to non-proliferation, a core policy that had helped get him elected. He would have to jettison it if he wanted to go to war in Afghanistan. To date, US funding of the Afghan resistance had been piecemeal—no more than $500,000—and came out of the annual CIA budget. The cash was delivered to Islamabad in the diplomatic bag and handed over to the Pakistanis by the CIA's station chief without Congress getting involved. But the large cash sums now being considered would have to be approved by Congress, and it had recently accused Pakistan of enriching uranium, invoked the Symington amendment and barred all US economic and military aid. The president was going to have break US law.

In Pakistan, Khan continued to wage a war of his own. Responding to an article in London's *Observer* about his theft of URENCO technology from Holland, he wrote to the newspaper's editor, Donald Trelford, in July 1980. "The article on Pakistan by Colin Smith and Shyam Bhatia was so vulgar and low that I considered it an insult to reflect on it." However, he managed to pull himself together sufficiently to write the letter. "It was in short words, a bullshit, full of lies, insinuations, and cheap journalism ... Shyam Bhatia, a Hindu bastard, could not write anything objective about Pakistan. Both insinuated as if Holland is an atomic bomb manufacturing factory where, instead of cheese balls, you could pick up triggering mechanisms. Have you for a moment thought of the meaning of this word? Of course not, because you could not differentiate between the mouth and back hole of a donkey."[73]

4

PEANUTS

In January 1980, the US president revealed the bare bones of his Pakistan deal. "We will provide military equipment, food and other assistance to help Pakistan defend its independence and national security against the seriously increased threat from the north," he said.[1] The lobbying had begun for a new US–Pakistan relationship and the president used his State of the Union address later that month to float the "Carter Doctrine," a policy that defined his late-found anti-Soviet credentials. "The US will take action consistent with our laws to assist Pakistan and resist any outside aggression," Carter said, mindful of Symington.[2] A Soviet attack on any part of the Persian Gulf region would be regarded as an attack on US vital interests.

Carter's thinking had jelled after listening to his National Security Council and the CIA, for whom Afghanistan was only a part of the broader Soviet game plan. An eyes-only memo from Stansfield Turner, the CIA director, reported that the Soviets "covet a larger sphere of influence in southwest Asia" and "a pro-Soviet Iran." The occupation of Kabul had enabled Moscow to place its forces on Iran's east and northern borders at a time when Iran "may be on the brink of political, social and economic chaos." Turner advised that the Afghan occupation brought Moscow within a hair's breadth of Iranian oil reserves.[3]

However, US law remained an obstacle to positioning the US closer to Pakistan and when both the Senate foreign relations committee and the House foreign affairs committee demanded to be brought into the discussion, the National Security Council, State and Defense Departments debated whether the new aid-for-munitions package could be disguised as debt relief, Afghan refugee assistance, or even channelled through a friendly Islamic country like Saudi Arabia.

Such an overt lie was indefensible, Carter argued, and he decided to proceed more subtly, seeking a waiver to the Symington amendment (and another amendment introduced by Senator John Glenn in 1977 barring any country from receiving US aid if it conducted a nuclear explosion) by certifying that Pakistan posed no known nuclear threat. Even this was tricky. Officials had already warned Warren Christopher, the deputy secretary of state, in a classified briefing that the US had considerable knowledge about Kahuta and A. Q. Khan. "Certification that we had received 'reliable assurances' from Pakistan that it was not constructing nuclear weapons would be extremely difficult to justify on the basis of information available to us. We must bear in mind that a waiver would cause the president extreme embarrassment if Pakistan subsequently exploded a device."[4]

As well as the US having to cover for Pakistan's nuclear program, General Zia was playing up. Moscow's intervention in Afghanistan had brought him back into the fold, and with his human rights record, his nuclear intent and the execution of Zulfikar Ali Bhutto all but forgotten, he was making the most of his moment. Zia argued about every last detail of the proposed US deal, insisting that a war in Afghanistan would cost far more than the US was proposing to spend and that Pakistan be placed in overall control.[5] Turning down Zia's demands for a face-to-face meeting, Carter asked Warren Christopher to attempt to clear the logjam by meeting Agha Shahi, Pakistan's foreign minister, who was due in New York for a special session of the United Nations General Assembly on Afghanistan.[6] Shahi was to be softened up before a White House session with President Carter on 9 January, in which Pakistan was offered $400 million, in military and economic assistance, to be spread over two years. The deal would include military hardware transfers worth $90 million, including "two or three Lockheed L100 Super Hercules transporters, six Chinook helicopters, six TPS-43 air defense radar, 10,000 rounds for Howitzer field-guns and 200 night vision devices," followed by ten more Chinooks and 200 armored personnel carriers a year later.[7] US newspapers reported that Pakistan could not believe its luck.

They were speculative. The truth for a military man like Zia was that there was nothing here that he needed. Pakistan required an advanced jet fighter that could take on Russian MiGs, rather than troop carriers which would be useless in the Afghan desert and at high altitude in the country's Tora Bora mountains. The Americans had turned down a specific request from Islamabad for advanced F-16 fighter aircraft, a weapon for the West that was embargoed for use by NATO powers only.[8] Zia resented being hustled. That was his specialty. He told journalists in Islamabad that he was not ready to sign any deal until Washington could "prove its credibility and durability" as an ally, dismissing the $400 million package as "peanuts" (digging at Carter's former career as a peanut farmer).[9] Security was something that Pakistan was not willing to compromise on and could "not be bought for a miserly $400 million," Zia railed. The White House was aghast. It was looking to steal a march on the Soviets within weeks and no one liked the sound of having to build confidence with Pakistan. Such an amorphous process was open-ended and would take as long as Zia wanted it to.

Carter dispatched Brzezinski and Warren Christopher to Islamabad with a sop: the promise of extra covert aid for Pakistan's ISI (to be delivered via the CIA). Before the meeting, Brzezinski flew up to the Khyber Pass, where he was photographed peering down the sights of an AK-47. But the brothers-in-arms photo opportunity failed to engage Zia, who met the Americans flanked by General Arif, Shahi and Ghulam Ishaq Khan, the finance minister. Brzezinski did his best to prick the tension. When the national security adviser inquired of Arthur Hummel, the US ambassador, what status the prickly General Arif held in Pakistan, he was told: "He roughly enjoys the same position as you do in the US administration." Arif recalled: "Dr. Brzezinski smiled wistfully and said, 'In that case he must be an unpopular person.'"[10] But the talks stalled. Brzezinski stressed that an enduring friendship with Pakistan was in the vital interest of the US. However, when President Zia countered, "Can you give us a guaranteed security umbrella that you will aid us unconditionally if we are attacked?" Brzezinski conceded that that was not possible, as "it would have to follow congressional approval and Congress may be against it."[11]

But Arthur Hummel remained confident. After lunch he sent an upbeat telegram to Washington.[12] However, when the meeting reconvened the mood on the Pakistani side was even darker. General Arif said: "What equipment can we buy for $400 million? Five to six aircraft? That's all. It's not possible. Sorry." Arif recalled: "We had a break and the Americans came back and rewrote the agreement, 'Nearly half a billion dollars.' We said, 'Where has this word billion come from? It's only marginally more than the old offer. You can change the words but it makes no difference.'" Even after the US delegation confided that President Carter was willing to waive the Symington and Glenn amendments, Zia remained intransigent. That night he rang up Carter and said, "Mr. President, we cannot make an agreement, as your delegation has a limited brief."[13]

The White House could not afford to give up. Brzezinski flew on to Riyadh to ask the Saudis to match its offer to Pakistan and leverage through the deal. He sought commitments from Japan, China and several Islamic states, as well as the International Monetary Fund and Asian Development Bank.[14] But even while he was lobbying, on 5 March, Zia went cold on the Brzezinski–Christopher package. The US could not be trusted to honor its security commitments, as had been evinced in 1965 when Washington had imposed sanctions on Pakistan in the midst of its war with India over Kashmir, and again in 1971 when it had failed to come to Pakistan's assistance during the disastrous war in East Pakistan. Turning the screw, Zia announced that to hold back the Soviet threat Pakistan would instead seek "political, moral and material support" from the Islamic and non-aligned powers—as well as its time-tested friendship with China.[15]

The deal was slipping away from Washington and then a series of calamitous events sunk the Carter administration's cause. In April 1980 a secret rescue mission to free the American hostages in Iran ended in disaster with the loss of eight American servicemen, who died after a US military helicopter crashed into a US military transport at a rendezvous point in the Iranian desert, failing to make it as far as Tehran, let alone rescue the hostages.[16] When, in May 1980, Carter wrote to Zia, offering to reopen negotiations on an Afghanistan deal "on a private and unpublicized basis," he was greeted with prevarication.[17]

Pakistan was also rocked by external factors. In June 1980 the BBC broadcast a documentary, "Project 706—The Islamic Bomb," the fullest investigation to date into Khan's illicit uranium enrichment program.[18] Days later it was shown in Holland, where Henny happened to be staying with her parents on an annual pilgrimage to renew her Dutch visa. Her recollection of a meeting she had with Dutch immigration officials the following day revealed how the authorities there were oblivious to the growing Khan scandal. "The clerk, after finding out that I came from Pakistan, started discussing the [television] program. He inquired if I knew this Dr. Khan. And before I could answer, he added that Dr. Khan must have earned millions through this game. With difficulty I managed to keep quiet and never gave the impression that I was 'that' Mrs. Khan. At that moment I wished I could tell him that, like any other

Pakistani senior government official, my husband was earning only 3750 rupees [$400] a month."[19] Khan was a wanted man in Holland and his wife should have been a prime asset, if not a lure to force him to return to The Hague. Instead, her passport was stamped and she got back on the plane to Islamabad.

By October, Iran was at war with Iraq, with Zia, who was at that time chairman of the Organization of the Islamic Conference, called on to intercede. He flew to New York on 3 October 1980 to brief the UN General Assembly on talks he had been having with Saddam Hussein, in Iraq, and Abolhassan Bani Sadr, the Iranian president. Carter, facing elections the following month, seized the opportunity for one last attempt to secure a deal. He invited Zia to the White House and offered him F-16s. It was too late. Zia commented flippantly that the matter could wait until after the US presidential campaign was over. With Carter at an all-time low in the ratings, the inference was obvious.[20] The Pakistan president was looking ahead to dealing with Ronald Reagan, who was likely to be a shoe-in at the White House in 1981.

Before the US polls even opened, the Republicans reached out to Pakistan, passing a message that should they get in a sea change would wash over US foreign policy. While he was in New York at the UN in October 1980, Zia received an unexpected call from former president Richard Nixon, who said he wanted to discuss the ongoing Afghanistan crisis. But during the hour-long conversation, Pakistan's nuclear program also came up. General Arif, who was at the meeting, remembered that Nixon made it clear he was in favor of them gaining nuclear weapons capability.[21] He did not say he was acting for Republican challenger Ronald Reagan, but as a former Republican president, his comments signalled the way ahead. Najmuddin Sheikh, then Pakistan's chargé d'affaires in Washington, also noticed the temperature warming when he met Alexander Haig, Reagan's secretary of state designate, at a reception. "Al Haig sidled over, charming as could be," remembered Sheikh. "He said: 'We have had problems, Pakistan and the US. But things are going to change.' "[22]

As soon as he took office, Reagan began broadcasting his intentions to a wider audience. Howard Schaffer, who was running the India desk at the Bureau of Near Eastern and South Asian Affairs in the State Department, recalled: "We knew they would take a very strong line on Afghanistan and therefore chummy up to Pakistan, which was going to be a problem for India.

For the Reagan people there was a willing suspension of disbelief about General Zia."[23] Robert Gates, who had worked in the Carter White House with Brzezinski and was then the CIA's national intelligence officer for the Soviet Union, described the change of guard as somewhere between a hijack and a hostile takeover. The incoming president "orchestrated a comprehensive battle plan to seize control of a city long believed to be in enemy hands. Main force political units, flanked maneuvers, feints, sappers, and psychological warfare all played their part as Reagan and company ... deployed their forces for a political blitzkrieg," Gates remembered.[24]

The Reagan election campaign had promised an end to the growing sense of national weakness as the US came out of Vietnam, the scandal of Watergate and the misery of a downed helicopter at a desert rendezvous point in Iran. The Reaganites, "breathing fire," as Gates recalled it, had lambasted the Carter White House for going soft on Moscow and raised the specter of a nuclear winter emanating from Red Square, creeping over Afghanistan and down into the Persian Gulf, swallowing up the Middle East and all of its oil reserves.[25] This was a critical and emotive trigger. Inflation and interest rates in the US were running at almost 20 percent, unemployment had skyrocketed and, along with much of Western Europe, the US was in recession, largely due to a price hike in crude oil. Reagan broadcast the news that the Soviets were on the march around the world, undermining Western-looking governments and supporting Marxist alternatives from Angola to Afghanistan. His people turned public opinion in favor of expanding spending on defense and intelligence.

Alexander Haig went even further, and the fix he got himself into illustrated the fate of intelligence for the next decade. The new secretary of state announced that the Soviets were behind all international terrorism and had to be stopped. Challenged in Congress and unable to supply any evidence, he asked the CIA to produce a national intelligence estimate. It came back with the broad finding that the Soviets fundamentally disapproved of terrorism and discouraged the killing of innocents, especially by groups they had trained and supported. Haig was in a fix. However, Bill Casey, the new CIA director, knew what to do. He rejected the report and Haig ordered another, this time written by the Defense Intelligence Agency, the military's intelligence arm. It concluded more ambiguously, suggesting that the Soviets were deeply engaged in the support of "revolutionary violence" worldwide.[26] It was the first of many occasions to come when intelligence would be renosed and politicized.

The fact that Casey got the CIA job at all was an indication of what was to come. He was an old Office of Strategic Services agent—a spook from the Second World War—who had never gone back to intelligence, making money instead as a Wall Street lawyer before becoming campaign manager for Reagan's victorious march on the White House. Like many Reaganites, Casey viewed the intelligence establishment as having gone soft on the Soviets under Carter, and he was imposed on the CIA with a view to kicking out what Republicans saw as a liberal Ivy League clique. A little over sixty-eight years old when he was sworn in, Casey was affluent, rigorous and unconventional, a risk taker with little regard for process who, as Robert Gates saw it, wanted to transform the agency into a mace with which to batter Moscow. He acquired a cabinet seat—a first for a CIA chief—and ensured that all other avenues of intelligence destined for the president were diverted, including the National Security Council, with the national security adviser moved into the White House basement.[27]

Next on the list was the State Department's Arms Control and Disarmament Agency (ACDA), whose director was supposed to be the primary adviser to the president on non-proliferation matters. ACDA had tracked Khan and alerted Carter to the full extent of the enrichment program in Kahuta. Now ACDA was decimated, its staffing levels halved and its director kept out of Reagan's way. Richard Barlow, then a student intern straight out of Western Washington University, who would go on to become the premier US intelligence analyst on Pakistan, arrived as the Reagan revolution tore the organization to pieces. "There were grown men crying around me in the office," Barlow recalled.[28]

Alexander Haig had singled out Pakistan as the means by which the US could contain the Soviet threat, with Afghanistan as the theater in which to do it. But the idea was not his own. It came from the US ambassador in Islamabad, Arthur Hummel, who suggested the US offer a dramatic increase in aid.[29] Potentially, it was a golden opportunity. Pakistan was desperate to act against Soviet aggression and the US had a chance to bleed the Soviets without putting troops on the ground. Here was a war the US could win. The only sticking point was Pakistan's nuclear program. The White House came up with an argument. The US would lavish aid on Pakistan and in return a secure Islamic Republic would be less inclined to build a doomsday device. The theory was let loose on Capitol Hill.

Hummel's plan came endorsed by powerful backers, including Prince Turki al-Faisal, son of the king of Saudi Arabia and head of the country's General Intelligence Directorate, who stated that it was both "urgent and important."[30] But that still left a Congress angry at Pakistan and its nuclear deception. No one there had forgotten the unmasking of the Kahuta project in 1978, or how the Pakistan program had been built taking advantage of Western equipment, technology and goodwill. Congressional and bureaucratic attitudes had to be realigned and amendments had to be got around before the Reagan White House could lubricate its new relationship with General Zia.

Even inside the Reagan administration people were unsettled by the idea of rewarding a country like Pakistan while it pursued an illicit nuclear program, and details about the plan on the table were leaked to the White House press pack in the first few days of February 1981, even before the State Department had had time to formulate a clearly-thought-out view on the policy.[31]

In Pakistan, Zia did what he could to help. A frank briefing on the state of the secretive Pakistan nuclear project from Dr. Ishrat Usmani, the former head of PAEC, found its way into an influential European nuclear publication. He revealed that, contrary to public fears, his country "faced severe challenges" in completing the Kahuta program.[32] Usmani had gone on to work at the United Nations in New York and had become a trusted face in the West. But although Usmani knew that in February 1979 Khan had succeeded in building several operational centrifuge cascades at Sihala, he told the reporter from *Nucleonics Week* that Pakistan faced severe technical challenges and was unlikely ever to be capable of producing even the crudest of nuclear devices.[33]

Such was the enthusiasm for a Pakistan deal that only three weeks after Reagan was sworn in, the State Department produced a classified action memorandum that delicately set the US desire to exploit Pakistan as a staging post to bleed the Soviets alongside the Islamic Republic's need for protection by America.[34] "Pakistan is a front line state under heavy Soviet pressure," it warned. "Its national integrity, its anti-Soviet posture are critical to our larger interests in the region ... Our credibility, fourteen months after the Soviet invasion is low, but Pakistani expectations of the new administration are high." The memo concluded: "We do not have much latitude for delay since the atmosphere could quickly sour."

Congress was to be rushed at. Money had to reach Pakistan by the next financial year, which involved the tightest of schedules—the proposals having to be presented to a congressional budget committee by 15 March for approval by the House and the Senate by 15 May. Even before anyone on Capitol Hill was forewarned, ambassador Hummel floated the details in Pakistan, inviting foreign minister Shahi to bring a delegation to Washington in April. Shahi had bad memories of the White House, after Gerard Smith had ambushed him with his valley of death speech. Even though Hummel's offer looked as if it would be several billion dollars over five years, Shahi remained cautious. "I knew that Pakistan would have to engage in a delicate balancing act," he said. "I counselled Zia that we needed to consider whether the US proposals would undermine Pakistan's sovereignty and most critically its nuclear program." Shahi also questioned American sincerity. "We needed to understand the subtext to the Hummel deal."[35]

In Washington the ire of those opposed to rewarding a nuclear-bound Pakistan began to grow, as did the feeling among some sections of Congress that they were being chivvied into making the wrong decision. More leaks from the White House revealed the magnitude of the proposed Pakistan aid package, which was now rumored to include F-16 fighters. Although the Senate had fallen to the Republicans, a small lobby of well-travelled internationalist congressmen got up a head of steam. They were led by Senator John Glenn (Democrat, Ohio), the Second World War ace and astronaut, the first American to orbit the earth, a genuine American hero and author of the 1977 amendment that banned US assistance to countries conducting a nuclear explosion. He was one of the few Democrats capable of taking on Reagan on matters of national security without looking like a Soviet sap.

Glenn's ears and eyes since 1976 had been Len Weiss, a former professor of electrical engineering, who had helped write the Nuclear Non-Proliferation Act of 1978, which threatened sanctions against any country attempting to acquire unauthorized nuclear technology.[36] Weiss knew well the parameters of US non-proliferation law and he reflected on how the Reagan people had bulldozed Congress.[37] "Afghanistan had a huge effect on the Hill, becoming a marker of patriotism. There were only two choices. You were against the Soviets and therefore for Pakistan. Or you were against Pakistan and somehow for the Soviets," Weiss said. "Nobody thought to tell us that we could be against Pakistan's bomb and against the Soviets too. That required too much work for the Reagan people. They were lazy and short-sighted. Glenn was one of the few who battled it out. He refused to see one nuclear nation enabled (Pakistan), in order to shut down the nuclear capabilities of another (the Soviet Union)."

One of Glenn's allies was Senator Alan Cranston (Democrat, California), a former *International News Service* correspondent in Europe and Africa, who was the Democratic whip. When he caught wind of the Haig–Hummel plan, he wrote to the secretary of state in private, warning him to be prepared for a fight. "I view our nation's leadership in international nuclear non-proliferation efforts as a <u>central component of our national security program</u> [*sic*]," Cranston wrote. The senator revealed that without much digging he had learned that "the Pakistanis—through continued purchases of sensitive hardware and dual use technology in Europe—have achieved swift progress towards making their new reprocessing plant operational and have continued development of larger reprocessing and enrichment plants."[38]

The knowledge was out there and easy to grasp. Representative Stephen Solarz (Democrat, New York), an equally global and savvy politician, who sat on the House foreign affairs committee, recalled: "Everyone could see where Pakistan was going. I said we should be telling them unequivocally, 'You want aid, give up your nukes.' Instead the messages coming from the White House were the opposite. Let's face it, we all thought Afghanistan was critical in bringing down the Soviets but we didn't expect the administration to bring down the entire skyscraper of non-proliferation too."[39]

The president's men were on the offensive. A senior official at the Department of State called Senator Charles Percy (Republican, Illinois), chairman of the Senate foreign relations committee, which would have to vet aid to Pakistan. Anticipating strong opposition, Percy was advised to say that Pakistan "faced an immediate and growing threat from the Soviets in Afghanistan" and its survival hinged on the Afghan freedom fighters.[40] A talking-points pack recommended that if the nuclear issue were to be raised he should acknowledge the Islamic Republic was "making a determined effort to acquire nuclear explosives" and that the punitive measures taken in the past had achieved nothing. Sanctions were a failure. The way to gain assurance that A. Q. Khan would roll back the nuclear program was to give Islamabad jets and money. The twisted logic of granting Pakistan security to buy off its nuclear program was getting some usage.

Far more worrying, Percy was advised that previous intelligence estimates that concluded Pakistan was "two to three years" away from getting the bomb, and was willing to sell it to its neighbors, had been wrong. Percy was instead told that Pakistan was far behind and "we believe [it] will exercise restraint in the transfer of sensitive technology to third countries."[41] However, this was in marked contrast to the active intelligence estimates in which Pakistan was described as being "within 12 to 18 months" of exploding a nuclear device.[42]

The White House was steering a perilous course, hanging its reputation on the Pakistan plan, and anyone who got in the way was trampled over. When the president's own Office of Management and Budget cast doubts, claiming the Pakistan proposals were politically dangerous and that there were insufficient funds for the war, the State Department whipped back a memo warning that "the establishment of a cooperative security relationship with Pakistan is critical to the success of the administration." It concluded, dramatically: "The Reagan administration is determined to improve the US defense posture and considers security assistance an essential element in achieving that objective. We need to tie this down before meeting with the visiting Pakistani foreign minister next Monday."[43] The clock was ticking. Haig and James Buckley, Reagan's under secretary for security, had already testified before the Senate and House foreign relations committees that only by "removing insecurities" could Pakistan's nuclear thirst be quenched.[44]

When foreign minister Shahi eventually arrived in Washington on 20 April, he was not surprised that the US side raised Pakistan's nuclear program. But he was not expecting the direction the conversation rapidly took. "We had thought we would be harangued and end up walking out. But Haig volunteered that the nuclear issue need not be the centerpiece of US–Pakistan policy. The only thing that he did warn us against was detonating a bomb. We got the message."[45]

General Arif, Zia's chief of staff, was also at the meeting and was bowled over by the US turnaround. "Haig characterized the Pakistan nuclear program as a 'private matter.' He told us the White House would not interfere in our internal affairs. The message was clear. The US never wanted Pakistan to have the bomb, but they were not going to get in our way now."[46] Deputy assistant secretary of state Jane A. Coon, the government's leading South Asia specialist, was at the same meeting and summarized Reagan's message, delivered via Haig, as being: "Reagan could live with the Pakistan bomb."[47] For General Arif the highlight of the trip was a meeting with the charismatic new US president. "Ronald Reagan entered the cabinet room of the White House with a broad smile and warmly greeted the delegation ... He spoke in a congenial, captivating style, optimism oozing from his words ... and expressed US support for [Pakistan's] security and stability," the general recalled.[48]

In eighteen months, the Pakistan nuclear program had gone from within a wing tip of being atomized by US or even Israeli bombers, to a low-level risk with little chance of succeeding, pushed to the back of US priorities.

5

THE TIES THAT BIND

Early in the morning of 1 May 1981, A. Q. Khan was woken by an urgent and unexpected phone call. Several weeks earlier he had sent word to General Zia that he had successfully enriched a small sample of uranium to weapons-grade strength, a colossal breakthrough on the path to manufacturing a nuclear bomb. Using European blueprints, he had modified URENCO's energy-supplying technology for use in a weapons program. Now Zia had decided to view the progress at Kahuta for himself, with an unscheduled visit that morning. Khan was thrown into a panic. He immediately called Brigadier Sajawal, told him to get into his dress uniform and join him in the staff car in half an hour.[1] Dr. Shafiq, then a thirteen-year-old schoolboy, tagged along. "When he arrived at Kahuta, Zia was shocked," he recalled. "He was expecting a school chemistry lab and here was a plant filled with fully functioning Western-style laboratories, cascades of gleaming centrifuges humming away in glass chambers all being monitored by scientists in pristine white coats. Nothing like this had ever been done in Pakistan before. I remember the look on his face. He was like, 'This is an empire.' He was overwhelmed."

Khan recalled the visit as a great morale booster for him and his colleagues. "During his flying visit to our laboratories Zia renamed our organization from 'Engineering Research Laboratories' to 'Dr. A. Q. Khan Research Laboratories,' a distinction that was unmatched in the scientific world since no living scientist had been bestowed the honor of the naming of an organization after him," Khan later wrote with characteristic immodesty.[2]

Zia presented Khan with citations, one of which he would frame and hang on the wall at Kahuta's administration block, still located in the ex-Royal Air Force workshops at Islamabad international airport, the first port of call for anyone new in town. "They would be brought into the office and pointed in the direction of the certificate as if to say, 'I am blessed by the Head of State,'" a former aide recalled.[3] Soon after, big, bold, gold lettering was erected above the gates to Kahuta, spelling out its new dedication. Zia now ordered Khan to pursue the design of a device ready for a cold or simulated test. He granted extra funding and called on Khan to redouble his efforts.

In Washington, the groundbreaking event passed unremarked. Instead, on 13 May 1981, a six-year waiver on the aid restrictions imposed on Pakistan under the terms of the Symington and Glenn amendments slipped through the Senate foreign relations committee by ten votes to seven, authorizing more than $3 billion in assistance to Pakistan as well as permission to sell the F-16 fighters.

Howard Hart, the CIA's new Islamabad station chief, arrived that month to find the burned-out US embassy still under reconstruction. A veteran of the Tehran CIA station, he chose an old USAID building to house the agency's enhanced Pakistan operation, and from here the war in Afghanistan would be directed. Hart had strict instructions from CIA headquarters that his agents were to ignore Pakistan's internal politics—including its nuclear program—as they were to be handled solely by the State Department.[4] Hart's liaison was Lieutenant General Akhtar Abdur Rahman, the ISI chief and a close confidant of Zia. It had to remain a low-level insurgency, Zia's mantra being that "the water in Afghanistan must boil at the right temperature"—and not boil over.[5] Pakistan could ill afford to provoke the Soviets into coming after them and the ISI needed time to decide which of the twenty-nine Afghan mujahideen factions to arm, train and set upon the Red Army.

But strong opposition to the Pakistan aid plan continued to grow. On 2 June 1981, Israel's permanent representative at the UN warned the General Assembly that "there is abundant evidence indicating that [Pakistan] is producing nuclear weapons."[6] Ambassador Yehuda Blum highlighted the potency of Khan's operation "at the Engineering Research Labs [sic]," saying, "Pakistan is secretly constructing a plant for the production of weapons-grade enriched uranium by centrifuges," based on technology "stolen from the URENCO plant in the Netherlands." Blum warned that Pakistan had established a chain of front companies in fourteen countries to acquire all the necessary components. They were close to having built a cascade of at least 1,000 centrifuges and intended to construct more than 10,000 "which in turn could produce about 150 kg of enriched uranium a year, sufficient for seven nuclear explosive devices every year." It was what the US had known for several years but had chosen not to share with the rest of the world.

The US State Department would provide Israel with a classified response. "We believe that the Pakistanis have so far been unable to make their centrifuge machines work and that they have not yet produced any significant quantities of enriched uranium." It was a blatant lie and the letter concluded in a similar vein: "Even if the Pakistanis do manage to eventually overcome their problems in the enrichment area, it would likely take them a few years of successful operations to produce sufficient fissile material to fabricate a single device."[7] The letter estimated that it would take Pakistan another decade before it had acquired a suitable missile system to wed to a warhead. Not only was the US misrepresenting the available intelligence, but it was also ignoring several articles published by Khan himself in Western nuclear gazettes in which he had explicitly laid out the hurdles his centrifuge construction program had overcome.[8] Moshe Ya'alon, a former head of Israel's military intelligence and until 2005 chief of staff to the Israel Defense Forces (IDF), recalled the stunned reaction in Jerusalem. "The US was glib on Pakistan. It was their weak spot. They knew we knew far more than that. After all, when the shah was toppled we became the primary source for a generous slice of US intelligence in the region."[9]

Back in 1979, the Israelis, according to a senior intelligence source in Israel, had been shown a classified US memo by their counterparts in RAW, the Indian foreign intelligence agency. Intercepted on its way from the US embassy in New Delhi to the secretary of state, Cyrus Vance, it confirmed that the US privately believed Pakistan would be able to explode a bomb within "two or three years"—most likely by 1981.[10] So shocked had the Israelis been by the massive advances made by Khan that they had begun planning a pre-emptive strike on Kahuta, a plan that had only been put on ice due to US pressure. Now both Israel and India picked up more worrying indicators, including signs that test tunnels were being dug in Pakistan's Ras Koh mountains.[11]

So certain were the Indians of Pakistan's intent that Lieutenant General Krishnaswami Sundarji, a future Indian vice chief of army staff, took the unprecedented step of publishing a war-gaming manual on the basis that Pakistan would imminently have a deployable bomb.[12] Israel was less cerebral in its response. On 7 June 1981, deploying US-supplied bombers, armed with US-manufactured munitions, targeting with satellite overheads supplied by the US intelligence community, Israel destroyed the Iraqi nuclear program, striking out its reactor in Osirak, sending a clear message that even if the US was willing to turn a blind eye to the activities of unauthorized nuclear powers, the Israelis were not.[13] Jerusalem would not stand by and allow realpolitik to arm Pakistan either, and a highly secretive bombing campaign orchestrated by the Mossad, Israel's external security agency, which had begun earlier in the year and targeted A. Q. Khan's European suppliers, was escalated.

The first victim had been Heinz Mebus, Khan's old friend from West Berlin Technische Universität, who, along with Albrecht Migule, had helped build Pakistan's fluoride and uranium conversion plants in 1979. A letter bomb exploded inside Mebus's home in Erlangen, West Germany. Mebus was out at work, but his dog died in the attack. European criminal investigators soon linked the bombing to another that had occurred in Berne, Switzerland, on 20 February, outside the home of Eduard German, managing director of CORA Engineering, the company that had exported the gasification and solidification unit to Pakistan in 1979. The company had been preparing to send another rig to Pakistan when the bomb went off.[14] The incident was followed by an anonymous caller demanding that CORA stop trading with Pakistan. Rudolf Walti, a CORA official, recalled that after his company was threatened again two months later it ended its association with Pakistan, having discovered that the US knew everything.[15] However, this information had been kept highly classified, lest it undermine the aid train that had started to leave for Pakistan.

Police in Berne could find no trace of any of the attackers, only references to a gang that called itself the Group for Non-Proliferation in South Asia. However, they soon discovered that similar attacks against Khan's European suppliers had been carried out by other equally untraceable groups, including one called the Committee to Safeguard the Islamic Revolution and another known as the League for Protecting the Sub-Continent, which had exposed secret contracts between Khan and a French nuclear supplier.[16]

Pooling resources through Interpol, the international police organization, the Swiss detectives learned of an Italian company trading with Khan that had also been warned off. Emanuele Poncini, deputy director of Alcom Engineering, which was supplying metal components to Pakistan, confirmed that his company had received a threatening letter and had backed away from its deal.[17]

Then, on 18 May 1981, another bomb exploded, this one planted in the southern German town of Markdorf outside a company that had been supplying Pakistan since 1976.[18] That November, Albrecht Migule was also targeted when a letter bomb was delivered to his house in Freiberg, West Germany. The Swiss police investigations floundered, although in private the detectives believed a sophisticated, state-backed group was behind the attacks, with Mossad the most likely candidate.[19] Peter Griffin recalled having the frighteners put on him, too, when he went to Bonn to pick up a payment from Ikram ul-Haq, A. Q. Khan's agent there. "I was in a bar when a stranger sat down next to me.[20] 'You're Peter Griffin,' he said. 'We don't like what you're doing, so stop it.'" Griffin started recording all his business dealings and movements in a diary, put all his company records into a bank vault, and advised his wife that if anything untoward should happen to him she should give everything to their son Paul.

In Washington, the administration insisted it remained as committed as ever to non-proliferation. After the Osirak attack, President Reagan was asked in a press conference to define where he stood. "We are opposed to the proliferation of nuclear weapons and do everything in our power to prevent it," he replied.[21] Publicly at least, Reagan was emphatic, as was James Buckley. He told John Glenn's government affairs committee in June 1981 that he had received "absolute assurances" from Pakistan that it would not develop or test a nuclear weapon.[22] That September, Buckley went on to testify before Congressman Stephen Solarz and the House foreign affairs committee that Pakistan was even more unlikely to progress with its nuclear program once it began receiving US assistance. He wrote to the *New York Times* that December: "In place of the ineffective sanctions on Pakistan's nuclear program imposed by past administrations, we hope to address through conventional means the sources of insecurity that prompt a nation like Pakistan to seek a nuclear capability in the first place."[23] Len Weiss, Glenn's aide, recalled: "It seemed highly unconventional to reward a country bent on becoming nuclear with extra funding and jets."[24]

However, over the months in which these speeches and testimonies were given, James Buckley and other officials were ordered by the White House to shuttle between Washington and Islamabad, refining the back-channel deal on the Pakistan nuclear program, making certain that both sides knew that when the president had signalled the US's intention to ignore Pakistan's bomb—through Alexander Haig—it had been no slip of the tongue.[25] General Arif greeted Buckley on one occasion and recalled that after discussing the delivery of Pakistan's F-16s, he had raised the nuclear question. "The Americans suggested there was no need to talk about Pakistan's [nuclear] program any more."[26]

In December 1981, the Senate rubber-stamped Pakistan's $3.2 billion aid package, making it the third largest recipient of US largesse, after Israel and Egypt. Congress was assured that the program was dependent on Pakistan desisting with its nuclear efforts. However, days later Agha Shahi received Buckley in Islamabad and recalled: "I mentioned the nuclear caveats and emphasized that if we had a bomb and wanted to test it there was nothing the US could do. Buckley shrugged his shoulders and said, 'I understand. Yes, we know.' "[27]

All the time, evidence was piling up as law enforcement agencies in Europe and North America uncovered strands of the Khan network. In August 1980 three Canadians of Pakistani origin were arrested allegedly trying illicitly to export nuclear components to Pakistan, among them Aziz Khan, A. Q. Khan's correspondent from Montreal. Customs officials recovered from Aziz's house a bundle of letters from Islamabad, painting the first picture of life inside the secretive Project 706. Spanning the earliest days in Sihala to the shift of Pakistan's enrichment facilities to Kahuta, they revealed the names of Khan's most trusted aides and suppliers in the West and identified many of Khan's employees. They provided a route map to the Pakistan nuclear industry—if anyone in the Reagan administration had cared. In one letter, Aziz had offered the prescient warning that if he and his friends were rounded up they "had nothing to be scared about," and when the case came before a court in Quebec, in October 1981, although Aziz and two others were charged with supplying sensitive electronic components to Pakistan, the hearings were closed, the evidence sealed.[28]

Ostensibly the gagging order was requested by the Canadian authorities in order to protect nuclear secrets, particularly details concerning components that US companies had allegedly supplied to Khan. But just as crucially it also prevented the US Congress from learning that many American firms had helped to facilitate Pakistan's nuclear project. Aziz was acquitted, having convinced the jury that he had supplied "harmless" Pakistani projects, including the now familiar "food-processing factory" and a textile plant.[29] A fat seam of intelligence was locked up in the trial material and kept away from investigators who were tracking Khan—material that would have revealed the existence of a series of dummy companies, such as the Institute of Industrial Automation, with its address in a smart residential suburb of Islamabad.[30] In Islamabad, Zia continued with the rhetoric, stating two weeks after the start of the trial that Pakistan's nuclear program was purely peaceful. "We will work, we will borrow, and we will beg for this technology. God willing we will never pass it to any other nation."[31]

The same month that Aziz's trial started, a 5,000-lb shipment of zirconium, a gray-white metal that resembles titanium and is commonly used to lag the fuel rods in nuclear reactors, was seized at Kennedy international airport in New York after a Pakistani passenger tried to check it on to a Pakistan International Airlines flight in a box labelled "climbing gear." The passenger disappeared when airline staff asked to see inside. It was later discovered that an American businessman had bought the zirconium in Oregon on behalf of a Pakistan-based company, S. J. Enterprises, and that the passenger who had vanished was in reality a retired Pakistan army officer and close friend of Zia ul-Haq. Pakistan International Airways promised an inquiry, which never materialized.[32]

The White House had a wellspring of intelligence on Khan, most of which never reached Congress. Much of it related to Khan's ongoing shopping operations in North America and Europe, which were needed in order to fit out the main centrifuge hall at Kahuta and finish off other essential workshops and research facilities at the plant. But out of the scores of classified cables seen by the State Department, one in particular stood out. It concluded: "We have strong reason to believe that Pakistan is seeking to develop a nuclear explosives capability ... conducting a program for the design and development for a triggering package for a nuclear explosive device."[33]

The CIA had picked up on Zia's instructions to Khan in May 1981 to get ready for a cold test. Pakistan had moved on to the next stage. Officially, Pakistan's warhead design was the responsibility of Dr. Samar Mubarakmand, a founding member of PAEC, who had attended the 1972 Multan conference and ran PAEC's Directorate of Technical Development (DTD), one of the most secretive organizations in the labyrinth of Pakistan's nuclear industry.[34] At a secret laboratory, the location of which was never disclosed, Mubarakmand worked with a team of scientists and engineers who had formerly been employed by the Pakistan army's ordnance complex at Wah, north of Islamabad. They had been shifted from conventional to nuclear weapons in March 1974 but had yet to perfect their warhead design.[35] In 1981, Zia decided to increase the pace by authorizing Khan to establish a competing weapons team at Kahuta.[36]

However, rather than act on the warnings, President Reagan invited General Zia to the White House. At a dinner held in his honor on 7 December 1982, the US president eulogized: "Differences may come between our nations or have come between our nations in the past, but they've proven to be transitory while the ties which bind us together grow stronger year by year."[37] The following day Zia admonished those who had accused Pakistan of insincerity. "There has been an orchestrated campaign to malign us by falsely attributing a non-existent military dimension [to our civil nuclear project]."[38] He appeared on NBC's *Meet the Press*, declaring: "There is no such thing as a peaceful nuclear device. It's like a sword. You can cut your throat. You can save yourself. We are planning neither."[39]

To cap off a year in which the formerly denigrated Pakistan had become a well-dined friend of the White House, Reagan delivered a televised speech to the American people on 26 December. "At this holiday season when most Americans are warmed and comforted by their family relationships and the blessings of this country," he told viewers, "it is hard for us to realize that far away in a remote and mountainous land a valiant people is putting up a fight for freedom that affects us all. No matter how far removed from our daily lives, Afghanistan is a struggle we must not forget."[40]

Behind the scenes, the Reagan administration was desperately struggling to suppress evidence that A. Q. Khan was designing a bomb. After British intelligence caught his network shopping in the UK for reflective shields made from beryllium, which could significantly boost the power of a nuclear device, Reagan sent a warning to Islamabad via his envoy, Vernon Walters, a two-star general and former CIA deputy director.[41] Robert Gallucci, who was then director of the Bureau of Near Eastern and South Asian Affairs at the State Department, accompanied him there in October 1982. "I'd been issuing démarches from State to Zia for months saying as politely as I could, 'I'm sorry to have to tell you that some people in your government are doing really bad stuff,'" recalled Gallucci.[42] "But the bad stuff had continued so we had to confront Zia face-to-face. Our evidence was incontrovertible. 'This is what your experts have been up to,' we said, as politely as we could, giving Zia a get-out. However, the president rejected our briefing, saying our information had come from the Indians." When General Walters showed Zia a satellite photograph of Kahuta, Pakistan's president brushed it aside, saying, "This can't be a nuclear installation. Maybe it's a goat shed." Gallucci recalled: "Afterwards as we were getting into the car, we discussed what we'd heard. Ambassador Walters didn't want to believe that Zia was lying to him, but there was no way this stuff could have been going on without Zia's knowledge."

What Gallucci was not privy to were secret White House instructions for Walters, who had been asked to warn the Pakistanis to do their nuclear trading more discreetly, rather than demanding from them a rollback. Walters confided as much to a senior State Department colleague on his return. "He came in looking miserable," the colleague recalled. "I said, 'What's up?' He said, 'I was told [by the White House] to tell Zia to get that nuclear problem off our radar.' I was shocked. It was the antithesis of what we were supposed to be doing. Instead of giving it to them with both barrels, Walters had told the Pakistanis they had better hide their bomb program, lest it humiliate Reagan."[43]

But Zia did not heed the warning and, as the months passed, the intelligence mounted. Robert Gallucci recalled: "We had human intel, electronic intel, intel of every conceivable nature using most of our agencies and facilities. We had wiretaps, satellite overheads, and highly sensitive on-the-ground intel, both human and technological. We expected a response from President [Reagan]. We did our jobs. We are not in the business of politics. However, the mantra that Reagan was the president most committed to non-proliferation was, to be frank, a fairy tale."

The intelligence was augmented by a US data-collecting operation made possible by the infiltration of a high-tech surveillance device into the arid area surrounding the heavily guarded Kahuta hills, a place no US or European spies could get near. The device was a resin boulder, molded and colored to look exactly the same as the red rock that surrounded Khan's secret plant. It had been transported on the back of a delivery lorry and was capable of transmitting intelligence through an array of sophisticated recording and air-sampling technology hidden inside the shell. Only a freak accident exposed the operation. General Arif recalled that a student travelling on the back of an open-backed truck had, while horsing around, fallen off and struck his head against a rock.[44] "He opened his eyes and realized that he was still alive and unbruised. The rock, however, had a hole in it and inside were all sorts of whirring and blinking bits. We took it away for analysis and later put it into our museum for trainee spies."

In the summer of 1983, four months after Reagan certified to Congress for the third year running that Zia was not involved in nuclear weapons design, Robert Gallucci compiled a damning review of Pakistan's program.[45] "There is unambiguous evidence that Pakistan is actively pursuing a nuclear weapons development program," he wrote.[46] Marked "Secret," with no distribution abroad or to security contractors, it continued: "Pakistan's near-term goal evidently is to have a nuclear test capability enabling it to explode a nuclear device if Zia decides it's appropriate for diplomatic and domestic political gains."

Most damaging was the section headed "Nuclear Explosives," which explained how Pakistan was working "on an electronic triggering circuit for nuclear device detonation ... as well as experiments on conventional as well as shaped charges"—the high explosives layer that surrounds a bomb's core and detonates a fission chain reaction.[47] Pakistan "has already undertaken a substantial amount of the necessary design and high explosives testing of the explosive device and we believe that Pakistan is now capable of producing a workable package of this kind," Gallucci reported. Some of this know-how had been obtained during the shopping expeditions that Vernon Walters had advised the Pakistanis to conduct below the US radar. Gallucci had even obtained copies of drawings given to suppliers by Khan's agents "which ... have been unambiguously identified as those of a nuclear device."

Gallucci also tripped over Pakistan's secret pact with China. Notes in Chinese and an operations manual, also from the People's Republic, that accompanied some of these drawings were analyzed by US scientists at Los Alamos, who concluded that they were remarkably similar to the device China had exploded in its fourth nuclear test, in 1964, at Lop Nor in the remote northwestern deserts of Xinjiang.[48] "China has provided assistance to Pakistan's program to develop a nuclear weapons capability," Gallucci concluded. It was an alarming development as the Chinese had already demonstrated their contempt for international non-proliferation agreements, supplying technical expertise and UF$_6$ to Pakistan in breach of the Non-Proliferation Treaty. The US now had so much data it even created a model of Pakistan's would-be bomb, the size of a soccer ball, which was kept in a vault at the Pentagon.[49] The warhead had multiple detonators placed around its surface and experts who set it off in a computer simulation found that it worked every time.[50]

US intelligence made another stark discovery. China had also shipped to Pakistan samples of weapons-grade highly enriched uranium to fuel a nuclear bomb if General Zia signalled he was ready to test before Khan had manufactured enough fissile material at Kahuta. Exactly how much highly enriched uranium Pakistan had received was unclear, but senior intelligence sources in the US and Israel confirmed that they thought that China had given Pakistan enough for two devices.[51] According to another US intelligence source, Khan's technicians had even converted the highly enriched uranium into a metal core which would be slotted into the Chinese bomb design that was now under construction.[52] If the design were the same as the one for China's fourth test device, its yield would be as high as 20–25 kilotons, giving it the power to kill as many as 100,000 people in a crowded city.[53]

Pakistan's enrichment cycle had been refined and problem-solved by China and Robert Gallucci underscored the significance of the relationship. With assistance from a proven nuclear power, nagging technical problems that had to date slowed down Pakistan's ambitions could no longer be counted on to act as a brake. However, in a classified report to Congress in 1983, backing his decision to waive the Symington and Glenn amendments, the US president stated: "We do not expect Pakistan to attempt a test of a nuclear device in the near future. Pakistan lacks access to fissile material for a device, since neither the Kahuta uranium enrichment plant nor the new labs [Pakistan Institute of Science and Technology, PINSTECH] reprocessing facility are in production."[54]

In Islamabad, Kahuta was thriving behind a vast security ring. Outside its main gates, with their glistening golden letters bearing Khan's name, ISI and Intelligence Bureau agents manned the busy road leading towards Islamabad international airport. Dr. Shafiq, the son of Brigadier Sajawal, recalled: "My dad was in charge and tracked everything moving along that road. Any shipment, day or night, was reported back to army headquarters."[55] The hills around the complex were alive with men and munitions. "There were three or four tiers of guards that included military intelligence, two brigades of 10,000 regular soldiers, one anti-aircraft battalion, a commando unit with dogs and also a signals battalion." At the center of this security cocoon was the facility partitioned into four self-contained areas: the central and highly sensitive centrifuge halls; the "B section," where missiles would be produced; the non-sensitive machine shops; and, in the outermost zone, a medical zone for employees, dealing with industrial injuries, particularly radiation sickness. "Staff could not travel between the zones," Dr. Shafiq said. "To confuse infiltrators, there were no signboards."

Brigadier Sajawal had built a series of guest houses for official visitors and technical advisers next to an artificial lake which fed the plant's air-conditioning system. Dr. Shafiq said: "Nationalities who had to be more discreet, like the Chinese, Iranians and North Koreans, stayed there."

Everything was building up for a cold test, and in March 1983, shortly after Reagan had hailed US efforts at "dissuading [Pakistan] from continuing its nuclear explosives program," work began in tunnels bored into the Kirana Hills near Sargodha, the Pakistan air force's largest base and its central ammunition depot.[56] The tests were to be conducted by PAEC, after Dr. Samar Mubarakmand's team at the Directorate of Technical Development finally produced a viable bomb design with input from Khan's teams at Kahuta. Mubarakmand, who oversaw the preparations, recalled how they first had to clear the site of wild boars, one of which had previously written off a jet as it landed by charging into its undercarriage. He then booted up the US- and German-manufactured supercomputers with which his scientists would monitor the triggering of a nuclear bomb that had had its fissile core removed.[57]

An armed escort arrived with the weapon. "The bomb was assembled in the tunnel. The telemetry was set up, checked and rechecked. Vans outside the test site would monitor the event from every angle."[58] The first test was designed to monitor the trigger mechanism and to see if it would generate sufficient neutrons to start a chain reaction. "The button was pushed and nothing happened," the report stated. Fearing the device had failed, a team entered the tunnel and, running every wire through their fingers, they found that two connections had come adrift. After conducting some running repairs the test went off successfully. Now Pakistan's dignitaries were invited to the site. A few days later, General K. M. Arif arrived, alongside Munir Ahmed Khan, chairman of PAEC, and Ghulam Ishaq Khan, the finance minister. "Only a few people in Pakistan knew. It was a red-letter day," recalled Arif.[59] "I can tell you we were all very excited. The tests went perfectly. Pakistan to all intents and purposes now had its bomb. The work of our scientists was nothing short of heroic. From now on there were twenty-four more cold tests to straighten out the triggering mechanism until we got the hang of it exactly."

A. Q. Khan's moment of triumph would be short-lived. On 18 October 1983, the Dutch ambassador in Islamabad delivered a subpoena to Pakistan's Ministry of Foreign Affairs, charging Khan with nuclear espionage at URENCO in 1975. Rather than alerting Khan, the ministry forwarded the subpoena to the Ministry of Law, which sat on the documents, failing to respond until November, by which time the Dutch had convicted Khan in absentia, sentencing him to four years.[60] "Khan was incandescent," Dr. Shafiq remembered. "He kept shouting that he had done nothing wrong and that the Dutch had not even served him with papers. Everything he got from Holland was more or less in the public domain. I recall him screaming: 'We'll give them hell. We'll make their democracy work against them.'"[61] Khan knew he could never return to Holland or to any other European country unless he could overturn the ruling. He asked Zia for permission to appeal. The president approved and, backed by Islamabad's deep coffers, Khan hired Sir David Napley, a celebrated and prohibitively expensive British lawyer, who had successfully defended Jeremy Thorpe, the former Liberal politician, on charges of conspiracy to murder.[62]

Khan's explosive temper and the tension of running such an elaborate project, coupled with the criminal proceedings, began to take their toll, bringing him into conflict with Henny. She could not stand it and asked for a divorce shortly after the Dutch court case. One friend confirmed: "Henny said Khan had threatened her, physically. He denied it vehemently."[63] At the insistence of Khan's family, the couple sought out Professor Haroon Ahmed, Pakistan's foremost psychiatrist.[64] "I'm for peace, pro-India, against the bomb—how did I end up with A. Q. Khan?" the psychiatrist sighed, recalling the years when Khan was his patient. "Khan and Henny were in a crisis. She was obsessive, stubborn. He was a perfectionist. It was a collision that had been building for some time,"

Ahmed recalled. "She said he had become insufferable. He flew into terrible rages and suffered from depression. He was classically manic."

Dr. Ahmed drew from Khan an admission. His stress levels were rising uncontrollably as he competed to be the first to give the Islamic world a bomb. "He was determined to better the PAEC people, and having succeeded with uranium, he wanted to be the first with the weapons design too." But in reality Khan was on the periphery, the source of fissile material, rather than the bomb designer designate. "He wanted to be the racing car driver, not the petrol pump attendant," said Ahmed. Khan also demanded that Henny embrace the whirlwind of the new life the nuclear business had brought him. "I became their marriage counsellor. I dug around the two of them. He was taking on new airs and graces. She was happy with reading, knitting and the dogs. He was gregarious—at least from the outside. A charmer. He was in fact deeply insecure." Khan became a regular caller. Dr. Ahmed recalled: "He would ring, 'It is v. v. v. important please come to Islamabad.' And I would say I was busy and then he would come down to Karachi anyway. It would then turn out to be nothing at all, just an ear to listen."

Khan wanted to repay his therapist. When he learned that Dr. Ahmed was attempting to open the country's first free mental health clinic and center for behavioral sciences in Karachi, he decided to become its patron. Dr. Ahmed recalled: "Khan sent a message, 'I'll give you a wonderful building.' He insisted. We inducted him into the governing body of the clinic. I could not refuse."

However, Khan's relationship with Henny worsened. "As he increased in power he increased in paranoia and Henny, the one thing in his life beyond his control, who did not climb as he climbed—and remember that this man was surrounded by 'yes men'—was again physically threatened by him. She believed he wanted to kill her or harm her. He confessed that he had had an ISI team following Henny and his daughters. He thought they were more loyal to Europe than they were to Pakistan. He imagined that they were going to sell him out." Dina and Ayesha, still teenagers, just wanted the kind of anonymous life they had enjoyed in Europe. "At one point Khan even conjectured his family would be kidnapped by the US or the Israelis and held hostage until Pakistan dismantled its nuclear program. Outlandish yes. But this was shortly after the Israelis had bombed Osirak and nerves were frayed."

Dr. Ahmed unravelled Khan's past. "He was deeply insecure with a poor self-image, snubbed frequently in his younger life by the authorities, by his fellow students in Karachi, by the military that he tried to emulate, a terrible experience that left a yawning gulf that he tried to fill. He felt as if he was never quite good enough. Then he had found something unique, something to trade, with the URENCO enrichment technology. Suddenly he became overbearing as if his heart was galloping faster than his body could control it. He had a Hitler complex—you know, poor artist rejected by the salons of Vienna invades Poland. Always overcompensating."

Dr. Ahmed wondered what Khan would do next. "The government was not going to stop him. He was above the government. The army was not going to stop him. He was joined at the hip to the military. The intelligence establishment was instructed to stay clear after the trailing Henny affair. There was nothing in the way of Khan's ambition. And he was his own worst enemy."

6

A FIGMENT OF THE ZIONIST MIND

Towards the end of 1983 there was an unexpected thaw in the nuclear winter. Having shunned the Western apparatchiks who administered the Nuclear Non-Proliferation Treaty (NPT) for almost two decades, China announced it was sending a representative to the IAEA in Vienna. Chinese premier Zhao Ziyang flew to the US in January 1984 and delivered an upbeat message about a nuclear program that until then the People's Republic of China (PRC) had rarely mentioned in public. "We do not advocate or encourage nuclear proliferation nor do we ourselves practice nuclear proliferation or help other countries to develop arms," Zhao pledged. Robert Gallucci at the State Department and his compatriots in the CIA balked. They had failed so far to get a reaction out of the White House from their keg of explosive evidence that showed that China was teaching Pakistan how to build a bomb.[1]

For those with insufficient clearances to get at the information the Reagan administration had on China's proliferation activities, premier Zhao's remarks seemed groundbreaking, and Reagan's people made the most of them. Paul Wolfowitz, then in the Bureau of East Asian and Pacific Affairs at the State Department, dwelt on the arduous work that lay behind extracting Zhao's twenty-two words, which were the product of three days of intensive wrangling by US officials locked away in discussions with their Chinese counterparts at the Madison Hotel in Washington.[2] In reality, a lucrative deal was hanging on these words, since in return for joining the IAEA, China had signed up to purchase US-manufactured nuclear technology worth billions of dollars with which it intended to modernize and expand its overworked power-generation facilities.

No one mentioned the bomb designs, UF_6, highly enriched uranium, manuals and scientific teams that flowed from Beijing to Islamabad to help build the Islamic Republic's bomb. A senior State Department official at the time recalled: "The White House faced a conundrum. If the US endorsed the Chinese as members of the IAEA, took their money and then it was revealed that all along the White House knew the PRC was helping Zia build a bomb, there would be hell to pay."[3]

But this was the path the White House chose—a diplomatic high-wire act, which had begun after the PRC declared an interest in buying US nuclear technology when Reagan entered office in January 1981. The following year, George Shultz, sworn in as secretary of state in July, had flown to Beijing to pursue this tantalizing request.[4] "The Reagan administration had jumped at the opportunity and, as with Pakistan, had come up with a form of words that combined the strategic and commercial advantages to the US of striking the deal while paying lip service to non-proliferation goals," recalled the former senior official at the State Department.[5] "We said to the Chinese, 'Yes, we will take your money and while we are at it bang the NPT gong—as we are required to do.' But this kind of twin track approach could only succeed if both sides were honest brokers and truly backed both levels of negotiations. The problem was that the Reagan administration saw non-proliferation as a duty rather than an abiding principle. And China? We had no idea what it thought."

It had taken five rounds of intricate negotiations to get to the draft agreement stage, but both sides failed to sign during Zhao's historic US visit, becoming bogged down by US demands to inspect sensitive Chinese facilities.[6] Instead, the White House pegged its hopes on an impending visit to China by President Reagan, planned for April 1984, the first such trip since President Richard Nixon had offered his hand to the Chinese premier Chou En-lai in February 1972; an historic rapprochement that had been brokered in part by Pakistan.[7] "But this was all dependent on a lid being kept on the Sino–Pakistan deal and of course on Pakistan staying absolutely quiet," the former State Department official said.[8]

In Pakistan, Khan was unconcerned about White House sensitivities. His Khan Research Laboratories (KRL) was filled with droves of conspicuous foreign visitors. "The Chinese were working on triggering mechanisms, the centrifuges, vacuum systems. They brought rocket propellant and super-hard metals like maraging steel," recalled Dr. Shafiq, who was then training to be a medical doctor and frequently visited the plant to see his father, Brigadier Sajawal.[9] "They brought in fissile material and Khan gave them the data on enrichment and metallurgy. They helped Pakistan import and experiment with high explosives and Khan gave them his work on the centrifuge rotors." To make them feel welcome the main guest house was hung with lanterns and done up as a Chinese hall.

The collaboration grew so immense that the Chinese requested Pakistan to change the old-fashioned way in which some deals were financed. Dr. Shafiq recalled his father and Khan discussing China's demands. "There would be no more suitcases full of cash delivered by high-ranking Pakistan army officers or ISI agents. China wanted a trustworthy and transparent line of credit. Dr. Khan had to get things regularized and get the government to deposit money into an account in one of its chosen banks, the Bank of Credit and Commerce International [BCCI], the Islamic Development Bank or the National Bank of Pakistan." These bank-to-bank transfers would attract the attention of Western intelligence, which began investigating Khan's finances in 1982, but they would not report back until much later and those involved in the investigations complained at the time of being largely ignored.[10]

However, despite the enormous sensitivity of what was going on at KRL, and the delicate nature of the US position regarding Beijing, combined with Washington's fears over being exposed in connection with both, it suddenly became hard to pick up a newspaper in Pakistan without reading about A. Q. Khan and how his research center had subsumed the village of Kahuta. In January 1984, Khan called a reporter at the *Qaumi Digest* and asked him to send a list of questions. Khan was so disappointed with them that he threw them away and drafted his own.[11] "What did the scientist think was his greatest achievement?" Khan asked himself and then answered: "Achieving in seven years what the West had taken twenty years to accomplish—the enriching of uranium to weapons grade." It was an astonishing claim to be making in public, given that on it hung US aid to Pakistan. Khan wanted everyone to know what no one was supposed to know and what the Reagan administration had repeatedly told Congress had not yet occurred. He then asked himself: "Did the government recognize his contribution?" He penned an answer: "I have been given increasing autonomy in running KRL." He was now in charge of recruitment at the labs, although ultimate control still rested with the Pakistan military. He wrote in his article that President Zia had appointed two major generals, Zahid Ali Akbar Khan and Anis Nawab, whom Peter Griffin had met in London in 1977 over dinner at the Kundan Restaurant, to oversee all operations.

In February 1984, Khan reached for the phone again, this time calling the Urdu-language *Nawa-i-Waqt*, a pro-army newspaper. It was the same format. Khan asked himself: "Do we have a bomb?" He answered (presumably with full military authority): "You have me cornered. I do not know whether to say yes or no, either way I get caught. First of all I must say that our atomic program is peaceful. The question is now one of ability. We have made major strides in this difficult field. And we have a team of patriotic scientists and extremely brilliant engineers. Forty years ago no one was familiar with the secrets of the atom bomb but American scientists did the job. Today we have ended their monopoly." It was a half-heartedly ambiguous response, but the message was clear.[12]

The following day Khan rang Tariq Warsi, editor of the *Daily Jang*, a newspaper read by Pakistanis around the world. Khan had a special message and raised the prospect of an Islamic bomb. "If in the interests of the country's solidarity the president of Pakistan in extreme need gives the team of my scientists and engineers any important task we will not disappoint the nation." But one thing was sacrosanct. He had done it all alone. "I must make one thing absolutely clear, contrary to the mischievous foreign propaganda, no foreign country has given financial [or] technical aid to us in this [nuclear] field. The 'Islamic bomb' is a figment of the Zionist mind."[13]

Deane Hinton, the US ambassador to Pakistan, called Zia's office in dismay. Was he about to destroy the trust placed in him by Washington and embarrass President Reagan just as he was trying to convince China to sign up to the NPT? Zia placated Hinton. He pledged to discipline Khan, who, he claimed, was speaking out of turn.[14] But according to Sharifuddin Pirzada, Zia's closest non-military aide, Pakistan's president was far from displeased with Khan's outpourings. Pakistan was doing what it always did: servicing its own interests and riding roughshod over US sensibilities.

A lawyer in the supreme court of Pakistan, Pirzada had been courted by every Pakistani dictator since 1958 and administered advice from an office in army headquarters, adjacent to one used by A. Q. Khan. The two of them would often sit down with a cup of tea and swap political tidbits while down the corridor Zia schemed. The president and Pirzada had drawn close in 1978 when the lawyer had laid the legal groundwork for the usurping of Zulfikar Ali Bhutto.[15] Out of the country when Bhutto was hung in 1979, and an expert on constitutional deviation and obfuscation, Pirzada came home in time to conceive a shiny legal construct that justified Zia's suspension of democracy, a provisional constitutional order which temporarily transferred the mandate of power without need to refer to the National Assembly. Zia used it for more than a decade.[16]

Still beloved by the powerful, Pirzada is today ensconced in a spacious bureau on the ground floor of the prime minister's secretariat, from where he counsels General Pervez Musharraf, as his principal legal adviser, and prime minister Shaukat Aziz, for whom he sits on Pakistan's National Security Council.[17] Pirzada has an encyclopedic recall of Pakistan's vast penal code, his mind so agile that he can instantly conjure and construe every codicil in it. A colleague once complained that in every episode of military rule where Pirzada was confederate, "the constitution was abrogated or suspended, fundamental rights were denied, the courts were degraded, arbitrary laws were promulgated, democracy was smothered, one-man rule imposed, human rights violated, and all norms of civil and civilian society put in jeopardy and threat."[18]

Pirzada remembered well Khan's proclivity for speaking out. The flurry of interviews in January and February 1984 had a purpose. "Khan found it hard to keep his trap shut. This is true. But these prolonged interviews were for a reason. Zia believed in nuclear ambiguity, a strategy whereby it could be inferred that Pakistan had the bomb without Pakistan losing its lucrative US aid. The plan was to give the impression that Pakistan's nuclear mission was unstoppable in order to bring about its international acceptance and to warn India that should they choose to strike we were ready to respond."[19] Khan had spoken out on Zia's instruction, the CIA having warned Islamabad that India had finally snapped and was planning a pre-emptive military strike against Kahuta.[20]

"The problem with Khan was that he always set out to do one thing and then invariably achieved another," Pirzada recalled. "Khan went further than his brief and sent our American friends apoplectic." Zia was advised to draft a clarification, carried by state television and the newspapers. Gilded in semantics, the president's statement made no mention of Khan's claim that Pakistan had enriched uranium to weapons grade and the president insisted there were no plans to build a bomb, even though Khan had been right to say that "Pakistan could build a bomb if it needed to."[21] The Pakistanis were masterful word-smiths and there were many in the West who were glad that they were.

The timing of Khan's outpourings could not have been worse. Reagan was due in Beijing. The aid package to Pakistan was up for renewal on Capitol Hill. In New Delhi, too, there was anger at Khan and at the US. The talk was that Washington had betrayed India's secret plans to strike at Pakistan's nuclear project. K. Subrahmanyam, chairman of India's joint intelligence committee, picked over the Khan interviews. "We knew we were being challenged by Islamabad," Subrahmanyam recalled.[22] "Our intelligence people also had evidence of the Pakistan air force increasing their levels of readiness, further proof, if any more were needed, that our covert intentions to hit Kahuta were not secret any more."

But what made India's joint intelligence committee livid was that it had been sitting on the plan to strike KRL for a year. A committee of soldiers and intelligence people had first come together to discuss what became known as "the Osirak contingency" in 1981, after Lieutenant General Krishnaswami Sundarji had published his Pakistan war-gaming manual. Indian prime minister Indira Gandhi had consented and placed Air Marshal Dilbagh Singh, chief of air staff, in charge of the operation. He had ordered Indian Air Force Jaguar squadrons to practice low-level flying, simulating runs with 2,000-lb bombs.[23]

In February 1983, with the strike plan at an advanced stage, Indian military officials had travelled secretly to Israel, which had a common interest in eliminating Khan, to buy electronic warfare equipment to neutralize Kahuta's air defenses.[24] On 25 February 1983, Indian prime minister Indira Gandhi had accused Pakistan of "covertly attempting to make nuclear weapons," and three days later, Raja Ramanna, director of India's Bhabha Atomic Research Center, had revealed that India, too, was developing a uranium enrichment facility.[25] Suspecting something was brewing, the ISI sent a message to their Indian intelligence counterparts in RAW that autumn, and as a result Munir Ahmed Khan of the Pakistan Atomic Energy Commission met Dr. Ramanna at the Imperial Hotel in Vienna.[26] He warned Ramanna that if India were to strike at

Kahuta, Pakistan would hit India's nuclear facilities at Trombay. It lay downwind from the teeming Indian city of Mumbai and an attack would result in the release of "massive amounts of radiation to a large populated area, causing a disaster."[27]

New Delhi paused. Israel stepped in, suggesting that it carry out the raid, using India's airbase at Jamnagar to launch Israeli air force jets and a second base in northern India to refuel. A senior Israeli analyst close to the operation recalled that the plan was to enter Pakistan beneath the radar, with jets tracking the line of the Himalayas through Kashmir. As Reagan's staff finalized arrangements for the president's visit to China in March 1984, prime minister Indira Gandhi signed off the Israeli-led operation, bringing India, Pakistan and Israel to within a hair's breadth of a nuclear conflagration. It was at this point that the CIA tipped off President Zia, hoping the chain reaction would defuse the situation. And after Khan's outbursts in the Pakistani newspapers, India and Israel had backed off. But these were high-stakes games, played between a known nuclear nation—India—and another—Pakistan—that Reagan continued to insist had no capability, the US deception bringing the region even further towards an apocalyptic conflagration.

Soon afterwards, Khan was at it again. This time sticking to a tight script, he contacted the *Daily Jang* and *The Muslim*. "Pakistan can set up several nuclear centers of the Kahuta pattern," he bragged, knowing that every one of his words was being read over the border. "In the event of the destruction of the Kahuta plant, more than one such plant can be set up in Pakistan."[28] To make things absolutely clear, Pakistan's ambassador in New Delhi approached the Indian foreign office, promising that they would make it rain fire if India went ahead.[29]

Indira Gandhi had her resolve to do something about Kahuta rekindled in March 1984, when, just weeks after the Chinese president Li Xiannian visited Pakistan and stated that China endorsed a nuclear weapons-free South Asia, the Indian foreign ministry learned that China appeared to have detonated a nuclear-capable device on behalf of Pakistan at its test site at Lop Nor, an event witnessed by Pakistan's foreign minister.[30] In Washington, the true nature of the China–Pakistan nuclear pact also began to surface. Len Weiss, Senator Glenn's staffer, recalled the congressional backlash as newspaper stories from the UK reached Washington claiming that US and Western intelligence had concluded that China had passed its bomb designs to Pakistan.[31] "This news for us came from nowhere and its consequences were obvious. It was no longer just inexperienced Pakistan striving for a bomb and the US turning a blind eye. It was Pakistan backed by a sophisticated and proven nuclear power with the US burying the bad news from elected officials."[32]

The long-predicted crisis over the US–China deal broke. Reagan aides began lobbying senators, advising that this was the worst of times to cut Pakistan loose. The US-backed war in Afghanistan had been getting bloodier, with the Soviet Union deploying helicopter gunships to slaughter the still poorly armed mujahideen. In February 1984, Bill Casey had flown to Islamabad, where for the first time President Zia had thrown aside his normal caution and his mantra of "don't let the pot boil over," asking for the US to step up its assistance. Rather than approach Congress for additional funding, the White House had agreed massively to increase covert CIA aid. In the first three years of the war, only $60 million in black assistance had been funnelled annually into Pakistan, every dollar of it matched by the Saudis, but now this sum leapt to $250 million a year to meet a Soviet offensive that was expected the following spring. By the end of 1985, the CIA would be contributing $300 million annually, unacknowledged funds that were moved through unnumbered bank accounts, a sign over the desk of the responsible officer at CIA headquarters reading, "War Is Not Cheap."[33] But the White House had misjudged the temperature on Capitol Hill.

Senators Alan Cranston and John Glenn proposed an amendment to the Foreign Assistance Act that barred aid to the Islamic Republic unless the US president certified that Pakistan did not possess a bomb and was not acquiring the technology to make one. The wording went to the heart of the legalistic dissembling that had enabled President Reagan to continue backing Pakistan by claiming that while Islamabad may have been striving for a weapon there was no proof that it had actually been assembled. The Senate foreign relations committee adopted the new and far tighter amendment, which closed down Reagan's options, on 28 March 1984, despite strenuous White House objections.[34] There followed a frenzy of bargaining and bullying with the Reagan administration threatening to withdraw all foreign assistance that finally, after an exhausting round of talks on 12 April, led to the surprise overturning of the amendment by a single vote.[35]

*

Less than three weeks later, Ronald and Nancy Reagan arrived in Beijing and were driven to Tiananmen Square for a twenty-one-gun salute outside the Great Hall of the People. Flanked by Chinese president Li Xiannian, 600 members of the press, aides and US secret service agents, Reagan talked in Chinese about "mutual respect and benefit" before signing the US–Chinese nuclear cooperation pact, while in Washington the row over China's involvement in the Pakistan nuclear program continued to escalate. Reagan arrived home to find a letter from Senators Alan Cranston and William Proxmire (Democrat, Wisconsin). "We [remain] deeply concerned by press reports that China has helped Pakistan develop a capacity to enrich uranium for nuclear weapons use and has provided Pakistan with sensitive information about the design of nuclear weapons," they wrote. "In particular we ask that you personally investigate those allegations and advise us as to whether or not they are true."[36]

All the while, the administration held Pakistan's hand, with Vice President George H. W. Bush flying to see President Zia in May, armed with a brief stating: "Your visit will both symbolize and further solidify the strong relationship with Pakistan we have successfully developed over the past three years, a major administration objective and accomplishment."[37] Like Brzezinski before him, Bush was flown through the Khyber Pass to peer at Soviet expansionism before lunch with Zia served in the cool Murree hills, where the Americans raised the nuclear issue. General Arif recalled: "Bush said that if we exploded a device, things would get difficult for Reagan. But his tone was conciliatory rather than hectoring. It was knowing."[38] Zia insisted that he was thinking of doing nothing of the kind, but while Bush accepted the assurances, he returned to find Washington engulfed in a furious row.

Senator Cranston's staff had been digging. On 21 June 1984, Cranston delivered an extraordinary salvo that questioned the principles on which the Reagan administration stood: security and the national interest. While on an election drive in Jacksonville, Florida, in January 1980, Republican challenger Reagan had apparently said of Pakistan's program, "I don't think it's any of our business if they build nuclear weapons."[39] Now Cranston questioned whether the president was qualified to defuse rapidly heightening tensions around the world. "Nowhere is war waging with fewer restraints and more serious threats to US national security interests than in the Middle East and South Asia," the senator said, citing Afghanistan, the Israeli conflict with Lebanon, and the ongoing Iran–Iraq war in which the US would soon be embroiled, backing Saddam Hussein. "The Reagan administration has not demonstrated a firm commitment to combating nuclear proliferation," he argued, but had instead subsidized the Pakistani nuclear weapons effort.[40]

Cranston warned of a nuclear stand-off in South Asia, advising that India and Pakistan were both preparing more test sites. No one on Capitol Hill yet knew that India and Pakistan were also a jet-wing away from striking each other's nuclear plants. This remained highly classified intelligence. Cranston argued that, contrary to what Reagan had told Congress, Pakistan was accelerating its nuclear program and expanding operations at Kahuta. "None of this information was volunteered to me in classified briefings," he fumed. "But [Pakistanis] now have what they need to produce nuclear weapons. Henceforth US policies must be prefaced on the fact that Pakistan has the designs, the hardware, the plants and the personnel capable of producing several nuclear weapons per year."[41]

Cranston said he had discovered that clandestine purchases made by Khan had increased over the past twelve months and 8,000 centrifuges were spinning at Kahuta, capable of enriching up to 120 kg of uranium per year, enough to fuel seven bombs. Then he turned to China and the delicate US civil nuclear deal. Pakistan had been given a nuclear device designed by Beijing, which had also helped troubleshoot its centrifugal enrichment program. "Pakistan now has the ability, if it so chooses, to export the nuclear technicians and highly advanced nuclear technology and perhaps even nuclear weapons to supportive colleagues in other nations," the senator predicted. "We stand on the brink of a fully fledged nuclear arms race."[42]

In a desperate bid to appear reactive to congressional concerns, Arthur Hummel, then US ambassador to China, was ordered to clarify Beijing's relationship with Pakistan. But he was also furnished with a question-and-answer sheet by the State Department that clearly steered him wide of the truth.[43] "Yes, we have seen the senator's speech and understand his concerns about the dangers of nuclear proliferation. No, we have no comment to make about the Pakistan program." And if anyone asked: "Addressing the charge that State Department officials have, 'Obscured, withheld or downright misrepresented the facts about the Pakistan nuclear program,' the department keeps the appropriate committees of Congress fully and currently informed."[44]

Privately, many within the State Department were worried about the ramifications of the Pakistan policy on US international standing. "American righteousness, for want of a better word, was being eroded," remembered Robert Gallucci, then in the department's Bureau of Politico-Military Affairs.[45] "We were turning up for negotiations with any number of high-handed countries like China or the Soviets, where we intended to extract strong resolutions on any number of critical subjects—arms control, non-proliferation, the test ban treaty—only to have the Pakistan situation raised with us again and again. It was becoming a stumbling block to our wider policies, although no one with access to the Oval Office could see it that way."[46]

Then Pakistan was caught red-handed again, this time on US soil. On 22 June 1984, US Customs agents arrested Nazir Ahmed Vaid, a thirty-three-year-old from Lahore, with two Pakistani accomplices, at Houston airport as they tried to export a box of krytrons, cold-cathode gas-filled tubes intended for use as high-speed switches. They were a critical component of a nuclear bomb's trigger mechanism and required an export license. Vaid did not have one and his attempted shipment suggested Pakistan's nuclear weapons program was entering its final stage.

Vaid and his accomplices had been under surveillance since the previous October, when a company in Salem, Massachusetts, the only US firm that manufactured a particular kind of krytron, the KN22, had contacted the FBI.[47] John McClafferty, customer manager at EG&G Electro Optics, had become concerned when Vaid had offered above the market price and asked if he could pay in gold via the Pakistan-founded Bank of Credit and Commerce International.

Asked why he wanted krytrons, Vaid said they were for the University of Islamabad. General Zia would later claim they were bought to illuminate the flashing lights used by ambulances. Vaid explained to McClafferty that he made ten trips per year to the US on behalf of the university and yet, wearing his creased *kurta pajamas*, it seemed to McClafferty that Vaid was "fresh out of the box" and likely to have been on one of his first foreign assignments. When McClafferty also discovered that Vaid lacked export licenses for Pakistan, he called in the FBI and US Customs. But by the time a case was registered, Vaid had disappeared.

Eleven days later, he turned up in Houston, Texas, and went straight to Eletrotex, an EG&G Electro Optics sales front—which no one other than a specialist would know about—and placed an order for fifty KN22 krytrons with Jerry Simons, sales manager, secured with a $1,000 cash deposit. Simons contacted his supplier in Salem, who asked whether the purchaser held an export license. Vaid did not, and the FBI was brought back in, concerned that the "characteristics of the krytrons ordered were so unusual and their practical use limited." They sat and waited for Vaid to collect his order.

Five months later, Salim Ahmed Mohamedy, a Pakistani businessman, called Eletrotex to clear Vaid's bill.[48] There was no sign of Vaid. Over the next few months, Simons met a dozen times with undercover agents as they waited for the shipment to be claimed. US law stipulated Vaid could only be arrested when he tried to get the package through US Customs. Acting on FBI instructions, Simons attempted to move things along by contacting Mohamedy about the pickup on 13 April 1984. On 19 June, Vaid finally surfaced, arriving in Houston on a flight from Pakistan. Three days later, he, Mohamedy and a third man, Ilyas Ahmed Mohamedy, made arrangements for the krytrons to be shipped.[49]

They were delivered to Houston intercontinental airport, where they were labelled "printed material and office supplies," and as soon as the package crossed into the sterile area of the airport US Customs agents arrested Vaid and his partners, indicting them for giving false statements to customs officials, conspiracy and violating US export laws governing munitions. The FBI was delighted, as was assistant US attorney Sam Longoria, who told reporters: "We strongly suspect Mr. Vaid is operating on the instructions of the Pakistani government and that the purchase of the krytrons was for Pakistani use in obtaining a nuclear bomb."[50]

Tempers boiled on Capitol Hill once again. Pakistan was asked for an explanation and issued a tame statement, refuting any knowledge of Nazir Ahmed Vaid.[51] It was enough for the president, who told Congress in his 1984 annual statement on non-proliferation that Pakistan posed no significant risk, insisting: "I continue to regard the prevention of the spread of nuclear explosives as a fundamental national security and foreign policy objective, and I remain firmly committed to the pursuit of policies designed to advance our non-proliferation goals."[52]

No sooner had the presidential declaration been made than a US reconnaissance unit reported it had lost sight of two Indian air force Jaguar squadrons normally based at Ambala in the Punjab. It was possible, CIA director Bill Casey advised the president, that they had been concealed or moved as a prelude to striking Kahuta.[53] Jittery, the White House instructed the CIA to brief the chairman and vice chairman of the Senate intelligence committee.[54] The State Department sent a strongly worded warning to India: "The US will be responsive if India persists."[55] Despite protests from military planners in New Delhi and Jerusalem, prime minister Indira Gandhi aborted the operation. General Arif recalled: "Our friends had let us know what the Israelis and Indians intended to do and so we let them know how we would respond. Both sides were harrying the other and were absolutely aware of the consequences of every move. In the end it was India that blinked."[56]

That September, with Capitol Hill still unaware of the nuclear catastrophe narrowly averted along the Pakistan–India border, a bill was passed granting a further $635 million to Pakistan, money that was officially for nation building but also rewarded Pakistan's efforts in the Afghan war.[57] Immediately afterwards, the White House launched a credibility campaign. Reagan wrote a private letter to President Zia in which he expressed his "deep concern" that Pakistan's efforts to attain a bomb could undermine its relationship with the US. Reagan requested that Zia not cross the "red line" of 5 percent enrichment, the level required for uranium used in civil applications such as power stations, lest he face "serious consequences."[58] The letter was simultaneously leaked by the White House to the *Wall Street Journal*, drawing positive coverage for Reagan, who was once again portrayed as striving to contain a quixotic ally and adhering to the spirit of the Nuclear Non-Proliferation Treaty. However, at the time of its writing, the CIA and the president had known for almost a year that Pakistan had twice successfully cold-tested its nuclear device, that A. Q. Khan had gone way beyond the red line, having achieved 95 percent enrichment, and that China was likely to have hot-tested a complete device on Pakistan's behalf. The White House even knew, as the Pentagon had modelled it for them, what Pakistan's bomb looked like.

As with many things in the Reagan White House, the Zia letter was theatrical. A classified briefing memo for George Shultz given by Arnold Raphel, then senior deputy assistant secretary in the State Department's Bureau of Near Eastern and South Asian Affairs, revealed that while the letter seemingly threatened Pakistan, Shultz was to emphasize that the president was determined to sustain the US–Pakistan relationship regardless.[59] Raphel warned Shultz that Senator Cranston was likely to propose yet another amendment to prohibit

Pakistan aid. He advised that Shultz should put at ease the Pakistani foreign minister, Sahabzada Yaqub Khan, who had taken over from Agha Shahi in 1982, by telling him that "the president can waive the prohibition if he determines in writing to the chairman of the Senate foreign relations committee and the speaker of the House." Above all, Pakistan was to deduce that the US would do it no harm.[60]

President Zia soon had a more pressing letter on his desk. Dated 10 December 1984, it was written by A. Q. Khan and required careful consideration. Everything was in place at Kahuta, Khan wrote, to detonate a real nuclear bomb—a hot test.[61] That in the closing months of 1984 Pakistan was on the brink of unveiling in public its nuclear program was verified by a second source, the Pakistani finance minister, Ghulam Ishaq Khan. "The nation owes a debt of gratitude to its scientists ... using weapons-grade enriched uranium, a product of KRL, they had developed by 1984 a nuclear explosive device which could be detonated at short notice," he wrote in a private letter sent to staff at Kahuta.[62]

General Arif recalled that Zia was thrilled, but in two minds. He was eager to witness Pakistan's nuclear ascendancy, but equally wary of losing the billions of dollars coming from the US. "Khan was told to wait. He was not used to being refused. He was devastated."

According to Zia's chief of staff, something other than US hard cash had led to Zia calling off the hot test: the imminent arrival of a US delegation that was visiting Islamabad to talk about the nuclear program and witness how the covert war over the border was being prosecuted.[63] "Pakistan could not detonate a bomb while the Americans were here. With the Soviets still in Afghanistan we needed them to go back home with a vision that we were winning that war with US support. We could afford to wait," Arif said.[64]

The visiting congressmen were to be treated to a show. Senator John Glenn was there along with his senior staff assistant, Len Weiss. "Ambassador Deane Hinton was with us, as he was then our man in Islamabad," Weiss recalled. "We were given a cordial welcome in Islamabad. But from the outset we were told 'no President Zia' and 'no A. Q. Khan.' "[65] Instead, Munir Ahmed Khan, the Pakistan Atomic Energy Commission chairman, was put forward. "Munir Khan was a face known to the West, quiet, intense and able to project being serious and honest. I listened incredulously as he said they had no bomb and were not seeking one. The senators, who had supposedly been sent to interrogate the Pakistanis on behalf of Congress, did not challenge him."

Weiss grew impatient. "I don't know why Glenn stayed quiet. Maybe he didn't want to reveal too much about our intelligence. But I decided to talk up, to stir things a little. I threw in a few hard questions," he said. "I mentioned the India crisis, the levels of enrichment rising, the Chinese bomb design, the triggering mechanism in development. Munir Khan just sat there smiling." Still the senators said nothing.

The meeting broke up and the delegation was flown into the jaws of the Khyber Pass, following the well-beaten path taken by dozens of representatives of the US government, towards the emotional heart of the US–Pakistan relationship. "We landed in Peshawar outside an Afghan refugee camp," remembered Weiss. "There were mullahs on a little platform, beneath a tent, all dressed up in silk finery. Senator Sam Nunn [Democrat, Georgia] spoke first and said he was pleased to support the freedom fighters. Just yards away I spied a makeshift hospital for sick refugees, all of them sprawled in the baking sun. Dirty, sick, they looked just terrible. I was appalled that all these women and children were waiting to be treated, parched and hot. There was no medicine or doctors while the talking shop, shaded under the tent, was discussing aid we had given, none of which seemed to have reached the people themselves. I felt outraged."[66]

The US delegation returned home buoyant. A classified cable from the State Department which summarized the visit made no mention of Weiss's outburst or his unconventional cross-examination of Munir Khan. "It had all gone just fine," said Weiss. "There had been no controversy. US aid was doing its job."

Unbeknown to Weiss, his frustration was matched by the CIA. Howard Hart, who was still running the Islamabad station, could not help but come up against Pakistan's nuclear program, with his well-developed sources turning up frequent intelligence on the burgeoning KRL and the increasingly frenetic lifestyle of its founder, Abdul Qadeer Khan. Hart reported his worries to ambassador Hinton, who dutifully communicated them to Washington, although he recalled thinking it was a thankless task. "I got to the point when I wished that Hart wasn't getting all this information [about Pakistan's nuclear capabilities]. It felt rotten that we were spewing the official line when the CIA was getting hard intelligence saying the opposite."[67]

*

Then yet more of the topsy-turvy world that comprised the US–Pakistan relationship was exposed. Shortly after the congressional delegation returned from Pakistan, it emerged that Nazir Ahmed Vaid, the smuggler who had tried to export nuclear triggers from the US to Pakistan, would not be spending time in an American prison. Weiss recalled the disbelief in John Glenn's office.[68] They called the district court in Houston for the file, only to be told that a gag order had been placed on it. Customs sources told Weiss that senior administration officials had sandbagged Vaid's case, ensuring it was downgraded. First, Vaid's indictment by a federal grand jury in Houston had been rewritten, removing all references to nuclear bombs, krytrons and Vaid's role as an agent of the Pakistan government. Vaid's attorney, William Burge, recalled being surprised at the eagerness of the federal prosecutor's office to redraft the indictment.[69] Then the charges of conspiring to ship krytrons without a license, deception and conspiracy were also struck down. Vaid, who was to have been tried under the Atomic Energy Act or the Export Administration Act, which carried a maximum twenty-year prison term, was instead convicted on only one, technical count: violating American export law. On 22 October 1984, taking into account time served, Judge James DeAnda, at the district court in Houston, awarded Vaid the smallest possible sentence, ruling that the accused was simply a businessman "trying to expedite what he thought was a business deal." Three weeks later he was on a plane back to Lahore.

Defense lawyer Burge was clear about what had happened. "I can only conclude that the Justice Department went along because we are friendly with Pakistan," Burge said.[70] As more facts concerning the Vaid case emerged and the assistant district attorney, Longoria, was pressed to respond, he made an alarming admission. "The evidence simply was not there," he said. Longoria did not mean that there had been insufficient evidence upon which to build a case against Vaid. Rather, evidence that had been gathered was withheld from the trial, including three letters linking Vaid to Sulfikar Ahmed Butt, whom the State Department and the CIA had both identified as a coordinator for the Khan network. Vaid had even addressed his letters to Butt, "Director for Research and Development, Pakistan Atomic Energy Commission, Islamabad." It was incontrovertible.

The US at best was shielding Khan's network and at worst appeared not to care that Khan's agents were shopping for nuclear components on US soil. US

Customs weighed in to defend its actions. It pleaded, weakly, guilty of a cock-up rather than a conspiracy, claiming to have misunderstood the significance of the letters, a defense that was barely credible given that its agents had understood the rarefied world of krytrons and their part in triggering a nuclear bomb. "This was one part, a lack of sophistication in Houston; one part, a lack of vigor in the State Department, where the case never got high-level attention; and one part, a poor decision by Justice to permit a plea bargain," a spokesman said.[71]

A Pakistan national caught trying to export a nuclear trigger mechanism from the US, a man who was in constant contact with the head of Khan's procurement network, had had his criminal file rewritten, his charges whittled pencil-thin, and had then been hastily bundled out of the country. Len Weiss, in Glenn's office, recalled the growing feeling of incredulity. "If US Customs was right and the State Department had declined to give the case proper attention then that in itself was scandalous," he said.[72]

Congressmen reasoned that if they could not trust US Customs, they would have to tighten up the law. Representative Stephen Solarz sponsored an amendment to the Foreign Assistance Act to prohibit aid to countries that attempted illegally to export nuclear components from the US. The Senate foreign relations committee passed it, but Peter Galbraith, then a senior committee adviser, recommended setting an even higher bar. "Existing law blocked aid to countries that possessed 'a nuclear device,' so everything came down to theological speculation as to what constituted a 'device.' To keep the aid flowing, the administration had been quibbling over the difference between components and the device itself. We had to tighten up the definition to include nuclear components," Galbraith remembered.[73] Senators Glenn and Cranston proposed the wording: the president would have to certify that "Pakistan did not possess a nuclear explosive device, was not developing a nuclear explosive device and was not acquiring the equipment or technology, covertly or overtly, for a nuclear device," or else suspend aid.

It was a pair of handcuffs the Republicans failed to see coming. Galbraith recalled: "When committee mark-up arrived, the administration was caught flat-footed and could not explain why they would oppose such a positive law."[74] To do so would have required senators to concede that aid to Pakistan was to be furnished at any cost and that the constraining of Pakistan's nuclear program was no longer a priority for the US. Glenn and Cranston's amendment to the Foreign Assistance Act was adopted unanimously for debate.[75] "The White House was incandescent. They could not let the amendment stand. They fought back."

Three Republican senators sponsored a substitute amendment to nudge out the first.[76] Charles Percy, who had been called on by secretary of state Alexander Haig in 1981 to smooth the passage of the original Pakistan aid package, Charles Mathias (Republican, Maryland) and Larry Pressler (Republican, South Dakota), the Senate foreign relations committee's most junior member, gave their names to it. This amendment only required the president to certify that Pakistan had no nuclear device and that US aid reduced the likelihood that it would acquire one. It slipped through by one vote.[77] Galbraith recollected: "I was furious. The Pressler amendment was a pro-Pakistan initiative to undermine a tougher non-proliferation regime."

In Pakistan, Pressler's amendment was met with jubilation. Sharifuddin Pirzada recalled: "Initially we saw Pressler as yet more Pakistan bashing. But Pressler was in reality a clever gift. It appeared to be against Pakistan when really it worked in our favor. We could continue to procure for our bomb and hone our nuclear program and the US aid could continue, as they would argue that we had no actual bomb. The definition of a 'bomb' was, legally and politically speaking, a mile long and two miles deep." Senior sources in the Pakistan foreign ministry even claimed that in redrafting the amendment Sahabzada Yaqub Khan, the foreign minister, had offered key suggestions that were adopted. Pirzada said: "Now we were repeatedly told by officials at State, 'Don't worry, Pressler will save you.' "

It was the season for getting off scot-free. But President Reagan, in his February 1985 statement to Congress on non-proliferation, stated: "It is my firm conviction that preventing the spread of nuclear explosives to additional countries is essential to world peace and stability ... It is no exaggeration to say that the future of mankind may well depend on the achievement of these goals, and I intend to pursue them with unflagging determination and a deep sense of personal commitment."[78]

By the end of 1985 even more barriers to Pakistan's procurement activities had been removed. Among the last to go were inspections for goods exported to Pakistan from the US defense industry. After Steve Bryen, deputy under secretary for defense technology security, complained to his superiors that he had been cut out of the review process for Pakistani exports, having questioned why the Islamic Republic was being allowed to buy components manufactured in the US and Europe that were clearly assisting its nuclear program, the Defense Department withdrew the requirement for licenses for military exports to Pakistan altogether.[79] An invisible tide of military hardware and software was heading for South Asia which was immune from investigation.

In 1985, Khan got off too. Despite overwhelming evidence that he had stolen suitcase loads of highly classified information from URENCO, the Dutch supreme court bungled the criminal case against him. Khan's expensive European lawyers argued successfully at appeal that having served him with a subpoena on 18 October 1983, then prosecuted him only thirteen days later, the accused had been given insufficient time to prepare a case. They also tore to pieces the central evidence cited by the prosecution, which relied on two letters written by Khan from Pakistan in 1976 and 1977 in which he requested assistance from colleagues at URENCO (including Frits Veerman) in identifying components used in the centrifugal process.[80] The prosecution was forced to concede that both letters were oblique and ambiguous, framed in language that made it difficult to verify exactly what Khan was asking for, and therefore equally hard to frame as evidence that he was fishing for parts for a process he had stolen from URENCO. Khan's principal Pakistani lawyer, S. M. Zafar, recalled: "The court's verdict was our complete victory. It proved that the Dutch courts upheld the law at all costs and that Dutch lawyers are very professional and respectful to the law. But most of all it proved that Dr. Khan knew how to fight for his rights and principles."[81]

Realizing the basic procedural errors they had made, and with new evidence in hand, lawyers for the Dutch government prepared to level new charges against Khan. But before they could be entered into court, an intervention killed the case outright. The then Dutch prime minister, Ruud Lubbers, recalled how the CIA asked his government to back off Khan: "The CIA argued that if Dr. Khan was left free they would be able to follow him and keep track of his activities ... They said this was far more useful than scoring points on a conviction that would go nowhere as we had no extradition agreement with Pakistan." Lubbers was furious. "Considerable pressure was applied and we eventually agreed. There might have been a CIA operation to monitor Khan but it was being used to ensure that nothing untoward in the Pakistani nuclear program jeopardized the aid being poured into Pakistan and hence Afghanistan. You could say we were duped by the [US] administration that allowed Khan to get off."[82]

The US was not interested in successful prosecutions that highlighted Pakistan's duplicity. Senior State Department officials, including Norman A. Wulf, then deputy assistant director at the Arms Control and Disarmament Agency, complained that US embassies in Europe were instructed to fire off only the mildest of diplomatic reproaches whenever a European company was spotted assisting Pakistan.[83] So ineffective were they that Richard Perle, then assistant secretary at the Pentagon, derided them as "démarche-mallows." Wulf remembered: "Pakistan was to be cherished, striving as it was for a bomb. Europe, too, was a touchy subject."[84] From 1983 onwards the Reagan administration had to deal with the increasingly hostile nuclear disarmament demonstrations sparked by the aiming of US cruise and Pershing missiles at the Soviet Union from within European bases. "It was not a good time to be scolding your allies."[85]

The Dutch legal system took another pasting that year when Henk Slebos was convicted of breaking Dutch export laws by attempting to ship US-made oscilloscopes, equipment that monitored the efficiency of the centrifugal process, via Sharjah to Pakistan. He was sentenced to a year in prison, only to have the conviction reduced on appeal to a fine and a six-month suspended sentence because prosecutors had failed to prove that the exports had been destined for Pakistan's nuclear program.[86] By the end of 1985 he was back in business, his two firms, Slebos Research BV and Bodmerhof BV, exporting large amounts of goods to clients in Pakistan.[87] Slebos continued networking and was spotted in December 1985 in the company of Gunes Cire, the fair-haired Turkish engineer who had formerly worked for Siemens in Germany and had a company in Istanbul (ETI Elektroteknik) that regularly did business with KRL.[88] In Germany, Albrecht Migule also got off with a fine and a suspended sentence after his company, CES Kalthof, was found guilty of breaching export laws by supplying millions of dollars worth of components to Khan.[89]

The customs and investigating agencies could not keep pace with the nuclear trades being made on behalf of Khan. There was also a lack of political will, with European governments reluctant to interfere in a lucrative industrial sector that generated tens of thousands of jobs. Khan still thrived on antiquated legislation to net container loads of dual-use components that had, by definition, no single, provable purpose. He also relied on the inability of the IAEA to update its trigger lists, the purchase of items from which was supposed to set off international alarm bells. Only in January 1983, after Khan had acquired most of what he needed for Kahuta, did the IAEA begin the lengthy process of reconsidering these lists, including on them centrifuge components and equipment.[90] By the time it was done, anything Khan still required he was manufacturing himself.[91]

It was not as if there were a lack of intelligence on Khan. Richard Barlow, a former CIA analyst who studied a great number of Khan-related smuggling cases, confirmed that Slebos, Cire and Migule were well known to the US intelligence community, which had deployed considerable resources in tracking them. "The CIA was up to the minute on this stuff," Barlow remembered.[92] "We had wiretaps. Phone intercepts. We read mail. The file was as fat as any I have seen. The difficulty was that no one in the administration or in the floors above me at the agency or in Defense gave a damn. And in Europe the US failed to exert any pressure in case governments pointed to the ambiguity of US policy regarding Pakistan."

When it came to advocating the US aid package for Pakistan in 1985, Reagan wrote with ease: "I am convinced that our security relationship and assistance program are the most effective means available for us to dissuade Pakistan from acquiring nuclear explosive devices."[93] Howard Schaffer, who until recently had been deputy assistant secretary at the State Department's Bureau of Near Eastern and South Asian Affairs, recalled: "They lied to us and to the American people and we took it. I became very cynical about Pakistan and my own government. You accept the policy but become cynical about senior people in your own government accepting lies. We all had to live with it."[94]

President Reagan's certification of Pakistan's nuclear status to Congress in November 1985 was done under the terms of the new Pressler amendment, but the form of words he used was the same one the administration had relied on since 1981. Only now they rang especially hollow because the intelligence teams monitoring Pakistan's procurement in Europe had gained a critical insight into a new stage in Khan's program. It appeared that Pakistan was working not only on strengthening its own nuclear capability but on creating a nuclear export program.

The alarm was raised after Western intelligence agencies began monitoring what looked like a routine smuggling mission by the Khan network. A British businessman who claimed to be called Ian Shaw arrived in Bonn in July 1985 where he had arranged to meet a courier company, Global International, that had been hired to move a consignment of super-hard and export-controlled maraging steel, manufactured by Arbed, a specialist company in Völklingen, in the Saarland, near Germany's border with France. Lizrose Ltd, a legitimate British trading company that specialized in innocuous exports to South Asia, had ordered the steel in October 1984. But given the volume, more than 800 kg, and the rarity—the metal was normally used only for components undergoing tremendous stress, like the rotor of a centrifuge spinning at 70,000 rpm—the German intelligence service approached Arbed and cautioned it to back off. The sale was abandoned.[95] Shaw was investigated and customs officers discovered that he was better known in the UK as Inam Ullah Shah. Although Shaw aka Shah claimed that using an anglicized pseudonym merely made it easier to deal with European customers, it also was clearly intended to prevent Arbed from becoming suspicious as to the potential end user for the restricted steel.

Two weeks later, Arbed received a second order for maraging steel from another Briton. This time no government agencies barred the deal, although the British caller in reality was a friend of Inam Ullah Shah.[96] Arbed delivered 800 kg of the controlled metal to a broker in Cologne, who held it until payment was made by a Pakistani, Azmat Ullah, whose name appeared on the receipt for DM1.3 million.[97] There was a blizzard of names involved in the transaction for intelligence agents to pursue, but the name of Azmat Ullah stood out. He was the commercial counsel at the Pakistan embassy in Bonn. The shipper used by Shaw/Shah and the British caller had an intriguing connection, too. Global International had been hired previously by the Pakistan government to move its diplomats' possessions around the world.[98] One more connection came to the surface. Some staff at Lizrose were found to be close friends of Colonel Rashid Ali Qazi, the head of Khan's production machine shop.[99]

According to an intelligence officer connected to the investigation, Arbed sent the sensitive consignment to Hamburg, where it was loaded aboard the container ship *Nedlloyd Everest*, labelled for London.[100] The container vessel set sail on 10 August 1985. But it was not bound for London. Its cargo arrived in Karachi, where import agents from Technical Assistance offloaded it. This name was also known by Western intelligence agencies as a company managed by Ikram ul-Haq Khan, formerly of the Pakistan embassy in Bonn, from where he had sourced numerous components for Kahuta and paid Khan's suppliers, including Peter Griffin. When ul-Haq Khan had left Bonn in 1982, Azmat Ullah had filled his position.

A. Q. Khan was the ultimate beneficiary of the steel and it appeared to far exceed his needs. At Kahuta, his cascade hall was already complete, and suspicions that he was now in the business of exporting centrifuge technology were highlighted when Western intelligence learned that another large consignment of centrifuge components had recently been delivered to Pakistan. The scheme involved Khan's old employer URENCO, which since the thefts of 1974 and 1975 had gone on to develop another four generations of technology at its state-of-the-art plant in Gronau, near Münster, in Germany. Khan had fought hard to get hold of these new designs, according to an intelligence source.[101]

He had contacted Gotthard Lerch and another manager at Leybold Heraeus. Lerch had previously supplied Leybold components that had ended up in the Pakistan nuclear program, including vacuum equipment and a gas purification plant in 1977, and a pumping system and welding plant costing DM6 million in 1982.[102] What Lerch and his colleague received from Khan in 1984 is not clear, but soon after he got in touch they sent a set of highly classified URENCO schematics to MWB, a Swiss engineering factory, along with a contract worth 2 million Swiss francs to manufacture components for a UF_6 feed-and-withdrawal system for a centrifuge plant.[103]

In January 1984, MWB received a threatening letter from URANIT, the German subsidiary of URENCO, advising that "certain technical documents for our plants in Germany are in the possession of MWB." Fearing for the provenance of the schematics, Helmet Elder, a senior MWB employee, called Lerch and his colleague to a meeting at Zurich airport.[104] Arriving on 27 January, they listened as Elder complained that a prosecutor in Cologne had begun investigating MWB's involvement in the alleged theft of classified blueprints from URANIT. Lerch and his colleague took the drawings back. They deliberated as to what to tell URANIT.

The German intelligence service would later claim that Lerch and his colleague had invented a fictional businessman thief, "Mr. Kotari," and fabricated a letter in which he offered the plans to MWB, writing "perhaps we could do business regarding the manufacture of containers shown in the enclosed diagrams." The Kotari letter was then placed where URANIT would find it, and soon "Mr. Kotari" was accused of having commissioned the theft.[105]

Lerch, who along with his colleague would ultimately be acquitted of having stolen the plans, waited for the fuss to die down. One year later, Lerch left Leybold and moved to Switzerland, where another company employed him and soon began to manufacture components similar to those that had featured in the URANIT schematics. Under pressure from an impatient Khan, who had waited more than a year for his feed-and-withdrawal system, the company worked throughout the Christmas holiday in shifts to finish the order. Finally, in early 1985, the unit was shipped via Basel to Lyon in France, from where it was divided and sent as three separate consignments, two to Kuwait and one to Dubai. The order was finally recombined at Kahuta.[106]

Only three items were lost, seized by Swiss Customs who opened a box marked "pressurized containers," a discovery that kick-started a far wider investigation. Inside the box customs agents found autoclaves, commonly used to heat UF_6 during the process of converting it into gas to feed through the centrifuges. As a result, Swiss public prosecutors raided MWB, where they discovered more blueprints belonging to URANIT. The seized plans were sent for analysis at URENCO, where engineers concluded that the basic design corresponded to that "of the Almelo and Gronau plants" but numerous modifications had been made to the drawings, evidently taking into account the needs of Khan.[107] The deviations made it difficult to prosecute MWB or Leybold for theft even though it was plain where the blueprints had come from, but what was without doubt was that equipment manufactured in Switzerland had ended up in Pakistan where it served to double Kahuta's enrichment capacity, giving Khan the capability to build far more centrifuges and refine far more fissile material, as one intelligence source noted, than any one country could have needed.[108]

The Swiss and German inquiries returned to Leybold. One of its former managers who had worked with Lerch was found to have had close connections to Khan. A note written by this man suggested that "for better cover" payment for the contract was to be divided between a Leybold branch in Belgium and another company in Liechtenstein. It was his decision how the company's revenues were divided, he claimed, when questioned. At MWB's headquarters, Swiss prosecutors discovered a document that cast a sharper light on what was being planned in Pakistan, a reference to a "P-2 factory," work for which was valued at DM33 million.[109] Lerch and his colleague had been entrusted with supervising the manufacture of a complete centrifugal plant for Khan to house the P-2 centrifuges that were being manufactured at Kahuta, using maraging steel imported via the UK and Germany. A party of twenty West German customs officials and state attorneys raided Leybold's offices in Cologne and in Hanau, outside Frankfurt, as well as the home of one of the company directors.

Khan's labs had expanded rapidly, as had his reach. "US and European intelligence agencies felt sure Khan was manufacturing an export stock," a senior German intelligence source said.[110] "As well as updating his own facilities at Kahuta, Khan was making parts, centrifuges and components, and possibly enriched uranium as well, to order." But there was no attempt to investigate who the clients might be.

There was no response from Washington either. Instead, Richard Murphy, assistant secretary for Near Eastern and South Asian affairs, testified to a Senate subcommittee: "Development of a close and reliable security partnership with Pakistan gives Pakistan an alternative to nuclear weapons to meet its legitimate security needs and strengthen our influence on Pakistan's nuclear decision making. Shifting to a policy of threats and public ultimata would in our view decrease, not increase, our ability to continue to make a contribution to preventing a nuclear arms race in South Asia."[111] Even to those who could not see all the available intelligence, it was obvious that this arms race was already under way. After Murphy finished testifying, Senator John Glenn quietly intervened. "Pakistan," the senator predicted, "is about to proliferate to the whole of the Middle East, if not the world."[112]

7

A BOMB FOR THE UMMAH

The Kahuta project was costing Pakistan a fortune. A classified analysis by Western intelligence agencies tracking Khan's deals in North America and Europe for the years 1984 and 1985 estimated that he had spent more than $550 million, perhaps as much as $700 million.[1] This ballpark figure was reached by totting up the deals Khan's agents had been observed making, with some latitude allowed for the additional backhanders and rake-offs that Khan's intermediaries would have had to pay and expected to receive.

However, one of those who was permitted to go through the closed books for the megalopolis that Khan Research Laboratories (KRL) had become, found that over the same period it only officially received $18 million per year from the Pakistan government. There was a yawning gulf between what KRL was spending and what the Islamic Republic could afford to pay. General Mirza Aslam Beg, who reviewed the financial data when he was elevated to the position of chief of the army staff in 1988, recalled: "The budget for KRL was separate from everything else. It was kept from the Cabinet and struck from the usual budgetary documents. When I was permitted by the finance minister Ghulam Ishaq Khan to take a look at the accounts, the figures astounded me, only $18 million a year." General Beg had an unlikely explanation: "Perhaps [Khan] survived due to the dexterity of our scientists and Pakistani enterprise."[2]

Subtracting KRL's estimated spending from Pakistan's direct budgetary contributions left a gaping hole that required far more than dexterity and enterprise to fill it. According to the International Monetary Fund, Pakistan in 1985 had no reserves into which it could tap. It also had no collateral against which to borrow.[3] It was only the wiles of Ghulam Ishaq Khan, the minister who remained in sole charge of the project's finances from 1973 until 1988, when he was elevated to president of Pakistan, that kept KRL afloat.[4] According to the European analysts who plotted Khan's spending, and Saudi intelligence officials also familiar with it, KRL was only able to advance by making frequent forays into the vast reservoir of US aid money intended for Pakistan's infrastructure and into the covert aid dispatched by the CIA to arm the mujahideen factions pitted against the Soviets in Afghanistan.[5]

General Arif, Zia's second-in-command, another member of the tiny, elite group who sat on the KRL board and had access to its inner workings, preferred to characterize KRL's funding as a "black art." "Look," he said, crossing and recrossing his long legs, "after a deliberately slow start to the Afghan operation, funding poured in from the US and Saudi. No one can say they didn't get value for money. The Soviets were bled. Some cash, inevitably, didn't hit its mark. But we are only talking as little as 10 percent."[6] Even if the rake-off was at the 10 percent level—and Western analysts vehemently contested Arif's figure—that would have given Khan an extra $90 million in 1985 alone, five times more than his official budget.[7] What Arif had described as value for money actually meant US taxpayers unwittingly funding Pakistan's nuclear weapons program.

KRL's turbocharged spending—in a country that was permanently on the verge of financial collapse—had prompted Western intelligence analysts to investigate as far back as 1982.[8] A seasoned British diplomat, who reviewed the intelligence, recalled: "We came across bank accounts connected to KRL procurement filled with cash that had been transferred from accounts supposed to be for the ISI and the Afghan campaign. KRL accounts were also being fed by fake Pakistani charities in receipt of US congressional aid; two sources of US money being skimmed to build a bomb. Instead of buying mules, pickups and weapons, building schools and hospitals, they were purchasing centrifuge parts and machine tools for their workshops."[9]

To access the CIA money was relatively easy. Bags of dollar bills were flown into Pakistan and handed over to Lieutenant General Akhtar Abdur Rahman, the ISI director. Rahman banked the cash in ISI accounts held by the National Bank of Pakistan, the Pakistan-controlled Bank of Credit and Commerce International (BCCI) and the Bank of Oman (one third owned by the BCCI).[10] KRL was also associated with these banks, enabling Rahman or Ghulam Ishaq Khan to dip into the CIA money and redistribute it to Khan without raising suspicion. The British diplomat said: "As far as congressional money went, a raft of charities, educational set-ups and health groups that were named as legitimate beneficiaries turned out to be covers, run by the military that skillfully drained, laundered and redirected the cash to the nuclear fund. Our best estimate for US aid going astray was in the hundreds of millions of dollars. The CIA diversion was of the same scale. The combined fraud might have, over the years of the war, come near to one billion dollars. Our compatriots in the US heard our concerns. We made them forcibly. But they did not want to turn off the tap or even pressurize Pakistan."[11]

From Pakistan, some of the cash was dispersed to BCCI branches in more than seventy countries or to branches of the National Bank of Pakistan from where embassy officials, military attachés and ISI station chiefs could withdraw it. Sometimes, according to one of Khan's ad hoc bankers, the money was physically carried to the United Arab Emirates, where it was converted to gold bullion, making it far easier to trade and far harder to detect.[12]

Beneath the eyrie occupied by finance minister Ghulam Ishaq Khan sat I. A. Bhatti, KRL's financial comptroller, who operated out of the old RAF hangar at Islamabad international airport which served as Khan's downtown office. Bhatti would make out an order chit for a foreign agent/supplier, who was then issued with a letter of credit by the National Bank of Pakistan, many of which were backed by Commerzbank in West Germany. Against this letter, machinery and equipment were commissioned, raw materials ordered. Once the delivery was ready, cash was released from BCCI or National Bank of Pakistan accounts by commercial counsellors working in embassy positions overseen by the ISI. The most prolific of these was Ikram ul-Haq Khan at the Pakistan embassy in Bonn, in West Germany, who, having been outed by the CIA and Western intelligence agencies as a principal in the Khan network in 1982, was recalled to Pakistan to run Technical Services, the company that took delivery of the maraging steel purchased by a Briton friendly with Lizrose of London and marked for delivery to the UK.

Western investigators later glimpsed some of the skimmed-off cash when a Price Waterhouse audit of BCCI found $49.9 million in unaccounted funds at its London headquarters, money that had been deposited by the Pakistan government and, according to one former bank employee, was intended for KRL.[13]

Other US money was funnelled to KRL through the BCCI Foundation, a Pakistan-based charity established by the bank's founder in 1981. Millions passed through it ostensibly for charitable purposes and yet the foundation presented no detailed or audited accounts. The foundation was supposed to be building schools, orphanages, colleges and hospitals, but it had been awarded tax-free status and was more frequently used to shelter BCCI profits and unaccountable funds, only a fraction of which were actually deployed for good causes. Ghulam Ishaq Khan, the finance minister who granted the tax-free status, served as its chairman throughout while simultaneously running KRL's books.[14]

A US Senate investigation after BCCI collapsed in 1991 found a cat's cradle of accounting dodges. "Unlike any ordinary bank, BCCI was from its earliest days made up of multiplying layers of entities, related to one another through an impenetrable series of holding companies, affiliates, subsidiaries, banks-within-banks, insider dealings and nominee relationships. By fracturing corporate structure, record keeping, regulatory review, and audits the complex BCCI family of entities … was able to evade ordinary legal restrictions on the movement of capital and goods as a matter of daily practice and routine … BCCI [was] an ideal mechanism for facilitating illicit activity by others, including such activity by officials of many of the governments whose laws BCCI was breaking."[15]

BCCI staff could be relied upon to keep quiet. All senior executives came from Pakistan, including founder Agha Hasan Abedi, who made sure he had a close relationship with every government in Islamabad. His mantra perfectly fitted the requirements of Khan. "The only laws that are permanent are the laws of nature. Everything else is flexible. We can always work in and around the laws. The laws change," he said.[16] When Abedi first went into business and, as a precursor to BCCI, formed the United Bank in 1959, he appointed as chairman I. I. Chundrigar, a former prime minister of Pakistan, who was a close confidant of the country's current prime minister, and soon to be dictator, General Ayub Khan.

When Pakistan was severed from East Pakistan in 1971, Abedi sought out Zulfikar Ali Bhutto, making political pay-offs on his behalf during the elections. A year later, Abedi founded BCCI, which rapidly became the seventh largest private bank in the world and in 1978, when Zia overthrew Bhutto, Abedi was one of the first to call on the new president, transferring 40 million rupees (then more than $3.6 million) as a personal gift.[17] Nazir Chinoy, a BCCI branch manager based in Pakistan, recalled: "Every time Mr. Abedi came, he always called on President Zia. President Zia did not meet Abedi during office hours, but in the night. They would finish official dinners first and I would be sitting with Abedi and Abedi would leave for two to three hours and meet with Zia. It was the president that he spoke to first before speaking to the finance minister. I think that Abedi used Zia and Zia used Abedi. It was a two-way street."[18]

Although the European intelligence community frequently warned of fraudulent activities between BCCI, the BCCI Foundation and KRL, the Reagan administration continually denied there was a problem. The British diplomat said: "The important thing for the White House seemed to be to frame the Pakistan diversion of US cash in a wider context. Firstly, the US was winning in Afghanistan—no mean achievement when tribesmen, muskets, and mules were pitted against the Soviets' 40th Army. Second, by the height of the war, the CIA was receiving a global budget of $30 billion a year, so several hundred million taken from here or there by Pakistan was small beer. No one who was interested in entrapping the Soviets in Afghanistan cared about a little side dealing. In retrospect this was a terribly naive position."[19]

It was something that CIA director Bill Casey was happy to let run, stymieing all attempts by Congress to investigate. However, it enraged Robert Gates, who had become CIA deputy director in April 1986. Gates conceded, in private, to a senior State Department colleague, "that I was pissed because not only had Pakistan been taking loads of money but they were also skimming money intended for the mujahideen."[20] The defrauding of US cash, Gates continued, had been endemic, and he regarded the Pakistan military's behavior as treacherous. On Capitol Hill, congressmen continually asked for reassurances that US funding was being spent wisely, as many suspected it was not. Stephen Solarz recalled: "There was this flickering suspicion that the Pakistanis were defrauding us, but whenever I asked I was fobbed off by the administration. If this had come out there would have been hell to pay."[21]

Two hours north of Islamabad, on the road to Taxila, towards the grease-rimmed heart of Pakistan's heavy defense industries, a small name plaque outside a high-walled compound identified it as the home of Brigadier General Mohammed Youssaf, a nationalist, soldier and spy, who ran the CIA's secret war in Afghanistan and continually warned his American counterparts that the mujahideen were not getting what they needed (as a result of fraud and theft).

For a former Pakistan army general and high-ranking member of Pakistan's elite intelligence service, Youssaf has little to show today. Pakistan's armed services were notoriously acquisitive, their loyalty paid for with houses and parcels of land, one for every corps they commanded, and after a career that would potentially span five or six reassignments a military man could normally retire with an appreciable portfolio of real estate. Youssaf had only a dog driven mad by ticks that thrashed about in his compound, from where the guttural rumble of bulldozers grading a new four-lane highway could be heard day and night.

Youssaf's sitting room was decorated with scores of military citations accumulated over his thirty-seven years of service. "I was hand-picked," Youssaf said, explaining how ISI director Rahman had singled him out in August 1983. "I was a brigade commander on divisional exercises in Quetta when they called and I couldn't believe they had the right Mohammed Youssaf." A bear-like man, he had spent his life scorched by the desert and frozen by the mountain passes that bordered Pakistan's habitual enemy. Youssaf felt as if he was more suited to soldiering than the ethereal world of espionage. "To my dismay the news was correct."[22]

Pakistan's civilian population regarded the ISI with fear and awe. But the military loathed "the directorate" as it was known. One of the ISI's functions was to monitor the loyalty of senior army officers, ensuring their support for the dictatorship. "In those days of martial law under Zia the fear was very real indeed," Youssaf said. "I took the posting in October 1983 and then, as far as my in-laws and friends were concerned, I vanished, like a diver flipping off the side of a boat and sinking into a deep trench."

Youssaf recalled the first time he met the CIA director. "I was introduced to 'The Cyclone' in 1984." The ISI revelled in its codename for Bill Casey. They thought it best described his anti-Communist tirades, which regularly disrupted meetings. "He flew into Rawalpindi's Chaklala airbase, in a black C-141 Starlifter that taxied to a desolate part of the airstrip," Youssaf remembered. The plane, which bore no tell-tale markings, had been refitted with beds and an array of electronic jamming equipment, and flew the 10,000 miles from Washington to Islamabad without stopping by refuelling in mid-air. Youssaf said: "There were no diplomats present. We deployed no immigration staff or customs men. Pakistan air force guards were stood down. In town, the US ambassador threw a dinner to distract the diplomatic corps."

After that first meeting, Youssaf would meet Casey several times a year. He recalled sitting opposite him at a long conference table at ISI headquarters: "Sometimes Casey appeared to be dozing off but then quick as anything he would snap a reply or call for vengeance against the Soviets, shouting 'those bastards must pay.' He was never squeamish about the methods used. He had a callous, combative streak to his character."

Youssaf contemplated the conundrum of Bill Casey. "He hated politicians back home. He was contemptuous of Congress. Casey bragged that he withheld information as often as possible, arguing that secret wars were just that—secret." Casey's critics accused the Office of Strategic Services (OSS) veteran of being obsessed with unorthodoxy, a condition archly described as "night-drop syndrome"—a reference to the OSS's preferred and perilous technique of parachuting teams into enemy territory at night.[23] "He did not care that cheats and con artists were all around him, as long as the Soviet bodies piled up," Youssaf recalled. But Casey's greatest mistake was to agree to ISI terms for funding of the war: "It was the cardinal rule in Pakistan that no American ever became involved in the actual distribution of funds or arms once the money had arrived. Pakistan did as it wanted to—or perhaps as it needed to." Cash was fungible. Covert wars demanded it. Anything else, checks or electronic transfers, created a paper trail that would have been exposed by the Soviets as proof of US involvement, risking an escalation of a regional conflict into something far more global and deadly.

Early in 1984, General Youssaf caught wind of a fraud. Despite the talk of money "pouring in from the US," insufficient funds were reaching the battlefront. Youssaf remembered: "We suffered a never-ending anxiety of running out. We required 35 million rupees [$1.5 million] every month just to move supplies from Pakistan into Afghanistan. What we got barely covered the basics. There was a constant howl of complaints that US cash was being stolen, but the fiddling was not at our end." Somewhere between the point of delivery, where the dollar bills were handed over to the ISI, and its distribution to the forward lines controlled by Youssaf, the money evaporated. Defeating the Russians was the sole US priority and to have made a huge stink about money being siphoned off by Pakistan would have brought the thorny subject of trust into the equation, and that was not something that President Reagan wanted to talk about.

There was another vulnerability that Pakistan exploited to KRL's benefit: the supply of munitions. The rules of engagement for the first half of the 1980s were that the mujahideen, so as to protect Pakistan and the US from accusations of interference, could deploy only Soviet-made weapons. Initially, the CIA used a store of Soviet weapons it had accrued over the years, but as the operation grew and more than 65,000 tons of weapons and ammunition were required annually, the CIA bought arms on the black market and delivered them to Karachi docks covertly, from where the ISI moved them to its Ojhiri arms depot, near Rawalpindi.[24] General Youssaf said: "Guns and bullets earmarked for the Afghan war offered ample opportunity for corruption. One method was for agents acting for Pakistan to secure a deal with the CIA and screw the agency by cheating on what was bought."

Youssaf recalled how one arms dealer of Pakistani descent found his way into the confidence of the CIA and offered to sell 30 million bullets for a .303 rifle at $0.50 per round. Under orders from Zia and Rahman, the dealer procured the ammunition from Pakistan army stores for free, securing $8 million from the CIA for the purchase. "A ship loaded with the ammunition left Karachi and sailed out to sea for a day, to ensure the deception worked. Then it docked and unloaded its supposedly imported supplies," Youssaf continued. The double-dealing backfired when the crates reached Ojhiri and Youssaf discovered that every round bore the stamp "POF," Pakistan Ordnance Factory. The entire shipment had to be returned to the POF to be filed clean, an operation that was prohibitively expensive and took three years.

Rahman also supervised a secret trade in CIA-supplied weapons which were sold on by Pakistan's agents, with the funds raised redirected to KRL, a precarious operation that went on until Washington demanded an independent audit of the Ojhiri arms depot in 1988.[25] What finally persuaded the White House to intervene was the appearance in Central Asian arms bazaars of US-manufactured shoulder-launched Stinger missiles, introduced to the Afghan war amid great controversy and secrecy to bring down Soviet Hind attack helicopters.[26] Weeks before US inspectors arrived to conduct the audit on 10 April 1988 the arms dump mysteriously exploded, sending shells raining down on Rawalpindi and Islamabad, killing 100 and injuring more than a thousand. General Youssaf recalled: "It was 10.10 a.m. and we thought India was attacking. Ten thousand tons of munitions were sucked into a devastating fireworks display. The crash and crump of secondary blasts could be heard miles away." One Stinger landed in the water tank of A. Q. Khan's neighbor's house.[27]

The official Pakistan government line was that faulty mortars bought from Egypt had sparked an unstoppable fire.[28] However, General Hamid Gul, then a senior ISI offier, who conducted a secret inquiry on behalf of ISI director Rahman, recalled "the blast was in reality a very effective act of sabotage." Two agents hired by the Pakistan military had been ordered to conceal the wholesale theft of munitions, including Stingers, and had chosen to do so by starting a small fire. "They had been over-eager and soon the blaze grew out of control," Gul remembered.[29] "The US stood by and could prove nothing." An indication of the monies that Zia was keen to realize by selling munitions to aid KRL was given by Arnold Raphel, then serving as US ambassador to Pakistan, who estimated that the destroyed ordnance at Ojhiri had been worth between $120 million and $130 million.[30]

More than anything, it was the methodology required for a secret war that had enabled Pakistan to defraud the US to the benefit of KRL, recalled General Youssaf. "Normal bureaucracy was suspended. Nothing was committed to writing." As a grand double bluff, the ISI even developed a cover story for Afghan operations, a reasoning that it believed would stymie all rumors and paper over its duplicitous dealings with the US. "Whenever the ISI had to work with civilians, or those who could not be completely relied on to keep quiet," said Youssaf, "we bound people up by telling them that whatever they were doing was related to a covert project for making Pakistan's nuclear bomb. Such was their nationalism and the romance that surrounded KRL that no one talked." In truth, these civilians were working for the secret war in Afghanistan which was being plundered, wholesale, to keep Khan's project in Kahuta afloat. But they would never know the difference.

President Zia was well aware that the US money and political goodwill keeping KRL alive was finite. "Zia began to see the truth in something I had long argued," recalled former foreign minister Agha Shahi.[31] "We were now deep inside the US pocket. Pakistan needed to win independence so as not to suffer when the inevitable happened and the US dropped us. Pakistan needed to broker new alliances and develop a revenue stream that was dependable and outside the scope of the US-run Afghan war."

Even in the mid-1980s, there were clear indications that America would soon be focused elsewhere. Soviet president Mikhail Gorbachev later claimed that the

Politburo had agreed, tentatively, to a withdrawal from Afghanistan in 1985, with a decision taken in November 1986 that the war should end "within one year or two."[32] When the ISI gleaned the news too, Zia began casting around for alternative sources of finance.

Shahi recalled how the president pushed for the country to act quickly to secure itself financially and strategically. KRL was Pakistan's money pit, costing hundreds of millions of dollars to maintain, but it was also potentially a cash cow, Khan's advances in the field of uranium enrichment being unique and extremely valuable. Out of the handful of countries that had mastered enrichment, including China, France, Pakistan, the US and the Soviet Union, only China and Pakistan were free to share it, having refused to sign the Nuclear Non-Proliferation Treaty (NPT). Thanks to Khan's determination, Pakistan was years ahead of China in its centrifuge technology and had got the process spinning right the way up to producing weapons-grade material. This technology was worth millions if Pakistan was able to sell it, and, according to senior military officers who served in Zia's cabinet, in early 1985 an elite group of principals, steered by the president, began at highly secretive meetings to explore trading KRL's skills and assets.[33]

The subject was first tentatively broached with potential customers in September 1985, when a delegation from Pakistan's foreign ministry met their counterparts from Iran, Syria and Libya to discuss strategic cooperation.[34] Although aware of the extreme sensitivity and implications of nuclear proliferation, which if discovered would instantaneously bring sanctions upon Pakistan and shatter the favorable relationship with the US, no one at Army House in Rawalpindi perceived it as immoral or considered the risk too large to take. "Having seen the US so flexible in the past, everyone doubted that it would sanction us at all," recalled General Arif.[35] "Also, few of us held the NPT in high regard. We referred to it as a monopoly, to service the West's interests. There were so many countries that had been allowed to arm and proliferate—Israel, South Africa, Argentina—countries that slotted into the US's foreign policy requirements and were allowed to do as they please."[36]

Part of the motivation to sell came from Zia's long-held view that Pakistan should share its weapons technology with the wider Muslim *ummah*, but as a devout Sunni and follower of the fundamental Deobandi sect he had serious misgivings about arming neighboring Shia Iran. However, back then Iran was on the defensive, hemmed in by its war with Iraq in the west, by the Soviets fighting in Afghanistan to the east and threatening to cross into Iran from the north. The Shias were a contained and localized minority, the underdogs to the US-backed Sunni elite of Islamabad, Amman, Cairo and Riyadh. No one contemplated a time when that Sunni strength and wealth would be threatened by war in Iraq and a Shi'ite awakening with its epicenter in Iran. Selling something as dangerous as a nuclear bomb to an unpredictable neighbor was a step too far, but selling Tehran uranium enrichment technology, the first stage in a long and difficult process, in the knowledge that Iran's scientific community had been severely depleted and possibly irretrievably damaged by the 1979 revolution, was something Zia could just about stomach—if he thought long enough about the millions of dollars that would flow from such a deal.

The West's determination to stop Pakistan from getting the bomb had been driven by a firm belief that if Islamabad did not lose it (through a breach of internal security) or use it (against India) it would sell it, unable to resist the lucrative profits offered by such a forbidden trade. But the last thing the analysts watching Pakistan's progress predicted was a nuclear relationship between Pakistan and Iran. That no one looked harder or seemed to take it seriously enough at the time might be explained by the unlikely nature of an alliance with Shi'ite Iran, which was theocratic and austere, while Sunni Pakistan remained spasmodically democratic and temperamentally autocratic. Iran regarded itself as an ancient civilization reflecting millennia of history, while it viewed Pakistan as a Sunni upstart formed in 1947. Pakistan's ISI feared Shia extremism within Iran and blamed it for fomenting unrest in Pakistan, while Sunni militant groups continually goaded Iran, which accused the ISI of aiding and abetting them. Pakistan had been wary of the Shia revolution in Iran, worried about the instability it induced in the region and the radical clerics it elevated. Iran, having made its hatred of "the Great Satan" a showpiece of domestic and foreign policy, was continually frustrated by Pakistan's tendency to fall back on the US.[37]

But beneath the surface there were common bonds. Iranian and Pakistani societies were both steeped in religious and mystical culture, sharing their music and writing. The Urdu and Persian languages shared many stories and myths, with the *Rubáiyát of Omar Khayyám* as likely to be on the shelves of a house in Islamabad as in Tehran. More than anyone before him, President Zia had elevated clerical Islam in Pakistan, ensuring that madrasahs flourished across a republic that was unmistakably remolded on the rules of Islam, and Pakistan had made efforts from the first few days of the Iranian Revolution to befriend its neighbor.[38]

In March 1979, Agha Shahi, Pakistan's foreign minister, had flown to Tehran for a meeting with Ayatollah Khomeini, which set in motion a process of confidence building which gained momentum after Shahi returned to Tehran that December to lobby for the release of the US hostages. Iran was soon caught in the middle of an apocalyptic war with Iraq and fighting a common enemy with Pakistan. Iran and Pakistan both needed to hold back the Soviet threat and they collaborated on the secret war plans, Iran even contributing to the Afghan war chest, although Tehran endlessly argued with Pakistan over which mujahideen leader they should back.[39] In February 1986 this confidence building resulted in Pakistan offering to help Iran with its stalled nuclear program, with A. Q. Khan flying to Tehran accompanied by Brigadier Sajawal.[40]

Iran's nuclear ambitions had begun in the 1950s when the shah had commissioned a nuclear research facility at Tehran University, and had continued in 1974 with work beginning on a German-supplied nuclear power station at Bushehr, a port city on the Persian Gulf coast. But that project had stopped in July 1979 when the new theocratic regime had been unable to pay its workers or German contractors from Siemens, who left claiming they were owed $450 million.[41] The ayatollah readdressed the nuclear issue again in December 1981 when Reza Amrollahi, head of the Atomic Energy Organization of Iran (AEOI), announced that significant deposits of uranium ore had been discovered in four locations.[42] By 1984 Iranian scientists were conducting experiments at a subterranean nuclear research center near Esfahan, and Western intelligence agencies received reports that Iran had also established a small pilot uranium enrichment centrifuge project at Moallem Kalayeh, northwest of Tehran.[43]

Iran's religious leaders had disparaged nuclear weapons as un-Islamic when they were swept to power in 1979, but they relented as the war with Iraq grew more apocalyptic. In March 1984 the Iraqis bombed Bushehr (where work had restarted) and one month later West German intelligence tapped a meeting of Iranian officials discussing a two-year deadline to obtain a nuclear device.[44] Within weeks, French intelligence reported that Tehran was debating whether to strike a deal with Pakistan to import enriched uranium or even the wherewithal to carry out its own full-scale enrichment program.[45] Soon afterwards, Iran announced that it had succeeded in mining "high-quality uranium," and that September the Pakistan proposal was firmed up by the Iranian delegation in Islamabad.[46]

Khan's trip to Tehran in February 1986 was a short one, but he was on the ground long enough to be spotted by Israeli intelligence and their Indian counterparts in RAW, who reported that Khan stayed at a state guest house before being taken on a tour of Iran's civil nuclear reactor project at Bushehr.[47] He was warmly received and accompanied on his travels by Mohammad Reza Ayatollahi, then deputy director of the AEOI.[48] However, the Bushehr visit was a cover. Khan was not in Iran to talk about nuclear power but uranium enrichment. Reza Amrollahi, the AEOI director, arranged another secret meeting for him. He was introduced to Brigadier General Mohammed Eslami of the Iranian Revolutionary Guard Corps.[49] Established by Ayatollah Khomeini in May 1979 as the guardians of the revolution, by 1986 the Revolutionary Guard numbered 350,000 recruits and 1 million volunteers. Organized into battalion-size units, they operated independently from the armed forces and, having recently acquired a small air force and a modest navy, they formed a private army of God which answered to the mullahs and sought new ways of fending off their neighbor, Iraq.

General Eslami, who was chief of the Revolutionary Guard's research group, asked Khan for a detailed presentation on the processes developed by KRL. "On his return, Khan was slightly dismissive," recalled Dr. Shafiq, whose father was on the trip. "He doubted Iran's vision or commitment to see it through. He was slightly contemptuous of the fact that what Iran wanted was to build its own enrichment facility rather than buy a ready-made one. He just could not see them doing it without an awful lot of help. But this was not his problem and the deal was not between KRL and the AEOI or even the Revolutionary Guard. This was government to government."

After Khan returned to Islamabad, Seyyed Ali Khamenei, the Iranian president and future supreme leader of Iran, visited Pakistan and discussed the issue of nuclear cooperation with Zia.[50] He gave a green light to the project, signing a secret accord to share KRL's assets with Tehran, a pact that signalled the last fizzling of the clerics' opposition to entering the nuclear arms race.[51]

Zia and Khan were right to doubt Iran's ability to see the nuclear project through. Iran had a dearth of experts, thousands having fled abroad even before the shah fell, and to draw them back the AEOI placed advertisements in the foreign edition of *Kayhan*, one of the oldest Iranian newspapers, which appealed for them to attend a conference in Iran just a month after Khan's visit.[52] Those who came home and were persuaded to stay would soon be given access to some of Khan's most sensitive technologies, not all of which came directly from Islamabad. China, which had been aiding the Iranian nuclear program on and off for many years, had recently passed on data and drawings relating to a revolutionary new process to smelt uranium, which it had obtained from KRL and which KRL had stolen from URANIT.[53] The smelting process, by which highly enriched UF_6 was cast into metal spheres which became cores for a warhead, was the last stage needed in the manufacture of a bomb. All that Iran needed now was the rest of the process: a uranium conversion plant to transform raw yellowcake into UF_6; centrifuges to provide a steady source of enriched uranium; warhead designs and missiles to carry them to their target.

8

THE PINEAPPLE UPSIDE-DOWN CAKE

If Iran had much to do, so did Pakistan, where Zia's plan to create a revenue stream independent of the US was marching ahead. To accede to his president's vision, A. Q. Khan needed to change the flow of the KRL network from procuring to proliferating, and to do this unnoticed he needed to spread his operations away from Kahuta to a more neutral zone. Pakistan had a special relationship with Dubai, one of the seven United Arab Emirates, whose markets and cafés brimmed with refugees from Iraq and followers of the vanquished shah of Iran, war-weary Shias rubbing shoulders with Sufis, Sunnis and salesmen from the Gulf states. Between them all, they stoked a raucous black market afloat with anything from which money could be made, Islamic or secular, living or dead, organic or inorganic.

Dubai had begun to grow rich on oil revenues in the 1960s and remained outwardly religious but instinctively pragmatic, while Zia's Pakistan was increasingly knitted together by an intolerant madrasah culture led by inflexible maulvis, or preachers. But the economies of the two countries were inextricably linked, as while Pakistan's industry dwindled Dubai's rocketed, fuelled by a tax-free climate that drew millions of working- and middle-class Pakistanis, whose wages and savings mostly returned back home. Many went on to settle permanently, dominating Dubai's gold trade and organized crime, as well as its armed forces. As theocratic rule spread like a murmur across Arabia and South Asia in the 1980s, travellers came to Dubai in droves to sate their vices while they dabbled in business, watched over by an army of intelligence agents from the Gulf, India and Pakistan, who came to listen in, blackmail and trade in secrets.

When Khan had first visited in the early 1970s, Dubai had been still little more than a fleet of dhows anchored in a drab harbor at the mouth of a creek. But even then there were things a Muslim could do there that were prohibited elsewhere in Islamic South Asia, and Khan had arranged, surreptitiously, to have a vasectomy. He was content with having had Dina and Ayesha, his two daughters, and having lived as an NRP or Non-Resident Pakistani in Germany, Belgium and Holland he had come to accept the values of the European nuclear family. Khan was also growing restless with Henny after a decade together. It was during this Dubai trip that he first betrayed her, beginning an affair with a businesswoman whom he called "R," and who was, inevitably, everything that Henny was not. "R" was Pakistani and had always lived in Islamabad, while Khan had had to forgo Pakistan for more than fifteen years. "R" was clever but deferential, while Henny, as a smart European woman, demanded that she be treated as an equal. A close friend said: "Henny was a little shouty. Intolerant. She argued the toss over everything. 'R' was demure. A minor wife. Khan's romanticized idea of Pakistan. The affair was as much to do with his homesickness as the differences between him and Henny."[1]

By the mid-1980s, having commuted to and from Dubai for several years, balancing his secret double life and continuing to see "R" as often as he could, Khan had developed well-embedded connections. One of his brothers came to live in the city and made money importing Daikin air-conditioning units from South Korea. Dubai was also the place to which the hub of KRL's procurement network had decamped after the Emerson Electric scandal of 1978 had awakened European customs, police and intelligence services to Pakistan's trade in dual-use components and machine tools.

Peter Griffin, who had exported tools for Khan in the 1970s, was already well ensconced. "Abdus Salam and I had decided to run the business out of Dubai," he recalled.[2] The only drawback was that all foreigners were required to find a local sponsor in order to open a company. Through his connections at Colindale mosque in north London, Salam had gained an introduction to S. M. Farouq, a Sri Lankan Muslim who, along with his brother, ran a thriving business importing fruit and vegetables. "They operated out of this dirty little room with one light bulb. But they knew everyone," Griffin said. "S. M. Farouq introduced Salam to a local sponsor Khalid Jassim, and together they set up Khalid Jassim Trading, whose registered offices were Farouq's apartment, just off Nasser Square.[3] I was not a partner but had a profit-sharing agreement with them." The company, Griffin claimed, began by importing building materials for

KRL. "I didn't ask what the bits and pieces were being used for. I mean," he said, in a recurring defense of his business, "if I was selling someone tires I wouldn't ask for reassurance that they were not going to be used on a getaway car."

S. M. Farouq was a tough negotiator and a prolific networker. He impressed Griffin and Salam. He was also a bully and a penny counter who rarely let go of a deal. At the first opportunity, Salam also introduced Farouq to A. Q. Khan. Griffin said: "Khan immediately took to him." They had much in common. Both were preternaturally superstitious. "Farouq always said 'with your blessing' whenever I wished him good luck in a project. I only found out later that his soothsayer had told him I was his guiding star and to be revered," Griffin recalled, and said that both Farouq and Khan rarely acted without first consulting their palmists. Khan's was a "greasy little man from Karachi," but whenever he was in Dubai he would also take advice from Farouq's Svengali.[4] Every minor event, for Farouq and Khan, was a consequence of divine providence. "One night we were walking home about 1 a.m. across Dubai, unable to find a taxi," remembered Griffin. "You could track our progress through town by the sound of the barking dogs. We were all tired and quarrelsome. Suddenly, Farouq fell over, got up and said, 'Please forgive me, Peter.' He then explained God had just punished him for harboring bad thoughts about me: if he'd not agreed to come out with us so late, he'd now be tucked up in bed."

Not only were they alike, but Khan realized that Farouq was exceptionally well placed to run the logistics for KRL. The fruit wholesaler understood everything there was to know about trade to and from Dubai, and KRL, which had been founded on import, was about to go into export. But things did not run smoothly in Dubai. Khan's network of import–export barons was full of sharp elbows, as eager to better each other as they were to service KRL. Griffin recalled: "In 1982 I said to Salam, you come back to the UK, it's my turn to go over to Dubai, to be tax-free for a couple of years. Salam made excuses. He claimed we had made no profit, when I had put hundreds of deals together for him." The company collapsed later that year after Farouq took out a case at the sharia court, claiming Salam did not own the company. He won, and Salam left Dubai and, according to Griffin, relocated to Florida, where he continued to sail close to the wind, persuading a local penitentiary to allow him to invest inmates' prison-shop earnings in the Bank of Credit and Commerce

International. Griffin alleged that all their savings disappeared when the bank went under in 1991 with $7 billion in unsecured debts.[5]

In Dubai, Griffin suggested forming a new company with S. M. Farouq, with Saeed Bin Belailah, Dubai's director of immigration, as sponsor.[6] Henk Slebos, Khan's old university chum, came over, eager for a piece of the action, having bumped into Peter Griffin at the KRL guest house and heard talk of the money to be made. When Farouq, Slebos and Griffin formed the Bin Belailah Trading Company, Khan was delighted and nicknamed Griffin "Butch Cassidy," as he was the shorter of the two Westerners and talked endlessly, while Slebos, with his luxuriant porn-star mustache and roving eye, was known as "the Sundance Kid."

The final member of the Dubai connection emerged out of a tragedy and a family feud. When Farouq's elder brother died, Farouq mounted a hostile takeover of the family's assets, including a mansion in Colombo, the Sri Lankan capital. He evicted his grieving brother's family and brought his nephew to work for him in Dubai. Known to everyone as Tahir (as his full name, Buhary Seyed Abu Tahir, was a mouthful), he had been visiting Dubai since 1981 when he was a sixteen-year-old schoolboy. Now working for his *chacha*, or uncle, he was consigned to sleep under the desk in the front room. "Tahir became a kind of house-boy or employee to his *chacha*," recalled Griffin. "Everyone felt sorry for him because he had wanted to study in the West." Only Khan spotted his potential, meeting him for the first time in 1985. He took Tahir under his wing and set out to transform the naive Sri Lankan teenager into a major player.

Those who knew Tahir said he was a quick learner, exchanging his *dhoti* and sandals for Western suits and handmade shoes.[7] Such was Khan's influence that Tahir soon adopted his mannerisms, rubbing his hands together and sitting cross-legged, as his mentor did. Exiles from the worries of South Asia, Tahir, Farouq, Khan, his aide Brigadier Sajawal and Sajawal's son, Dr. Shafiq, longed for good food and frequently crossed the sandbar on the strait in a boat to reach the cold markets on the other side.[8]

Then the Bin Belailah business imploded. Slebos was not a team player, Griffin alleged. "He grew bored and walked away, leaving us with all the start-up costs, £30,000 in my case." Slebos went back to Holland, but his former partners prospered. They abandoned the apartment off Nasser Square and converged on a new, upmarket apartment block more suitable to the high-stakes world Khan was entering. Tahir and his *chacha* rented flat 604 on Sheikh

Rashid Road, with floor-to-ceiling windows and balconies that overlooked the Dubai creek.

Khan, who was by then visiting Dubai a dozen times a year, rented flat 910, a four-bedroom apartment on the ninth floor, where his wife and daughters stayed whenever they came shopping in Dubai and which was used for entertaining KRL suppliers. Down the corridor, Griffin rented flat 904 as staff accommodation for the newly formed partnership, al-Abbar General Trading, born out of the ashes of Bin Belailah.[9] People from all over the world began flying in to see Khan at his new base of operations in the Sheikh Rashid building, which became known among nuclear component suppliers as "Mummy & Me," after the children's store that was located on the ground floor.

Securely ensconced in Mummy & Me, the various factions began to settle down. Farouq went into semi-retirement in Singapore, leaving Tahir to run the fruit and vegetable business, which had already expanded into importing and exporting computers and would soon source centrifuge components and machine parts for Khan, too. In the summer of 1987, satisfied with his Dubai operation, Khan called an extraordinary general meeting, introducing Tahir and his uncle to Mohammed Farooq, head of foreign procurements for KRL, and two Germans: Heinz Mebus, the engineer who had survived a letter-bomb attack; and Gotthard Lerch, the former Leybold Heraeus executive, who had relocated to Switzerland, where he was under investigation in connection with blueprints stolen from URANIT. Also there was Colonel Qazi, the head of Khan's production machine shop.[10]

Khan talked excitedly about a new customer and swore everyone to secrecy. They were going to do business with Iran. He laid on the table a handwritten list of what the Iranians had asked for: "a sample machine (disassembled), including drawings, specifications, and calculations for a 'complete plant' and material for 2000 centrifuge machines."[11] Khan explained that early successes at KRL had led to his team abandoning the basic P-1 centrifuge design based on the URENCO technology stolen in 1975. Pakistan had begun working on a more advanced P-2 centrifuge, an adapted version of the German G-2, which could spin twice as fast because it was fitted with super-strength steel rotors. That left KRL with a warehouse full of spare P-1 machines and components. It was these that Khan, at the behest of General Zia, intended to sell to Iran. The Iranians need not know the technology was outdated, and as he had serious doubts that they had the expertise to put it all together anyway, the Pakistan government was happy enough for them to try. Mebus and Lerch would be needed to source other items on the list that were not available in Pakistan but that they had supplied before, such as "auxiliary vacuum and electric drive equipment and uranium reconversion and casting capabilities," the entry and exit processes for a centrifugal cascade.[12] Against every item were suggested prices, which began in the hundreds of thousands of dollars and ranged into the millions. Even if the Iranians bought the bare minimum, the deal would net KRL (and that meant the Pakistan government) in excess of $2 million.[13] The list drawn up at the Mummy & Me meeting would be shown to General Mohammed Eslami of the Revolutionary Guard at a rendezvous later that year in Switzerland.[14]

In Pakistan everyone was delighted with Khan, except Khan. He was by now regularly visiting Dr. Haroon Ahmed, his psychiatrist, in Karachi, who recalled: "Regardless of his apparent success—and don't get me wrong, I had no idea what specifically Khan was up to—he seemed eaten up. It was as if he was unable to sate his ambition."[15]

One of Khan's most significant ongoing problems was his relationship with his wife. While he continued to see "R," for whom he had bought a new apartment in Islamabad, he believed Henny had gone mad, something he divulged to Peter Griffin. "He was worried about her. I told him it was the menopause. He froze. He said he could never suggest such a thing to her as she would eat him alive. It all had to come from Henny herself."[16]

Dr. Ahmed asked Khan if he thought that he was a contributory factor in Henny's apparent madness. The psychiatrist recalled: "He was a handful and prone to grandiloquence. He was becoming insufferable to be around. This once mild-mannered guy had taken to booming, 'Jinnah built Pakistan but I saved it.'" Khan had begun to seek out awards and titles. In 1984 it was two honors: a gold medal from the people of Kahuta, whose village had been engulfed by KRL; and another, the Justice Hamood ur-Rahman gold medal, named after a resolute former chief justice of the Supreme Court.[17] "So uncertain was Khan of Khan that he expressed himself most clearly by giving to charities and mosques and schools, all of which would then have to bear his name as testimony to his greatness," Dr. Ahmed remembered. "I often thought that this was not generosity in the real sense. He really did this so that if he was driving down the Peshawar Road, let us say, the chances are he would pass a building bearing his name—and it would remind him that he was indeed the great Abdul Qadeer Khan." Having had to keep quiet for so many years, he now craved public recognition.

Soon Khan found a method of replicating himself. In December 1985, he opened the Ghulam Ishaq Khan Institute of Engineering Sciences and Technology in the hills of Topi, in the Northwest Frontier Province, appointing himself as the director, hoping to mass-produce a legion of metallurgists and engineers honed in the image of their benefactor, naming it after the man who as finance minister had solidly backed KRL since its inception.[18] Khan did not pay for the institute himself but approached Agha Hasan Abedi, the founder of the Bank of Credit and Commerce International, who so helpfully funded KRL by redirecting US aid and CIA cash. Abedi found $10 million from the charitable funds held by his BCCI Foundation, and within a short time another of Khan's resolute backers was rewarded by being made rector of the institute: Professor Martin Brabers, his old mentor from the Catholic University of Leuven, who had helped get him the job at URENCO.

However, Dr. Ahmed recalled that sometimes Khan's generosity was barbed. "My own small psychiatric hospital project, to provide free mental health care to people in Karachi, became gathered up in his pathology. I could see it happen and stupidly I did nothing. Khan could be really quite charming. A capable, convincing persuader. He came to my consulting room one day and announced that he had begun collecting money, fund raising, on my behalf. And then slowly and imperceptibly he began to exert small amounts of pressure. It was little things really. Little things that would lead to big things. But it began by Khan suddenly becoming my 'very good friend,' and I use this phrase wisely. He was my 'best friend.' And I was just a little scared of what would happen next."

In 1986, when the Iran deal was at its most tense, Khan invited a friend to come to Kahuta. No one outside a very small circle of scientific staff, generals, Chinese technicians, European suppliers and a Saudi prince or two, had been permitted to visit KRL. What made this invitation more surprising was that the man invited was a journalist who wrote occasionally for *Hurmat*, a small-circulation weekly Urdu digest.[19]

This meeting was to be "live," a face-to-face with Khan. Until now, everything Pakistan's journalists wished to ask had to be written down and submitted to the KRL chief or the military as a Q&A. But Khan even allowed the writer to bring a photographer, promising to pose in his office. The journey to KRL was unforgettable for the journalist, who wrote: "Anti-aircraft guns and missiles were aiming towards the sky. With our onwards journey the number of them as well as radar antennae and missiles increased. The summer had begun but it didn't warrant air conditioning and yet the brigadier travelling with me in the car had switched it on. Perhaps he also felt, like me, the heat of the atmosphere we were travelling through." They drew up at the first checkpoint. "The brigadier slowed down the car. Two security officials glanced into the vehicle and saluted. Then a second checkpoint and a third. And then a fourth checkpoint as we passed into the danger zone. After a couple more yards we stopped and were greeted by another brigadier who took us to Abdul Qadeer Khan. He was sitting at his desk with an open attaché case before him in which, clearly visible, sat a black revolver."[20]

Khan was in fear of his life. He had been terrified by news that Mossad assassins had killed one of the leading scientists working on the Iraqi nuclear program, Yahya al-Meshad, an Egyptian by birth, who had travelled to France to examine critical components that Baghdad intended to purchase for its Osirak reactor.[21] On the day Yahya was due to fly home he was found stabbed and beaten to death at the Meridien Hotel in Paris; the last person to have seen him alive, a prostitute known as "Marie Express," was also found dead a few weeks later following a hit-and-run accident.[22] The *Hurmat* journalist wrote: "In these days of most modern automatic and telescopic weapons what is the utility of a revolver? Dr. Khan is the most important symbol of Pakistan's progress. It would not be wrong to say that today he is one of the few extremely valuable Pakistanis ... His personality is assuming a mythological stature. He is being labelled as the James Bond of the nuclear world and also Pakistan's biggest and most valuable personality." A man like this had to be better protected by the state, and Khan had taken his own measures to secure his health, appointing as his personal physician Lieutenant General Dr. Riaz Chowhan, a former surgeon-general to the Pakistan army.[23]

The scribe was shocked that Khan had had to take his own safety precautions. "In my view the doctor sahib is not receiving the respect and honor due ... the government and also the nation is guilty of negligence," he wrote. "An organization in Lahore has given the doctor a gold medal for his superior services, but is it enough? The president should give to the doctor the highest honor in the country at a ceremony attended by federal ombudsmen, ministers, chiefs of the armed forces, chief justice of the Supreme Court, governors of the four provinces and other personalities. In addition, he should be encouraged and honored in every way possible. Every Tom, Dick or Harry is patronized in every manner—why this coldness to doctor sahib?"

Finally, the article revealed what lay behind Khan's invitation to the man from *Hurmat*; he was soliciting for Pakistan's top nuclear job. "In order to overcome the energy crisis in Pakistan," the journalist wrote, clearly regurgitating Khan's own thoughts, "the Pakistan Atomic Energy Commission should be overhauled and its leadership should be handed over to this *Marde Momin of Iqbal* [a real believer of Islam]." As well as his own job, A.Q. wanted Munir Khan's chair at PAEC. He was furious that Munir Khan continued to run the country's plutonium program and was still technically in charge of weapons research and design, the most sensitive and high-profile aspect of Pakistan's armament program. Via an act of ventriloquism, A. Q. Khan spoke directly to the president of Pakistan: "The present PAEC has assumed the position of white elephant and this organization cannot be expected to relieve the nation from the increasing energy crisis." Dr. Khan, on the other hand, had performed a miracle. "He has invaluable knowledge and experience. He is a courageous and a great patriotic personality. At the moment he is managing thousands of employees at Kahuta very efficiently. He is extremely courteous and tolerant and possesses tremendous management capabilities."

A. Q. Khan's public outbursts, combined with rumors of ever-expanding nuclear cooperation between Pakistan and China, again began to fuel talk in India of a military strike against Kahuta. Rajiv Gandhi, who had succeeded his mother, shot dead by Sikh militants in 1984, flew to Washington in June 1985, determined to make headway, warning the administration that he was struggling to control an intense lobby calling for the destruction of Pakistan's nuclear weapons program.[24] But the press briefing ahead of his visit revealed that the White House was still sitting on the fence and was likely to be deaf to his appeals. "We have made it clear to the Pakistanis that our ability to continue our security assistance program presumes restraint in the nuclear area. They have assured us that they have no intention of developing a nuclear weapons program."[25]

When Gandhi returned home empty-handed amid rumors that Khan had again petitioned his president to hot-test a nuclear device, the Indian parliament demanded military action and the US administration felt compelled to send a high-level firefighting team to Islamabad and New Delhi to calm tempers: Michael Armacost, under secretary of state for political affairs, and Donald Fortier, the third-ranking White House official in the National Security Council.[26] The pre-trip press briefing was baffling. "Q. Why are Armacost and Fortier travelling to South Asia? A. They will review the full range of bilateral cooperation. Q. But isn't the primary purpose of the visit the nuclear issue? A. We would expect the subject to come up. Q. Do we have any new and special concerns about nuclear problems? A. No. Q. What is the likelihood of an Indian strike against Pakistani nuclear facilities? A. I am not going to address such a highly speculative question."[27]

The visit achieved nothing. Just weeks later, with New Delhi and Islamabad edging towards a nuclear stand-off, President Reagan again certified to Congress that Pakistan had no nuclear device.[28] In July 1986 the White House announced that it intended to increase aid to Pakistan to $4.02 billion, $1 billion more than the previous package.[29] The State Department prepared another stalling brief for administration officials facing tough questions. Drafted by Arnold Raphel, and cleared by Armacost, it outlined a surreal Q&A. "Q. Does Pakistan have the bomb? A. … I am not prepared to provide any details about what intelligence tells us that the Pakistanis are doing in the nuclear field." To end further damaging speculation, Raphel added: "For the future, I am not going to get involved in giving daily or weekly assessments of the Pakistan nuclear program."[30]

When Reagan certified that Pakistan had no bomb in October 1986, there was a rebellion inside the White House and the State Department.[31] Professor Stephen Cohen, a Hindi-speaking academic, who having spent many years researching the military in Pakistan and India had developed strong contacts with both, grew concerned. In 1985 he had been drafted on to the policy planning staff at the State Department, which was expected to stand back from the day-to-day grind and analyze the bigger picture. By 1986, Cohen felt he could no longer watch US–Pakistan policy dictate relations with India. "I grew worried," recalled Cohen. "White House policy was irrational and potentially dangerous. I started writing memos on reversing this situation, on how relations could be continued while more actively trying to stop Pakistan going nuclear at the same time. I was brought into a briefing at a very high level where we tried to square the circle, curtailing Pakistan's nuclear program while appeasing those behind the aid program."[32]

Cohen recalled that Mort Abramowitz, an assistant secretary of state for intelligence, was also present at this meeting and conceded that the administration had got it wrong.[33] Cohen said: "Mort insisted that there were to be no official papers on this discussion. Everyone was sworn to secrecy. That's how touchy a subject this was."

But Cohen and others lost. "The bottom line was that nobody could stand up and do anything to frighten the relationship with Pakistan and I was told by one very senior person at State that if we did what I wanted to do—for example, try and rescind US military aid, like pulling back the F-16s—we would never get it through government. I was warned that we would lose our jobs tomorrow. One senior official in the Reagan administration told me, 'Why are you talking about this? Keep your head down.' It was not a suggestion."

Norm Wulf, the deputy assistant director at the Arms Control and Disarmament Agency (ACDA), recalled the tense atmosphere after the 1986 certification. "It was an outright lie. The president lied," Wulf said. It was the job of the ACDA team to review all US intelligence on KRL and Wulf confirmed that the National Security Agency, with its globe-spanning ability to intercept and eavesdrop, had for years been reading virtually every communication sent between the Khan agents in Germany, Switzerland, the UK, France, Turkey and Dubai. They had even secured the floor plans for KRL and its supply lists.[34] "The US knew Pakistan had the bomb. Not just the pieces of a bomb. It was assembled and ready to go." Within a few months, the 1986 certification nearly choked the administration.

The Indians had had enough. Rajiv Gandhi had a new and assertive army chief, Lieutenant General Krishnaswami Sundarji, who had been the first Indian strategist to war-game a nuclear conflagration with Pakistan, in 1981. In the autumn of 1986, Sundarji recommended resorting to more forceful means to let Pakistan know New Delhi had reached its limits: a vast military exercise in Rajasthan, in which India's tactical nuclear weapon would be maneuvered into position along the border—a potshot away from Pakistan. In December 1986, Rajiv Gandhi gave the go-ahead and Sundarji launched the largest war-game ever seen on the subcontinent, a walk-through larger than any launched by NATO since the Second World War, bringing together all branches of the armed forces, more than a thousand armored vehicles and 400,000 troops. It was a model for a full-scale invasion, codenamed Brass Tacks.[35]

Zia immediately understood the message. Sundarji was viewed in Islamabad as a hawk, a general capable of persuading even a peacenik like Rajiv Gandhi to allow an exercise to become a reality. With the 1971 East Pakistan crisis imprinted on everyone's mind, Zia ordered mechanized divisions and artillery to amass on the Pakistan side of the border. By January 1987 the two armies of Pakistan and India were facing off, 100 miles apart, a three-hour tank ride away from combat—wholly due to the US-sponsored nuclear program at KRL. Knowing Pakistan's armed forces were no match for India's firepower, Zia decided to deliver a threat that would force India to back down.[36] A. Q. Khan was to be the messenger and it should have been his finest hour. Zia asked Khan to arrange an interview that would play loudly in India, in which he would reveal just a little more of the secret work at KRL—in particular, the state of readiness of his program and Islamabad's willingness to assemble and deliver a bomb should it be sufficiently provoked.[37] But Khan had to remain ambiguous enough for Washington to continue funding Pakistan.

Khan approached Mushahid Hussain, a well-respected journalist and editor of *The Muslim*, an influential and pro-government daily. Mushahid Hussain could be relied upon to be discreet. Hussain was casting around for a journalist of suitable gravitas to conduct the interview when he received a telephone call from over the border in India. An old friend and syndicated columnist of *The Muslim*, Kuldip Nayar, was on the line. The Indian journalist wanted a sponsor to get him over to Pakistan. Although Zia had not considered giving the story to an Indian, Nayar was exactly the kind of journalist that he needed.[38]

A humanist Hindu born in Sialkot, a part of the Punjab that is now in Pakistan, Nayar had been raised among Muslims talking Urdu and English, before fleeing to New Delhi in 1947, where he learned Hindi and made his home among Hindus. Torn between his cultural roots in Pakistan and the emancipation of being a Hindu living in India, Nayar had become a writer whose columns were syndicated across the subcontinent. His New Delhi apartment bore the signs of his mixed ancestry as well as his success: shelves filled with books and clippings; the walls hung with the iridescent abstract paintings of M. F. Hussain, the most sought-after (and controversial) Muslim artist in the subcontinent.

Nayar recalled how Mushahid Hussain had jumped at the chance to get him over to Pakistan.[39] To his surprise, within twenty-four hours of the telephone call, he had a visa, a ticket and was on his way, arriving on 29 January 1987. "Mushahid met me at the airport and said he had got me a very big present." Hussain told Nayar he was taking him to meet A. Q. Khan. "I could not believe it. He was one of the most famous people in Asia and among the most infamous in India. There were two conditions: no tapes and no notes." Nayar consented and they drove to Khan's house.

"As we reached the house, my mind was working overtime," remembered Nayar. "Was it a put-up thing or just for show? There were no surprised faces among the guards at an Indian having arrived in the most sensitive location in Pakistan." Khan's house was wood and stone with a sweeping veranda and a garden filled with brilliant red Dutch tulips. "I looked up and Khan was standing on the veranda. He waved and beckoned me up. He said, 'I am a great fan of yours. I read your column regularly.'"

Henny was waiting in the drawing room with a trolley laden with teacups and a large pineapple upside-down cake. Nayar recalled: "It was my favorite. I asked her how she knew. She smiled." The Khans were going to an awful lot of trouble to set him at ease. "She didn't stay to pour the tea. I could tell Khan wanted to say something. But I broke the ice. 'In the subcontinent there was really no one who had achieved his level of fame,' I said, knowing how to massage his ego. 'I would like to know about your background.'"

Khan handed over an Urdu magazine in which he had previously talked about his family history. "He didn't want to waste any time. He said I should read it later." Nayar swung the conversation awkwardly to the subject of KRL. "I said that I had seen the road to Kahuta on the way in from the airport and surely the Indians must have tried to get down it. Khan replied, 'They have tried. But we rebuffed them. No foreigner has ever been inside.'" Sensing he was getting nowhere, Nayar decided to rile Khan. "Suddenly I said, and I confess that this was a fiction, 'Khan sahib, see, when I was coming over from Delhi to Islamabad I ran into Dr. Raja Ramanna—I named one of the fathers of the Indian bomb. Ramanna asked me, 'Where are you going?' I said, 'To

Islamabad to meet with Dr. Khan.' Ramanna said, 'Don't waste your time. They don't have anything. No bomb, no men, no rationale.' "

Khan's face fell. "This really hurt," Nayar recalled. He went off like a cooked mortar, banging the table with his fists and screaming, "'Tell them we have it. Tell them. Tell them.' I pressed on. 'Khan sahib, it is very easy to claim these things but you have not tested.' He jumped up. 'You don't have to test in the ground any more. You can test in the lab. Let me assure you, we have tested.' He was furious now. His face was purple. 'We have it and we have enriched uranium. Weaponized the thing. Put it all together.' Mushahid looked dismayed. Now we were getting somewhere."

Nayar poked and nudged. "I said, 'If you have tested it would be a tremendous warning for India.' Khan stared at me coldly. He spoke very clearly. 'Mr. Nayar, if you ever drive us to the wall, we will use the bomb. You did it to us in East Bengal. We won't waste time with conventional weapons. We will come straight out with it.' " Nayar had his story and got out as quickly as he could. On the way back to the hotel, Mushahid Hussain pleaded with Nayar not to print Khan's claims that Pakistan had assembled a bomb. "He seemed shocked Khan had gone so far," Nayar recalled.

As soon as he was back in India, Nayar called an old colleague in London, Shyam Bhatia, a journalist on the *Observer*. The paper was so worried about the ramifications of Khan's alleged statement that it spent more than a month checking out Nayar and his story. Everything inched forwards until eventually, convinced that he was telling the truth, the *Observer* splashed with it, "Pakistan Has the A-Bomb," on 1 March 1987, quoting Khan as saying: "What the CIA has been saying about our possessing the bomb is correct. They told us Pakistan could never produce the bomb and they doubted my capabilities, but they now know we have it." Kuldip Nayar was paid a miserly £350 for his scoop which raced around the globe.[40]

The news slapped on to the pavements and the phone lines to Washington and Islamabad trilled, with politicians and journalists desperate for confirmation that Pakistan had a nuclear bomb and was preparing to use it. President Reagan was advised to continue with the business of the day, which happened to be delivering his annual statement on non-proliferation to Congress. "A central objective of my administration has been the prevention of the spread of nuclear explosives to additional countries," he said, presenting what was by now a standard text. "I intend to continue my pursuit of this goal with unflagging determination and a deep sense of personal commitment."[41]

Behind the scenes there were furious discussions. Zia had done the unthinkable and embarrassed the US president by going back on his promise never to build a bomb. The US–Pakistan relationship was now up in the air. Pakistan panicked. Zia's plan had been to deliver a subtle and speedy message to India but everyone had overlooked Khan's short fuse. Having been rubbed up the wrong way by the sly Nayar, Khan had blown off and abandoned the carefully honed script, bragging that Pakistan had assembled a nuclear bomb, something no one was supposed to know. To make matters worse, while the *Observer* was sitting on the story, Zia had resorted to diplomacy to defuse tensions on the Indo–Pakistan border and had travelled to New Delhi where he and Rajiv Gandhi both agreed to pull back.[42] With the Indian army back in barracks and Operation Brass Tacks over by the time the *Observer* went to press, the story served no purpose other than to embarrass Zia and destroy the lucrative Pakistan–US relationship before its time.

Zia's first task was to mount a major damage limitation exercise. As an incredulous White House searched for explanations, Khan claimed Nayar had tricked him into giving the interview, adding, "the government of Pakistan has made it abundantly clear that it has no desire to produce nuclear weapons."[43] It was insufficient for Rajiv Gandhi, who attacked the US for failing to stop Pakistan's nuclear weapons program and for continuing to supply Pakistan with economic and military aid.[44] Wasim Sajjad, Pakistan's minister for science and technology, countered with a categorical denial about the bomb, addressing Pakistan's National Assembly: "Today Pakistan does not possess an atomic bomb, has no desire to have a bomb, and cannot afford to manufacture an atomic bomb."[45] Soon Pakistan's foreign minister, its ambassador to the US and its president all issued similar denials, Zia claiming that Pakistan "has neither the desire, nor the intention, nor the capacity to develop a nuclear weapon" and that he was not about to break his gentleman's agreement with the US president to honor this commitment.[46]

However, the Nayar story would not go away. In Pakistan, Khan called Zahid Malik, an influential journalist who had become his memoirist, a man through whom Khan frequently fed stories into the public domain, many of them untrue or exaggerated. Together they concocted a poisonous smear. Nayar was "a scummy RAW agent." Shyam Bhatia was "a Hindu dog in the pay of Jerusalem."[47] To get "their lies" into a serious and credible newspaper like the *Observer* these two spies had deployed a device beloved of intelligence agencies around the world—a honey trap. Her name was Pamela Bordes, a former House of Commons researcher in London. Malik wrote a diatribe in which he bastardized a real scandal unfolding in London where Donald Trelford, the *Observer*'s editor, had had a well-publicized affair with Bordes, who created a stir by simultaneously dating the editor of the *Sunday Times*, Andrew Neil, resulting in an undignified public spat between two journalists who between them represented the somber end of the British press.

Now rewriting the gossip, by placing the love interest in the pay of RAW or Bhatia, Khan and Malik maliciously described Bordes as an "Indian call girl who played a key role in the publication of the concocted interview." Malik wrote on behalf of his mentor: "The lady ... of Indian origin ... took a special interest in the publication of the sensational interview ... Shyam Bhatia also played an important role. He knew that Dr. Donald Trelford (nicknamed Dirty Don) could be easily tempted by the call girl. He also knew that the Indian call girl was well equipped with sexual weapons. As their meetings continued and Pamela obliged him fully, Donald Trelford agreed to buy the story ... Our hats off to you Mr. Trelford ... the readers will now realize how a network of intrigue was woven around the most reputed and invaluable son of Pakistan, Dr. A. Q. Khan, the man who totally destroyed the Hindu dream of black-mailing and subjugating Pakistan." It was a mischievous piece of black propaganda which was gobbled up in the cafés of Islamabad. In a city where maulvis stifled joy, gossip was oxygen.

However, Khan's admission to Kuldip Nayar continued to fizz and whirr like a firecracker, infuriating Zia, who demanded answers and a scapegoat. He called in all Khan's deputy directors, including Mohammed Farooq, the head of foreign procurement.[48] Khan had suggested Farooq had been behind a plan to reveal everything to the Indian journalist. But Farooq was not in Pakistan, having decamped to Mecca on haj with his family.

As Washington continued to berate Zia, he got Arif to call Pakistan International Airlines. Arif demanded a plane and a pilot. They were dispatched, along with a military team, to bring back Mohammed Farooq from Saudi Arabia. "But the military team did not know what Farooq looked like. No one had thought to give them a photograph," recalled Dr. Shafiq, the son of Khan's aide, Brigadier Sajawal. "They dared not fail. They did what all terrified men would have done and seized every Farooq holding a Pakistan passport they could find on haj." A planeload of Farooqs was flown back to the Chaklala airbase in Rawalpindi, where they were met by General Arif and a phalanx of ISI officers. Arif demanded that Khan's deputy step forward and he nervously emerged from the crowd of namesakes.

KRL scientists had their movements restricted. Everything they did had to be cleared through the army. The Iranian deal that was running at speed was to be chaperoned at every stage by Zia's men. "Their passports were impounded. They kept very quiet. No one went anywhere without a military escort for many months," Dr. Shafiq said. But in the midst of the chaos everyone had forgotten to bring back the wives and children of all the Mohammed Farooqs, who were abandoned to make their own way back from haj.

Kuldip Nayar got on with his own work back in New Delhi, resolving that in future he would charge more for his stories. A few weeks after the scandal broke, there was one more call, from Washington. "Senator John Glenn rang. He asked me: 'Sir, is it all true?' I said: 'Senator Glenn, every word of it is as Abdul Qadeer Khan told it to me. The whole dangerous, angry, cantankerous truth.'"

9

THE WINKING GENERAL

Kuldip Nayar had given a truthful account of his meeting with Khan and the CIA knew it. Regardless of the political environment in Washington, within the agency there was a unit that still doggedly tracked weapons of mass destruction. The Office of Scientific and Weapons Research (OSWR), based at the Directorate of Intelligence in Langley, Virginia, had as its chief Gordon Oehler, an electrical engineer from upstate New York.[1] He was pedantic and principled and would soon become the national intelligence officer for science, technology, and proliferation, the pre-eminent member of the US intelligence community on matters of proliferation.[2]

Under Oehler's leadership, and despite the inclinations of Reagan officials, the OSWR had kept a special watch on Pakistan. Such was Oehler's concern with the volume of accumulating intelligence that he recruited a new analyst in 1985 specifically to track Pakistan's nuclear program. Richard Barlow was given free rein. Oehler awarded Barlow code-word clearances that gave access to material filed according to the methodology used in its capture.[3] *Humint* stood for a living source, *photint* for material gathered by satellite or aerial reconnaissance, *comint* for intercepted communications, *techint* for anything gained through technical means, and *royal* signified intelligence so volatile, using methods so secret, that it was shared with very few.[4] Barlow could see almost all of it.[5]

The CIA's new boy consistently maintained a high score rate. Barlow's material on Pakistan was regularly included in the national intelligence daily, a summary of the main intelligence items from the previous day, and the president's daily brief, the most restricted of assessments, viewed only by the president, the vice president, the secretaries of state and defense and a handful of senior aides. Reagan et al. already had a pretty clear picture of what was happening in Pakistan and with Barlow's material piled on top, by the summer of 1987 the US had an unparalleled and exacting insight into Pakistan's nuclear program, making the administration painfully aware that its policy on the Islamic Republic was buckling daily under the pressure of ground realities.

The administration had just about weathered the firestorm of the Kuldip Nayar affair, Congress having been badgered and bullied to play it down in favor of pursuing victory against the Soviets, when yet another crisis reared. A Canadian businessman of Pakistani origin was arrested in Philadelphia attempting to buy twenty-five tons of maraging steel, not realizing that the men he was doing business with were undercover FBI and US Customs agents.[6] The repercussions of the arrest in July 1987 would not have been immediately obvious to anyone apart from on Capitol Hill and at the State Department, especially its legal team headed by Abraham Sofaer, who warned that if the buyer was proven to have links with Pakistan's government the Solarz amendment would be invoked, severing US aid.[7]

The White House had known about this operation since the previous November, when Arshad Pervez first pinged on to the radar trying to buy a consignment of the super-strength metal from Carpenter Steel in Reading, Pennsylvania.[8] Suspicious of the buyer, Albert Tomley, Carpenter's international marketing manager, had immediately contacted the Department of Energy, which controlled the export of such materials.

An affidavit filed in July 1987 at the Philadelphia district court by John New, a US Customs agent, was spartan but marked out the parameters of the case.[9] FBI and US Customs agents had replaced Carpenter's salespeople soon after Pervez's initial approach and as they cozied up to him he had jabbered about his client in Pakistan, a "Mr. Inam," working for a corporation in Lahore. The indictment alleged that in an attempt to secure an export license for the steel, Pervez had offered to bribe a Commerce Department official to the tune of $5,000, made a down payment of $1,000 to an undercover federal agent, and agreed to provide a further $2,000 if and when the license was approved.

Over the following months, Pervez repeatedly switched stories concerning the end use for the restricted metal. It was needed for turbines, he said on one occasion, later claiming that his client in Pakistan, "Mr. Inam," was "dealing with compressors." He also suggested that the steel was for rocket engines, even for an engineering project run by Karachi University, and, later, was to be melted down to be sold as ingots. As he grew more confident, he eventually let it slip during a conversation taped by US Customs agents that his real client was Kahuta.

The admission confirmed the suspicions of Richard Barlow at the OSWR, who was managing the operation from CIA headquarters.[10] Pervez had ordered from Carpenter a specific type of maraging steel called 350-gauge which, being super-strong, was used almost exclusively to manufacture components that moved at tremendous speed, generating excessive heat. Key among them were tubular rotors for a P-2 centrifuge of the kind being developed by Khan.

Pervez wanted more than one order of steel. He claimed he had $2 million to spend on eleven additional shipments and he also wanted beryllium, a grayish, super-light, flexible metal which could be machined into a shell for a nuclear device, a thick layer of it encasing a core of highly enriched uranium and acting as a neutron reflector, which would enable scientists radically to reduce a device's critical mass while retaining the scale of the blast, ensuring a bomb retained its bang even when it had lost its breadth.[11] Smaller devices suggested Pakistan was looking to drop a bomb from a plane, Barlow suspected.[12]

Pre-empting Pervez's conviction for exporting banned materials from the US to Pakistan, the administration went on the offensive, demanding that Congress think very clearly about the ramifications of suspending aid.[13] By the summer of 1987 the mujahideen had turned the war in Afghanistan around and were winning. Cutting Pakistan off now might compromise the mujahideen's position and maybe even persuade the Soviets to stay on. The administration contended that in the Pervez affair no one had proved Pakistan's intent, or even that Pervez was working for the Pakistan government. When the assistant district attorney in Philadelphia agreed, stating that federal investigators had yet to nail those who had hired Pervez, Reagan officials breathed easy.[14] Michael Armacost, under secretary of state for political affairs, who in 1985 had tried unsuccessfully to placate India and Pakistan as they edged towards a nuclear showdown, presented a classified testimony to the Senate foreign relations committee that asserted there was no clear evidence linking Pervez to the Zia regime.[15] The head of the Philadelphia customs office backed him up.[16]

Pressure from Capitol Hill mounted. Solarz, whose Damoclean amendment hung over the White House, warned Reagan: "Pakistan's actions are creating a dilemma for the United States. But if the Department of Justice has sufficient evidence to seek an indictment then presumably the president has ample justification for triggering the law."[17] Senator John Glenn agreed: "We have short-term interests in Afghanistan," he said. "But we have long-term interests in trying to keep our finger in the dike to prevent the spread of nuclear weapons. That is more important than anything else."[18] The chairman of the Senate foreign relations committee, Claiborne Pell (Democrat, Rhode Island), got straight to the point. Describing Pakistan as "in contempt" of US law, he called for the $4.02 billion aid package to be revoked.[19]

But the White House maintained its course and took the fight to Pakistan. Michael Armacost flew to Islamabad to demonstrate US resolve, the press brief claiming he intended to "impress on President Zia the need to crack down on private procurement networks."[20] The word "private" here was critical. It was the escape hatch, skillfully inserted by Armacost and the State Department lawyer, Abraham Sofaer.[21] Privateers were responsible for running Pervez and absolutely not the government of Pakistan. The US needed to create as much space as possible between the smuggler and the Islamabad regime if they were to prevent the Solarz amendment from being invoked. It was a defense that would become extremely useful in the years to come.

Pakistan played along, issuing an arrest warrant for Pervez and a press briefing from its foreign ministry that suggested the US would accept Zia's denials of any involvement in what it termed "the export conspiracy."[22] Incredulous, Stephen Solarz demanded to see the raw intelligence on the Pervez case. Under congressional rules, having put his name to an amendment that was potentially to be triggered, it was his right to receive a classified briefing.[23] However, the caliber of that briefing under the Reagan administration's highly politicized Departments of State and Defense was not guaranteed.

The acting Director of Central Intelligence picked General David Einsel to address Solarz and his congressional colleagues, a significant choice.[24] A Pentagon heavyweight, coaxed by Bill Casey to join the intelligence community in 1985 after a long career dedicated to warfare and promoting the use of nuclear weapons, Einsel served as the national intelligence officer for non-proliferation, an ideal representative for an administration that had no time for non-proliferation. Einsel had survived the bloody battle for Heartbreak

Ridge in Korea and had gone on to become a chemical officer working with Agent Orange in the First Cavalry Division (Airmobile) during the Vietnam War. In peacetime, he had taught chemistry at the US military academy at West Point and run an army program testing and manufacturing munitions, explosives and propellants. From 1980, Einsel had worked for defense secretary Caspar Weinberger on the development, deployment and planning of US nuclear and chemical weapon systems and was later hand-picked by Reagan to become executive director of the Star Wars program. He could be relied on to douse a liberal-led fire.

Gordon Oehler in the OSWR and Deputy Director for Intelligence Richard Kerr were extremely unhappy with the choice, recalled Richard Barlow.[25] Einsel's involvement guaranteed that the Solarz briefing would become gladiatorial, and Oehler and his deputy Charles Burke grew more worried as the day approached.[26] "Burke called me saying, 'We're very concerned about what Einsel's going to get up to at Congress,'" Barlow remembered. "As the CIA's top expert, I was selected by my superiors, including Bob Gates [then Deputy Director of Central Intelligence], to testify."

With all the facts of the Pervez case at his fingertips, Barlow was asked to backbench, to be the voice in Einsel's ear. "The problem was," Barlow said, "that Einsel was also the national intelligence officer in charge of everything to do with the mujahideen." Einsel had been drafted in to reconcile the potential clash between the covert Afghan war being coordinated and funded by the CIA with the data being gathered by the intelligence community about Pakistan's nuclear program. "Einsel was known as the 'winking general.' He was going to play it all down," Barlow recalled.

Barlow went into a frenzy of preparations and took out some insurance. "I went down to State with Charlie Burke and got talking points cleared by their number one man, Steve Aoki."[27] Initially it went well. "They gave me a list of things I was allowed to say if needed. He signed me off," Barlow said.

A code-word room in Congress, used for hearings involving intelligence, was booked. Solarz attended alongside his fellow subcommittee members, accompanied by a handful of staffers who had sufficient clearances. Barlow recalled: "There was a big table behind which Einsel and myself sat ourselves down." Beside them was a woman from congressional affairs who babysat agency people when they encountered politicians on Capitol Hill. It was one of the Chinese walls built into the system, designed to prevent the CIA from becoming an arm of Congress rather than a resource to be deployed by the executive. There was one more agency man there too: John Serabian, head of the CIA's Nuclear Proliferation Branch.[28] "Across the other side were the congressmen, about twelve in all, two subcommittees' worth," remembered Barlow. Standing at the back was Robert Peck, the deputy assistant secretary of state for South Asian Affairs, and Richard Murphy, assistant secretary for Near Eastern and South Asian Affairs—both of them following the proceedings on behalf of the White House.

Einsel got up to speak as Barlow watched nervously. "I'm sitting beside him with my cleared talking points laid out before me on the table. It was tense. We were in the middle of the Iran–Contra scandal and there was a hearing going on next door. People were very twitchy." In December 1986, an independent council had been appointed to investigate the National Security Council's Colonel Oliver North, among others, for his role in a CIA "black operation" in which the US covertly sold arms to Iran in order to secure the release of thirty hostages captured in 1983 by the Tehran-backed Hezbollah. The profits had been illicitly diverted to the US-backed Contras, right-wing guerrillas fighting to topple the communist regime in Nicaragua.

Iran–Contra was illicit on two fronts: done at a time when Iran had been officially shut off from US aid and the CIA had been barred by Congress from funding the overthrow of the Nicaraguan government.[29] What worried the White House more than anything else was that Afghanistan, which by then accounted for more than 70 percent of the CIA's budget for covert operations, might also become snarled up in the current climate of suspicion where everything covert was perceived as potentially illicit.[30]

The code-word room for the Solarz hearing had been swept for bugs before the session started. An armed guard stood outside. Barlow recalled the first question from the congressmen: "Were Pervez and 'Mr. Inam' agents of the Pakistan government?" Einsel answered, "We're not sure. It is certainly not cut and dried." Barlow gulped. It was a felony offense to lie before Congress, as the Iran–Contra hearing down the corridor was making clear to Reagan officials, including national security adviser Admiral John Poindexter and defense secretary Caspar Weinberger—both of whom would soon face indictments.[31] Barlow recalled: "I was, 'Like fuck Pervez and Inam are not Pak agents.' Einsel had seen everything I had seen. We knew. All the high value stuff I got hold of went across Einsel's desk."

According to paperwork recovered from Pervez, "Mr. Inam" was Inam ul-Haq, a retired brigadier general in the Pakistan army. He had exhorted Pervez in writing to clinch the steel deal "for the good of Pakistan." Inam was on a CIA watch-list, having been identified in the early 1980s as one of A. Q. Khan's key procurement agents. A decorated war hero, he was close to Zia and favored by the ISI. "He was not as high as Henk Slebos but he was pretty high on our list of Khan aides," said Barlow. Inam's presence in the deal, given his track record and the extensive intelligence the CIA had on him, marked out the Carpenter operation as an official Pakistan government buy. "And yet Einsel claimed not to know." Given that Michael Armacost had also seen this CIA material, his statement before Congress that the administration knew of no linkage between Pervez, "Mr. Inam" and the Pakistan government was also incorrect.

Inam ul-Haq was also well known to Khan's European suppliers. Peter Griffin recalled bumping into him in Dubai, Europe and Islamabad. Inam even invited Griffin to attend the wedding of his son in the late 1980s.[32] When, in 2004, one of his daughters was married, a phalanx of ISI generals turned up to honor their comrade, and in April 2006, still living in Lahore, Inam recalled: "These things we had to do were matters of grave national importance, matters of the highest security that guaranteed the future for Pakistan. Even today they are state secrets and to go into them would undermine the republic for which I served for so many years."[33]

But there was Einsel giving Solarz and his fellow congressmen the brush-off. Charles Burke had told Barlow, "If Einsel starts to lie, get up and stalk out of the room." Instead, Barlow froze. "I just sat there nodding my head." Barlow realized that the audience was in the dark. None of the material he had collated, the intelligence he had fed to the administration, had filtered down to anyone in the room. "The lying had been going on for years. They had no idea what was really going on in Pakistan and what had been coming across my desk about its purchases in the US."[34]

Solarz and others suspected as much. Barlow recalled: "He turned to me and said, 'I think we need to hear from Mr. Barlow.' I stammered and muttered, remembering what Burke had told me: 'Tell the truth.' So I said that it was clear that Pervez was an agent for Pakistan's nuclear program. Everyone started shouting. Einsel got back up and said, 'Rich doesn't know what he's talking about.' One of us was lying.

"Then Solarz quieted everyone down. He asked, 'Have there been any other cases since 1985?' Einsel thought for a moment. 'No.' I thought, 'Oh fuck, here we go again. I wish I wasn't here.' I started nodding my head again. A congressman said, 'I think we need to hear from Mr. Barlow again.' Solarz said, 'I don't care if this stuff is being bought through mail order or through some third country like Germany—does it originate in the US and are there many other US cases?' There were scores of cases in front of me and Congress knew about none of them. I'd been cleared to talk. I had cleared my responses with Aoki at State and Burke. I was terrified. I got up and said, 'Yes, there have been scores of other cases since 1985.' "[35]

Richard Murphy's face fell. Robert Peck's, too. They looked at Einsel and he slowly got to his feet, claiming the additional cases were yet to be proven and as yet were only assumptions and allegations, insinuations and lines of inquiry. Barlow was referring to intelligence that was unsorted and unrefined, he suggested. Corroboration and analysis was the job of the CIA, which would only report back when it was sure. Einsel's statement was a smoke bomb designed to cloud the hearing, but it had the opposite effect.

"When Einsel said he didn't know about any of the other cases, the shit really hit the fan," remembered Barlow. The congressional affairs babysitter whispered across the desk to Barlow: "Shut up. Let Einsel run the show." Another handwritten note came over from the other side of the room: "Can Rich clarify when he says 'scores of violations of export laws since 1985'? Several staffers want to be briefed on this. State is NOT happy."

Barlow remembered swallowing so hard he almost lost his tongue. "All I could think about was the list of cases in front of me, the ones I'd cleared with Aoki." But Barlow kept quiet. "It was too much. I was just too inexperienced. I'd only been in the agency two years. For God's sake, Ollie North was being cut to pieces along the hall. I really believed that Congress already had enough from our hearing for an independent counsel to be appointed. I had only done what I was told to do."

Fractious and embittered, the meeting broke up. Peck stormed out calling Barlow "an s.o.b. who has messed it all up."[36] He also shouted at a colleague to "get back in there and get the congressmen back on track." But the room had already spilled outside, jockeying and shouting, with staffers racing to reach

Barlow, who was bundled into a CIA car and sent on his way back to Langley, while the congressmen gathered in scrums whispering about whether they now had enough to sever the umbilical cord to Islamabad.

Sitting in the car with Einsel, Sarabian and the congressional affairs officer, Barlow remembered a silent journey across the Potomac river back to CIA headquarters. When they arrived, the entire agency already knew what had happened. "The phone was ringing off the hook," remembered Barlow. "People were running around saying Congress wanted to terminate aid to Pakistan. Charlie Burke and Gordon Oehler asked Sarabian for an update. John said, 'Oh, Rich has just been impertinent to Congress.' That was it. I went from golden boy to traitor in eight words." Barlow tried to get into Burke's office but was turned away. "He refused to discuss anything until he got a transcript of the hearing." When it arrived soon afterwards, Burke locked himself away for hours. "Afterwards, he called me in and said I'd done the best job I could. Then he called in Sarabian. I could hear screaming. I was caught in the middle of a furious dispute."

Part of the problem was that this was not the first time the executive had been caught lying to Congress. Just before Barlow tripped up David Einsel, a diplomat many government service grades above Barlow also found himself in a similar position. Robert Gallucci, then working for the Bureau of Politico-Military Affairs in the State Department, was asked to backbench at a classified briefing about Pakistan for William Schneider, the under secretary of state for security assistance, science and technology. Gallucci recalled: "I went to the Hill. Schneider briefed and what he said was not accurate. I got all antsy in the back. And when I get antsy it comes out in a physical manifestation. Someone said, 'It looks like someone at the back has got a problem.' We were in this small code-word room. Everyone was looking at me and so I spoke and gave a much darker description of the situation regarding that country. The under secretary didn't contradict me but afterwards he walked out without saying a word and one staffer said you'll never be going up to the Hill again."[37]

There was another incident, a little later. "Pakistan, what we liked to call a good, friendly country was caught mid-trans-shipment of something they shouldn't have been buying," remembered Gallucci. He saw a memo that had been rewritten to remove the negative evidence. "I wrote a dissenting footnote. Everyone went apeshit. It was not just sympathy I felt for Richard Barlow, it was empathy." The rewriting of history would soon become a key issue in the Pakistan imbroglio.

Behind Barlow's back, Einsel, Peck and others up to assistant secretary of state level began haranguing his line managers at the CIA. They even protested to Dick Kerr, the deputy director for intelligence. For the Cold War warriors the only way to save the Pakistan program was to discredit the young agency analyst. They wanted Barlow fired. "I should have jacked it in there and then," Barlow said. "I would have saved myself a lifetime's worth of agony."

Born in Upper Manhattan, New York, Richard Barlow grew up feeling as if he saw too little of his father. Dr. Carl Barlow was a surgeon who spent several years with the US army, before settling in New York. Then Richard Barlow lost his mother, who died when he was six. But Dr. Barlow remarried and sent his son to Fieldston, the Ivy League feeder school in New York for unconventionalists, which counted among its alumni Robert Oppenheimer, architect of the Manhattan Project.

Motherless and rudderless, Barlow didn't care much for his father's new wife and when he finished at Fieldston, leaving with the strong moral and ethical sense that the school specialized in instilling, he fled New York to the other side of the US and the northwest coast. He enrolled in Western Washington University, with its campus concealed by a thick blanket of pines that petered out into the waters of Puget Sound.

A science major for three years, Barlow came under the influence of a professor whose lectures on nuclear proliferation intelligence prompted him to switch subjects. As a political scientist, Barlow did his senior honors thesis in counter-proliferation intelligence and learned about diplomatic pragmatism, how the US could know things and yet decline to act upon them. "I got my material from newspapers, books, I went to congressional hearings, did lots of interviews in Washington. That was when I first came across the name A. Q. Khan," he said. "I discovered that we ignored tons of intelligence about countries that proliferated like Pakistan." Barlow found this hard to fathom, especially when the administration was dealing, theoretically, with the end of the world.

He graduated in 1980, keen to set it right. He was zealous, stubborn and filled with a great sense of righteousness. Offended by doublespeak and hypocrisy, he saw himself as intellectually independent and began rebuilding himself in the mold of an American pioneer. Later on in life, he would buy an array of handguns and a hunting rifle and take to keeping dogs. He would roll his own cigarettes from a pouch stuffed with American Spirit tobacco which he kept tied around his waist.

Barlow applied to graduate school at the University of Oregon but immediately won a professional, paid internship at the State Department. In 1981 he accepted an offer from the Arms Control and Disarmament Agency (ACDA). "I just loved it. I was the intelligence officer for the proliferation bureau in ACDA covering all countries, but Pakistan took up almost all of my time. I quickly learned how Pakistan built its program exploiting dual-use components, commercial greed and blinkered governments." Barlow was in his element, energized by his proximity to secrets, taxed by having to calm a whirlwind of documents, trainspotterish in his obsession with order, someone uniquely qualified to reach into the global turbine of the half-heard and intercepted and draw from it a picture of what was really going on.

But ACDA was getting in the way of the White House. Two years after Barlow started, Reagan took it apart. There was a hiring freeze and Barlow was forced out in 1982.[38] He ended up working in a food store in Connecticut before jumping from job to job. He married his girlfriend Cindy in a simple pauper's ceremony in Connecticut where the only guests were the witnesses. All the time he plotted how he could get back to Washington.

Then, in 1985, Barlow got a call from the CIA. They wanted to hire him for the Directorate of Operations, the DO or clandestine branch, which conducted covert action, recruited and managed the agency's human intelligence assets. Barlow attended secret recruitment meetings in an assortment of hotels and after six months learned that he had been selected to work as an analyst on the Pakistan brief at the OSWR. Delighted, and on a salary once again, Barlow, now thirty-one, moved to Virginia and married Cindy all over again, throwing a party for all their friends.

But Washington was not everything Barlow expected it to be. "By the time I arrived there was a split in every agency of the Reagan government between those concerned about proliferation and those more concerned by the Cold War." It was often described as the regionalist–functionalist divide, with the former seeing themselves as the guardians of long-term US relationships while the latter perceived themselves as safeguarding the future of the world. "In OSWR, we believed proliferation by countries like Pakistan would pose an even greater long-term threat than the Soviet Union. But this was not a good time to be talking like that." Barlow was assigned to look at the vast gray market in dual-use components. "There was tons of it. Pakistan was buying here, in the UK, Germany, all over the world. We had the most superb intelligence."

Asked to share it with the agency's European partners, Barlow reached out to MI6 in London. "I used to call my contact 'John Steed' after the character in the *Avengers*." John Steed booked him into the Travellers' Club in Pall Mall, where they debated the direction the Khan network was taking. The British had been looking at a company called Lizrose, the London export firm that had ordered a shipment of maraging steel for KRL. But there was also time to get to know each other. "We'd do the business side and then get drunk out of our minds," Barlow recalled. "One time, John Steed took me fly-fishing on the royal estates in Scotland."

Back home, Barlow was becoming something of a minor prodigy. He was also a pain in the ass. Burdened with a pedantry that drove his line managers to distraction, he was self-obsessed.[39] While he demonstrated accomplished investigative and analytical skills, he bridled when he saw his material going unactioned. Barlow had little experience of the politics of a combative institution like the CIA and no tolerance for government departments that cherry-picked from the raw mass of intelligence analyzed by the OSWR. For Cold War warriors, a man like Barlow was best kept in the back room, out of sight and beyond reach of Capitol Hill.

Burrowing through cables and files on Pakistan and A. Q. Khan, Barlow made his first startling discovery, a pattern of behavior that greatly disturbed him. "There was a serious case of 'clientitis' going on," he recalled. Barlow discovered that the State Department was sitting on intelligence about the Pakistan nuclear program, preventing other agencies like the Commerce Department (which approved export licenses) and US Customs (which enforced them) from doing their jobs.

Barlow lobbied to create an inter-agency group. "We needed to share our knowledge. The Pakistan Atomic Energy Commission and Khan's people were remarkably open and often had components from abroad sent to their home addresses. I had lists of road names and house numbers in Islamabad, but because we did not share data the names and addresses did not mean anything to US Customs officials who were coming across them in export documents."

Then Barlow chanced on a tendril of the Khan network that reached into the small Californian town of Grass Valley, from where an unassuming couple, Arnold and Rona Mandel, had shipped $993,000 of hi-tech goods—computers, oscilloscopes, programmable digitizers and other electronic equipment—to Hong Kong. A man called Leung Yiu Hung had picked up the crates and forwarded them to a private address in Pakistan.[40] No one in US Customs had interceded, even though many of the items were exported without a license. They had also not appreciated the significance of the name and private address of the consignee: Dr. Samar Mubarakmand, the head of the PAEC warhead design workshop.[41]

In 1986, Barlow won his argument and the top-secret Nuclear Export Violations Working Group came into being, with Fred McGoldrick, a senior non-proliferation official in the State Department, as chairman.[42] Then Barlow made a second, unsettling discovery. In addition to keeping back intelligence, he later discovered that the State Department had been facilitating back-door procurement, issuing scores of approvals for the Pakistan embassy in Washington to export hi-tech equipment for its bomb that the Commerce Department had refused to license for proliferation reasons.

Barlow dug deeper. Analyzing US cable traffic in and out of Pakistan, he realized critical details about CIA or US Customs operations were somehow always discovered by Pakistan before the trap was sprung. "We would learn that the Paks, for example, were using a company in Oklahoma and we would get there to raid it and find everyone had already flown." Matching incidents with cables, Barlow discovered that the State Department had been sending detailed démarches tipping off contacts in the Pakistan government. "This was treachery."

The source of the tip-offs had to be someone very senior at the State Department who had clearance to view the most sensitive operational material. Barlow narrowed it down to a handful of players and approached Dick Kerr, the deputy director for intelligence, who summoned senior State Department officials to a meeting at Langley. "He told them that there was a steady pattern of démarches to Islamabad revealing classified material," Barlow recalled. Kerr was effectively accusing his colleagues of sabotage but tried to do it as nicely as he could. He said he understood the State Department "was trying to change Pakistan's behavior" rather than seeing it shut out by US sanctions.[43] A good mediator, Kerr said he would drop any plans for an internal investigation if the State Department guaranteed that it would stop working against the agency. The

State Department people consented, but soon afterwards a Pakistani-born Canadian walked into a trap sprung by Barlow in an operation that would test the strength of this new CIA–State Department understanding.

Barlow recalled the call from the Department of Energy: "A guy was asking for a specific type of maraging steel. His name was Arshad Pervez. I contacted Customs. We had a secret meeting in Fred McGoldrick's office and decided not to tell the State Department about the operation. What a turn of events—not trusting your own guys. US Customs agents inserted themselves at Carpenter Steel, met Pervez and then told me what the deal was. Eventually he said something about 'the Kahuta client.' But we knew Pervez was just the legman. We had to get the Pakistanis to break the law through signing a letter of credit so that we could prove it led back to the nuclear program."[44]

A trap was sprung. "The deal was that Pervez and, more importantly, his handler, Inam ul-Haq, would show up at a hotel in Pennsylvania, where there would be cameras and other recording devices planted to capture the moment they handed over the letter of credit." Barlow was confident that Inam was already in the US and gave the go-ahead for the final hotel meet to occur. The State Department was informed at the very last moment, as the law required. Barlow said: "Pervez arrived, blabbed and was arrested. The police raided his house in Canada and sent down his paperwork, which proved I'd been right. But the main man, Inam, didn't show, even though we had been tailing him right up until the sting."

Before Barlow could investigate he was pitched into the classified and explosive Solarz briefing. Only later, when an IG at State asked him to prepare an overview of the Pervez case and the others he had raised on Capitol Hill, did he discover what had happened. Trawling through piles of NODIS (no-distribution) cables and reports, Barlow found compelling evidence that the Pervez operation had, like others before it, been sabotaged from within the State Department. Inam ul-Haq had been tipped off.

Kerr once again contacted the State Department, where the inspector general too had become concerned by the machinations of a few senior officials. Abraham Sofaer, the departmental lawyer, was told of the allegations, responding that to fully examine them he would need to "see the computer traffic at the time."[45] According to Funk, what Sofaer subsequently saw was a "smoking gun," evidence that two high-ranking officials within the State Department had alerted Pakistan's government to the Pervez sting. It had been done in a legalistic manner, the tip-off buried within the lawyerly language of a démarche to Islamabad, subtly phrased so as to protect those who had sent it.[46] The CIA claimed that its aim was as clear as the repercussions of the action.[47]

Dick Kerr looked over the evidence.[48] Abraham Sofaer for State reviewed it too. Both had little appetite for another inquisition, and yet the men accused of blowing the Pervez sting were extremely close to the White House: Robert Peck, the deputy assistant secretary of state for Near East Affairs, and another official at the under secretary level. The accusations were devastating. The lawyer dryly put his thoughts to a criminal investigator working for the State IG: "I am fully aware of the cable traffic and documents on this issue." There was cold proof of sabotage from within the State Department.[49]

The State Department's lawyers considered their position, and eventually would argue that a Justice Department probe into Peck or his colleague would necessitate the spilling of state secrets and possibly invoke an independent counsel's investigation. While they dumped the probe, the president made his annual Pressler amendment certification to Congress in December 1987, saying, "Pakistan does not possess a nuclear explosive device."[50]

The following day a jury convicted Arshad Pervez of conspiracy illegally to export maraging steel and beryllium to Pakistan, invoking the Solarz amendment—although no one mentioned the crisis going on inside the State Department.[51] But in the end all Solarz, Barlow and Oehler's efforts came to nothing as on 15 January 1988 President Reagan waived the Solarz amendment, citing reasons of national security. "There is no diminution in the president's commitment to restraining the spread of nuclear weapons in the Indian subcontinent or elsewhere," Reagan said.[52] There would be no cut-off and there was nothing Congress could do about it. The cases against Peck and his colleague were quietly dropped.

Richard Barlow was feted—awarded a Certificate of Exceptional Accomplishment "for services of extreme value to the Central Intelligence Agency."[53] He received a commendation from Richard Clarke, the deputy assistant secretary for intelligence, for his "outstanding assistance in long and complex investigations."[54] Even Abraham Sofaer expressed his "appreciation for the important contribution" made by Barlow, whose analysis was "clear, well organized and well documented."

Yet despite the awards, Barlow found himself cold-shouldered at the agency, with Einsel working hard to discredit him. Barlow, the brilliant analyst, and the United States' foremost expert on Pakistan's nuclear program at a time when the administration was desperate to prove it didn't exist, had no future in the CIA. He was spurned in the canteen, harassed by people including Einsel and Serabian. Barlow came to the terrible realization that he was going to have to abandon the thing he loved.

At home he fared no better. His marriage was in crisis. Barlow was miserable and Cindy found it hard to live with his moods. "I couldn't bear it," Barlow said. "I was going to have to quit, but as news got around of my fight with Einsel and the clash at State the only post anyone would offer me was a GS12 job with a Kevlar vest and a magnum in Seattle, working for US Customs." It was like going from being a spook to a cop. Barlow began to fall to pieces.

Out of desperation, he called someone on the classified working group he had established whom he had always thought of as a friend, Gerald Brubaker, the Department of Defense representative.[55] He seemed friendly enough on the phone and threw Barlow a line. "He offered me a job as an intelligence analyst at the Pentagon," Barlow recalled. "I took it. Cindy and I went into marriage counselling. I hoped for the best. Boy, was I stupid."

On 25 March 1988, President Reagan made his annual statement on non-proliferation.[56] A new administration would take over following elections later that year, so this would be the last time he addressed Congress on the matter, and it was no different from any other. Having read the traffic on Pervez that concluded he was run by Pakistan, having waived Solarz despite being warned that Pakistan continued to shop for its nuclear program, and having had some of his most senior officials accused of passing intelligence to Pakistan, Reagan wrote: "My central arms control objective has been to reduce substantially, and ultimately to eliminate, nuclear weapons and rid the world of the nuclear threat. The prevention of the spread of nuclear explosives to additional countries is an indispensable part of our efforts to meet this objective. I intend to continue my pursuit of this goal with untiring determination and a profound sense of personal commitment."[57]

In private, the president was advised that his non-proliferation policy was in tatters.[58] So anxious was the National Security Council (NSC) about the prospect of a nuclear showdown in South Asia that it pressured Reagan into confronting Pakistan in one last attempt to get it over to them: the bomb program had to stop. Robert Oakley, the NSC's senior director for the Middle East and South Asia, recalled that the opportunity came when defense secretary Frank Carlucci visited Islamabad that spring to discuss the proposed terms of a US-brokered agreement with the Soviet Union to end hostilities in Afghanistan. "He was going to have to tell Zia to stop lying about the bomb. But all Zia cared about was getting a good deal in Afghanistan," Oakley recalled.[59]

Washington's main interest in Afghanistan was getting the Soviet troops out, pulling its funding and leaving the country to its own devices. But Zia felt that after eight years of war Pakistan was entitled to run the show in Kabul.[60] In a telephone conversation with President Reagan, Zia had said he was happy to sign the Afghanistan agreement but had no intention of abiding by Moscow's condition to stop arming the mujahideen after the Soviet withdrawal. When Reagan warned him that this amounted to lying, Zia retorted: "We've been denying our activities there for eight years, Muslims have the right to lie in a good cause."[61] And he wasn't just talking about Afghanistan. Frank Carlucci, reporting back to Washington after meeting Zia in Islamabad, said Pakistan's president had adopted the same line with him, telling him, "I'll lie to them like I have been lying to them for the past ten years." Carlucci responded: "Just like you've been lying to us about the nuclear business."[62]

In an interview with the *Wall Street Journal* on 26 April 1988, shortly after the Afghanistan accords were signed in Geneva, Zia was positively flip about the Islamic Republic's nuclear ambitions: "Having seen that Pakistan has gone and succeeded the best thing now is to enjoy and relax."[63] Zia went further with a visiting delegation from the US Carnegie Endowment, a think tank based in Washington, telling them that Pakistan had attained a nuclear capability "that is good enough to create an impression of deterrence."[64]

Reagan had to make his point more forcefully, and during a trip to Washington that summer Sahabzada Yaqub Khan, Pakistan's foreign minister, was asked why KRL operations were expanding rather than contracting.[65] Robert Oakley recalled: "Yaqub Khan launched into a series of face-saving denials. Pakistan was enriching. But KRL had never exceeded the red line of 5 percent, a benchmark set by Reagan in his 1986 letter to Zia."[66] Oakley recalled taking Yaqub Khan over to the Department of State where he was shown maps of KRL, a site plan and overheads, as well as reams of technical data that demonstrated the level of electronic snooping of which the US was capable. "Yaqub Khan was horrified," Oakley said. "He had never asked too much about the nuclear program so that he was rarely forced to lie. And here he was being called a liar by his erstwhile friends in the US and then proved a liar with our intelligence."[67] Oakley also suspected that Pakistan was now hawking its nuclear technology around the Middle East, but he did not yet have enough evidence with which to confront Yaqub Khan.

Oakley's suspicions were right. While negotiating the Afghanistan accords in the spring of 1988, Zia had been seeking out new strategic and military partners who he hoped would replace the US when it ultimately dropped Pakistan, the date of which was fast approaching. To frame this move, he had commissioned a strategic rethink from within the armed forces, asking his new vice chief of the army staff, General Mirza Aslam Beg, and his new ISI chief, General Hamid Gul, to put the volte-face in writing.

They prepared a "regional strategic consensus paper" proposing that Iran, Pakistan and Afghanistan come together in a pact lubricated by nuclear cooperation.[68] Afghanistan had been liberated and would have to be forced into forming a post-Soviet government favorable to Islamabad, while Iran was already a signatory to a nuclear deal, having bought the first shipment of P-1 centrifuges from KRL the previous year, and would have to be coaxed into greater proximity.

Co-author General Beg recalled: "I wrote that Pakistan should also link up with Turkey, at the southern end of NATO, creating an Islamic crescent from Europe to Asia. This strategic consensus would provide security for all of us."[69] He did not, in the consensus paper, mention the significance of Pakistan's nuclear bomb. "At that time the nuclear thing was not completely out of the bag and we could not risk writing about it, but it was there in the background. The bomb was what lay behind everything myself and Hamid Gul put down." Shortly after the position paper was circulated, Zia sent General Beg to Tehran. He was to air the new strategic consensus and follow up on the KRL sales.[70] In the years to come Beg would become a crucial conduit in the Pakistan–Iran nuclear relationship.

In Islamabad, A. Q. Khan was also cogitating his future, concerned that he had outlived his usefulness.[71] KRL had shone by enriching uranium, but had amassed enough weapons-grade material for forty or more bombs, more than enough even for Zia. KRL would have to broaden its horizons if it was to stay on top, and Khan knew his weakness was weapons design, an area still dominated by Dr. Samar Mubarakmand of PAEC and his team of scientists from Wah. PAEC also had a head start on Pakistan's missile program, buying technology from France and borrowing it from their old ally China.[72] The Space and Upper Atmosphere Research Commission (SUPARCO) had already completed cold tests on the Hatf 1 and Hatf 2 missiles, both of them "a home design but produced with the assistance of Chinese experts," and was preparing to let them off in the Thar Desert, predicting that they were capable of striking Mumbai or New Delhi.[73]

It would only get worse for Khan. Zia had teed up a massive secret contract for Munir Khan's men at PAEC. Pakistan had agreed to act as an interlocutor between China and Saudi Arabia over the sale of thirty-six long-range Chinese CSS-II nuclear-capable missiles. Beijing had been keen to sell them at an exorbitant $3 billion to offset US military aid to nuclear-capable (but undeclared) Israel. It was also keen to undermine Saudi Arabia's allegiance to Taiwan. After Zia made the introductions, the House of Saud jumped at the chance of buying the weapons and in return formally established diplomatic relations with Beijing in the summer of 1990. There would be payback for Pakistan, not only in terms of getting closer to China, a proximity that would bring with it far more nuclear assistance in the years to come, but also a massive cash deal.

In exchange for its part in the deal, Pakistan would win renewed financial assistance for its nuclear program from Saudi Arabia. Riyadh had an ulterior motive. The CSS-II missile was notoriously inaccurate and only really made sense when it was armed with a nuclear warhead which could cast a wide irradiated footprint. Zia had agreed that as soon as Munir Khan's team had completed its warhead design, the Saudis would be secretly supplied with the same. Pakistan was proposing the sale of a nuclear bomb. "The Saudis did not want the process, unlike Iran. They were not interested in centrifuges," an insider at PAEC said.[74] "Riyadh did not have the scientists or infrastructure for these things. Saudis getting into enrichment would also have sparked a massive row with the US. They wanted the finished product, to stash away in case of emergency, and Pakistan agreed to supply it in return for many hundreds of millions of dollars."

But before any of these deals could come to fruition, on 17 August 1988 a camouflaged Pakistan air force C-130 transport plane plummeted from the sky, killing President Zia, his joint chief of staff and former ISI chief General Rahman, as well as US ambassador Arnold Raphel, US military attaché Brigadier General Herbert Wassom, and twenty-seven others. The disaster decapitated a nation with an undeclared and well-developed nuclear weapons program, which had begun to sell to one and all, and sent the US State Department into a paroxysm of hand-wringing.

10

GANGSTERS IN BANGLES

General K. M. Arif was on the passenger list to board the C-130. But he had cried off. Arif, who had served Zia for the best part of a decade and had often stood in for the overstretched dictator as Pakistan's de facto number two, had recently been retired, hurried out of his career. There had been no fanfare—a dinner in every mess at each of the bases where the general had served—and he felt deprived of the traditional hoopla that should have accompanied a dignified end to thirty-nine years of military service. So on 17 August 1988, General Arif had stayed at home in Rawalpindi.[1]

President Zia was not supposed to have flown on the plane, having been warned just days earlier of a plot to kill him which would probably occur during a military flight. But, persuaded by his own officers that the great and ambitious from the US and Pakistan would be in attendance at the military display, Zia had reluctantly agreed to board. He had an autocrat's compulsion to be seen by his officers and his powerful US allies, whom he relentlessly inspected for signs of indifference and treachery.[2]

For years, General Arif had found his good fortune hard to reconcile and refused to discuss the significance of the disaster. Recently, however, he relented. "Zia was called up by Major General Mahmud Ali Durrani, on August 14th, to attend a demonstration of the American M1 Abrams tank," he said.[3] Zia had been reluctant to fly anywhere that week, but Durrani, an artillery commander (and today Pakistan's ambassador to the US), had been insistent. "He said: 'We need to show our US partners that we are taking the demo seriously,' Arif remembered. 'We need to keep them on side, especially with Afghanistan coming to an end. Everyone is coming to the show.' Zia was persuaded."

The president flew from Islamabad to Bahawalpur, more than 300 miles south of the capital, aboard Pak 1. The C-130 was a rudimentary and reliable workhorse but when mechanics rolled into its carcass a plywood and aluminum passenger tube, fitted with seats and air conditioning, it made a reasonable VIP carrier too.

The chairman of the joint chiefs of staff committee, General Rahman, was also not supposed to have been on the flight. Arif reasoned: "Rahman rarely attended military sales pitches." However, several days before the crash, Rahman had learned that Zia was preparing to make radical changes within the armed forces and he needed to know where he stood. The journey would give him the chance of a full briefing. Thus, Pakistan's two most senior military officers, along with a dozen more of Zia's staunchest allies, were on the doomed flight.

From Bahawalpur, the presidential party took a helicopter to a firing range at Tamewali, where the M1 Abrams flunked, snarling in the desert sand and missing all ten of its targets. After a quick lunch, Zia had knelt down for the Zohr prayer on a mat laid beside Pak 1, in one of his frequent shows of humility and religious zeal. Then he had reboarded the plane, followed by Rahman, who sat beside US ambassador Arnold Raphel and his attaché, Herbert Wassom.[4]

Pak 1 taxied down the runway at 4.30 p.m. Two minutes later, having suddenly lost contact with the control tower, the turbo-prop lurched into a nosedive, before climbing rapidly over the village of Basti Lal Kamal. With an alarmed crowd gathering, Pak 1 porpoised across the horizon for two agonizing minutes before it crashed with such force that the propellers, still churning, were buried several feet below ground. The impact ignited the 20,000 pounds of fuel in the wings, sending a ball of flame hurtling high above the splintered wreckage, creating an inferno that burned for four hours, incinerating everyone aboard.

General Arif reflected on how he had struggled to gather as many facts as he could. "No rocket was seen to hit the C-130. It didn't explode mid-air. There was no fire until it hit the ground. Later, we would also rule out any kind of mechanical failure. That left only two explanations: an act of God or the pilots had been got at. We sensed foul play and found in the wreckage chemical traces that were consistent with a small explosive charge."[5] Arif worked on the theory that a canister of nerve gas had been smuggled aboard, fixed with a timed charge which blew it open once the plane had taken off, asphyxiating the flight crew and leaving Pak 1 in free fall. The plane was fitted with a device in its tail to compensate for such a spin, a piece of equipment that forced the nose up into the air, which would have explained the see-sawing flight path observed from the ground. However, with no one able to rectify the plane's trajectory—the passengers were far back in the plywood tube—it had fallen from the sky. The general learned that two crates of mangoes and a box of model tanks had been loaded at Bahawalpur before the plane took off. Neither had been inspected. "Anything could have been in them. If this was sabotage, we needed to look at who would benefit," said Arif.[6]

There were plenty with motives, even if the method as yet remained obscure. An increasing number of officers in Pakistan's carnivorous military viewed their president as having become irascible. Many had come off worse in fights with Zia, who had had a tendency to micromanage Pakistan. The country's economy was in a parlous state despite the billions in US aid, prompting accusations that Zia's inner circle was corrupt and profligate. And Pakistan was now facing a future without that aid as the war in Afghanistan entered its final stage. Zia was accused by some of having sold out to the US over the Geneva accords, and many in the military wanted different relationships with Pakistan's Islamic neighbors than the ones being proposed in Zia's strategic consensus paper.[7]

Outside Pakistan, too, as a result of the nuclear program and the war in Afghanistan, there was a cavalcade of Zia haters. The KGB and its ruthless Afghan surrogates had a deadly record of infiltrating Pakistan's establishment and had already demonstrated that they had the means with which to carry off a hit like this, having become practiced in the use of VX gas, a quick-acting and fatal nerve agent, in Afghanistan.[8]

But this was also the kind of conspiracy favored by the Israelis. In fear of Zia's nuclear ambitions, they had repeatedly contemplated striking Kahuta—as recently as 1987.[9] They had already covertly attacked, threatened, bombed, and blackmailed many of A. Q. Khan's procurement agents in Europe. They had also goaded India into considering similar assaults on KRL as New Delhi, too, grew tired of Pakistan's dissembling, its religious zealotry and its increasingly bellicose president.

Arif said the US was also suspected: "The CIA and US State Department also had much to gain from Zia's death." There was the constant and embarrassing lying over the KRL project, as well as a new fear that Pakistan was neck deep in graft. Zia had been privately accused of redirecting US aid and weapons to KRL as well as to militant Islamic factions within the mujahideen, which Saudi intelligence had repeatedly warned the US and Europe were likely to turn round and attack the West. Particularly irksome was Zia's relationship with Gulbud-din Hekmatyar, the rabid chief of Hizbi-i-Islami, the most radical of the seven parties that made up the fractious alliance of anti-Soviet forces in Afghanistan.[10] The mujahideen leader did not hide his disdain for America. Refusing to meet President Reagan in 1985 during a visit to the UN in New York, Hekmatyar would in the near future align himself with the most radical and warmongering fringe elements of the global jihad that was gathering in Afghanistan.[11]

Political opponents in Pakistan were also suspected, particularly followers of Zulfikar Ali Bhutto. Under the leadership of Bhutto's son Murtaza, a hard core had formed a gonzo terrorist outfit known as al-Zulfikar (The Sword), which lusted for revenge. From its base in Kabul, al-Zulfikar had made several attempts on Zia's life already, using Soviet SAM-7 missiles with which it endeavored to shoot down Zia's jet on two occasions.[12] The authorities had hushed up both of these attacks and Zia was thought to have responded in kind, the Bhutto family claiming that he had sent a hit squad to poison Murtaza's younger brother, Shah Nawaz Bhutto, who was found dead in his apartment in the south of France in 1985.

However, while Arif refused to name his chief suspect, others were less circumspect. Sharifuddin Pirzada, Zia's lawyer, was at home when he heard news of the crash. He had half been expecting it and knew what to do. Pirzada, who had seen dictators come and go and had serviced all of them, rang around to secure information and began to anticipate what would happen next. A quick tally of who was where at the time of the crash focused him in on General Mirza Aslam Beg, Zia's vice chief of army staff. "Beg had somehow missed the crash," Pirzada recalled.[13] "It smelt like a coup." In early August, Pirzada had returned from a tour of the Middle East with a warning for Zia. Senior intelligence sources in Saudi Arabia had picked up a whisper that an assassination plot was brewing and he should not travel in military planes. If he had to fly in civil aircraft he should leave the selection of the pilot until the very last minute before he boarded. According to Pirzada, the president had been so worried he had called a meeting of the military top brass on 15 August 1988. It had lasted for more than five hours. "Don't fly," Pirzada had exhorted.

"Treat your friends as enemies until the threat passes." But then Zia's own officers had entreated him to come to the firing range and board Pak 1.

Only General Mirza Aslam Beg had bucked the carefully laid preparations for the tank display, making excuses so as not to board the Pak 1 return flight and taking instead a circuitous route from Bahawalpur in a jet-prop plane which flew to Dhamial, a military base in the Punjab, from where his staff car was waiting to take him to army headquarters.[14]

Over the eighteen years since the crash, General Beg has insisted that his absence aboard the fated C-130 proved nothing. Sitting in his office, tucked away down a back lane of the Chaklala army cantonment in Rawalpindi, a stone's throw from President Musharraf's official residence, Beg recalled the day of Zia's death with a stone-cold face, speaking so deliberately that he was almost somnambulant.

Stopping only for the muezzin whose call to prayer from a neighboring mosque caused his windows to rattle, he pooh-poohed claims that he had fled the scene of the crash with undue haste, heading for Pakistan's seat of power. "We overheard a helicopter pilot telling the control tower about a crash," Beg said.[15] "We saw the wreckage on the ground was blazing. There was no point in hanging around." His face was expressionless. "I was persuaded by others to get back to Rawalpindi, to take a grip on the political crisis. I needed to secure Pakistan. But I never wanted the top job for myself. My first thoughts were: seek advice, gain a consensus, keep everyone calm."[16]

However, remembering the events that unfolded over the next few hours, Sharifuddin Pirzada kept coming back to a single thought: "General Beg would do well out of Zia's demise. Zia was army chief and upon his death Beg would automatically take the top job." Upon landing at Dhamial, Beg did just that, assuming position as the chief of army staff. Certain that Beg would also make a move on the office of president, Pirzada determined to stop him, putting forward a civilian candidate for the post.

While Beg tore towards Rawalpindi, where the military top brass was being corralled, another of Pakistan's immutable forces travelled to Rawalpindi from a different direction. Driving from Islamabad was Ghulam Ishaq Khan, the former finance minister, chairman of the BCCI Foundation, champion of A. Q. Khan and, since 1985, chairman of the senate, Pakistan's upper parliamentary house.[17] Pirzada said: "There was a feeling that the people would not tolerate yet more army rule. Some called me and asked if I would become the caretaker prime minister. I refused. I preferred to remain in the background. I did offer some advice though." Pirzada did what he did best, riffling through the Pakistan constitution looking for a way to stop General Beg. "I found a provision that allowed for the chairman of the senate to accede to the post of president in the event of a power vacuum." General Beg folded. Ghulam Ishaq Khan was president. A lawyer with an uncanny ability to survive once again shaped Pakistan's future.

President Ishaq Khan made peace with General Beg that evening and, with the army's backing, addressed the people of Pakistan, announcing a period of ten days' mourning. He arranged for Zia's funeral to be held on 20 August and, in an act loaded with symbolism, chose to lay the former president to rest in a place never intended as a burial ground: the Shah Faisal Masjid in Islamabad, the largest mosque in the world, built by the Saudi royal family.[18] Zia had forged a special relationship with the Saudis, who had financed a whole host of Pakistan's causes, most especially the nuclear project which they hoped would produce a warhead for the Chinese-supplied missiles whose delivery had been so discreetly brokered by the dead president.

As his body was interred, the Lahore high court announced that the dictator's suspension of democracy had been illegal.[19] Now he was dead, the lawyers were emboldened and they decreed that a general election would be held.[20] But in Pakistan democracy rarely had a free hand. This time General Beg and President Ishaq Khan made certain of it.

Once Ishaq Khan and General Beg were bound together, they found they had common beliefs. Both set store by the righteousness of the military establishment (left badly creaking after ten years of dictatorship), both harbored a deep-seated desire for exacting revenge against India, coming from the generation that felt the loss of East Pakistan in December 1971 most acutely, and both recognized the significance of Pakistan's nuclear capability and held a great affinity for A. Q. Khan. General Beg regarded him as a national hero. More than that, he and A.Q had been born in India and spoke the same Urdu dialect. Beg and Ishaq Khan believed that Pakistan's nuclear project would enable the country to shore up the military while exacting revenge against India.

The bomb was already wooing new friends—China, Saudi Arabia and Iran.

There was a third hand in the new leadership who would steer a radical plan for change, a soldier and éminence grise—the country's new spymaster, General Hamid Gul. Inducted into the Pakistan army's armored division, he had graduated from the British army's staff college, becoming a three-star general after returning to Pakistan. He had taken over at the ISI from General Rahman in March 1987 to see through the final stages of the Afghan war. "I thought, wonderful, there's bound to be some action here," Gul recalled.[21] To his CIA counterparts in Afghanistan and Pakistan, General Gul appeared sanguine. He dressed like a Westerner, his rough features set off with a luxuriant mustache, his starched kurta and tweedy suits giving the impression of a clubbable officer. He was even feted by West German chancellor Helmut Kohl, who sent him a piece of the Berlin Wall inscribed "With deepest respect to Lieutenant General Hamid Gul, who helped deliver the first blow." Today this memento sits beneath a coffee table in Gul's lounge at his home in Askari Villas, Rawalpindi.

In truth, Hamid Gul regarded himself as an ideological warrior. In the early 1980s he had begun to gather like-minded soldiers and religious leaders around him, drawing close to the radical *ulema*, the conservative Islamic scholars who had prospered under Zia, replacing the secular principles of Pakistan's founding father Muhammad Ali Jinnah with a quest to create a strict Islamic state.

Almost twenty years later, Gul recalled how he had always found working with the West distasteful. "The CIA were only useful in Afghanistan to counter Communist expansionism," he said wryly. His real world view was that the US offered at best an unreliable friendship, freighted with preconditions that more often than not resulted in Pakistan being left high and dry. "I told my clerical and military friends that until Islamabad achieved independence from Washington it would always be enfeebled and colonized. Its fortunes—like those of other countries in the Islamic world—were continually undermined by the US preoccupation with Israel. The Muslims and Arab peoples were beholden to a global Zionist conspiracy. Our fate chopped and changed as the US wavered over Israel and Palestinians. We had to release ourselves from this influence."[22] The general would invoke this theme time and again, a theory that he would place in the mouths of those he came to influence and control.

Before Zia's death it had been only talk. However, after Pak 1 went down, Gul began to play an increasingly significant role. With his connections to the Islamic throng, Gul argued that the madrasahs could be militarized to make

India bleed. He had a vision of creating an Army of God, with Pakistan's religious schools transformed by the ISI into training camps where the instructors would be war-hardened jihadis from Afghanistan and the pupils soldiers of Allah. General Beg agreed and planned to place the training camps out of sight, high up in the hills of Muzaffarabad, the capital of Pakistan-administered Kashmir.

Gul recalled: "We wanted to mirror the mujahideen's successes in Afghanistan by sending them into Indian-administered Kashmir to manipulate the Kashmiri people's anger at India's refusal to grant them autonomy. We would train the freedom fighters. We would arm them." It was for Hamid Gul a campaign that worked on every level: turning the screw on India, reviving the Pakistani military, while promoting an increasingly zealous and chauvinistic home-grown Islamic movement.

Gul also suggested that Ghulam Ishaq Khan should accelerate Pakistan's nuclear program.[23] There would be no rollback, as the US had requested. Instead, Gul argued that Pakistan had to wield the bomb that the US had enabled it to build, refining missiles and other delivery systems that would leave India in no doubt about Pakistan's capabilities. Until now Islamabad had created uranium cores and devised a device, yet had not taken the final leap of mating a warhead to a missile or developing the technology to drop a bomb from a jet. Most significantly, A. Q. Khan was to be encouraged to share his knowledge with the Islamic world, as Zia had suggested as far back as 1985. The KRL industry would be allowed to market its wares, generating the hard cash needed to make the Islamic Republic independent of US largesse and capable of running the new and prohibitively expensive manifesto.

General Beg, who was consulted about this plan, recalled: "We had to stop hiding our bomb. We needed others to see that we had it and knew how to use it. We needed to terrify, to create fear of the consequences of a Pakistani bomb going off. We also needed missiles with which to launch them or planes from which we could drop them."[24]

But the military was not yet in complete control. Having promised a return to democracy, a general election was scheduled for 16 November 1988 and, for all or any of this master plan to work, Generals Gul and Beg, watched hawkishly by Ghulam Ishaq Khan, would have to get their candidate for prime minister past the post. They would have to do it with cunning so as to camouflage the military's intent. There was a well-known political dictum in

Pakistan that the military was only able to rule when the people perceived it as "a mythical entity, a magical force, that would succour them in times of need when all else fails."[25] Spy chief Hamid Gul knew that after more than ten years of Zia, Pakistan's people no longer thought of the army as a magical force. Together with Beg, he drew up a plan to conceal the military's ambitions behind a coalition of Islamic political parties that would stand together under the banner of the IJI, an acronym that in Urdu stood for Islamic Democratic Alliance. The IJI would contest the elections and be directed, funded, bullied and manipulated by Beg, Gul and Ishaq Khan.[26] Only one person stood in their way, someone the army feared and abhorred, a candidate who had the support of the civilian masses and was favored by the US, Zulfikar Ali Bhutto's thirty-five-year-old daughter, Benazir.

Milton Beardon, the CIA station chief in Islamabad, had advised Washington to keep its specialists away from the Pak 1 crash site. US spies, technicians and investigators crawling through the wreckage would give credence to conspiracy theorists who were already accusing the US of having had a hand in the tragedy.[27]

Stunned by a calamity that had claimed a much-loved and highly regarded diplomat in Arnold Raphel, the US also realized that there had been no plan B. With Zia dead, the people emerging as Pakistan's new leaders were potential enemies of America whose loyalties lay with the radical *ulema*. According to the chatter emanating from Islamabad, they were also intent on hijacking the nuclear button. In the White House Situation Room, Colin Powell, who the year before had been promoted to President Reagan's national security adviser, chaired a crisis meeting.[28] He called on considerable collective experience on Pakistan: Richard Armitage from the Pentagon, Michael Armacost, the under secretary of state for political affairs, Thomas Twetten from the CIA's Near East Division, and Robert Oakley, the National Security Council's senior director for the Middle East and South Asia.

The first move, according to Oakley, who had no idea that many in Pakistan suspected that General Beg was responsible for Zia's death, was to secure US interests in South Asia. "There was anxiety about the future of the war in Afghanistan, with the makeup of a future government in Kabul still a serious bone of contention that could yet choke the whole covert campaign after billions of dollars had been plowed into it," recalled Oakley.[29] "We were worried, too, about elements within the Pakistan military, and the Indian Army were lobbying to manipulate the chaos to spark a conflagration across the border. We had to influence and guide the outcome."

In the State Department, Pakistan experts including Teresita Schaffer, soon to become deputy assistant secretary of state for South Asian affairs, lobbied for a new US approach.[30] While some in the US had preferred dealing with a dictator, as it simplified the decision-making processes, Schaffer had repeatedly emphasized that the only permanent solution to the Pakistan problem—especially with the growing concerns over the Islamic Republic's unsecured nuclear program—was to foster a stable and long-lasting democracy. The US had to support the forthcoming elections in Pakistan and needed to back a candidate who was pro-Western and credible. Benazir Bhutto, ex-Oxford and Harvard, where she had acquired the nickname "Pinkie" due to her rosy cheeks, was the obvious choice.

With the outline of a plan, and having mourned the loss of Arnold Raphel at a boozy wake at a bar in Dupont Circle, Washington, Oakley took a phone call. "The secretary of state was on the line," Oakley recalled. "George Shultz said, 'I'm leading the Zia funeral delegation tomorrow; the plane's leaving for Pakistan at 12:00. Bring two suitcases because you're not coming back. You're the new ambassador.' "

Shultz had a reputation for obduracy. But Oakley relished the opportunity of sorting out the crisis in Islamabad. A Texan with a reputation for balling out people who crossed him, Oakley would be direct, authoritative, a face known in Pakistan and trusted at the White House. He recalled the journey to Islamabad sitting beside Armacost and Armitage. "We talked of the need to reassure Pakistan," he said. "We had to stabilize the situation." When the plane set down, Shultz told Ghulam Ishaq Khan and General Beg: "'I'm leaving Oakley behind, he's our man. We're going to give Pakistan all of our support.' " Oakley immediately reached out to Benazir Bhutto, who was already being buffeted about in an ISI-powered whirlpool.

Fuelled by a potent mixture of patronage, tribalism, backstabbing, side-dealing, blackmail and straightforward medieval feudalism, politics Pakistan-style made Washington look like a pajama party, Bhutto recalled thinking.[31] She should have been better prepared for the dogfight of the 1988 elections, having had prior first-hand experience of the brutality of the establishment. After watching her father usurped and hanged in 1979, she had narrowly escaped death herself while under house arrest in 1982. "That nasty tin-pot dictator Zia tried to infect me with blood poisoning, sending a doctor to inject a dirty needle into my ear," Bhutto recalled. Luckily, the resulting infection had burst out of her ear on to a pillow and she had been given permission to travel to London for an operation at University College Hospital. "I was rearrested when I returned to Pakistan. Zia wanted to certify I had mental health problems so he could lock me away forever. But my friends in the US campaigned for my release."

Peter Galbraith, Bhutto's Harvard classmate, who had led calls for clemency for her father in 1978 and 1979, contacted Zia in 1984 after he had addressed the Oxford Union, where he was quizzed about the jailed Benazir Bhutto. Zia had told the students: "She's not under house arrest. You can visit her any time. You can ring her up."[32] Afterwards Galbraith had called Zia to take him up on the offer. "It worked," Benazir Bhutto remembered. "Zia was embarrassed into letting me go." Released in 1984, Bhutto spent two years in exile before returning to Pakistan to become the figurehead of the Pakistan People's Party (PPP), her father's old political machine.[33]

Then Zia's plane had fallen from the sky. Benazir recalled thinking: "This is God's will."[34] She was so certain of it and of the political future that awaited her that she wrote the lines down and used them in the first volume of her memoirs. *Daughter of the East*, which she published in 1989 in London and Washington, with one eye on her image, the other on business.[35] She was fully aware of the allure and value of her exotic provenance as the daughter of the hanged Zulfikar. It was a pedigree that also made her a hate-figure for the military in Pakistan, where the book was banned.

In October 1988, Generals Beg and Gul got to work on her. First, the new chief of army staff disenfranchised almost a fifth of traditional PPP voters, impoverished farmers and working-class town settlers, by changing the election rules so as to ban those who did not possess a national identification card from participating.[36] Then Hamid Gul fed the IJI political coalition with insinuations that its candidates regurgitated, honing in on and magnifying Benazir Bhutto's perceived weaknesses: a woman in an Islamic state, a friend of the US, educated in the West. Most potent was the nuclear issue. Gul ordered candidates to attack Bhutto as a security risk. He told them: "Pakistan needs a bomb. Bhutto cannot be trusted with it. Her loyalties are with the country that educated her—the US. She is going to sell us out to the Americans. She is a spy who will give up our nuclear secrets. She will not stand up to India."[37]

IJI candidates distributed crude leaflets that warned the electorate of Bhutto's nuclear sell-out policies and questioned whether it was permissible within Islam for a woman to become prime minister.[38] Hamid Gul tightened the tourniquet. Crude posters appeared with humiliating slogans. Bhutto and her mother were "Gangsters in Bangles," their heads superimposed on photographs of models immodestly riding bicycles in their swimsuits.[39] To make sure everyone got the point, one of General Beg's friends rented training aircraft from the Lahore Aero Club and dropped leaflets over Pakistan's major towns and cities.[40] Short of actual dirt on Benazir Bhutto, Imtiaz Ahmed, an ISI general, was tasked with digging into the Bhutto family archives. He eventually found an innocent but symbolic photo that would do to make Hamid Gul's point. It featured Benazir Bhutto's mother dancing with President Gerald Ford on a visit to Washington in 1975, when she had been Pakistan's first lady. As Gul put it to IJI candidates, under the PPP, Pakistan would forever be in a clinch with the US. General Beg could see nothing wrong with these tactics and recalled: "It was one of Pakistan's fairest ever elections. Not one man was killed."[41]

Beg and Gul began to transform the campaign into a poll on Pakistan's nuclear program—the driving force for their secret manifesto. Everything began sliding in a direction that set off alarm bells in Washington. Oakley reported in a classified cable in October 1988: "The [nuclear] issue surfaced again when [Benazir Bhutto's mother] was widely quoted in the press as willing to accept US inspection of the Kahuta nuclear facility." In truth, the quote was fabricated by the ISI. Oakley continued: "Although the most influential Pakistani political parties do not openly advocate the acquisition of nuclear weapons, the current highly charged political atmosphere may induce more parties to get on the nuclear bandwagon ... At the IJI's kick-off rally in Karachi on October 28 ... the leader ... said that becoming an atomic power was necessary to Pakistan's survival."[42] A second cable from Oakley a few days later warned that even Washington-friendly Bhutto was being forced into taking a more extreme stance on the nuclear issue to shore up her election chances: "In this atmosphere, voices of moderation will be rare."[43]

The polls closed on 16 November 1988 and Benazir Bhutto's PPP appeared to have won a slender majority. But having secured only ninety-two out of a possible 215 seats in Pakistan's lower house, she still had insufficient muscle to claim outright victory. Generals Beg and Gul persuaded President Ishaq Khan to suspend the results while the ISI strove to knit together a coalition of vanquished forces. Benazir Bhutto recalled: "I waited for more than a fortnight and Ishaq Khan refused to see me. He was hostile. I had won the majority and had the largest number of seats but he refused to call me to form the government. He called others, people with one vote and two votes. He did everything to scuttle my chances. I thought I had lost."[44]

The US did too. It attempted to stop the slide away from Bhutto by tilting external factors in her favor. In Washington, the annual wrangle over certification, the presidential declaration that Pakistan had no bomb in order for aid to flow, was due. Robert Oakley argued that it was critical for the US to demonstrate its support for Pakistan if the inexperienced Bhutto was to have any chance. "This was no time to cut Pakistan free," he remembered.[45] The White House listened. Reagan certified in favor of Pakistan. Even though the Islamic Republic was currently rudderless, the president assured Capitol Hill that Islamabad had no nuclear bomb and continued to be entitled to US aid. He was backed by president elect George H. W. Bush, the former vice president, who had just won the US election and sent a separate letter endorsing continued support for Pakistan.[46] Norm Wulf, the deputy assistant director of the ACDA, was horrified, as was Gordon Oehler at the CIA and many in the State Department.[47] In the months preceding Zia's death, nuclear procurement had accelerated, with agents working for A. Q. Khan and PAEC spotted all over Europe, and now in Islamabad radical Islamists were trying to grab power (and the bomb).

Benazir Bhutto's proximity to the US worked in her favor. More than $600 million was hanging on her confirmation as prime minister and Sharifuddin Pirzada recalled how he was brought in to calm Beg and Gul's nerves. "The military would allow Bhutto to assume power but she would be hobbled."[48] Surrounded by the remnants of her father's cabinet, they knew Bhutto would be unable to shine a light into the dark corners of Pakistani politics. While Generals Gul and Beg and President Ishaq Khan had the whole establishment at their fingertips, Bhutto had as one of the last loyalists left to counsel her, her father's dentist, Dr. Zafar Niazi, who had fled Pakistan in 1979 and had been living in a flat in London paid for by A. Q. Khan. She recalled a meeting hosted by Niazi, who had returned to Islamabad shortly before the election, in which he brought a few friends from the PPP together. In a downstairs room sat Air Chief Marshal Hakimullah, Air Chief Marshal Zulfiqar Ali Khan and an old ISI agent, General Iftikhar Ali Shah, who would go on to become the governor of the Northwest Frontier Province. "These old men simply said I should retain Ishaq Khan as president and sit back. 'He was bureaucratic and would accord to the law,' they said. I had no choice," Bhutto remembered.[49]

Bhutto knew that whatever course was chosen for her, she would have to find someone else to help her deal with the military men and the president. With little political experience beyond a handful of trips she had made with her father to the United Nations in the early 1970s, it was not a prospect she relished. She needed an intermediary to negotiate on her behalf and chose Happy Minwalla. Darayus Cyrus Minwalla, popularly known as "Happy," had been born into an old Parsee family and had been educated at Karachi Grammar School. After the death of his father in 1967, Happy had taken over the city's prestigious Hotel Metropole. Eloquent and charming, he was also well connected all over the subcontinent and the Middle East. Bhutto persuaded him to become her ambassador-at-large.[50]

It was a one-sided discourse. "Ishaq Khan told Happy the PPP should promise not to rock the boat," Bhutto recalled. "He agreed. Ishaq Khan said I should respect the army. Happy agreed. Ishaq Khan asked me to keep away from the nuclear issue altogether. Happy agreed. Finally Ishaq Khan called me in." He said he wanted to dictate who Bhutto chose as foreign minister. Sahabzada Yaqub Khan's name was put forward, the man who had served Zia. Bhutto agreed.

The president was still not satisfied and asked Sharifuddin Pirzada to determine how he could further tether the PPP. Pirzada called Benazir Bhutto directly. "I just want you to know I did not hang your father," he told her, before explaining that she would have to learn how to do business with the military establishment. He recalled: "But Benazir was nothing more than a queen. She was immature, naive and impulsive."[51] Another compromise was reached. The Punjab was one of the largest and richest states in the republic and its governor was a key figure in Pakistan. "Normally the Punjab governor had to be of the same party as the prime minister or the country pulled in different directions," Pirzada observed.[52] "But we saw to it that someone from the IJI remained in the Punjab. After some squabbling we chose Nawaz Sharif." Sharif, the son of a hard-nosed Punjabi industrialist, had stood as the IJI candidate in the general election. He was Hamid Gul's man and was ordered to make things as rough as possible for the new prime minister.

Benazir Bhutto was in power but disempowered. She had a president above her who openly despised her and retained power under the 8th amendment of the Pakistan constitution to dismiss her whenever he saw fit. She faced a calculating Punjab governor in Nawaz Sharif, who was backed by the army and was about to engage in a sniping war against her. Her foreign minister's loyalties lay elsewhere too, with the Zia generation.

So unsure was Bhutto that she called up Robert Oakley, the US ambassador, to accompany her on her first meeting with Generals Beg and Gul. "She was scared stiff and they made it crystal clear that she would only be allowed to serve if she agreed not to meddle with the army, stayed out of Afghanistan, and kept out of the nuclear issue," Oakley recalled.[53] Benazir Bhutto remembered the meeting as a fait accompli. "I got to be a prime minister—but over nothing much. I was frightened. This is Pakistan. Many of us don't say much even today, as the establishment has the capacity to kill. You are dealing with mass killers."

In December 1988, Bhutto, accompanied by her advisers, entered the prime minister's secretariat to find she had been physically constrained. "My office had been stripped," she remembered.[54] "There were no pens, pencils, not even a sheet of paper. I had only one staff officer. How was I supposed to run a country? I rang up General Beg and asked why I had no official files. 'The president asked for all files to be sent to him," Beg said. I said, 'I'm the prime minister and I want them back.'" What she read when the paperwork was finally returned filled her with gloom. Bhutto, who had attained a degree in political science from Harvard and an MA in philosophy, politics and economics from Oxford, recalled: "President Zia had hijacked the country. Pakistan spent only 2.6 percent of GNP on education while 6.7 percent was handed over to the military. The year I came in, they were preparing to import $2.693 billion in arms. Soldiers outnumbered doctors by 10 to 1. With the Pakistan military, it always was a case of total detachment. They didn't contest elections. They had no relations with the people. They carried out the worst kinds of adventurism. Pakistan imploded while they meddled and I was throttled."[55]

Bhutto was strong-willed. She got together a team and sent them to Downing Street in London where civil service mandarins showed them how the British prime minister's office was run. But it would take more than gestures to win the war against Generals Beg and Gul, and far more worrying for Pakistan's fledgling democracy was the fact that they and President Ishaq Khan had not even bothered to tell the prime minister that they had already set the agenda for Pakistan's immediate future: consolidate the army, drag India into an Afghan-style insurgency in Kashmir, and protect Pakistan from reprisals with its new nuclear capability (that was also going to pay for it all).

Oblivious, Bhutto decided to launch out on her own with what she saw as a vote-winning policy. Conscious of her image as a youthful, progressive politician from a much-loved dynasty, Bhutto called Indian prime minister Rajiv Gandhi, the scion of another great house. They agreed to sign a no-strike pact against each other's nuclear facilities. It went against everything that Gul and Beg stood for.

Next, Bhutto proposed a plan that could only have seemed workable to someone sidelined by her military, a policy that also cut across the deal she had made with her president. She offered Gandhi talks over the disputed territory of Siachen, an uninhabitable 19,000-ft, ice-bound pass in the Karakoram mountains which bordered Kashmir. As far as Bhutto was concerned, it was not worth spilling blood over. However, for military men like Beg and Gul, who had left ancestral homes in India in 1947 to join the fledgling Pakistan army only to see half their country torn away by the Indian army in 1971, every inch of the Islamic Republic was to be cherished. Twice in the previous five years the two countries had fought over the inhospitable glacier. In 1984, India had antagonized its neighbor with Operation Meghdoot, which sent mountaineering specialists from the army, unseen by Pakistan, to seize the high ground. Three years later, Pakistan had responded by creating a specialist snow-warfare commando force, led by a young artillery officer, Pervez Musharraf, who counter-attacked, taking the Indian position at Bilafond Pass, before losing everything.[56] Even as Bhutto made overtures to Gandhi, the army was preparing for another secret assault on Kashmir.

Bhutto's third blunder was an attempt to force her way into Pakistan's nuclear program. "I contacted Munir Ahmed Khan [at PAEC] and A. Q. Khan and asked them to come to my office. I told them, 'You are old friends of my father. He set you up and now I pay your salaries.' They were polite on the phone. Long silences. But they refused to visit me."

After several weeks, Bhutto received a call. "Munir Khan and A. Q. said they were planning to see the president and if I should happen to call by at the same time, then perhaps we could all meet together." Knowing that this might be her only chance, Bhutto played along. "I turned up and there was the usual to-ing and fro-ing. But eventually it was agreed that the prime minister had to have a role in the nuclear program. We created 'the troika'—Ishaq Khan, General Beg and myself would create a Nuclear Command Authority. We decided on a strategy. Although we had all the components for a bomb, we would tell Washington we would refrain from putting it together. I argued that to be trusted we needed to give some real ground and I pressed for a reduction in the levels of uranium enrichment at Kahuta. I was surprised when they all agreed. We called it the Benazir doctrine." General Beg, who described the same meeting, said the troika was "a sham" and he had only agreed to its formation because he had been invited to visit Washington in February 1989 and needed to show that Islamabad was making progress in stabilizing its nuclear program.[57]

While Beg appeared to give with one hand, Hamid Gul took away with the other. Just as Bhutto felt she was winning over the military, the ISI launched a plot to weaken her umbilical cord to the US, buying up copies of a book that had yet to be noticed by the Islamic world. Salman Rushdie's *The Satanic Verses*, a novel set in Bombay which contained loose echoes of the life of the Prophet Muhammad, had just been published in the US and Europe. After General Gul's agents read it, highlighting incendiary paragraphs, they sent a marked-up copy to the cleric Maulana Kauser Niazi, Zulfikar Bhutto's old information minister and a great supporter of A. Q. Khan. Lately, Maulana Niazi had split with the PPP, drifted towards radical Islam, and was down on his luck. A gifted propagandist, he understood the significance of Gul's gift and began to write in Urdu against Rushdie, finding immediate support for his views.

In Pakistan, the word of God was inviolable and the Koran was physically cherished. Blasphemy, the desecration of a Koranic text or the lambasting of its meaning, was tantamount to treason. Thanks to Maulana Niazi, Hamid Gul soon had a ready-made revolution on his hands. Within days there were violent protests, led by a clerical lobby already distanced from the prime minister which chanted slogans damning an American–Zionist conspiracy. Bhutto was forced to go against her democratic instincts and ban the book. But the crowds continued to swell. Then, on 12 February 1989, to the delight of the ISI, a mob attacked the US Information Service building in Islamabad, laying siege to those working inside, invoking memories of the painful scenes of Tehran and Islamabad in 1979.

The fuse was lit. In Tehran, Ayatollah Khomenei issued his infamous fatwa against Rushdie. That only left Gul to make one last, sneering connection, revealing that the publisher of *The Satanic Verses* in the US was the same as for Bhutto's *Daughter of the East*. Bhutto appeared as a woman of poor judgment, unsuited to the cloisters of an insular Islamic state.[58]

When Benazir Bhutto and the new US president, George H. W. Bush, met for the first time in February 1989 it was in Tokyo, where both were attending the funeral of Emperor Hirohito. Robert Oakley recalled that beside the smoldering fires lit by *The Satanic Verses* the nuclear program was high on the agenda. Bush had backed Reagan's certification that Pakistan had no bomb, but was uneasy with intelligence he had seen showing an unrelenting shopping program for KRL and PAEC. In Tokyo, Bhutto assured Bush that she understood his concerns. Meanwhile, General Beg was in the US, meeting with Colin Powell, the outgoing Reagan administration national security adviser, and General Brent Scowcroft, Bush's incoming national security adviser. Television pictures from Pakistan showed chanting mobs burning the American flag, and his reception was less than accommodating. Oakley said: "They gave it to him with no frills. 'Here's where you are with the nukes. If you continue you will have three or four weapons and then we will be obliged to invoke the amendments. Look at everything you will lose. Unless you are going to go to war with India you should think about it.' "[59]

However, Beg was unperturbed. He was planning to go to the brink of war with India and already had his sights set on new alliances beyond the US. Returning home, he called on President Ishaq Khan. "I said that things had gone well in the US," remembered Beg.[60] "I said we had told them we would freeze the enrichment program. It cost us nothing. We had enough uranium for our weapons program already." Benazir Bhutto met Ishaq Khan on her return from Tokyo. "I said, 'I need to know about the aid money that will come in this year. How is it being spent?' He said, 'I am not telling you. It's a nuclear issue. You need to know nothing.' "[61]

It dawned on the prime minister that rather than tiptoeing around the establishment she would have to wreck it and rebuild it. In the summer of 1989, she made her first move, sacking Admiral Iftikhar Sirohey, chairman of the joint chiefs of staff, whom she replaced with a PPP ally. President Ishaq Khan insisted that only he retained the constitutional right to hire and fire officers and the appointment was rescinded. Bhutto tried again, promoting Lieutenant General Alam Mahsud, the Lahore corps commander, to full general and making him the army's deputy chief. With General Beg due to retire in August 1991 this placed the pro-Bhutto General Mahsud in prime position to take over, rather than Beg's chosen successor, Hamid Gul. The military stamped on this plan too. A new corps commander was dispatched to Lahore and General Mahsud was retired early.

The prime minister tried once more. She appointed a new chief justice of the supreme court and a chief election commissioner. However, the president insisted on maintaining this power too, and, as in so many of the conflicts, Bhutto was forced to fold.[62]

The constant warfare between the military and the prime minister, and the angry noises coming from the US, set A. Q. Khan on edge. Not only did he fear KRL's obsolescence and PAEC's domination of bomb design, but he also worried that Bhutto was going to wreck the nuclear program altogether by doing a deal with Washington. He called a friend, Husain Haqqani, formerly a journalist at *The Muslim*, and a man of many hats. Haqqani had worked for the ISI and Hamid Gul, helping to assemble the IJI coalition that had fought to stop Bhutto at the polls. He also had influence with Nawaz Sharif, the Punjab governor. "Khan was irritable," Haqqani recalled.[63] "He wanted the forces opposed to Benazir to place her under increased pressure. He was worried. He said that he had contacted Hamid Gul personally to end the enrichment freeze. He wanted to turn up the program and advance once again."

Khan need not have worried. The ISI was by then convinced it needed to get rid of Bhutto. Having promised to stay out of Afghan politics, she had lectured Hamid Gul on the need to stop the war and start a permanent peace process, arguing for a fixed border to be negotiated and for the mujahideen to hand back their ISI-supplied weapons.[64] It was too much for Gul, who in the spring of 1989 began plotting to take Bhutto's life. He approached a mujahideen fighter and financier based in Peshawar, the gateway to the Khyber Pass. As yet unknown in the West or South Asia, Osama bin Laden, a Saudi dissident, whose family had made their fortune in construction, had many prosperous and powerful political connections. He was bored, looking for a new purpose. Gul, who had got to know him via the ISI bureau in Peshawar, had a job in mind.[65]

Husain Haqqani was let into the plan. "Hamid Gul took Osama to see Nawaz Sharif. I was there when he did it. He wanted to put the two of them together so that they could mount a coup and overthrow Benazir." The meeting took place at the Jamaat-e-Islami office in Mansehra, Northwest Frontier Province. Two further meetings took place in Jamaat-e-Islami offices in Peshawar and Lahore.[66] "Gul wanted Osama to pay for the overthrow, preferably with Benazir finished off." There was a huge war chest assembled, with Osama bin Laden raising $10 million, against which he set one precondition. Nawaz Sharif, who would take over as prime minister, was to transform Pakistan into a strict Islamic state, administered solely by sharia law, an austere theocracy of the type that would shortly rise under the Taliban in Afghanistan. "Sharif agreed," Haqqani said. "The money was already in Pakistan."

11

A GUEST OF THE REVOLUTIONARY GUARD

On 1 January 1989, Richard Barlow, the top US analyst on Pakistan's bomb program, moved from Langley to the Office of the Secretary of Defense (OSD) at the Pentagon. His enemies at the CIA and the State Department were legion. Bringing with him a folder-full of citations and awards, Barlow buried himself in his work. He was the OSD's first intelligence officer and his job description was broad, part diplomat—representing the OSD to the board of governors of the IAEA—and part investigator—he was instructed to pursue proliferation vigorously. However, he was in a department that was steeped in realpolitik, balancing the commercial needs of the domestic military industry with US foreign policy. Within weeks, Barlow had amassed a stack of evidence on the advancing Pakistani program and had caught sight of Hamid Gul's plans. Pakistan was being taken to the next level by acquiring a delivery system for their nuclear bomb. They were building missiles and adapting US-supplied jets to drop a bomb.

But nothing Barlow did seemed to stimulate interest at the OSD. It was as if his reports were falling into a deep void, until April 1989 when he was introduced to Edward "Skip" Gnehm, the new deputy assistant secretary of defense.[1] Gnehm, who had had a long career at the State Department, where he was a Middle East expert, had just returned from Jordan where he had served as deputy chief of mission. Highly respected, he worked closely with another high-flyer, Stephen Hadley, assistant secretary of defense for international security policy.[2] Hadley's portfolio was to look after NATO, Western Europe and US policy on nuclear weapons, missile defense and arms control. Everything Barlow handed in ended up with Gnehm or Hadley.[3]

When Gnehm showed a personal interest in Barlow's work, the former CIA analyst jumped at the chance to give a full briefing, paying little attention to office politics. A bloodhound, Barlow's head rarely rose above the trail. "I expressed specific concerns," he remembered. "Pakistan was getting ready to launch or drop its bomb and was still shopping for parts. But the intelligence was being manipulated to prevent Pressler, the Solarz amendment and the Non-Proliferation Act from coming into play. It was different from what the Reagan people had done. The Cold War warriors around Bush shielded the president from learning about Pakistan's real aims. This had serious security ramifications that went beyond Pakistan getting aid. Concealing evidence from the president hindered his ability to understand the threat or make smart decisions to act against it." The new president had a very different attitude to the truth, which Robert Oakley, the US ambassador in Islamabad, noted too: "President Bush cared about the law and wanted a good relationship with Congress—much more so than President Reagan who rode roughshod over the Hill. Different man, different outlook."[4]

Gnehm listened to Barlow in disbelief. He appeared to have no knowledge of the previous clashes between the CIA and State Department in Reagan's second term, in which the latter was accused of undermining the former, even tipping off Pakistan to criminal and investigative proceedings. "Gnehm was furious," Barlow recalled.

Michael MacMurray, the OSD's Pakistan desk officer, the man in charge of military sales to the Islamic Republic, overheard the conversation. He blew up, accusing Barlow of talking out of turn because it was his job to brief Gnehm. But it was too late for recriminations, as Gnehm had the bit between his teeth. The new deputy assistant secretary hated deception. Convinced by Barlow and the evidence, he began to hawk the analyst and his files around the Pentagon, getting the message out to all of those who needed to know: Pakistan was working on new ways of delivering its nuclear bombs. It was behaving like a nation getting ready to wage a war. It had to be stopped.[5]

Barlow was commissioned to write a full intelligence assessment on Pakistan for Dick Cheney, George Bush's secretary of defense, who was about to attend a National Security Council meeting on the subject. Gathering all available evidence, Barlow contacted the highly secretive Defense Intelligence Agency (DIA), the Pentagon's coordinating intelligence agency.[6] Barlow was already well known to the DIA, having frequently accessed its products while at the CIA. The DIA was asked to write up a technical assessment of the Pakistan program:

where Islamabad was at and where it was going. In particular, the DIA focused in on Pakistan's American-supplied F-16s, the first of which had landed at Sargodha airbase in Pakistan on 15 January 1983 as part of a package of six aircraft released to cement the deal between Reagan and Zia. The Islamic Republic had then received another thirty-four by way of an enticement to stay the course in the war against the Soviets.[7] These sales had all been preconditioned by pitches from the Defense Department in which Congress had been assured that it was impossible for Pakistan to adapt the jets to drop a nuclear bomb.

However, the DIA and Barlow discovered the reverse. "Our conclusions were stark," Barlow remembered. "Pakistan had found a way to modify the F-16s to carry a nuclear bomb. They not only knew how, but they had actually done it. They were shopping for components that were obviously for a nuclear-capable missile. And the program was being accelerated as if something significant was being planned."

This was not what many in the Pentagon wanted to hear, especially the offices that dealt with military sales. While Barlow's report placed the prior F-16 deal in an appalling light, the Defense Department was, unbeknown to Barlow, considering selling sixty more F-16s to Pakistan as part of a new agreement that had yet to be made public. General Dynamics, in Fort Worth, Texas, the jets' manufacturer, badly needed the contract, which was valued in excess of $1.4 billion.[8]

Barlow admitted: "I didn't know what was going on. MacMurray started breathing down my neck. Officials at the OSD kept pressurizing me to change my conclusions." They wanted Barlow to erase whole sections of his report, including the paragraphs explaining how Pakistan had already taken action to utilize their F-16s as a nuclear strike force and those detailing how the Islamic Republic was repeatedly in breach of he Solarz and Pressler amendments. "This was a straightforward piece of engineering that had been confirmed in multiple technical studies by top experts in the government," Barlow said. "The intelligence was rock solid." Barlow was not alone in his findings; the Department of Energy, too, had been analyzing the F-16 issue as well as Pakistan's breach of Pressler and Solarz.[9]

The following month, Skip Gnehm was transferred to the State Department.[10] His job at the Defense Department was taken by Arthur Hughes, who came over from the State Department. Barlow continued to work, hoping there was nothing significant about the personnel changes above him.

"I spotted another terrible act of collusion. Pakistan was using the F-16s as a cover. They would claim they needed a piece of kit to work on the fighter as a matter of routine maintenance when that same equipment was also integral to transforming the fighter into a nuclear-capable jet. Everything had been rubber-stamped in the US. We were sending the kit over to them. US components were helping build their delivery system."

Then Barlow noticed a curious thing. Bits of information, files and reports, started going missing. A secretary tipped him off. An official above Barlow had been intercepting papers that contained information on procurement cases he was working on, including an ongoing criminal inquiry.[11] Barlow dithered. He was upset and confused. He said nothing, not even to his supervisor. When his acting boss, Gerald Brubaker, asked him to set up a meeting on Capitol Hill, he followed orders—even though last time he had backbenched he had got his fingers burned. "I went right ahead," Barlow said. "Brubaker was my manager. I had no idea that they were getting ready to screw me."[12]

In Pakistan, General Mirza Aslam Beg unveiled a silo full of surprises in Sargodha: two nuclear-capable ballistic missiles. In the US, the DIA informed the Bush administration that Pakistan had test-fired the missiles, the Hatf 1 and Hatf 2, over the Thar Desert in May 1988 and that they had a range of between fifty and 200 miles, bringing Pakistan within striking distance of New Delhi and Mumbai.[13] Manufactured by PAEC using Chinese designs, PAEC chairman Munir Ahmed Khan had christened them Hatf, a familiar Arabic word meaning lethal and the name given by the Prophet to his sword.[14]

Addressing students at Pakistan's National Defense College in February 1989, General Beg congratulated Munir Khan and confirmed that the Hatf 1 and 2 had just been tested again, this time from mobile launching pads on Pakistan's Mekran coast. They were "extremely accurate" and could carry 500-kg payloads, he said.[15] He also revealed that Pakistan was well on its way to developing a tank, a pointed announcement aimed at the US, letting the Pentagon know that there was less and less that defense sales could do for the Pakistan army. No more demonstrations of the M1 Abrams would be needed. "No lollipops to throw to the Pakistanis. Not now," General Beg recalled.[16]

There were more revelations. Working on the basis that a concealed weapon failed to terrorize and therefore held no deterrent value, General Beg called a friend on *The Muslim.* A. Q. Khan had made another breakthrough, he advised. "Pakistan has now produced a surface-to-air missile and a laser rangefinder," General Beg told the newspaper. "The SAM has a range of 150 to 5000 meters."[17] This was another calculated piece of spite, aimed squarely at the US. In 1986, after much hand-wringing, the US had supplied hand-held Stinger missiles to the mujahideen and changed the face of the Afghan war. Pakistan had no need for them now, as it had gone into production with its own version at KRL, using technology supplied by Khan's European agents.[18] Khan had called his missile the Anza, from a story in the Sura about a companion of the Prophet who killed his enemy with a striking lance.[19]

Benazir Bhutto learned about the breakthroughs from the newspapers. Frequently she found herself having to catch up this way, issuing congratulatory telegrams about yet more developments that the army had forgotten to brief her on.[20] "The missile launch enhanced the self-respect and esteem of the Pakistani people," she wrote in a hastily released press statement. "It is the blessing of Allah."[21] The US bridled. She was weak. The prime minister they had backed was unable to control the army, which was moving towards open defiance of the US. Washington realized that it could no longer rely on Bhutto's assurances that Pakistan had no bomb.

Over the border India fumed. New Delhi felt obliged to unveil something new of its own. It test-fired its first intermediate nuclear-capable missile. Named Agni, after the Sanskrit word for fire, the 18-meter-long, 7.5-ton colossus had a range of up to 1,500 miles (enabling it to reach southern China). Before Robert Oakley's weary eyes—with General Beg eager to trump prime minister Bhutto and Pakistan keen to eclipse India—a perilous nuclear arms race had begun, while the Bhutto–Gandhi-inspired peace process had all but collapsed.[22]

Bhutto was being squeezed. She finally made her move in May 1989 after learning of the plot to kill her initiated by Hamid Gul, backed by Nawaz Sharif and paid for by Osama bin Laden. She called on General Iftikhar Gillani, an old PPP retainer from her father's days.

"I was terrified," she remembered.[23] "I asked him to visit the king of Saudi Arabia. We needed to know if he was giving the money and backing Osama bin Laden. If this was the case then we were finished. But the king said, 'No, Benazir is like a daughter to me.' Next time I was in Saudi I saw all of these construction signs with the bin Laden name on them and I thought to myself, 'This is the family of the man who tried to kill me.'" Bhutto fired General

Hamid Gul as her ISI chief, replaced him with Lieutenant General Shamsur Rehman Kallue, an old PPP loyalist, and held her breath.[24] Within days, General Beg countermanded his prime minister, ordering loyal officers to remove from ISI headquarters all sensitive material, files and tape transcripts, as well as dossiers on political leaders, taking them to his lair at Army House in Rawalpindi.[25]

All the time the military was working hard to destabilize Bhutto's rule across the country, fuelling sectarianism, encouraging local PPP offices to commit corrupt acts which it then revelled in bringing into the open. After Nawaz Sharif's Punjab was wracked by bomb blasts which caused the deaths of scores of bystanders, rumors spread that Bhutto's PPP was to blame, although many of the explosions were actually the work of agents provocateurs in the pay of Generals Gul and Beg.[26] In Karachi, the country's economic powerhouse, the ISI stoked indiscriminate killing and violence between opposing political parties, closing factories and shops, wiping an estimated $48 million per day off the economy.[27]

The chaos surrounding the prime minister was wearing down even her most loyal supporters.[28] When she flew to the US in June 1989 for her first visit to the White House, she found President Bush noticeably reserved. The CIA was also less than happy with her. William Webster, who had come from the FBI to become the new CIA director after Bill Casey's death in May 1987, vowed to straighten out an agency tarnished by its reputation for deceit. Webster turned up the temperature on Pakistan by showing Bhutto exactly what the US knew about Islamabad's nuclear program, including a mock-up bomb. Bhutto recalled: "It was daunting. Half of this stuff I did not know. Missiles. Jets. Shopping for components to deploy our bombs. What could one say? So much had been withheld from me but I could not use that as an excuse. I was prime minister. The message I took away was the need to wrestle back control of Khan and the program."[29]

A prime minister who was weak was still better than a cabal of Islamist generals who were beyond Washington's reach. The day after she was shown the bomb mock-up, Bhutto met Bush again and they discussed a deal. In return for allowing US aid to continue, she would provide assurances that her scientists would stop weaponizing uranium. "Bush told me that he knew of my difficulties and as a result was prepared to certify Pakistan had no bomb to allow aid to flow in December 1989," recalled Bhutto. "He wanted me to provide guarantees that Pakistan would desist from producing cores for its nuclear bombs." To sugar the pill, the White House announced it would sell Pakistan sixty F-16 fighters, something positive to take back to army chief General Beg. "I thought I had got a good deal here," Bhutto said. "We had the jets and the US money. We agreed to tone down activities at Kahuta for a while. I was sure I had done well."

But in Pakistan, there was no good news for Bhutto. Newspapers, following the lead of Hamid Gul, who remained an influential corps commander, lambasted the prime minister. "Pakistan's nuclear weapons capabilities simply cannot be safe under the leadership of a westernized woman," railed one, quoting the words of cleric Maulana Sami ul-Haq, leader of the radical group Jamiat Ulema Islam. "She cares more for American approval than for ensuring the *ummah*'s first bomb."[30]

General Beg also notched up the pressure. With Bhutto having promised the US peace, in November 1989 he gave them a vision of war. The general unveiled plans for Pakistan's largest military exercise to date, code-named Zarb-e-Momin or The Blow of the Believer, a militaristic striptease in which General Beg would reveal more from the arsenal of weapons in the Pakistan army's basement.[31] "I needed to raise the tempo," the general recalled without remorse.[32] "I was letting people know the truth for the first time. We had missiles. We had a capability. We had gone nuclear. There was no longer any point pretending we hadn't."

US Pakistan policy was once again in tatters. Nuclear Pakistan, certified by President Bush as having no weapons, about to receive the third highest level of US foreign aid in the world and sixty F-16 fighters in return for suppressing its uranium enrichment program, was conducting military exercises and turning the jets into a platform for nuclear weapons. If it made no sense to demand a rollback in Pakistan's nuclear program while offering the Pakistanis a new military deal that would have seen the same program escalated, that was because of the scandal brewing at the heart of government in Washington.

On 25 July 1989, Richard Barlow had noticed a story in a Pentagon magazine which he thought his boss Gerald Brubaker should see before anyone else from the OSD talked to Congress. German intelligence had concluded that the Islamic Republic had learned to adapt its existing F-16s to carrying nuclear weapons and had tested the newly altered fighters in wind tunnels to make sure that they were aerodynamic.[33] "I told Brubaker that this matched the highly classified assessments written by myself and the DIA for Dick Cheney. And I told him I was going to call my colleagues at the CIA to see what they knew. He flipped out."

Within a day, Barlow was hauled into a meeting with Colonel James Hutchinson of the OSD's acquisitions office, one of the Pentagon's top military salesmen. According to allegations later made in an inquiry by the department's inspector general, the colonel suggested that Barlow was sabotaging the new F-16 deal. Barlow said: "His worry was that my information would impact negatively on the sales. They were all going mad at me. Screaming and shouting. They ordered me to stop all investigations."

Eight days later, with the new F-16 deal to Pakistan finally unveiled to the public, Arthur Hughes, the deputy assistant secretary of defense appeared before the House foreign affairs committee.[34] Asked by Representative Stephen Solarz, by then a veteran of the deceit over Pakistan, if the jet could be adapted by Pakistan for its nuclear program Hughes said: "No." To Barlow's amazement, when he was handed the transcript by MacMurray later that day, Hughes had also told Solarz that adapting an F-16 to drop a nuclear bomb was beyond "the state of the art in Pakistan."[35]

Next on the stand was deputy assistant secretary of state Teresita Schaffer, a polyglot whose opinions about Pakistan and the need for permanent democracy were revered at the State Department and by the House. She told the committee: "None of the F-16s Pakistan already owns or is about to purchase is configured for nuclear delivery. Pakistan, moreover, will be obligated by contract not to modify its new acquisitions without the approval of the United States."[36]

Barlow was horrified. He could not believe that officials of the caliber of Hughes and Schaffer would mislead Congress. They had to have been briefed incorrectly by officials at the Pentagon. He sought out MacMurray on the Pakistan desk, who had read his original report to Dick Cheney. Barlow said: "I warned MacMurray that Congress had been told a pack of lies. I asked him who had drafted the replies for the officials. He said, 'The people above me, my bosses.' " Barlow went to see his boss, Gerald Brubaker. He claimed that the State and Defense department was behind a widespread campaign of misinformation. Barlow immediately filed a complaint with Brubaker. "I wanted out of the OSD. The whole place stank. Given what I had written for Secretary Cheney, I felt there was a deliberate and widespread conspiracy at work to lie to Congress so that a billion-dollar fighter deal could go through."

On 4 August 1989, one month after Barlow had been promoted yet again for "outstanding investigative work," Gerald Brubaker fired him. Confused and suspecting his intelligence was the root cause, Barlow challenged him. "Brubaker told me he was acting for Stephen Hadley," recalled Barlow. Whether or not that was true, Hadley's departmental secretary, James Hinds, had approved Barlow's termination, with no notice given or pre-warning, by signing the order.[37] Barlow tried Hadley's office directly. He was barred. Eventually he got hold of Hadley's military assistant, who confirmed that his boss had signed off the termination notice and told him not to call back again.[38]

Brubaker, meanwhile, had called the DIA, having them strike down all of Barlow's security clearances, telling the agency that Barlow could no longer be trusted. On 8 August, Barlow was ordered to see the OSD's security director, who told him that all his top-secret clearances had been revoked. These were Barlow's tools and without them he could do nothing. Barlow had not even been told what he had been accused of. "I asked what on earth was going on. And they told me they had received credible information that I was a security risk." Barlow demanded to know what they had been told and by whom. "They said they could not tell me as both of these pieces of information were classified too." All they would tell him, as his world caved in, was that "senior Defense Department officials," whose identities were also classified, had supplied "plenty of evidence."

Barlow went home to Cindy, barely able to explain to her what had happened. "We were in marriage counselling following my fall-out at the CIA—something I had already had to tell my employers about. We were getting our relationship back on track. And now I had to explain to my already upset wife that not only was I being fired from the Pentagon but that I stood accused of being some kind of double agent." It was only when Barlow managed to get his head straight for a moment and hired a specialist government lawyer that he discovered Brubaker had told the OSD chain of command he believed Barlow intended to blow state secrets to Congress. Brubaker had written a fictitious "memo of conversation" to substantiate the charge, in which he recounted a meeting on 11 August 1989 that had never taken place. In it, Barlow was supposed to have told Brubaker of his intention to go to Congress to "straighten them out" on the F-16 deal and how Congress had been lied to about the Pakistan nuclear program.[39]

Barlow and his lawyer dug some more, catching a glimpse of the mountain they would have to climb. OSD security had been told by Brubaker and officials far more senior that Barlow was receiving psychiatric care and was "a psychotic suffering from delusions in which non-existent people were supposed to have lied to Congress."[40] Barlow said: "We learned that my file reached up to the under secretary level. Some officials were using my marriage to try and destroy me. Invading our marriage and manipulating our counselling sessions as evidence of my insanity."[41]

More documents surfaced in which a stellar cast of officials connected to the sacking of Barlow and its aftermath was revealed. Barlow's case had been handled by Mervyn Hampton, an assistant to under secretary Paul Wolfowitz and director of administration at the Pentagon.[42] Wolfowitz's military assistant, Admiral John Scott Redd, thirty-six years in the US Navy before coming to the Pentagon, had also become involved, having been contacted by the Pentagon security division, which asked the rear admiral to re-employ Barlow. But Redd refused, claiming that Barlow had been ousted due to a "performance-related issue," something that the Pentagon had already determined to be untrue.[43] Eric Edelman, acting on behalf of I. Lewis "Scooter" Libby, Wolfowitz's principal deputy under secretary for strategy and resources, would also become involved, as Barlow appealed to all levels of the Pentagon hierarchy for justice.[44] A memo from the Pentagon security department reported that although Barlow had had his security clearance restored and had been "exonerated," the OSD "does not appear to intend to re-employ him unless we force the issue ... Edelman said, 'No ... he would be a real awkward fit.' "[45]

Within days Hadley's department confirmed Barlow's dismissal. He was told by Hinds that the reason for his termination "remained classified" but that it was Hadley's intention to "remove you from government permanently."[46] Another of Barlow's line managers at the OSD came in to gloat. He told Barlow that they all knew what this would do to his marriage to Cindy and "that this was part of the punishment."[47]

Barlow said: "If I had been allowed to confront my accusers it would all have been over in minutes. But the charges remained classified; the identity of the accusers who planned to threaten, smear and destroy, too." However, Barlow refused to roll over. Instead, he went back to the security office at the OSD and demanded that its chief investigate. This inquiry, too, was classified. Barlow now faced a covert investigation into secret charges by nameless officials as high as Wolfowitz. America's most experienced intelligence analyst on Pakistan's nuclear program was redeployed to the OSD secretarial department and put on the job of arranging lunch appointments.

Eventually, the OSD security office came back to Barlow—with a whole host of new allegations. He was a tax evader, an alcoholic and an adulterer who had been fired from all of his previous government jobs. His marriage counselling was a cover for a course of psychiatric care in which he was receiving treatment for bouts of delusion. Barlow was pressured to sign a release form permitting the investigators to interview his marriage guidance counsellor, dragging Cindy into the inquiry. "This would be it for our marriage," Barlow said. "But I was told if I did not sign it would be over for me. I got home from work and had to explain to Cindy that her private fears were to be trawled by the OSD." Then the smear kicked in. "I discovered that news of the inquiry and the subsequent unsubstantiated claims had been broadcast around the government to friends and old employers. People thought I had done something terrible, like talking to the Soviets. I was a spy, a pariah. My life, professionally and personally, had been destroyed."

Barlow would some years later make another, far more astonishing discovery, the fact that the intelligence assessment he had written for defense secretary Dick Cheney on Pakistan's F-16s had been pulped. As he had suspected, the reason why Hughes had misled Congress was that he knew no better. Richard Barlow's full intelligence assessment, commissioned by Skip Gnehm, a document that was to have been presented at the National Security Council and used to brief the president, had been shredded and rewritten.[48]

Pakistan desk officer MacMurray had taken Barlow's highly classified findings and changed them to omit any references to the F-16s being adapted by Islamabad for nuclear warfare.[49] MacMurray later admitted to having also struck from the intelligence assessment all material that showed the Pakistan government to be in breach of the Solarz and Pressler amendments.[50] What the principals had ended up reading on Pakistan and its program and had advised the president was that continued US military and financial aid was the course most likely to ensure that Pakistan would act with restraint. But the rewriting had another, unforeseen consequence. It would lead to a massive and near-calamitous underestimation of what the Islamic Republic was capable of, as Pakistan and India came the closest that two nations have come to a nuclear war since the Cuban missile crisis.

Benazir Bhutto struggled to explain to the White House that she was still in control of Pakistan's nuclear program after General Beg took reporters aside at the war games in November 1989 and told them of Pakistan's nuclear arsenal.[51] That month he also came to find her. Over the previous three years resentment over Indian rule in Kashmir had escalated to the point where a home-grown uprising was now in full swing.[52] In addition to the Zarb-e-Momin exercise, Beg wanted to launch the Kashmir operation he and Hamid Gul had long planned.

Benazir Bhutto recalled: "Local separatists had launched a war in Kashmir, the Indian army had responded with brutal force and the state was in crisis. The general gave me a briefing on the situation."[53] Major General Jehangir Karamat, Beg's director general of military intelligence, attended too. Bhutto said: "They said we had to seize the opportunity. The Kashmiri people had spoken. They were battling India of their own accord and we could intensify the insurgency."

Specifically, the generals wanted freedom to strike whenever they needed, without recourse to the prime minister. "Beg had a plan," Bhutto remembered. "Kashmiri freedom fighters from our side would take to the peaks, cross into the Indian sector unnoticed and be followed by 100,000 battle-hardened mujahideen from the Afghan war. Pakistan would capture Srinagar [the capital of Indian Kashmir] and I would wear the crown of victory and glory." Bhutto said she was horrified. "We wanted liberty for the Kashmiris. Of course we did. I had given speeches saying as much earlier in the year when the Kashmiris rose up. But can you imagine General Beg's vision? All-out war triggered by military leaders with no reference to the elected government. Can you think what it would be like to wear that crown of victory and glory? They wanted me to change the rules of engagement and have me take the blame for their folly. It was a very heated meeting. Everyone with me, including my defense adviser, Brigadier Imtiaz Ali, told General Beg that civilians had superiority. His request was denied. Beg was furious." The Pakistan army and ISI were not given sole charge of the war button. As a compromise they were authorized to stoke a low-level insurgency.

Beg had a second, more sensitive request. Waiting until he was on his own with the prime minister, he warned that the rebellion Pakistan was starting to support in Kashmir would be inordinately expensive and that Pakistan was broke. Its GNP per capita was only $370, with one third of the population, almost 37 million people, living below the UN poverty line. The general needed money for the mujahideen, for the training camps and to arm the graduates. He needed cash to send weapons to the freedom fighters in Indian Kashmir. "This was when I first heard Beg's proposal to sell off KRL technology," Bhutto recalled. "I simply could not believe it. This shadowy circle led by Generals Gul and Beg said they wanted to create a cash flow that was independent of the US and the world banking system, from which we borrowed heavily. General Beg suggested that we didn't need International Monetary Fund (IMF) money, as all we needed to do was sell our nuclear weapons or the technology. I pointed out the IMF gave us $200 million a year. 'How many will buy our nuclear technology?' I asked him. I could only think of Iran, Iraq and possibly Libya. I said, 'Who will pay us $200 million? And even if they do, what happens after two or three years when they have all they need? Where do we get the money from then?'"

Bhutto rebuffed General Beg and reflected with incredulity on his audacity. She claimed she knew nothing of the ongoing deal with Iran or the nuclear warheads promised the Saudis. "Of course I had my suspicions," Bhutto remembered. "Oakley had already warned me that something was going on at KRL, with scientists and the military going away on unexplained trips in cargo planes."

However, the scandal of nuclear sales soon slipped her mind as the Kashmir operation promised by Beg quickly bore startling results, turning Indian-administered Kashmir into a bloody and chaotic mess with the heavily armed Indian security forces lashing out, unable to control increasingly sophisticated demonstrations, ambushes and assassination attempts. New Delhi accused Islamabad of fuelling war. On 19 January 1990, in desperation and anger, the Indian government imposed direct rule in Kashmir, rounding up hundreds of militants. In Pakistan, the ISI, with Bhutto's tacit approval, escalated, increasing the number of training camps and the volume of fighters that were being secretly sent over the line of control. Then, as up to 100,000 Pandits, Hindus who lived in Kashmir, fled the fighting, General Beg unilaterally decided on a course of action, going against the wishes of his prime minister. The Persian-speaking chief of army staff secretly flew to Tehran as a guest of the Revolutionary Guard.[54]

Robert Oakley saw General Beg before he left and described him as nervous and shifty. He was a changed man on his return. "Beg was full of it," Oakley recalled.[55] "He said he'd got support from the Iranians for his proxy war in Kashmir and that in return Pakistan would help out the Iranian nuclear program." Oakley was a little mystified as to how Iran, with its third-rate army and air force, was going to aid Pakistan, or why Pakistan would sell something as dangerous as a nuclear weapon to its unpredictable neighbor. But he filed an urgent report to Washington, warning of the nuclear component to the deal. He heard nothing back. "This was big news and potentially extremely worrying, but no one seemed to bite on it. It was a major oversight."

General Beg then repeated the same claim to Harry Rowen, the assistant secretary of defense for international security affairs, who visited Islamabad in January 1990. Rowen recalled: "Beg said something like, 'If we don't get adequate support from the US, then we may be forced to share nuclear technology with Iran.'"[56] Rowen told Beg that Pakistan would be "in deep trouble" if it went ahead. "There was no particular reason to think it was a bluff, but on the other hand, we didn't know." A few weeks later Beg said it again, this time to General Norman Schwarzkopf, the head of US Central Command, which had responsibility for the Middle East and parts of South Asia.[57]

General Beg was being slightly disingenuous. He did not need military support from Iran, since he already had F-16s adapted to carry the Pakistani bomb—a deterrent he felt sure would hold India back from invading. What Beg had really offered the Revolutionary Guard was a step-up in sales of uranium enrichment technology from KRL in return for hard cash and oil to pay for the Kashmiri jihad.[58]

Pakistan continued to increase the pressure on India. "I wanted to fully unfurl our nuclear umbrella," General Beg recalled.[59] "I ordered the F-16s we had adapted to be armed. We had also recalibrated our French Mirage jets so that they, too, could be used to carry a nuclear device. Our few rockets similarly had warheads attached to them and were placed on alert. Our panoply, although at this stage fairly crude, of nuclear weapons was activated. This was what I meant by a nuclear umbrella. Now India would have to be convinced of our intent and in the face of our new-found strength would surely not risk an attack—even though we were stirring the pot in Kashmir."

US ambassador William Clark in New Delhi, who had arrived at his posting in December 1989, recalled the rise in temperature. "I think it is fair to say that the US embassy and the Indian government were taken by surprise by the intensity and rapidity with which the violence escalated in Kashmir."[60]

By March 1990 the Indian army had amassed 200,000 troops there and, with Kashmir writhing, New Delhi ramped up the pressure, launching a large military exercise at Mahajan in the Rajasthan desert.[61] Five brigades of its most sophisticated attack unit, the Strike Corps, were stationed fifty miles from the Pakistan border. Recalling the Indian-orchestrated Brass Tacks exercise from 1987 which Zia had feared was a prelude to an Indian invasion, Pakistan ordered military exercises too, openly deploying its main armored tank units along the border. Ambassador Clark in New Delhi recalled: "There was a great deal of chest-thumping and drum-beating in New Delhi and other parts of India as well. The army itself became concerned that an inadvertent escalation could go forward. It started to ratchet up."[62]

In Islamabad, ambassador Oakley, too, felt the heat. "A lot of screaming and shouting had been going on in 1989 but nothing really serious. But in 1990 things began to worsen." Afghanistan had left the Pakistani military emboldened and also skilled at making an insurgency work, he thought. "There were more people and more materials going over the border into Indian-administered Kashmir and it did begin to look like the start of another Afghanistan."[63]

However, with Richard Barlow's report to Dick Cheney suppressed, the US ambassadors on both sides of the line of control completely underestimated what was going on. Ambassador Clark recalled seeing one report claiming the Pakistan air force had been practicing a maneuver that was sometimes associated with dropping a nuclear bomb. But his attaché cautioned that the intelligence showed that it was unlikely Pakistan had such a weapon.[64] Oakley was more emphatic: "So far as I can recall we never had any credible evidence that the F-16s were fitted out to deliver a nuclear device."

Barlow knew different. The DIA analysts too. All of them had come together to draw a picture of a rapidly advancing nuclear weapons program in Pakistan which was deployable in rocket form and in bomb form mounted on

F-16s and French Mirage jets. Strangely, Dick Kerr, then the deputy chief of intelligence, number two at the CIA, also seemed to have seen the Barlow files, as he told the investigative reporter Seymour Hersh three years after the crisis: "It was the most dangerous nuclear situation we have ever faced since I have been in the US government. It was far more frightening than the Cuban missile crisis."[65]

Then the Indians threatened to take out Pakistan's training camps, with General Vishwanath Sharma, India's new chief of army staff, warning that Islamabad was about to be given a "boot up the backside."[66] Oakley said: "The military in Pakistan was surprisingly calm but unrealistically confident, I thought. The Iranians had assured Pakistan of their strong support and this was interpreted by General Beg as something meaningful."

In a calculated act of defiance, General Beg ordered A. Q. Khan to restart the centrifuges at KRL. As forces on both sides of the border gathered, Pakistan began producing weapons-grade uranium again. Without knowing that the centrifuges were humming, Bhutto was pressured by the military into making a patriotic gesture which she was advised would further enrage India. It was also aimed at the US. On 23 March 1990, the prime minister presented A. Q. Khan with the Hilal-i-Imtiaz, Pakistan's second-highest civilian honor. "Pakistan is proud to have a man of Dr. A. Q. Khan's caliber," Bhutto said. "I hope the country will have more men of such eminence. He has made an invaluable contribution, not only in the nuclear field, but also in other fields, including defense production."[67]

Ambassador Oakley grew more worried by the day, even if he knew nothing of Beg's decision to take Pakistan's nuclear arsenal out of the basement. "Our sensors picked up on what was happening in Kahuta. We feared that if the momentum of this ratcheting up was not stopped by the fall, the prime fighting season, the two armies might be face to face again and the momentum would be so strong that it could not be stopped." Washington decided to take a closer look, adjusting the orbiting paths of American satellites to increase the hour-to-hour coverage over South Asia, and committing extra resources for the US–British eavesdropping station at Diego Garcia in the Indian Ocean. By May the situation looked so bleak, with intense military activity on both sides of the border, that ambassador Oakley sought out Bhutto, who recalled: "Oakley told me the whole thing had gone mad. He was worried. Really worried. He said, 'Sit tight and I'll get back to you.'"

Frustrated at being able to do nothing, sidelined by Beg and then by Oakley, Bhutto left Pakistan in the midst of the crisis for a tour planned by her foreign ministry. In reality, she reflected, it was a ruse devised by the president to keep her out of the way as a new set of talks began. Unbeknown to Bhutto, the US had just dispatched a middleman to calm the rapidly rising tensions—even though the nuclear dimension of the growing conflict was still misunderstood. On President Bush's orders, Robert Gates, the deputy national security adviser, was hauled out of Moscow, where he was preparing for a presidential summit, and flown to South Asia. Ambassador Oakley recalled: "Gates and I alone met with President Ishaq Khan and chief of army staff Beg. Gates presented a very sober assessment of what would happen in the event of war." Bhutto rang in from abroad to find out what was going on. "I only learned what was happening because Oakley told me," Bhutto said.[68] "But even he said everything was being taken care of and so I stayed away."

The talks seemed to end successfully. Gates and Oakley believed they had convinced Beg to back down or that the general had himself reasoned that Pakistan was still incapable of defeating India. The US was satisfied either way. However, General Beg saw it differently. "We did not need Gates," he recalled. "What the US worried was going to happen, would never have taken place. We never intended to fight India. We only intended to show our enemy that we had the capability. This would have been enough to stop them coming after us when we nipped away at them elsewhere. We had established our minimum credible deterrence—although Gates had no idea."[69]

Bhutto was only let in on the discussions in July 1990, after Gates had gone home and the crisis had passed. "Oakley told me that war had been averted but that the nuclear issue was making waves in Washington," she recalled.[70] "KRL was enriching again and I had to try everything I could to prevent the US from cutting off aid. I sought an immediate meeting with the president, A. Q. Khan and Munir Khan from the Pakistan Atomic Energy Commission. I wanted to tell them we were about to be sanctioned. They had to turn off Kahuta. The meeting was cancelled." With no commitment coming from Bhutto's office, Oakley was losing his cool. "Enrichment was going through the roof and we asked and got no answer," he remembered.[71] "Every month I would call the prime minister, the president and Beg and tell them that on 1 October 1990 we were going to have to invoke the Pressler amendment and cut off aid. Beg kept saying to me, 'But we've had the bomb for many years and you've never cut us off. So why be different now?'" Bhutto sought another meeting with the president and A. Q. Khan. The message came back that it had been rescheduled for the end of July. "Then they chose another date," she recalled. "This time I was out of the country on official business. Ishaq Khan said, 'You come back on schedule and then we'll discuss it.' When I got back I sought yet another date." By the time that day came around, the Pakistan president had already decided on a different strategy. He invoked the 8th amendment and on 6 August 1990 sacked Benazir Bhutto without any reference to the millions who had voted for her. The date for her removal had been chosen purposefully to lessen the expected backlash from the US. It was three days after Saddam Hussein had invaded Kuwait and, with the US preoccupied with the Gulf, there was barely a flicker of interest in Washington when she walked out of the prime minister's secretariat.

On 9 March 1990 the secret inquiry, to which Richard Barlow had not been allowed to be a party, into allegations that remained classified, was completed by men he never met.[72] "I was called in and was amazed to hear that I had been completely exonerated," Barlow remembered.[73] "My top-secret clearances were restored. The head of security said he had concluded the entire thing had been a fabrication. He told me he had had a fierce battle with people at very high levels of the OSD. He told me he was going to see Wolfowitz's people to get me reinstated immediately." But nobody wanted to give Barlow a job.

He hired another lawyer and in the autumn of 1990 was offered a $20,000 compensation payment, attached to a gagging order. On his lawyer's advice, he declined and filed a counter-claim. However, as the papers worked their way through the system, Barlow found himself under caution once again, this time at the behest of the Department of Defense's inspector general (IG), the internal watchdog for the Pentagon. "I showed up for work only to find guys standing with their warrant badges out," Barlow recalled. "They said I was not going to work anywhere until I cooperated with their inquiry." The IG's office had heard a rumor of a criminal conspiracy at the highest levels in the OSD but could not find out from anyone what had happened, other than that it involved Richard Barlow. "They said I was to tell them everything or I would be arrested. I was pressed into revealing what had happened to me."

They drew from Barlow the entire story, how senior State and Defense Department officials had misled Congress, how information on Pakistan's nuclear-capable

F-16s had been withheld, as well as the constant breaches of Solarz and Pressler, how Barlow had been smeared and then cleared in a nightmarish inquiry with no end which more befitted a Soviet state than the United States.

"The agents were agog," Barlow remembered. "They said: 'You did nothing wrong. You played by the book.' They sat down and drafted criminal allegations against the people who had persecuted me." But without explanation the inquiry with its charges was suddenly dropped. "No one would tell me why but I learned from a very angry lead investigator that the criminal inquiry into Wolfowitz's office had been shut down as a result of political pressure. I was on the verge of a nervous breakdown. I took leave without pay, drove off to see friends in Seattle and tried everywhere to find a job. But whenever anyone took references from the OSD, the job would evaporate." Cindy filed for divorce. "She wanted stability and babies. My life was totally destabilized and she realized then that this was not going to end for a very long time."

12

PROJECT A/B

Upon his inauguration in 1989, President George H. W. Bush had been lobbied to plot a new course for US–Pakistan policy. Among the most influential voices beseeching him to get a grip on Islamabad was a former diplomat and hard-bitten negotiator who had risen to become America's foremost authority on non-proliferation, Gerard Smith. He had served under Eisenhower, Nixon and Carter, and in October 1979 had ambushed Pakistan's foreign minister Agha Shahi in a White House side room to warn him that by reaching out for nuclear weapons the Islamic Republic was entering the valley of death.[1]

Smith's warning to Bush came through an article he wrote for *Foreign Affairs*, one of the premier US journals on matters international, in which he accused the Carter and Reagan administrations (and sections of Congress) of pulling a confidence trick on the American people.[2] They had been deceived wholeheartedly about Pakistan's nuclear program, hoodwinked into thinking that there had been no choices. "Rolling back the Soviet presence in Afghanistan superseded the US interest in preventing nuclear proliferation ... there was little or no public debate over the relative value of these two goals," Smith wrote.[3] There had also been no acknowledgment that both could have been achieved simultaneously, rather than the bomb being dropped to elevate victory against Moscow.

In Smith's eyes, US–Pakistan policy was a dismal failure. The White House had adopted "a frequently permissive attitude towards ... Pakistan" which had a "significant ripple effect in eroding the credibility of the Nuclear Non-Proliferation Treaty (NPT) regime." As Pakistan had been aided by the US in building its nuclear bomb, a nightmarish scenario presented itself whereby other would-be nuclear nations were now likely to strive for the same in the knowledge that the US had lost the moral high ground. The essence of the NPT, the fear of the mass opprobrium that would be heaped on a rogue nuclear state by the licensed nuclear powers, had been shot to pieces.

Smith's article concluded: "The arguments that made building the NPT regime seem worthwhile in the 1960s have lost none of their relevance. Quite the contrary. Those arguments centered on the uniquely destructive properties of nuclear arms and the international linkages that gave any incident of nuclear use the potential to catapult all humanity into a global nuclear holocaust. They must still, like all matters in the nuclear realm, take precedence in American national strategy over all lesser considerations."

More warning signals that something had to be done about Pakistan came in the autumn of 1990, when Bush received a CIA report revealing that US export controls aimed at preventing the sale of hi-tech equipment to Pakistan's nuclear program were being ruthlessly exploited by Islamabad.[4] The consensus was moving towards censure. Ambassador Oakley in Islamabad recalled: "President Bush and I told President Ishaq Khan and General Beg, 'We know that you've reactivated your nuclear program. We don't like the tone of things. We are going to be obliged to apply sanctions.' "[5] There was no response, and on 1 October 1990 President Bush announced he could no longer provide Congress with Pressler amendment certification that Pakistan did not possess a nuclear weapon. The $564 million economic and military aid program that Congress had already approved for 1991 was frozen and thirty F-16s that Pakistan had ordered from General Dynamics were put into storage at a US Air Force base near Tucson, Arizona.[6] For the first time in ten years, Islamabad was cut adrift.

The decision suited Washington just fine. With the US-leaning Benazir Bhutto out of office in Islamabad and the war in Afghanistan over, the last Soviet soldier having left in February 1989, the US had had just about enough of the region and had a growing crisis in the Gulf to attend to, with Saddam Hussein having invaded Kuwait. But this new US–Pakistan strategy was not what Gerard Smith had envisaged. He had argued that the US should use its proximity to exert pressure on Islamabad to curtail its bomb program. Smith had called for an end to the double-dealing at the State Department and in the White House and had suggested that, to demonstrate its seriousness, the White House should initiate a punitive break in aid while the State Department and US military continued to bully, cajole and, most importantly, contain

Islamabad. Instead, the drawbridge was pulled up on a nuclear state with an undeclared arsenal, travelling rapidly in the general direction of fundamentalism and with a desire to share its technology with like-minded allies the world over. For more than a decade everything had been made available to Pakistan and now there was to be nothing from Washington at all—until the first US cruise missiles slammed into the Afghan desert in October 1998.[7]

Norm Wulf, deputy assistant director at the Arms Control and Disarmament Agency (ACDA), recalled: "No one would be looking at Pakistan. Our attempts at inhibiting its nuclear program took a back seat."[8] In Pakistan, the caretaker government imposed by President Ishaq Khan was so shocked that it sent foreign minister Sahabzada Yaqub Khan to Washington with an offer to freeze Pakistan's nuclear program. But Yaqub Khan was turned away after he said he could not promise his government would adhere to US demands for Pakistan to destroy its nuclear bomb cores and "roll back its capability to the other side of the line."[9] He returned empty-handed to Islamabad, where the democratic process was taking another beating.

Politics in the Islamic Republic was becoming a self-fulfilling prophecy: hobbled, the politicians failed; unfettered, the military saved the day. This would be the pattern imprinted on successive civil administrations in Pakistan for a decade to come. Husain Haqqani, the former ISI confederate who had helped run the stop-Bhutto coalition in 1988, but whose disillusionment with the ISI would lead to him becoming a counsellor to successive prime ministers, recalled: "We were entering a dangerous spiral. The civilian parties were being prevented from growing by the military and had no knowledge of how to build strong, grass-roots organizations. Instead, they fielded weak and venal candidates, ripe to be smeared, manipulated and toppled by the ISI and military that magnified their sins."[10]

President Ishaq Khan, following his dismissal of Benazir Bhutto on 6 August 1990, had called a general election, and the military, religious and intelligence factions were cutting each other's throats. Whoever was allowed to cross the finish line on 24 October, the election day, would be so beholden to the military that he or she would have little chance of making any impact on the predestined course chosen for Pakistan by the president and Generals Beg and Gul. Haqqani said: "The new prime minister would be expected by the army to ignore the mounting hard-line Islamic forces in Afghanistan and also the nuclear program. This prime minister might intend to pursue peace with India but he or she would also have to support the ISI's insurgency in Kashmir."

The election campaign demonstrated Haqqani's point in truly dismal fashion. Benazir Bhutto decided to run again, but without US backing. Opposing her were IJI candidates fielded and nurtured by General Gul, whom she had ousted from the intelligence service, and along with General Beg, who had just over a year left to serve as chief of army staff, he took complete charge of annihilating the PPP leader. Beg had a new bagman, Lieutenant General Asad Durrani, who had served as Pakistan's defense attaché in Germany from 1980 to 1984 during a period in which KRL had made Germany the pivot of its nuclear procurement operations. Durrani always denied involvement in A. Q. Khan's world, but whether or not he was complicit, his performance won him promotions and eventually the job of director general of military intelligence, from where he had been plucked by General Beg to run the ISI just after Bhutto was sacked.[11]

Generals Beg and Durrani plotted to hijack the vote. They approached a banker, Younis Habib of the Habib and Mehran bank, who claimed he loaned them 150 million rupees ($3 million) for a slush fund kept by military intelligence and its commander, Major General Javed Qazi.[12] Scores of religious candidates and radical Islamist groups were lavished with money to batter Bhutto, introducing a fundamentalist tone to the elections. She had taken on as her adviser Mark Siegel, a former Carter administration official and an accomplished lobbyist, whose clients had included Israel. In Pakistan this was political dynamite, with Siegel ridiculed by the IJI as "Benazir's Jew," while she was denigrated for fronting a US–Zionist conspiracy.[13] Unsurprisingly, Bhutto's election campaign drowned in the soup of innuendo on 24 October, while the former Punjab governor, Nawaz Sharif, backed by Generals Beg and Gul, was ushered in as prime minister.

Born on Christmas Day in 1949, Nawaz Sharif was the second son of a wealthy Punjab industrialist, Mohammed Sharif, and was outshone in his father's eyes by his ambitious younger brother Shahbaz. The doe-eyed Nawaz was seen as just a little dull, lacking in charisma, and had shown no sign of ambition until General Malik Ghulam Jilani, an ISI agent and confidant of Zia, came calling at the family's home in Model Town, Lahore, in 1980.

The spy Jilani, who was also Punjab governor, was looking for a successor. He had his eye on Shahbaz Sharif but his father refused to part with him.

Instead, he offered his younger boy who, out of his elder brother's shadow, surprised everyone by blossoming. Nawaz Sharif found the political world to his liking. He and Jilani saw eye to eye, with Jilani making him the Punjab's treasurer in 1981 before enabling him to succeed as governor in 1985. When he became prime minister in October 1990, Sharif was eager to make an impression—if Generals Beg and Gul would allow him.

But the generals were first out of the trap and pointedly set the tone, announcing that it had been "an anti-American election" and that the new prime minister was answerable only to Pakistan, a welcome relief from Bhutto who had been so intimidated by the military that US ambassador Oakley had sometimes accompanied her to government meetings. However, Sharif was not anti-American or a zealot, as Husain Haqqani, his former adviser, recalled. "Nawaz had the canny ability of holding two opposing views simultaneously— for the army and against it. He also had a tendency to feign deafness and an ability to allow others to make the call on contentious issues, a contrived air of vagueness that some—to their chagrin—mistook for stupidity." Sharif also understood the power of religion and the necessity of appearing pious; he wore a traditional *kurta* and prayed openly five times a day. But having been helped into office by the forces of reaction, the new prime minister was hoping to make his mark as a pro-business, Western-looking, center-right nationalist leader.

Pakistan, as its new ambassador to the US quipped, was now so far at the back of the queue for America's affection that its relationship with the White House was akin to that which Pakistan had with the Maldives.[14] For good measure, the US had fallen out of love with Afghanistan, too, and was in the process of withdrawing its legal authority for action, preventing the State Department from intervening in the UN-led negotiations to create a moderate government in Kabul.[15] The Soviet-leaning prime minister, Mohammed Najibullah, who had been placed in position in 1986, was weakening and Pakistan was keen for the US to use its political muscle to influence the choice of successor.[16] However, there would be no US embassy or CIA station in Kabul until 2001, and the only sanctioned operation was an attempt by the CIA to buy back unused US shoulder-launched Stingers, with agents offering cash rewards for every piece turned in.

A hands-off policy for Islamabad, Gerard Smith had warned, would lead Pakistan even further astray, while the CIA forecast that Afghanistan, abandoned by Washington, was likely, with Pakistan's interference, to turn against the West and become a staging post "for terrorism in the region and beyond."[17] The country was weakened by veteran mujahideen fighters who, unemployed and bored, had become warlords, pitching Afghanistan into a brutal civil war, with more small arms in the country than in the combined arsenals of India and Pakistan.[18] Afghanistan was awash with weapons and mullahs, with the ISI dealing in both.

In Islamabad, Generals Beg and Gul were consolidating Pakistan's new strategic partnerships and the means of continuing to finance the military's covert agenda—which would run with or without the assistance of the new prime minister, Sharif. Zia might have preferred talking Muslims and morals, how a crescent of nuclear-armed Islamic nations would match NATO in power and influence, but Beg believed that money was king. He argued fervently that to possess nuclear technology was every nation's right and that the Nuclear Non-Proliferation Treaty was nothing short of racketeering on behalf of those developed countries that had got into the technology first.

Writing in Urdu for small and select Pakistan-based publications, articles that no one in the US administration was looking out for, Beg revealed an *Alice through the Looking-Glass* version of Eisenhower's resonant Atoms for Peace manifesto. "Why the commotion if a country wants to sell its atomic technology for good and positive purposes and to earn foreign exchange?" Beg asked.[19] "This is the best way for Pakistan to pay off her debts." The Islamic Republic had every right to market its nuclear capability, he argued, just as the US, France and Britain had done, making fortunes out of trading with each other and with China, South Africa, Iraq, Israel and so many others bent on a nuclear program. "Pakistan was attempting to earn its foreign exchange in an honorable way."

While the US was indifferent (or even asleep) to the seismic shift in Pakistan's nuclear program—its sales network having been made to change direction, from incoming to outgoing—General Beg, in collusion with A. Q. Khan, who advised the military which countries were after what kinds of technology, began ramping up covert operations, twisting the blade in America's back.[20] To help lubricate the foreign deals, Beg reached out to the ISI, which had another new director general, who had been radicalized by the war in Afghanistan. Just as General Gul had had his faith renewed in President Zia's newly religious army, so the incoming ISI chief, Javid Nasir, had become a born-again Muslim while in the military, growing a long flowing beard as an external sign of his devotion in an army whose uniform was short-clipped mustaches. He had recently become head of Tablighi Jamaat (TJ), a revivalist movement whose name meant "proselytizing group," which had a mission to win Muslims to the strict Deobandi sect to which Zia had belonged. TJ wrapped into its folds many senior Pakistani politicians, army officers and intelligence agents, and its annual congregation, where one million devotees from around the world converged on Raiwind in Pakistan, was the second largest Islamic get-together after the haj in Mecca. TJ's intent was to destroy all agencies of the civil state and replace them with a clerical one.[21]

General Beg had a sensitive mission for the zealous Nasir. He sent him to North Korea with a gift. A. Q. Khan had advised that a channel he had opened to Pyongyang in the 1980s, with the blessing of President Zia, selling some basic enrichment technology from the Kahuta labs, had never been fully exploited. The machinery had lain unused, as the North Koreans had insufficient technical expertise to master enrichment alone, and the pact between the two nations had stalled. It was hoped Nasir could reinvigorate the relationship by bringing with him an American Stinger missile and its battery (one of many the ISI had hoarded instead of assisting the CIA in reclaiming them from Afghanistan). The North Koreans had been after the technology for years, and Nasir was to ask them if they could help reverse-engineer the Stinger's battery. Those provided by the US had a limited shelf-life and would soon expire. Without functioning batteries, the Stingers were useless. Beg intended the missile as an hors d'oeuvre for the North Koreans, softening up Pakistan's relationship with them, alerting Pyongyang to the possibility and advantages of further technological exchanges. And the cloned Stingers would be made to work twice, as they were also intended for cash export by Pakistan to another of its allies, Iran.[22]

But since Beg did not care where Pakistan's money or political patronage came from, he simultaneously reached out to Saddam Hussein in Iraq, authorizing a KRL agent to approach Baghdad just as the UN Security Council authorized the use of "all means necessary" to eject Iraq from Kuwait and a US-led coalition prepared to insert ground forces into Kuwait to repel Saddam's army.[23] Beg's man offered the Iraqi secret service something special, a nuclear bomb.[24] The Iraqi nuclear weapons program—code-named PC-3—had been all but destroyed by Israel's attack on the Osirak reactor in 1981, and for the following decade, against a backdrop of censure from the international community, Saddam and his scientists had struggled to rebuild it. But here was pragmatic and impoverished Pakistan offering Saddam the whole package, a complete product or the blueprints to manufacture one (along with advice and drawings on the creation of a uranium enrichment plant). PAEC in Islamabad would machine the former, and the latter would come from A. Q. Khan at Kahuta, who planned to recycle bomb designs given to him by China in the 1980s.[25]

If intelligence about this offer had filtered out at the time it would have radically transformed the approach to the Gulf War, as no US president would have willingly put thousands of American troops into a maverick state armed with a nuclear weapon. However, another five years would pass before the West glimpsed the Pakistan–Iraq deal, after IAEA inspectors raided a farm outside Baghdad belonging to General Hussein Kamel, Saddam Hussein's son-in-law, who, as director of the Military Industrialization Authority, had been in charge of the country's weapons program. Briton Gary Dillon, who led this inspection team, recalled how they recovered boxes of documents, among which was a tantalizing reference to the offer made by Pakistan.[26] Dillon's team was so shocked by the contents of the one-page memo that for some time they presumed it was a fake. Headed "Top-Secret Proposal," it referred to something with the code name "Project A/B." Dillon said: "The memo appeared to be from the Mukhabarat, the Iraqi intelligence service, and dated 6 October 1990 it was an account of a meeting that had taken place in the offices of the Technical Consultation Corporation, a procurement organization used by the Mukhabarat." Addressed to an unnamed link man in PC-3, it reported: "We have enclosed for you the following proposal from the Pakistani scientist Dr. Abd-el-Qadeer Khan [sic] regarding the possibility of helping Iraq establish a project to enrich uranium and manufacture a nuclear weapon." On offer were project designs for a bomb, with the necessary components supplied by European companies operating through the nexus of Dubai. The report noted that a meeting could not be arranged with Khan himself, due to the chaos surrounding the invasion of Kuwait, so instead a rendezvous was proposed with a trusted intermediary in Greece. As to Pakistan's motives, the Mukhabarat was clear: money.

Poring over the documents, Dillon's team found a second reference to

Pakistan, something that resembled the offer KRL had made to Iran in 1987. It was a menu of items for sale, with a request by Pakistan's intermediary for an initial fee of $5 million, with 10 percent commission payable by Iraq on every purchase. Dillon recalled: "We also discovered a response from PC-3 to the Mukhabarat that warned of their fears of a possible sting operation. Iraq's nuclear specialists were unsure." It was such an extraordinary offer, someone proposing to sell a nuclear bomb to a malignant Arab state, that even an adventurist like Saddam was skeptical. But then, he had seen what the forces pitted against his nuclear plans were capable of—like the undercover Mossad hit men who had killed one of his top scientists in a hotel room in Paris.

Dillon said: "Hedging their bets, PC-3 suggested that Iraq obtain samples from Pakistan before agreeing to go-ahead." But there the paper trail ended. Dillon later tracked around the world to identify the parties involved and traced an Iraqi who had participated in the negotiations to Australia, where he was living as a refugee. "He refused to discuss the Iraqi nuclear project," Dillon recalled. "He said, 'I know my rights and if you pursue this I will disappear and you will never be able to find me.' We registered our extreme concern at the IAEA and I tried to prick the US interest too, but no one in Washington wanted to talk about it or share any intelligence." Dillon scrutinized the documents. "I believed that they were an accurate representation of what Pakistan had put on the table—although we could never know for sure. As for the overall code name, Project A/B, I puzzled over this for some time until I realized what the letters stood for: Atom Bomb. The truth is often far simpler than one thinks."

There was a morbid conclusion to the uncovering of the Iraqi bomb-for-sale plot. Dillon explained: "We had been led to the farm where we found the Pakistani bomb proposal by General Hussein Kamel and his brother, Colonel Saddam Kamel, after they had defected to Jordan on 8 August 1995, bringing with them their wives, Saddam's daughters Rana and Raghad, and Saddam's nine grandchildren." Saddam would never forget the treachery, and the following February he lured the Kamel brothers back to Baghdad, only to have them and many of their in-laws shot dead in their own home.

The cash deal with Iraq faltered, but General Beg worked hard to get the Islamabad–Baghdad relationship on track. As US troops entered Kuwait in

February 1991, General Beg called on prime minister Sharif and, without mentioning the Mukhabarat negotiations, reasoned that Pakistan should stand beside Saddam Hussein. Sharif was startled. He recalled: "Pakistan had already pledged to be part of an Islamic coalition formed to defend the Middle East against Saddam and we had offered to send soldiers to Saudi Arabia. I had been touring Arab states pulling the coalition together. Saddam had occupied an Islamic state, Kuwait, and was threatening to attack our sponsors, Saudi Arabia. I said to Beg, 'No, we won't support Saddam.' He left disgruntled and no doubt sowed dissent in the military against me."[27]

A. Q. Khan also heard about Beg's proposal to stand by Saddam and was horrified, even though he had been only too happy to sell KRL technology to Baghdad. More than anyone, he understood how precarious the export program was and how financially dependent KRL was on its Saudi benefactors. Husain Haqqani, then Sharif's counsel, recalled: "Khan contacted me. He wanted to make sure the prime minister stuck with the Saudis even if it meant siding with America. I passed his comments on but Sharif needed no persuasion."[28]

Prime minister Sharif had been right to worry about the repercussions of standing up to the military. Immediately after he rebuffed Beg's Saddam plan, Generals Gul and Beg began agitating within the IJI to portray him as insufficiently fervent. Protesters, corralled by the intelligence directorate, took to the streets calling for victory for Saddam, a posture that further enraged Washington. The rallies also served another purpose. Allies of the prime minister warned him that if he did not clamp down, Generals Beg and Gul would use the mob as a cover to mount a coup. The prime minister had to neutralize them both before they were successful in unseating him.

When it became obvious that Saddam was losing, General Beg effortlessly switched sides again. He approached Nawaz Sharif and the finance minister, Ishaq Dar, and proposed a different strategy, in a meeting that bore echoes of one General Beg had had with Benazir Bhutto shortly after she was elected in 1988. Ishaq Dar recalled: "Beg came straight out with it. 'We should transfer nuclear technology to a friendly state, for the sum of $12 billion.' By 'friendly state' he meant Iran, and with that figure Beg could have underwritten the defense budget for the decade to come."[29] Beg beseeched the finance minister to become part of the secret technology exchange program, Project A/B. Sharif recalled the approach too. "Like Dar, I was flabbergasted. We rejected it outright," he said.[30]

Beg would not take no for an answer. He sought out Chaudhary Nisar Ali Khan, Sharif's minister for petroleum and natural resources. Ali Khan's brother was a senior officer in the Pakistan army and his family thus straddled two worlds.[31] Ali Khan recalled: "General Beg called me for a cup of tea. He said, 'Don't you realize we are on the brink of economic collapse? I can change that by selling what we are good at. I can offer this country a lot. Six, eight, ten billion dollars.' I laughed. I said, 'You can't be serious.' The general said, 'I am very serious.' He then mentioned selling our bombs to Iran. He said, 'Nisar, you can argue with me but that's not your job. You tell Nawaz Sharif that this is a good idea. It's the prime minister's position to decide.' "[32]

Ali Khan passed the message on. Sharif recalled: "Beg was insistent. I realized then that we had to change the way that power worked in Pakistan, to break the stranglehold that kept the politicians on a military leash."[33]

General Beg cared little what Sharif thought—or about anyone else outside the military or KRL hierarchy. He had only approached Sharif, as he had Bhutto, to implicate the civil establishment in his Iran plan, hoping to spread the blame around in case the military's role was ever exposed.[34] Just as he did with Bhutto after she rebuffed him, he did with Sharif, and flew to Tehran anyway. By 1991 the supply of P-1 centrifuge parts had been completed and KRL had also furnished Iran with several fully functioning centrifuges.[35] Now Beg had something new to offer—along the lines of his failed Baghdad deal.

However, he had a shock waiting for him when he arrived in the Iranian capital. Tehran was hosting Husayn al-Shahristani, the former chief scientific adviser to the Iraq Atomic Energy Commission, who had been imprisoned by Saddam in 1979 for refusing to participate in a secret program to produce an atomic bomb. Shahristani had just escaped from Abu Ghraib prison in Baghdad and was spilling details of Iraq's nuclear weapons program.[36] He said that Saddam Hussein would have been able to produce a nuclear bomb if he had delayed his invasion of Kuwait by only six months and that most of the project was located in the Al-Tuwaythah district of Baghdad.[37] Iraq had come close to enriching uranium to 93 percent with assistance from Western companies, Shahristani said, having established during the 1980s fifteen "major nuclear installations" capable of enriching uranium through centrifuge, electromagnetic separation and laser techniques. Western companies helped the

Iraqi military develop detonation devices crucial to the successful explosion of a nuclear weapon at the Military Industrialization Authority complex near Al-Hillah run by Saddam's son-in-law.[38]

Although he was in detention throughout this period, Shahristani appeared to know so much that it was just possible he had heard of Beg's offer to sell a bomb to Baghdad, too. However, he said nothing about Pakistan's role and, according to an Iranian opposition group, whose vast network of informers included members of the Iranian nuclear establishment, General Beg went ahead with his pitch, offering the Revolutionary Guard a complete nuclear warhead or blueprints for a weapon.[39] Tehran agreed on a price "in the many hundreds of millions of dollars" for four devices, and also suggested the shipment should be made via Kazakhstan, a former Soviet state that was attempting to sell off its own weapons stockpile and was therefore open to any and all shady nuclear business. The route via Kazakhstan was off the West's surveillance map, unlike the port at Karachi and all of Pakistan's airports which were regularly spied on by US satellites.

Iran certainly had money to spend, having allocated $4.2 billion for its nuclear program from 1991 to 1994.[40] The existence of the Beg deal was also testified to by Kazakhstan's head of nuclear security, who later became the Kazakh ambassador to the US and claimed that he had been consulted about the proposal (flatly denied by Generals Beg and Gul). Before General Beg's visit, Tehran had sent an Iranian nuclear physicist and intelligence officer to Kazakhstan to investigate an offer of assistance with the Iranian weapons program.[41] The agent was said to have returned and reported directly to President Rafsanjani that the Kazakhs were happy to help Iran in its procurement efforts.[42] Leonard Spector, then a senior official in the US Department of Energy's National Nuclear Security Administration, caught wind of the allegations, too. "Although Pakistan has told the US that it will not share nuclear technology with other nations, Pakistan has been implicated in transferring sensitive nuclear technology to Iran and Iraq," he alleged.[43]

However, while the Pakistan–Iran warhead deal dissolved, ultimately because of President Ishaq Khan's concern at selling nuclear bombs to a neighboring country run by a radical clerical Shia regime, other sales went through. Pakistan had pledged to supply the Saudis with nuclear warheads for their Chinese CSS-II missiles, in a deal that senior KRL sources maintained was completed around this time.[44] When the Israelis and Indian intelligence services caught a whisper about this trade they were so horrified that they began lobbying for the CIA and White House to investigate. The rumor about Saudi Arabia was pervasive and also reached the IAEA in Vienna, where Marvin Peterson, a US government specialist on the nuclear programs of Iran, Iraq and North Korea, heard it and reported as much to Washington. But he found little enthusiasm to follow through.[45]

Peterson had every reason to be taken seriously. He had gained his top-secret clearances back in 1970 and built a career out of gathering credible intelligence. A decorated Vietnam veteran and linguist, Peterson had started off in the office of the assistant secretary of defense as a foreign affairs analyst before being attached to the State Department, which posted him to Vienna in August 1990.[46] Soft-spoken and athletic, Peterson was obsessed by details and ferreted away for intelligence in the most obscure corners of the IAEA headquarters. "I raised my concerns over the Saudi purchase of a bomb from Pakistan with Washington but my government took Riyadh's response at face value. The US asked the Saudi foreign ministry simply to confirm or deny the allegations of nuclear cooperation with Pakistan. It is widely known that the Wahhabi form of Islam authorizes the faithful to lie to non-believers, especially in matters dealing with national security and state sovereignty. But when the Saudis said there was no Pakistan deal, our side, without any further investigation, accepted the answer. We took an entirely different approach when the guy across the border in Iraq said: 'I have no WMD.' "

As the Saudi–Pakistan pact was placed off-limits, so that officials like Peterson at the IAEA were prevented from investigating, other elements of the covert Pakistan technical exchange program remained obscure. Peterson said: "Prising the lid off the Saudi warhead deal might well have exposed strands of Pakistan's nuclear export network in other countries, and its nexus in Dubai, allowing us to interdict it before it was too late. Instead the Pakistan military sold anything to everyone."[47]

Back from Iran, General Beg began lobbying Nawaz Sharif to allocate more funds to A. Q. Khan and the PAEC, even though defense spending had already reached 8 percent of GDP and was absorbing almost 27 percent of Pakistan's federal budget.[48] With a manifesto appealing to an aspirant but as yet minuscule Pakistani middle class, and an eye to mending the broken Pakistan economy,

Sharif refused. More wily than Bhutto, he also moved against his enemies in the Pakistan army.[49]

In a move taken from the ISI strategy book, on 16 August 1991 Sharif published General Beg's date of retirement, as well as the name of his replacement.[50] Beg had not been due to leave office for another three months and was planning to appoint his own successor—the redoubtable General Gul. Once Beg had been publicly humiliated, and therefore irreparably weakened, the prime minister struck again. This time he took on the ISI, appointing an ally to a senior position in a competitor agency known as the Intelligence Bureau (IB), Pakistan's equivalent to Britain's MI5. Sharif intended to wield the IB against his ISI opponents and his man, Brigadier Imtiaz Ahmed, had proved himself in the past, having run the smear campaign against Benazir Bhutto in 1988, digging out photos of her mother waltzing with Gerald Ford.

The prime minister had one more score to settle. He had General Gul reassigned from corps commander to commandant of the Pakistan army's tank refit factory in the industrial wasteland of Taxila. It was a dead-end job and, as Sharif hoped, General Gul refused it, forcing him to accept compulsory retirement in January 1992. "Nawaz Sharif and America were desperate for me not to become the army chief," Gul recalled.[51] "But they could not crush my spirit or ideology." He pledged to wield his significant influence from the margins. It sounded like a threat. "My biggest contribution was jihad," he recalled. "I strongly believed that jihadis were going to take over Pakistan. Everyone else, from the politicians to the army, had repeatedly disappointed the nation."

Having weakened the grip of the military, Nawaz Sharif attempted to reconcile Pakistan with the US by attempting to wrest control over the nuclear program. In an unorthodox move, he did it by announcing the existence of the Pakistani bomb. Husain Haqqani recalled: "It was as if to say, 'Look, it's out there. It's done. Let's not let it come between us any more.' "[52] A bomb in the basement would always be a burr in Pakistan's side, but a declared weapon would have to be negotiated over. Shahryar Khan, the new foreign secretary, told the *Washington Post* that Pakistan had the components to assemble "at least one device."[53]

Unsurprisingly, the Bush administration was outraged and winced when Sharif went on to play the nuclear card back home, touring the Kahuta complex with A. Q. Khan in August 1992, making him the first elected prime minister to do so. Sharif addressed a crowd of scientists and technicians, saying: "We salute the dedication of Dr. A. Q. Khan (a national hero) and all his team members for giving a sense of pride to our nation. May Allah shower his blessing on us."[54] Nawaz Sharif then bestowed a make-believe title on Khan that would forever be associated with him, sidelining the work of his nemesis, Munir Ahmed Khan, who had retired as PAEC chairman the previous year. It was a certificate embossed with the words "Father of the Bomb," and however meaningless and inaccurate it was, Khan's certificate took pride of place next to the one given to him by Zia in 1981.

Khan's new title got little play back in the US or in Europe, where everything to do with Pakistan was suddenly "news in brief"—even the conclusion to an episode that had grabbed headlines in 1987. Retired Pakistan army general Inam ul-Haq, who had been extradited to the US from Germany in 1991 following a two-year manhunt, was tried in the summer of 1992 in a court in Philadelphia for attempting to export beryllium and maraging steel to Pakistan.[55] Although the charges he faced carried a ten-year sentence and a $500,000 fine, District Judge James Giles, who had presided over the case involving ul-Haq's agent Arshad Pervez in 1987, was again lenient, sentencing Inam ul-Haq to time already served and a $10,000 fine.

No one mentioned the fact that ul-Haq had escaped the CIA's sting operation in 1987, eluding Richard Barlow (masterminding the operation from agency headquarters in Langley) and US Customs agents (waiting in a Philadelphia hotel room), or the fact that he had been tipped off by two presidential appointees in the State Department (including Robert Peck). "I was a victim of a conspiracy," ul-Haq maintained. "I have been a victim of the pro-India, pro-Israeli, anti-Pakistan lobby."[56]

In Pakistan, however, nothing that Nawaz Sharif did addressed his country's growing instability. Islamist factions in the ISI and military continued to campaign against the prime minister even after he had deposed Generals Beg and Gul, manipulating the country's ethnic and religious divides to create chaos and terror which threatened Pakistan's future—giving the military the pretext it needed to intervene and secure its hold over the nuclear weapons program, should it wish to do so.[57]

A bomb blast thousands of miles away from Islamabad would highlight all of these complex strands and the dangers they posed not just to Pakistan but much further afield. It would also demonstrate how America's blinkered approach to Pakistan's nuclear program had left the West vulnerable to potentially catastrophic consequences. On 26 February 1993 a van crammed with explosives blew up in the parking lot beneath Tower One of the World Trade Center in New York, killing six and injuring more than a thousand. It could have been far worse, as those behind the bomb had intended to bring the tower down. The evidential trail led back to Pakistan and a key suspect, identified by the FBI as Ramzi Yousef, who claimed to be an Iraqi refugee. The FBI had discovered passport records and fingerprints kept in a government record center in Kuwait showing that Yousef was a pseudonym for Abdul Karim, a Pakistan national, whose parents were from Balochistan.[58] An analysis of calls made by Yousef prior to the bombing found that he had dialled numbers in Balochistan—telephone calls that equated to a broad geographic corridor along which he would escape after fleeing the US. Informers and associates revealed that Yousef was not only of Pakistani descent but had been trained by the ISI in Afghanistan, alongside Arab and Pakistani fighters. After the Afghan war he had gone on to run seminars on bomb-making in the ISI-run Kashmiri camps near Muzaffarabad. The device that had gone off at the World Trade Center was simple and effective, but there was also evidence that Yousef had been experimenting with a dirty bomb, attaching radioactive material to high explosives to create a device that would be capable of contaminating an entire city.[59]

While the foreign ministry in Islamabad was emphatic that Yousef was not from the Islamic Republic and was not being sheltered there, the US did not believe Pakistan.[60] The World Trade Center bombing for the first time marked out Pakistan as having become the epicenter of global instability. Washington demanded that Sharif shut down the terror camps. Keen to ameliorate the US, Sharif readily agreed. But when he tried, the ISI simply moved them. Bands of fighters were shifted from the Pakistan sector of Kashmir to new holding centers in the anonymity of Afghanistan's eastern deserts in an operation run by the ISI branch known as Joint Intelligence North (JIN). Sharif recalled: "I did not have the power to rein in the ISI, who refused to believe—or possibly care—that Washington would punish Pakistan."[61]

Chaos in Afghanistan helped cover the ISI's tracks. The last vestiges of Soviet rule had finally given way in 1992, when prime minister Mohammed Najibullah had been ousted and replaced by General Hamid Gul's protégé, the virulently anti-American Gulbuddin Hekmatyar. By 1993, Hekmatyar was out of control and fighting the leaders of the coalition with whom he had formed a government the previous year.[62] Waves of incendiaries rained down on Kabul, leading to the deaths of more than 1,800 civilians, with 500,000 forced to flee from a city that would be besieged by Hekmatyar for the next three years.[63] Pakistan had had a prime opportunity to push a government of its choosing into place and reap the economic benefits of peace along its borders. But instead, with assistance from the ISI and the Pakistan military, Afghanistan was allowed to free-fall into war once again, with Shia Hazaras taking the center of the country, while the Pashtuns and Hekmatyar fought from the south, and the Uzbeks and Tajiks occupied the north.

Rather than deal with this crisis, Nawaz Sharif returned to what he did best: wiring traps and fixing plots in Pakistan, ensuring his own survival.[64] But he made one move too many, gunning for Ghulam Ishaq Khan, fearing the president's power to wield the 8th amendment. In April 1993, Ishaq Khan responded and with a familiar and partially correct chorus of accusations of maladministration, nepotism and corruption, Nawaz Sharif was slung out of office after the 8th amendment was invoked.[65] Sharif lobbied the supreme court and managed to get the president's ruling temporarily overturned. The two men battled until General Wahid Kakar, Pakistan's chief of army staff, who had entered office in January 1993, weighed in and forced both men to resign in July 1993. New elections were tabled, the third since 1988, the political anarchy further disguising the slowly escalating, secret technology transfers emanating from KRL.[66]

The whole world could see that Pakistan was falling to pieces and the situation in Afghanistan was even worse. But even a new Democratic government in Washington, where President Bill Clinton had been sworn in, had nothing to bring to the South Asian melee. In Pakistan, among the civil service establishment, particularly those with long memories, the advent of a Democrat in the White House was viewed with a shudder. "We remembered what had happened with the Democrats last time around," said Agha Shahi, Pakistan's former foreign minister.[67] Under Carter, Pakistan had first been subjected to sanctions, then ostracized, before the two countries fell out over an offer of aid that Zia had denigrated as "peanuts." Shahi said: "The new Clinton administration did itself few favors. Immediately secretary of state Warren Christopher, who I knew from the Carter days, lumped Pakistan together with Burma as two pariah states where human rights abuses were rife." Shahi shook his head. "Christopher, who had never visited us, and never would, evidently saw Asia as a blur. Even if it was a slip of the tongue, it was revealing."[68]

The Clinton White House struggled to form a coherent Pakistan policy. After the bomb went off in the World Trade Center, James Woolsey, Clinton's new CIA director, zeroed in on Islamic terrorism and advised the president that Pakistan was on the brink of becoming a terrorist state. Arnold Kanter, under secretary of state for political affairs, bluntly conveyed the message to Islamabad. "If you get hit with this on top of Pressler," Kanter said, "that will end the US–Pakistan relationship."[69]

But in a bizarre attempt to tackle Pakistan's nuclear program, the Clinton administration revived a piece of discredited Reaganite logic: offering Islamabad F-16 jets in exchange for a nuclear rollback. Four years after Zia had ordered thirty fighters and Pakistan had put down $200 million as a deposit, the US had yet to deliver them.[70] The new administration argued that the jets might entice Pakistan into freezing or even abandoning its nuclear program. Perhaps they would also entice the military into reining in the fundamentalists.

However, first Congress had to be satisfied that the F-16s had no nuclear capability. This time the task fell to John Glenn, chairman of the Senate governmental affairs committee, who cross-examined Rear Admiral William Pendley of the Pentagon.[71] Senator Glenn reminded Pendley how in 1989 the Department of Defense had been clear-cut that Pakistan would have had substantially to modify the fighters if they were to carry a nuclear device, using skills and equipment that its scientists did not possess. Was that claim true?

The rear admiral was adamant. Nothing had changed. Reading from a brief prepared for him by the Pentagon, he said that Pakistan remained incapable of making an F-16 carry a nuclear device.[72] The State Department made ready to send Strobe Talbott, Clinton's deputy secretary of state, to Islamabad in the spring of 1994, offering the trade. Norm Wulf, deputy assistant director at the ACDA, recalled: "It was as if time had stood still."[73]

Richard Barlow watched the new round of perambulations over the nuclear/non-nuclear F-16s with astonishment. More than three years after his intelligence estimate had been spiked at the Office of the Secretary of Defense (OSD), with its conclusion that Pakistan had already adapted its first batch of US-supplied F-16s to drop nuclear bombs, the lie had continued to flourish. Barlow recalled his lawyer sending him a copy of the Glenn committee hearing. "It contradicted the view of all of the technical experts in US government. Every single statement the Pentagon made was false."[74]

It was galling for Barlow to see how well the OSD had covered up the F-16 issue. But then, he had also witnessed close up how effective the Pentagon was at playing rough, how skillfully it had destroyed him. Congress did manage one tangible act, in calling upon the Defense Department inspector general (IG), an ombudsman with wide-ranging powers to investigate the Pentagon, to launch a second inquiry into the Barlow case in 1991. It, too, had ultimately skirted around many of Barlow's specific complaints and refused even to go into his allegations that Congress had been misled and the Pakistani government tipped off by senior officials, although admitting "there is some indication that such a notification took place."[75] These were concerns for the State Department and the CIA, the IG had ruled, but subsequent disclosure by Barlow's legal team resulted in some startling findings about how far the Pentagon was prepared to go to shut Barlow up.[76]

These discoveries might also explain why in 1993 false intelligence continued to win new friends. In preparation for his legal fight, Barlow had contacted the OSD and requested sight of his original research files and reports from 1989. Judy Miller, the Defense Department's general counsel, had replied that "the DoD has found no record of Barlow's views [regarding Pakistan's nuclear program]."[77] Critical documents appeared to have been shredded and Barlow's tenure as the foremost Pentagon expert on Pakistan's nuclear weapons program had been virtually erased. When the IG's inquiry had wrapped up, Barlow was unsurprised to read that the ombudsman had found no case for the Pentagon to answer.[78] A review of closed and open sessions on Capitol Hill had "revealed no indications of willful, misleading testimony" by officials leading congressmen astray.[79]

Barlow could not believe it. Committee staffers and others said they had no idea they had been misled because the intelligence had been rewritten and Barlow neutralized, his conclusions reworked in support of the $1.4 billion F-16 deal, resulting in the Glenn hearing of 1993 in which the committee was told that the F-16 was locked tight and incapable of dropping Pakistan's bomb. Barlow said: "It was a whitewash."

Barlow's lawyers went to work on the congressmen involved in signing off the 1993 F-16 deal. The Senate armed forces committee, the Senate select committee on intelligence and the Senate governmental affairs committee all became involved. They wrote innumerable letters to the defense secretary, the replies to which dodged around the issue. Finally, Barlow's legal team won a combined inquiry by the IGs for the Defense Department, the CIA and the State Department. In September 1993 a draft of their findings was circulated among the three IGs for review and Sherman Funk, the State Department IG, sat down to read it microscopically. Funk disapproved of everything in it. He submitted his thoughts to his colleague at Defense, a vivid and frank letter marked "For Official Use Only," and insisted the IG report be rewritten to reflect more accurately what he had discovered.[80]

Funk had found that Barlow had been sandbagged by his superiors, who made him appear to be lax at work, as well being wrongly accused of intending to leak highly classified information on the Pakistan program to Capitol Hill.[81] It was these charges that had resulted in Barlow losing his clearances. "This belief," Funk wrote, "turned out to be an error not supported by a scintilla of evidence. The truth about Barlow's termination is, simply put, that it was unfair and unwarranted."[82]

Funk also identified something far more insidious: the campaign of rumors started by the Defense Department shortly before and after Barlow was sacked. The IG found no evidence of Barlow's alleged mental health problems, or of his treachery. There was no sign of delinquency or rulebreaking. He was not an alcoholic or a philanderer. Barlow was so obsessed with his work that he had eschewed R&R (rest and recreation), as his now ex-wife Cindy often complained. Funk concluded that Barlow's security clearances "had been revoked erroneously." He had been ambushed. "I recognize that it is difficult for investigators to highlight something which is not easy to touch, hear or smell. I recognize also that non-events can be documented as well as events. If I were Arthur Conan Doyle, I would write: 'I call your attention to the curious incident of Barlow's security clearance.' 'But Barlow can't get a security clearance.' 'That is the curious incident.' "[83]

The whole affair for Funk was "Kafka-like and grievously unfair," Barlow was sacrificed for "refusing to accede to policies which he knew to be wrong."[84] These findings should have been incorporated into the triple IGs' report. However, having signed and sent his copy back, Funk discovered, to his horror, that his own report had been rewritten and neutered. Funk wrote immediately to his colleagues, "Yesterday, I received a copy of the Barlow report I had co-signed. Reviewing it I was startled and dismayed to realize that the summary of conclusions had not been revised to reflect the changes we had made."[85]

While Barlow remained in limbo, Funk immediately wrote to his colleague in the Department of Defense: "I signed the report ... and I should have read it more carefully ... I frankly don't know what to do about this, now that the report has been distributed."[86]

Shocked, Funk tried to head the report off, writing to the Senate: "I regret that I must withdraw my approval of the investigative report on Mr. Barlow."[87] However, when Barlow's lawyers called the Pentagon, the OSD counsel Miller told them the department was in the clear. There would be no apology. No need. The triple IGs' inquiry had found no evidence of wrongdoing—endorsing the wrong intelligence on Pakistan, making the Islamic Republic seem incapable of dropping a nuclear bomb, let alone modifying an American-made F-16 to do so.

To the Father of the Bomb, the US debate on whether the F-16s were or were not nuclear-capable was hilarious. A. Q. Khan was by now completely out in the open, his presence required at every opening and social gathering in Pakistan, his program pelting ahead. Khan's psychiatrist, Dr. Haroon Ahmed, in Karachi, noticed how the adulation impacted on his client. "It was dramatic," recalled Ahmed.[88] "Khan thought everything he had done and was planning to do was legitimized by his new title. He saw himself as the benefactor to the nation."

In reality, the establishment was finding Khan increasingly difficult to control. ISI chief Asad Durrani, who ran Khan's personal security, recalled how the scientist could not keep his mouth shut even though he headed a project that remained classified and was engaged in a deeply sensitive export trade.[89] General Durrani said he received an early warning of what was to come when an informer dropped in to see him. "We had a man who ran the garages for

President Ronald Reagan receives General Zia ul-Haq in Washington in 1982 (Reagan Library)

Ghulam Ishaq Khan (right), then Pakistan's finance minister and a keystone in the country's nuclear program, talks to A. Q. Khan (Author archives)

Peter Griffin (right), Khan's former supplier, in front of A. Q. Khan's house in Islamabad with Khan's gatekeeper, taken during the 1980s (Peter Griffin)

Anna Griffin with Henny Khan, A. Q. Khan's wife, in front of Khan's house on Hillside Road in Islamabad, taken during the 1980s (Peter Griffin)

Peter Griffin and Dr. Shafiq ur-Rehman, former supplier and son of Khan's aide Brigadier Sajawal (both center), in Dubai, taken during the 1980s (Peter Griffin)

Peter Griffin (second right) at the home of KRL procurement chief Colonel Qazi Rashid Ali (right) with Qazi's son Khalil (left) and Henk Slebos (second left), taken during the 1980s (Peter Griffin)

A. Q. Khan and his wife, Henny, with their daughters Dina (left) and Ayesha, taken during the 1980s (Peter Griffin)

Richard Barlow during his first internship at the State Department, Washington, 1981 (Richard Barlow)

B. S. A. Tahir, Khan's principal agent and protégé, on a mission to Paris, France, taken during the 1980s (Peter Griffin)

Agha Shahi, Pakistan's former foreign minister and a member of its first Nuclear Command Authority (Catherine Scott-Clark)

General Mirza Aslam Beg, Pakistan's chief of army staff (second left), with A. Q. Khan (right) examining a shoulder-launched missile manufactured by the Khan Research Laboratories in 1990 (Author archives)

A. Q. Khan and Nawaz Sharif, prime minister of Pakistan, at a press conference in 1991 (Author archives)

(left–right) Prime Minister Benazir Bhutto, President George H. W. Bush, First Lady Barbara Bush, and Azif Zardari (Benazir Bhutto's husband) at a White House state dinner, June 1989 (George Bush Presidential Library)

Lt. General Javid Nasir, former
director general of Pakistan's Inter
Services Intelligence (ISI) agency
and leading figure in Tablighi
Jamaat (Reuters News Agency,
Pakistan)

Maulana Masood Azhar, formerly the chief of
the banned Harkat al-Ansar and later the head of
the Sunni extremist group Jaish-e-Mohammed,
attending a rally in Pakistan-administered Kashmir
(Reuters News Agency, Pakistan)

A. Q. Khan, second right (clapping), attends a press conference called by Benazir Bhutto
(Author archives)

A. Q. Khan's centrifuge plant at Kahuta, Pakistan (IKONOS satellite imagery courtesy of GeoEye, 2007)

A. Q. Khan giving lessons on making nuclear bombs (Author archives)

A. Q. Khan in the test tunnels before the explosion of Pakistan's first bomb in 1998 (Simon Henderson, Washington Institute for Near East Policy)

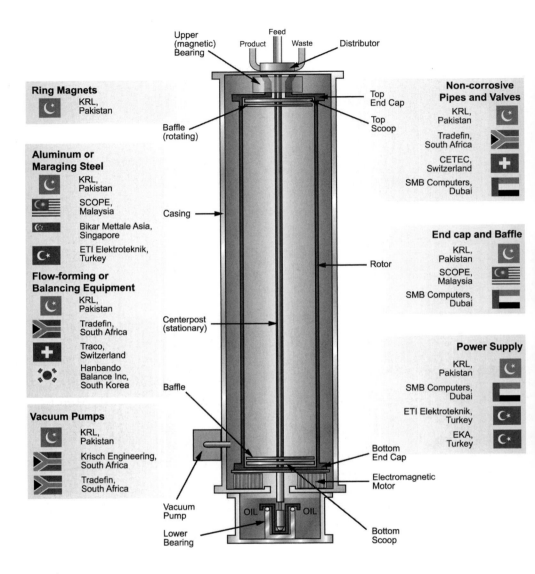

Cross-section of a Pakistani uranium enrichment centrifuge with parts listed by supplier
(Mark Rolfe Technical Art)

A. Q. Khan (second from right) and colleagues at the Pakistan nuclear test site, 1998 (Simon Henderson, Washington Institute for Near East Policy)

The logo of the labs, which were renamed in 1981 in A. Q. Khan's honor at the behest of General Zia ul-Haq (www.hetnet.nl)

A commercial uranium enrichment plant (Author archives)

A. Q. Khan presented with the
Nishan-i-Imtiaz, the highest
civilian honor in Pakistan, for
the second time in 1998 after the
country carried out its nuclear tests
(PA Photos)

President Pervez Musharraf (left) shakes hands with General Mahmood Ahmed, his
new director general of the Inter Services Intelligence agency (Reuters News Agency,
Pakistan)

President George W. Bush inspects part of the haul of centrifuge components (manufactured by Pakistan and seized on their way to Libya) at the Oak Ridge nuclear laboratory in Tennessee, 2003 (PA Photos/AP)

President Pervez Musharraf with President George W. Bush in Washington, 2006 (PA Photos/AP)

A neo-Taliban cadre, from the ranks of a resurgent movement that decamped to the tribal areas of Pakistan, celebrates the stringing up of an alleged criminal (behind left) in the lawless Miram Shah area of Pakistan, 1996 (Newsline, Pakistan)

Suleiman Abu Gheith, an al-Qaeda spokesman who issued a threat to kill millions of Americans with a nuclear device (www.globalsecurity.org)

Abu Khabab al-Masri, al-Qaeda's former WMD chief, killed in eastern Pakistan in January 2006 (www.cnn.com)

Abu Musab al-Zarqawi, the former Jordanian gangster who became the leader of "al-Qaeda in Mesopotamia," in a videotaped warning to the West (www.washingtonpost.com)

Abu Musab al-Suri, author of *The Call for Worldwide Islamic Resistance*, photographed in London where he worked for an Arab newspaper before leaving for Osama bin Laden's camps in Afghanistan (US State Department)

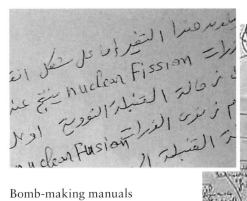

Bomb-making manuals recovered from an al-Qaeda safe house in Kabul, used by Abu Khabab al-Masri: one manual entitled "Super Bombs" (above) contained the words "nuclear fission," "nuclear fusion" and "isotopes" written in English (CNN/Institute for Science and International Security)

General Mohammed Aziz, President Musharraf's long-term ally and, until 2004, chairman of Pakistan's Joint Chiefs of Staff (Reuters News Agency, Pakistan)

After his arrest and televised confession in 2004, when A. Q. Khan claimed to have single-handedly sold nuclear technology to "Axis of Evil" powers, his image is held up high by his supporters (PA Photos)

official events who would give us useful bits and pieces," Durrani recalled.[90] "This humble garage man was troubled by Khan's chattering. He said to us, 'Khan's job is secret, so what business does this chap have to be at every single reception where he blabs to everyone.' The garage man had tried to tell Khan, 'You can't talk so much all over the place.' But being a lowly garage man he had been ignored. I tried to warn Khan too, 'Keep quiet. Your project is supposed to be secret.' But it was difficult to censor a person whom we needed more than he needed us."

Khan continued to collect awards and honors, many of them invented at his request. Dr. Ahmed recalled: "He became addicted to it." Between 1984 and 1992, the KRL chief scored eleven gold medals from organizations as diverse as the Lions Club of Gujarat, the Institute of Metallurgy and the Citizens of Rawalpindi. He awarded himself the "Man of the Nation" medal given by the Pakistan Institute of National Affairs in Lahore, and even wangled a commendation out of the Abbasi Shaheed public hospital in Karachi, which, after receiving an envelope stuffed with cash, had a gold medal cast glorifying its benefactor.

Dr. Ahmed said: "Khan was thrilled to be at the very heart of the establishment and all of its dark and murky dealings, but he knew no boundaries. Everything became his concern. He began collecting money, fund-raising, looking for a reward out of whatever cause he attached himself to, even my family. In the 1990s, my daughter was running an anti-nukes charity. She felt strongly. One day Khan walked into my house and saw her. 'Come here,' he said and pulled $50,000 in cash out of his jacket pocket. 'Ban the bomb,' he said, handing the money over."

Dr. Ahmed's psychiatric hospital in Karachi attracted renewed attention from Khan, too, who sent over scores of expensive air-conditioning units when Ahmed was away. "Over the week I had been absent a huge porch had also been built, the sort grand cars would drive under so the top brass could be sheltered from the rain. Khan called. He told me that he had ordered the porch and that the air conditioners had come from S. M. Farouq [the uncle of Khan's protégé in Dubai, B. S. A. Tahir]. He insisted they be installed. 'This is a free hospital,' I told him. 'We cannot afford to run these air-conditioning units, let alone install them.' 'Do it,' Khan ordered. More and more equipment turned up, the sort of stuff needed by five-star hotels. I was losing control of the hospital."

Khan was hard to refuse and intolerant of anyone who contradicted him. Peter Griffin, who had supplied machine tools to Khan since 1977, witnessed the change and was chastened by the experience. One night at the KRL guest house, in 1993, Griffin recalled how Khan turned on him in front of a crowd of KRL executives and military officers.[91] "He was picking on other people in the room. It was cruel and I protested. It was just impolite and unfair. I warned him, 'You should be careful.' He stopped as if he had been threatened: 'Why?' he asked. I said, 'Because there are many things that I could say about the way you have changed too, Qadeer.' He froze, clicked his fingers and everyone in the room stood still. They were terrified. I got up. 'I'm off to bed,' I said. 'I think I prefer the company of my book.' " Griffin stalked off while Khan fumed and the room around him twitched in embarrassment. So quixotic had the Father of the Bomb become that it could have been any of them.

But Khan's special wrath was reserved for Pakistan's leading theoretical nuclear physicist, Professor Pervez Hoodbhoy at Quaid-i-Azam University in Islamabad, a man with an equally honed sense of self-importance. After Hoodbhoy wrote an article in 1993 questioning the security of Pakistan's bomb, in which he described a system known as Permissive Action Links (PALs)—command-and-control mechanisms used in the West to prevent a bomb from being hot-wired or triggered accidentally—Khan launched a vindictive campaign to destroy him. The professor received a call from General Shamin Alam Khan, chairman of the joint chiefs of staff. "He asked me to come to his office," Hoodbhoy recalled.[92] "As I went in his secretary told me to wait as he had an important visitor. After a few minutes Khan walked out and glowered at me. Shamin Alam Khan sat me down. He was quite candid and asked how PALs worked. I was horrified. He revealed that none of them, A. Q. Khan included, knew anything about PALs or had even thought about securing Pakistan's bomb. We were a country that had raised coups to a national sport and here was an army chief in charge of a nuclear arsenal telling me he had not worked out how to make it safe from saboteurs or terrorists."

Hoodbhoy heard nothing more until he learned that the KRL chief had joined the board of Quaid-i-Azam University.[93] "Now he was on my patch. I learned he was supporting the selling off of large chunks of the university's valuable campus." It was as if Khan had begun to dismantle his enemy's territory. Established in the green belt of Islamabad, in the shade of the Margalla hills, the university grounds were prime real estate and worth hundreds of millions of dollars. But they had been given in perpetuity to the students and lecturers and Professor Hoodbhoy campaigned against the sale. "Big posters appeared calling me 'a snake in the grass,' saying I was 'against Islam and against Jinnah' and that I was 'with the Israelis and pro American.'"

Then Hoodbhoy's sister called to tell him he was on the exit control list, prevented from leaving the country. "I called the airport and they confirmed it," Hoodbhoy recalled. "I called the interior minister who said, 'Yes, you are on the list but we cannot disclose the reasons.'" Stuck in a loop, subject to a classified inquiry triggered by anonymous sources and backed by invisible evidence, Hoodbhoy went to see the minister and asked to see his file. "It was two inches thick. Page one was a handwritten complaint penned by A. Q. Khan. The minister flicked through and said, 'You have written against our bomb.' I said, 'Yes, but it's only an opinion.' He looked at me blankly and shrugged. He was taking instruction from someone else. The Father of the Bomb had people on remote control."

13

CHESTNUTS AND STEAMED FISH

With another general election imminent in the autumn of 1993, Pakistan, with its unsecured nuclear weapons program, writhed, pulling the covers off incendiary forces who were actively canvassing for the *ulema* of radical jihadis to have control of the Islamic bomb. Benazir Bhutto had decided to try her luck again, running for prime minister, and as she campaigned over the summer, Ramzi Yousef, who had blown up the World Trade Center in February, a man who Islamabad's foreign ministry continued to insist was not in Pakistan, turned his attention to influencing the outcome of the vote. Emboldened by his success in New York, Yousef accepted a contract to kill Bhutto from Sipah-e-Sahaba (SSP), the Army of the Companions of the Prophet, a Sunni extremist group created by Zia in the early 1980s to weigh into Pakistan's wealthy, landowning and politically influential Shia community.[1] Later the SSP had sent its cadres to fight in Afghanistan and it was there that Ramzi Yousef had first made contact with them.

Aggrieved at Bhutto's perceived liberalism and her mother's Shia ancestry, the vitriolic SSP gave the World Trade Center bomber $90,000 to get rid of her.[2] More money came from Yousef's uncle, Khalid Sheikh Mohammed, who would go on to plot a second much more deadly attack on New York in 2001.[3] Yousef recruited two friends, Abdul Hakim Murad and Abdul Shakur, sending Shakur to Pabi, an Afghan refugee camp and jihadi hideout in the Northwest Frontier Province to pick up detonators and a wireless set, part of a cache left over from the Afghan war.[4] Early one morning in late July, the gang drove to Bhutto's home in Karachi's prestigious Clifton district and Yousef lowered the bomb into a drain outside the gate.[5] But they were interrupted, spotted by the police, and as Yousef hauled the bomb back up one of the old Soviet detonators went off, sending a plume of shrapnel into his hands and face, forcing his two co-conspirators to throw him, unconscious, into a taxi which was lost by its pursuers in the maze of streets. Groups like the SSP, nurtured by the military for so many years, were getting bolder inside Pakistan, but there were new challenges for them that the ISI and the army were about to unveil.

Refusing to be intimidated, Benazir Bhutto won the election in October and, having been unceremoniously turned out of office in 1990 after only twenty months in power, and wary of the murderous pathology of the extremists pitted against her, she returned with a new strategy. President Ishaq Khan, her old foe, had been retired by the military in July 1993 after sacking Sharif, and for once Bhutto was in charge. She chose as Ishaq Khan's successor a former PPP loyalist, Farukh Leghari, who was installed, retaining the constitutional 8th amendment power to sack a prime minister but with a promise never to use it. To pacify the military, Bhutto handed the entire foreign affairs portfolio to President Leghari. Dabbling in foreign policy, she believed, was most likely to get her killed. "I intended to look after the economy, regeneration, schools and the power supply," Bhutto recalled.[6] "I wanted to get foreign investors to come back to Pakistan. Hopefully, this time I would survive a little longer." But Pakistan's foreign policy would dominate Bhutto's second term.

No sooner had she entered office than the military called on her with a special briefing. The subject was Kashmir, where the insurgency ignited by Generals Beg and Gul had fallen into a lull. Bhutto had a new director general of military operations, Pervez Musharraf, an ambitious and wily officer, who requested permission to revive and escalate the campaign. Musharraf had been Hamid Gul's artillery pupil and had made his name battling it out in Kashmir. He had fled India as a child with his family in 1947, leaving an ancestral home in New Delhi to be occupied by Hindus, and he bore a deep-seated hatred of India's attempts to encroach on Pakistan's territory, particularly in Kashmir and Bangladesh. Musharraf had advanced through the ranks by focusing on all of the military's non-negotiables, as defined by Gul's secret manifesto penned in 1987. At the behest of army chief General Beg, in 1987 Musharraf had led a newly formed alpine commando unit in a pre-emptive strike on Indian positions in Siachen, only to be beaten back.[7]

Undaunted, Musharraf had in 1988 been called on by General Beg to put down a Shia riot in Gilgit, in the north of Pakistan. Rather than get the Pakistan army bloodied, he inducted a tribal band of Pashtun and Sunni irregulars, many from the SSP which had recently put out a contract on Bhutto, led by the mercenary Osama bin Laden (who had been hired by Hamid Gul to do the same four years earlier). Bin Laden's militia mounted a savage pogrom, killing more than 300, and when the fighting had subsided Musharraf opened an office for SSP extremists in Gilgit, helping spread their influence across Pakistan.[8] After Zia's death in August 1988, Musharraf had got closer to Generals Beg and Gul, and played the extremist card many times.[9] In October 1993 he suggested to prime minister Bhutto that she change the rules of war and give the army sole responsibility for deciding the timing of conflicts, as Beg had argued, suggesting the move would enable the Pakistani military to react quicker if there was ever a pre-emptive strike by India. But Benazir Bhutto refused again, fearful of what an unfettered army would do.[10]

Unfazed, Musharraf moved on, setting out his special plan for Kashmir. "He told me he wanted to 'unleash the forces of fundamentalism' to ramp up the war," Bhutto recalled. Musharraf wanted to recruit from among the Sunni extremists cultivated by Zia in the Punjab and the remote Northwest Frontier Province, many of whom had already tasted war in Afghanistan.[11] According to the military's own tally, dipping into these groups could fetch as many as 10,000 new jihadis to send over the border into India.

Bhutto gave Musharraf the go-ahead. She needed the military on her side. "Second time around I did not want to rock the boat," she said. Her director general of military operations worked alongside the ISI's Joint Intelligence North division, which ran the Afghan camps, to begin the recruitment drive. The operation would further demonstrate the proximity of Musharraf to Pakistan's extremist forces—not that anyone in the West was looking.

First the general approached Jamaat-e-Islami (JI), one of the largest and oldest Islamic organizations in Pakistan, whose founder, Maulana Maududi, had failed to unseat Zulfikar Ali Bhutto in 1977. Maududi had died in 1979 but the JI had thrived and had a massive following among the middle classes and had also involved itself in the anti-Soviet coalition. The JI agreed to supply cadres to be trained as fighters. Next, Musharraf called on the Jamiat Ulema Islam, the Assembly of Islamic Clergy, whose nebulous-sounding title belied the fact it was a radical and chauvinist Sunni organization which, under Zia, had come to run the largest number of religious schools, or madrasahs, in the country. The Jamiat agreed to funnel its students into military training, too.

Then Musharraf won support from the Markaz Dawa Al Irshad (MDI), the Center for Preaching and Guidance. Three university graduates from Pakistan, who had been in awe of Osama bin Laden, had founded it in 1987 and built a university campus thirty miles north of Lahore in which to indoctrinate teenagers in the way of the Deobandis, with bin Laden contributing $1 million.[12] The MDI had already formed a military wing known as Lashkar-e-Taiba (LeT), formed in 1990 in Kunar province, Afghanistan, with a goal of restoring Islamic rule to the whole of South Asia, Russia and even China. Under Musharraf's plan, all MDI's graduates were to be handed over to LeT and trained for Kashmir and whatever other duties he had in mind. LeT was already proficient, running guerrilla warfare courses, specializing in small arms training, the sniper's craft, plotting and ambush, the manufacture of improvised explosive devices and even hijacking.[13] Through Musharraf's patronage, LeT would become the largest jihadi organization in Pakistan.

The remaining factions to emerge, who were to produce fodder for Kashmir and elsewhere, were entirely the creation of Musharraf himself and included Harkat-ul-Ansar (HuA), formed by the merger of two armed Sunni factions founded in the era of the Afghan war in order to oust the Soviets.[14] HuA was to become the most vicious and unscrupulous of all the militant groups.

Over the border in India, the recruitment drive was immediately obvious, its story told in the bloodshed that soon catapulted Kashmir into crisis. The joint intelligence committee in New Delhi estimated the Pakistani military was spending $7.5 million per month to reinvigorate the proxy war.[15] They presented a file of evidence to the US, warning that fundamentalists were being infiltrated into Kashmir and Musharraf was at the helm. They asked the US to consider where these fighters would go next, when they grew bored with the Kashmiri war or had been forced from the territory by the military reprisals that India was now planning. Naresh Chandra, India's former ambassador to Washington, recalled: "The US was not interested. I was shouting and no one in the State Department or elsewhere could have cared less."[16]

The Clinton administration stood back. Pakistan escalated. The Islamic Republic's strategy in Kashmir dovetailed with another of Musharraf's policies, the promotion of the Taliban. In Afghanistan the warlords were still pitted against each other, nowhere more obviously than in the southern city of Kandahar, which was beset by street-by-street fighting. Gathering on the city outskirts, elsewhere in Kandahar province, and in the madrasahs of the neighboring Pakistani province of Balochistan, were hordes of Islamic students, many of them refugees from the war with the Soviets, who seemed to offer a pious antidote to the anarchy. In their flowing black turbans and austere beards, they emerged as moralistic vigilantes: threatening, kidnapping and bribing their anarchic enemies to submit to the teachings of the Koran. Against the warlords they were ruthless, their medieval values manifested in a vengeful crusade. But their emerging leader, Mullah Omar, a former mujahideen fighter who had lost an eye during the Soviet war, had established a reputation as an Afghan Robin Hood, standing up for the warlords' victims. Noticing their success, in early 1994 Pervez Musharraf turned to these "Taliban," a Dari word meaning student, a seeker of knowledge, using the ISI's Joint Intelligence North division as interlocutor, offering the bearded wraiths money, weapons and training to subdue Afghanistan.[17]

Musharraf was head of military operations and, brought up with the idea of strategic defiance authored by Generals Beg and Gul, he viewed Afghanistan as a critical northern buffer. Only a Pashtun government, put in place by Pakistan and therefore indebted to Islamabad, would offer the kind of loyal kinship, open to manipulation by the ISI, that Musharraf desired. With Gulbuddin Hekmatyar, the ISI's principal mujahideen leader, going nowhere, Musharraf, as director general of military operations, recognized the potential of the Taliban as a client army that could become a client government. An expert in sectarian politics, Musharraf also recognized them as a righteous Sunni army, akin to the Deobandis of Pakistan and the Salafists of Saudi Arabia. If necessary, they could be called upon to declare war against Pakistan's Shias, or at least to act as a buffer against Iran.

Bhutto's government was in step. Interior minister General Naseerullah Babar wholeheartedly backed the Taliban plan. A die-hard Pashtun and former confidant of Zulfikar Ali Bhutto, General Babar was said to have single-handedly captured a seventy-strong company of Indian soldiers in the 1965 war, for which he was awarded the Sitara-e-Jurat or Star of Courage. Unlike the ISI, his interest was not in religious war. General Babar saw the Taliban as a tool to impose peace. "They looked useful," the general recalled.[18] "When one compared them to the horses we had backed in Afghanistan already, they were pedigree. The Taliban would bring order, restore morality and more important than any of these things, the peace they imposed would enable us to open up trade across the region into Central Asia and beyond. They were intended as a poultice: drawing out the bad blood."

With the involvement of Jamiat Ulema Islam, the only Islamist faction in Bhutto's coalition government, which was close to the merchants and shipping agencies based along the Pakistan–Afghan border, General Babar sanctioned a broadening of Musharraf's secret supply operation for the Taliban, which city by city was marching eastwards. Bhutto wrestled with the decision. Although backing the Taliban went against her secular instincts, she knew it was impossible to survive in Pakistan without engaging with sectarian forces. She recalled: "But to be frank none of us, General Babar included, had any idea where these Talibs had sprung from or where they were going."[19]

Benazir Bhutto had made another decision upon starting her second term: to stay out of A. Q. Khan's way. Her involvement in trying to defuse the enrichment crisis of 1990 had cost her many friends in the US, in Islamabad, at KRL, in the military, and ultimately her job. However, she could not fail to notice just how much Khan had changed. "He was not the man I had met in my first term. The humility was gone. He was stubborn. Diffident. Rude. He was, having been awarded that strange title, 'Father of the Bomb,' now quite insufferable." Khan was also more religious, more conservative, a little fanatical even. "It was rather like listening to Hamid Gul. Khan had become quite the maulvi," she said.

Bhutto soon heard talk of Project A/B and Khan's secret sales. Anxious that nuclear technology was being illicitly sold on her watch, in late 1993 she broached the subject with General Wahid Kakar, her new army chief. "Of course Kakar denied everything, but he suggested a solution that ultimately played into the military's hands and weakened my own. He advised me, 'Why don't we set up a command and control for KRL so the scientists can't go in and out without passing through the army ring?' It seemed like a good idea. Cut the labs off. Put the military in charge of their perimeter. If KRL was airtight, then anything coming out could only be done with the permission and close co-operation of the army. I agreed. Kakar even proposed a man for the job, General Khawaja Ziauddin. I didn't know him. It was only later I found out that he was connected to the ISI and the forces pitted against me." General Ziauddin was the nephew of General Jilani, the former ISI chief who had plucked Nawaz Sharif out of obscurity and elevated him to take over as Punjab governor in 1985. Ziauddin was a close ally of Generals Beg and Gul and would become critical in Project A/B.

In the winter of 1993, the Pakistan army rewarded Bhutto for giving them what they wanted by involving her directly in an act of proliferation. The initial approach came from A. Q. Khan. "He called me up," Bhutto remembered. "Frankly, I was shocked. I had got used to not hearing from him. He said he had a couple of favors to ask. First, we talked about the People's Steel Mill in Karachi. It had been closed down due to corruption and poor management and Khan had designs on it. He said he could do something really hi-tech there that would aid all aspects of life but particularly his program at KRL. I said, 'Yes, provisionally. I would take a look at it.' " The steel mill, the same one whose bosses had refused to give Khan a job in the 1960s, would soon become critically important to Project A/B.

Khan's second request was more sensitive. Bhutto said: "He wanted me to go to North Korea. Pakistan used to send cultural exchanges every year—a legacy from my father who had striven to build a friendship with them. Pyongyang had always kept in touch with the PPP and every time they had a conference they would invite our party. But I had never been."

Bhutto had been pressured by the PPP to fly to Pyongyang in her first term but had resisted, fearing adverse publicity in the West. "Khan already knew I was scheduled to pay a visit to Beijing in December 1993 and he said, 'It's only a short hop to Pyongyang and we need their help.' He got me on my own. In a flurry. He said to me, 'We need better missiles. We cannot yet reach into the depths of India with the missiles we are already developing.' To tell you the truth, I had no idea of what we could and couldn't do, as the military never let me near any of it. But I wanted it to be known that I would not stand in the military's way, and when Khan told me that only a country like North Korea could provide the kind of intercontinental missiles we needed, I thought there was no harm in it. But I did tell him I would not give him the money to develop these missiles. I believed in parity. India had not escalated by creating such missiles, I thought, so Pakistan would not do so either. On that understanding I said, 'OK, I'll stop for a little while in Pyongyang.' "

What Khan did not tell Bhutto was that he had already made overtures to North Korea. Having forced his way into missile production in order to compete with his nemesis, Munir Ahmed Khan, he was trailing badly, with his home-grown designs and the missile workshops at KRL inferior to those at PAEC. His products had a shorter range and were as yet completely untested, but North Korea had a long-range ballistic device that was already manu-factured and tested, the No-dong liquid-fuelled missile. With Khan having opened the channel to Pyongyang in the 1980s, giving them a US Stinger missile in 1990, he had privately discussed purchasing the No-dong or exchanging it for KRL technology, with Kim Yong-nam, the North Korean foreign minister and deputy prime minister, who had visited Pakistan in August 1992.[20] Yong-nam was on a tour of friendly countries which also took in Syria and Iran, and the conversation with Khan was lubricated by their common interest in selling weaponry to Iran, Pyongyang having supplied 160 Hwasong 5 missiles to Tehran at the start of the Iran–Iraq war.[21] Since then, technicians from North Korea and Pakistan had been working together on the Iranian missile program, and as a result of the meeting between Khan and Kim Yong-nam, the KRL director, accompanied by Brigadier Sajawal, was invited to North Korea in May 1993 to witness the test firing of the Nodong—which was said by the North Koreans to have a range of 800 miles and could carry a 1,000-kg payload.[22] It was exactly what KRL needed, and although not yet capable of carrying a nuclear warhead, Khan was confident he could mate it to a warhead. But Khan needed the request to buy it to come from his head of state and so he had knocked on prime minister Bhutto's door, hoping to exploit her family connection to the North Korean regime and entangle her in his secret plan.

The Pyongyang trip immediately sounded alarm bells among those close to Bhutto. Husain Haqqani, then her counsel, recalled: "North Korea was an outlaw state, with few morals or qualms about trading in anything illicit, and it was at loggerheads with the US. I told her the military and Khan were trying to trick her and that we should not be doing arms deals with Pyongyang. But she ignored me and asked me to accompany her. I cried off. I let a colleague go in my place. I let him think I was giving him a chance when I was actually watching my own back. All I kept thinking was, what happens many years down the line when this trip to North Korea is gone over? Such a thing could ruin a career. There was this bad smell about it."[23] Bhutto flew into Pyongyang on 29 December 1993 as the Democratic Republic of North Korea wrestled with the US over its nuclear program.

*

The Democratic Republic of North Korea's nuclear aspirations reached back to 1959. Shortly after a hair-trigger demilitarization zone had been established as a buffer between the Pyongyang regime and that backed by the US in Seoul, Kim Il-sung, North Korea's prime minister, had signed an agreement with the Soviet Union on the peaceful use of nuclear energy. Moscow agreed to build a nuclear complex in Yongbyon-kun, in North Pyongan province, 100 miles north of the capital. Besides a research center, the Soviets assembled a nuclear research reactor which was used to produce radioisotopes and train personnel.[24] However, after the Cuban missile crisis of 1962, the North Korean leader had grown disappointed in the Soviets, who he believed had shown weakness by backing down. Kim Il-sung, whose name literally meant Behold the Sun, decided to go it alone with his nuclear program, as Moscow could not be counted on.[25]

Pyongyang had followed the plutonium route and in the 1970s began importing reprocessing technology, most of it from the Soviet Union. In 1977 it agreed to bring its research reactor under IAEA safeguards in order to win access to technology from other countries too.[26] By the 1980s, North Korea had acquired uranium milling facilities, a fabrication complex for fuel rods, and a full-scale nuclear reactor. The IAEA began to suspect that Pyongyang was interested in weapons when inspectors reported North Korean scientists were conducting explosive tests for a bomb-triggering mechanism.[27] The IAEA had been in this situation before. The tests were identical to those that Pakistan had conducted as a prelude to assembling its nuclear device in 1984.

North Korea denied everything. Its conventional nuclear program continued to grow, with a larger nuclear reactor commissioned in the mid-1980s. To assuage Western suspicions, Pyongyang also agreed to sign up to the Nuclear Non-Proliferation Treaty in December 1985, which bound North Korea to put stronger safeguards in place, installing cameras and allowing permanent access to IAEA inspectors at all its facilities. But Pyongyang failed to meet the safeguards deadline, claiming insecurity because of the presence of nuclear weapons in the south of the peninsula, and it called for Washington to remove US nuclear missiles from South Korea. On 18 December 1991, Pyongyang's wishes were finally acceded to, America's last nuclear weapons were removed, and North and South Korea signed a pledge "not to test, manufacture, produce, receive, possess, store, deploy or use nuclear weapons" or engage in nuclear reprocessing and uranium enrichment.[28]

In 1992, Pyongyang finally signed the IAEA safeguards agreement, enabling inspectors to visit Yongbyon-kun and other nuclear sites to verify that what had been declared was correct.[29] However, by February 1993, IAEA inspectors were convinced that Pyongyang was misrepresenting its program, building secret sites hidden from inspectors in remote mountain regions. Under pressure, North Korea admitted that it had reprocessed some plutonium. But it claimed it was less than 100 grams and had come from damaged spent fuel rods. IAEA inspectors disagreed, citing evidence that showed North Korean scientists had reprocessed on at least three occasions: in 1989, 1990 and 1991. The IAEA requested an inspection of waste sites. The North Koreans declared them "military areas" and out of bounds.

As Bhutto planned her visit, the US sought a tough new inspection regime. Pyongyang's response was bullish. It announced its withdrawal from the NPT, a threat it held in abeyance while intense negotiations continued in Washington and Vienna. To cover its tracks and save face, North Korea came up with a compromise: it would enable inspections of its current facilities but only if all probes into its historic research activities ceased. With the deal on the table, the prime minister of Pakistan's plane touched down at Pyongyang Sunan international airport.

The state-run media proclaimed Bhutto was greeted by premier Kang Song-san, the vice premier and foreign minister and "100,000 citizens of the capital who lined the route from the approach to Yonmot-tong to Kumsong Street."[30] Kim Il-sung, then the president, extended his personal welcome to Bhutto and "exchanged warm greetings at 15.01 GMT as they reviewed a guard of honor."

Bhutto recalled being mystified, baffled and surprised. "You read so much about him, but President Kim was none of those things. Rather than being the evil dictator, he was very garrulous. He talked through an interpreter. He was open and even chatty."[31] Prime minister Bhutto was awed by the scale of the state banquet arranged in her honor at the Kum Susan Hall and stood to address the diners, evoking her father, who had framed the Pakistan–North Korea relationship. He had planned for her to visit North Korea when she finished her studies in 1977, she said, only for Zia's coup to swallow up the trip.[32]

Bhutto praised Kim's "astonishing progress in rebuilding the country ... that embodied the principles of self-reliance," before touching on an issue far more delicate. Two republics denigrated in the West for their undeclared nuclear weapons programs were sitting down to eat with one another. "Nuclear non-proliferation should not be used as a pretext for preventing states from exercising fully their right to acquire and develop nuclear technology for peaceful purposes geared to their economic and social development," she told the diners.[33] "Pakistan is committed to nuclear non-proliferation both at global and regional level. It is not fair to cast doubts on Pakistan's intentions and to subject Pakistan to discriminatory treatment." She recalled that Khan's request for her to ask for missiles was pounding in her head. "The Asian people, as the masters of Asia," Bhutto concluded, "must carve out Asia's future independently."

Then it was Kim's turn. He evoked a "road of friendship pioneered seventeen years before by Zulfikar Ali Bhutto" and, describing Benazir as his "close friend," praised her "unfaltering conviction."[34] Kim said: "Despite a variety of storms and stress and repeated tribulations you are working energetically to maintain independence, promote national unity and build a progressive and democratic Pakistan."

The two leaders sat and the feast began: chestnuts, steamed fish and lotuses. Bhutto could hardly eat. "I was quite nervous," she remembered.[35] "I leaned over to Kim and said, 'You were very close to my father.' He nodded. I continued: 'But there is one thing I really need for you to do for me.' He smiled. I had to get to the point. 'Give my country No-dong blueprints, please,' I said, straight out. He looked shocked. I said, 'We need those missiles.' He stared at me in amazement. I was not sure if he understood and repeated my request. I could see the translator was trying to find the right way to express it. Suddenly Kim nodded his head and said: 'Yes. Let's set up technical teams and they can discuss the details.' And we continued with our dinner."

The next day, Kim and Bhutto returned to the subject of missiles. Bhutto recalled: "His people said they would have to put the information about the missiles on computer disks. They gave me a bag of materials. Kim said the teams each side selected would do the deal, whatever the deal was to be. I really had little idea of what they were discussing. I did wonder, though. Was it only missiles? They said it was to be a cash deal. In charge on our side was General Khawaja Ziauddin, who now worked closely with Khan on all the arrangements."

With only a few hours left in North Korea, Kim had a surprise for Bhutto.

"He whisked us all off on a trip to his home village," she remembered. "They had reconstructed it. There were beautiful gardens. It was a lovely place. Only something was wrong. I found it hard to concentrate, worrying about the bag I had been given, but also outside, everything seemed surreal. There were very broad roads, upon which the snow slowly fell. Thick wafts soon covered everything. Only there were no snowplows, simply crowds of people with small brooms who swept away as more snow fell." Bhutto felt that she had glimpsed something morbid, a snapshot of the real North Korea. "Everywhere we went the population seemed so poor and thin." Bhutto reflected on her speech of the previous evening. "I began to feel dreadful. I was pained by the plight of the people. Their clothes were drab. They evidently had no food. They were very thin. We were eating sumptuous food. It made me feel guilty. Then someone said, 'The snow is so thick, you might not be able to fly.' And Kim said, 'Yes. Please stay.' And I thought to myself, I have to get out of this place. Right now. I could not stay there one more night."

Husain Haqqani was waiting for Bhutto's plane to land in Islamabad. "She told me she had peeked inside the bag and seen the disks and other things she obviously had no understanding of," Haqqani recalled.[36] "They could have been anything. It horrified me and I said so. She sensed then that the military had framed her. Her fingerprints were all over whatever their plan was for North Korea."

Bhutto handed the materials over to General Khawaja Ziauddin and began to worry. "As far as I knew, the deal involved buying No-dong missiles for cash. But when I requested more information, the military clammed up." Military budgets were still closed, even to the prime minister. The cabinet was also prevented from accessing military purchasing arrangements. "KRL was even more opaque, seeming to be run out of thin air," recalled Bhutto. "I was pushed to the margins. I was no longer useful to KRL or the military." Khan, General Ziauddin and Musharraf were dealing with it, she was repeatedly told. The ISI, too, was getting involved, with Major General Shujjat, who had been assigned to the clandestine procurement division of the ISI, known as Joint Intelligence Miscellaneous, placed in charge.[37]

What Bhutto could see was how the military activity between the two countries soon heated up. In January 1994, Pakistan, China and North Korea signed a formal technical assistance pact.[38] Khan began to commute between Islamabad and Pyongyang, making more than a dozen trips in all, supervised by General Ziauddin and accompanied by Brigadier Sajawal.[39] In April 1994 a North Korean foreign ministry delegation, led by Pak Chung-kuk, deputy to the Supreme People's Assembly, visited Pakistan—en route to Iran.[40] In September 1994 another high-ranking North Korean delegation arrived, this one led by the chairman of the State Commission on Science and Technology.[41] It was followed in November 1995 by a delegation headed by Choe Kwang, vice chairman of the National Defense Commission. Choe Kwang was also minister of the people's armed forces and marshal of the Korean people's army, and as such was responsible for North Korea's nuclear procurement program. The marshal was treated to a first-class reception in Islamabad, meeting President Leghari, the defense minister, Aftab Shaban Mirani, as well as the chairman of the joint chiefs of staff, commander of the air force and chief of naval operations.[42]

Pakistan's army chief, General Kakar, even took Marshal Kwang on a rare tour of KRL and its enrichment halls.[43] He visited Pakistan's secret missile production facility, run by Dr. Samar Mubarakmand, near Faisalabad and a missile test site at Jhelum. During this visit North Korea signed a further agreement to provide Pakistan with fuel tanks, rocket engines and between twelve and twenty-five complete No-dong missiles. The armaments would be produced by the Fourth Machine Industry Bureau of the 2nd Economic Committee and delivered to KRL the following spring by North Korea's Changgwang Sinyong Corporation (also known as the North Korea Mining Development Trading Corporation), which was a front for Pyongyang's arms and technology procurement network.[44] In return, Khan agreed to host North Korean missile experts in a joint training program. "For at least eighteen months it was missiles that everyone was interested in," recalled Dr. Shafiq, whose father, Brigadier Sajawal, was at Khan's side throughout the negotiations.[45] "But then Pakistan ran out of money."

The military and KRL were motoring ahead, but Bhutto lost track of the North Korean deal as she struggled to keep a grip on power. The Taliban had succeeded in wresting control over large sections of Afghanistan and Kashmir was once again burning. Overly confident, the Pakistani military began to up the pace. In July 1995 six Western tourists were kidnapped from the ski slopes of a resort in Indian-administered Kashmir. One of the hostages, John Childs, an American, escaped to describe "a well-disciplined unit" using radios which rounded up the tourists like cattle and relentlessly bullied them.[46] After it made specific demands for the release of named Pakistani militants who had been jailed in India, the kidnappers were unmasked by the CIA as working for Harkat-ul-Ansar, the extremist group formed at Musharaf's bidding in 1993 to produce fighters for the insurgency.[47]

The recovery of the body of one of the kidnap victims in August 1995 defined the full scope of the crisis.[48] Hans Ostro, a Norwegian, had been decapitated and on his chest was scored the name of the kidnap gang.[49] A note pinned to Ostro's shirt explained in Urdu: "We have killed the hostage because the [Indian] government has failed to accept our demands. In forty-eight hours, if our demands are not met, the other hostages will meet the same fate." The four remaining captives, two Britons (Paul Wells, aged twenty-three, and Keith Mangan, thirty-three), an American (Donald Hutchings, forty-two), and a German (Dirk Hasert, twenty-six), would never be found and the killing of Ostro and the method used evoked universal horror. Back then, a beheading appeared uniquely extreme. Bhutto said: "We were living in an age of innocence, before the Taliban's hold in Afghanistan consolidated. Then, as al-Qaeda and its offshoots grew, they would come to film themselves beheading hostages like Daniel Pearl for the benefit of cable TV."[50]

Ostro's death and the unresolved kidnapping became an open wound for Pakistan and Kashmiris, who were shocked by what had been done in their name. The fury these events generated in the US and Europe forced Bhutto to confront the price she had paid to hold on to power: giving the military a free hand in engaging with the militants as she turned her back on foreign policy. Bhutto claimed she felt as if she was waking from a dream: "The US had been sending démarches for some time, concerned at our support of militant activities in Pakistan and Afghanistan. Now as I reread this correspondence, I suddenly realized our military had gone too far." Bhutto sent emissaries to negotiate with jihadi groups for calm to be restored in Kashmir and demanded Musharraf rein in the more extreme factions in the Pakistan militant camps. But for all Bhutto's new-found evangelism, she still had radical Islamists in her coalition government, including Maulana Fazlur Rehman, the leader of Jamiat Ulema Islam, whom she had made chairman of the National Assembly committee on foreign affairs.[51]

One step ahead, Washington was increasingly concerned that the various elements of terror emanating from Pakistan had a common denominator: Osama bin Laden. In 1992, while many Arab fighters had left Afghanistan for home, bin Laden had been unable to return to Saudi Arabia, having lambasted the Saudi royal family, who revoked his passport. He had gone to Sudan instead, accompanied by a hard core of fighters, established two training camps there and started a construction business to fund his plans.[52] In the winter of 1995, after British police raided the home of Rachid Ramda, an Algerian wanted in connection with bomb blasts in France, they discovered records for bank transfers which they traced to Osama bin Laden's new office in Khartoum. Further digging led the US authorities to point to bin Laden as the financier of a number of terrorist attacks, from the bombing of US troops in Aden in 1992 to an explosion at a Saudi National Guard barracks in Riyadh in November 1995. There was also evidence linking Osama bin Laden to Ramzi Yousef: a bank transaction that showed he had paid Yousef's guest-house bill in Pakistan after the World Trade Center blast.[53]

In Pakistan, the US informed Bhutto that bin Laden was also meddling in Kashmir, a crisis managed by Musharraf and the ISI, that was growing into a revolving door for foreign insurgents who entered from all over the Islamic world—from Chechnya, Saudi Arabia, Yemen, Bosnia and North Africa—before leaving fully trained to fuel terror in the Middle East, Africa, Europe and North America. "I called in my ISI chief, General Javed Ashraf Qazi," Bhutto recalled.[54] "I asked: 'Why were there armies of foreigners being sent into Kashmir and being trained in our camps?' Qazi, with a straight face, told me, 'Because the Indians have killed all the Kashmiris.' These military guys and the intelligence agencies were living in a world of their own."

If Bhutto needed more proof of the growing distance between her and the military, it was now that the PPP learned of the existence of the ISI slush fund wielded to defeat her in 1990. General Naseerullah Babar, the interior minister, had been tipped off about the black operation run by Generals Beg and Durrani and raised the scandal in the National Assembly. His allegations touched many serving officers, including ISI chief Qazi, who was in 1990 head of military intelligence and had looked after a secret bank account "Survey Section 202" in which the fund had been deposited. Babar's allegations formed the basis of a criminal case taken to the supreme court by the former chief of the Pakistan air force Air Marshal Asghar Khan, who was appalled at what he had heard and keen to see the generals indicted. But for the vast majority of the military it was as if the civilian arm of government had declared war against it. Taking the military on, they were about to demonstrate, yet again, was a perilous strategy. The key witness in the slush-fund scandal, Younes Habib, the banker who had come up with the millions needed to run the fund, suddenly clammed up. On 10 September 1995, Zeba Habib, his wife, was shot dead as she walked through Clifton in Karachi by a gunman riding pillion on a motorcycle. She had been on her way to visit her husband who had been sentenced to seventeen years' imprisonment for misappropriating—on behalf of the ISI and himself—$37.6 million in dollar bearer certificates from the Pakistan State Bank.[55]

To rein in the ISI and win back US support, Bhutto acted rapidly on a piece of raw intelligence that dropped into her lap. On 7 February 1995 crack troops answerable only to the prime minister raided an Islamabad guest house and seized Ramzi Yousef, who had been living there secretly under ISI protection for two years. Waiving legal formalities that would have allowed the case to drag on indefinitely (and enable Yousef to be sprung by his supporters in the army), Bhutto had him immediately extradited to the US. One month later, on 8 March, after Yousef's supporters had responded by shooting dead two Americans who worked at the US consulate in Karachi, Bhutto ordered a tentative crackdown against the extremists, placing Maulana Azam Tariq, the second in command of the Sipah-e-Sahaba, which had paid Yousef to kill Bhutto, and Maulana Masood Azhar, a leader of Harkat-ul-Ansar, which had kidnapped the tourists in Kashmir, on an exit control list.[56]

Even this mild response drove sections of the military wild. In September 1995, Bhutto uncovered plans for a coup led by Major General Zahir-ul-Islam Abbasi, director general of infantry corps at the army high command.[57] A born-again Muslim, allied to the strict Deobandi sect, Abbasi believed in fighting for a caliphate to subsume Pakistan. He was a zealot who had been sent on attachment to the Islamic militias formed by the ISI to fight the Soviets, and in Afghanistan had worked closely with the fledgling Taliban, passing on guns and money. Abbasi's reward had been to serve as ISI station chief at Pakistan's embassy in New Delhi, a plum job in the directorate given the range of operations available deep inside enemy territory. He had recently returned to Pakistan to take up a senior position in the army and also at the Tablighi Jamaat (TJ), the umbrella organization for followers of the fanatical Deobandi sect, which called for Bhutto's removal and an Islamic state to be raised after her fall.[58]

When Bhutto began to investigate the plot against her, she discovered strands of it linking thirty-six army officers and twenty civilians, including Lieutenanat General Ghulam Mohammad Malik, the commander of Rawalpindi's 10 Corps, one of the most elevated positions in the army. All the plotters, including Malik, were followers of Mufti Sufi Iqbal, a TJ preacher from Taxila who had frequently spoken at 10 Corps headquarters, where he had called for followers to take up arms in the name of Islam and Pakistan and against Bhutto.[59]

The ISI was everywhere and Bhutto was losing control. Then she received an uncomfortable call from Washington: her military attaché had been caught running a counterfeit currency racket. Brigadier Khalid Maqbool, who was in reality the ISI station chief, had been passing fake $100 bills so sophisticated that the US Treasury was later forced to change the design of the note.[60] Maqbool refused to explain to his prime minister what he had been doing or under whose authorization he had done it and was deported from the US back to Pakistan. "It was hugely embarrassing," recalled Bhutto.[61] "We made up a story in the end to cover the scandal and said the bills had come from Afghanistan after the US contingent left. No one believed us. We behaved like gangsters and our credibility was shot to pieces."

Back home the terror unfolded with a massive truck bomb detonating outside the Egyptian embassy in Islamabad on 19 November 1995, killing seventeen people. Interior minister Babar gathered intelligence connecting the explosion to supporters of Ramzi Yousef, who wanted to punish Egypt for pressuring Pakistan into expelling jihadis left over from the Afghan war. On 21 December another massive explosion went off in Peshawar, killing fifty-six. It, too, bore all the hallmarks of a Sunni group connected to Yousef. But this time no organization even bothered officially to claim the blast or to deliver a demand. Bombs also rocked Sindh province, the prime minister's stronghold, where Pervez Musharraf, now a lieutenant general and commander of the elite strike corps at Mangla, in Rawalpindi, had introduced the vicious Sipah-e-Sahaba in 1994.[62] The extremists worked hard alongside other ethnic and religious factions to foment violence and destabilize Bhutto's term in office, and it was rapidly becoming clear that no civilian government would be strong enough to remedy the crisis.

It would take more than phony dollar bills to save Pakistan. By 1996 the Islamic Republic was broke. Industry had fallen idle, inflation climbed to almost

14 percent, while Pakistan's foreign reserves fell to a low of $500 million, the equivalent to two weeks' worth of imports.[63] The Karachi stock exchange looked as if it was about to plummet into free fall. An inspector from the International Monetary Fund who visited Islamabad blamed "stop-and-go policies" for the crisis and called on the government to rope in the military and prevent them from implementing a "substantial increase in spending." But Pakistan had become a stop-and-go country, a cavalcade of violence interrupted by the occasional moment of peace. There was no money at home, but the military remained solvent because they continued to look abroad to fund their excesses. Bhutto caught only occasional glimpses of what was going on and was never able to join together all the dots, to picture the extent of the military's secret sales project.

If she had been allowed to visit KRL, things would have been a little more obvious. Dr. Shafiq, the son of Khan's military aide, Brigadier Sajawal, recalled: "The two guest houses beside the lake were chock-a-block with foreigners. It was Babel. We were up to our necks in North Koreans, Chinese, Iranians, Syrians, Vietnamese and Libyans. Dr. Sahib never ceased to amaze me how he got these people in and out with no questions asked."[64]

Pakistan's military airstrips and its docks were also busy with C-130 transport planes and container ships on unspecified missions, giving fuel to Bhutto's worst fears. Many of the rumors reaching her were not to do with North Korea but pointed to some kind of trade with Iran, stories that had become so heightened and persistent that the year before she had raised them with the Iranians personally. A state visit had been planned and she joined President Leghari on it. Bhutto recalled: "Leghari visited Ayatollah Khomeini's tomb, and gave all the speeches, stating that working closely together Iran and Pakistan 'can serve Islam.' We then met Iranian president Rafsanjani. Leghari once again pledged 'all-out cooperation between Iran and Pakistan to resolve the Muslim world's regional problems.' I waited for a quiet moment. I asked Rafsanjani: 'Is there something going on? Is there a nuclear exchange?' Rafsanjani looked surprised. He said he suspected it too but he said he knew nothing. I was told later the Revolutionary Guard were running the Iranian nuclear program."[65]

Bhutto was frustrated. But when quizzed about the Pakistan nuclear sales program in a televised interview conducted by the broadcaster David Frost she kept her concerns about sales to Iran and North Korea to herself. "We have neither detonated one nor have we got nuclear weapons," she told an incredulous Frost.[66] "Being a responsible state and a state committed to non-proliferation, we in Pakistan, through five successive governments, have taken a policy decision to follow a peaceful nuclear program." It was a lie. She knew it. But she was not sure what she was dealing with or how far the military had gone.

The dust being kicked up by KRL in Iran pricked interest further afield, particularly in Israel, where the intelligence community had been studying the Pakistan–Iran nuclear pact since its inception in 1987. Unit 8200, the top-secret military intelligence corps of the Israel Defense Forces (IDF) responsible for listening in to enemy chatter, had cracked the encryption used in communications between Pakistan and Iran, and the conversations it monitored suggested Islamabad had done the unthinkable and given Tehran a nuclear weapons factory. General Moshe Ya'alon, a future head of the IDF, who in the mid-1990s acted as Israel's intelligence liaison in Washington, recalled how the drumbeat grew louder: "Pakistan was broke. Khan was flying around the world alongside his military escort. Our people overheard him dealing and many of these deals came back to Iran, to whom he was offering KRL stock."[67]

The Iranians had come back to Khan and told him that technology he had sold them during the 1980s, P-1 centrifuges and spare parts from his stockpile, was no good. By the early 1990s, Tehran had learned that the P-1 had been superseded in Pakistan by far more reliable centrifugal technology, the German-designed P-2 with its maraging steel rotors. The Iranians wanted it too, and Pakistan obliged them, supplying P-2 blueprints in 1995.[68] Israeli spies then spotted Khan even closer to Israel—meeting a senior Syrian government official in Beirut, accompanied by a Pakistan army official (almost certainly Brigadier Sajawal).[69] General Ya'alon recalled: "Khan had a menu with him. He was offering nuclear assistance. But we do not know if the deal went through. What we determined was that although Khan was intent on selling to Damascus, he was also keen to use Syria as a conduit to deliver nuclear assistance to Iran. Nobody was looking at Syria in those days from a nuclear perspective."[70]

The radio chatter revealed yet more horrors. Pakistan owed North Korea $40 million for the 1993 Nodong missile deal and by 1996 officials were telling Pyongyang the bill could not be met.[71] With no means of paying, Pakistan offered Pyongyang a uranium enrichment plant in lieu, a proposal A. Q. Khan had discussed with North Korea's deputy prime minister in August 1992. Ya'alon said: "I remember saying to the Americans some time in 1995 or 1996, 'How do you think Pakistan is going to pay for all those No-dong missiles?' But I was shouting myself hoarse. Nobody wanted to know."

What helped to cloud the issue was the fact that China, North Korea's neighbor, had also been supplying Pakistan with M-11 missiles since 1991—with barely a murmur from the White House. Despite overwhelming evidence from satellite overheads, human intelligence and reconnaissance aircraft, Washington had held back from intervening, fearing an impasse at a time when the White House was trying to better relations with Beijing, with an eye on the rapidly expanding spending power of the Chinese consumer who, it was hoped, would be allowed to purchase imported US goods. At home, the trade versus proliferation tight-rope that the Clinton administration tottered along (turning a blind eye to one in the hopes of making ground on the other) gradually eroded all confidence in the White House among even the most experienced officials at the CIA and the State Department. Soon there were murmurs that the Clinton administration (as the Reagan and Bush administrations had done, too) was manipulating intelligence, in an episode which also evoked the Richard Barlow affair.

Gorden Oehler, Barlow's former boss at the Office of the Secretary of Defense (OSD), had begun to track Pakistan's missile deals with China in 1989 after he had left the OSD to become national intelligence officer for WMD. In June 1991 the Bush administration had imposed sanctions on two Chinese companies when Oehler reported that Pakistan had acquired a "training M-11 ballistic missile" from Beijing, only for the sanctions to be waived in March 1992, with China promising to sign the Nuclear Non-Proliferation Treaty (NPT) and restrict its missile sales.[72] The issue with these missiles was not simply that their supply by China to a country like Pakistan contravened treaties on the proliferation of such weapons, but that they were yet another—and deadly—vehicle for Pakistan's nuclear program.

In April 1992, Oehler became director of the CIA's Center for Weapons Intelligence, Non-Proliferation and Arms Control, a position that brought him significantly closer to the White House.[73] The M-11 sales had continued, Oehler warned, Pakistan receiving thirty-four missiles from Beijing just weeks after

China had signed the NPT. He even knew where the weapons were—US spy satellites having photographed crates at the Pakistan air force base at Sargodha.[74] Intelligence mounted and was regurgitated for Clinton in vivid detail.

China should not be trusted, Oehler warned. Since the early 1980s it had given Pakistan nearly everything it had needed to make its first atomic bomb—most of it for free.[75] In August 1993 the Clinton administration briefly bowed to Oehler's advice and applied sanctions.[76] But they were lifted again in October 1994 when China weakly pledged to comply with US law. Even then, as the pledge was made, Beijing's loyalty to Islamabad superseded it and the missile exports secretly continued, with Oehler picking up another alarming development: Beijing had moved from supplying nuclear-capable M-11s to helping Pakistan build its own plant to manufacture a generic version of the missile near Rawalpindi.[77] Activity there was "very high," and if the Chinese continued with their current rate of support the plant would be ready for production by 1998. At this stage the exchange did not benefit A. Q. Khan but the PAEC, with the M-11 program coming under the direct control of Dr. Samar Mubarakmand, who used Chinese blueprints as a basis for a new ballistic missile, the 150-mile-range Hatf 3. There was also growing evidence that Pakistan was attempting to mate this version of the M-11 to its nuclear warheads, warned Oehler.

His analysis put Clinton in an awkward position. If the president accepted the assessment, he would have to impose sanctions that would potentially cost American companies billions of dollars in lost revenue if Beijing lashed out at being censured by Washington—particularly Boeing, which was negotiating a major contract with the Chinese aviation industry, and Westinghouse Electric Corporation, which had a valuable deal with the China National Nuclear Corporation.[78] However, not to act on Oehler's analysis, backed as it was by hard intelligence, would have enhanced Pakistan's nuclear capability, to the detriment of India. Oehler had also warned, more significantly, that whatever Pakistan gained it could not be trusted to keep. If it learned to manufacture the Hatf 3 and mate it with a warhead, the technology would be sold to others whom the West had reason to fear. This was not a bargain anyone should make.

The US stalled, see-sawing between its appetite for the Chinese market and the need to peg down Pakistan. China revelled in the confusion and widened its client base, selling medium-range nuclear-capable missiles to Saudi Arabia and missile guidance components to Iran. In early 1996, Oehler also uncovered evidence that China was once again directly involved in the Pakistan nuclear program. This was the clincher, he thought. Sanctions would have to be imposed. Clinton had to do something now. Oehler had seen intelligence that showed that China was manufacturing centrifuge parts for A. Q. Khan. The China Nuclear Energy Industry Corporation had shipped to Karachi 5,000 ring magnets, used in the suspension bearings of centrifuge rotors. But the Clinton administration did nothing.[79] No one was prepared to take on Pakistan or to get firm with China. Officials in the State Department familiar with the deal lamely recalled: "China did not respond well to sanctions. We tried: they achieved nothing. So, we did—well, nothing."[80]

Only after the ring magnet sale and ongoing missile cooperation were leaked into the public domain was there movement. In February 1996, Congress demanded an inquiry. But in May 1996 the State Department announced that China and Pakistan would not be sanctioned after an investigation found "no evidence that the Chinese government had willfully aided or abetted Pakistan's nuclear weapon program through the magnet transfer." It flew in the face of the truth—in the same way that Bush officials had claimed F-16s could not be used to deploy a nuclear bomb. Oehler was infuriated. He refused to back down, reporting that China had also sold a "special industrial furnace" for molding uranium and "hi-tech diagnostic equipment" to KRL, where Chinese technicians were currently working to install the equipment.[81] Seth Carus, a visiting fellow at the National Defense University in Washington, warned the Senate: "Everybody knew the M-11 missiles went to Pakistan. But because of the implications of that decision, the intelligence process was corrupted. This is simply because if the executive branch decides that they do not want to impose sanctions, they will start corrupting the intelligence process to make sure there is never a determination that some egregious event has happened."[82] It was the same old story. "It was shades of Reagan and Bush," said a former senior official in the State Department. "Why, when it came to the destruction of the world, did these guys find it so hard to play it straight?"

In April 1997, Oehler had had enough. There was no consistent policy emerging. There was no strategy even. There was no considered attempt to rein China in or to tackle Pakistan, which was getting increasingly out of hand. There was just the steady drip, drip of doomsday technology from China to

Pakistan and from Pakistan to—no one was exactly sure how many countries. The view from where Oehler was sitting was of an increasingly sophisticated Pakistani nuclear program that was steadily growing out of control. Oehler had to do something. He appeared at a closed hearing of the Senate governmental affairs committee and warned of a government cover-up involving Chinese missile deals to Pakistan. He found the softest way he could to contradict his superiors short of becoming a whistle-blower. It was akin to the Barlow strategy—although Oehler, far more senior than Barlow, had more chance of surviving.

Oehler's views won support. Gary Milhollin, a law professor and director of the Wisconsin Project on Nuclear Arms Control in Washington, told a separate Senate hearing: "We are simply watching the Chinese shipments go out, without any hope of stopping them. All our present policy has produced is a new missile factory in Pakistan, an upgraded nuclear weapon factory in Pakistan and new chemical weapon plants in Iran."[83] But Clinton still refused to take action, preferring to side with Beijing. In October 1997, exhausted and cynical, Gordon Oehler took early retirement, testifying to the Senate foreign relations committee the following year that "analysts were very discouraged to see their work was regularly dismissed."[84] Others who knew him said he had "kind of set down an ultimatum" that was ignored "and he felt he had to walk."[85]

Throughout this period, the relationship between Pakistan and North Korea was there to see and yet nothing was done. In March 1996 a North Korean ship bound for Pakistan had been held in Taiwan carrying 15 tons of rocket propellants.[86] That summer US and UK intelligence agents had warned their respective governments that Pakistan was "readying itself to sell or was selling already" to North Korea and possibly Iran.[87] Wajid Shamsul Hasan, Pakistan's high commissioner in London, recalled getting an angry phone call from the British authorities. "They said the ISI had been buying and selling for the nuclear program," Hasan recalled.[88] "One official at my embassy, Mohammed Saleem, was accused of proliferation of WMDs." Saleem had been employed as a clerk five years before, but was actually an ISI agent working for the nuclear project. "The British said Saleem was the new and primary European agent for Khan. I called up the ISI guys and asked them: 'What are you doing?' They told me to keep my nose out of it. Khan was not acting alone. He never acted alone. He was trading, using the ISI and the military. Both were untouchable."

So confident was Khan that he had even touted for business on the open market, representing KRL at the 5th Defense Services Asia conference in Kuala Lumpur, Malaysia, in April 1996, with a brochure that concluded: "Keeping pace with the emerging demands of the competitive international defense products market, KRL ventures to offer its expertise in the shape of services and products not only to the domestic consumer but also to an international audience of friendly countries ... KRL has earned credibility not only in Southeast Asia but also in the Middle East and West Asia."[89] Three weeks later, on 29 April, customs officers in Hong Kong intercepted a convoy from China bound for KRL that was carrying 200 crates of rocket-fuel propellant.[90] The CIA and MI6 refocused their resources on Pakistan. By September 1997, UK and US satellite imagery showed regular flights between Pyongyang and Islamabad, mostly involving bulky Ilyushin-76 transport planes.[91] Something was being delivered or taken away. Gnawing away at analysts in Whitehall and in Washington was the rapidly growing realization that Khan and the Pakistani military were brazenly selling nuclear technology to all the West's enemies, Gary Milhollin warning one Senate hearing: "Most of the countries that worry Washington are interconnected, so the failure to confront proliferation by one usually means there will be a failure to confront proliferation by others."[92] But there was also mounting evidence that a voracious demand for nuclear material had been pricked among individuals as well as states.

On 10 January 1996, John Deutch, the CIA director, confirmed that six Lithuanians and a Georgian had been detained in Visaginas, Lithuania, as they attempted to sell 100 kg of uranium. It had been smuggled from another former Soviet state, Kazakhstan, which had previously offered its services to Pakistan as a conduit for nuclear sales to Iran. Those arrested claimed the uranium was for an anonymous buyer in Pakistan.[93] The CIA concluded that Sunni extremists, possibly allied to Osama bin Laden, were behind the purchase. A short time later these fears were reinforced when British and US intelligence learned that uranium ore was being hawked around the Pakistani city of Peshawar, the gateway to Osama bin Laden's new camps.[94] Someone was looking to construct the dirty bomb that Ramzi Yousef had failed to build in 1993.

But in Islamabad, where A. Q. Khan had a certificate endorsing his claim to be Father of the Bomb, he was being maneuverd into ever more rarefied positions. A growing lobby demanded that the prime minister award him another title. General Jehangir Karamat, the new chief of army staff, had even issued a statement: "[A. Q. Khan's] achievements to date are a source of strength and pride for the whole nation."[95] Khan's friends began calling Bhutto's office demanding tangible recognition for his "invaluable work." "They kept pressuring me," remembered Bhutto. "There was no modesty about it." Eventually she buckled and on 14 August 1996 President Leghari pinned the Nishan-i-Imtiaz, Pakistan's highest civil honor, on Khan's jacket.

One month later, the turmoil in Afghanistan and Pakistan merged, with thousands of recruits from the extremist groups, including Sipah-e-Sahaba, the Lashkar-e-Taiba (LeT) and Harkat-ul-Ansar, re-entering Afghanistan in support of the Taliban, which took the eastern stronghold of Jalalabad. The victory was witnessed by Osama bin Laden, who had left Sudan to slip back into Afghanistan in May 1996, transiting through Pakistan with the army's blessing.[96] On 26 September 1996, Kabul fell to the Taliban, with Pakistan's brutal Sunni militias participating in a massacre of Afghan Shia to underscore the triumph. Bin Laden, who had given substantial financial support, left Jalalabad for the Taliban stronghold of Kandahar, taking up the reins of the training camps established there by the ISI and the leadership of their well-funded and heavily armed Armies of God.

These jihadi groups included Sipah-e-Sahaba and LeT, the armed wing of the dogmatic Markaz Dawa Al Irshad, which ran the militant Islamist university near Lahore inspired and funded by bin Laden—and egged on by General Musharraf.[97] Some had been forced to change their names, such as Harkat-ul-Ansar which became Harkat-ul-Mujahideen after being proscribed by the US in 1997 for the kidnappings in Kashmir and its close links to bin Laden.

The last to come to bin Laden's camps was a group called Jaish-e-Mohammed (JEM), the Army of Mohammed, led by Maulana Masood Azhar, who had a long jihadist pedigree. An obstreperous Islamist, Azhar had been general secretary of Harkat-ul-Ansar until Indian security forces arrested him as he crossed into Kashmir in February 1994. To secure Azhar's release, his men had kidnapped the six Western tourists in July 1995. When India refused to release Azhar and the hostages vanished, he remained in jail until December

1999 when his men hijacked an Indian Airlines flight with 155 passengers on board. This time India relented, the passengers were released, and Azhar was handed over to Pakistan.[98]

But none of this was clearly visible from Islamabad, where Bhutto was overthrown by her hand-picked president. On 5 November 1996, invoking the notorious 8th amendment which he had promised never to use, Farukh Leghari sacked Bhutto, citing corruption, instability and nepotism. On 4 February 1997 a general election returned Nawaz Sharif to power as prime minister. But the people of Pakistan had grown tired of the military's version of democracy and largely failed to vote. Sharif immediately revoked the 8th amendment, ridding himself of the threat from President Leghari. He planned to take on all comers who would challenge him and blithely set off on a collision course with America—and his armed forces.

14

A NEW CLEAR VISION

Within weeks of the start of President Bill Clinton's second term in January 1997, Nawaz Sharif was also returned to power in Pakistan.[1] Clinton had won a sweeping victory in the November 1996 elections, while Sharif's mandate had been greatly reduced by an electorate fed up with the military's version of doctored democracy.

Clinton was determined to bring a fresh approach. Foreign affairs would come to the fore and in particular South Asian relations. Incredibly, no US president had visited the region since Jimmy Carter's trip to India in January 1978. Warren Christopher, Clinton's secretary of state, had also not bothered to visit India or Pakistan, despite the growing instability, the increasing evidence connecting the ISI to extremist organizations that were perpetrating terrorism around the world, and the Islamic Republic's proximity to Osama bin Laden at a time when its nuclear proliferation activities should have been causing extreme concern.

However, when the new administration began talking up South Asia in 1997, what it really meant was India, President Clinton having become intrigued by the country after Hillary and Chelsea had visited it in 1995 and inspired him with their impressions of the largest democracy on earth. Karl "Rick" Inderfurth, Clinton's incoming assistant secretary of state for South Asia, a National Security Council staffer under Carter and a former *ABC News* anchor, who had reported on the ground the Soviet withdrawal from Afghanistan in February 1989, recalled: "India was what drew Clinton spiritually and intellectually. The upshot was new management on the seventh floor at the State Department and a review of US policy towards India and Pakistan by the National Security Council."[2] To signal his intent, Clinton replaced Christopher with Madeleine Albright, former US representative to the UN, and chose Tom Pickering, a former US ambassador to India, as his new under secretary of state. As Pickering put it: "We want to show that we don't consider South Asia the backside of the diplomatic globe."[3]

But there could be no reconsideration of where America stood on India without having to tackle its neighbor. "Pakistan was a whole bunch of things: non-proliferation, extremism, terrorism, hostilities with India, the list went on and on," recalled Inderfurth. "The great missing ingredient with the US–Pakistan relationship was trust. When we needed them we'd worked closely and when we didn't we'd shut the door. Until we could demonstrate we deserved their trust, they would continue to hedge their bets. And you didn't have to be Henry Kissinger to figure out why they had pursued the nuclear option."

In Clinton's first term, policy on the Islamic Republic had foundered as the country was threatened with being proscribed and simultaneously offered delivery of long-promised nuclear-capable F-16s. That policy had collapsed with Pakistan rejecting the jets and demanding their down payment back. Ultimately, the administration had done no more than fall behind a Republican senator who had proposed an easing of sanctions, which led to a few million dollars being dispatched to a handful of Pakistan-based charities.[4] It was not a remedy and did nothing to bolster the fragile democracy that had gone ten rounds in the ring with the military and its ISI.

Deciding what to do about Pakistan in Clinton's second term was made far harder by intelligence that A. Q. Khan's Dubai operation had massively expanded and that Khan was circumnavigating the globe. In February 1998 he kicked off a series of trips to Africa, taking with him many of his Dubai contacts and European agents, among them Henk Slebos, B. S. A. Tahir and Brigadier Sajawal. Also in the party were senior scientists from KRL.

A sanitized account of Khan's African sojourn was written up as a monograph by one of the KRL chief's oldest friends, Abdul Siddiqui, a chartered accountant who attended the mosque in Colindale, in north London, from where Khan had recruited many of his earliest suppliers. Siddiqui had been asked along because his son, Abu Bakr, was a business partner in B. S. A. Tahir's company, SMB Computers. "In February 1998 I was in London and received a call from Tahir [in Dubai]," Siddiqui wrote.[5] "He said that Dr. Khan is planning a visit to

Timbuktu and 'you are invited to join him.' My joy knew no bounds at the prospect of spending some time with Dr. Khan."

By 1998, Tahir was the undisputed king of Khan's Dubai operation, making a fortune importing and exporting centrifuge technology for Pakistan through SMB, a company set up by his uncle Farouq in the early 1980s, originally to trade fruit from Sri Lanka and later to bid for the Dubai dealerships from major computer corporations. Peter Griffin, who became SMB's unpaid business manager in 1992, recalled that Tahir had not won a significant computer dealership until he came on board. "Tahir wasn't comfortable talking to Western businessmen, his English was poor and he felt embarrassed," Griffin recalled.[6] "He got me in to do the talking and I made him millions, negotiating with companies like Epson, Hewlett-Packard and Intel."

But Abu Bakr was Tahir's official European business partner, running SMB Europe from an office in the Ritz Plaza in Ealing, west London.[7] At the time of the Africa trip, Tahir was in the process of ejecting his uncle Farouq from the board of SMB through a court case in Dubai in which he accused Farouq of contributing nothing to the business, having gone into semi-retirement in Singapore.[8] In reality, Tahir was no longer interested in computer dealerships either, having found a much more lucrative business sourcing nuclear technologies for A. Q. Khan. Leaving his brother Saeed to run the computer side of the business, Tahir had opened offices in several former Soviet states, including Kazakhstan, Azerbaijan, Turkmenistan and Uzbekistan, running millions of centrifuge parts from Europe and North America through them to SMB in Dubai and on to Pakistan. Peter Griffin, who said he believed the company was still only importing computers, noticed something strange was going on when Tahir asked him to audit SMB's accounts in 1997: "I discovered Tahir's export manager, who was paid on turnover, was selling stock at less than the purchase price. Tahir would not prosecute him. I also found significant deficiencies between stocks bought and stocks sold. So much so that I asked Tahir how he kept his head above water. He did not give me an explanation."[9]

The 1998 trip to Africa by Tahir, Khan and Siddiqui was no holiday. While Siddiqui senior's prose lingered on tourist sites and the remarkable taste of sweet mint tea, he also revealed how the team travelled with all of the razzmatazz of an official Pakistani government delegation. Siddiqui joined the party in Dubai, arriving on 19 February 1998, where Khan introduced him to "Mr. Hanks, a Dutch businessman dealing in air filtration systems, solar energy, metallurgical machinery and materials." This was, of course, Henk Slebos. Siddiqui then met Lieutenant General Dr. Riaz Chowhan, Khan's personal physician, the former surgeon general of the Pakistan army, who had been employed when Khan first became paranoid about being assassinated. Brigadier Sajawal, Khan's faithful shadow, was there too. Siddiqui wrote that they would fly to Timbuktu via Casablanca in Morocco and Bamako, the capital of Mali. The red carpet treatment started the moment the party landed in Africa. "At Casablanca, the first secretary of the Pakistan embassy, Mr. Inayatullah Kakar received us," Siddiqui wrote. "The honorary consul general of Pakistan in Morocco, Hussain bin Jiloon, gave a dinner in honor of Dr. Khan, which was also attended by our ambassador, Azmat Hussain."

The following day, the party caught a Royal Moroccan Airlines flight for Bamako and then chartered a plane for Timbuktu. Khan told Siddiqui he wanted to see Mali, which had once been a center of Islamic publishing. However, Khan never took holidays. According to Khan's closest business associates, he was actually looking for new bases for operations. Peter Griffin, who was not involved in these trips but was intimate with Khan's methodology, said: "Around this time Dubai was coming under the spotlight. Anything I sent there would immediately get picked up by Dubai Customs. Khan must have been having the same problems. So I guess to divert stuff via Africa would take the heat off a little."[10] At this time Khan could least afford heat since, following orders from the military, he was in the throes of expanding the most sensitive operation of all—Project A/B.[11]

In Mali, Khan established a cover for himself, a reason to be travelling, by buying into a small business in Timbuktu, which he named after his wife, the Hendrina Khan Hotel. Griffin said: "It was classic Khan. Make things appear as open as possible. You can't get more open than naming a project after Henny. It was a great diversion from his official business there, whatever that was."[12]

To make things harder for Washington, less than two months after Khan returned from Africa, Pakistan got stuck into yet more nuclear missile controversy, supervising the test firing of a nuclear-capable long-range missile, the Ghauri.[13] Based on the No-dong, it was the product of all of those years of networking with the North Koreans which had culminated with Bhutto's trip in December 1993. At last, Khan had bettered his rivals at PAEC and, never shy, he had named his missile after Sultan Muhammad Ghauri, the twelfth-century Afghan king, whose army commander was, according to Khan, an ancestor. But there was a chauvinistic theatricality to the name as well. India had pipped Pakistan to the post, testing the first medium-range nuclear-capable missile in South Asia in February 1988.[14] The Prithvi missile had been named after Prithvi Raj Chohan, the twelfth-century ruler of Ajmir and Delhi, who, Khan knew, had been vanquished by Sultan Ghauri. The naming of a missile bore far greater significance for these two nations on a hair trigger than it did in the West, where it appeared petty, for ancient history would always resonate throughout the modern-day Indo–Pakistan rivalry.

The US took notice. Pakistan's Ghauri could carry a payload of 1,300 kg for 1,000 miles and brought New Delhi within reach of a nuclear strike. Such was Pakistan's delight that prime minister Sharif sent Khan a message describing the launch as "a major breakthrough because this missile ... provided Pakistan with a real deterrent against India's growing missile capability."[15] What no one apart from the KRL team knew was that in his eagerness to thwart India, and to preserve his own reputation, Khan had not in fact fired a Ghauri on 6 April 1998 but a real North Korean No-dong. KRL technicians had been unable to perfect the technology, so Khan had simply ordered his men to repaint the North Korean weapon in the livery of the Pakistani military. "The paint was barely dry, but nobody noticed, such was the excitement," Dr. Shafiq recalled.

India did not know and bridled. The Hindu nationalist Bharatiya Janata Party (BJP) had come to power in March 1998 on a platform of putting a stop to Pakistan's terrorism and sabre-rattling. Atal Bihari Vajpayee, the new BJP prime minister, had been lobbied from the moment he took office to sanction a hot test of India's nuclear bomb, and on 11 May 1998 India did just that, in the Pokhran Desert in Rajasthan, the location used when New Delhi had first tested in 1974. Clinton's team was wrong-footed. The CIA had failed to tip off Washington about preparations for a test. India had used stealth and knowledge of US resources, waiting for a short daily window in which US satellites were out of range before preparing the Pokhran site. Then they sat still while the US intelligence community pored over the live images.[16]

Following five blasts which sent Clinton apoplectic, prime minister Vajpayee announced that India would go further. He unveiled a "proactive" policy that would see the Indian army do what it had to, end Pakistan's meddling in Kashmir. As elements within the BJP government demanded that India occupy the divided state and invade Pakistan, Vajpayee warned Islamabad to realize the "new geopolitical realities in South Asia." With one act, India had deflated the Pakistan nuclear umbrella championed by Generals Beg and Gul, and there was clearly only one way for Pakistan to respond. In Washington, all thoughts of a measured unfurling of a new strategy for South Asia were dashed. Instead, the Clinton administration would have to firefight. What had been an ideal for his second term, bringing peace and renewed US interest to South Asia, was now recast in the State Department as "Mission Impossible."[17]

Pakistan could not be allowed to follow suit and hot-test its nuclear bomb. Clinton telephoned Nawaz Sharif. With nothing new to offer, he suggested that the failed F-16 deal from 1993 be revived, added to which he offered aid and, more importantly for Nawaz Sharif, a coveted invitation to the White House. Clinton recalled, after hanging up the phone: "You can almost hear the guy wringing his hands and sweating."[18] But it would take more than a phone call to get Sharif on board. A high-level delegation led by Strobe Talbott, Clinton's deputy secretary of state, accompanied by Karl Inderfurth and Anthony Zinni, a Marine four-star general who was in charge of US Central Command, was sent to Islamabad on 13 May 1998.

On the twenty-two-hour flight, Talbott, Inderfurth and Zinni honed an argument that would rest on the maxim "restraint and maturity." This, plus the F-16s, was what they were going to offer Sharif. It was a simplistic and patronizing homily which represented a complete underestimation of millennia of enmity. And the F-16s no longer had the allure they once did. The package was thrown back in their faces the minute they touched down in Islamabad, Pakistan's foreign minister Gohar Ayub, a son of the former dictator General Ayub Khan, ridiculing the US proposal as "rotting and virtually obsolete." He jibed that the F-16s were "shoddy rugs you've tried to sell us before," adding that the Pakistani people would take to the streets in protest if Sharif accepted them.[19] When Talbott suggested Pakistan was already able to deter its enemies without testing nuclear weapons, a reference to the fact that for many years the US had known and kept quiet about Islamabad's bombs in the basement, the foreign minister was derisive: "As any military man knows, before a weapon can be inducted into military service—even a water bottle—it must be tested."[20] Inderfurth recalled: "Short of making Pakistan the fifty-first state of the US there was no way to turn them around. It looked hopeless."[21] But it was a little late to be getting hot under the collar, given that the US had aided Pakistan in building its bomb, sold it the delivery system (the F-16s), and then ignored it for a decade.

The US delegation decamped to Rawalpindi, Zinni to talk strategy and consequences with his opposite, General Jehangir Karamat, Nawaz Sharif's new, US-trained chief of army staff. The urbane Karamat said his government was still "wrestling" with the question of how to respond. Picking up on the general's apparent lack of finality on the issue, Talbott and Zinni together sought out Sharif. The prime minister appeared "diminutive and roly-poly," according to Talbott. "It was hard to see how he had come out on top of a rough-and-tumble political system."[22] Obviously, no one had briefed Talbott on how Sharif had been raised by the ISI.

Talbott found the prime minister "nearly paralyzed with exhaustion, anguish and fear," and yet this was a well-worn Sharif ruse—the manipulated figurehead, deferring responsibility. Sharif told the US team that his greatest fear was whether he would remain in office long enough to make the critical nuclear decision. The only thing that had pricked his interest, Sharif's visitors recalled, was the offer of a state visit to Washington. Clinton was already making plans to come to South Asia that autumn and Talbott suggested the president could use it to "dramatize" the world's gratitude, paying a visit to Islamabad where he would invite Sharif to the US, if Pakistan refrained from testing its bomb. But Sharif was capricious. He wanted a promise that Clinton would cancel his New Delhi plans and only come to Pakistan. That was clearly out of the question, given the president's determination to visit India, and Talbott declined, recalling: "Sharif looked more miserable than ever." In reality, Sharif was delighted to be at the center of world events and recalled getting ever more urgent calls from the White House. "Clinton rang me five times asking what we were doing, asking for assurances that we were not going to test. When Strobe Talbott came, he thought he had it in the bag. Clinton thought he had it in the bag. Only we knew what we would do."[23]

At the end of the meeting, Sharif called Talbott aside. He claimed that if he were to do as the US wanted and hold back from testing, Talbott would find that next time he came to Islamabad he would not be "dealing with a clean-shaven moderate like himself, but with an Islamic fundamentalist 'who has a long beard.'"[24]

The consequences of such a seismic shift in Pakistan were brought home to the US team later that day when Osama bin Laden, wanted for a range of bombings on US forces in Aden and Saudi Arabia, as well as his apparent connection to Ramzi Yousef and the World Trade Center attack, issued a statement from his headquarters in Kandahar, Afghanistan: "We call upon the Muslim nations in general, and Pakistan and its army in particular, to prepare for the jihad imposed by Allah and terrorize the enemy by preparing the force necessary ... This should include a nuclear force to raise fears among all enemies led by the Zionist–Christian alliance."[25] Given that nuclear material had recently shown up in the gateway to the Khyber Pass, and fundamentalist demonstrators at madrasahs across Pakistan had greeted India's test blast with placards calling for the Pakistani army to hand them nuclear weapons, bin Laden's threat had to be taken seriously. A coalition of Islamist groups calling for global jihad had declared war on America in January 1998, and in an interview broadcast by ABC News two months later bin Laden warned: "I predict a black day for America; a day after which America will never be the same ... I am declaring war on the United States. I'm going to attack your country."[26] However, plenty of people in Washington thought otherwise and bin Laden was still only receiving minor attention there, perceived as a loud-mouth who had not yet demonstrated his apocalyptic potential.[27]

While the US team was still in town, on 15 May 1998, Sharif double-crossed them. Secretly, he called the defense committee of the Cabinet to the prime minister's secretariat in Islamabad. The finance minister, foreign minister, foreign secretary and the three armed forces chiefs, including General Jehangir Karamat, were to be briefed by PAEC and KRL. Dr. Ishfaq Ahmed, the PAEC chairman, was out of the country, so it was left to Dr. Samar Mubarakmand, who had been involved in the nuclear program since Zulfikar Ali Bhutto's conference in Multan in 1972, to represent PAEC. For KRL there could only be one spokesman: the Father of the Bomb, A. Q. Khan.[28]

While Talbott's team debated how persuasive their arguments had been, Sharif's War Cabinet discussed a two-point agenda: should Pakistan conduct nuclear tests, and if so, would it be PAEC or KRL that supervised them? The debate went on for several hours and focused largely on the latter, as there was only one voice of dissent, finance minister Sartaj Aziz, who warned that testing would cripple Pakistan's economy by invoking sanctions. Now that Sharif's War Cabinet had decided to sanction a hot test, PAEC and KRL fought over who would run the show.[29]

Dr. Mubarakmand claimed that PAEC had analyzed India's tests and found that their devices had only the same yield as the ones detonated by India in 1974. He claimed that if his men were allowed to use one of their devices they would provide a far more robust performance, with high-yield bombs of 30–40 kilotons, larger than that dropped on Hiroshima. Mubarakmand concluded that "the PAEC was fully prepared and capable of carrying out these nuclear tests within ten days."[30]

A. Q. Khan also claimed that KRL could be ready to go in ten days. He claimed the right to supervise the blast, as PAEC had failed in its duty to deliver Zulfikar Ali Bhutto a bomb in the 1970s, wasting many years and billions of rupees on the plutonium route. Khan reminded the Cabinet that "it was KRL which had first enriched uranium, converted it into metal, machined it into semi-spheres of metal, designed their own atomic bomb and carried out cold tests on their own," as far back as 1984.[31] Most importantly, KRL had come to Pakistan's rescue as recently as April 1998, when, in the face of BJP aggression, the team from Kahuta had unveiled a missile that could shake the windows of India's parliament buildings in New Delhi. However, PAEC had one clear advantage. It had ready-made test tunnels at Chagai in Balochistan. Nawaz Sharif's indecision saved Khan. Unable or unwilling to give clear orders, he allowed the meeting to break up without a final decision.

The American team left Pakistan the following day with Inderfurth resigned. "At least they didn't set the thing off while we were there," he recalled. As they left, Dr. Ishfaq Ahmed, the new PAEC chairman, returned from his foreign trip and sought out Sharif. "Mr. Prime Minister, take a decision and, insha'Allah, I give you the guarantee of success," Ahmed urged.[32] The following morning, on 18 May 1998, he was summoned back to see the prime minister and told, "dhamaka kar dein" (conduct the explosion).[33] PAEC was to run things—not A. Q. Khan, who now sent a formal complaint to army chief General Karamat. Unwilling to see an embarrassing public spat between Pakistan's foremost nuclear experts ruin the tests, Karamat conceded that Khan and senior KRL personnel could also witness them. Sharif recalled the compromise: "Many in Pakistan saw Abdul Qadeer Khan as the father of the nuclear program.

I coined the phrase. His team was not best placed to conduct the tests but of course he had played a crucial part, so we could not ignore him."[34]

On 19 May 1998, more than a hundred PAEC technicians were flown in two Pakistan International Airlines Boeing 737s to Chagai, where the test tunnels were being unblocked. More men and equipment were transported by road and by Cobra helicopter gunship. Ishfaq Ahmed and Samar Mubarakmand had decided to use five test tunnels plus an extra facility beneath the nearby Kharan Desert—six blasts in all. While the US still held out hope of heading off the tests, believing it still had leverage, the Pakistani scientists camouflaged their secret plans. Tunnel entrances, instruments and control cables were covered with canvas and netting as teams of soldiers erased the tracks of incoming and outgoing trucks and jeeps. Dr. Mubarakmand recalled: "The facilities were made to look like a small hamlet using adobe huts so as to deceive satellite surveillance. Just before the tests Sharif spoke to me and said: 'Dr. Sahib, please do not fail. We cannot afford to fail. IF WE FAIL WE CANNOT SURVIVE. This is an hour of crisis for Pakistan.' He was sure that if we failed, Israel would have attacked our nuclear facilities immediately."[35] Dr. Mubarakmand was referring to a cover story that had just been invented by Sharif and his advisers to justify the test to the West.

Sharif recalled the Israeli imbroglio. "We said that Pakistan had picked up intelligence about several countries looking to destroy our nuclear assets. We were very worried about the Israelis—a direct strike. We could not allow anything to come between success in our nuclear vision." However, the US realized there was nothing to the story. Bruce Riedel, on Clinton's National Security Council, called the chief of the Israel Defense Forces for an authoritative denial which was patched through to Pakistan's ambassador in Washington to underscore that the US was not prepared to "take the horseshit."[36] Pakistan would have to have the stomach for whatever punishment followed.

However, PAEC took no chances. It transferred Pakistan's nuclear devices from Chaklala airbase in Rawalpindi on two C-130 transport aircraft in a "semi-knocked-down form." The bomb mechanisms, HMX explosive lenses and casings were flown separately from the uranium components: beryllium/uranium-238 shields and the uranium-235 cores. Four Pakistan air force F-16s armed with air-to-air missiles escorted the aerial convoy with instructions to shoot them down in the event of hijack or if the transports left Pakistan airspace.[37]

Once at Chagai, the components for each bomb were taken to a "Zero Room" located at the end of a tunnel, where the devices were assembled under Mubarakmand's supervision. "There was so much responsibility on the shoulders of a few," he recalled.[38] "One would expect us to become tense, abusive, quarrelling with each other and bad-tempered. But you would be surprised to find us there all smiling and in good spirits." Cabling connected all the devices to a command and observation post seven miles away and on 26 May, after the tunnels had been plugged with 6,000 bags of wet cement and 12,000 bags of sand, the scientists were ready.

On 27 May 1998, after the cement had dried in the desert sun, Sharif telephoned President Clinton to apologize for disappointing him, putting it all down to the pressure being heaped on his head. In the early hours of 28 May the automatic data transmission link between Pakistan's seismic stations and the outside world was switched off. Personnel, apart from the firing team, were evacuated from Ground Zero. At 2:30 p.m. a Pakistan air force Mi-17 helicopter carrying Ishfaq Ahmed, Samar Mubarakmand, A. Q. Khan and his two long-term deputies, Farooq Hashmi and Javid Mirza, withdrew to the observation post. To avoid further disputes between Khan and his PAEC competitors, neither team was invited to press the button. Instead, the honor was given to a young scientific officer, Muhammad Arshad, who had designed the trigger mechanism.[39]

At 3:16 p.m. Arshad uttered: "All praise be to Allah." He initiated a six-step firing sequence which led from the observation tower to the nuclear bombs located in the heart of the Ras Koh mountains. Each step in the sequence was supplied with an independent power source which was controlled and shut off by computer as the previous step was completed, sending an electrical current pulsing across the desert, up the foothills, into the tunnels and down wires into the HMX lenses formed around the five nuclear devices. Thirty seconds after Arshad pressed the button, the HMX detonated, sending a shockwave into the spherical beryllium/uranium-238 shields which protected the grapefruit-sized uranium-235 cores, imploding each shield into each core, compressing each core to the size of a plum. In a microsecond the uranium went from sub-critical to super-critical density, the initiator at the center of the core was similarly squeezed and the atoms began to fission, or split apart. When neutrons released from the initiator began striking and bombarding the uranium-235, each uranium atom split, creating two more neutrons, which in turn hit two more atoms, creating four more neutrons, which hit four more atoms, creating a runaway train, a chain reaction releasing a lethal variety of atomic particles into the subterranean atmosphere.[40]

The Ras Koh mountains trembled. The observation post shook as millennia of dust and grit were dislodged. And in the intense heat of the radioactive furnace, growling deep inside, the granite rock face of the mountain transformed from dark gray to white. "Allah-o-Akbar." The cries rose up from the gathered scientists, including Mubarakmand, who declared: "Our life expectancy is 122nd in the world; in literacy we are 162nd ... Now in nuclear weapons we are seventh in the world."[41] As the dust settled, the scientists, technicians, engineers and soldiers posed for the cameras, A. Q. Khan beaming at the center of the group, a full head taller than the rest of his colleagues—no trace of the animosity that coursed between them.

In Washington, President Clinton called an urgent press conference in the Rose Garden where he described the tests as "self-defeating, wasteful and dangerous" since they would make the people of Pakistan and India "poorer and less secure."[42] But in Pakistan they understood exactly the immeasurable value of the event. Nawaz Sharif appeared on television and, in stark contrast to his contrite telephone conversation with Clinton, declared: "Today we have settled the score!" Pakistanis had "full faith in their destiny."[43] People poured onto the streets, strapping life-sized cardboard cut-outs of A. Q. Khan to lamp posts and government buildings. A stone's throw from his home in Hillside Road, prayers were held at the Faisal mosque in thanks for the man whom Sharif had re-created as the Father of the Bomb.

Khan was reasonably measured even though he was at his zenith, telling reporters that Pakistan had given India "an appropriate response." In an interview with *The News* he said: "One was a big bomb which had a yield of about 30–35 kilotons, twice as big as the one dropped on Hiroshima. The other four were small tactical weapons of low yield. Tipped on small missiles, they can be used in the battlefield against concentrations of troops."[44] But the political establishment was less reserved in its response. Pakistan's new president, Mohammed Rafiq Tarar, wrote to the KRL chief, saying: "The restoration of the strategic security balance would not have been possible but for your brilliant work and superb leadership ... I congratulate you and your team on my behalf and on behalf of the whole nation for one of the greatest achievements in our history."[45] Tarar awarded Khan another Nishan-i-Imtiaz, Pakistan's highest civil honor.[46] Khan's mentor, former president Ghulam Ishaq Khan, joined in the congratulations, writing to the Pakistan *Observer*: "The nation owes a debt of gratitude to its scientists ... using weapons-grade enriched uranium, a product of KRL, as fuel they had developed by the second half of 1984 a nuclear explosive device which could be assembled and detonated at short notice."[47]

The street party showed no signs of ending, with 140 million guests who normally had so little to celebrate. They made banners and papier-mâché models, outdoing each other with ever more elaborate ways of praising the blasts, even constructing scale models of the Ras Koh test site which were erected at strategic points in Islamabad, Karachi and Lahore. Newspapers published special nuclear supplements, which transformed a stepping-up of the voices for war into a jamboree. "New Clear Vision: Marching Towards a Better Tomorrow," screamed one supplement, with the words "New Clear" super-imposed on a picture of a Ghauri missile blasting into space.[48]

Pakistan was deliriously nuclear. It was also planning on being provocatively generous. The US was in no doubt that the Islamic Republic was selling its wares. More than a decade after it had been warned of the existence of Project A/B, Washington at last took seriously the claim often repeated by the Israelis, Indians and West Germans that Khan and the Pakistani military were staging a big, fat nuclear bazaar. Yet the manner of the realization was more jigsaw-like than a eureka moment, with several strange events unfolding that when put together painted a somber picture for the CIA and the White House.

One week after Pakistan's nuclear tests, a North Korean woman was shot dead at point-blank range outside the KRL guest house on Hillside Road in Islamabad, just yards from Khan's front door. Islamabad is a sterile and largely crime-free zone, which made the shooting headline news. Government officials were quick to dismiss it as a tragic accident, claiming bizarrely that the woman, Kim Sa-nae, had been caught in the crossfire of an unfortunate domestic spat.

However, when the US discovered that the dead woman had been shot execution-style and was the wife of Kang Thae Yun, economic counsellor at the North Korean embassy, a man already on the nuclear watch-list, questions were asked about the killing and its connection to Pakistan's proliferation trade.[49] The most believable logic, based on interviews conducted by the CIA, was that Kim Sa-nae had been silenced by the ISI for preparing to pass on sensitive material relating to the Pakistan–Pyongyang nuclear pact to Western contacts.

What gave this reasoning credibility was that the more US and British intelligence agencies dug, the more they unravelled about the strange world of Kang, who, in addition to his diplomatic duties, secretly represented the Changgwang Sinyong Corporation (CSC), aka the North Korean Mining Development Trading Corporation, which had supplied No-dong missiles to Pakistan in 1994. According to defectors, the most important job of North Korean embassies around the world at this time was to facilitate a plan to "seek nuclear technology."[50] And in Islamabad, this was Kang's primary role.

Western intelligence sources discovered that Kang had been a frequent visitor to Khan's house in Hillside Road and, according to Peter Griffin, teams from Pyongyang were semi-permanently lodged at the guest house next door. Griffin frequently saw them when he was supplying building materials to Khan in the mid-1990s, although the North Koreans spoke insufficient English to take part in any conversation. Griffin's insider knowledge matched what the CIA was seeing on its overheads.

In February 1998, US spy satellites had photographed North Korean technical and telemetry crews arriving at the Pakistan air force base at Sargodha, home to Pakistan's F-16 fleet and a forward weapons storage facility. From Sargodha, the Pakistan air force had launched low-flying exercises to test its F-16 pilots' ability to drop dummy nuclear weapons in 1989—fighter jets that Congress would be told had no nuclear capability, thanks to the Barlow conspiracy. Then, in March 1998, the North Korean chief of staff and the head of North Korean strategic forces also visited Sargodha, leading the CIA to conclude that the North Koreans had won access to Pakistan's range facilities, making the deal between the two countries more explicit.[51]

The US Defense Intelligence Agency (DIA) spotted more collaboration when Pyongyang flight-tested what they called Taepodong 1, a solid-fuelled missile that in every way resembled the technology Pakistan's technicians used in their Hatf range, designed by PAEC and based on the Chinese M-11.[52] Technology was now flowing both ways, with Pakistan using Shaheen Air International, an airline run by Pakistan's Air Chief Marshal Kaleem Saadat, or Pakistan air force C-130 transporters to make their deliveries.[53]

But more than missiles were on the agenda. The CIA learned that in April 1998, counsellor Kang and special technical teams from Pyongyang had witnessed Pakistan's nuclear tests in Balochistan and there was considerable and alarming evidence that North Korea was more than just a passive observer. Highly classified analysis by the US Los Alamos nuclear laboratory of air samples obtained by specialist US sniffer aircraft flying above the blast sites revealed that plutonium had been deployed in the final test, conducted away from the others beneath the Kharan Desert, leading to speculation that what had been detonated there was a plutonium bomb (whereas all those at Ras Koh had been fuelled by enriched uranium). As North Korea and not Pakistan was working on this kind of technology at the time, the conclusion drawn by the US was that that test had been conducted by Pakistan on behalf of its nuclear partner.[54] In terms of nuclear readiness, this placed North Korea far ahead of where the CIA had thought it was, since Pyongyang had yet to conduct any hot tests of its own.

There were other reasons to be concerned. US investigators learned that in the days after Kang's wife's death, he had disappeared while her body was flown back to Pyongyang on a Boeing 707 operated by Shaheen Air International. Senior sources in the Pakistani military and close to Khan maintained that the mercy mission served a double purpose. A. Q. Khan had also boarded the flight, with five pieces of luggage, including two large crates, which nobody was allowed to check, in which were P-1 and P-2 centrifuges as well as drawings, technical data and drums of uranium hexafluoride, the feedstock needed to get the enrichment process going.[55] North Korea was now a major headache, alongside Pakistan, and if the intelligence was to be believed, it was actively involved in building a uranium enrichment plant in addition to its plutonium program.

The Clinton White House convened a small team of senior officials to get behind the North Korean operation and focus on Khan, since, travelling to Pyongyang several times a month, he was the most visible common denominator in the Islamic Republic's sprawling nuclear operation, a flag to be followed.

This would represent the first serious attempt at interdicting the Pakistani operation—but Clinton's team consisted of officials so overworked that a key member characterized it as "the five minute [info] dump on Khan."[56]

Those called on board had all the necessary clearances and sufficient experience within government to work the covert resources deployed by the intelligence community. They included Robert Gallucci, who had become Clinton's special envoy on ballistic weapons and WMD, and had monitored Pakistan's nuclear growth for more than twenty years. Since growing tired of the Reagan and Bush administrations, which he characterized as having turned non-proliferation "into a fairy tale," Gallucci had negotiated the North Korean Agreed Framework in 1994, in which Pyongyang had promised to stop reprocessing fuel rods in exchange for US assistance with its nuclear power program. Gallucci was one of the few US officials to have first-hand experience in dealing with Pyongyang.[57] Working alongside him was Robert Einhorn, assistant secretary for non-proliferation, a skeletal figure, as dry as he was quick-witted. Karl Inderfurth would also participate, as would Gary Samore, a long-time State Department official, who had seen most of the highly classified stuff on Pakistan over the years and was then working as senior director for non-proliferation at Clinton's National Security Council.

There was a surfeit of material, much of it higgledy-piggledy, since over the years no organized overview had been taken of Pakistan's illicit trade. Instead, a multiplicity of agencies in intelligence, defense and foreign affairs had all assigned analysts to work on the Khan conundrum, stovepiping what they discovered, so no one agency knew everything. High on the new working group's tip sheet was a piece of intelligence gathered by the British. MI6 had become certain that Khan was using his North Korean connections to purchase materials for Kahuta, rare metals, magnets and other difficult-to-source items which were being used to amass an export stock, a storeroom of nuclear equipment for Pakistan to hawk. In 1997, UK Customs officials at Gatwick airport had intercepted a shipment of maraging steel on a British Airways flight from Moscow en route to Kang Thae Yun at the North Korean embassy in Islamabad. A little digging led to Customs discovering that Kang had brokered a deal with the All-Russian Institute of Light Alloys in Moscow to buy maraging steel, and the purchase had been made on behalf of Pakistan. In February 1998, Kang had been spotted again, this time involved in negotiations between the Tabani Corporation, based in Pakistan, and a second Russian company which manufactured mass spectrometers, lasers and carbon fiber.[58] When the intelligence also revealed that Kang was negotiating with this factory to supply maraging steel to his own government, the purchase showed it was highly probable that North Korea had entered the field of uranium enrichment. MI6 and the CIA redoubled their efforts to see if Pyongyang had established a cascade to weaponize uranium, using A. Q. Khan's P-1 or P-2 technology, both of which required maraging steel in their manufacture.

Robert Einhorn, today a senior fellow at the Center for Strategic and International Studies (CSIS), an affluent Washington think tank, recalled: "In 1998 we began to get some information of North Korean–Pakistani deals that went way beyond missiles. There was a nuclear dimension to this arrangement. There were Pakistan and North Korean weapons specialists getting together, including people from KRL. There was a pattern to the interactions." Einhorn said that démarches from the US began to flow but he was told specifically not to identify A. Q. Khan. The CIA wanted the network to keep running, in the hopes of winding up more of it. As he got to work, Einhorn reported that by January 1998 the US was observing at least nine flights per month between Islamabad and Pyongyang.

Robert Gallucci was not surprised to see North Korea ping up on the uranium enrichment radar. He had expected the North Koreans to seek out Pakistan's nuclear technology after they had agreed to freeze their plutonium activities as a result of the Agreed Framework. "Back in 1994 there wasn't a whiff of interest about Pakistani enrichment technology in Pyongyang. But by 1997 we began to focus on information about enrichment shopping by the North Koreans. Khan was an exceptionally busy person. And believe me, we knew the difference between missile deals and enrichment parts as well as the generals did in Pakistan. It was parts for gas centrifuges that Pak was trading and the North Koreans were buying, simple as that. We were on to them even though it was not yet a large-scale operation. But the CIA always said, 'let it run.' "[59]

Einhorn stepped up pressure on the Pakistanis. "At the assistant secretary level we established a US–Pakistan experts group. We met in Washington, Islamabad, New York, at least twice a year from 1998. On the Pakistan side there was a foreign ministry official who did the greetings but the military men were always in charge." The first time Einhorn broached the possibility that Pakistan was supplying enrichment technology to North Korea, the Pakistani general reacted furiously: "He got red in the face. He was incredibly angry. He was deeply chagrined, let us say." More often than not the man Pakistan selected to field Einhorn was General Feroz Khan, the head of the Combat Development Directorate, who was a close family friend of General Pervez Musharraf. However, since the Americans were unwilling to be too specific with their information, claiming it would reveal what Einhorn described as a prohibitive "human source within the KRL hierarchy," Pakistan always found ways to stall. One Pakistani official said the conversations were so vague that they wondered if the US really knew anything—or was just bluffing to trick them into revealing more.[60]

But even as Einhorn batted away, unable to tell Pakistan what he knew, the CIA, too, worked hard, trying to identify where Khan's uranium enrichment technology had been installed in North Korea. "The North is constructing a plant that could produce enough weapons-grade uranium for two or more nuclear weapons per year when fully operational."[61] North Korea certainly had the wherewithal for a uranium plant as it had numerous sources of yellowcake, having established uranium mines at half a dozen sites around the country since the 1960s. There was a uranium processing facility with a daily capacity to put through 300 kg of ore.[62] The agency also knew of a uranium concentration facility.[63] However, what was needed to make the process work and produce enough weapons-grade uranium for two bombs, roughly 50 kg of highly enriched uranium, was a cascade of at least 1,000 centrifuges.

Hwang Jang-yop, a former aide to President Kim Il-sung, who became the highest-ranking North Korean official to defect when he fled in 1997, confirmed to investigators during a debriefing that there had been a deal to trade Nodong missiles for enrichment technology after a technical delegation from KRL visited Pyongyang in the summer of 1996.[64] He claimed that the secret enrichment plant was based in a series of caves at the head of a small valley near the town of Kumch'ang-ni, 100 miles north of Pyongyang and thirty miles northwest of North Korea's nuclear reactor at Yongbyon-kun.[65] However, when in March 1999 the US government reached agreement with North Korea to visit Kumch'ang-ni, inspectors found only hollowed-out caverns.[66]

Other defectors suggested the US look at sites that included Yongjo-ri, Taechon, Pyongyang, Mount Chonma and Ha'gap, twenty miles northeast of Yongbyon-kun, where satellite photographs showed tunnel entrances being built.[67] However, Washington could not pin down an exact location, leaving the

White House to ask Islamabad to explain and assist.[68] Pakistan sat back. Einhorn kept at them: "I recall a meeting at the residence of Nawaz Sharif where we raised the North Korean centrifuge connection. It was raised at the Strobe Talbott level, at the Clinton level too. Eventually the Pakistanis said, 'We'll look into this.' They knew that they had to do something as we were not going to go away."

A. Q. Khan, Islamabad's greatest asset, was becoming a liability because of his ubiquity and ego. One of those on the Pakistan side recalled: "It began to dawn on everyone that perhaps Khan had done enough. It was time for others to take over—who were a little less public and whose anonymity suited the secret program better."[69]

For his part, Khan did not feel the least bit overexposed. This was the time he had patiently waited for, an age of A. Q. Khan in which everyone knew his face and deeds. It made up for the years of rejection and enforced silence. But his aides recalled that reacting to US pressure, the Pakistan military told Khan to move his network out of the limelight. Dubai was becoming a spent force, crawled over by Western and Israeli spies, and the last thing the Pakistan army needed was accusations that it was collaborating in nuclear proliferation.[70] It was time to make use of Khan's contacts in Southeast Asia and Africa, where he planned to relocate elements of Project A/B.

A. Q. Khan needed to get his various agents together. A wedding on 27 June 1998 provided that opportunity. The groom was B. S. A. Tahir, Khan's Dubai don, who was getting married in Kuala Lumpur and had paid for everyone to attend, including 300 staff from SMB Computers in Dubai, 100 scientists from KRL, and all Khan's old European suppliers, including Peter Griffin and Henk Slebos. Everyone's wedding outfit had been paid for by the groom, as had their airline tickets and the rental of a black limousine for their own personal use for the five days of celebration.[71] Peter Griffin recalled: "There were sightseeing trips laid on every day there wasn't a formal event and all guests were given a cigar box and an inscribed pewter jewelry box to take home."

The reception was held at the Sheraton Hotel. "It was his favorite chain since the early Dubai days when it was the only hotel in town," Griffin recalled. The bride, Nazimah, was the daughter of a former Malaysian diplomat, and Tahir's aunt, who lived in Kuala Lumpur, had brought them together, matchmaking at

Tahir's request. Nazimah wore a traditional cream and gold wedding dress and stared demurely at the floor as Khan and his agents took their seats round a table at the back. Only Griffin bucked the plan. "When I arrived at the Sheraton with my wife Anna I was led past the five-tiered wedding cake over to Khan's table: Khan, Slebos, Sajawal, Hashmi, Mohammed Farooq, General Chowhan. There were two places for myself and Anna, but I refused to sit down because of Slebos." While Griffin and his wife sat elsewhere, at Khan's table there was plenty to talk about.

Griffin noticed that Khan kept a low profile. "He made no mention of the recent nuclear tests in Pakistan and kept in the background throughout the celebration." There were uninvited guests at the wedding too, spies working for the British and US intelligence agencies, who fed back accounts that those on Khan's table spent most of the day planning their business relocation and debating a list of new clients for KRL, even though Griffin recalled that Tahir complained to him during the wedding that KRL business was drying up and he had to find something new to do.

London accountant Abdul Siddiqui was at the wedding too, and later wrote: "It was decided to visit Timbuktu again because the last visit was short and we could not see much of the city." The hotel excuse was rolled out again, the cover of monitoring progress on the Hendrina Khan Hotel a plausible way of getting them all to wherever they needed to be without raising too much suspicion. But while Siddiqui made no reference to the real purpose of the second trip, in February 1999, he listed the travellers, demonstrating the punching power of the delegation: A. Q. Khan, Brigadier Sajawal, Lieutenant General Dr. Riaz Chowhan, Dr. Farooq Hashmi, Khan's deputy, Brigadier Tajwar, director of KRL security, and Dr. Nazir Ahmed, director of KRL science and technology. "Dr. Khan told us that this time we would take a different route to Timbuktu," wrote Siddiqui. "We will fly there via Sudan and Nigeria." Snapshots taken by Siddiqui showed the most important men in Pakistan's nuclear establishment and generals from the Pakistan army squashed together inside a light aircraft, the military men in their uniforms knocking knees with the scientists. All expenses were paid for by the Pakistan government.[72]

Khan and his party arrived in Khartoum on 21 February 1999, where they were met by Sudan's education minister and "lodged at the state guest house."[73] By 24 February, Khan's party was back in Timbuktu, where they stayed for two days while Khan supposedly oversaw the construction of the Hendrina

Khan Hotel. Afterwards they headed to N'Djamena, the capital of Chad, and Niamey, the capital of Niger. Abdul Siddiqui wrote that "Niger has big uranium deposits," and in the 1970s the country had been a major supplier of yellowcake to Pakistan in deals negotiated by Zulfikar Ali Bhutto. When the CIA learned about Khan's visit to Niamey from Valerie Plame, an undercover non-proliferation officer at the CIA who had previously lived in several African countries with her diplomat husband, it was so concerned that it launched an investigation. Maybe Khan was in Niger buying yellowcake too, the CIA warned, sending Valerie Plame's husband, Joseph Wilson, to take a look. Wilson, a former US ambassador to Gabon, had good contacts with Niger's ministry of mines and knew the prime minister. However, he reported back nothing significant, concluding illicit uranium sales were highly unlikely since the French had operated Niger's mines and international uranium sales since the mid-1980s and adhered to the terms of the IAEA.[74] Wilson would be sent back to Niamey in February 2002 to investigate claims that Saddam Hussein was also sourcing yellowcake from this African country.

Next, Khan's party headed back to Khartoum, where Siddiqui finally conceded that "Dr. Khan attended to some business," something of significance since Khan was feted by the Sudanese president. Another bizarre and disturbing connection came out of this Sudan visit, spotted by the US intelligence community. During their stay, Khan's party toured the site of the al-Shifa pharmaceutical plant which was owned by Osama bin Laden and also, it appeared, according to documents procured by Israeli intelligence, co-owned by Khan.[75]

The once anonymous al-Shifa factory was then in ruins as US Tomahawk missiles had targeted it six months earlier, in August 1998, blowing it up days after two bloody attacks on US embassies in Kenya and Tanzania in which truck bombs had killed more than 200 people and injured thousands. The FBI had immediately honed in on Osama bin Laden as having funded and orchestrated the attacks, carried out by al-Qaeda.[76]

American targeters (who simultaneously decided to bomb al-Qaeda training camps in Khost, Afghanistan) had been led to the al-Shifa plant by Jamal al-Fadl, a Sudanese man who had worked for Osama bin Laden when he lived in Khartoum for four years from 1992. Al-Fadl insisted (it transpired incorrectly) that the plant had been used by bin Laden to develop chemical weapons. A. Q. Khan's visit to the al-Shifa bomb site and his links to other businesses run by bin Laden—including a bizarre claim that one of bin Laden's construction companies was erecting the Hendrina Khan Hotel in Timbuktu— led the CIA to ponder what else Khan shared with the terrorist, by then holed up again in Afghanistan.[77] Their fears of a KRL–al-Qaeda nuclear nexus, the ultimate terrorist nightmare, were fed by informer al-Fadl, who, right on many things other than al-Shifa, told interrogators that he had witnessed al-Qaeda's attempts to acquire uranium technology:

I remember Abu Fadhl al-Makkee [a bin Laden aide related to Osama by marriage] called me and he told me we hear somebody in Khartoum, he got uranium, and we need you to go and study that. We went to another office in Jambouria Street in Khartoum. [The seller] told me, "Are you serious? You want uranium?" I tell him, "Yes, I know the people, they very serious, and they want to buy it." He say, "We need $150,000. We need the money outside of Sudan." I went to Ikhlak Company, in Baraka building, in Khartoum City, and I told [al Qaeda member Abu Rida al-Suri] about the whole information and he say, "Tell him we have our machine, electric machine, we going to check the uranium, but first we want information. We want to see the cylinder and we need information about the quality." And after a few minutes they bring a big bag and they open it, and [it is a] cylinder like this tall [indicating two or three feet tall]. A lot [is] written in the cylinder. The information was like engraved.[78]

15

THE WINDOW OF VULNERABILITY

After al-Qaeda bombed the US embassies in Africa in August 1998, a US president confronting a new global terrorist threat with terrifying nuclear overtones summoned Nawaz Sharif to Washington.[1] But, as Clinton greeted Sharif at the White House on 3 December 1998, he was distracted, facing his own personal excoriation as result of the Monica Lewinsky affair and the prospect of becoming only the second president in US history to be impeached. The president offered a weak deal: the US was willing to refund most of the $470 million it owed Pakistan for the undelivered F-16 fighters and wanted in return reassurances that Pakistan would close down A. Q. Khan, its nuclear business and the terror camps in Afghanistan, many of which had survived the US missile attacks of August 1998 unharmed.[2]

Sharif agreed and then returned to Pakistan, where he did nothing at all. The prime minister was secure at home and sensed Clinton's distraction. Letting off nuclear bombs had cost Pakistan little. US sanctions had been watered down even before they had been introduced, with US agricultural aid released in July 1998 and US military and technological assistance following three months later. The International Monetary Fund, too, had offered extra financial assistance to Pakistan, worried that a new nuclear nation with foreign debts of $30 billion would fall to pieces, with the obvious consequences.[3]

Rather than reining in the nuclear program, Sharif took pleasure in vaunting KRL and, worryingly, opened it up to the leaders of like-minded Islamic states, fulfilling the manifesto penned by Generals Beg and Gul. In early May 1999, Prince Sultan bin abd al Aziz, Saudi Arabia's defense minister, held up traffic on the road from Islamabad international airport to Kahuta for four hours when he flew in for a tour of the KRL plant.[4] Sharif was also on hand when a few weeks later KRL was opened to Sheikh Abdullah bin Zayed Al-Nahyan, minister for information for the United Arab Emirates (UAE). That the second visit was connected to Project A/B was testified to by A. Q. Khan, who told the Urdu-language *Jasarat* newspaper: "Prince Abdullah bin Zayed also asked Dr. Qadeer Khan what help he could give them. Dr. Qadeer replied that Pakistan would not present the atomic bomb or a missile on a platter but could train UAE manpower."[5]

Then Pakistan reverted to type, reducing all of its policies to a single imperative, "screw India," as Sharif's counsel, Husain Haqqani, liked to put it.[6] In February 1999, Sharif had invited Indian prime minister Vajpayee to Lahore, an historic event that marked the resumption of a symbolic bus service between the two countries—the first time in years that Indians and Pakistanis would be able to cross the border. Simultaneously, thousands of Pakistani soldiers disguised as insurgents slipped across Kashmir's line of control, concealed by the winter snow, and into the Indian-administered sector in a secret military operation instigated by Sharif's new chief of army staff, General Pervez Musharraf. By May 1999, Pakistan dominated the heights above Kargil, an Indian town on the sole road link between Srinagar and Ladakh, threatening to cut off the northernmost end of Kashmir. When India's forward forces realized the insurgents were actually Pakistan army units, Vajpayee exploded. Sharif had betrayed him, making the hawkish BJP leader look like a foolish peacenik. This was an invasion and India launched a counter-attack. For the first time in Kashmir, the Indian air force was deployed to bomb Pakistan's troops off the peaks, while both countries sent thousands of soldiers scrambling into the foothills. After an Indian helicopter and two jet fighters were downed over Pakistani territory, India threatened to cross the border, raising the doomsday scenario of two nuclear powers going head to head.[7] When President Clinton learned of satellite overheads that appeared to show Pakistan unveiling nuclear-tipped missiles from bunkers at its air force base at Sargodha, he summoned Sharif back to Washington.

The Kargil operation was the brainchild of army chief Pervez Musharraf, who was obsessed with Kashmir. Having led an attack on Indian positions in Siachen in 1987, he had been among those out front in 1988 asking Bhutto to change the rules of war so as to enable the army to launch surprise attacks in Kashmir without her say-so. The strategy had been rejected and then put again to Bhutto directly by Musharraf in 1992, when she appointed him director general of military operations, and although he had been refused, Bhutto had allowed the general to send thousands of infiltrators into Kashmir, creating turmoil. The roots of this new war lay in October 1998, when Sharif had sacked General Karamat as his army chief.

General Karamat's mistake had been to lobby for Pakistan to form a national security council, which the paranoid Sharif read as a bid by the military to take over politics. Having got rid of Karamat, the soldier least likely in Pakistan to mount a coup, Sharif was quickly convinced by his new man, General Musharraf, that India was "creeping forward" towards the line of control demarcating Pakistan-run Kashmir from that administered by India. Musharraf wrote: "We know the Indian army had procured large quantities of high-altitude equipment, special weapons, and new snow scooters and snowmobiles."[8] In reality, India was not planning a pre-emptive strike and Sharif later insisted he was never consulted about the Kargil infiltration until it was a fait accompli. "We went to the Indians and they thought we were friends," he recalled.[9] "Then our army invaded and India called and said, 'You've stabbed us in the back.' But all the time it was me who was being stabbed in the back by Musharraf. I knew nothing about Kargil until after the soldiers had marched over the line of control. Then, when our soldiers were in place, I had to accept we were at war and of course we understood that everyone was now worried that things could go nuclear very easily."

Whether Sharif was in reality pushed into a war by Musharraf, or was attempting to diminish his role in the crisis as Musharraf later claimed, when he flew to Washington on 4 July 1999, the Americans were unsure as to who was really in control in Islamabad. The Saudi ambassador, Prince Bandar bin Sultan, a long-term Sharif ally, was asked to soften up Pakistan's prime minister in the car ride over from Dulles airport. Bruce Riedel, at the National Security Council, recalled: "Bandar called me up and told me the PM was distraught. He was deeply worried about the direction the crisis was going towards, but equally worried about his own hold on power and the threat from his military chiefs."[10] The US was right to be worried, as Sharif doubted his ability to call off the war. Equally worrying, Sharif had brought his wife and children with him to the US, suggesting that he was prepared not to go back or that there might be no Pakistan to return to.[11]

When Clinton met Sharif at Blair House two hours later, the president began by saying he had just read John Keegan's new book on the First World War and the Kargil crisis seemed, to him, eerily like 1914: armies mobilizing and disaster looming with no one capable of calling it off.[12] Riedel recalled: "Clinton asked Sharif if he knew how advanced the threat of nuclear war really was? Did he know, for example, that his military was preparing to use nuclear missiles?"[13] Sharif shook his head. The president warned that he had a statement ready for release that would pin all the blame for Kargil on Pakistan if the prime minister refused to pull his forces back. Clinton questioned whether he could trust Sharif on anything since, despite his promising to help bring Osama bin Laden to justice in December 1998, the Americans knew that the ISI had continued to work with bin Laden and the Taliban to foment terrorism.

Sharif briefly left the room to seek advice. He returned and Riedel recalled: "He was getting exhausted. He denied that he had ordered the preparation of their missile force, said he was against war but was worried for his life in Pakistan." There was a break in the middle of the day: Clinton lying down on the sofa at Blair House while Sharif went to his hotel room for a nap. When they reconvened, Clinton placed the prepared statement on the table. Sharif left the room again to read it to his advisers and then returned finally ready to order a volte-face and call for his troops to withdraw back to the line of control. "The mood changed in a nanosecond," recalled Riedel.[14] "Clinton told Sharif that they had tested their personal relationship hard that day but they had reached the right ending." Sharif posed for photographs with Clinton at the White House before returning to Dulles airport. "His mood was glum," said Riedel. "He was not looking forward to his trip home. The PM knew he had done the right thing for Pakistan and the world, but he was not sure his army would see it that way."

Sharif pulled back the troops. But two months later his brother Shahbaz Sharif turned up in Washington. Inderfurth recalled meeting him at the Willard Hotel: "We were hoping to see what new thinking there might be in engaging India. But after lunch Shahbaz took me off to a corner table and confided that his brother was under intense pressure."[15] A few days earlier, while attending the funeral of his father-in-law, Nawaz Sharif had been warned by Pakistan's attorney general that he was about to be unseated in a military coup.[16] "The domestic situation was very difficult," remembered Inderfurth. "They were bringing their forces back from the line of control. There was endless footage of soldiers trudging home. Shahbaz didn't ask for anything, he just wanted to inform us of the tensions. But the message was clear."

The following month, Nawaz Sharif came out fighting. He decided on a high-stakes game, one that he had first played in 1991 against Generals Beg and Gul, when he had rounded on them before they had time to oust him. In October 1999, he waited for his army chief to leave the country. Musharraf had been invited to a military conference in Sri Lanka, and when he returned on 12 October aboard a Pakistan International Airlines flight from Colombo bound for Karachi, prime minister Sharif ordered that Karachi international airport be closed as PK 805 made its final approach. The runway lights were dimmed. Three fire trucks blocked the tarmac. The Airbus was full of children returning for the new school term and Musharraf later remembered how he had been watching the winking lights of the city below him when he was called to the cockpit.[17]

The pilot told him the plane had been ordered out of Pakistani airspace but had only one hour's worth of fuel remaining, saying, "Sir, I think it has something to do with you."[18] Musharraf recalled: "I could only guess that prime minister Nawaz Sharif was moving against me; he was endangering a lot of lives. Since India was the country closest to us we would have no option but to go there ... This would put us in the hands of our most dangerous enemy, against whom we had fought three full-blown wars." Musharraf ordered the pilot to stay in the air.

After a series of furious mobile-phone calls to the civil aviation authority, army headquarters and the prime minister's residence, Nawaz Sharif relented and PK 805 was given permission to land. Suspicious of how quickly Sharif had rolled over, Musharraf, still in the sky, made radio contact with a personal friend in Karachi, a major general who told him it was safe to land as the army had taken control of the airport and senior officers were on the way to arrest Nawaz Sharif in Rawalpindi. "I still wanted to make doubly certain," said Musharraf, asking the major general to name his two dogs.[19] "I asked, because I knew that he knew them. If it was someone impersonating him or if he was under duress, he would not have given the correct names. 'Dot and Buddy, sir,' he replied without hesitation." PK 805 landed with just seven minutes' worth of fuel to spare, forcing Nawaz Sharif out of office. "Musharraf charged me with plane-jacking," Sharif lamented later.[20] "But how can you hijack a plane when you're standing on the ground?"

Sharifuddin Pirzada, lawyer to successive presidents and dictators, got the call at 2 a.m. "I was alarmed," he recalled.[21] "I picked up the phone and it was a general who introduced himself as Pervez Musharraf. To be frank, I had never heard of him. He said, 'Never mind, turn on the television.' There was a looped interview playing on PTV, Musharraf explaining that Sharif had been deposed and that the army was in control."

Pirzada met his new boss that afternoon at 4.30 p.m. "He had the same plans as Zia. He wanted to declare martial law and become a martial law administrator. I told him times had changed and he shouldn't pursue the Zia route." Musharraf asked the generals who accompanied him and the stenographers who attended every high-level meeting to leave the room, before closing the door. "Now we were one to one," remembered Pirzada. "I told him to be more modern, perhaps a 'chief executive.'" Musharraf liked this idea and, calling his generals back in, announced he was now Pakistan's chief executive, as well as retaining his military ranks as chief of army staff and chairman of the joint chiefs of staff committee. Only the lesser positions were to be shared around.

Lieutenant Generals Jamshed Gulzar, Mohammed Aziz and Muzzaffar Usmani—three confirmed jihadists who had been involved intimately with Afghanistan, the Taliban and Osama bin Laden—were all given senior positions in the new military administration.[22] General Mahmood Ahmed, the commander of 10 Corps which guarded Rawalpindi, was rewarded as the new ISI chief for having secured the capital and arrested Nawaz Sharif. He was another born-again, a convert to radical Deobandi Islam, his faith found while in Zia's newly religious army. He was also an avowed ally of the Taliban and sympathetic to Osama bin Laden. General Ghulam Ahmed Khan, a former cavalry commander, became chief of staff, and Brigadier General Salahuddin Satti, the commander of 111 Brigade and a former brigade major from Musharraf's Siachen days, would assist. Musharraf told them he was to be chief executive but they were his equals and he would take counsel from them. His next action was to pardon Major General Zaheerul Islam Abbasi, a leading figure in the radical Tablighi Jamaat whose coup plot in September 1995 had failed to oust Benazir Bhutto.

In November, Pirzada flew off to launch the coup on the world, seeking support from Japan, the Gulf, Egypt, the UK and the US. In London, Musharraf's emissary met with Lord Goldsmith, the attorney general, and members of Tony Blair's cabinet. "The rights of citizens will remain intact, the country is still functioning," Pirzada pledged. "I got full support extended by the UK with one proviso—don't take us for granted. Hold elections, do something about the transfer of power, take care of the nuclear issue."[23] The following month Musharraf turned to the nuclear issue. President Clinton was coming over and Musharraf asked Pirzada: "Should we sign the NPT?" Pirzada replied: "If India signs we will sign too." India was planning to do nothing of the sort, so Pakistan's unsecured nuclear weapons program passed into the hands of a military dictator.

Karl Inderfurth was one of the first foreign diplomats into Islamabad after the coup, visiting in January 2000, accompanied by Michael Sheehan, the State Department's counter-terrorism expert. One notable absentee was Robert Einhorn, Clinton's non-proliferation specialist. Inderfurth said: "The fact that Mike was included and Bob was left out showed our priorities at that time. Our agenda was counter-terrorism, al-Qaeda, Taliban and democracy. We had somehow divorced these from the nuclear threat and A. Q. Khan. Of course, the first thing Musharraf wanted to talk about was how Pakistan had never had real democracy. What had passed for democracy during the 1990s was a sham."[24] Benazir Bhutto had spent much of her second term filling the Supreme Court with actions against the Sharif family company Ittifaq, which was accused of tax evasion, fraud, smuggling and corruption, and Nawaz Sharif had spent much time in his second term ordering investigations into similar allegations against Bhutto and her husband, Asif Ali Zadari. Musharraf told the Americans: "Things are going to change. I intend to bring true democracy to Pakistan."[25]

Chief executive Musharraf also had his own ideas about the terrorist threat over the border in Afghanistan. Before the coup, Nawaz Sharif had agreed to support a CIA operation to send an elite Pakistani commando team into Afghanistan to kidnap Osama bin Laden from his base at Tarnak Farms, an al-Qaeda training camp near Kandahar, and turn him over to the Americans. He would have been secretly flown out and held in a third country inside a commercial shipping container fitted with a dentist's chair with restraints. When the search parties had given up, the shipping container and its contents would have been loaded into the back of a C-130 and flown to a landing strip at El Paso, Texas, where bin Laden would have been interrogated in his container, still strapped to the chair. The Americans would have admitted to having him only after he had been charged.[26] "But from the start, Musharraf made it clear he was not going to pursue that option," recalled Inderfurth, adding that Pakistan's new chief executive was also unwilling to act on US intelligence that Abu Zubaida, al-Qaeda's chief recruiter, was living openly in the Pakistan city of Peshawar.[27]

Inderfurth warned Musharraf that the view from Washington was that Pakistan was actively supporting al-Qaeda and the Taliban. Musharraf became irritated. Inderfurth recalled: "He said, 'I'm going with my knapsack to Kandahar to see Mullah Omar [the one-eyed Taliban chief]. I'll sleep on the floor and talk to him, military man to military man.' Of course, he never went, he knew he didn't have a chance of persuading Omar to give himself up and didn't want to be associated with a failed mission. But he did send Mahmood Ahmed, his ISI general." Given Ahmed's sympathies with the Taliban, no one was surprised when nothing came of this mission.

While Musharraf, with his center-parting and neatly clipped mustache, did not come across as a fundamentalist to officials like Inderfurth, the Clinton administration was worried that a significant number of senior generals in Pakistan's new military structure owed their allegiance far more to men like bin Laden than to the West. There was firm intelligence that showed proximity between these military leaders, KRL and al-Qaeda, with nuclear material being offered for sale in Pakistan and Afghanistan, further cementing the idea that, due to the unsecured nature of the Pakistan nuclear program, terrorists might get their hands on a doomsday device. Such was the fear that in the spring of 2000, CIA director George Tenet established a national security advisory panel, a team of security analysts, chaired by Admiral David Jeremiah, a former vice chairman of the joint chiefs of staff. It was asked to think the unthinkable. Robert Gallucci, who sat on the panel, recalled: "It was all sources, all clearances. Of the fifteen people with me, ten to twelve were flag officers [generals]. I was the nuclear freak and got briefings set up on the nuclear terrorist thing. Every single scenario was extremely scary, and entirely believable. There was lots and lots of intelligence. Put it this way, the US number one enemy was looking more and more like Pakistan."[28]

Much of the material presented to Jeremiah's panel came from a highly classified CIA program which since 1996 had been tracking bin Laden's attempts to get his hands on nuclear material. The program operated from a "virtual" station located in government offices near CIA headquarters in Langley, Virginia. Technically it was a subsection of the CIA's counter-terrorist center, but the office appeared on organizational charts identified only as "Terrorist Financial Links." To the small team who worked there under chief Mike Scheuer, it was Alec Station, named after Scheuer's son, and one of its first successful operations had been to turn the Sudanese al-Qaeda operative Jamal al-Fadl into an informer.[29]

By the time Musharraf took over as Pakistan's chief executive, al-Fadl's claim that bin Laden aides had been pursuing uranium in the early 1990s had been backed up by another founding al-Qaeda member, arrested in Germany. In September 1998, Mamdouh Mahmud Salim was charged with conspiracy to use weapons of mass destruction. An affidavit filed by the FBI concluded: "In late 1993, after bin Laden had issued a private fatwa to al-Qaeda members and associates indicating that the United States was an enemy that needed to be attacked, members of al-Qaeda made efforts to procure enriched uranium for the purpose of developing nuclear weapons." Documents showed that the proposed purchase was "routed to Salim for his review ... and he indicated that the project ... should proceed."[30] The source of the enriched uranium was not given, but Pakistan was in the frame. Then Scheuer's unit learned that al-Qaeda even had a WMD chief, Abu Khabab al-Masri, who conducted crude chemical weapons experiments at Darunta training camp, outside Jalalabad.[31] Al-Masri poisoned dogs with chemical or biological agents and then videotaped them as they died. In one of the most alarming written instructions, recovered by Scheuer's unit, al-Masri referred to connections between al-Qaeda and Pakistan's scientists. "As you instructed us you will find attached a summary of the discharges from a traditional nuclear reactor, amongst which are radioactive elements that could be used for military ends. One can use them to contaminate an area or halt the advance of the enemy. It is possible to get more information from our Pakistani friends who have great experience in this sphere."[32] What al-Masri was considering was a dirty bomb, and he was looking actively for help to build it from Pakistani scientists working in the nuclear industry.

*

In March 2000, Bill Clinton became the first US president to visit Pakistan in thirty years—despite the concerns of Bruce Riedel that Musharraf had done nothing to deserve it. He had failed to show he was willing to rein in the Taliban or al-Qaeda.[33] Clinton also brushed aside CIA reports that al-Qaeda was planning to assassinate him in Islamabad, joking that he would invite Newt Gingrich to fly over with him and let him disembark first—wearing a Clinton mask.[34] In the end, Clinton entered the country aboard an unmarked Gulfstream jet, with a decoy painted with Air Force One colors leading the way.[35] In an hour-and-a-half session with Musharraf at Army House on 25 March, Clinton laid it out for the general: if the US was to warm to him he had to show restraint in Kashmir, exert pressure on terrorist groups and help apprehend Osama bin Laden. Musharraf was slippery, according to Inderfurth, claiming it was difficult to convince "people who believe that God is on their side."[36] No one was entirely clear if he was referring to the religious ideologues within his own ranks or al-Qaeda. Inderfurth recalled that A. Q. Khan was mentioned— but way down the agenda.[37] To make sure Musharraf got the nuclear message, Clinton addressed it in a live broadcast on Pakistan TV: "I ask Pakistan to be a leader in non-proliferation in your own self-interest and to help us prevent dangerous technologies spreading to those who might have no reservations about using them."[38]

As with everything else, Musharraf was dismissive. He told Clinton he already had the A. Q. Khan situation in hand, while refusing to expand upon the "situation" that Pakistan needed to deal with. Pre-empting Clinton's visit, Musharraf had instigated an overhaul of Pakistan's nuclear weapons program that included the re-establishment of a National Command Authority, of which he made himself chairman. Musharraf told Clinton these measures proved that Pakistan could be a responsible custodian of nuclear weapons, by relieving the PAEC and KRL directors of many of their duties, including control over accounting and auditing, foreign travel, security and the screening of personnel. All staff in nuclear-related jobs would in future have to undergo "personal reliability tests."[39] Officially the National Command Authority was run by a secretariat, the Strategic Plans Division. Musharraf appointed his close friend, General Feroz Khan, as its director.

Husain Haqqani, counsellor to three former prime ministers, slung into jail by Musharraf for many months after the coup, recalled: "It was another takeover and nothing more than that. Here was yet another dictator shoring up his personal power over a useful nuclear trophy. This was nothing to do with Clinton's requests for moderation or an end to proliferation."[40] The army had made sure its control over KRL was watertight during Bhutto's second term, when General Ziauddin had been foisted on Khan as the overall head of security. Chief executive Musharraf planned to go even further and take over KRL completely, and in the process knock out the one person in Pakistan most likely to eclipse him: the Father of the Bomb.

But first Musharraf would need to make an overt display of strong-arm tactics to get the US off his back. After Clinton returned to Washington, Musharraf's new man, General Feroz Khan, met Einhorn's special group and assured them that his namesake A. Q. Khan would have to abide by the new regulations of the National Command Authority along with everyone else.[41] He also advised that Lieutenant General Syed Mohammed Amjad, head of Pakistan's National Accountability Bureau, had been ordered to quiz A. Q. Khan over allegations of corruption and private profiteering. Nawaz Sharif had used the same ruse in 1998, telling the US that the ISI was investigating Khan, despite the fact that the spy directorate's chief knew of no such investigation.[42] Amjad's report would never surface and he later resigned, disaffected with his brief. The elusive inquiries—which got nowhere or never happened—coincided with a handful of high-profile, theatrical raids conducted by the ISI, including the storming of a C-130 plane that was supposedly chartered by Khan and heading for North Korea. When nothing incriminating was found, Musharraf claimed: "We got some suspicious reports ... [but] unfortunately, either you know, he was tipped off or whatever ... we just could not catch them red-handed."[43] One of those who led the raids was more candid. "We rang KRL first and checked the coast was clear. This was meant to demonstrate a point."[44] Husain Haqqani was incredulous. "It was a lot of hot air. The military had been in sole control of KRL and PAEC since Zia's days. They had always been in charge of Khan—in that all of his activities were governed by their orders. And now he was being portrayed as operating beyond the state. It was a put-on show for the US."

It was to the military orders that governed Khan that Musharraf next turned. Since Zia's time, every sale had been sanctioned by the military and now Pakistan's chief executive decided to legitimize nuclear proliferation altogether. Musharraf ordered the publishing in national newspapers of the secret menu that A. Q. Khan had long been touting around Iran, Iraq, North Korea, Africa and the Middle East. Everything on the menu would still be available, the government announced, the only difference being that in future a permit would be required from the Defense Control Committee, chaired by Musharraf and whomever he picked as his prime minister. The advertisement hit the streets on 24 July 2000, and Washington was horrified by what it read:

The items listed in the advertisement can be in the form of metal alloys, chemical compounds, or other materials containing any of the following: 1. Natural, depleted or enriched uranium; 2. Thorium, plutonium or zirconium; 3. Heavy water, tritium, or beryllium; 4. Natural or artificial radioactive materials with more than 0.002 microcuries per gram; 5. Nuclear-grade graphite with a boron equivalent content of less than five parts per million and density greater than 1.5 g/cubic centimeter.[45]

It was the whole shebang, everything anyone needed to make a nuclear bomb. Listed was equipment "for the production, use or application of nuclear energy and generation of electricity," including "gas centrifuges and magnet baffles for the separation of uranium isotopes" and "UF_6 mass spectrometers and frequency changers." They made it appear that Pakistan was for the first time applying rigorous export controls to a prohibited trade that was to be governed by the Pakistan authorities. In reality the advertisement blew to pieces the Nuclear Non-Proliferation Treaty and decades of arms controls which had to date kept the nuclear club down to five declared and a handful of undeclared nuclear powers—and was Musharraf's clumsy bid to find a get-rich-quick scheme for Pakistan.

Former army chief General Beg saw the advertisements for what they were and, writing in an Urdu newspaper, championed them as the Islamic Atoms for Peace. "This is the best way for Pakistan to pay off her debts," he argued, conceding that Pakistan "used to sell atomic material and equipment quietly and secretly."[46] Beg bemoaned the fact that his country had always been singled out for harsh treatment, compared to "the former Soviet Union whose atomic technology found its way on to the market after its break-up and there was no ban or hurdle on it. Who got hold of this atomic material nobody knows but Pakistan is attempting to earn its foreign exchange in an honorable way." It was all so un-extraordinary now, this conspiracy to hawk nuclear weapons on the black market, that General Beg felt quite secure in admitting in public that Pakistan had long been flogging off its KRL stock in secret.

The Clinton administration was shocked and demanded that Islamabad withdraw the advertisements.[47] Pakistan's ministry of commerce set to it and in a matter of hours retracted the notices, pulping newspapers that had yet to be sold, lamely claiming that the sales procedures laid out in the advertisements were "under reconsideration." But the message conveyed to the wider world was striking: new boss, but business as usual.

The dummy investigations had done nothing to convince the US that Musharraf was taking proliferation seriously. The advertisements confirmed that belief. In the CIA's biannual report to Congress on the acquisition of WMD technology for the year 2000, Pakistan was for the first time described as a potential supplier of black-market nuclear technology. "As their domestic capabilities grow, traditional recipients of WMD and missile technology could emerge as new suppliers of technology and expertise. Many of these countries—such as India, Iran and Pakistan—do not adhere to export restraints."[48] It was tentative and highly dampened, given what was really known by the CIA as well as the groups under Admiral Jeremiah and in the White House that were tracking A. Q. Khan. But in the mute language of diplomacy, a discourse of heightened sensitivities, it constituted what Gallucci described as "a serious bollocking" for an Islamabad that was up to no good—and had to stop. However, rather than rollback, KRL and Project A/B went into overdrive, reaching beyond its existing customers to a new one in the Middle East, offering to sell it a ready-made centrifuge enrichment plant.

Colonel Muammar Gaddafi's interest in Pakistan's nuclear program went back the early 1970s, when he had offered to fund Zulfikar Ali Bhutto's early attempts to build an atomic bomb. But supplying enrichment technology to Tripoli was something altogether new. Gaddafi had been pleased to be the sponsor of an Islamic bomb that would counter the hegemony of the licensed nuclear powers, and by the late 1990s the notoriously quixotic and wayward leader was seeking his own. To meet his request, KRL began importing large consignments of maraging steel from China, quantities that went way beyond Pakistan's own needs. When the US first heard a whisper of this trade in the summer of 2000, the information was shared with Pakistan—which did nothing, pointing to the new National Command Authority as evidence of a root-and-branch reform. Clinton's non-proliferation adviser, Robert Einhorn, flew to Islamabad to warn the Strategic Plans Division director in person: "Either you're not on top of this or you are complicit. Either one is disturbing."[49]

Although the Americans had still not named A. Q. Khan in any of their reports, the response to Einhorn's roughing up of General Feroz Khan came directly from the Father of the Bomb. Shortly after Einhorn's visit, he told an interviewer that Pakistan was in a position to "hit almost all the major Indian cities" and had a "stockpile of missiles and atom bombs." It included a new nuclear missile with a 1,550-mile range.[50] "It is ready for testing," said Khan. "We are waiting for orders."[51] These were not the words of a man frozen out of Pakistan's nuclear weapons program or of someone beyond Musharraf's control.

If any more evidence were needed that Khan's proliferation activities were being actively promoted by Musharraf's military regime, it came in November 2000 when the Pakistan army staged "IDEAS 2000," an international munitions fair in Karachi.[52] The central exhibit was a large Khan Research Laboratories booth promoting the sale of centrifuges with an after-sales consultancy service that included "installation, repair and maintenence" thrown in. Alan Coke, a senior editor from *Jane's Defense Weekly*, who visited the KRL booth, recalled: "They were handing out glossy brochures offering the kind of technology that would be directly applicable in a nuclear weapons program, the whole kit and caboodle, all in one." When Coke asked a KRL representative if everything in the brochure was cleared for export he was told: "Of course, it wouldn't be on the shelf if it wasn't."[53]

In November 2000, with the Lewinsky scandal having tarred Clinton as mendacious and untrustworthy, a venerable and seemingly dignified Republican dynasty snatched victory, pushing George W. Bush into office as president along with an aggressive and apparently well-seasoned foreign policy team, chosen to counter the new commander-in-chief's perceived lack of experience.

Most of those in his "dream team" had long-running and intertwined careers in government and several had spent considerable time in the Pentagon. Colin Powell, the new secretary of state, and Richard Armitage, his deputy, had both served in Vietnam. Donald Rumsfeld, the new defense secretary, having been elected as a Republican to Congress under Nixon, for whom he also acted as the director of the Office of Economic Opportunity and ambassador to NATO, had also run the Defense Department for Gerald Ford, with Dick Cheney as his administrative assistant. Cheney, who had gone on to be defense secretary in the George H. W. Bush administration and was now vice president, had brought up Colin Powell, appointing him as chairman of the joint chiefs of staff in 1989. Richard Armitage had also worked with Powell before, when the two men helped run the Pentagon in the Reagan administration, Powell as deputy national security adviser and Armitage as assistant secretary of defense. Paul Wolfowitz, Rumsfeld's new deputy, had also worked closely with Armitage in the Reagan years (as assistant secretary of state) and had once been Dick Cheney's top aide. Condoleezza Rice was the only outsider, a protégée of Bush senior's national security adviser, Brent Scowcroft. A tight-knit team, with a common belief in military superiority, its members famously revelled in the nickname of the Vulcans, bestowed upon them during the presidential election, which referenced the Roman god of fire—and was soon mocked, after Bush got in, when the Vulcans were rechristened the "retreads."[54]

But one area that many at the State Department and the CIA hoped the Vulcans would surely not revisit was the stone-cold bullying that had triggered the Richard Barlow conspiracy, the evasion of truth and hoodwinking of Congress, the papering over of Pakistan's nuclear capabilities in support of the Afghan conflict and a $1.4 billion fighter deal. Many of those in the new inner circle had actively participated in the undermining of Barlow and the rewriting of intelligence that had thrown US non-proliferation policy off-kilter for a decade, something that Wolfowitz would come close to admitting at his nomination hearing for the job of deputy defense secretary, saying, "I specifically sensed that people thought we could somehow construct a policy on a house of cards, that the Congress wouldn't know what the Pakistanis were doing."[55]

The Vulcans immediately set about ushering in a profoundly new and uncompromising approach to US foreign policy. Their vision was of an unchallengeable America set free from empathy and moral equivalence, a military power so brutal it no longer needed to make accommodations to international treaties it did not believe in or to political correctness which, the Vulcans warned, had lamed US foreign policy. Instead of engagement, America would take pre-emptive action. "Now is not the time to defend outdated treaties but to defend the American people," Bush had declared in his acceptance speech at the Republican convention in 1999, foreshadowing an age in which America's rights and other nations' wrongs would dictate policy.[56]

For too long America had been too conciliatory, too understanding and too accommodating. A focused and vastly improved US military fighting force would spend less time observing and more time prosecuting the nation's future wars. From the start, this new administration cast aside traditional policies of containment and deterrence. It adopted a more confrontational approach and, critically—and to the dismay of large sections of the State Department, who had watched Pakistan prove the case for proliferation being the number-one policy consideration—non-proliferation was viewed with pronounced skepticism.

Instead of talking about ridding the world of dangerous weapons, the Vulcans talked of eliminating dangerous regimes. Norm Wulf, one of America's most senior diplomats, who had worked for years at the Arms Control and Disarmament Agency (ACDA) and had gone on to play senior roles in the flashpoint of North Korea, recalled: "It was a clear shift away from the architecture of non-proliferation and into the world of regime change. We can't stop the spread of the bombs, the Bush team immediately said, but we can get rid of the bad people wielding them."[57]

It was a policy that owed much to Albert Wohlstetter, a political science professor at Chicago University, who had been Paul Wolfowitz's PhD dissertation adviser in the 1960s. A former Rand Corporation analyst, who had done contract work for the US Air Force out of Rand's Santa Monica headquarters, Wohlstetter had become one of America's leading experts on the theory and strategy of nuclear war and focused attention on the concept of America facing a "window of vulnerability." A sudden threat from a rapidly advancing opponent, such as the Soviet Union, would leave only a short time in which to frame a reaction and act decisively. Wohlstetter, an ardent anti-Communist, believed that long-term policies such as détente and containment were doomed, as potential enemies could never be trusted and had to be neutralized by pre-emptive action as quickly as possible.[58]

These ideas had a profound impact on Wolfowitz, the son of a Jewish refugee from Poland, who in the summer of 1969 had been persuaded by Wohlstetter to go to Washington to work for the Committee to Maintain a Prudent Defense Policy, a think tank that was lobbying Congress to construct an anti-ballistic missile defense system for the US. While there, Wolfowitz had met Richard Perle, an up-and-coming staffer on Capitol Hill who also held hard-line views on arms reduction, and the two young men cemented a friendship that would lead to them becoming among the US's most powerful voices for pre-emption in the decades to come.

In 1973, Wohlstetter recommended Wolfowitz for a job at ACDA, which had just been taken over by another former Rand strategist, Fred Ilké, who was equally unenthusiastic about arms control. Ilké and Wolfowitz were among a group of hawks deeply skeptical of the Anti-Ballistic Missile Treaty that had been signed by US president Nixon and Soviet premier Leonid Brezhnev the previous year.[59] Three years later, Wolfowitz became involved in Team B, a group of independent experts who were invited by CIA director George H. W. Bush to review classified data about the nuclear intentions of the Soviet Union. They concluded (incorrectly) that the Kremlin believed it could win a nuclear war against America.[60]

Wolfowitz took to Wohlstetter's empirical view of the world and would return to the image of a window of vulnerability after the US was, for the first time in its history, subjected to a terrorist attack at home in 2001. Moving on from ACDA, Wolfowitz had worked at the Pentagon under Carter, and while the Reagan administration finished off ACDA he became director of the policy planning office, then assistant secretary of state for East Asian and Pacific affairs, and finally US ambassador to Indonesia. Appointed under secretary of defense by George H. W. Bush, Wolfowitz rode out the Clinton years in academia, as dean of international studies at Johns Hopkins University, before returning to Washington with the Republicans in 2000.

By late 2001, Wolfowitz was among the officials in the George W. Bush administration pushing hardest for the US intelligence community to come up with stronger information on America's enemies. But not on Pakistan or the nuclear ambitions of bin Laden and al-Qaeda. Not on the Islamic hard-liners within the Pakistan army and its nuclear establishment, who were linking up with radicals in the desert around Jalalabad and Khost. Wolfowitz wanted to focus resources on Iraq and its ties to terrorism and WMD. Iraq was unfinished business, after the Gulf War in 1991 had left Saddam Hussein in power. It would be a test of America's new strength to wipe out the old tyrant, who, Wolfowitz believed, was becoming increasingly irascible. The Vulcans, particularly Condoleezza Rice—who had once mocked herself, saying, "For much of my career ... I was one of the high priestesses of arms control—a true believer"—backed the Wolfowitz line.[61]

Donald Rumsfeld, too, had consistently argued against détente and for an invasion of Iraq, long before he joined Bush's team. In January 1998, as a congressman, he had been among the signatories of a letter urging President Clinton to "eliminate" Saddam Hussein, warning, "The security of the world in the first part of the twenty-first century will be determined largely by how we handle this threat."[62] The letter was co-signed by R. James Woolsey, the former CIA director, and William Schneider, Jr., chairman of the Defense Science Board, a federal advisory committee established to provide independent advice to the secretary of defense, and was issued by a then little-known conservative Washington think tank, the Project for the New American Century. The project produced many of the neoconservatives who would go on to take key official and unofficial positions under Bush, including Richard Armitage, Richard Perle, Paul Wolfowitz, John Bolton (Bush's future adviser on non-proliferation policy and later US ambassador to the UN), philosopher Francis Fukuyama, Robert Kagan (co-founder of the Project, former speechwriter for George Shultz and neoconservative scholar) and Zalmay Khalilzad (Bush's future US ambassador to Afghanistan and later Iraq). All of them signed the Clinton letter about Iraq.

Later that year, Donald Rumsfeld headed the Commission to Assess the Ballistic Missile Threat to the United States, the so-called Rumsfeld Commission, which counted among its members Paul Wolfowitz, R. James Woolsey and William Schneider, Jr. They, along with five other members, concluded in July 1998 that the threat was far greater than the CIA and other intelligence agencies had so far reported: "Concerted efforts by a number of overtly or potentially hostile nations to acquire ballistic missiles with biological or nuclear payloads pose a growing threat to the United States, its deployed forces, friends and allies."[63] Pakistan was nowhere on the list. The three most worrisome countries for Rumsfeld et al. were Iran, Iraq and North Korea—the future "Axis of Evil" powers. Rumsfeld in particular focused on Iraq, and when the Republicans came to power in 2001 he would make sure this was Bush's focus.

Soon after Bush took office, the Vulcans did broach Pakistan. But as Richard Clarke, the national coordinator for counter-terrorism, described it, only "a box was ticked."[64] In the spring of 2001, George Tenet gathered together a small group of senior officials, including Colin Powell, Richard Armitage, Powell's deputy, Stephen Hadley, the deputy national security adviser, John McLaughlin, the deputy CIA director, and Robert Joseph, non-proliferation director at the National Security Council, to go through the "known knowns." North Korea was undoubtedly a client of the Pakistan nuclear trade. There was also the Pakistan–Iran pact, which appeared to be still functioning, and evidence of offers Islamabad had made to sell nuclear weapons to Iraq. There were also the recent rumors of a deal between Pakistan and Libya.[65]

Robert Einhorn, who had agreed to stay on as Bush's assistant secretary for non-proliferation in order to ensure continuity, recalled: "A very small number of people got involved. Any names added to the list had to be sanctioned personally by Tenet."[66] Meeting once a month, the group tracked Khan by logging flights and meetings, intercepting letters and phone calls, while they tried to build the bigger picture. "The CIA guys would grudgingly come over to share anything new with us policy types," remembered Einhorn. "State was always making the case to roll up the network now, to stop it doing more damage. The CIA would make a plausible case to keep watching, let the network run so eventually we could pick it up by the roots, not just lop off the tentacles. We'd debate and always decide to continue following. The policy people were nervous about leaving it too long." Einhorn's colleagues accused the CIA of being "addicted" to collecting intelligence rather than using it to act quickly. Senior analysts at the agency believed only they understood the breadth and depth of the problem and should dictate when to act.[67]

Einhorn was the only one who was edgy: "I kept looking behind me. There was nobody covering my back. I went to Armitage and said, 'You need to take this one on. I can't do it alone.' He told me, 'Go see Bob Joseph.' It went on like that, displacing responsibility, until I left in September 2001." The Bush administration was not interested in acting on Pakistan, or had no idea of how to act. They were far more interested in eliminating Pakistan's clients: Iran, Iraq, Libya and North Korea.

Robert Einhorn was not the only worried long-termer. Soon after Bush took office, Richard Clarke briefed Condoleezza Rice, Dick Cheney, Colin Powell and Stephen Hadley on the al-Qaeda threat and its links to Pakistan. "My message was stark," Clarke recalled. "Al-Qaeda was at war with us, it is a highly capable organization, probably with sleeper cells in the US, and it is clearly planning a major series of attacks against us."[68] Clarke recommended going on the offensive with decisive actions and suggested that a principals' committee hold an "urgent discussion."

Instead, Cheney requested a briefing from George Tenet at CIA headquarters and Colin Powell met with the counter-terrorism security group, made up of senior counter-terrorism officers from the National Security Council, State Department, Defense Department, CIA, FBI and military. Clarke recalled that when he first mentioned bin Laden and al-Qaeda to Condoleezza Rice she had not even heard of them, and in the spring of 2001 she downgraded Clarke.

Now he would no longer report directly to principals but only to deputy secretaries. Accustomed to having had face time with his previous president, Clarke would instead have to beg at the door of the cabinet.

While he waited for the first deputies' committee meeting to be scheduled, in the spring of 2001 Clarke organized an intelligence summit on the terrorist threat, and high on his agenda was a question: could al-Qaeda obtain a nuclear weapon? The conference was attended by three dozen analysts and took place at the top-secret National Reconnaissance Office, in Chantilly, Virginia, a $350-million complex from where most of America's spy satellites and listening stations were run, located beyond the southern perimeter of Dulles international airport beside the headquarters of Lockheed Martin, designer of the F-16.[69]

Evidence that al-Qaeda posed a real threat had been compounded the previous October when the USS *Cole*, a billion-dollar guided-missile destroyer, had been holed in a devastating but off-the-wall attack, rammed with a bomb-filled fiberglass fishing boat in Aden harbor, with the loss of seventeen US lives.[70] Then, Clarke had proposed a retaliatory strike against al-Qaeda's camps in Afghanistan, but the FBI and CIA would not accept that al-Qaeda was necessarily responsible for the USS *Cole* attack. But Clarke was sure, and he could barely bring himself to imagine what al-Qaeda would do if next time the bombs were of the nuclear variety. "We thought the highest probability of their getting anything would be to buy a weapon full up," he recalled.[71] He pointed to a corrupt or ideologically allied insider in the chain of custody in a nuclear state. Pakistan was at the top of the list.[72] It remained there after a classified assessment for President Bush, prepared soon after the Chantilly conference, identified the Islamic Republic as among those posing the "highest risk" of enabling black-market sales.[73] But Clarke was isolated. He felt as if only he really understood what Pakistan was up to and where it might lead.

When Clarke finally got to his first deputies' committee meeting on terrorism, it was in April 2001 and held in a small, wood-panelled situation room in the White House. But he found that Paul Wolfowitz, Donald Rumsfeld's deputy, was more interested in talking about Iraq than Pakistan, Osama bin Laden or al-Qaeda. "I just don't understand why we are beginning by talking about this one man bin Laden," Wolfowitz said.[74] Clarke replied: "Al-Qaeda plans major acts of terrorism against the US. It plans to overthrow Islamic governments and set up a radical multi-nation caliphate and then go to war with non-Muslim states." However, when Clarke added, "They have published all of this and sometimes, as with Hitler, in *Mein Kampf*, you have to believe that these people will actually do what they say they will do," Wolfowitz seized on the Hitler reference and snapped: "I resent any comparison between the Holocaust and this little terrorist in Afghanistan."

By the spring of 2001, Pervez Musharraf was ready to make his move on A. Q. Khan. He saw the Father of the Bomb as a spent force, someone who just got in the way of his own plans for Pakistan's nuclear weapons program. But among the more radical elements within the military elite there was a vociferous campaign to do nothing. Leading these calls was General Mahmood Ahmed, Musharraf's ISI chief, General Zaheerul Islam Abbasi, the Islamist and former Benazir Bhutto coup plotter, and General Javid Nasir, ISI director from 1991 to 1993, who had been sent to North Korea by Nawaz Sharif with a Stinger missile. Nasir, who had held the title of emir of the radical Tablighi Jamaat while in government office in the 1990s, had been sacked by Sharif under pressure from the US, which suspected that not all Stingers had been given back to the CIA after the Afghan war.[75] Since then, Nasir had harbored a deep hatred of everything American and saw the pressure to rein in A. Q. Khan as US meddling. Men like Ahmed, Abbasi and Nasir had inherited General Hamid Gul's world view: hurt India and hurt America. Robert Einhorn understood Musharraf's conundrum: "Musharraf had high incentives to humiliate and punish Khan but he had to tread carefully to keep the generals onside and he also needed to buy Khan's silence."

Musharraf claimed that he agonized over the best approach. "We had to deliberate for hours how to handle the situation ... this had to be done as a gradual process ... it was extremely sensitive. One couldn't outright start investigating as if [A. Q. Khan is] any common criminal."[76] In the end, he decided to handle it the old-fashioned Pakistani way, by first softening the ground, sullying Khan's reputation with a series of newspaper leaks. For many years Khan had frequently used journalists to write positive stories. His favorite scribe was Zahid Malik, long-term editor of the *Pakistan Observer*, who in 1992 published a hagiography of Khan in which the scientist was glorified while his nemesis Munir Ahmed Khan (along with everyone else who had crossed Khan) was trashed.[77] All over Islamabad and Karachi, reporters assigned to different political parties and military persuasions sat in their offices waiting for a telephone call from their benefactor, and when Musharraf's aides began ringing round in March 2001 there was no shortage of newspapers who had taken the military's rupee and were willing to spread the muck.

The Urdu-language *Jasarat* newspaper began the campaign. It reported that KRL employees were using staff cars for personal use. Petty but hurtful. Another newspaper wrote that Khan was about to retire due to probes into financial corruption at KRL. Incorrect but stinging. A third accused Khan of using KRL funds to boost his image as Father of the Bomb. False but pungent in a country that had elevated corruption to a national sport. Some reporters were called in for a presentation where they were shown copies of checks that Khan was said to have received from foreign customers. One journalist recalled: "Musharraf had been so keen to associate with all the positive aspects of Khan and the nuclear tests, that as soon as the first negative stories began emanating, we knew something dramatic was about to happen."[78]

Khan counter-briefed, making egotistical pronouncements in his favorite newspapers, *The Muslim, Hurmat* and the *Daily Jang*, about ambitious new technical advances at KRL. He claimed KRL scientists were developing a revolutionary satellite launch vehicle.[79] He said Pakistan was preparing to test a nuclear missile with twice the payload of anything ever before seen in Asia.[80] The message was clear: Khan was too busy running projects vital to Pakistan's national security to think about anything else.

But in the battle for newsprint, Musharraf claimed the first victory, borrowing Nawaz Sharif's strategy by announcing to the world that A. Q. Khan was retiring from KRL after twenty-five years in service. Musharraf made sure the details were mapped out in private, where, out of view of the US, he could fete Khan, lavishing him with praise and new titles, including "Special Adviser to the Chief Executive on Strategic and KRL Affairs," a sinecure that had the status of a federal minister but authority over nothing. Replacing Khan at the helm of KRL was Javid Mirza, an electrical engineering graduate of Glasgow University who had worked with Khan since Kahuta's inception. Mirza too had participated in the covert Project A/B and would continue to do so. But unlike Khan, Mirza was not a household name and Musharraf would be able to exert far more pressure over him.

For reasons of parity, Musharraf also announced the retirement of Dr. Ishfaq Ahmed, chairman of PAEC, writing later that "the sad truth is that Ishfaq became a decoy to forestall the impression that A. Q. Khan was being singled out." Musharraf put out a semi-official story that the measures were designed to end decades of infighting between KRL and PAEC which were unhelpful to Pakistan's international reputation. But privately he and A. Q. Khan had fought over the terms of the scientist's withdrawal, particularly over his new ceremonial title, Musharraf suggesting "Adviser to the Chief Executive" but Khan insisting on something that recognized his ongoing role in Pakistan's nuclear affairs. In the end Musharraf had agreed on a compromise. Whatever it took, he was determined to cut Khan "off from his base."[81]

To further pacify Khan, on 27 March 2001 Musharraf hosted a lavish dinner for him at the Serena Hotel in Islamabad, where he eulogized the former KRL chief. "The nation is grateful to you for what you have done for us, today and for all times to come. You are our national hero and an inspiration to our future generations. Nobody can ever take that away from you and your place in history is assured. You will always be at the very top. We salute you and thank you from the depths of our hearts." To thunderous applause, Musharraf rounded off: "These men of science, these mujahids have put Pakistan in the exclusive nuclear club, they have made Islamic nations proud."[82]

Musharraf would go even further. He prepared a statement for a special private pamphlet issued to celebrate twenty-five years of work at Kahuta. "Dr. Khan and his team toiled and sweated day and night against all odds and obstacles, against international sanctions and sting operations, to create literally out of nothing, with their bare hands, the pride of Pakistan's nuclear capability, the Kahuta research laboratories." Compared to "the general sea of disappointments" that was Pakistan's lot, Khan's development was "a unique national success story ... of selfless devotion, unbridled dedication, scientific brilliance, technological mastery and above all supreme patriotism and religious fervour."[83] Musharraf was killing him gently, but Khan was devastated. His official retirement date was 1 April 2001, his sixty-third birthday.

After the party, Musharraf awarded himself a new title, becoming president of Pakistan in July 2001.[84] But he stuck to the script with Khan. Khan was gone, Musharraf told the US, as he secretly mounted an audit of KRL nuclear stock, one that led to an alarming discovery. "What they were most interested in was the highly enriched uranium canister store, the nucleus of KRL. Most of the fissile material KRL had produced over the years was still stored there under lock and key, in a reinforced chamber, and some guys on the inside became very concerned that canisters had gone missing."[85] For an aspirant nuclear power, a canister of highly enriched uranium was an invaluable asset, enabling its scientists to leapfrog the enrichment process altogether and begin weapons design. On the black market, the canisters were worth tens of millions of dollars and there were forty missing. "They could only account for eighty out of a supposed 120 canisters. Only Dr. Sahib might have been able to explain where they had gone, but now when Musharraf approached him, Khan pointedly told his adversary: 'I have retired.' " Some of the drums had probably gone to North Korea, the ISI reasoned, and some to Iran and probably Libya.[86] But what worried Musharraf more, and what he dared not tell the US, was that enough highly enriched uranium remained at large to fuel 1,000 dirty bombs, and for a skilled team of zealots with access to proficient scientists to manufacture a sizable nuclear device.

Musharraf need not have worried. The White House was not looking in his direction, but instead scrabbling around for evidence of Saddam Hussein's WMD program. The Bush administration was positively muted about Pakistan. When asked about Khan, Richard Armitage, the deputy secretary of state, responded with an anodyne statement: "US concerns are centered on people who were employed by the Pakistani nuclear agency and have retired."[87] However, just weeks after the Serena Hotel dinner, American spy satellites photographed missile components being loaded into a Pakistani C-130 outside of Pyongyang, with intelligence reports concluding that the cargo was a direct exchange for nuclear technology coming from Kahuta.[88] Khan may have gone but the proliferation was continuing, on Musharraf's watch.

Throughout that spring and summer, the US intelligence community continued to pick up signals that al-Qaeda was planning a major strike against an American target, intercepting more than thirty communications that emanated from Pakistan, Afghanistan and al-Qaeda cells around the globe. They referred variously to "zero hour" or "something spectacular."[89] Early in the summer, George Tenet made a secret trip to Islamabad to urge General Mahmood Ahmed at the ISI to trade information on Osama bin Laden. But the Taliban-supporting general had no intention of cooperating.[90]

There was much he was already withholding from the CIA. In August 2001, the ISI had proof positive that Osama bin Laden had received in person two retired nuclear scientists, Sultan Bashiruddin Mahmood and Chaudiri Abdul Majeed, at his secret headquarters in Afghanistan. Mahmood, who had studied nuclear physics in Britain in the 1960s, had been a junior technician at the time of Zulfikar Ali Bhutto's 1972 Multan conference and had vowed to dedicate his life to helping Pakistan develop the bomb. He specialized in enrichment technology and had helped A. Q. Khan establish Kahuta in 1975, spending two decades working there in a senior position. In the early 1990s, Mahmood and Khan had fallen out. The former went to work at PAEC instead, where he designed the Khushab nuclear reactor.[91]

Mahmood was highly regarded in Pakistan's nuclear physics community. But outside the lab he was entering a strange metaphysical world, becoming a follower of the Lahore-based pro-Taliban cleric Israr Ahmad. Mahmood praised the virtues of the Taliban government for sponsoring a renaissance in Islam and suggested that Taliban rule should serve as a model for Pakistan. He published a pamphlet entitled "Mechanics of Doomsday and Life after Death" in which he argued that natural catastrophes were inevitable in countries that succumbed to moral decay, and predicted in another treatise that "by 2002 millions may die through mass destruction weapons … terrorist attack, and suicide."[92] When Mahmood had described Pakistan's nuclear capability following the tests of 1998 as "the property of the whole Muslim ummah" and publicly advocated that KRL should provide gas centrifuges and enriched uranium to arm other Islamic states, he had been forced to retire.[93]

Chaudiri Abdul Majeed had also retired in 1999, after a lengthy and illustrious career which had begun in the 1960s at a Belgian plutonium facility associated with A. Q. Khan's alma mater, Leuven's Catholic University. Majeed had gone on to study at the International Center for Theoretical Physics in Trieste, Italy, founded by Pakistan's most famous nuclear physicist, the Nobel laureate Abdus Salaam, and had then worked for many years at the nuclear materials division of the Pakistan Institute of Nuclear Science and Technology (PINSTECH). With both scientists entertaining increasingly radical views, in 2000 they set up Ummah Tameer-e-Nau, Reconstruction of the Muslim Community, a charity that purported to conduct relief work in Afghanistan.[94]

At the meeting in Afghanistan in August 2001, Osama bin Laden allegedly told the two scientists that he had made great headway in advancing the apocalypse of which Mahmood had written.[95] He had succeeded in acquiring highly enriched uranium from the Islamic Movement of Uzbekistan and he wanted their help to turn it into a bomb. Mahmood and Majeed were amazed, but they explained that while they could help with the science of fissile materials, they were not weapons designers. Bin Laden passed them over to Ayman al-Zawahiri, his Egyptian deputy, who quizzed them about which of Pakistan's weapons experts could be approached. The ISI chief General Ahmed had learned of these meetings through military contacts, several of whom sat on the board of Ummah Tameer-e-Nau, including General Hamid Gul, his predecessor at the ISI. Gul was the charity's honorary patron and had been in Afghanistan when the two scientists were meeting bin Laden.[96] This information, added to the missing canisters of highly enriched uranium, might have been sufficient to redirect the Vulcans. But Pakistan withheld it.

Instead, when on 4 September 2001 Richard Clarke, Bush's national co-ordinator for counter-terrorism, finally got to brief the principals on al-Qaeda, nine months after he had called for an urgent meeting, the CIA claimed it could not find a single dollar to transfer to the anti-al-Qaeda effort and argued against proposals to fly an armed Predator drone over Afghanistan to take out bin Laden and his aides. Donald Rumsfeld was more concerned about Iraq and its role in supporting terrorism, and the meeting ended without a strategy or any sense of purpose. Condoleezza Rice had only one request for Clarke: write up a lengthy presidential directive.[97]

Pervez Musharraf was in Karachi on 11 September 2001, inspecting the gardens at the mausoleum for Muhammad Ali Jinnah, when he learned that a hijacked plane had flown into the World Trade Center in New York. "Little did I know that we were about to be thrust into the front line of yet another war, a war against shadows," he recalled, without so much as a passing reference to the active role he and Pakistan had played in helping al-Qaeda grow. Musharraf returned to his Karachi residence to watch a second plane hit the South Tower on CNN. "I could not believe what I saw. Smoke was billowing out of both towers ... people were jumping out of windows. There was sheer panic, utter chaos."[98]

There was also chaos at the National Reconnaissance Office in Chantilly, Virginia, where John Fulton, the CIA's chief of strategic war gaming, had been preparing the final countdown for "a pre-planned simulation to explore the emergency response issues that would be created if a plane were to strike a building." Fulton's simulation was to consist of "a small corporate jet crashing into one of the four towers at the agency's headquarters" and the simulation had been due to begin within minutes of the real attack.[99]

Donald Rumsfeld was having breakfast in the private dining room at the Pentagon with a group of Republican congressmen, discussing how to get more support on Capitol Hill for his long-running bid for a US ballistic missile defense system. America should be prepared for surprises, he said, just as the first plane struck the North Tower. Eighteen minutes later another plane plowed into the South Tower and then a third struck the Pentagon itself, Rumsfeld emerging briefly to help with the rescue effort before disappearing back inside to the National Military Command Center, where he remained throughout the day.[100]

General Ahmed also happened to be in Washington that day, having been flown over from Islamabad on a CIA jet to update George Tenet, who had asked him where Pakistan stood on interdicting al-Qaeda and bin Laden. It was like asking bin Laden to find al-Zawahiri. The general was having breakfast in a room on the White House side of the Capitol, with Senators Bob Graham and Porter Goss, the chairmen of the Senate and House intelligence committees. They were talking about a recent trip Goss and Graham had made to Pakistan, where they had discussed with Musharraf the possibility of extraditing Osama bin Laden in connection with the US embassy bombings in Africa in August 1998. Musharraf had told the delegation that there was really nothing he could do. As General Ahmed repeated the same, New York descended into chaos.

The air traffic shutdown kept General Ahmed in situ and the next morning Richard Armitage summoned him to his office.[101] Armitage was furious and suddenly very focused on Pakistan. "Are you with us or against us?" Armitage repeatedly asked, claiming Pakistan had been the prime supporter of the Taliban. It was the only country maintaining diplomatic relations with its leader, Mullah Omar, relations that were personally run by General Ahmed. Armitage said it was not clear yet what the US would ask of Pakistan. But the requests would force "deep introspection." Pakistan "faces a stark choice, either it is with us or it is not." This was "a black and white choice with no gray."[102] When Ahmed wryly pointed out that for many years the US had paid the mujahideen via the ISI to wage war against the Soviet Union, Armitage cut him off. "History starts today," he growled. Pointing to a military citation sitting on a shelf, which he had received in Islamabad, he said that if Musharraf did not act now he would return it and no American would want to be decorated by Pakistan ever again.

Armitage and Colin Powell spent the rest of the day compiling a list of demands. That night, Powell called Musharraf. It was already morning in Karachi and Musharraf was chairing a meeting at Governor's House. "I said I would call back later, but he insisted to my staff that I come out of the meeting," recalled Musharraf.[103] Powell was quite candid, repeating what Armitage had told Ahmed: "You're either with us or against us." Musharraf said: "It was an ultimatum. I told him that we were with the US against terrorism ... and would fight along with his country against it. We did not negotiate anything."

The next morning, Ahmed was back in with Armitage, who presented seven demands, including stopping all al-Qaeda operatives from crossing Pakistan's borders, providing the US with blanket overflight rights, cutting off all shipments of fuel, aid and military hardware to the Taliban and a promise to "assist the United States ... to destroy Osama bin Laden and his al-Qaeda network," which was already being accused of orchestrating the 9/11 attacks. Armitage and Powell had debated whether A. Q. Khan should appear on the list of demands, too. But they backed off from pursuing the nuclear question, reasoning that the priority was to get Musharraf's commitment to fighting terrorism. The ISI director called Musharraf. He said Armitage was warning Pakistan that if it chose to side with the terrorists then "we should be prepared to be bombed back to the Stone Age." Musharraf saw it as a "shockingly barefaced threat" and pondered Pakistan's options.[104]

Two days later, General Ahmed was back in Rawalpindi. Musharraf recalled that the ISI chief, along with other senior officers, was called to a meeting at which Musharraf "made a dispassionate, military-style analysis of our options," aware that on his decision hung "the fate of millions of people and the future of [my country]."[105] But for six hours Ahmed, Lieutenant General Usmani, the deputy army chief, and two others argued against giving America any aid at all. "Let the US do its dirty work. Its enemies are our friends," Ahmed argued. Musharraf did not disagree. He was no US lackey. Like many others, he had never forgiven Bush the elder for cutting Pakistan adrift in 1990 and resented the way America had snapped its fingers in the hours after 9/11. According to his closest advisers, Musharraf said: "Pakistan has been deluged by terrorism for decades. We have learned to live with it. The Americans, too, should get used to the taste of blood."[106]

But the clinical Musharraf, an officer who was practiced in manipulation and who had set the hunting dogs of the Sunni extremists to work in Afghanistan, Kashmir and elsewhere, spotted an opportunity. Pakistan was the only country that could offer the US a launch pad into Afghanistan and could pry open the closed world of Osama bin Laden. Musharraf's counsel, Sharifuddin Pirzada, recalled the dawning realization. "Musharraf saw that for Pakistan it was 1979 all over again. 'We should offer up help,' Musharraf said, 'and, mark my words, we will receive a clean bill of health.' "[107]

16

MUSH AND BUSH

At the outset of his presidential campaign George W. Bush had been unable to name the leader of Pakistan (having been challenged to do so by an interviewer).[1] But in the weeks following 9/11, Pakistan once again became America's closest regional ally, with President Bush later describing General Pervez Musharraf as "one of my best friends."[2]

"Mush and Bush," Pakistan's press corps dubbed them. It was a strange match, given the US president was on a warpath to crush the extremism that had catapulted terrorists from Afghanistan into the heart of America, while Pakistan's president had helped author the rise of the Taliban regime and was responsible for loading the jihadi toolbox with an array of sharp Sunni blades, militant groups armed, trained and manufactured to bring bloodshed to Kashmir.[3] More worryingly for the US, the Pakistan army—and Musharraf—had overseen Project A/B, the covert arming of Iran, Iraq, North Korea, Libya and Saudi Arabia (at the very least) with nuclear weapons, setting the agenda for future wars.

But none of these concerns, which continued to preoccupy the CIA and State Department, as well as virtually every intelligence agency around the world, seemed overly to concern the Bush White House, which was impressed by the apparently Western-leaning Musharraf, photographed cuddling his Pekinese dogs.[4] His well-groomed manners and pressed suits lent him the air of a convivial officer and belied his Machiavellian streak. Musharraf could do no wrong for Bush. After 9/11, all sanctions imposed following the nuclear tests of 1998 and the military coup of 1999 were jettisoned, Pakistan receiving a $2.64-billion bounty of aid (military and civil) to join the US fight against Osama bin Laden and al-Qaeda.[5] The US made other compromises, too. To the dismay of ordinary Pakistanis, the country's courts, politicians and industrialists, Washington stayed silent when Musharraf amended Pakistan's constitution and extend his "presidency" for another five years without having to hold elections.[6] Combined with Musharraf's right to dissolve parliament, this sent democracy in the Islamic Republic back to the Dark Ages.[7] The Bush administration argued, new times, dominated by a faceless enemy, necessitated extreme actions. The US, too had changed course, hamstringing democracy with a raft of draconian domestic legislation. It had begun just forty-five days after 9/11 with the Patriot Act, which gave the government the power to access medical records, tax information, details about the books Americans were buying or borrowing, "and the power to break into your home and conduct secret searches without telling you for weeks, months, or indefinitely."[8]

To bolster the case for Pakistan as a key ally, Bush officials stopped talking in public about nuclear proliferation, Ari Fleischer, the White House spokesman, conceding in one press conference that the administration was no longer even unduly concerned about the Pakistan–North Korea connection: "Well yes, since September 11, many things that people may have done years before September 11 or some time before September 11, have changed, as September 11 changed the world and it changed many nations' behaviors along with it. And don't read that to be any type of acknowledgment of what may or may not be true."[9] There was absolutely no mention of George Tenet's top-secret working group which had Pakistan's relationships with North Korea and Libya in its sights (as well as all the other nuclear misdeeds committed by Pakistan). History had begun all over again, according to the administration, much as it had done in 1981 when the Soviets rolled into Kabul.

But behind the scenes there was bitter wrangling over the appropriate response to 9/11. Secretary of state Colin Powell focused on Afghanistan, the logical choice, he said, as it played host to bin Laden and much of al-Qaeda.[10] However, Paul Wolfowitz, number two at the Pentagon, and Scooter Libby, Dick Cheney's chief of staff, stuck to the Vulcan agenda of pre-emptive action against Iraq, even after a trawl of 19,000 documents obtained from the Iraqi National Congress, the exiled opposition group, failed to find a single reference to Saddam Hussein's WMD program.[11]

Wolfowitz and Libby argued that the forces of terror in the Middle East were all connected and that as Saddam Hussein was the most powerful godfather of all, he was evidently the éminence grise. The administration should take him out first, closing a "window of vulnerability," an act that would lessen the remaining threats too.[12] It was an argument that failed to take into account the complex and factional religious make-up of the region or the goals of pious al-Qaeda and Osama bin Laden, detested by the avowedly secular Saddam Hussein, who would gladly have strung them all up. Terrorism in the Middle East was not all the same—some Sunni, some Shia, some Armageddon and some mystical, and much of it muddled.[13] As yet, many elements were far from interlinked—although they would become so after Wolfowitz got his way and the US attacked Iraq in March 2003, soon after which he was placed in charge of military operations there.

Initially, Bush trod cautiously, sanctioning only Colin Powell's plan of attack on Afghanistan. On 7 October 2001, American and British forces unleashed Operation Enduring Freedom, with air strikes and cruise missiles targeting al-Qaeda training camps—sending a message to the Taliban that harboring terrorists would no longer be tolerated. The operation immediately resounded in Rawalpindi, where potentially devastating intelligence emerged suggesting a link between Pakistan's ISI, Pervez Musharraf and the terrorists behind 9/11. Foreign agencies discovered that Mohammed Atta, who had flown American Airlines flight 11 into the World Trade Center, had received $100,000 in a Manhattan bank account from the United Arab Emirates. The sender was Ahmed Umar Sheikh, aka Saeed Sheikh, a convicted Pakistani militant and a man who was also known to the West as an important ISI asset. Released by the Indian government from jail in 1999 after jihadis seized an Indian Airlines passenger jet, threatening to kill everyone on board, Ahmed Umar Sheikh and the Harkat-ul-Ansar general secretary, Maulana Masood Azhar, also released as a result, had worked for Pakistan ever since. General Mahmood Ahmed, the ISI chief, was in the frame.[14] He was also known to have sent ISI operatives to the Taliban's stronghold of Kandahar in September 2001, ostensibly to persuade Mullah Omar, the Taliban leader, to hand bin Laden to the US. However, there were strong indications that he had simply warned them to prepare for a US onslaught.[15]

Musharraf sacked the ISI chief Mahmood Ahmed. Washington applauded. But far from it being an attempt to come clean with the US, it was a move that further entrenched the extremist element in the military, as well as strengthening the hand of Musharraf. The night of Ahmed's departure, with US missiles raining down on Afghanistan, Pakistan's nine corps commanders, the most influential figures in the Islamic Republic's army, met with Musharraf to rejig the power structure. Announcing Mahmood Ahmed's removal, Musharraf had knocked out one of the few officers capable of standing up to him. There was perhaps one other officer of Mahmood's caliber and experience, Lieutenant General Muzzaffar Usmani, the commander of 5 Corps (Karachi). Musharraf had him sidelined, too.[16] On 8 October, Musharraf promoted two of his most loyal and long-standing colleagues, Lieutenant General Mohammed Aziz, the commander of 4 Corps (Lahore), and General Mohammed Yusaf, the chief of general staff.

Their military records explained what lay behind the move. Musharraf and Aziz had trained together as commandos in the 1960s and, together with Yusaf, had played critical roles in the training of the Afghan mujahideen in the 1980s under the tutelage of General Hamid Gul. Musharraf, Aziz and Yusaf had run the proxy war in Kashmir in the early 1990s, and Aziz, a Kashmiri by birth, had been on the ground handling Musharraf's disastrous Kargil operation in 1999.[17] Aziz was so close to Pakistan's sponsored jihadi organizations that when Musharraf had tried to promote him to commander of 10 Corps (Rawalpindi) in October 1999 as a precursor to making him army chief, a job that would have brought him back to the capital, Jamaat-e-Islami and Maulana Fazlur Rahman of the Jamiat Ulema Islam protested, warning it would weaken the jihad in Kashmir. Musharraf subsequently backed down.[18] Aziz held great influence over Pakistan's president. He persuaded Musharraf against clamping down on the Taliban and Osama bin Laden as a result of Clinton's visit in 2000, and he also vetoed US demands for action against the Pakistan-based activities of organizations such as the Harkat-ul-Mujahideen and Lashkar-e-Taiba.[19] Aziz was promoted to chairman of the joint chiefs of staff, a position that until then Musharraf had retained for himself.[20] Yusaf was promoted to vice chief of army staff, the second most important job in the Pakistan army. Both men were known for their strict adherence to the Koran, praying five times a day, even in battle, and giving all their spare time over to the Tablighi Jamaat movement.[21] Talking to the people of Pakistan, Musharraf denied the changes had any connection to America or 9/11, saying glibly: "In fact, I was wearing too many hats. Some changes had to take place within the army, which I was actually contemplating for a number of months."[22]

Those in Musharraf's inner circle saw the moves for what they were. Sharifuddin Pirzada, the president's counsel, recalled: "Although Musharraf had been presented to the outside world as leader since the coup of 1999, it was really a cabal of generals who had pitched in and elevated him. But after 9/11, those who had acted as balances and power breaks were disposed of or died accidentally, leaving Musharraf pre-eminent."[23]

If the Bush administration truly understood what Musharraf was about, it kept it to itself. However, Bush officials evidently—and privately—understood the consequences of Pakistan's nuclear sideline. On 11 October 2001, George Tenet brought alarming news to Bush's daily intelligence brief: a CIA agent code-named Dragonfire had picked up chatter that al-Qaeda terrorists were about to decimate New York City with a 10-kiloton nuclear bomb. The source said the compact device was already being driven around Manhattan in the back of a van. If it was detonated in the heart of the city, at a busy public location such as Times Square, it would generate a fireball of tens of millions of degrees which would immediately engulf the 500,000 people who worked within a half-mile radius and destroy every well-known landmark from the Guggenheim Museum, on the Upper East Side, to the Flatiron Building at Broadway and Fifth Avenue.[24]

There was nothing against which to test the Dragonfire report. However, the CIA warned the administration that bin Laden had been attempting to acquire nuclear materials as far back as 1992. Many of these attempts had involved Pakistan and had been amateurish, but the evidence that they were trying to procure was overwhelming. Now was not a time to hesitate. When the US intelligence community had failed to take seriously the signals about a terrorist plan to hijack planes and fly them into prominent US landmarks, it had cost almost 3,000 lives.[25] The president made a snap decision. Vice President Dick Cheney was ordered to leave Washington immediately and head for an undisclosed location with hundreds of federal employees to form an alternative government in case the unthinkable happened. Nuclear emergency support teams descended on New York. No one outside central government was informed, not even New York mayor Rudolph Giuliani. If the story had got out, the impact on Wall Street would have been calamitous. America could ill afford another mass panic.[26]

In the end, no bomb was found and Dragonfire was discredited. But rumors that terrorists were shopping for a nuclear weapon were irrepressible and the source of many of them was Pakistan, where an unsecured black market in nuclear material and a pool of scientists disaffected with the West and sympathetic to the goals of al-Qaeda, were growing. In mid-October 2001, George Tenet secretly flew to Islamabad, particularly concerned by intelligence that two Pakistani scientists had been spotted meeting Osama bin Laden shortly before 9/11, an event that Musharraf had not bothered to report. Sultan Bashiruddin Mahmood and Chaudiri Abdul Majeed were still living comfortably in their KRL-supplied retirement homes, thanks to the largesse of A. Q. Khan and the former ISI director General Ahmed.

Tenet insisted Musharraf take action, and on 23 October 2001, Mahmood and Majeed were arrested and questioned by a joint ISI–CIA team. Only the day before, Mahmood had bragged to *Nida-i-Millat* newspaper that under the Taliban, Afghanistan was well on the way to becoming a fully industrialized nation until the US had attacked it on 7 October. Now both men played dumb, claiming they had never met bin Laden or anyone connected to al-Qaeda. But after Mahmood repeatedly failed polygraph tests and his son Azim helpfully bragged to reporters that bin Laden had asked his father "how to make a nuclear bomb and things like that," Mahmood's memory was jogged.[27] He admitted to his interrogators that he had met the al-Qaeda leader, but said the discussions had been "academic." Literally, this had been true, as while the two scientists had been keen to offer their services as nuclear advisers, what Osama bin Laden had been looking for was a bomb builder.

The Americans knew Mahmood and Majeed had multiple contacts within Pakistan's nuclear community, and as a former divisional chief at KRL and former director of a large reactor project, Mahmood would have known how to import large quantities of sensitive technology without alerting the authorities. Since leaving the nuclear establishment and setting up the charity Ummah Tameer-e-Nau (UTN), the two scientists had had further opportunities to procure on behalf of al-Qaeda or the Taliban. UTN's declared projects in Afghanistan had been medical or humanitarian in nature, making any imports made by it exempt from the UN embargo.

As a result of Tenet's intervention, the charity's board was stripped down and found to include two senior officers in the Pakistani military and a former PAEC scientist, Mirza Yusef Baig, who had gone on to become one of the country's leading industrialists and who was known to have extensive Taliban links, winning contracts in Afghanistan to build hospitals, government offices, a flour mill and schools.[28]

Further digging led to the discovery that other Pakistani scientists had met with al-Qaeda as a result of Mahmood's August 2001 discussions, including Mohammad Nasim, who had co-authored an article opposing Pakistan's signing of the test-ban treaty with Mahmood in 1999, Humayun Niaz, a former PAEC employee, who had been assisting the Taliban to explore Afghanistan for natural uranium and plutonium, and Sheikh Mohammed Tufail, the owner of one of Pakistan's leading engineering companies. These men were brought in and questioned. However, two other scientists whom the US wanted to interrogate, Muhammad Ali Mukhtar, who had a PhD in nuclear physics and had gone on to work for PAEC as a weapons expert, and Suleiman Asad, who had been employed at KRL in its weapons design division, evaded the ISI–CIA team. Even though the US reasoned they were most likely to have been the bomb designers Osama bin Laden was searching for, Musharraf's government claimed they were working on a sensitive and until then highly classified government-to-government project and could not be brought back. Both men had been sent by Musharraf to Burma.[29] Everyone was so hyped on getting bin Laden that no one asked why Pakistan's nuclear experts, especially KRL men, were assisting the military junta in Rangoon.[30]

There was one more name on the list: General Hamid Gul, the former ISI director and UTN's honorary patron. But to appease the military, Gul was not pulled in, although intelligence showed he had regularly met Mullah Omar and had rendezvoused with Sultan Bashiruddin Mahmood in Kabul in August 2001, when the scientist was due to meet Osama bin Laden.[31]

The US's private fears of a nuclear-terrorist plot, with Pakistan at its epicenter, heightened when the US-backed forces of Afghanistan's Northern Alliance marched into Kabul on 13 November 2001, putting the Taliban to flight. Western intelligence agencies and journalists discovered a trove of information on al-Qaeda's nuclear ambitions from offices previously used as Taliban ministries and safe houses. Most had been located in Kabul's upmarket Wazir Arkvar Khan neighborhood, where the Taliban had been in such a hurry to leave, surprised by the speed and force of the US-inspired invasion, that they had got no further than stuffing incriminating paperwork into black plastic garbage bags, which had been abandoned in situ. As soldiers and journalists combed the rubbish, they discovered that here had been a virtual campus, a terrorist university, much of it hiding behind official fronts, like a Saudi-financed orphanage that doubled as an al-Qaeda explosives training department, where among the children's books and ID documents were trip wires, explosives, grenades, a rocket and bomb-maker's manuals.[32]

The CIA headed for the headquarters of Mahmood's UTN, a house in central Kabul, where they recovered hundreds of documents, some of which showed that UTN had been helping in Afghanistan with road building, erecting flour mills and distributing educational materials, as Mahmood had claimed. But others clearly suggested that al-Qaeda had "an appetite for WMD" which was being fed by UTN.[33] There was a drawing of a crude device for delivering anthrax, boxes of gas masks and containers of chemicals. In a second-floor workshop was a disassembled rocket beside a cylinder labelled "helium." Someone had been planning to float a balloon loaded with anthrax over a city. In another building were multiple copies of a document, *Biologic Warfare: An Imminent Danger*, which accused the US government of planning to conduct experiments on the international Muslim community using anthrax. There were also documents linking UTN to the Pakistani militant group Jaish-e-Mohammed, formed by Harkat-ul-Ansar chief Maulana Masood Azhar upon his release from an Indian jail in 1999 (when he was thought also to have entered the pay of the ISI). Also among the debris were found homemade stickers celebrating the bombing of the USS *Cole*. UTN, alQaeda and Pakistan's militant groups, backed by Musharraf, were inextricably linked.[34]

CIA and ISI interrogators returned to scientists Mahmood and Majeed and, confronted by the documentation, they admitted to having had long and detailed discussions about nuclear, chemical and biological weapons with al-Qaeda officials. One ISI interrogator characterized the men as "very motivated" and "extremist in their views."[35] President Bush announced the proscription of UTN as a terrorist organization, with the assets of its members, Mahmood, Majeed and Sheikh Mohammed Tufail, frozen.[36] But he looked no further into the games being played by the ISI or Musharraf.

However, Pakistan still refused to act against Mahmood and Majeed, preferring instead to underplay the mounting evidence that they had assisted al-Qaeda in its goal of going nuclear. "For that kind of operation you need dozens and dozens of people and millions of dollars," said one senior member of PAEC, rolled out by Musharraf. "That sort of technology transfer takes fifty to sixty years. The chance that [two scientists] gave the Taliban nuclear arms is zero—

less than zero."[37] But it was not the Taliban they were aiding, but al-Qaeda, and it was not looking to implement an A. Q. Khan–style state-of-the-art uranium enrichment program. All it wanted was a bomb, or some fissile material strapped to high explosives, to contaminate a city.[38] Later, Mahmood claimed that he had collapsed and been rushed to hospital during his interrogations and that he had only failed lie-detector tests because he was an old man with high blood pressure, suffering from extreme stress. Musharraf, concerned at what Mahmood or Majeed might reveal about Pakistan's secret nuclear activities, refused to put either man on trial—or to question A. Q. Khan.

By the end of 2001, Bush's goal of capturing Osama bin Laden "dead or alive" had got nowhere and more than a thousand al-Qaeda fighters were holed up in the cave complexes of the Tora Bora mountains on Afghanistan's eastern border with Pakistan. Soon, Gulbuddin Hekmatyar, the virulently anti-American mujahideen leader and Hamid Gul's man in Afghanistan, would arrive to lead them to freedom in Pakistan.[39] However, the hunt for WMDs had only just begun.

The US targeted fifty sites across Afghanistan and recovered tens of thousands of documents, booklets, personnel records, videos, equipment and other materials. Among the trove were instruction manuals on how to make and use a wide variety of conventional explosives, schematics of intended targets including nuclear power plants, training manuals in guerrilla warfare, and instructor and student notebooks describing techniques for kidnapping and assassination. Nearly all of this material was the detritus of the ISI, used under Musharraf's guidance to train militants bound for Kashmir.

In Kabul too, there was much still to discover. Residents led CIA agents to a house in Wazir Arkvar Khan where the "big Arabs had lived."[40] Inside were signs of another hasty retreat: a large cache of discarded documents, including part of a letter dated 12 January 2001 to Abu Khabab al-Masri. This was a name the CIA not only knew but feared: the WMD chief for al-Qaeda. The sender's name was missing, but the letter began: "Most respected Abu Khabab, I am sending some companions, who are eager to be trained in explosives or whatever they want. All of them are trustworthy. Concerning the expenditure, they would pay you themselves. I hope that you would not disappoint me."[41]

From other paperwork found in the building it soon became clear that this was where al-Masri, formerly an Egyptian chemist, had run his training workshops.[42] Student notebooks lay scattered around, depicting crude atomic bomb designs using plutonium or uranium: dirty bombs that Western scientists who studied the pictures said could have functioned. One twenty-five-page booklet, handwritten in Arabic and missing its cover and first pages, read: "... anyone desiring to obtain a nuclear weapon must set up a plant for enriching uranium." The odd phrase was spelled out in English in fat blue marker pen to draw students' attention to something significant: "super bombs," "nuclear fission" and "isotopes." The body of the text detailed various types of nuclear weapons, the physics of nuclear explosions, the properties of nuclear materials needed to make them, and the smelting temperature for uranium-235 as well as various shortcuts on making crude nuclear explosives.

Former IAEA weapons inspectors who studied the "super bombs" document said it showed knowledge of nuclear explosives far more extensive than was available in the public domain. There were other equally worrying textbooks in al-Masri's library, including an eleven-volume "encyclopedia" on WMD. The final volume was a remarkably up-to-date assessment of the latest explosives research and included notes on where to source RDX and Semtex, high explosives that could be used in "shaped charges" to compress the nuclear core in an implosion-type nuclear device.

While there was no indication that the al-Qaeda instructors had reached anywhere near the level of technical expertise to design a nuclear weapon like that tested by Pakistan in May 1998, explosives experts concluded after studying several hand-drawn diagrams that it was entirely conceivable that al-Masri's class might have been capable of constructing a gun-type nuclear bomb, in which a propellant would fire a slug of highly enriched uranium down a barrel into another lump of highly enriched uranium, creating fission.

Arab-language specialists, who translated passages on behalf of the CIA, suggested the authors were probably Egyptian and likely to have been university professors rather than technicians: people who had theoretical rather than practical knowledge. Other documents hinted at al-Masri's attempts to elicit outside help, one memo dated June 1999 stating that the program should seek to place al-Qaeda people into educational institutions, which "would allow easy access to specialists, which will greatly benefit us in the first stage, God willing."[43]

As the Taliban's seven-year hold over Afghanistan was deconstructed, the Bush administration, realizing what it had uncovered, began to warn in public of the distinct possibility that al-Qaeda had obtained weapons of mass destruction (WMD), Donald Rumsfeld saying that it was "reasonable to assume" Osama bin Laden already had access to some kind of device. Speaking at the UN General Assembly, Bush, too, suggested that terrorists were "searching for WMD, the tools to turn their hatred into Holocaust."[44] This time there were no complaints from Paul Wolfowitz about facile comparisons between Hitler's treatment of the Jews and a "little terrorist in Afghanistan."

Then, in the spring of 2002, al-Qaeda confirmed its apocalyptic capabilities. Khalid Sheikh Mohammed, accused by the US of being the chief planner of 9/11 and placed on the FBI's most-wanted terrorists list, told Yosri Fouda, an al-Jazeera television reporter, who was driven blindfold to a secret location in Karachi to interview him, that he was the head of al-Qaeda's military committee and that while planning 9/11 the initial targets had been "a couple of nuclear facilities." However, Khalid continued, "it was eventually decided to leave out the nuclear targets—for now." When Fouda asked what Khalid meant by "for now," he snapped: "For now means for now."[45] Khalid claimed that al-Qaeda had intended using conventional explosives on a nuclear facility, but from the documents and designs found in Afghanistan it was clear that al-Qaeda was also considering the deployment of crude nuclear weapons themselves, or was perhaps seeking fissile material with which to arm a weapon. Khalid Sheikh Mohammed would eventually be seized by the ISI, who raided a house in a middle-class suburb of Rawalpindi in March 2003. He was swiftly turned over to the Americans, who rendered him on a secret CIA flight to an undisclosed location, mirroring the CIA's covert plan for capturing bin Laden, strapping him in a dentist's chair and flying him in a shipping container to El Paso. Later, he would be transferred to Guantanamo Bay.

Others issued threats, too, including Suleiman Abu Gheith, a self-styled spokesman for Osama bin Laden, who posted a four-part essay on a mujahideen website closely affiliated to al-Qaeda. "We have the right to kill four million Americans—two million of them children," he declared. "And to exile twice as many and wound and cripple hundreds of thousands."[46] His suggested means for revenge on this scale was nuclear.

Concern about dirty bombs would only intensify after the seizure in Pakistan on 28 March 2002 of Abu Zubaida, who the US Justice Department described as al-Qaeda's "lead operational planner and organizer." He had been living openly in Peshawar for the previous two years, despite US requests for his arrest stretching back to January 2000. But Zubaida had not been captured with Pakistan's help. The US National Reconnaissance Office, in Chantilly, Virginia, had traced him through mobile-phone calls he had made from a house in Faisalabad, in the northern Punjab. Zubaida was rendered to a secret US detention facility, where he was questioned by the FBI and allegedly told his interrogators that al-Qaeda was interested in producing a dirty bomb and now knew how to do it.[47]

Nine days after 9/11, President Bush had told the American people in a televised address: "Our war on terror begins with al-Qaeda, but it does not end there. It will not end until every terrorist group of global reach has been found, stopped and defeated." This was one of the first outings for the slogan "war on terror" and it was aimed at alerting the world to the notion that the US was in the midst of a rolling campaign of pre-emptive action. Phase one was Afghanistan. Initially, there was much debate over where the US would launch phase two.

For a few weeks in the autumn of 2001, there had been talk of US forces going back into Somalia, a failed state, with a minority of Islamists, where al-Qaeda had operated before and where it was thought to be regrouping after fleeing Afghanistan via Pakistan or Iran, an idea promoted by Colin Powell. Powell had also considered Sudan, Yemen and the Philippines, countries that many al-Qaeda recruits had passed through. Sudan was the largest Muslim-dominated country in Africa and had played host to several leading al-Qaeda figures during the 1990s, not least Osama bin Laden, who had been welcomed by Khartoum in 1992. But the US was hesitant about starting a war in Africa, destabilizing another continent, and there was a fear of the legacy of "Black Hawk Down," the US Somali misadventure in October 1993 when two helicopters were downed, leading to the deaths of nineteen US servicemen.[48] The Philippines, too, was problematic as it was an ally and any action against its Islamic separatist movement, known as Abu Sayyaf, which had turned the southern island of Mindanao into its headquarters, would have to be carried out under the auspices of the Philippines army. Colin Powell's operations would not see the light of day.

Rumsfeld, Wolfowitz, Armitage and other leading neoconservatives close to Bush already knew where the US should go, having campaigned for it since 1998. Most of them had signed the letter in January 1998 urging President Clinton to depose Saddam Hussein and some had sat on the Rumsfeld Commission later that year, identifying the world's most dangerous regimes as Iraq, Iran and North Korea. In his state of the union address of January 2002, President Bush duly unveiled the "Axis of Evil," a distillation of Rumsfeld's 1998 Commission and Vulcan ideals, as expressed by presidential speechwriter David Frum who referenced Reagan's old phrase from the Cold War days, the "evil empire."[49] Three countries—North Korea, Iran and Iraq—that Rumsfeld, Wolfowitz, Armitage, Richard Perle, Zalmay Khalilzad, William Schneider, Jr., John Bolton and R. James Woolsey had first identified in 1998 as hostile nations posing the greatest threat to "the United States, its deployed forces, friends and allies," were put on notice.[50] President Bush warned that "we intend to take their development of weapons of mass destruction very seriously," and those that did not yield to US military supremacy would be targeted. In this new American era there was no room for non-proliferation treaties or Agreed Frameworks. From now on, the world would be reduced to good and evil; the former would have to choose to be with America, while those who did not so choose would be denounced. However, Pakistan, whose scientists had recklessly armed these rogue regimes, and continued to trade in doomsday weapons, did not even merit a mention.

Pakistan was not mentioned in June 2002 either, when Bush announced pre-emption as a new national strategy, unveiling it before graduating cadets assembled on the football field at West Point, the heart of the US military. This was something that a Defense Department team consisting of Paul Wolfowitz, Scooter Libby and Zalmay Khalilzad had first recommended in 1992, only to have their controversial report quashed, such was the outcry it prompted.[51] Now, in 2002, and departing from 200 years of US military tradition, Bush declared: "We must take the battle to the enemy, disrupt his plans and confront the worst threats before they emerge ... If we wait for the threats to fully materialize, we will have waited too long."[52] This was just what the US and Britain proceeded to do with Pakistan's proliferation program.

*

In London, the intelligence community's concerns about A. Q. Khan were so intense by 2002 that he became the topic of discussion at a Wednesday afternoon meeting of the joint intelligence committee (JIC) at the Cabinet Office in Whitehall, the forum in which the combined British intelligence services met to discuss the most pressing threats to the UK. In March 2002, the British intelligence community was asked to provide a detailed assessment of everything it knew about Khan and Pakistan's proliferation activities. It was two years since the JIC had last discussed the subject. Having decided to do nothing in 2000, what was then an "incomplete picture of the supply of uranium enrichment equipment to at least one customer in the Middle East, thought to be Libya," had evolved by 2002, on Musharraf's watch, into a "widespread network" based in Dubai and assisted by "certain African governments"—the ones Khan had visited in 1998, 1999 and 2000 under the guise of fixing up the Hendrina Khan Hotel. Khan had also "established his own production facilities in Malaysia," which were being run by "a network of associates and suppliers," led by B. S. A. Tahir, Khan's Sri Lankan protégé.[53]

Calling in intelligence from abroad, the JIC found that Khan had made forty-four visits to Dubai since Tahir's wedding in June 1998, an event at which, the British officials were informed, Khan had fixed his plan to move out of Pakistan, to Dubai, Southeast Asia and Africa. In fact, as Peter Griffin recalled, Khan had been in Dubai since the 1970s, and what the British had spotted was simply an intensification of his activities there.[54] Although the British were still unclear as to the range of customers being supported through this newly revived network, several of Khan's original suppliers were being followed by the security services, including Peter Griffin, a Dubai resident since 1997, where he had established Gulf Technical Industries (GTI) to import and export engineering parts and machine tools.

By 2002, Griffin knew he was being trailed, but claimed his business with Khan had all but ceased.[55] "They were following the wrong man," recalled Griffin. "It was Tahir who was up to his neck in it." Tahir had come a long way from sleeping on the floor of his uncle Farouq's apartment, helping run the family fruit and vegetable business in a corrugated hut behind Dubai's Nasser Square. By 2002 his firm, SMB Computers, was booming, with more than 200 employees, and the day-to-day business was being run by his brother Saeed Buhary, while Tahir used SMB as a cover to supply Khan's proliferation operations in Libya, Iran and North Korea.[56] He also had a new manufacturing base.

Tahir's relationship with and subsequent marriage to Nazimah Syed Majid, a Malaysian diplomat's daughter, had brought him influence, respectability and permanent residency in Malaysia. The year before they married she had introduced him to Kamal Abdullah, the son of Malaysia's future prime minister, Abdullah Badawi.[57] Kamal owned SCOMI, an up-and-coming petroleum and gas company which had yet to find its feet, and in 1997 Tahir helped SCOMI rise, buying a 25 percent stake as a silent partner. In December 2000, Kamal asked Tahir to join his venture capital business, Kaspadu.[58] All the while the patient Tahir was edging closer to his real goal, establishing a manufacturing front in Malaysia. Tahir and Kamal had much in common. After thirteen years in Dubai, Tahir had learned a lot about the oil and gas industry, and by 2000 SCOMI was riding high on the Malaysian stock exchange, and looking for new investment opportunities. Tahir had a few ideas—that would work for him and also for his mentor in Pakistan.

Khan needed to supply Libya, Iran and North Korea with nuclear-related components which were increasingly difficult to source in the West, where customs authorities immediately investigated any shipments connected to KRL and Pakistan. He could make most of these things at the KRL workshops, but getting them out of Pakistan was also problematic. Malaysia was virgin territory. With no nuclear program, it was ignored by the IAEA and had virtually no laws against the manufacture and export of dual-use components that could be deployed in a nuclear program. Malaysian engineers were adaptable and had a reputation for being able to copy anything cheaply and reliably. Shoes, Sony Walkmans, or centrifuges, it was all the same to them. It was the perfect location for the kind of low-key operation that Khan needed.

In December 2001, Tahir approached SCOMI with a formal business plan, a precision-engineering plant to manufacture aluminum components for oil and gas producers in Dubai. Tahir had identified a disused plant in Shah Alam, an industrial town fifteen miles north of Kuala Lumpur, where skilled labor was cheap and space was plentiful. Engineers from Europe were ready to fit it out and Tahir had negotiated for a German company, Bikar Metal, to supply top-grade aluminum. The plant would produce fourteen components to European standard but for a much cheaper price. Tahir had negotiated with two companies to handle the export side of the business. The Aryash Trading Company would dispatch goods from Malaysia and Gulf Technical Industries (GTI), Peter Griffin's company, would receive them in Dubai, something Griffin said he knew nothing about.

In December 2001, Tahir established SCOMI Precision Engineering (SCOPE), in which Kamal Abdullah, the deputy prime minister's son, was a partner. Tahir brought in Urs Tinner, a Swiss technical consultant and son of Friedrich "Fred" Tinner, the former export manager of a Swiss firm that had supplied vacuum pumps for Khan's uranium enrichment plant as far back as 1977.[59] Urs Tinner went to work fitting out the new Shah Alam factory, importing precision-engineering equipment from the UK, USA and Taiwan through Traco, Switzerland, a company owned by his brother, Marco Tinner.[60]

Urs Tinner also brought with him European blueprints for the aluminum components the factory was to produce. Workers at the plant noted that he was always careful to take back the technical drawings once they had copied them down. But no one was suspicious, as they were told the factory was manufacturing components for the petroleum industry in Dubai and Tinner was only advocating caution to protect European patents. But unbeknown to the manufacturing line in Shah Alam, to Kamal Abdullah and the upper echelons of Kuala Lumpur society, Tahir was producing dual-use components for the illicit nuclear weapons industry. With Malaysia as the point of production, Swiss engineers running the factory, German and Swiss companies supplying the raw materials, and not a Pakistani name in sight, it was invisible to the intelligence community.

Tahir was prescient. He had shifted to Malaysia just in time. In October 2001 the British courts moved against his UK business partner Abu Bakr Siddiqui, prosecuting him for evading export restrictions and shipping nuclear-related equipment to Pakistan. Bakr was sentenced to a twelve-month suspended sentence with a £6000 fine; SMB Europe was dissolved and Tahir turned his back on the UK.[61] In March 2002 the British authorities decided not to tackle the "illicit network" head-on. Like the CIA, the British intelligence community advised the government to do nothing, on the understanding that if the network were left to run while under close surveillance, more detailed information would emerge that would lead to the winding-up of a global trade—headed by Pakistan.

*

The decision suited British prime minister Tony Blair, who was keen to talk down Pakistan and its proliferation and talk up the case for war with Iraq, meeting with President George W. Bush at his ranch in Crawford, Texas, in April 2002 to discuss the battle plan.[62] Blair came out of the Crawford meeting stating: "the issue of weapons of mass destruction cannot be ducked, it is a threat, it is a danger to our world and we must heed that threat and act to prevent it being realized."[63] The argument for eliminating Saddam Hussein was founded on the eradication of his WMDs. However, A. Q. Khan, who had by then been named by British and American spies as "the Typhoid Mary of nuclear proliferation," formed only "part of the background" to these discussions, according to Downing Street aides.[64] Five years after Khan had become the focus of a White House special working group which had determined that Pakistan was selling nuclear weapons technology, the network was still running. And every day that the shut-down operation was held in abeyance gave Pakistan an opportunity to strike another deal.

How would Blair tackle the obvious disparity in leaving Pakistan to its own devices while Iraq was to be obliterated, given that the new campaign was to be based on eradication of WMDs? Downing Street advisers came up with a formulation that the British prime minister promoted, stating that "September 2001 ... had changed the paradigm within which I thought these things through. My thought then was look: Iraq is the place to start on WMD, it's not that you don't have Iran, North Korea, and Libya and the network of A. Q. Khan and others who were a big WMD problem. But the place to start was Iraq."[65] Blair reasoned that for many years Saddam Hussein had ignored successive UN resolutions concerning his country's WMD capability and had frustrated efforts by the IAEA to carry out weapons inspections. "I thought you had to send such a clear signal across the world that regimes from then on would know that they had to comply with international obligations and terrorists would have a reduced chance of getting hold of those weapons."[66] Never mind that Pakistan was the source of them all—and continued to proliferate.

Killing off a client would not throttle the trader. It was Pakistan that had offered to sell nuclear warheads to Iraq, Iran and Saudi Arabia. It was Pakistan that had bred terrorism like other nations farmed rare breeds or cured special sausages. It was Pakistan that had brought the nuclear and terrorist worlds close together, ushering in a nuclear winter that had already seen Khan's scientists meeting with Osama bin Laden. And yet Saddam Hussein was in the frame and Iraq was configured as "the place to start."

In London, several members of Blair's cabinet were concerned the evidence against Iraq just did not stack up, including Jack Straw, the foreign secretary, who voiced his unease at a Downing Street meeting in July 2002. "Bush had made up his mind to take military action, even if the timing was not yet decided," Straw said, according to a report written after the meeting. "But the case was thin. Saddam was not threatening his neighbors, and his WMD capability was less than that of Libya, North Korea and Iran."[67] Straw warned that discussions over Iraq were seriously impeding the West's ability to tackle proliferation. That month, the JIC discussed Khan again, concluding that Pakistan was not only selling technology to enrich uranium but also nuclear warhead designs (if not warheads as well). "This was the first case of a private enterprise offering a complete range of services to enable a customer to acquire highly enriched uranium for nuclear weapons," the JIC warned.[68] And that private enterprise (or the customer) was not Iraq.

For the Iraq campaign to gather momentum, Bush and Blair had to hope the Khan network would not throw up any undue surprises to distract the public from "target Saddam." Then in August 2002, the National Council of Resistance of Iran (NCRI), an exiled Iranian group, summoned reporters to Washington's Willard Hotel for an extraordinary briefing. The group's spokesman, Alireza Jafarzadeh, revealed that Iran was building two secret nuclear facilities in the desert south of Tehran: a heavy water plant near Arak, and a large uranium enrichment facility outside the town of Natanz.[69] Four months after the Crawford summit and one month after Jack Straw had warned that the West had taken its eye off the ball regarding nuclear proliferation, another of Pakistan's clients went public.

Cameramen and reporters jostled for space as Jafarzadeh pointed out the nuclear sites on a large map of Iran. As far as the world was concerned, the country's nuclear ambitions to date had been limited to the Bushehr nuclear power plant, a long-running civilian project, supported first by Germany and later by Russia. News of the two new sites was worrying, but it was Jafarzadeh's second allegation that was astonishing: Iran had a well-advanced uranium enrichment centrifuge facility (which anyone with an overview of the nuclear weapons business would have immediately known could only have been built by Pakistan). Iran had distracted the IAEA by drawing its attention to the country's plutonium program, while its scientists proceeded unhindered with a far more sophisticated project to enrich uranium to weapons-grade.[70]

Pointing his laser pen at an area of central Iran that appeared empty except for a scattering of villages, Jafarzadeh revealed that the Atomic Energy Organization of Iran (AEOI) had been building two large subterranean centrifuge halls, sunk 8 meters into the ground and protected by concrete walls 2.5 meters thick, behind the façade of a "desert eradication project" run by the Kalaye ("Good") Electric Company. "The nuclear project has reached a point where the regime would be capable of a nuclear test in the next few years and could obtain nuclear weapons," Jafarzadeh said. Mohammad Khatami, Iran's president, was personally supervising the project through his Supreme Security Council, day-to-day management came under former Iranian prime minister Mir Hossein Moussavi and the centrifuge expert was Dr. Mohammedi, a senior official in Iran's Defense Industries Organization. The press pack went to work, spinning headlines around the world. The avowedly anti-Western Iran was building a nuclear bomb.

The timing could not have been worse for Bush and Blair. When asked about Iran that afternoon, a State Department spokesman brushed off suggestions that the dangers revealed by the NCRI were comparable to those posed by Saddam Hussein in Iraq. He casually noted that the NCRI's military wing, the Mujahedin e-Khalq (MEK), the People's Mujahideen of Iran, was on the State Department's terrorist list and had ties to Saddam Hussein. The focus was on the messengers and not the message.[71]

A series of weblogs pinged on to the Internet and revealed how, behind Alireza Jafarzadeh's slick appearance, there was a secret past. After leaving Iran in 1979, he had joined the MEK, which stood accused of helping to massacre Iraqi Kurds and Marsh Arabs in March 1991 after the first Gulf War and of cooperation with Iraqi intelligence in hiding WMDs from UN weapons inspectors. The weblogs noted that Jafarzadeh had once volunteered as a suicide bomber and had spent time in a terrorist training camp in Iraq. He was a Saddam Hussein lickspittle and could not be trusted.[72] The NCRI was banned in the US soon after the press conference. But Jafarzadeh, who was comfortable in Washington's corridors and held a green card, stayed on, renting a small office at the National Press Club from where he worked a slot as an Iran analyst for Fox News.[73] A credible orator, he recalled breaking the bomb story: "My 2002 revelations came at the height of preparations for Iraq. They knew my information came from inside the regime, from people who had been inside the facilities. Until I went public, there were even senior officials inside the Khatami regime in Tehran who didn't know about these sites."[74]

What Jafarzadeh did not realize was that he had forced into the open highly classified information about Iran's nuclear program that the West had known and had been sitting on for more than a decade, blowing apart the current administration's argument for pre-emptive action against supposedly WMD-armed Iraq. The CIA was well aware that Pakistan had forged a nuclear pact with Tehran as far back as 1987, the year that Iranian scientists and Brigadier General Mohammed Eslami of the Revolutionary Guard had met A. Q. Khan, Tahir and his uncle Farouq at a hotel in Dubai, and Eslami had agreed to pay $3 million for Khan's obsolete P-1 centrifuge machines, with some of the parts sourced by Khan's European contacts, Heinz Mebus and Gotthard Lerch. That year, Reza Amrollahi, director of the AEOI, also signed an agreement with Munir Ahmed Khan, chairman of PAEC, while both men were attending a meeting of the IAEA in Vienna, for six Iranian scientists to get training at the Pakistan Institute of Nuclear Science and Technology (PINSTECH) in Islamabad.[75] Soon afterwards, a sample P-1 centrifuge and parts for 2,000 more had been sent to Tehran. But then the war in Afghanistan was still playing and nothing negative could be said about Pakistan, even after General Mirza Aslam Beg had bragged to the American about his nuclear pact with Tehran in January 1990 and returned to Tehran the following year to sell the Iranians weapons designs too.

British and US intelligence always suspected that Pakistan had followed up its P-1 centrifuge sales and sold weapons designs to the Revolutionary Guard. But it had been left to Israel to act unilaterally and get to the bottom of the arrangement, which it did in the early 1990s when the Israel Defense Forces (IDF) intelligence corps, Unit 8200, hacked into Iran's communications and listened to discussions about its nuclear deals with Pakistan. General Moshe Ya'alon, who became head of Israeli military intelligence in 1995 and later served as IDF chief, recalled he had "shouted himself hoarse" trying to get Washington to act on Pakistan–Iran.[76] He fared little better in Europe. "Once, when I paid a visit to Berlin, the foreign minister told me that Germany also knew about the Iranian program and that 'We should accept nuclear Iran' and that 'Europeans know how to deal with it.' We should not try to prevent it." In exasperation at the West's reticence, Mossad had leaked intelligence on the Iranian uranium program to the NCRI, which then fed it to Alireza Jafarzadeh, who, believing his information had come from a hot source inside the Iranian nuclear program, gladly shared it with the rest of the world on 14 August 2002 at the Willard Hotel.[77]

With the allegations about Iran out in the open, the story became unstoppable; a commercial imaging firm soon released satellite images of Natanz to sate a public desire for knowledge about the Iranian program. Remarkably detailed pictures showed an extensive complex where construction was clearly moving at an intensive pace.[78] Clearly visible were two enormous square voids dug into the earth and thought to be the subterranean centrifuge halls, each offering a floor space of more than 30,000 square meters. According to calculations made by a former IAEA weapons inspector, together they could accommodate at least 50,000 centrifuges, each machine needing roughly 1 square meter of floor space.[79] Uranium enrichment is measured in "separative work units" (SWU), a measure of the increase in concentration of uranium-235 each time the material is passed through a centrifuge cascade. Commercial centrifuges, such as those developed by Khan, had a capacity of around 5 SWU per year, which gave the massive Natanz project kitted out with Khan's centrifuges a possible output of 250,000 SWU per year, enough enriched uranium to arm seventy-five nuclear weapons.[80] It was an alarming prospect, and such was the detail then available about Natanz that Iran conceded to the IAEA that it had installed uranium enrichment technology—but only as part of a nuclear power program. Mohamed ElBaradei, director general of the IAEA, demanded a site visit and Iran was in no position to refuse.

Iran had been kitted out by Pakistan, which had also tried to sell Iraq a completed nuclear bomb, but on 12 September 2002 President Bush addressed the UN General Assembly for twenty-six minutes about the "grave and gathering danger" of WMDs in Iraq, as delegates were handed copies of the national security strategy for the USA, a document that formalized the new US pre-emptive doctrine. "We cannot let our enemies strike first," Bush said. The world was put on notice that the US military would "detect and destroy an adversary's WMD assets before these weapons are used." The strategy mapped the way ahead for war in Iraq, but it should also have focused America on all WMD threats, enabling the military to prioritize and remove them in order of severity. "We will not permit the world's most dangerous regimes and terrorists to threaten our nation and our friends and allies with the world's most destructive weapons," declared Bush—without a mention, of course, of Pakistan.

The trouble for the Bush people was that they wanted Congress to focus only on Iraq, as this was where the Vulcans were determined that US forces should go. All other threats, especially those greater than Iraq, would have to be concealed, defused or downplayed. In this regard, a top-secret CIA analysis that had been passed to the president in June 2002 became a major problem, as it confirmed that for the past year North Korea had been enriching uranium in "significant quantities," and that Pakistan was to blame, having sold centrifuges and data on how to build and test a uranium-fuelled nuclear weapon.[81] The CIA reported that, despite assurances that travel restrictions had been imposed on Pakistan's scientists, including A. Q. Khan, and pledges that the atomic trade had ceased, Pakistan was still sending teams to Pyongyang, where they were even helping North Korea to conduct a series of cold tests using supercomputers and giving Pyongyang advice on how to "fly under the radar," hiding nuclear research from American satellites and global intelligence agencies.

The CIA report on North Korea had to be buried. It was already classified as Top Secret SCI (sensitive compartmentalized information), enabling the White House to keep it under wraps, even from officials at the Arms Control and Disarmament Agency (ACDA). Norm Wulf, who was then deputy assistant director at ACDA, and others alleged that among those who orchestrated the diversionary tactics was John Bolton, a working-class Lutheran neoconservative from Baltimore, who had got the job of under secretary of state for arms control in May 2001, making him the top proliferation official in the State Department. Bolton was uncompromising and intimidated his staff in the non-proliferation bureau to look away from areas he deemed not to be in their purview.[82] He had also been a signatory to the 1998 letter to President Clinton urging the elimination of Saddam Hussein. Norm Wulf, who had been a frequent visitor to Pyongyang during the Clinton administration, recalled that before Bolton arrived intelligence on Pakistan's involvement in North Korea's uranium enrichment program had been piling up on his desk for three years: "The Pakistanis would happily lie to your face and continue to do what they were doing."[83] But Wulf believed that by 2002 he was only getting a partial picture of what the US really knew. He relied on intelligence passed down to him via Bolton, and there were concerns that the under secretary, or those between him and Wulf, were not handing on all they should. "I became less and less trustful of the evidence and the more clever people who saw it in its original form. Between the raw intelligence and me were several filters. There were hostile relations between Bolton, his staff and the non-proliferation bureau."[84]

Bolton would also attempt to undermine international figures who blocked the new US thinking on proliferation, including the Muslim leader of the IAEA, Mohamed ElBaradei, whose organization relied on negotiated settlement and engagement. ElBaradei, who was seeking a third term as IAEA director, had to be hobbled, and the Bush administration ordered the bugging of his office phone to fish for incriminating evidence to use against him.[85]

But while some US officials dodged the threat from North Korea, or trounced capable exponents of negotiation, Condoleezza Rice, the president's national security adviser, plumped for ignorance. In a letter she wrote to congressmen just weeks after the CIA's North Korea report landed on the president's desk, she advised that the administration would continue to provide North Korea with shipments of heavy fuel oil and nuclear technology, even though Pyongyang had, by starting uranium enrichment, broken the terms of the Agreed Framework and hence forfeited its right to any US assistance.[86] Days later, US intelligence tracked a C-130 transport plane, which Washington had provided to Pakistan to help fight the war on terror, as it flew to North Korea, where it picked up missile parts before returning to Pakistan.

One former intelligence expert on North Korea said that while Rice seemed not to care, senior non-proliferation specialists like Bolton were so reluctant to discuss Pyongyang's program that it was difficult to decipher what American policy was. "We couldn't get people's attention ... the administration was deeply, viciously ideological," he said.[87] Bush and Bolton were particularly contemptuous of efforts that had been made by the Clinton White House to engage Pyongyang, and, anyhow, for the scions of Wohlstetter, engagement smacked of moral equivalence and had to be discouraged. President Bush had been quoted as saying that he "loathed" Kim Jong-il and had "a visceral reaction to this guy, because he is starving his people."[88] His attitude to the regime was blunt and to the point: no deals, no compromises, no attempt at negotiation, this despite it being one of the most militarized nations in the world, with more than 40 percent of its population under arms, an enemy that could not be crushed through conventional warfare. Bolton, too, did not want to empathize with Pyongyang—or even talk to them. While supposedly engaged in talks with President Kim Jong-il, he described the North Korean president as a "tyrannical dictator" in a country where for many "life is a hellish nightmare," triggering the inevitable response from a government spokesman that "such human scum and a blood-sucker is not entitled to take part in the talks."[89] It was a self-fulfilling prophecy: the US goaded, the North Koreans responded and nothing was achieved.

In early October 2002, shortly before Congress would have to vote on authorizing military action in Iraq, the White House finally sent a delegation to tackle Pyongyang on its uranium enrichment program. It was a mission set up to fail. James Kelly, assistant secretary of state for East Asia, a former ambassador to South Korea, arrived with strict instructions that the North Koreans were to be made to shut down their uranium enrichment program before any negotiations could take place—a hard-nosed position to which no country would ever agree. During an all-night session with Kang Suk Ju, the first vice foreign minister of North Korea, Kelly confronted his counterpart with evidence about Pakistan's involvement in the Pyongyang program. "The North Koreans were stunned," said one Japanese diplomat who spoke to some of the participants.[90] "They did not know that the US had cottoned on to the Pak–Pyongyang deal." Backed into a corner, Kang Suk Ju warned Kelly that North Korea possessed even "more powerful weapons" than the Americans had suggested, and the discussions came to a halt.

The North Koreans suspected that the talks had been set up to go nowhere and, believing that President Kim Jong-il was to be targeted after the US had finished with Saddam Hussein, Kang Suk Ju was instructed to return to the table with an incredible offer. The North Koreans offered to shut down their enrichment program in return for a promise from the Americans not to attack.[91] It was tantamount to an admission that North Korea had a uranium program, supplied by Pakistan. But the Bush administration refused to negotiate, James Kelly returned to Washington and the US president sat on the information for five days, during which time Congress voted to authorize military action against the WMD in Iraq.

When news of North Korea's admission was eventually broken, with some in Congress bridling at the thought that they had been manipulated into backing the wrong war, Condoleezza Rice was called on to explain. "Saddam Hussein is in a category by himself," she said, denying the North Korea offer had been deliberately withheld until after the Iraq vote.[92] But by the time Rice spoke, the US had formally rejected Pyongyang's advances and it was left to President Kim Jong-il to write to President Bush the following month, a last futile attempt to open up dialogue. When no one replied, the nonplussed North Korean leader decided to escalate. He announced that he would resume long-range missile tests and step up armaments sales.[93] In December 2002, the North Koreans announced that they would also be restarting work at their Yongbyon-kun plutonium reactor—closed for eight years—reprocessing 8,000 spent fuel rods that had been left over from 1994, enough fissile material for scores of nuclear weapons.[94] Then, in January 2003, North Korea withdrew from the Nuclear Non-Proliferation Treaty, too. An exasperated Robert Gallucci, who had negotiated the Agreed Framework in 1994, recalled: "Now we had no carrot, no stick and no talks."[95] All the administration had won was a congressional mandate for a war in Iraq to counter the threat of WMDs—that were so far proving elusive.

For his part, General Musharraf denied that his country was in any way responsible for the Pyongyang program, telling the *New York Times* that "there is no such thing as collaboration with North Korea in this nuclear area."[96] US secretary of state Colin Powell publicly took Musharraf at his word, but warned that "any ... contact between Pakistan and North Korea we believe would be improper, inappropriate and would have consequences. President Musharraf understands the seriousness of the issue."[97] It was a mirror of the nonsensical relationship between Zia ul-Haq and George Shultz in the late 1980s, when Pakistan's president had offered repeated denials that were accepted for the record by the secretary of state—although in private the CIA had unequivocal intelligence showing the opposite.[98]

There was more unfinished business from the 1980s to deal with in 2002 and it concerned former CIA and Pentagon analyst Richard Barlow. After the controversy surrounding the three inspector general inquiries of 1997 (in which Sherman Funk, inspector general for the State Department, had backed Barlow and accused the Pentagon's deputy inspector general of misrepresenting the truth), Barlow had won another high-level investigation by the Government Accountability Office (GAO), Congress's audit arm, after convincing the Senate armed forces committee, the Senate select committee on intelligence and the GAO there had been a Pentagon conspiracy to cover up evidence about Pakistan's nuclear readiness. The following year the GAO recommended that Barlow should be compensated for the loss of his job, marriage and professional reputation. It looked as if at last there would be some recompense for telling the truth.

"The Senate armed services committee, led by chairman Thurmond and senators Nunn and Levin in particular, convinced that I had been irreparably and unjustifiably harmed, committed to pass a private relief bill for $1.1 million," Barlow recalled.[99] "They explained that this is what private relief bills were for—when someone is harmed by government and where there are no other legal options. They made it very clear that this case was viewed as extraordinary, not just because of my interests but the constitutional interests of Congress itself."

Before the bill could be passed it needed presidential consent. Barlow went to see Alan Krezco, an old lawyer colleague from the State Department, who had become chief counsel to the National Security Council. "Alan was horrified at what had befallen me. He met with President Clinton personally and explained the situation. Clinton said, 'Inform the Senate to send up the bill. I'll sign it right away.' The idea was to let me try to resume a normal life as quickly as possible."

But nothing was straightforward about Barlow's life. When Senator Jeff Bingaman (Democrat, New Mexico), a member of the armed services committee and Barlow's senator, tried to introduce the bill for a vote, he was advised of a procedural error.[100] Barlow remembered: "In a sequence of events that I believe could only occur in the US Congress, it now emerged that certain senators did not like private relief bills in general, even though they had supported my case vigorously. They objected to it, my bill died, sending a message to the Office of the Secretary of Defense that they could get away with anything."[101]

Barlow's compensation claim was referred instead to the Court of Federal Claims.[102] "It was for no apparent reason other than to pass the buck. We would now be trapped in years more hell." Barlow's lawyers preparing his case spent over a million dollars, and when the court finally heard it in February 2000, his legal team subpoenaed intelligence going back to 1987 to prove the US government had covered up for Pakistan. But before the case could be determined, CIA director George Tenet and Michael Hayden, director of the National Security Agency, the US eavesdropping organization, asserted "state secrets privilege" over all evidence, preventing Barlow's team from referring to any of it, citing a threat to national security. Refusing to back down, Barlow's legal team obtained sworn affidavits from Dick Kerr, the recently retired CIA deputy director, and Barlow's two former bosses, Gordon Oehler and Charles Burke, who all backed him, claiming that Congress had been lied to about Pakistan's nuclear program. But the CIA and Justice Department officials seized these statements too, claiming they were secret. The judge agreed, blocking the affidavits, and when Richard Barlow finally got his day in front of the judge in June 2002, after fighting for fifteen years to clear his name, his case was rejected for lack of evidence.

Destroyed and penniless, former CIA golden boy Barlow spent his last savings on a third-hand silver Avion trailer, packed up his life, and drove off to start anew in Bear Canyon campground in Bozeman, Montana. At last he was where Washington had always wanted him to be, just about as far away as possible from causing trouble, his only contact with the outside world being the constant stream of emails he sent to his lawyers, former friends and work colleagues, tapping away day and night in his trailer on a borrowed computer, with only his dogs, guns and a half-empty pouch of American Spirit tobacco for company. Robert Gallucci, who had followed Barlow's case as well as proliferation in Pakistan, recalled: "I felt kind of guilty. Both Rich and I had tried to tell the truth about Pakistan. The difference was he had been taken apart and somehow I survived."[103]

In Washington, it was still only Iraq that was on the president's mind. "The dictator of Iraq is not disarming," he warned in his state of the union address in January 2003. "To the contrary, he is deceiving ... We will consult, but let there be no misunderstanding: if Saddam Hussein does not fully disarm, for the safety of our people, and for the peace of the world, we will lead a coalition to disarm him."[104]

Bush even presented crucial evidence of the Iraqi threat. Citing British intelligence, he revealed that Saddam Hussein's agents had bought yellowcake in Niger, as a first step to obtaining the fissile material with which to fuel a nuclear bomb. It was a resonant allegation repeated around the world, which had come through John Bolton's office. Unfortunately it was not true, and high-ranking US diplomats and military officials who watched the speech on television that night were incredulous. Joseph Wilson, the former US ambassador to Gabon, who had recently returned from Niamey, the capital of Niger, sent at the behest of Vice President Dick Cheney, had concluded the exact opposite. Having gone there in 1999 to investigate suspicions that A. Q. Khan was buying yellowcake, he had been sent back in 2002, told that Iraq was trying to secure a deal, something attested to in documents allegedly recovered by Britain's MI6. However, after his trip, Wilson warned the administration that the MI6 documents—a memorandum of understanding between the Iraqi and Niger governments—were clumsy forgeries, signed by people who no longer held office.[105]

Since Wilson had given the White House fair warning about the dead-end Niger deal, the ambassador could only conclude that the president knew he was lying. Wilson went public, claiming the Bush speech was a deliberate attempt to deceive Congress and the American people. A four-star general who also visited Niger in 2002 backed him. Marine General Carlton W. Fulford, Jr., had come away "assured" that the country's stocks of yellowcake were secure and passed his findings up to the chairman of the joint chiefs of staff. "I was convinced it was not an issue," Fulford said.[106] After Wilson wrote a column in the *Washington Post* detailing the truth, his wife, Valerie Plame, then serving undercover as a CIA agent, found herself exposed in several newspapers by conservative columnists who, it was alleged, had been tipped off by senior sources close to the president and Dick Cheney. The unveiling of Valerie Plame, a wife wielded against a husband, was a device that had been used before, and some of those involved had had a hand in the discrediting of Pentagon WMD analyst Richard Barlow in 1989, turning his wife, Cindy, against him after Barlow had uncovered evidence that senior Pentagon officials were lying about Pakistan's nuclear capabilities.

As for proliferation, there was no mention of Pakistan in the state of the union address, although Bush claimed (in full knowledge of the dirty tricks campaign mounted against ElBaradei): "We are strongly supporting the IAEA in its mission to track and control nuclear materials around the world. We are working with other governments to ... strengthen global treaties banning the production and shipment of missile technologies and weapons of mass destruction." Iran, Bush hinted, was ripe for regime change, but only after the Iraqi dictator had been brought to book. "Iranians, like all people, have a right to choose their own government and determine their own destiny," Bush said. "The United States supports their aspirations to live in freedom." The recent breakdown in communications with North Korea was glossed over, Bush simply saying that the "regime will find respect in the world and revival for its people only when it turns away from its nuclear ambitions."[107]

On 5 February 2003, Colin Powell was sent, clasping a tiny vial, to the United Nations Security Council. Backed by satellite photographs, he presented "irrefutable and undeniable" evidence that Iraq had been deceiving UN weapons inspectors. Saddam Hussein was hiding banned weapons—including chemical agents, a small pinch of which could snuff out the life of a city. Powell detailed links between Iraq and al-Qaeda, claiming Hussein had offered the terrorists a haven in northeastern Iraq and pooled expertise on poisons. There was no hard evidence of this unlikely union, or any reference to the al-Masri library found in Afghanistan, which linked Pakistan's scientists to the al-Qaeda WMD program. There was also no mention of the $1.5 billion in US exports to Iraq that had made Hussein's weapons program viable in the early 1990s, sales that had been approved by the US Commerce Department in the full knowledge that the components would be used in Iraq's military programs.[108]

All the while, bubbling beneath the surface were two genuine WMD crises: North Korea in virtual meltdown, announcing it had restarted reprocessing 8000 spent fuel rods at Yongbyon-kun; and Iran, where President Mohammed Khatami revealed that teams had started mining uranium near the city of Yazd and were developing the wherewithal for a complete nuclear fuel cycle.[109]

Washington had to do something. White House spokesman Ari Fleischer admitted the Natanz and Arak facilities reinforced US fears about Iran's "across-the-board pursuit of weapons of mass destruction and missile capabilities." While ElBaradei lobbied for a site inspection of Natanz, two senior US officials approached the Iranians at the United Nations in Geneva—one of them, Zalmay Khalilzad, the highest-ranking Muslim in the Bush administration, a neoconservative advocate of regime change, who, like many of the Vulcans, regarded nuclear disarmament with disdain and had signed the 1998 letter to Clinton advocating the elimination of Saddam Hussein. An ethnic Pashtun born in the northern Afghan city of Mazar-e-Sharif, Khalilzad had studied with Paul Wolfowitz under Albert Wohlstetter at Chicago University in the 1960s. In the 1980s he had worked closely with avowedly anti-Communist Zbigniew Brzezinski, supporting the Soviet war in his homeland as well as advising on the conflagration between Iran and Iraq. Khalilzad approached the Iranians with an uncompromising agenda—back down on the nuclear weapons program or face annihilation.[110] Two tracks on Iran: one, emanating from the IAEA in Vienna, which was old school and believed in dialogue, while the other, the Vulcan school, was tired of talking.

Khalilzad achieved nothing, but on 21 February 2003 Mohamed ElBaradei finally gained access to Natanz. Only hours before he arrived, Alireza Jafarzadeh, the spokesman for the NCRI, announced that the building ElBaradei was about to be shown was not the enrichment complex. "I held a press conference in DC, tipped ElBaradei off and he located the correct build-ing, discovering inside 164 centrifuge machines and lots of parts. He was stunned."[111]

What the Iranians reluctantly showed the IAEA inspectors was Natanz's pilot enrichment plant, due to begin operating in June 2003. The inspectors reported that "over 100 of the approximately 1000 planned centrifuge casings had already been installed."[112] The main cascade halls, designed to hold more than 50,000 centrifuges, would be ready by early 2005. The IAEA officials were "taken aback" by the advanced state of the facility.[113]

ElBaradei had brought along Trevor Edwards, a British metallurgist who had worked for URENCO in the early 1970s—at the same time as A. Q. Khan. He concluded that Iran's centrifuges were based on the CNOR blueprints stolen by Khan in 1975. "I knew how the Iranians had made their great leap forward. Every single detail of the centrifuges, down to the millimeter, the exact tolerances of the different parts, was identical to models I remembered from my work in Capenhurst and Almelo."[114]

In early March 2003, with the world waiting for bombs to fall on Iraq, a Palestinian man contacted MI6 at Vauxhall Cross in London to pass on a message that Colonel Muammar Gaddafi of Libya wanted to discuss his country's WMD. Improbable as it sounded, the Libyan leader was preparing to send his son, Saif al-Islam, as an emissary. Gaddafi had been watching the run-up to the US-led attack on Iraq, and, fearing that he would soon become a US target too, had, according to a US diplomatic cable, been calling "every Arab leader on his Rolodex."[115] But Saif Gaddafi at first denied that his father had been prompted by the looming war. He recalled: "We started negotiating before the beginning of the war, and it is not because we are afraid or under American pressure or blackmail."[116] He did, however, recognize the extraordinary nature of this meeting that saw the thirty-five-year-old ensconced in a Mayfair hotel suite facing "people whom I had regarded for a long time as the devils, enemies."[117]

Libya had been designated a state sponsor of terrorism in 1979 and in 1984 had proved its credentials after policewoman Yvonne Fletcher was shot dead outside the Libyan embassy in St. James's Square, London. Two years later, US planes had killed Saif's two-year-old sister and badly injured two of his brothers when they bombed the Gaddafi compound in Tripoli in retaliation for an attack on a Berlin disco for which Libya was blamed (and in response to intelligence received by the CIA that Libya was contemplating assassinating Ronald Reagan). Saif, then fourteen, was paraded before cameras with his arms in bandages, and after December 1988 relations between Tripoli and the West had been dominated by the blowing up of Pan Am 103 over Lockerbie in Scotland, an attack that killed 270 people. The attack had been linked to a Libyan intelligence officer through pieces of clothing found in a suitcase in the wreckage. The present discussions in Mayfair had only been made possible after Libya had agreed in 1999 to hand over two suspects in the Lockerbie bombing, leading Tony Blair and Colonel Gaddafi to exchange a series of letters.

Saif Gaddafi, who had graduated from the London School of Economics, was no stranger to navigating between the Islamic and Christian worlds. Unlike his father, who clung to nomadic traditions, Saif had been schooled in the ways of the West and headed the Gaddafi International Foundation for Charity Associations, which had successfully negotiated the release of several European hostages held by Islamic groups in Southeast Asia and Africa. Saif had also represented his father during talks with Israel in Jerusalem. But what the British negotiating team did not yet know was that Saif also had a more personal involvement in his father's nuclear dealings.

Wajid Shamsul Hasan, who served as Pakistan's high commissioner to London during Benazir Bhutto's second term, recalled meeting a colleague in Islamabad in 2001, who had been involved in the protocol of a recent trip to Pakistan by Saif Gaddafi. He alleged that "there had been a huge kerfuffle because Saif had arrived loaded down with suitcases crammed with cash. He had to clear these suitcases through the diplomatic channel. Our government had booked him a whole floor of the Marriott, in Islamabad, only for the ISI and military to complain that it was far too dangerous, packing him off to a secret guest house. My contacts said the cash was for uranium enrichment technology."[118]

Now, in Mayfair, Saif Gaddafi began by announcing that his father wanted to work with the UK and US to launch a new initiative to reform the Middle East. However, MI6 cut him short. "Talk to us about WMDs," they said. Saif Gaddafi was circumspect. He was the messenger and not the message. All he had to offer was the prospect of talks on WMDs, but as to what his father wished to reveal, he claimed to have no idea. A call was put through from the Mayfair hotel to Sir David Manning, Blair's foreign affairs adviser, who suggested that before making any commitments, the British government needed to hear from Colonel Gaddafi himself.[119]

Three days later, on 20 March, as Operation Shock and Awe engulfed Iraq in a storm of munitions and the hunt began for WMDs, a small team of British officials took off from RAF Northolt, in northwest London, bound for Libya. Gaddafi was waiting for his visitors inside a vast tent erected on an army parade ground in Tripoli. But he, too, did not want to talk details. Instead, the British team was told to negotiate with Musa Kusa, Libya's head of foreign intelligence.[120] The diplomats were wary. Musa Kusa was well known in London as an uncompromising hard-liner, part of Gaddafi's old guard, having been expelled from the UK in 1980 when he was head of the Libyan mission, after openly discussing the assassination of Libyan exiles. Musa Kusa was also a wanted man in France, where the authorities were keen to question him about the blowing up of a French passenger jet in 1989 at the cost of 170 lives.

The British team bit their tongues and entered into a series of meetings with the intelligence chief. They told Musa Kusa there were rules: they would have to visit all of Libya's nuclear sites and had to be allowed to talk to all of the scientists involved in the WMD program before any kind of diplomatic deal could be discussed. But extracting details from Musa Kusa proved as difficult as eliciting information from the Gaddafi clan, the British officials reported back to Downing Street after returning home without having made any significant progress. Libya was still working out what it wanted and what it was prepared to hand over in exchange.

By the time Tony Blair met President Bush in Washington on 26 March 2003, events were unfolding so rapidly in Iraq that the US was happy for the British to take the lead on Libya. Blair imposed one condition: the acerbic John Bolton was to be kept away from the negotiations.[121] The US president was, however, to be kept in the picture at every stage and in April 2003, as coalition forces fought to dislodge Saddam Hussein's Revolutionary Guard from the outer suburbs of Baghdad, a senior member of the MI6 Libya team flew to Washington to brief George Tenet. With him was Sir Richard Dearlove, the head of MI6, who suggested that it was time to bring the Libyans and American negotiators together for direct talks. Sir Richard arranged for Musa Kusa to meet a senior CIA official, Stephen Kappes, in Geneva. Kappes, a former station chief in Moscow, spoke Russian and Farsi and was an agency old hand. He asked Kusa to bring with him a breakdown of Libya's WMD activities as a sign of good faith. But when the two men met several weeks later, the Libyan once again turned up empty-handed, claiming to have run out of time. It was going to be a long-drawn-out process. Musa Kusa was in no hurry. It was as if Gaddafi could not bring himself to go through with a deal that was far more about self-preservation than it was about coming to an accommodation with the West.[122]

However, the need to strike a deal with Gaddafi would only intensify, as Pakistan, it seemed, was popping up wherever US satellites were trained. US and UK intelligence showed KRL was doing yet more business with China, in a government-to-government contract that saw Chinese M-11 nuclear-capable missiles delivered to Islamabad, while Islamabad also continued to pursue a close relationship with the Changgwang Sinyong Corporation, North Korea's nuclear procurement cover company. US spy satellites had captured a ship flying the star and crescent moon flag of Pakistan docking in Pyongyang and off-loading ten Scud missiles, while on 3 April 2003 German intelligence had intercepted a cargo vessel in the Suez Canal carrying aluminum tubing headed for North Korea with specifications suggesting just one likely purpose: the manufacture of outer casings for P-2 centrifuges. Colin Powell called up Pervez Musharraf and came up with a diplomatic solution. KRL and the Changgwang

Sinyong Corporation were to be sanctioned as private entities, rather than punitive measures being slapped on America's regional ally, Pakistan. This was exactly the strategy that the Reagan White House had used in August 1987 when Arshad Pervez had been caught buying maraging steel in the US. Then the administration had put the buy down to a "private procurement network," in order to create as much space as possible between the smuggler and the regime in Islamabad. Now Powell did the same, and Pakistan agreeably played along.[123]

A. Q. Khan's former suppliers were well aware that the net was closing in. Peter Griffin recalled flying to Islamabad at the end of March 2003: "My son Paul was doing some business there and asked me to come along. I contacted Colonel Qazi, my old KRL contact, who was delighted to hear from me and said, 'You must come to stay.' " Griffin was keen to catch up with Khan too. "I said to Qazi, 'Let's go to see Qadeer.' " But Qazi was firm. " 'Under no circumstances,' he told me. Khan had given instructions that I was not to see him, or attempt to contact him. I think he was trying to protect me."[124]

It was too late for that. Griffin flew on to Dubai, where he had arranged to meet a new sponsor for his company, Gulf Technical Industries (GTI), and while he was away his home in France was raided.[125] Anna, his wife, was at home on her own and answered the door in her bikini to find eight French police officers and a British customs official standing on the doorstep. "It was a Friday," recalled Anna.[126] "I was about to go down to the pool. They said I was under arrest and they produced a warrant to search the house."

For nine hours, the police and customs agent scoured the property. "They went through everything, including love letters and personal things. I had to accompany them through every room. There was no explanation, they wouldn't show me any paperwork and I wasn't allowed to call Peter. They took all our mobile phones, Peter's Filofax, a commemorative cigar box given to us by Tahir and Nazimah at their Malaysian wedding." Griffin had amassed a trove of keepsakes from his work with Khan, including a copy of *The Islamic Bomb*, the book that had first outed the KRL chief in 1981 and which Khan had then published in Pakistan at his own expense. This was vintage Khan, turning the book that demonized him into a vehicle for his own publicity, and he had dedicated one copy to Griffin, signing the endpapers with a facetious comment. More pertinently, the police bagged up Griffin's two computers and a third machine used by his wife, as well as their CDs. Anna Griffin recalled how the customs official lingered over an old copy of *Time* magazine. She could see how it appeared: "It was an edition about 9/11. He wanted to know why I'd kept it. The truth was mundane. We'd not had a TV at that time and wanted to read about the destruction of the Twin Towers. They made notes. About everything."

Peter Griffin returned to France two days later and was arrested at Nice airport. "As I got off the flight, I was seized on a judge's warrant. I asked on suspicion of what? They said, 'Don't you know?' I said, 'No.' They refused to say any more. I got taken to the security area and there was this British guy sitting there with his feet up. I remember he was wearing Doc Martens and was badly sunburnt. He'd obviously been lying around, waiting for me to get back. He wouldn't speak either. It was only when they all left the room for a moment that I was able to glance at the warrant lying on the table and saw that the requesting authority was Her Majesty's Customs and Excise."[127]

Griffin was released several hours later and contacted the British consul in Marseilles. "She said she would get back to me but after three months I'd heard nothing about why I'd been questioned, my wife harassed and my home raided. I went back to her. The consul said she couldn't discuss it and couldn't help me further. She put me on to an English-speaking lawyer who got no response from the British authorities. Even my lawyers in the UK hit a blank. I was being wrapped up—but no one wanted to say for what and on whose orders."

By the summer of 2003, Olli Heinonen, a senior IAEA inspector from Finland who had been tracking Iran's nuclear weapons program since the mid-1990s, was convinced that Pakistan was to blame, with modest assistance from China. But the IAEA was not privy to US and UK intelligence that would have confirmed Heinonen's suspicions, and he and his colleagues had to go about proving their case through what they saw with their own eyes.[128] Not only had Heinonen's IAEA colleague Trevor Edwards noted the remarkable similarities between the Iranian centrifuges and those acquired and then adapted by Khan, but swipe samples taken from the pilot plant at Natanz revealed particles of highly enriched uranium that could not have been produced inside Iran, as they were enriched well beyond the capabilities of the Iranian rig. To Heinonen, they looked remarkably similar to samples from centrifuge components originating from Pakistan which had been intercepted elsewhere.

But the Iranians said nothing, even as IAEA inspectors returned to Iran in

March 2003, where they visited the workshop at the Kalaye Electric Company in Tehran, a place where the Iranians admitted centrifuges had been tested before Natanz was built. The Iranian authorities refused access to one of the workshop buildings, claiming it was only a storage facility to which they had lost the keys. When the IAEA returned to Kalaye on a subsequent occasion, the inspectors "noted that there had been considerable modification to the premises since their [last] visit." Heinonen suspected that Pakistan-sourced material had been stored inside, including Khan's most advanced centrifuge— the P-2.[129] They had been removed and concealed elsewhere.

With ElBaradei's blessing, Heinonen wrote to KRL, PAEC and Musharraf's Strategic Plans Division, asking for senior representatives to come to Vienna. This was tricky for Musharraf. He could not be seen by his own people to be caving in to an organization like the IAEA, but he needed to demonstrate his integrity to the West. Instead of a scientist, he sent a diplomat who was ill versed in the nuclear program but well versed in prevarication. The emissary agreed to talk on the basis that he would not answer any questions about Khan. It was a wasted meeting which left Heinonen frustrated, but in Tehran the Iranians had reluctantly revealed a little more about equipment the IAEA had discovered. They admitted that the highly enriched uranium particles swiped by Heinonen's team were not home-processed. If they had been, Iranian scientists would have had to explain how they were capable of achieving this level of enrichment when all the equipment they had demonstrated a much lower yield capability. In the end, Tehran admitted it had imported used components, although the Iranians refused to say from where.

Iran, meanwhile, was looking for a way out. It sent word to the Americans, via the Swiss ambassador in Tehran, that it was ready to discuss its nuclear program.[130] More than twenty years after the 1979 hostage crisis, the Swiss embassy was still the only diplomatic channel between Iran and the US. The offer was drafted with the blessing of all the major political players in the Iranian regime, including the supreme leader, Ayatollah Ali Khamenei. It was an incredible deal: in return for the United States addressing Iran's security concerns, the lifting of economic sanctions and normalization of relations, including support for Iran's integration into the global economic structure, Tehran was offering to cut off support to Hamas and Islamic Jihad and to convert Hezbollah, its sponsored political, military and welfare front in Lebanon, into a purely political organization.

Powell and his deputy Armitage could see no wrong in any of it. They argued in support of the talks, believing it was time to move on from 1979. Iran could be helpful in stabilizing post-conflict Iraq, given that the long-oppressed Shia population was in the majority and would need to be mobilized to heal the country once Saddam was eliminated. But a lobby led by Rumsfeld, Cheney and Bolton blocked all discussions. "They were saying we didn't want to engage with Iran because we didn't want to owe them," recalled a senior adminis-tration official.[131] "They demanded instead that the Iranians pass over information on high-ranking al-Qaeda fighters detained by Tehran, a side issue that the ayatollahs were baffled by." When the US agreed to send an emissary to listen to Tehran at a round of talks in Geneva, the staunch Zalmay Khalilzad, who had previously threatened Iran with annihilation, was sent.

The dialogue went nowhere. The State Department was directed by the White House to rebuke the Swiss ambassador for having passed on the Iranian offer. The Pentagon, already thinking beyond Iraq and to the Vulcans' agenda and the "Axis of Evil," called for the destabilization of a rogue nuclear nation by "using all available points of pressure on the Iranian regime, including backing armed Iranian dissidents and employing the services of the Mujahedin e-Khalq (MEK)."[132]

The MEK was, of course, the same Iranian opposition group that had been denounced after Alireza Jafarzadeh revealed the Iranian nuclear program at Natanz, at the wrong time in the wrong place, just as the US was girding itself for war in Iraq. Now the MEK was apparently back in favor in Washington as the Vulcans zeroed in on Iran.[133]

But the Bush people were even-handed in the dispensing of rough treatment. It was not only the Iranians who were sandbagged. The same treatment was to be meted out to Bush's favorite ally, Britain, which foolishly believed it could finally get some momentum behind an operation to put an end to Pakistan's covert nuclear sales.

17

MISSION ACCOMPLISHED

In late June 2003, President Pervez Musharraf set out on a three-day visit to London. Government ministers attended dinners thrown in his honor. The Lord Chancellor, Lord Falconer, feted him. Musharraf was even introduced to Prince Charles. What had been agreed between the US and British governments behind the scenes was a softening up of the Pakistan president before the next leg of his tour, meeting President Bush at Camp David, where he was, Tony Blair had been assured, to be skewered over Pakistan's secret nuclear sales and in particular the mounting evidence—kept from Capitol Hill and the British parliament—that Project A/B now encompassed not just North Korea and Iran but Libya and, everyone suspected, many other countries and individuals too.[1]

In London, Musharraf revelled in the high-class reception that the British establishment liked to bestow on impressionable guests whom they regarded as low-class. The president responded by becoming positively convivial in the face of all of the razzmatazz, sounding with every day he spent in the British capital more and more like an enlightened despot. "We are striving to build a modern, tolerant, progressive Islamic state," he told an invited audience at Lancaster House, the mansion used by the Foreign Office blue bloods for doling out hospitality—perhaps not appreciating that the mandarins who were studying his every move were the descendants of a civil service line that stretched right back to Robert Clive, who first scored a foothold on the subcontinent by defeating a Bengali nawab at the battle of Plassey in 1757. They knew exactly who Musharraf was and where he came from: the manipulator of the home-grown Sunni mob, the sectarian pogroms and massacres of Shias, a nasty little war in Kashmir, the rise of the Taliban and the birth of al-Qaeda. But after they had feted the dictator, and then sent him on his way to the US from Heathrow on 20 June, an astonishing call came through to Downing Street from the White House. The discussions about the nuclear sales had been struck from the agenda. There would be no talks about proliferation.[2]

When Musharraf arrived in the US he had time on his hands. He called on his son Bilal, who ran a hi-tech start-up company in Boston, and when President Bush welcomed him on the lawn at Camp David four days later, on 24 June, he eulogized: "President Musharraf is a courageous leader and a friend of the United States. Today, our two nations are working together closely on common challenges. Both the United States and Pakistan are threatened by global terror, and we're determined to defeat it." The president was on a high, having announced the end of combat in Iraq one month earlier. "Mission Accomplished," he had declared aboard the aircraft carrier USS *Abraham Lincoln*, moored off the coast of San Diego (rather than the Persian Gulf).[3] Now, he dumped the British request for a joint approach to crack down on proliferation. It was bad leaders and not bad weapons, corrupt regimes and not their arsenals, who were to be addressed in this new age. And Bush had evidence of Pakistan's commitment. He told reporters that since September 2001 the Islamic Republic had apprehended more than 500 al-Qaeda and Taliban terrorists. For this assistance, the US was rewarding Pakistan by cancelling a $1 billion debt and instigating a new $3 billion military and economic assistance package. The only reference to Pakistan's nuclear program came during a question-and-answer session when Musharraf was quizzed by a Pakistani journalist about his country's nuclear intent. "Pakistan follows a strategy of minimum deterrence," the president demurred. "We are not into any arms race, but we do maintain forces to ensure this strategy of minimum deterrence." It was all the CIA could do, according to one senior analyst, not to curl up and cry.[4]

British intelligence, however, had not given up on proliferation. They had the bit between their teeth. The team attempting to coax the Libyans into unravelling their program now received a critical tip-off from Kuala Lumpur. Aluminum parts that had been manufactured at a factory owned by B. S. A. Tahir in Malaysia had arrived in Dubai's free-trade zone, from where they had been loaded on to a German ship, the *BBC China*, that was destined for Tripoli. The parts were said to include rotors about 6 feet high, designed to fit inside a P-1 or P-2 centrifuge, and they were manufactured to specifications identical to those used in Pakistan. If they were interdicted, these components would offer compelling evidence of a Libyan nuclear program, bolstered by the Islamabad regime, and might be the clincher in forcing the pace of the Gaddafi negotiations.

But it was a race against time. MI6 had received the information a little too late. Customs officials in Dubai discovered that the *BBC China* was already at sea. After a frantic search, it was found making its way through the Suez Canal, and while its progress was closely monitored the British intelligence community debated what to do. The ship had to be stopped and searched. Now, all the spooks had to figure out was where to board it and how to go through its numerous containers without raising suspicion. Nothing should alert the Libyans or Pakistan. MI6 got in touch with their counterparts in Germany, who made contact with the ship's owners in Hamburg. They claimed to know nothing about the destination or contents of individual containers, but agreed to cooperate if a friendly port could be found. At a meeting in Rome, in late September 2003, the UK asked Italian officials for assistance, as the *BBC China* would be passing close to Taranto, a major shipping destination in southern Italy. MI6 and customs officers needed only a few hours to inspect the vessel. The Italians agreed. Hamburg radioed the ship's captain, who mapped in an early-morning stopover in Italy, set for three weeks hence.

Only now, with evidence of Pakistan's continuing proliferation floating down the Suez Canal and into an open port in Italy, did President Bush accede to the British request to discuss nuclear sales face to face with Pakistan's president, who was due in New York for a UN summit. Bush would draw him aside for a private tête-à-tête, his officials assured the British. The venue would be the $7,000-a-night suite on the thirty-third floor of the Waldorf-Astoria Hotel where Bush always stayed when on UN business.[5] The press brief would simply state that the meeting between the two presidents was to discuss the war on terror, Iraq, Kashmir and dialogue with India.

A senior White House official recalled: "President Bush kicked things off. He warned that proliferation was rife and had to stop. 'It is extremely serious and very important from your point of view,'" he told Musharraf on 23 September.[6] George Tenet called at Musharraf's hotel suite the next day with a sheaf of incriminating evidence, in a meeting that a senior Musharraf aide described disingenuously as "the most embarrassing moment in the [Pakistani] president's life."[7] Musharraf was surprised, but not about the issue of proliferation. His aides said that he had been certain that the US would not confront him, as

Pakistan was now on a long leash (on proliferation and many other issues), given how integral the country was to the war on terror. "Now the leash was being wound in, but Musharraf got over his surprise. He moved on and thought, 'So be it.' He was a survivor. Pakistan was a survivor. We would adapt to a new reality," the source said. "Musharraf would play dumb until he ascertained what the US knew and whom we could blame."[8]

On the polished wooden table, Tenet laid out detailed drawings of Pakistan's P-1 centrifuge, with part numbers, dates and signatures. Musharraf later claimed: "I immediately recognized them as our centrifuges ... a version that we were no longer using but had developed in the early stages of our program under A. Q. Khan." There were details of A. Q. Khan's travels around the world, bank statements, even paperwork showing what KRL had offered for sale and to which countries. Musharraf feigned ignorance. "I did not know what to say ... My first thoughts went to my country—how to protect it from harm. My second thought was extreme anger toward A.Q.—he had endangered Pakistan."[9]

Given that Project A/B had been a military imperative from its inception under Zia in the mid-1980s, and that the US knew that Musharraf had known about the nuclear trade all along, everyone in the room knew that everyone was lying. But the consensus in Washington was that what mattered more than prosecuting the guilty was saving Pakistan's vulnerable (and valuable) president. "Whatever suited him," a senior British Foreign Office source said. "He would come up with his own framework for survival and we would help him get through it, as long as the dirty deals were wound up. It was a compromise struck in the world of realpolitik."

Although the sourcing had been disguised, Tenet had made sure the evidence he presented was complete and compelling so as to persuade Musharraf that this was the tipping point. In fact, Tenet had overdone it and there was so much to wade through that Pakistan's president missed his next meeting, with the Russian leader Vladimir Putin. Musharraf would later claim: "There could be no doubt that it was [Khan] who had been peddling our technology, even though Tenet did not say so and the papers did not include his name."[10] It was another part of the retrospective rewriting, part of the shadow-puppetry between Pakistan and the West in which Musharraf began to refashion Pakistan's proliferation from a military prerogative to the act of a small group of renegade scientists.

In the early hours of 4 October 2003 the *BBC China* dropped anchor at Taranto, where a small MI6 and CIA search party was waiting. They had just two hours to identify and scour five 40-foot containers out of more than two hundred on board, before the ship resumed its journey. Using serial numbers given them by their Malaysian source—a European nuclear supplier—they quickly located the containers and discovered inside them hundreds of wooden crates stamped with the logo "SCOPE," B. S. A. Tahir's factory in Shah Alam.[11] The MI6 team had hit pay dirt. They pried open the crates and found inside aluminum casings, pumps, flanges and positioners—the brackets needed to hold fast centrifuge components. Everything was impounded—at least they thought this was the case—before the ship was allowed to continue its journey, so as not to alert Pakistan to the fact that its network had been penetrated.

However, A. Q. Khan and Tahir knew about the bust right away. Without liaising with MI6, Foreign Office officials clumsily contacted Musa Kusa to ask him why, with negotiations ongoing, a Pakistani shipment of dual-use nuclear components, sufficient to manufacture up to 1,000 centrifuges, had been intercepted on its way to Libya. Musa Kusa immediately called Tahir, who contacted Islamabad. But the Libyan spy chief remained cool. He was a man whose career had been spent under fire. When the British called back again he claimed the shipment was part of a regular delivery and he had been planning to hand it over to his British and American friends as evidence of Colonel Gaddafi's good faith. Suddenly the blockage, whatever it had been—nerves, anxiety or plain revulsion at dealing with the West—vanished. The Libyan intelligence chief agreed to coordinate the first Western site visits to Libya's top-secret nuclear facilities.

Two days later, Richard Armitage and Christina Rocca, assistant secretary for South Asia, flew into Islamabad for a secret meeting at Army House to advance "the save Musharraf" plan. Armitage could not reveal the ongoing Libyan operation, but his job was to hammer the message home that proliferation had to stop. It was a delicate moment for Armitage, who had known Musharraf since the war against the Soviets and was mindful of America's need to keep the general close, set against the imperative of shutting Pakistan's Project A/B down. There was going to have to be a trade here, a way for Musharraf to act without appearing to undermine Pakistan's best interests. However Armitage looked at it, if Musharraf was to be kept alive, one of Pakistan's national heroes would have to be sacrificed in his place. Armitage planned to make certain Musharraf understood the severity of the situation by also reaching out to his inner circle, and so while he talked tactics with Pakistan's president, General John Abizaid, the US CENTCOM commander, simultaneously briefed General Mohammed Yusaf, the Pakistan army's Taliban-supporting number two.[12]

Armitage and Rocca presented Musharraf with yet more detailed evidence, and after they left, Musharraf called up his closest friends, including Humayun Gauhar, the editor of *Blue Chip*, an exclusive business magazine that had been launched after Musharraf came to power to represent a new and aspirational Pakistan of industry, money, and Western-style savvy (one that for now mainly existed in the enclaves of expatriate Pakistanis the world over). Gauhar was a mountain of a man who lived in one of the scores of vast villas that had sprouted up in the exclusive lanes falling off the broad expanse of Islamabad's Margalla Road.[13] It was rumored that he was being considered as Pakistan's next ambassador to Washington, following in the footsteps of Altaf Gauhar, his father, who had been a close confidant of Ayub Khan (the general who had been Pakistan's dictator for most of the 1960s). Altaf Gauhar had ghost-written Ayub Khan's memoirs, *Friends, Not Masters*, and Humayun Gauhar was in the middle of scripting what would become Musharraf's *In the Line of Fire*.

Chain-smoking cigars, his maid bringing in cool glasses of freshly squeezed juice, Gauhar served as the president's sounding board. Convincing in the West and at ease in the East, men like Gauhar, who had lived in many different continents, were able to explain to the institutionalized Musharraf (who knew well only the inside of an officers' mess) what sounded credible in London or Washington, what chimed with the thinking in Paris and Berlin. Gauhar recalled that the A. Q. Khan affair had been "exceptionally well managed." He said: "Those days were very tense days. After 9/11 we had no choice. Blood was in America's eyes. They were not thinking straight. But we had to back the US horse or it would kick us in the teeth. The proliferation thing was something the US had known for a long time. We responded in the way we should have done. When Musharraf had his suspicions confirmed he brought Khan down."[14]

Gauhar recalled how Musharraf first called him in to discuss the crisis in late 2003. The meeting was part of the president of Pakistan's strategy to deal with the West's complaints, a soft opening for the Musharraf gambit—that Khan, already retired, was blamed solely for the ongoing proliferation. Musharraf was canvassing—testing the water before he attempted to string up one of the great Pakistanis, perhaps the greatest living Pakistani.

Gauhar was shown a PowerPoint presentation of evidence. "There were checks, lots of them, for large amounts of money. Different countries, I seem to remember Saudi Arabia was involved. Libya too—although later the whole thing there was overblown. The North Korea deal too. It was No-dong missiles, I was told, and not as significant as the US made out. We didn't need No-dongs as we had all the missiles we needed from China already." What he had been shown was enough to clear the military of any involvement in Project A/B and make the plan look improvised by A. Q. Khan and his team. Gauhar was convinced. But others who were similarly briefed at the prime minister's secretariat were horrified by Musharraf's intended broadside against "a truly heroic Pakistani."[15] Many had been uneasy with Khan's enforced retirement in 2001, and this smacked of cowardice and complicity with America. "Khan was worth a hundred Musharrafs," one of those in the room had muttered.

Gauhar, however, was adamant: "Musharraf was convincing. He had turned to us younger guys and said something like, 'We know things you don't know. There are things I cannot tell you. But take it from me, things have to change.'"

The situation was changing at such a pace that the IAEA could barely keep up. On 16 October 2003, its director, Mohamed ElBaradei, was invited to Tehran for urgent discussions about the country's nuclear program. Dr. Hassan Rohani, secretary of the Supreme National Security Council of Iran, had decided to come clean. He had offered the IAEA "a full disclosure of Iran's past and present nuclear activities." As a result, a dialogue began to open up, with Gholam Reza Aghazadeh, the Iranian vice president, travelling to Vienna the following week, where he, too, issued a declaration.[16]

For the first time since the 1979 revolution, and apparently in response to behind-the-scenes work at the IAEA as well as international pressure, Iran officially confirmed it had begun work on a centrifugal enrichment program. It had started in 1985, with Tehran receiving drawings of a centrifuge from a foreign intermediary officials declined to name, two years later. The program had three phases: 1985 to 1997—with all work located at the Plasma Physics Laboratory of the Tehran Nuclear Research Council; 1997 to 2001—when the project was relocated to the Kalaye Electric Company in Tehran; 2001 onwards—when Iran had begun construction of enrichment facilities at Natanz, in the central desert.[17]

Iran handed over crates of documents to the IAEA which had to be translated, sifted, filed and analyzed. However, ElBaradei revealed that while trawling through the paperwork his analysts found references to five middlemen who had aided the program, providing Tehran with key drawings, including designs for Pakistan's P-1 centrifuges, as well as components. While the blueprints were clearly based on the designs stolen from Holland by Khan in 1975, the labels were in English, not Dutch and German, suggesting they were prototypes modified by Pakistan. According to the Iranians, the middlemen, three of whom were German nationals, had arranged several important deliveries to Iran, including a flow-forming lathe obtained from the engineering company Leifeld in Ahlen, West Germany, in 1985, a machine capable of fashioning rotors from aluminum tubing.[18] A country with such a lathe needed only to order the raw materials to outfit its enrichment plant, rather than fishing for dual-use items on the international market.

The Iranians were loyal to those who had helped them. "The information had to be dragged out of them. They refused to name the middlemen, although eventually they showed the IAEA a one-page, handwritten sheet that appeared to be the earliest known record of a business transaction between Pakistan and a foreign government," one of those involved in the mission recalled.[19] It was dated to 1987 and appeared to be Khan's menu of what was for sale, from which Brigadier General Mohammed Eslami of the Revolutionary Guard had cherry-picked, buying frugally at the meeting in a Dubai hotel that year.[20] The Iranians claimed they had purchased P-1 centrifuge blueprints and components. They had initially planned to reverse-engineer an enrichment plant, angering Khan, who believed they were not capable of completing the job and could afford to spend more on better equipment. He was right. A second deal was struck with Eslami in 1994 to buy from Pakistan 500 completed P-1 centrifuges. But this deal soured too. The Iranians suspected they were being fobbed off with inferior goods. By 1997, when the majority of the centrifuge program had been relocated to Kalaye Electric, due to fears that the West was about to uncover it, they had all but given up. The Atomic Energy Organization of Iran had only been able to operate small cascades of ten to twenty machines because of "machine crashes attributed to poor quality components."[21] They went back to Pakistan, looking to spend, and asked for more sophisticated equipment. They also began to import UF_6 from Pakistan to test their machines, which explained why they had been reluctant to show inspectors around their workshops.[22] Pakistan was generous. It is claimed that it threw in some highly enriched uranium, drums of which were piling up in the storerooms of KRL, an irresistible sweetener that would have enabled the Iranians to leap ahead and experiment with manufacturing a nuclear weapon while they perfected the cascades. The IAEA would have been horrified—but it did not know.

According to what the Iranians told the IAEA, by 2001 Iran had returned to the idea of machining its own centrifuges, as the war on terror had made international supplies even more difficult to come by. It was now that they also began secretly to construct a pilot enrichment plant, slated to hold 1,000 centrifuges.[23] That had gone so well that by 2002 they had begun building a production-scale fuel enrichment factory at Natanz, to hold 50,000 centrifuges in two huge subterranean halls. Having already obtained the bulk of the manufacturing equipment it needed, a centrifuge assembly line was also set up at Natanz.

Iran's confession was a promising start.[24] "We are in a new phase," said ElBaradei, enthused, on 10 November 2003. "I look forward to working with the Iranian authorities in the next few weeks to resolve the outstanding questions and to bring to closure this issue that has been the subject of a good deal of international concern." ElBaradei was also conscious of the fact that he had succeeded where the US had failed and he was determined not to lose his advantage over John Bolton—who was still tapping his phones.[25]

A week later, IAEA inspectors returned to Natanz. Scientists there had restricted their centrifuges to low-level enrichment and it occurred to the IAEA that perhaps the Iranians had a second secret site where the more advanced P-2s had been configured to manufacture highly enriched uranium. The IAEA was certain that Pakistan had sold Iran P-2s at some stage in the 1990s, an allegation that Tehran had so far denied. At the back of the inspectors' minds was a thought placed there by the US that what Tehran had willingly shown represented only a fraction of the real Iranian program, a red herring to distract their attention away from this second "secret plant," a concealed centrifuge hall running P-2s that were four times as efficient as anything seen at Natanz.[26] It was too much of a temptation for the Iranians not to have tried it, Bolton argued.[27]

On 19 October 2003, as the IAEA began its talks in Tehran, a joint CIA–MI6 team flew out of RAF Northolt for their first meeting with the scientists running

Libya's WMD program. The mission was highly classified. In Washington, only the president, Colin Powell, Richard Armitage and William Burns, assistant secretary of state, knew.[28] John Bolton, who had predictably called for regime change in Libya when he learned of the interception of the *BBC China*, was, as the US had pledged, not informed. Even Mohamed ElBaradei and the handful of senior IAEA officials who would be responsible for inspecting Libya's facilities if a deal was ever signed and sealed, were not told about what was happening.

The Anglo-American team covered every eventuality. Its members included one nuclear specialist, a missile expert and a chemical/biological investigator. The CIA's Stephen Kappes and a senior MI6 agent completed the crew who arrived in Tripoli for a meeting with Musa Kusa, who immediately introduced them to the men who would be their guides, each of them supposedly the head of a strand of Libya's covert doomsday program. Musa Kusa promised co-operation, but the British nuclear expert got off to a bad start. Matoug Mohammed Matoug, secretary of the National Board of Scientific Research and supposedly the head of Libya's nuclear program, a man known as "Triple M," refused to meet him and passed the baton to a junior scientist who did not have the authority or experience to carry off the visit.

The available intelligence showed that Libya probably had up to a dozen secret research sites. But the junior guide insisted that Libya's facilities were all located at the Tajoura Nuclear Research Center, on the coast east of Tripoli, where the Soviets had built a 10-megawatt research reactor in the 1980s. Fuelled by enriched uranium, it had been subject to IAEA inspections for many years and was barely functioning. It was an inauspicious start, and the guide would go on to deny that Libya had been attempting to obtain anything connected to a full nuclear fuel cycle: yellowcake, a uranium conversion facility or even centrifuges. He also pretended not to have been told about the *BBC China* raid, an embarrassing incident of which all of Libya's WMD experts would have been aware. Once at Tajoura, a place the IAEA was familiar with, the British expert was raced through its halls without being able to talk to any of its staff and was barred from taking photos.

All the visits were painfully slow. Twelve-hour days. Report writing into the early hours. "But the team felt as if it was pushing against an open door and finally a story about the history of the Libyan program tumbled out," one of those who participated recalled.[29] The authorities admitted that in the early

1980s an unnamed German intermediary had assisted Libyan technicians with research into centrifugal uranium enrichment. It had been carried out at Tajoura, using a centrifuge design that the German expert had brought with him. In 1984 they had ordered a pilot uranium conversion facility from an unidentified source, designed to provide the UF_6 for a working enrichment plant. The facility had been fabricated in portable modules, according to specifications provided by Libyan scientists, so that it could be broken down and moved around in the event of an inspection or a military strike against Libya. These modules had been received in 1986 and stored in various locations around Tripoli, but, according to Libyan officials, they had never been put together.[30] The story bore all the hallmarks of a Pakistani operation, but the Libyan officials refused to confirm it or to identify the German. All they would reveal was that by the time he stopped assisting them, in 1992, Libya had not produced a single operating centrifuge and had not conducted any experiments using nuclear material.

On 29 October the Anglo-American team flew home. Although there was clear evidence that Gaddafi had commissioned some sort of uranium enrichment project with foreign help, the experts had not seen anything that confirmed that Libya had progressed to anything close to a real WMD program. If they were going to get to the bottom of it, many more trips to Tripoli would be needed, or additional help canvassed from outside Libya.

Components that investigators had seen at various warehouses in Libya had clearly come from countries outside Africa. The crates bore markings that suggested Dubai was the port of transit. This placed them, at least, within the orbit of Khan's supplier, Tahir, then living in Malaysia. The team decided to trace the Libyan program backwards to see where it led. On 10 November 2003, Stephen Kappes and his MI6 counterpart flew to Malaysia to seek assistance from the Malaysian special branch. Mohamed Bakri Omar, Malaysia's inspector general of police, recalled: "The focus of their discussion was the so-called international network that was suspected of transferring nuclear technology to third countries. Of course we cooperated, although we were dubious at first."[31]

Kappes and his colleagues briefed Omar on Khan, Libya, and what they knew about the role of Tahir. But there was a sticking point, something immediately obvious to Malaysian special branch officers. Tahir's factory was co-owned by Kamal Abdullah, the son of the Malaysian prime minister, Abdullah Badawi. He had to be kept out of it. A halt was called for two days while the prime minister was briefed, after which Kappes was given the go-ahead. The agents visited the Shah Alam factory, but it was by then an abandoned lot. The SCOPE logo had been taken down. All that was left inside it when police eventually broke open the lock in 2003 was a museum relic, a turning machine made in Switzerland in 1948, which had never been used.[32] Tahir, with his society connections, was slightly easier to track down and volunteered himself for questioning when police found him at his in-laws' house in Kuala Lumpur, although he feigned surprise at the accusation that he was at the center of an international WMD conspiracy.[33]

Tahir was good at that. He looked so innocent and conventional, not anyone's idea of a mafia don or nuclear smuggler. But under closer scrutiny Tahir's story was a little garbled. According to his Malaysian interrogators, he confessed to having done business with Libya and claimed the deals started in 1997, when he had travelled to Istanbul with Khan to meet two of Gaddafi's agents in a café. One was introduced as "Triple M," a former revolutionary who had gone on to become secretary of the National Board of Scientific Research. The other was referred to only as "Karim." Tahir recalled how he had sat at a side table while Khan, "Triple M" and Karim got down to business. Later, he claimed, Khan had told him to ship centrifuge units to Colonel Gaddafi's nuclear program. A container with twenty used P-1s was to be sent via Dubai to Tripoli, along with spare parts for 200 more. The Libyans were charged several million dollars, which Tahir recalled thinking "was money for old rope," given that the P-1s were regarded as scrap in Pakistan. But this, he claimed, was none of his business.

The following year Tahir and Khan met the Libyans again, this time in Casablanca.[34] The Libyans were polite but clearly vexed. "Triple M" advised Khan that the components previously sold had been useful but insufficient to establish a program. International sanctions prevented Libyan scientists from studying abroad and they did not have the technical expertise to set up their own production line. "Triple M" had learned that Pakistan had a far more sophisticated centrifuge design which to date it had failed to offer Libya—a polite way of letting Pakistan know that Libya knew it had been sold shoddy goods. Gaddafi had the cash, "Triple M" said. He wanted the P-2s. "Triple M" claimed he had been authorized to bid for an entire centrifuge facility of 10,000 machines based on the advanced P-2 blueprint.[35]

Tahir was amazed, he told the Malaysian authorities. Sourcing, building and shipping a state-of-the-art centrifuge facility would represent a demanding new challenge even for Khan's network. However, when "Triple M" mentioned that his government was willing to pay $140 million for the plant, Tahir's worries evaporated. "For that money, we would sell them the prime minister's secretariat," a friend recalled him joking.[36] Khan asked Tahir to drop all of his existing tasks. The Libyan deal was now Pakistan's (and his) top priority. Tahir told Malaysian detectives that he personally met with the Libyan agents in Dubai to refine his role in the ambitious deal.

Millions of components were needed to assemble 10,000 centrifuges, and to avoid the attention of the IAEA and Western security agencies, Tahir planned to source them from many different countries, collect them at the free-trade zone of Dubai, or possibly Kuwait, and ship them on to Tripoli. According to receipts, and shipping documentation later handed over to the British, by late December 2002 Tahir was trading with thirty companies in twelve countries to source the necessary parts.[37] It was a cat's cradle designed specifically to baffle the watchers.

Some of what the Libyans needed could be manufactured in Malaysia and Tahir's SCOPE factory in Shah Alam, and Kappes and his colleagues learned that it had been set up specifically for the Libyan job. The Libyans had paid him $3.4 million for his contribution, with which Tahir had employed Urs Tinner to oversee production. The components were delivered in four consignments, beginning in December 2002. A second contract went to another Tinner family business, Traco, the Swiss company owned by Urs's brother, Marco. Then one of Tahir's contacts in Turkey was called on to collaborate, Khan's old supplier Gunes Cire.[38] Tahir told Malaysian detectives that the five containers seized from the *BBC China* in October 2003 had been the last of the Shah Alam consignments, and that after they were dispatched Tinner had returned to Switzerland, shutting down the Malaysian factory.

Tahir was keen to demonstrate that he was cooperating. "His new in-laws heaped pressure on him to do so," a Malaysian friend said. The file from the Malaysian investigation revealed how Tahir blabbed, naming scores of his contacts in Europe and South Africa.[39] They included Gotthard Lerch, who had supplied Khan with vacuum technology via Leybold Heraeus, in Germany, in the 1970s. Gunes Cire, the electrical engineer from Turkey, who had met Khan while studying in Hamburg in the early 1960s, allegedly procured aluminum-casting and dynamo equipment, while Selim Alguadis, another Turkish engineer, sourced electrical cabinets and voltage regulators via Traco in Switzerland. Tahir revealed that he had arranged for the Turkish crates to be sent along with his Dubai components aboard the *BBC China*. This meant that when MI6 had raided the *BBC China* and impounded five containers, all of them connected to Malaysia, they had missed one. Not tipped off to look for Turkish goods, the British had enabled Cire's components to reach Tripoli.[40]

Tahir had another confession. He said that, as well as centrifuges, in 1999 the Libyans had demanded 20 tons of UF_6 with which to feed their machines. Pakistan obliged here, too, as they had done with other countries, also throwing in drums of highly enriched uranium so that Libya, like Iran, could get on with the business of designing a bomb. The drums of UF_6 and highly enriched uranium had been delivered on a commercial Pakistan International Airways flight from Islamabad "in 2001 or 2002," according to Tahir.[41] It was later claimed that these canisters had been driven through Dubai in the back of Tahir's maroon Lexus on their long journey through Khan's shadowy netherworld.[42] But Tahir claimed not to remember that detail.

Then Tahir was prompted into revealing another major strand to the Libyan deal. Gaddafi's scientists had asked him to open a workshop to manufacture their own centrifuge components. The Libyans wanted it stocked and their staff trained to European standards. Tahir claimed the deal was code-named Project Machine Shop 1001.[43] The machines for the workshop would be obtained from Europe, including flow-forming lathes for extruding aluminum tubes to form the rotors of a P-2 centrifuge, and a special annealing furnace from Italy. Colonel Gaddafi allegedly planned to locate the factory at Janzour, an idyllic seaside resort on the Mediterranean a few miles west of Tripoli, famed for its golden sandy beaches and orange groves.

Peter Griffin heard about the Malaysian inquiry, and that its investigators were probing his affairs too, in late 2003. "A Dubai sponsor who had helped us start up a company arrived on my doorstep in France in November or December 2003," recalled Griffin. "He just turned up out of the blue. He had an important message from Tahir in Kuala Lumpur. He wanted me to destroy all records of our business together. I rang Tahir and asked what was going on. He said, 'I can't say, I can't talk to you. Just destroy everything.' I said, 'No, these documents are my only insurance.' "[44]

Griffin learned soon afterwards that Tahir had betrayed him, telling Malaysian detectives that the Briton was the main middleman involved in fitting out Project Machine Shop 1001, and that the work was to have been done through Griffin's company, Gulf Technical Industries (GTI). Griffin claimed he had been framed and there was no such thing as Project Machine Shop 1001. "The number 1001 came from the next job number in our order book at GTI." He produced a well-thumbed photocopy of a factory logbook from Dubai, on which item 1001 was described as: "Repair machine shop for Libyan National Oil Company."

Griffin recalled how he was reeled in. Tahir had called him to his flat on the sixth floor of the Mummy & Me apartment building in Dubai in May 1994. "I was not living in Dubai at that stage, just passing through on some business," remembered Griffin. "Tahir and his uncle Farouq asked me to cost various machines to set up a workshop in Dubai. I said, 'Is it nuclear?' They said, 'No.' So that was dealt with. They said it was for the Libyan National Oil Company that wanted to replace its burnt-out machinery. They wanted to be able to manufacture their own spares in Dubai, where sanctions did not apply. I saw no problem in that and sent over a container-load of catalogues, all the usual stuff for a standard machine shop."[45]

Griffin heard nothing. He thought the project had been dropped, until in 1997 Tahir came back to him and asked him to do a new estimate. "Tahir called me up and said, 'Let's do it, the Libyan thing. Can you revalidate the quotes?' I said I'd have to charge him commission again. He said he'd pay." Griffin said that when Tahir told him the Libyan contract was worth $10 million, he decided to give it his full attention. "I moved to Dubai with Anna in August 1997 and set up GTI." But as far as Griffin was concerned this deal was with the Libyan National Oil Company only.

Tahir made all sorts of requests, but none worried him at the time, recalled Griffin. First, Tahir put $2 million into GTI's bank account, allegedly to buy equipment for the Dubai workshop. Griffin continued: "In came the money in about July 2000, although there were few signs that the workshop was about to be built." Instead, Tahir, who was now a father and lived in Kuala Lumpur full-time, called regularly, asking Griffin to transfer money to different accounts. "He'd say, 'I promised to send some money, can you send it for me to Lerch, to Gunes, to Nauman Shah [A. Q. Khan's son-in-law].'" Griffin did not ask any questions and recalled making at least nine payments. "I did point out to Tahir at one stage that this money was coming out of the Libyan National Oil Company cash. He said, 'Don't worry, I'll pay you back,' and he did. The only problem, as I realized to my cost later, was I had no paperwork for these deals. Nothing to protect myself with."

What Griffin claimed not to know was that these payments were part of the Libyan nuclear deal that was being tracked by MI6 and the CIA. Griffin admitted to having been suspicious, but not unduly so. He had known Tahir for years. He trusted him back then. He said, "I was asked later if it had not appeared unusual to use money set aside for one thing to pay off another, without making any official receipts. But I said, 'Tahir was a good friend. It was like a mate asking to borrow a fiver.' But since there was nothing in writing I could not prove that Tahir had lied to me. I was disappointed. I'd known Tahir since he was a kid."

In 1999, Tahir asked Griffin to supply two flow-turning lathes from Spain, in another deal that would incriminate him and enrich the Khan network. "Again, he said they were for the Libyan National Oil Company. They were 15.6 tons each, enormous machines as big as my living room, each costing $350,000. I delivered them to Dubai in July or August 2000. Tahir asked if I could rent some factory space and set them up so his clients could see them running. I rented space in the Al Ghoz industrial estate." But Tahir did not show. A month later, he called Griffin to say that the clients were coming to take the lathes away. "I didn't care," said Griffin. "I was glad to see the back of them." Griffin said that the next time he heard about the machinery was in February 2004, when Tahir told the Malaysian authorities that the lathes, too, had been part and parcel of the Libyan nuclear deal. Griffin flew back to Dubai to confront Tahir's staff. "It was chaos, hundreds of people running around trying to get hold of Tahir. But he was hiding." Suspecting he had been set up, while Griffin was in Dubai in 2004 he also visited the customs authorities, searching for paperwork that could show what had happened to the equipment.

Griffin discovered that in November 2000, instead of delivering the lathes to the Libyan National Oil Company, Tahir had sent at least one of them to South Africa, using a forged GTI invoice. Griffin claimed not to have known anything about the transaction. The freight was paid in Dubai, allegedly by Griffin's company, and the delivery address was Tradefin Engineering, a South African metalworking company based in an industrial park at Vanderbijlpark, a mining town forty miles southwest of Johannesburg. According to the documents, the lathe spent thirteen months in South Africa before being dispatched back to Dubai in transit to Malaysia. Griffin said: "It was possible that it had been adapted while away in South Africa, modified to be able to perform very fine definition work, something that it couldn't do when it left my warehouse." The lathe arrived back in Dubai on 12 December 2001 and, according to shipping documents, days later was re-exported to Malaysia under the instructions of a Mr. Hussain of GTI. Griffin said: "I didn't employ any Mr. Hussain. My company had been exploited to cover up a deal. I had to find out what Tahir was up to." It wasn't too hard. The contact number for "Mr. Hussain" rang through one of Tahir's companies in Dubai—SMB Distribution. Tahir had framed his friend. Griffin could not fathom where the equipment with his name on had ended up. He would have to wait to find out. He had been suspicious about SMB's real activities since 1997, when Tahir had asked him to audit the company and he had discovered major discrepancies between what was being bought and sold.[46]

In August 2001, Griffin decided to pack up and return to Europe. Tahir called him before he left. "He asked if he could use GTI to import things, as I was leaving Dubai. I said if he cared to send GTI inquiries they would be dealt with on a commercial and legal basis. We only spoke about it once and then I forgot it." Griffin and his wife Anna bought a villa in southern France. But then, in November 2001, Griffin received a call from his then office manager in Dubai: "He said he'd been advised by a shipping company there was a consignment of aluminum tubes that had just arrived at Dubai docks for GTI but he could not find any record of us having ordered them." Aluminum tubes were more than likely to be used by Tahir to manufacture nuclear parts. "I sensed right away it was Tahir. I said, 'Tell the shippers that they're not ours. Quickly.' I phoned Tahir up. He said, 'Yes, the tubes are for me. You don't mind?' I was furious. I said, 'Yes, I do. This is the end of it. If you do anything like this again I'll take you to court in Dubai. Do you hear?' But I still did not know what was really going on. I was out of the loop. GTI was going under. I was in France. Only later, when they pulled in Tahir, could I see how he had set me up as the fall guy for the Libyan nuclear deal. What crap."[47]

In France, Griffin kept himself to himself after Tahir had spun his stories.

Others were less lucky. Tahir's younger brother, Saeed Buhary, who had acted as chairman for SMB Computers, found himself locked up in the central prison in Dubai, without a proper trial. It was known as the Jumeira Hilton and had a reputation for harsh conditions.[48] Gunes Cire, Khan's former supplier from Turkey, was arrested in Istanbul and interrogated by the Turkish secret police for several months until he died during one particularly vigorous session.[49] "He had a heart murmur," said Griffin, who considered Cire a close friend. "The poor guy could not take the questioning. I felt so bad. He had been so good to me." Griffin had had a lucky escape.

In Pakistan, no one would escape as Musharraf prepared the ground before sacrificing A. Q. Khan. On the evening of 23 November 2003, Dr. Mohammed Farooq, KRL director and one of Khan's long-standing deputies, disappeared from his home in Islamabad. A rumor immediately raced around town that Farooq, who for many years had acted as intermediary with Khan's many foreign suppliers, had been arrested and taken to ISI headquarters for questioning over a matter of national security. Dr. Badar Habib, a senior KRL engineer, who had been at Farooq's home at the time of the arrest, also vanished. Neighbors, paranoid and frightened, claimed that those who took the two men away included Westerners dressed in civilian clothing, setting alarm bells ringing in the Pakistani press that the operation had been coordinated by the CIA. Later that night, more KRL scientists disappeared, including Dr. Yasin Chohan, head of the production line, Dr. Saeed Ahmed, head of the centrifuge design office, a technician called Shameem, Dr. Abdul Majid, director of KRL's health and physics department, and Dr. Zubair Khan, a KRL engineer. But officials from the interior ministry and the ISI issued flat denials that the authorities had arrested any of them, claiming that whatever was going on was an internal matter for KRL. In the confusion, Musharraf's plan remained obscure, even as the rumors of CIA renditions of Pakistan's leading scientists swirled around Islamabad.

Worried Khan employees and their families began to mill around the entrance to the KRL staff colony on the Islamabad highway. In the early hours of the next morning a government official drove up and pinned a directive to the gates, warning that foreign travel was banned with immediate effect, before driving away, refusing to answer questions. Over the following days, the government eventually admitted that an investigation was under way, but strenuously denied that anyone had been arrested. All Musharraf's spokesman would say was that the men were being "debriefed," normal procedure at KRL. Every person who had been pulled in was being put through a personal reliability test—although no one would confirm what these PRT tests were.

The families knew that was not the truth. But Dr. Shafiq, who was with his father, Brigadier Sajawal, when the round-ups began, recalled that Khan initially appeared unconcerned. He had no idea what was coming. "After Badar Habib and Dr. Farooq were picked up, Khan sahib's secretary, Major Islam, visited us," remembered Dr. Shafiq.[50] "But the discussions were not serious. There was no warning. No panic signals. We did not consider, even remotely, that it was serious. They were all so senior. We were the establishment. The ruling class, do you see? What could happen to us? We were heroes of Pakistan and had done the bidding of the military for decades. Everything Khan had done was for his country and based on an order. Only cowards sacrifice their friends and allies, after all. Isn't that true?" Khan was so relaxed he went on holiday to Bani Gala Lake, a beauty spot thirty minutes outside the capital and the source of Islamabad's drinking water. The area was green belt and it was supposedly prohibited to build on it so that the watercourse would remain pure and unadulterated. But Khan had built a weekend mansion on the pristine shoreline and his sewage ran untreated into the water.

18

THEY HAVE FED US TO THE DOGS

On 1 December 2003, the Anglo-American team was back in Tripoli, armed with Tahir's allegations of how Pakistan (and its European suppliers) had constructed a nuclear program for Libya. They asked to meet "Triple M," whom Tahir had identified as the lead negotiator in the deal struck with A. Q. Khan at an Istanbul café in 1997. But the Libyans insisted that he was unavailable. Instead, Musa Kusa announced that the investigators were to be allowed to tour several new sites that had previously been inaccessible. In the suburbs of the Libyan capital and then out in the desert, the fifteen-man team was ushered in and out of more than a dozen buildings. One team member recalled: "There was a centrifuge R&D workshop at Al Hashan and another at Al Fallah. There was a disused uranium conversion facility at Al Khalla and a new one at Salah Eddin. There was a yellowcake storage facility in the central desert at Sabhah and the foundations at Janzour for a building said to be the future Project Machine Shop 1001."[1]

Many of the facilities had been assembled and then dismantled, repeatedly packed up and moved to avoid detection. Not only were there new locations to search, but the Libyan guides were far more frank, conceding that following a "July 1995 strategic decision to reinvigorate its nuclear activities" Libya had approached Pakistan to assist with a uranium enrichment program. This was what the British team had been waiting to hear, but the details that followed were politically explosive.[2]

Islamabad, they revealed, had sanctioned Khan to proceed, working alongside a minder supplied by the Pakistani military. However, the Libyans still declined to name the "foreign expert" who had assisted Gaddafi to procure a prototype centrifuge in the 1980s, although the CIA and MI6 team had narrowed his

identity down to one name: Gotthard Lerch.[3] Already much had been discovered that starkly contradicted the official cover story being assembled by
Washington—that the Pakistani military was in the clear while corrupt scientists
at KRL and elsewhere had betrayed the Islamic Republic. A British Foreign
Office source connected to the investigation alleged: "Whoever was running the
show, when it all broke, would have to be careful to tailor the evidence so as to
keep Musharraf and his men out of it, and that wasn't going to be easy."

The Libyans confirmed that a deal with Pakistan had been thrashed out in
1997 in Istanbul, when they had ordered twenty preassembled P-1 centrifuges
and components for 200 more. But only one machine was test-run at the Al
Hashan R&D facility in Tripoli, and it had not produced any enriched material.
In September 2000, after the Libyan scientists complained at the quality of
what Pakistan had exported, Tripoli took delivery of two demonstrator P-2
centrifuges. They were sent on an ordinary Pakistan International Airlines (PIA)
flight from Islamabad to Dubai, from where Tahir had arranged the onward
journey to Libya.[4] And here again, the British team on the ground discovered
evidence of how the Pakistani military had supervised the Libyan project. The
delivery of P-2s had been shrouded in a cover story, with President Musharraf
visiting Tripoli in May 2000 to announce a conventional weapons deal between
Pakistan and Libya. No one was surprised therefore, when cargo, accompanied
by military permits which removed it from the normal customs procedures,
was loaded onto the PIA flight four months later and ultimately delivered to
Tripoli. Inside were the centrifuges.

Libyan technicians began installing more P-1s in a large hall at Al Hashan,
with the intention of building a cascade, although, try as they might, they could
only get nine machines running before the authorities decided to shift their
facility to a building at Al Fallah, in another part of the capital. By late
December 2002, according to Tahir's evidence, some of which was now backed
by the Libyans, millions of components also began to flood in for the centrifuge
assembly line at Janzour, coordinated through shell companies that consisted
of nothing more than a postbox on Dubai's main business artery, the Sheikh
Zayed Road.

While most components came via suppliers already identified by Tahir in his
special branch debriefing, the British discovered another source. For the first
time, MI6 understood the significance of Khan's visits to Africa, which had
commenced in 1998. Initially, they had focused on Niamey, the capital of Niger,

suspecting that he had been fishing for a new supply of yellowcake. But now it became clear that it was Khartoum that had been critical, as Khan had been negotiating to use the country as a warehouse for hi-tech engineering equipment. Examining Sudan's imports, investigators discovered that between 1999 and 2001 Sudan had imported £320 million worth of machine tools, gauges and hi-tech processing equipment from Western Europe. "The suspicion arises that at least some of the machinery was not destined for Sudan," an intelligence assessment concluded. "Among the equipment purchased by Sudan there are dual-use goods whose use there appears implausible."[5]

The CIA–MI6 team unearthed allegations that Gotthard Lerch might be in on the Libyan project, suspicions that hardened when the Mannheim district attorney's office conducted an investigation into Lerch's affairs. Having worked as Khan's deal-maker since the late 1970s, when he was sales manager for Leybold Heraeus, he owned property and businesses in Switzerland, Germany and South Africa, and had channelled millions through a bank account in Monaco. Documents recovered in Tripoli seemed to show that some of this money was payment for building Libya's ready-made and state-of-the-art centrifuge plant, a project to which Lerch had allegedly signed up in July 1999, when he was said to have met Tahir in Dubai. Tahir had told Malaysian investigators that he had been unable to manage the enormous Libyan project by himself and that Lerch had suggested he take over half of the contract, using South Africa as a staging post. In the 1980s, Leybold had worked with South African engineering companies to manufacture parts for the country's secret nuclear weapons program. When that was scrapped at the end of the apartheid era, many of Lerch's South African partners had been left struggling to stay afloat. In July 1999 they had jumped at the chance of a lucrative contract to build a complete centrifuge plant—with no questions asked.

Lerch introduced Tahir to Gerhard Wisser, Leybold's former representative in South Africa, at a Dubai dinner party in 1999. Wisser, a German national, still lived in South Africa, where he ran Krisch Engineering and at the time of this party he was in the middle of a costly divorce.[6] Wisser claimed that he could arrange for the construction of a complete five-stage cascade consisting of 5832 centrifuges, along with a feed-and-withdrawal system to pump UF_6 gas into and out of the plant.[7] Pakistan had come a long way from slipping the odd blueprint to a rogue state or shipping boxes of centrifuge components to an ally. Now the Islamic Republic was embarking on the construction of a replica

KRL for an unstable regime that had a nasty habit of sponsoring terrorism. Since the contract was also to equip a production line, there was no stopping Gaddafi from passing on the technology, or the highly enriched uranium it would produce, to anyone who could pay. The prospect terrified British investigators.[8]

Johan Meyer, an old friend of Wisser, who ran Tradefin Engineering, a South African metalworking company in Vanderbijlpark, was to carry out the work. This was the company that would take delivery of one of Peter Griffin's vast Spanish lathes, equipment that Griffin maintained he had been asked to supply for the Libyan National Oil Company project.[9] The CIA–MI6 team learned that in April 2001 Tradefin's Meyer had travelled to Dubai with Wisser to discuss the contract. Meyer claimed he was never told the destination of the plant. Wisser later claimed that he thought they were building a refinery intended for the UAE. But both Wisser and Meyer referred to the plan in all correspondence as "Project X," a subterfuge that suggested both men suspected an ulterior—and shadier—motive. There were other names for the job that also demonstrated a level of knowledge, one of the engineers working at Tradefin later telling investigators that many of them referred to it as the "A.F. Project," short for "Arab Fuckers."[10]

When work began on the cascade in several three-story metal buildings at Vanderbijlpark, another Krisch employee, Daniel Geiges, a Swiss engineer who had lived in South Africa since 1969, supervised it. Geiges claimed that he worked to German blueprints that had come from Lerch's old company, Leybold Heraeus, formerly a supplier to URENCO. Lerch had been accused on two previous occasions of stealing secrets.[11] However, the test data and calculations for the plant being built in Vanderbijlpark came from Pakistan.[12] Documents from the deal appeared to implicate all three men. A fax sent on 14 June 2001 from Wisser informed Geiges that Lerch was planning to visit the factory the following month. In another, Wisser informed Geiges that "GL is coming around 30/8/2001–1/9/2001."[13]

Such was the ambition of this project that many visitors wanted to see its progress, including Tahir and Dr. Farooq Hashmi, the KRL deputy director. On another occasion, two men who called themselves "Abdul" and "Ali," and claimed, implausibly, to be Ethiopians, inspected the plant. "It's possible they were Libyan, but I'm by no means certain," said Geiges, who claimed that he soon understood that he was working on a uranium enrichment cascade, because "Lerch told me so."[14] Geiges recalled that the project was completed in May 2003, when it was tested, taken apart and then packed into eleven 40-foot-long containers ready for shipping. Johan Meyer opened a bank account in Switzerland and large sums were funnelled into it from shell companies, except for one payment that was carelessly wired from an address in Libya.[15] This payment and a second move by Meyer, who had used a dummy company to purchase sensors and valves from Germany, eventually attracted the attention of the German federal public prosecutor's office in Karlsruhe, which had Lerch arrested.[16] He was accused of having received £20 million from Libya, half of which he cleared as profit.[17]

In Libya, the Anglo-American team uncovered another facet of the Pakistan deal that truly staggered them. The Libyans showed their visitors canisters at the Al Fallah storage facility in Tripoli that contained 1.7 tons of UF_6 from Pakistan, a gift to get the Libyan enrichment factory up and running. No mention was made of the highly enriched uranium.[18] They also discovered worrying evidence that some of what Pakistan had exported had gone missing en route from Dubai to Tripoli. Two shipping containers, one filled with centrifuge components and a ton of high-strength aluminum, the other containing precision tools and parts for two specialized lathes, had last been seen in Turkey and Malaysia shortly before the BBC China seizure.[19] A British Foreign Office source said: "We now began to worry that we had let the project run on too long and it was now too late to wrap it all up, as its tentacles were reaching everywhere."

But still the Libyans withheld information. If Pakistan had agreed to supply the entire process to Gaddafi, where, the British team asked, were the weapon designs? In the early hours of 12 December 2003, as the MI6–CIA team walked out to their unmarked plane at Tripoli airport, Libyan officials rushed on to the tarmac. They handed over half a dozen brown envelopes. Inside one were blueprints for a nuclear bomb. Another contained instructions on how to manufacture and assemble a device. They were written in a mixture of English and Chinese. As the world learned that US special forces had dragged the former Iraqi dictator, Saddam Hussein, from his spider-hole beneath a farmhouse near his home town of Tikrit, the covert team in Tripoli finally got to the bottom of the real story of the Pakistan–Libyan trade in WMDs.[20]

Four days later, the final pieces of the Libyan recanting were hammered out in London at an all-day meeting at government offices in Whitehall. On the

British side were two MI6 officers and, from the Foreign Office, William Ehrman, the director general for defense and intelligence (who was also acting deputy chairman of the joint intelligence committee), and David Landsman, the head of the counter-proliferation department.[21] Representing Washington was Robert Joseph of Bush's National Security Council, and two CIA officials, including Stephen Kappes. Musa Kusa was present for Libya, sitting alongside Abdul Ati al-Obeidi, the Libyan ambassador to Rome, and Mohamed Azwai, Libyan ambassador to London. "It was very much a 'nothing is agreed until everything is agreed' negotiation," one of those present recalled.[22] On the table was the text of an announcement that Britain hoped Gaddafi would make, surrendering his WMD program. Every word was being contested and the Libyans were not sure if Gaddafi would speak at all. Eventually, they reached a compromise. If Libya's leader wished to duck out, then Libya's foreign minister would make the statement, endorsed by Gaddafi.

On 18 December a rough transcript of the text was sent to Downing Street. For the first time, Blair and Gaddafi spoke on the telephone, and agreed that the announcement would be made on Libyan television at 9 p.m. the following night. But at 9 p.m. on 19 December there was no announcement. Instead, a football match was screened. Worried that the deal had fallen through, even at this late stage, an anxious Foreign Office official called the British ambassador in Tripoli. But he, too, had no idea what was going on. He counselled patience. Then suddenly, at 9.30 p.m., Gaddafi's foreign minister appeared on screen and declared that Libya was renouncing its WMD program. Gaddafi released his statement soon afterwards, and Blair, who was at home in his constituency in County Durham, rushed a statement through in time for the evening news.[23] "We must work now to create new partnerships, across geographical and cultural divides, backed by tough international rules and action," Blair said. "September 11 showed the world this new form of terrorism knows no limits to the innocent lives it will take."[24]

Blair made no mention of Pakistan, which had been only too happy to raise another KRL in a far-off land even less secure than its own, but in a jibe directed towards John Bolton and the Vulcans who had, on several occasions, almost blown the Libyan deal, Blair added: "Today's announcement shows that we can fight this menace through more than purely military means; that we can defeat it peacefully, if countries are prepared, in good faith, to work with the international community to dismantle such weapons." A few days later, Gaddafi sent Blair a gift, whose message was in the eating: boxes of succulent dates and oranges from Janzour, the fruit bowl of Libya and also the proposed secret site for Project Machine Shop 1001.

In South Africa, Gerhard Wisser, who would soon be accused by prosecutors of having commissioned Tradefin to manufacture half a cascade for Pakistan to send to Libya, sent a text message to company director Johan Meyer: "They have fed us to the dogs." The entire plant was still sitting in containers outside Meyer's workshops waiting to be shipped to Tripoli—only Tripoli had now turned them over. It was only a matter of time before the cargo was found and they were done for. Wisser fell to pieces. He sent another message later the same day: "The bird must be destroyed, feathers and all."[25] Meyer did not follow through. He was convinced they could ride it out. All he could think about were the months of hard work—and the money. He bundled up incriminating documents and concealed them inside a disused gold mine.[26]

But Wisser's prediction came true and he, Meyer, Geiges and Lerch were all brought in for questioning as part of a law enforcement operation that spanned four continents. Geiges and Wisser would later be charged under South Africa's Non-Proliferation of Weapons of Mass Destruction Act and the Nuclear Energy Act for their activities in connection with the Khan network. At the time of writing the court case was in abeyance while the court decided whether to hear the proceedings in camera.[27] The Swiss authorities arrested Fred Tinner and his sons Urs and Marco, who were asked to explain what contribution to the Libyan program had come from Traco and Tahir's Malaysian complex in Shah Alam.[28] All maintained their innocence but remained in custody.

More fireworks went off in Vienna. IAEA director Mohamed ElBaradei had not even been told the Libyan announcement was in the offing, his only warning a vague suggestion from American and British IAEA board members "not to go on annual leave" as "something was about to come up." It was not until the day after Tripoli's announcement that senior British officials finally briefed him, leaving him to pick up the trail. Squeezed by the US, bugged by Bolton, ignored by Gaddafi, ElBaradei, an Egyptian diplomat used to public jousting, was furious. "It becomes unpleasant when you apparently cannot even have a private phone conversation with your wife and daughter," the IAEA director complained, as an investigation into the phone tapping revealed

Bolton's hand, drawing a tepid excuse from Washington that it was only trying to keep tabs on the IAEA's dealings with Iran.[29] However, no one in the international community was surprised. The US and UK were openly hostile to anyone who questioned the WMD agenda. Three weeks before the invasion of Iraq in March 2003, the *Observer* newspaper in Britain had revealed a secret directive from the National Security Agency ordering increased eavesdropping on UN diplomats, especially those who had argued against war in Iraq. Later Clare Short, the international development secretary, accused MI6 of having spied on UN secretary general Kofi Annan, who was also opposed to the war.[30]

On 20 December 2003 ElBaradei attempted to save face by announcing a meeting with a Libyan delegation headed by "Triple M"—who had refused to see anyone else. But the situation was further complicated when the uncompromising Bolton stepped up his campaign against the IAEA director, citing the secret Libyan program as evidence that ElBaradei had no idea what was going on right under his nose. Bolton, of course, had not known either— as all parties had insisted on keeping Bush's junkyard dog out in the cold—but that part of the story was not mentioned.[31]

In the end, the White House succeeded in ambushing the Libyan deal. According to a strict reading of the founding principles of the IAEA, only nuclear weapons states were permitted to see nuclear weapons designs, and so, despite its limited role, the US insisted the Libyan haul be shipped to the Oak Ridge National Laboratory, a nuclear weapons facility, in Tennessee, where President Bush was photographed inspecting it on 12 July 2004. "To overcome the dangers of our time, America is also taking a new approach in the world. We are determined to challenge new threats—not ignore them, and simply wait for future tragedy," President Bush declared, as if the interdiction of Gaddafi's program was evidence of a triumph for the administration's non-proliferation policy.[32] Bush said nothing about the source of Libya's uranium enrichment program. There was no mention of the wider conspiracy steered by Musharraf and the Pakistani military to profit from the sale of nuclear materials, as enshrined in Project A/B. No talk of the deal hammered out by Richard Armitage and Christina Rocca to cleanse Musharraf and hang Khan out to dry. There was also no whisper of the thirty years of failed US diplomacy on Pakistan or the intelligence cover-ups from within the State Department which had seen federal investigations into Pakistan's proliferation blown by presidential aides, no mention of the Pentagon officials who had rewritten intelligence to make way for a multi-billion-dollar arms deal with Pakistan—all of which had cumulatively enabled the Islamic Republic to arm itself with nuclear weapons and sell them on to countries like Libya. This spectacular and at times criminal conspiracy from within the heart of Washington made the accusations of a limp-wristed IAEA appear nothing more than petty, and Bush's promise "to challenge new threats" rang hollow.

However, in Pakistan, Musharraf's gamesmanship, his apparent outmaneuvering of the fundamentalist generals he had cosseted and his treacherous clampdown on the nuclear scientists upon whom the Islamic Republic had for so long depended, almost cost him his life. On the evening of 14 December 2003, the president's heavily armed motorcade was targeted in a bomb attack as it crossed a bridge in Rawalpindi. The 551 pounds of explosives were activated by a mobile-phone call from the bomber, who was hiding near by. He missed the president's vehicle by seconds, injuring no one, and managed to escape. Investigators quickly tracked him down to the lawless Pakistani city of Quetta, where "Mushtaq" confessed to having been put up to the job—by officers in the Pakistan air force. A hit from within the military. Further investigation by the intelligence agencies found that the air force group responsible was allied to Jaish-e-Mohammed, the terrorist group formed by Maulana Masood Azhar, once Musharraf's prodigy, a man who had served as chief of the banned Harkat-ul-Ansar. Azhar and his sponsors were said to have been angered by Musharraf's perceived duplicity, his cozying up to the Americans in the war on terror and concessions to Washington over Pakistan's nuclear program, particularly his attempt to dump on A. Q. Khan.

But, if anything, the assassination attempt hardened Musharraf's resolve. The following day, the ISI raided Khan's house on Hillside Road with instructions not to let anyone in or out. Right away, news of the security cordon spread through Islamabad. The Father of the Bomb's home was soon surrounded by reporters, who also besieged the foreign ministry, demanding answers. Was it true that Musharraf was accusing Khan of having run a private nuclear bazaar? It took seven days for the government to make a statement and then, on 22 December, Masood Khan, a foreign ministry spokesman, refused to confirm what everyone could see. Khan was apparently "not under arrest, he is not under detention, he is under no restriction." Masood Khan suggested that instead "some questions have been raised with him in relation to the ongoing debriefing sessions." After all, Khan was "too eminent a scientist to undergo a normal debriefing session."[33] And what was being discussed with the Father of the Bomb had nothing to do with statements emanating from Washington about Iran and Libya. Musharraf was trying to bluff his way through the cold-faced plan to sacrifice Khan. But the crowds were building and their anger was palpable.

However, Khan's hand was not yet bust. Dina, his eldest daughter, had slipped out of the country with a document that, the ISI learned, was an exhaustive account of Project A/B written by Khan for his wife Henny, with instructions that she should publish it in the event of his disappearance or death. It was said to make a compelling case for the military, Musharraf and senior government officials having always run the secret sales program. Musharraf could not afford to let this go, even though he had no idea what Khan had actually written. A senior ISI source recalled: "Dina made one stupid mistake. She blabbed on her mobile phone about the document, calling Islamabad from Dubai, enabling us to trace her to the Khan family apartment." But when the ISI broke in, Dina was already gone, on a flight for London—with the document her father had written. Shafiq recalled: "Dr. Sahib told me he had a dossier of incriminating evidence made up of twelve pages of written material, audio and video cassettes and that the ISI made a terrible mess of the apartment in Dubai looking for it. Dina lost her mobile phones, jewellery, cash and her father's Bohemian crystal was smashed. Luckily, the dossier was now out of their reach." When Dina Khan arrived in London she was debriefed by MI5, keen to know what secrets she had brought with her. However, while Musharraf claimed that Dina had taken out of Pakistan state secrets, tipping off British intelligence to intercept them, Dina had none, only her father's detailed affidavit—which for now would remain under wraps. "The truth will come out eventually," Dina later said. "It always does."[34]

This was a dogfight and Musharraf, a self-confessed bully, who relished telling everyone a childhood story of how he had bloodied himself falling out of a mango tree, an event that had caused him not to fear death, was good at these.[35] Pre-empting Dina, the president sent word to Khan. A close family friend recalled: "His people called in on Hillside Road and made it explicitly clear. They did it coldly and with menace. It did not matter who Khan was but if he ever wanted out of this—he would have to promise his daughter would never release her incriminating document."[36] Khan refused but Dina backed off and remained in the UK.

Publicly, Musharraf was filmed looking grave and perplexed, but then he had a lot of balls in the air: assuaging the West, cleansing the Pakistani military, fending off attempts on his life from the disaffected, keeping the people onside while dispatching the Father of the Bomb and his aides. He launched a damage-limitation exercise. "The government of Pakistan has never authorized or initiated any transfers of sensitive nuclear technology," his spokesman said. "The government of Pakistan has never proliferated and it will never proliferate," Masood Khan reiterated, as the focus began to shift away from institutions in Pakistan and towards a handful of individuals. Pakistan was fully cooperating with the IAEA, he said. The president had "given 400 percent assurance and commitment that no violation or infraction of Pakistan's commitments would ever take place." He added that only "a very small number" of individuals were under investigation. The plan to separate Khan and his KRL allies from Pakistan and the institution of the military was now at full tilt. Information minister Sheikh Rashid Ahmed weighed in with a commitment that "Pakistan and its state institutions and entities would distance themselves from any individuals if they are found responsible at the end of these debriefing sessions."[37]

But it was a delicate balancing act. While distancing himself from his nuclear fall guy, Khan, Musharraf also had to tackle persistent rumors that Washington was masterminding the operation against the KRL scientists, with families of those arrested claiming to have seen Westerners in plain clothes lurking in cars outside their homes. None of Pakistan's citizens would be handed over to a foreign power, Musharraf declared. "These are purely in-house investigations. No foreigners or foreign agencies are associated with the debriefing sessions in sensitive organizations," the president's spokesman reiterated. In an attempt to calm the hysteria, Dr. Mohammed Farooq, one of the first to be seized, briefly emerged from the ISI black hole. He had been officially registered as missing by his family, but now his daughter said her father had returned home from "a special official visit," although she could not discuss the details. No sooner had Farooq been released than a government spokesman linked him and others to an investigation into the selling-off of nuclear technology. "Some individuals might have been motivated by personal ambitions or greed," the spokesman said. "If they are found responsible at the end of debriefing sessions, we shall take action." Farooq was sucked back into custody the following day, as government-supporting newspapers reported that he had been known as the "King" of the KRL labs and had multiple bank accounts containing millions of dollars hidden away in Dubai.

Musharraf's supporters were testing the waters. The response from the grass roots was incendiary. On Christmas Day, suicide bombers driving a van and a car packed with explosives rammed the presidential convoy, killing seventeen but narrowly missing Musharraf once again.

The evidence of Pakistan's hand in nuclear proliferation was everywhere. IAEA inspectors returned from a trip to Tehran in early January 2004 with a new set of admissions. Iranian negotiators had confessed to having received blueprints for the sophisticated P-2 centrifuges from Pakistan in 1994.[38] Speculation mounted that the intermediary had been B. S. A. Tahir, but he was lying low in Kuala Lumpur, his movements restricted by the authorities, with the Malaysian special branch inquiry having concluded that he had not broken any domestic laws. Tahir would not be helping the IAEA, his lawyers said. He would not be regurgitating any of his allegations for fear of being extradited to give evidence to the forthcoming trials of Khan's European agents. To complicate matters, Iran insisted it had done nothing with the P-2 blueprints, due to "shortage in professional resources and changes in the management of the Atomic Energy Organization of Iran [AEOI]."

The Iranians claimed that in 2002 the AEOI had hired a contractor to conduct experiments on the P-2.[39] But the only man available was a young and inexperienced scientist who had joined the organization to dodge compulsory military service.[40] When the IAEA interviewed him, he in turn said he had simply made adjustments to the existing designs, as Iran "was not capable of manufacturing maraging steel cylinders with bellows."[41] He had made inquiries of European firms about purchasing 4,000 ring magnets, which held the P-2 in place as it spun, and he had told these companies of the possibility of a much larger second purchase, in order to get a good price. But he had never followed through. His contract had been terminated in March 2003.

But although the paperwork matched the deposition, it did not suit Washington, where Bush officials were eyeing life after Iraq. Even though David

Kay, the head of the Iraq Survey Group, convened in 2003 to search for WMD, had resigned in January 2004, having found no evidence of any WMD stockpiles in Iraq and telling the Senate arms services committee that "we were all wrong," John Bolton had moved seamlessly around the admission, clinging instead to another potential WMD crisis, this time in Iran.[42] He let it be known that he was disinclined to believe Iran's denials. Bolton began to argue vociferously that Iran had constructed a secret second plant where a cascade of P-2 centrifuges was humming, making it extremely likely that Iran would have a bomb sooner than anyone thought. A senior IAEA source recalled: "Bolton and those who thought like him began reviving the P-2 story despite the lack of credible evidence. A hunch became a certainty for the administration and its attack dog."

In Tripoli, there was incontrovertible evidence that Pakistan had authored Libya's program. "Triple M" had a gift for the inspection team, which was led by ambassador Don Mahley, a former US Army colonel, and David Landsman, the British Foreign Office counter-proliferation chief. In a bizarre ceremony that took place in a meeting room of the Libyan National Board of Scientific Research in late January 2004, "Triple M" emerged with all of the nuclear warhead blueprints, schematics and manuals that Libya had bought from Pakistan. He handed them over to the IAEA, stuffed into a plastic bag emblazoned with the logo of a well-known Islamabad gentleman's outfitter— Good Looks Fabrics and Tailors. It was a store beloved by Khan, where he had bought his favorite safari suits for the past twenty-five years and to which he had sent his friends, including Henk Slebos and B. S. A. Tahir, to get kitted out during KRL's heyday. The schematics had arrived from Islamabad in the Good Looks Fabrics and Tailors bag—and it was then handed over to the IAEA.

From the carrier bag to a briefcase, locked shut with seals, IAEA official Jacques Baute took charge of the paperwork, which appeared to be for a nuclear bomb weighing around 500 kilograms. Also in the bag were instructions and notes, some in English, others in Chinese. One comment in the margin appeared to make reference to the age-old rivalry between Khan and Munir Ahmed Khan at PAEC, with the note-maker boasting, "Munir's bomb would be bigger," a reference to the KRL allegation that PAEC had manufactured a cumbersome device too large to fit on a missile or be dropped from a jet. Baute took the locked case to Tripoli airport where a US aircraft was waiting to fly it to Washington. From Dulles airport, armed couriers transferred the designs to a high-security vault at the Department of Energy. Further trophies were given up by the IAEA, including centrifuge components discovered in Libyan warehouses which were still packed in crates marked "KRL." Beside them were missile parts shipped from Pyongyang—completing the circle of proliferation. Musharraf would later write: "We stood before the world as the illicit source of nuclear technology for some of the most dangerous regimes ..." and the picture was "not pretty."[43] The picture was of an export industry so vast, complex, indiscriminate and complete that no one individual could have assembled it.

On 17 January 2004 another wave of "disappearances" swept Pakistan's capital as five more KRL employees were plucked from their homes by the ISI. They included Brigadier Sajawal, who had been in Khan's employ since 1976, who was taken away shortly after 9 p.m. His son, Dr. Shafiq, recalled: "Two vehicles belonging to the ISI approached our house. One person entered. He introduced himself as a major in the ISI. My father was directed to accompany him for 'interrogation at an ISI set-up.' He complied. My dad was a military guy."[44] Dr. Shafiq was upstairs. He heard a car speed off. He grabbed a mobile phone and called Khan. "Dr. Sahib, my dad has been taken. The others too," Dr. Shafiq recalled saying. But Khan was vague and appeared not to know that all over Islamabad KRL employees were being bundled into unmarked cars.[45]

Dr. Shafiq rang round family friends and the KRL Kids, as the children of the nuclear workers were known. They frantically tried to get mobile numbers for barristers who would be prepared to come out in the dark and raise petitions against the ISI. Then, shortly before midnight, Khan called back. This time he was agitated. His principal staff officer, Major Islam ul-Haq, had been snatched too. The paranoia had now reached Hillside Road and inside Khan's front door. Dr. Shafiq recalled, "Dr. Sahib said he had been eating a late supper with Major Islam when a servant came into the dining room and informed them that some army personnel wanted to see the major outside." Ul-Haq went out and never came back. Nilofar Islam, his wife, told Dr. Shafiq, "We have had no contact with him. We don't know where he is and what he is being asked."[46] Suddenly Khan understood that the end was approaching, according to those around him. Musharraf was turning them all in to save himself.

The KRL Kids began to mobilize. They had to head off Musharraf. "Nobody in the government would tell us what was happening," Dr. Shafiq said. "Dr. Sahib was not getting any answers. Every family was told something different. But even then it was in no one's mind that this was the end." As staff doctor to many KRL employees, Dr. Shafiq was best placed to demand access to the missing men and he volunteered to coordinate the response: "We went immediately to the court. We lodged writs of habeas corpus." Two days later, on 19 January 2004, Dr. Shafiq got an answer. According to the government's lawyers, his father had been held on the request of Sheikh Rashid Ahmed, the information minister, as part of a normal KRL "debriefing."

Dr. Shafiq balked: "This was extraordinary. No one was under arrest." This made matters far worse, as if they had all been dropped down some kind of ISI crevasse. Major General Shaukat Sultan, the intelligence services' public relations chief, insisted that no one was under arrest. It was a "normal process in a nuclear country to debrief scientists." But the courts were at a loss to understand what the government was doing. Having received Dr. Shafiq's petition, the deputy attorney general conceded that he was unable to determine where the nine detained men were being held, "despite having contacted a range of government departments and agencies."[47]

Pressing further and threatening to go public with unsavory details about Musharraf, Dr. Shafiq received a response from the government's lawyers in which Brigadier Sajawal was accused of having been in "close association, involvement and connection with persons engaged in and activities relating to nuclear proliferation and passing on to foreign countries and individuals secret codes, nuclear materials, substances, machinery, equipment, components, information, documents, sketches, plans, models, articles and notes." At least Musharraf's hand was out in the open. "After all the tiptoeing around, it was confirmed that my dad and the others were being investigated in connection with a nuclear smuggling ring," recalled Dr. Shafiq.[48] Even while it had been obvious that Musharraf had been building up to this, there was disbelief that he had "scythed the entire nuclear establishment to save himself." Dr. Shafiq recalled: "We kept saying to each other, 'Our fathers had for years gone about their daily jobs in the full belief that they were doing their country's bidding.' KRL etc. was not some part-time peripatetic operation. This was full-blown country-to-country stuff and now all of them were being accused of acts of personal greed and treachery."

The families came together at Dr. Shafiq's house, sitting round a table with a pad of paper: the son of Mohammed Farooq, the wife of Major ul-Haq, the children of Dr. Badar Habib, of Dr. Yasin Chohan, of Dr. Saeed Ahmed, of Dr. Abdul Majid, and even the in-laws of technician Shameem.[49] Their notes testified to the trance-like state of those overcome by a growing sense of desperation. Across the top right corner of the pad, someone had scribbled down "0333 5159486," the telephone number for a barrister who might help. Beneath, they scrawled subheadings, the names of the protagonists in the crackdown and what each of them had said. "*Musharraf*: initially claimed that this was a private issue. Subsequently told all of the families that he was under a lot of pressure from the US. Pleading for pity. Later claimed too that IAEA was kicking him and even Japan (infuriated by the North Korean trades). He is trying to dump everything on us. *Sh. Rasheed*, info minister: initially maintained that 95 percent of the debriefing was over. Later said that after two weeks, 90 percent was over. And eventually claimed that debriefing would be over before Eid [1 February 2004]. *DG intelligence service PR*: initially spoke as if he was handling things, then he was edged out by Sh. Rasheed. This is nothing but a stunt."

The hastily scribbled notes calculated the threat to the families, writing, "severe, shocking, painful—we are all taken aback and terribly disappointed," emotive words by which they hoped to illustrate to their constituency, the people of Pakistan, how they were being sacrificed. They would record how the families had suffered and smuggled statements to favored journalists working on Pakistan's many newspapers. Worried that those arrested would be rendered to the US, Dr. Shafiq chased up on the writ of habeas corpus until his lawyer got a clear answer. A detention order had been issued under the 1952 Security Act of Pakistan, which gave the ISI another three months to hold them all.[50]

The process of disclosure triggered by the multiple court actions began to throw up clues as to who was behind the move and how it was seen from abroad. Notes from an unidentified US State Department official turned over to Dr. Shafiq's lawyers described the scandal as the "mother of all terrorism."[51] Khan and his inner circle were "more dangerous than bin Laden and Saddam Hussein," which yet again begged the question as to why a war supposedly fought over WMD had kicked off in Iraq and not Pakistan.

The KRL Kids tried to pry apart Musharraf's arguments. Dr. Shafiq wrote down: "Despite America's misgivings, Kahuta was a closely guarded establishment with tight rules and regulations, ringed by the Pak military and by legions of intelligence agents, from multiple bureaus, the road to it protected by anti-aircraft positions, jets and soldiers. How did the scientists get around all of these tiers of security? Suggestions that anyone could wander in and steal a canister of UF_6 or even highly enriched uranium, perhaps also a warhead design, without being noticed were absurd. Given that the transfers were made using military C-130s, as Musharraf has conceded that many of them were, how did these transport aircraft fly in and out—in such large numbers and so regularly—without the military and its chief, knowing??? [sic]"

The families wrote an open letter to the Pakistani government: "We are insulted by the president's claims that these people are guilty and are involved in proliferation for personal greed. What hurts is that we all live humbly and lead modest and simple lifestyles. We cannot afford foreign vacations and trips and have often sacrificed education from leading Pakistani as well as foreign institutions for lack of funds." There was no reply from Army House, although the families saw an article that seemed to do all the talking. Shaukat Aziz, the finance minister, announced that the Bush administration had just approved a $395 million economic assistance package for Pakistan which had been delayed the previous year.

Suddenly, websites for all of the nuclear facilities and government departments in Pakistan went offline, with "site under construction" messages appearing. Newspaper sites followed, their online libraries inexplicably drained of clippings and taken "off air." Bookstores were raided, copies of Abdul Siddiqui's Urdu monograph on his trips to Africa with Khan, Zahid Malik's hagiography of the KRL chief, and republished copies of Steve Weissman and Herbert Krosney's The Islamic Bomb were seized. Men with black felt-tip pens went through the pages of English-language volumes on sale in the Saeed Book Bank in Jinnah Market, scrubbing out references to Musharraf, North Korea, General Jehangir Karamat, al-Qaeda, General Mirza Aslam Beg, General Hamid Gul, Osama bin Laden and the Taliban. And those held incommunicado were visited by far meaner men with darker purposes. Dr. Shafiq recalled: "Now they were less polite. 'Shut the fuck up,' they said. 'You sons of bitches are bringing us down.' 'We are going to squeeze you and your children and their friends unless you play ball.' People's houses were broken into. Their cars attacked. Men followed us everywhere." Outside Dr. Shafiq's window, every night the dull glow of a mobile handset illuminated a dark corner of the cul-de-sac, where faceless men chattered about his every action.

Then the ISI produced Dr. Zubair Khan, a KRL scientist who had been disciplined by A. Q. Khan on corruption charges and who bore a grudge. Dr. Zubair had gladly agreed to take over the interrogations. He knew what to ask and could, unlike Sheikh Rashid and the ISI, tell one end of a centrifuge from the other. Dr. Shafiq recalled how the families held a late-night meeting at the KRL colony. "Dr. Zubair Khan had been removed from service by Dr. Sahib. He could make mischief. The authorities said, 'Be quiet and it will all be over soon.' "[52]

However, the man at the center would not be quiet. A. Q. Khan was being questioned on a daily basis in his red-carpeted living room. He managed to slip a note to Dr. Shafiq. "Why is no one talking about the retired and serving generals who sanctioned the nuclear deals, such as Mirza Aslam Beg, who actively promoted sales to Iran when he was chief of army staff in 1990, and General Jehangir Karamat, Musharraf's ambassador to Washington, who negotiated a missiles-for-enrichment technology exchange with North Korea. No debriefing is complete unless you bring every one of the military men here and debrief us together," Khan wrote.[53] "Including Pervez Musharraf."

On 23 January, Musharraf held a briefing of his own. While attending the World Economic Forum, at Davos, in Switzerland, he offered an interview to Christiane Amanpour, CNN's high-profile chief international correspondent. Dressed in a navy business suit, his center-parting primped, he looked every bit the chief executive of a nation well under control. But his language was vitriolic. Pakistan had found evidence that "violators" and "enemies of the state" had sold nuclear secrets abroad "for personal financial gain." Musharraf said: "This I know, there is no official of the state or government involved at all. These are individuals ... There is no such evidence that any government or military personality was involved in this at all."[54] But Amanpour was no easy ticket. She recalled how Musharraf had bragged the previous weekend in Pakistan's parliament that the military was omnipresent. "You said even a bolt of a rifle cannot go missing without the highest levels of command knowing about it. So how can nuclear technology transfer take place without the highest levels of government or military command knowing about it?" It was the same argument being made through the courts by the KRL scientists under detention.

Without flinching, Musharraf responded. Since nuclear technology was "in computers, on paper and in the minds of people" it was far more difficult to control. He seemed to have forgotten the 5,832 centrifuges, each the size of a washing machine, ordered by Pakistan from Tradefin, that were still sitting in containers in an industrial park north of Johannesburg. He made no mention of the five containers seized by the MI6 team in Taranto, Italy, or the Libyan WMD program, now broken down in pieces and on display like booty in Oak Ridge, Tennessee, a shipment that followed his personal visit to Tripoli. Or, far more worrying, the forty missing canisters of highly enriched uranium, the largest of which was supposed to be the size of a small car. Musharraf wanted to spread the blame: "Let the world not imagine that it is Pakistan alone which has done that. I would like to say there are European countries and individuals involved, so let it not be said that there were only Pakistanis involved."⁵⁵

Three days later, on 26 January, Musharraf finally came out with it. Abdul Qadeer Khan was to blame and he was under house arrest. Opposite the front gate of 207 Hillside Road, in view of the beds of Dutch tulips that Khan had lovingly planted as bulbs mail-ordered from Amsterdam, a permanent guard hut was erected and neat signs were knocked into the grass verges: passers-by should not linger or take photographs.⁵⁶ A brazier was lit as a cold night slipped in, around which many pairs of battle-hardened hands, roughened by cordite and webbing, warmed themselves.

Twenty-four hours later, the Islamabad press corps was called to the prime minister's secretariat. Lieutenant General Khalid Kidwai, head of the Strategic Plans Division, was waiting with overheads and a slide projector to finish Khan off. The disgraced KRL chief had apparently signed a twelve-page confession, the startled audience was told, in which he admitted to providing Iran, Libya and North Korea with technical assistance and components. No foreign press had been admitted to hear (or challenge) Kidwai's claims that Khan was the mastermind of an elaborate and wholly unauthorized smuggling network, involving chartered cargo flights, clandestine overseas meetings and a Malaysian factory that reconditioned centrifuge parts discarded from Pakistan's nuclear program for sale to foreign clients. Kidwai spent the next two and a half hours skimming over technology transfers that had begun in 1989 and were brokered by a network of middlemen, including three German businessmen and a Sri Lankan, identified as "Tahir." No matter that none of the dates stacked up or even tallied with those logged by the CIA and MI6 which had traced Project A/B back to at least 1985.⁵⁷

Khan was taken to a face-to-face meeting with Musharraf. The president would write in his memoirs that he confronted Khan with evidence of his crimes and that the KRL chief "broke down" and admitted that he felt extremely guilty. "He asked me for an official pardon," Musharraf wrote. "I told him his apology should be to the people of Pakistan and he should seek his pardon from them directly." It was decided that the best format would be a televised confession. However, Khan's closest friends, to whom he slipped notes after this meeting, told a resolutely different story. It was the president who was apologetic. He bargained for a trade. Khan would go on television and make a brief confession, everything would be forgotten, and he would be able to go back to his old life. "You are still my hero," Musharraf assured the bitter Khan. Seeing no way out of the deadlock, Khan agreed to do the president's bidding.

On the morning of 4 February, the National Command Authority met again to agree on the wording of Khan's formal apology, after which the KRL chief was ushered in to see Musharraf. Photographs of that meeting taken by *Dawn* newspaper showed a tense president prepped for war in his combat fatigues, with Khan leaning back on a sofa in a beige silk and wool blazer and navy slacks.[58] That afternoon, Khan was driven to Pakistan Television headquarters and shown into a studio. At Washington's insistence, Musharraf had asked him to speak in English so his message could be understood across the world. But at the last minute Khan refused to use the teleprompter, insisting on reading the prepared statement from notes. Was he attempting to send a signal to his friends that these were somebody else's words? Dr. Shafiq thought as much.

The president ordered that the broadcast go out with a time delay, in case Khan suddenly broke away from the text. Such were the stakes that even at this late stage the two adversaries did not trust each other. Khan declared: "My dear brothers and sisters, I have chosen to appear before you to offer my deepest regrets and unqualified apologies to a traumatized nation. I am aware of the high esteem, love and affection in which you have held me for my services to national security, and I am grateful for all the awards and honors that have been bestowed upon me. However, it pains me to realize in retrospect that my entire lifetime achievement of providing foolproof national security to my nation could have been placed in serious jeopardy on account of my activities which were based"—Khan drew breath—"in good faith but on errors of judgment related to unauthorized proliferation activities."[59]

Sources at Pakistan Television later revealed that Khan had amended his statement at the last minute to add that he had been acting "in good faith," supporters claiming these three words were offered as a signal that Khan had always been working for the government and was motivated solely by patriotism. He continued: "I wish to place on record that those of my subordinates who have accepted their role in the affair were acting in good faith, like me, on my instructions. I also wish to clarify that there was never ever any kind of authorization for these activities by a government official. I take full responsibility for my actions and seek your pardon. I give an assurance, my dear brothers and sisters, that such activities will never take place in the future. I also appeal to all citizens of Pakistan, in the supreme national interest, to refrain from any further speculations and not to politicize this extremely sensitive issue of national security. May Allah keep Pakistan safe and secure."

The impact of Khan's confession was electric. Banners appeared on the streets of Islamabad and Karachi declaring: "We want Qadeer Khan as president not prisoner." Qazi Hussain Ahmad, the firebrand leader of Jamaat-e-Islami, went on al-Jazeera to demand that Musharraf step down, saying Khan had confessed only after the authorities threatened him with torture. Sticking to his part of the deal, Musharraf pardoned Khan the following day at a crowded press conference at Army House. "He is my hero," Musharraf somberly reflected. "He always was and still is." Asked if the world would pardon Dr. Khan as he had done, the president said: "Leave it to me. I am standing between Dr. Khan and the world community. Nothing will happen to him."[60] Contrast this with what Musharraf would write in his memoirs in 2006, when he bitterly noted of Khan: "The truth is that he was just a metallurgist, responsible for only one link in the complex chain of nuclear development. But he had managed to build himself up into Albert Einstein and Robert Oppenheimer rolled into one."[61] The truth was even more complex and this televised apology was just the start of a bitter war between Musharraf and Khan, who, rather than giving in, began to sit up and fight back.

For the moment, none of this was seen, although soon after Musharraf had smugly eulogized Khan, the Pakistani press broke ranks. Reporters thronged around Musharraf demanding answers to allegations that he and his government had known about the proliferation all along. Musharraf, caught out, was furious. He had not contemplated a rebellion. "Even if for the sake of argument it is accepted that the government and the army were involved in the affair, do you think it will serve our national interest to shout about it from the rooftop?" he responded. Pakistan was already in danger of facing UN Security Council sanctions. "Then we will be declared a rogue state and finally our vital interests would come under imminent physical danger." But the press would not back down, a foreign correspondent challenging Musharraf to hand over all documentary evidence, allowing a full and independent investigation. The president lost his cool. "Stop saying this," Musharraf shouted. Pakistan was a sovereign country and it would not hand over its nuclear program to the US or anyone else. "I have seen death very closely, not once but six times. We are not one of the cowards ... This country will never roll back its nuclear assets, its missile assets. I will be the last man doing it."[62]

The deal was done and in Washington there was a warm glow, with Condoleezza Rice issuing a statement that summed up the surreal semicolon placed after this crisis: "A. Q. Khan, in a sense, has been brought to justice because he is out of the business that he loved most." The phrase "in a sense" encapsulated the Armitage deal with Musharraf, and the US now had to hope that Musharraf would stick to his end of the bargain and that the truth would remain buried. Richard Boucher, the State Department spokesman, said he was "impressed with the seriousness of the [Pakistan] investigation" and expected that Pakistan would share everything it gleaned with the international community.[63] Armitage himself praised Pakistan for being "very forthright in the last several years with us about proliferation."[64] Colin Powell hailed Musharraf's uncovering of the black-market nuclear network as a success, too: "The biggest proliferator is now gone and so we don't have to worry about proliferation from A. Q. Khan or his network."[65] There was no evidence, he added, of government involvement in the scandal.

One week later, President Bush gave his reaction at the National Defense University in Washington. Congratulating Musharraf for his decisive action, Bush said: "A. Q. Khan has confessed his crimes, and his top associates are out of business. The government of Pakistan is interrogating the network's members, learning critical details that will help them prevent it from ever operating again. President Musharraf has promised to share all the information he learns about the Khan network, and has assured us that his country will never again be a source of proliferation." In an extraordinarily partial reading of the recent past, Bush hailed "a great coalition [that] has come together to defeat terrorism and to oppose the spread of weapons of mass destruction— the inseparable commitments of the war on terror." Particularly noteworthy was the "high-risk" work of America's "fine intelligence professionals" who had "shadowed members of the network around the world ... recorded their conversations ... penetrated their operations [and] uncovered their secrets."[66]

But the risk remained that Khan's associates were at large around the world, Bush warned. "These dealers are motivated by greed, or fanaticism, or both. They find eager customers in outlaw regimes, which pay millions for the parts and plans they need to speed up their weapons programs. And with deadly technology and expertise going on the market, there's the terrible possibility that terrorist groups could obtain the ultimate weapons they desire most." One by one, they would be found and their careers in the weapons trade ended, Bush pledged. "Our message to proliferators must be consistent and it must be clear: We will find you, and we're not going to rest until you are stopped."[67] Now that Iraq had been wrapped up and Pakistan (never a target) was playing ball, the White House was signalling that its attention was switching towards Iran.

However, those who were not a party to the Armitage–Musharraf deal could barely contain their skepticism. Mohamed ElBaradei, the IAEA director, bruised from his battle with Bolton, described A. Q. Khan as "the tip of an iceberg" who "was not working alone."[68] He was qualified to know, as he had read most of the classified intelligence on Khan. UN secretary general Kofi Annan, too, described the TV apology as "odd," and asked why Pakistan had been pardoned for selling atomic secrets to Iran, Libya and North Korea.[69]

Musharraf's aides laughed when they read the text of Bush's speech. One recalled: "We were back in the old relationship, you know the one, where we do as we please, and they do as we please."[70]

The truth had been scattered in pieces all over Pakistan, in safe houses and dank cells controlled by the ISI. Dr. Shafiq was virtually the only person outside the immediate family still permitted to visit A. Q. Khan. Khan was, according to Dr. Shafiq's slightly hysterical notes, "suffering from very high blood pressure and side effects, as well as needing anti-hypertension medication, and treatment for depression, constipation, etc., rendering him a ticking time bomb." But apart from these visits, for Khan there was nothing. The telephone line to his house had been cut. No more newspapers would be delivered, and he was not even permitted to watch television. Instead, he sat in his armchair in the lounge, talking to himself, studying the Koran, or occasionally practicing yoga in his garden.

His youngest daughter, Ayesha, who lived a few houses down, called by, as did Tanya, Dina's fourteen-year-old, who came once a week to accompany her grandmother on trips to the local market. Dina was stuck in London, refused permission to visit her father for more than a year.[71] "Henny was sick with worry," said Dr. Shafiq. "Khan was going out of his mind. He was convinced that President Bush's war on terror had become a crusade that was developing into a war between Islam and Christianity." But then he picked himself up. "He now vowed to stop talking to the ISI, to the military, to any of those who had betrayed him," said Dr. Shafiq. "He was plotting his revenge."

A close Musharraf aide recalled: "It was around now that we decided we had done enough. There would be nothing else volunteered to the Americans about the nuclear issue. Deal or no deal, for us it was over, and we were just waiting for the right time to announce that we had closed the door on the scandal."[72]

19

NEW THINK

Nobody knew where the KRL men were being held, or that their "debriefing" would turn into a two-and-a-half-year ordeal. In safe houses across Pakistan, the ISI minded its catch. Dr. Farooq, once the second most important man in Pakistan's nuclear industry, now aged fifty-four and suffering from diabetes and hypertension, spent most of his days and nights in darkness, shifted from town to town. Brigadier Sajawal's hulking frame had shrunk, his son claimed, and he had acquired a shaking condition akin to Parkinson's disease, after repeated interrogations.[1] The others followed similar paths. They were old men who had become frail overnight, falling to pieces in a limbo beyond the law, in the underbelly of a militarized state for which the only imperative was survival. Occasionally the families received a brusque call from the ISI informing them that a visit would be allowed. Then they would be driven blindfolded to a safe house, where they would be allowed a brief reunion with their loved ones, while Musharraf's agents scanned every word for any hint of betrayal.

There were persistent rumors in Pakistan that the detained were desperate to speak out about the complicity of the military and Musharraf in Project A/B. But hearing these views first-hand was impossible. The scientists were in limbo, their homes bugged, their phone lines severed. There were the sons and daughters, the KRL Kids, who mostly lived in the company compound set back from the Islamabad–Rawalpindi highway. But their cantonment had also become a virtual prison, heavily guarded by the ISI and a phalanx of other military and security personnel, who nestled behind checkpoints and tank traps, making an impromptu interview unlikely.

There was one last option. A small number of the families lived in Rawalpindi, a hectic maze of crowded streets that made up the country's largest army garrison, which in itself offered the legions of government-paid watchers plenty of opportunity to keep track of them. In a metropolis of strangers, jam-packed with job-seekers, many from the most distant quarters of Pakistan, a Hydra-headed city which talked in many different tongues, from Arabic and Urdu through to Farsi, Pashtun and Dari (and even some of the guttural dialects of the Central Asian steppes), everything that moved was potentially worth money, and virtually nothing came in or out of Rawalpindi without someone telling somebody about it.

Since Musharraf had come to power, any number of people squeezing up against the counter in a café might try and overhear enough of a conversation to recoup a couple of paisas from their eager controller. Every call a taxi driver made to his supposed sister or cousin, while his ride chatted merrily in the back, was as likely to have been to an agent-handler to whom he would narrate overheard conversations and chart destinations. No hotel room in the new Pakistan was secure from hackers. They drained guests' hard drives and opened email attachments. Restaurant waiters made up their tips by eavesdropping. The ISI worked like that, getting to work on those driven by poverty and fear, the main motivators for recruitment. Even if it took them a while, the spies made everyone work for them. That was what the intelligence guys did, coming between people and their hunger, relentlessly, professionally—and with great gusto.

Asim Farooq, son of Dr. Mohammed Farooq, the former head of KRL foreign procurement, rarely talked to anyone now. He was frightened. And when he did leave the family's home in Rawalpindi, there was always the chance that he would miss a call from the ISI to visit his father. The Farooq family house, down a twisting and sandy side road, was far from the lavish palace belonging to a "King of KRL," as government spokesmen had denigrated Mohammed Farooq in the days after he was arrested—an image that had jarred with those who knew Mohammed Farooq best, including Peter Griffin, who recalled an entirely different man, wide-eyed when he had travelled to the UK on KRL business, his only vice a brief excursion to Marks & Spencer on Baker Street, where he had bought sweaters and underwear for the family back home.[2]

The Farooqs' was an ugly modern villa. The only detail that made it stand out from any of the others was the amount of attention it was getting from the men dressed in beige *kurtas* idling on a wall opposite. It would be impossible for Europeans to knock on this front door unseen. We decided not to and thirty minutes later, while we waited around the corner, a Pakistani companion volunteered to trudge back and ring the bell.

After checking the street in both directions, Asim Farooq had reluctantly let him into the compound. But Farooq was too frightened to go into much detail. "We are bugged," he had immediately complained, refusing to let his visitor enter the house. "It has been a nightmare. We are all terrified of what might happen," he said. Farooq was a doctor and was used to blood and guts in a spit-and-sawdust hospital which thrived on pressure. But the A. Q. Khan affair, he said, had nearly done for him. "Everything written in the papers here and in the West is a distortion of the truth. My father was not a spy or a thief or a profiteer. He's a scientist who did what his country asked him to do. And now he is being made to take the fall. We have been told by the ISI to keep quiet and only if we do, will my father eventually be freed. There is much more to say. But I can't help you now."

The secret police had done their job well. It was the same story at the houses of other KRL families, who were terrified that if they spoke out their fathers would be committed to a lifetime of incarceration, or worse. The clampdown was happening at every level of society, including those closest to Musharraf.[3] Sharifuddin Pirzada, who loved nothing better than to reflect on a life spent close to the jugular, was reticent: "Khan is a very dangerous subject. I would rather not discuss it. Too near the knuckle. Things must settle down."[4] Humayun Gauhar, the *Blue Chip* editor, chose his words carefully. "These are tense days and it's been very painful for Pakistan," he offered, as the conversation rapidly broadened into less controversial areas.[5] Outside the country, too, there was reluctance to talk openly about Khan. Benazir Bhutto voiced the scale of the threat from the ISI: "These military guys have the capacity to kill," she said. "I cannot believe that the international community still thinks I am crazy when I say it."[6]

Even Karachi psychiatrist Dr. Haroon Ahmed received a surprise visit. His relationship with A. Q. Khan had broken down irretrievably in December 2002 when Qaiyum Khan, the scientist's brother, had arrived to take over Dr. Ahmed's Institute of Behavioral Sciences, accompanied by a retired general, two colonels and fifty armed men. "They told me to leave as A. Q. Khan was now chairman of the governing body. He'd plowed in so much money he wanted to run the show and he wanted me out," Dr. Ahmed recalled. "I was dragged to the gate along with all my staff and the nurses in front of our patients. We were barred from our own project."[7]

Dr. Ahmed had launched a case in the Sindh high court to eject the ex-KRL chief and get his hospital back, attempts that had turned into a well-publicized legal battle, in which Khan had been accused of contempt, having ignored a judge's ruling to give back that which he had illegally seized. But after A. Q. Khan's arrest in January 2004, Dr. Ahmed was visited by the ISI. "They said my court case was preventing the healing process between the government, Musharraf and A. Q. Khan. They did not want anything more appearing in the newspapers about him. They said, 'Sit tight, be quiet, drop the case, and everything regarding Khan will be cleared up. We know where his cash is. It is in gold bullion, at the ARY Bank in Dubai. Just bide your time.' And then they left my house. But I will not drop the case. We are continuing to push for justice."[8] However, to increase the pressure on Dr. Ahmed and to make sure the message hit home, the ISI had also visited a senior editor at *Dawn*, a close friend, who had seen to it that the legal case was doggedly reported. Next time the editor turned up for work, he found his possessions in a cardboard box with instructions not to bother coming back.

Musharraf had bagged up all of the pieces of the Khan affair, calculating that with Khan and his affiliates kept quiet, the West would forget about the scandal and the military's role in it. The official line was: nine KRL men arrested; Khan and his private network busted. No further detentions were needed or sought. The only other names to emerge were of people no longer alive, including Dr. Zafar Niazi and General Imtiaz Ahmed, the former a political confidant and the latter a military secretary to Zulfikar Ali Bhutto. It was no coincidence that both had also been aides to Bhutto's daughter, Benazir. She was the force behind the plan to sell nuclear technology to Iran in the 1990s, Islamabad alleged—something that Bhutto vociferously denied.[9]

But as far as the international community was concerned, the wrapping-up of Khan and a handful of KRL scientists mattered little so long as the greatest nuclear scandal of our age had been stopped. The US had taken the lead position on that issue, a deal having been struck between Armitage and Musharraf in which Pakistan's president had pledged to give Washington unlimited access to Khan (albeit via ISI interrogators).[10] However, by the summer of 2004, it was clear to British intelligence, the IAEA and many on Washington's non-proliferation circuit that Musharraf had reneged on his promise. Khan and his colleagues had vanished into a black hole and nothing asked of them by the West via intermediaries had been adequately answered. Robert Einhorn, a key player in the State Department investigations into Khan, recalled: "Once they were under house arrest, as far as I can gather, we got nothing of much value from Islamabad. Our people were being kept away from all of the key players. This was not what we had agreed. The US looked weak."[11] A senior State Department official who had been involved in liaising with the Pakistan foreign ministry said: "There we sat, with our list of a thousand questions, while our favorite ally in Islamabad told us to go jump. We were left hanging."

After a polite pause, Musharraf pulled the plug on the Khan probe altogether, the government announcing that the inquiry was over and the matter resolved. No other revelations would be forthcoming.[12] Tasnim Aslam, foreign ministry spokeswoman, said that the IAEA and the US were fully satisfied with Pakistan's handling of the issue. "As far as we are concerned the chapter is closed," she said in May 2006, adding that at no stage were Western officials or organizations allowed direct access to Khan. In one fell swoop, Musharraf claimed to have stopped Project A/B in its tracks. A thirty-year procurement and proliferation network, involving thousands of scientists, middlemen, agents, suppliers, importers and exporters, of a kind never seen before, had been boiled down to less than a dozen protagonists. Those arrested were banished to life under house arrest—keeping them beyond the arm of US law and the West's intelligence community.[13] Tasnim Aslam confirmed that Dr. Mohammed Farooq was the last of A. Q. Khan's team to be freed, technically, from ISI detention, although he would never again be allowed to leave his house without an ISI escort.[14]

No charges preferred. No intelligence shared. Robert Gallucci, who had spent the best part of three decades following Khan, was incredulous. "Our ally in Islamabad had proven to be dishonorable. There were many, many reasons for the US and Europe to be exceedingly unhappy."[15] However, while news of the collapse of the Khan deal horrified European governments, Israel and India, it suited the Bush administration fine. Its agenda revolved around shoring up Musharraf as an ally in the war on terror, which had another country in its sights.

US brinkmanship over Iraq had led the world down a cul-de-sac, with the US appearing to follow the diplomatic and negotiated route, signing up to and then triggering UN resolutions—and yet all of this process had been predicated on dubious intelligence that skewed the vote. Now the administration was muscling in on another "rogue regime" that it alleged had WMDs: Iran. It did not want any distractions from its pursuit of doomsday weapons there by having to explain, courtesy of a fountain of intelligence emanating from Khan, that the source of them was a major ally in the war on terror: Pakistan.

Washington's absolving of the Khan network and its military controllers—and its shift of attention to Iran—had been made possible by a political cleansing of the US State Department which had seen seasoned diplomats and weapons experts exiled and replaced with neophytes allied to the Vulcan way. Having foundered for the first years of the Bush presidency, by the time the Khan inquiry was shut down in Pakistan, in the US non-proliferation policy was dead in the water.

When John Bolton was shoehorned into the State Department as under secretary of state for arms control and international security in 2001, it was against the wishes of Colin Powell and State Department long-termers, who saw the move as the first of many attempts by Bush officials to bring the department more in line with White House thinking. Norm Wulf, then Bush's roving ambassador on disarmament, recalled: "Bolton was not Powell's first choice. The secretary did not want to work with Bolton and so he would bypass him and work directly with John Wolf, one of his deputies. Bolton had a reputation for demoting people who disagreed with him and promoted Bush loyalists."[16]

Bolton had come to the State Department two years into a massive reorganization of its arms control mechanisms which had seen the Arms Control and Disarmament Agency—first created by President John F. Kennedy—divided into three separate bureaus of "Arms Control," "Non-Proliferation" and "Verification and Compliance." As Bolton had openly declared that he doubted the value of US treaties and international institutions (like the IAEA), his natural ally in the new order was the verification chief, whose stated mission included identifying weaknesses in non-proliferation treaties and institutions.

The Non-Proliferation Bureau soon began to suffer. Dean Rust, then its acting deputy director, recalled: "Throughout 2003 and 2004 the three bureaus were frequently in conflict." At a time when the US was meant to be tracking the nuclear weapons programs of Iran and North Korea and wrapping up

Project A/B in Pakistan, with Armitage in Islamabad hammering out the secret deal with Musharraf, arms control staff were distracted by a turf war in Washington—with the non-proliferationists coming off worst. Rust evoked a department that was blighted by cabals, "secret meetings" and "back-channel messages." He said: "Bolton did not seek to ameliorate the situation. If anything he encouraged it. He had come to view the Non-Proliferation Bureau as untrustworthy because it occasionally took issue with his views. Daily bureaucratic battles broke out. Policy was sidetracked and drawn out ... Other governments and even US agencies wondered who was in charge."[17]

Such was the crisis that the inspector general (IG) for the State Department was called in to investigate. In September 2004, seven months after Khan had been placed under house arrest, the IG recommended another restructuring, merging two of the three disarmament bureaus—"Arms Control" and "Non-Proliferation"—spawning a super-bureau for international security and non-proliferation. But before it could be staffed and set to work, secretary of state Colin Powell resigned, ending more than four years of clashes with the Pentagon over the direction the war on terror had been taking.[18] Within two days Bush had replaced him with Condoleezza Rice, his national security adviser, a move that was seen as an attempt to suppress dissenting voices in the war cabinet. Soon, arms control chief John Bolton was also gone, nominated by the president as US ambassador to the UN, where it was feared that he would wreak more havoc. "There is no such thing as the United Nations. There is only the international community, which can only be led by the only remaining superpower, which is the United States," Bolton would go on to say about the institution he was set to join, reiterating a long-held neoconservative view that the UN was venal and ineffective.[19]

Any hopes the State Department's beleaguered non-proliferationists held that with Bolton gone things were about to get better were dashed when Rice announced that she was replacing him with Robert Joseph, who had been in on the negotiations with Libya.[20] A former Reagan administration official, Joseph had long argued in favor of offensive strategies against "evil" empires like the Soviet Union. He had established a reputation for undermining arms control treaties, promoting a military strategy of acting pre-emptively and unilaterally, marking a shift away from the historic US position of only fighting wars forced upon the country. Although not publicly aligned to the Vulcans, Joseph represented a new breed of militarist, a nuclear warrior who envisaged a world order even starker than that of his predecessor. Joseph's thinking was that in the face of rogue proliferators the US had to bolster its own WMD arsenal and then use nuclear weapons first before America came under attack. It was a terrifying take on Wohlstetter's idea of closing a window of vulnerability.

There were other commonalities. Joseph had been a member of the 1998 Rumsfeld Commission that had identified Iran, Iraq and North Korea as the greatest threats. In 2001, he had contributed to a controversial paper proposing that tactical nuclear weapons be treated as an essential part of the US arsenal, "for those occasions when the certain and prompt destruction of high priority targets is essential and beyond the promise of conventional weapons."[21] In 2003 it was Joseph, along with Bolton, who had repeatedly pressed for the inclusion in the president's state of the union address of the erroneous intelligence about Iraq's attempts to buy uranium from Niger—which would subsequently lead to the outing of Valerie Plame.[22]

Back in government, Joseph brought a new buzzword to the State Department: counter-proliferation. In plain English, that meant using pre-emptive military (potentially nuclear) strikes to counter the actions of proliferators. It was a concept he had developed and refined while founder and director of the Counter-Proliferation Center at the National Defense University in Washington.[23] Counter-proliferation was already a critical aspect of Bush's national security strategy, unveiled at the UN General Assembly in September 2002, and it would also become a founding principle of the president's proliferation security initiative (PSI), a multinational sea- and airborne strike force, launched in May 2003, which would operate outside the UN and was charged with intercepting nuclear terrorists and proliferators.[24]

In July 2005, secretary of state Condoleezza Rice finally rolled out her new super-bureau for international security and non-proliferation. Highlighting how the restructuring would bring the State Department—which under Colin Powell's tenure had come to be regarded as "renegade"—far closer to the Pentagon, Rice said: "We must also go on the offensive against outlaw scientists, black-market arms dealers and rogue-state proliferators."[25] The time had come for more than deterrence and arms control treaties, and Rice revealed that alongside its existing duties the super-bureau would have three new priorities: counter-proliferation, strategic planning and WMD terrorism.[26] The wrapping-up of US non-proliferation policy into the new US pre-emptive military strategy was complete.

It would be Robert Joseph's job to oversee the staffing of the massive Bureau of International Security and Non-Proliferation (ISN), a task he immediately delegated to his chief of staff, Frederick Fleitz, whom he had inherited from Bolton.[27] A former WMD apparatchik at the CIA, Fleitz had been hand-picked by Bolton and suited Joseph just fine.[28] His best-known public face was as the author of *Peacekeeping Fiascos of the 1990s*, a book that argued that peacekeepers almost always failed.[29] Now he brought together a panel of political appointees who had all served under Bolton and sat in judgment— and in secret—on the State Department's existing non-proliferation staff.[30] Former director Dean Rust recalled: "It was inevitable that paybacks would be part of this process." With three decades of government service behind him, a disillusioned Norm Wulf described the atmosphere: "They met in secret, deciding who to employ, displacing career civil servants with more than thirty years on the job in favor of young like-thinking people, right-wingers who would toe the administration line, so Bush could keep control post-2008." Rust saw it even more starkly: "Beyond cronyism and the influence of political factors in the selection of personnel, there was also a presumption by some in the administration that the State Department's seasoned WMD experts were only capable of 'old think' and that post-September 11, 'new think' was needed." "New think," in this context, meant doing away with talking, consensus-building and negotiation—and in with crack squads in wetsuits shimmying on to container vessels, or possibly even jets dropping strategic nuclear weapons on countries including Iran.[31]

Wulf described how one colleague, Michael Rosenthal, among the top non-proliferation experts in the US, returned from a two-year secondment to the IAEA in Vienna to find that a job he was supposed to take up as director of US diplomacy over the nuclear stand-off with Iran and North Korea had gone to a junior officer who was known as a Bolton ally. At least fifteen senior officials at Rosenthal's level resigned after they were demoted or pushed sideways.[32] Proof positive of overt political bias emerged in the shape of an email from Thomas Lehrman, head of the ISN's new WMD terrorism office, who wrote to universities and research centers seeking applicants for jobs that required loyalty to Bush and Rice as essential qualifications.[33] Wulf said: "Everyone is fleeing. People used to stay on until they were sixty or sixty-five years old but now they go as soon as they can. We have lost all the really bright people. We have to start all over again." The way had been left clear for Joseph to stamp his authority on all emerging conflicts.

Under his stewardship and Fleitz's management, five of the ISN's twelve office directorships went to people with no relevant experience, including the posts dealing with the Nuclear Non-Proliferation Treaty, the IAEA, and critically Iran and North Korea.[34] Rust was dismayed and warned: "The architects of this reorganization have weakened the administration's overall diplomatic resources needed to carry out its goals in coping with such threats as Iran and North Korea." But then, that was Robert Joseph's plan.

Robert Gallucci, a master of "old think," who had successfully negotiated the Agreed Framework with North Korea in 1994, recalled: "In the days of Robert Oppenheimer, the world thought the way to control nuclear weapons was to control the technology and the components. This involved diplomacy, patience and coercion. Given that over the last fifty years there still are only five licensed nuclear weapons powers—something obviously went right. We even got the old warhorses in North Korea to talk. But suddenly the choice words in Washington were 'interdiction' and 'pre-emptive strike.'"[35]

Gallucci warned that Joseph's philosophy had left the US and the world more vulnerable. Not only had the administration lost international goodwill by turning down and actively undermining diplomacy, but it was also having to confront a threat it was ill equipped to handle: an unknown number of nuclear sites hidden deep below ground (Iran) and bands of terrorists (al-Qaeda) who were shopping for fissile material, acting in cells or disparate groups. Gallucci said: "How are we going to penetrate a subterranean nuclear site if we don't know where it is? By launching a full-scale invasion? How are we going to know when a little black globe of highly enriched uranium is leaving Pakistan in a suitcase? How can we strike it? How the hell are we going to know when it's out there? The answer is we won't. This is pure bullshit wrapped around lazy thinking."[36]

But it was the counter-proliferationists who secured the most face time with the president and what they were chanting was: Iran. Pentagon and White House officials, too, claimed that Iran was intent on having a bomb and would be quite willing to sell it on. Iran, it was argued, was more likely than any other state to use such a weapon, pre-emptively and indiscriminately, with America's primary Middle East ally, Israel, a likely target.[37]

For the American people, Iran was inscrutable, if not evil, a country that had gone from being a most favored ally to most avowed enemy in 1979, dragging the US through the Tehran hostage crisis when the embassy was ransacked and its officials held until 1981. For the Bush administration, there was only one Iran: a fanatical and unipolar clerical regime that held its own people virtually hostage while secretly trying to build a bomb that it intended to wield against Israel and others. More than twenty-five years on, US policy remained stuck, with no diplomatic relations other than through the Swiss embassy in Tehran. Iran was perceived as marching on a predetermined course to collide with the West. But those who knew Iran better (and who had been talking to its leaders since the revolution of 1979) saw a fractured and secretive nation with no transparent goals, to which nothing could be so easily ascribed, since there were many competing political and religious forces, a good number of them progressive and sympathetic to the West.[38] Iran had demonstrated its ability to act pragmatically several times before, including during the Iran–Contra scandal of 1986, when it had secretly embraced Israel as an intermediary to buy weapons from the US.[39]

US misconceptions about Iran, and Vulcan strategy, had to date only served to strengthen the ayatollahs' hand. The US had removed the Taliban, Shia Iran's greatest Sunni threat to the east, and Saddam Hussein, its deadliest Sunni enemy to the west, and had then gone ahead and installed an Iran-friendly Shia government in Baghdad. Gary Sick, an Iran expert at the National Security Council under Ford, Carter and Reagan, and today a professor at Columbia University, argued: "The US virtually assured that Iran—essentially without raising a finger—would emerge as a power center rivalled only by Israel."[40]

Iran had yet to do many of the things of which it was being accused by Bolton, Joseph and countless Israeli intelligence officials—building a secret P-2 plant, arming a nuclear bomb, threatening to use one, or selling on the technology. But applying the pre-emptive Vulcan logic, the US had to act before Iran did. Gary Sick argued that such was "the [US] antipathy to Iran as a result of the hostage crisis" that even something as drastic as regime change would curry favor with some Democrats as well as the expected Republican hawks.

*

In 2003, France, Britain and Germany had begun negotiating with the Iranians to roll back their nuclear program, a diplomatic policy the Bush administration never warmed to, demanding instead that Iran be referred to the UN Security Council. While Bush officials counselled the world not to believe anything emanating from the Iranians, the European effort won Tehran over, leading to the suspension of its enrichment program. In response, Washington produced satellite overheads in June 2004 showing the Natanz facility, where two large centrifuge halls designed to house 50,000 centrifuges had been roofed over. Now they lay under 75 feet of earth and rock, reinforced with concrete, in a facility that was so vast, the White House claimed, that it was probably designed to manufacture fissile material for a weapons program. Iran had plenty of other means to generate power (most notably its massive oil reserves, which produced 4 million barrels per day), and the evidence of its malicious nuclear intentions was also provided by exiled groups committed to regime change. In February 2005 these partisan organizations claimed Iran had been attempting to import maraging steel, another clear sign that it was preparing to build thousands of centrifuge machines.[41] But there were widely differing estimates of how long it would take the Iranians to complete the program—or get their machines humming to the level where they could weaponize sufficient uranium to build a bomb.

The IAEA was clear that Iran was at least five years off—an estimate derived from former URENCO scientists. WMD old hands, including Robert Gallucci, were even more cautious, arguing that it was more like eight years. But the US took sides with Israel, which put the date for Tehran reaching the point of no return at anything from one year to three months—an accelerated estimate based more on politics, given that Israel was a front-line state keen quickly to snuff out the nuclear ambitions of its near neighbor.[42] Israel also bolstered Bolton's claim regarding a second secret plant stocked with the sophisticated and super-fast P-2 centrifuges. "There are two parallel nuclear programs inside Iran—the one declared to the IAEA and a separate operation, run by the military and the Revolutionary Guard," said a Mossad source.[43] There were two worlds of analysis on Iran, one based on intelligence emanating from Vienna and another based on US and Israeli preconceptions. The IAEA, the UN Security Council and virtually every European government made it clear that until hard evidence of the secret second plant was produced they could not act.

In July 2005, Bush officials announced that an Iranian scientist had walked into an unidentified US embassy in Europe with a laptop computer containing more than a thousand pages of technical drawings of weapons systems and designs, among which was long-awaited evidence of the second secret plant. In fact, despite briefing the IAEA and leaking the highly classified operation to the world's press, spreading fear that Iran was closer to a nuclear bomb than previously thought, the US was later forced to admit that the computer contained no more than "rough sketches" for a re-entry vehicle for a conventional missile.[44]

Then, in August 2005, events in Iran appeared to conspire in America's favor. Mahmoud Ahmadinejad, a forty-nine-year-old blacksmith's son from the city of Garmsar, north of Tehran, unexpectedly won the Iranian elections, edging out Hashemi Rafsanjani, a reformist who was seeking a third term as president. An arch-conservative from the school of Ayatollah Khomeini, Ahmadinejad had already surprised the electorate by becoming mayor of Tehran in 2003.[45] He had stolen a march on the far more experienced Rafsanjani by appealing to the pious working-class throng, emotionally denouncing the anti-Shia bloodshed over the border in Iraq. In late 2004, foreign fighters under the leadership of Abu Musab al-Zarqawi had begun a civil war between Iraq's Shia and Sunni populations and in October 2004 Zarqawi had pledged allegiance to Osama bin Laden, who had made him his deputy in Iraq, forming a new organization the name of which translated as "al-Qaeda in Mesopotamia." It orchestrated a kind of harrowing violence never seen before: beheadings, indiscriminate massacres and suicide bombings.[46] The fighting engulfed many of Shia Islam's most revered mosques and shrines in Iraq, killing thousands of Shias on pilgrimage from Iran in the process.[47]

After the election, Ahmadinejad began to unveil an agenda that superficially gave credence to the Vulcan warnings that Iran had to be dealt with soon. He immediately announced that Iran's nuclear program would be a national priority, revealing that Iran had reopened its uranium conversion facility at Esfahan. Ali Larijani, Iran's new chief nuclear negotiator, declared they had every right to make uranium fuel under the terms of the Nuclear Non-Proliferation Treaty. Technically he was correct, but the statement was deliberately provocative.

Not content with pushing the nuclear button, Ahmadinejad repeatedly and publicly made the West squeal. He questioned the scale of the Holocaust, calling a conference of deniers and revisionists to debate the hold this Second World War "myth" had on international politics. He called for the Jewish state to be wiped off the face of the earth. But while he intended his comments to reach out to his Sunni neighbors (and erstwhile enemies) in the Arab states and Iraq, appealing to them in the kind of language they understood, hoping to distract them from paying too much attention to the unstoppable rise of Shia Iran, it was Israel and the US that jumped.[48] Senior Bush officials began describing Ahmadinejad as a potential Adolf Hitler. "That's the name they're using," one senior intelligence official told the investigative reporter Seymour Hersh. "They ask, 'Will Iran get a strategic weapon and threaten another world war?'"[49]

Ahmadinejad's outbursts consolidated a serious policy review on Iran with the State Department, Pentagon and CIA, pressed by the White House into redoubling their efforts at gathering intelligence and analysis with which to pave the warpath to Tehran. They also began, via like-minded Washington think tanks, the American Enterprise Institute (AEI) and the Washington Institute on Near East Policy included, to talk up regime change—drawing up lists of potential successors; "a long scroll of Chalabis" as one State Department insider described it, referring to Ahmed Chalabi, the much-denigrated executive of the Iraqi National Congress who had been the source of much of the administration's flawed intelligence on Saddam's WMD.[50]

These think tanks had been active on Iran since the Tehran student riots of 1999, pounced on by some in the US as the first sign of a resurgent Iranian reform movement. Then the AEI and Washington Institute had encouraged the US government to fund a Farsi TV station in Los Angeles, where 600,000 expatriate Iranians lived, having fled the revolution of 1979. The station's footprint enabled it to be seen also in Iran, and in September 2000, Reza Pahlavi, the forty-five-year-old son of the deposed Shah, for some still a resonant figure, was put on air and regally called for Iranians back home to rise up. No matter that Pahlavi had been in exile for twenty-one years and had no idea of the limits placed on everyday life back in Iran. Five months later Pahlavi spoke at the Washington Institute, where he reiterated his call. CIA analysts watching him recalled thinking, "He's clean and has not killed anyone," cynically reflecting on the long list of opposition figures around the world who were courted by the CIA but wanted in their own countries for murders, blackmail and rape.[51] The fact that Pahlavi, who portrayed himself as a constitutional monarch in the mold of King Juan Carlos of Spain, was prone to making excitable and inappropriate statements, which necessitated employing a minder to keep him on track, was but a small problem.

When Bush named Iran as part of the "Axis of Evil" in his state of the union address of 2002, Pahlavi excitedly told friends he was "going home."[52] But for those living in Iran, according to one Tehran-based writer, the Bush speech served to generate a sense of torpor and pessimism, marking a deterioration in relations with the US that was compounded the following year when the American-led coalition invaded Iraq.[53]

Iran was right to be afraid, as the US was now more intent than ever on regime change. In 2003 the Pentagon began reaching out to other opposition groups, including the controversial Mujahideen e-Khalq (MeK) which had unmasked Natanz the previous August. The Pentagon prepared a draft national security presidential directive that recommended giving communication devices to students in Iran, buying off and neutralizing the Revolutionary Guard, and supporting the burgeoning exiled satellite media operations based in LA.[54] Senator Sam Brownback (Republican, Kansas) signed a bill calling for $100 million to be channelled to opposition groups active inside Iran.[55]

The rhetoric from Washington continued to mount. In the winter of 2005, White House officials described the Iranian president as belonging to the terrorist outfit that had executed the deadly bombings of the US embassy and US Marine barracks in Beirut in April and October 1983, in which 304 were killed and hundreds injured. This was surmise passed off as fact, and Pentagon insiders increased the pressure by talking up the prospect of an Osirak-style raid to knock out Natanz and the uranium conversion facility at Esfahan. The arguments melded together the war on terrorism with the buzzword of counter-proliferation, one Pentagon adviser warning: "We cannot have nukes being sent downstream to a terror network. It's just too dangerous."[56]

Officials talked up the US president's vision, how Bush had to do "what no Democrat or Republican, if elected in the future, would have the courage to do." Saving Iran was going to be his legacy—given that Iraq had by now descended into a sectarian bloodbath that no leader wanted as his epitaph.[57] Despite sending in Zalmay Khalilzad, the administration hard-liner, as US ambassador to Iraq in June 2005, the killing had continued unabated, leading to senior US government officials admitting that they no longer expected to see "a model new democracy" in Iraq.[58] The scale of the Iraq crisis was even beginning to worry US allies in the Middle East, with the normally tight-lipped Prince Saud al-Faisal, the Saudi foreign minister and son of King Faisal, warning during a visit to the US in September 2005 that "Iraq was hurtling towards disintegration."[59]

US Air Force planning groups identified 400 targets inside Iran, using intelligence derived from undercover American combat troops secretly ordered over the border from Iraq by Donald Rumsfeld. Much of this data was dubious, having been bought with cash from local tribesmen and shepherds, in a controversial operation that conveniently sidestepped Congress. Rumsfeld had exploited a loophole in oversight rules that allowed the military to run covert missions without congressional approval if they could be broadly classified as preparing the battlefield or protecting troops.[60] If the Iran data collection plan had been masterminded by the CIA, Rumsfeld would have required a presidential finding, making it unlikely that it would have been sanctioned.[61]

The White House found other ways to circumvent Congress, Bush briefing a select group of politicians on his Iran plans, most of them already backers of the war in Iraq.[62] There were few objections, but they raised incisive questions that teased out an alarming insight into the direction Pentagon war planners were taking. Asked how US forces intended to hit all of Iran's nuclear sites at once and penetrate deeply enough to destroy all of the underground nuclear facilities, Donald Rumsfeld revealed that his advisers were recommending the use of B61-11 bunker-buster tactical nuclear weapons, and that American naval aircraft had already begun simulating rapid ascending maneuvers known as "over the shoulder" bombing from US carriers positioned in the Arabian Sea.[63] This was a policy drawn straight out of Robert Joseph's radical strategy paper from 2001, when he had raised the idea of pre-emptively dropping a nuclear bomb. The B61-11 was his perfect weapon. Designed to burrow, fitted with what weapon designers called an earth-penetrating warhead, before deploying a nuclear explosion capable of destroying multiple layers of reinforced concrete—such as those that enclose subterranean nuclear facilities—it could be fitted with variable loads from 0.3 to 340 kilotons. The same weapon had been advanced for use against Libya's subterranean chemical weapons factory but was so controversial that the proposal had been stood down.[64]

Joseph's proposal divided even the most battle-hardened flag officers. "We're talking about mushroom clouds, radiation, mass casualties and contamination over years," one senior intelligence official told Seymour Hersh. The nuclear option was a "juggernaut that has to be stopped."[65] After senior military chiefs gave Bush formal notice of their opposition, advisers on the Defense Science

Board—the defense secretary's independent panel of experts, chaired by neo-conservative William Schneider, Jr.—recommended that the B61 could be redesigned "with more blast and less radiation."[66] All the while Mohamed ElBaradei at the IAEA continued to stress that dialogue was the only option. On 8 March 2006 he warned that the Iran crisis required "a comprehensive political settlement that takes account of all underlying issues."[67] Bush ignored the entreaty, warning: "I made it clear, I'll make it clear again, that we will use military might to protect our ally Israel."[68]

Bravado aside, US military might was failing over the border in Iraq. Since January 2006, the UN had been openly describing the conflict there as "civil-war-like," when all around US commanders and politicians refused to use the phraseology. The increasingly sectarian crisis had been made all the worse in February 2006 when the al Askari mosque in Samarra, the holiest site in Shia Islam, was blown up by al-Zarqawi's suicide bombers, killing hundreds of Iranians, fulfilling the fears raised by Ahmadinejad during his election campaign, triggering a spate of vicious reprisals against Sunni communities and mosques, and leading ultimately to Iraq, formerly wealthy and stable, albeit tyrannically governed, being listed as fourth on a US schedule of failed states (beaten only by Sudan, the Democratic Republic of Congo and the Ivory Coast).[69]

Sensing that the US was in a corner, Iran announced that it was starting up its centrifuges at Natanz, forcing the IAEA board to discuss US demands that Tehran be referred to the UN Security Council.[70] Robert Joseph travelled to Vienna, where he delivered an uncompromising message to Mohamed ElBaradei. "We cannot have a single centrifuge spinning. Iran is a direct threat to the national security of the United States and our allies, and we will not tolerate it."[71] But ElBaradei, who had recently been awarded the Nobel Peace Prize, was not receptive. He had not seen in Iran "any diversion of nuclear material to nuclear weapons or other nuclear explosive devices"—although he remained worried about the ambiguous "role of the military" in the uranium program.[72] The same was true of European delegates. One high-ranking diplomat warned the US: "You must bite the bullet and sit down with the Iranians."[73] The IAEA agreed to report Iran to the UN Security Council, but the Bush administration refused to talk.[74]

Washington wanted regime change, Condoleezza Rice going to Congress in February 2006 for an extra $85 million funding for radio and TV broadcasts from the US into Iran. Government officials travelled to California to see the twenty-five media outlets (twenty TV and five radio) that had sprung up there, one of them, Radio Farda, capably demonstrating its purpose in January 2007 when it broadcast news that a Mossad hit squad had killed a prize-winning Iranian nuclear scientist, Ardeshire Hassanpour.[75] The physicist, who worked at the uranium conversion facility in Esfahan, was said to have died from gas poisoning, with US sources pointing the blame in the direction of the Israelis. Who was to say what Israel would do next? Strike Iran's nuclear facilities with conventional missiles, or worse. Unverified but difficult to contest, the Radio Farda story thrived on the Internet, spawning debate in chat rooms and on bulletin boards, falling within the realm of classic US psychological operations.

The US remained intransigent, especially about talking. In March 2006, Nicholas Burns, under secretary of state for political affairs, dismissed the notion that direct discussions would be an effective way of dealing with Iran's nuclear program.[76] Gregory Schulte, the US ambassador to the IAEA, expanded on the no-talks plan, adding that the only discussion the US was prepared to engage in was about Iran's contribution to the chaos in Iraq. "We have no intention to open direct negotiations with Tehran on the nuclear issue," he said. The linkage between Tehran and the bloodshed in Baghdad—Revolutionary Guard-trained jihadis accused of aiding insurgents who were attacking US and UK forces—would be a theme constantly advanced by the US from this point on, despite a paucity of trustworthy intelligence. It was a tactic that, according to former Carter national security adviser Zbigniew Brzezinski, sought to portray Iran as an aggressor, paving the way, by providing a motive, for a strike by the US on Iran as part of a broader attempt by Bush to stabilize the careening war in Iraq.[77]

Ahmadinejad's response was predictable. In April 2006 he announced that uranium enrichment at Natanz had reached 3.5 percent, a breakthrough that demonstrated Iranian scientists had mastered the difficult process. Plans were on schedule for 3,000 centrifuges to be up and running within a year, raising the possibility that Iran would press on to reach higher levels of enrichment.[78] Four weeks later, Iran duly announced it had reached 4.8 percent—from where it would not be too technically challenging to make the leap to the levels at which fissile material would be created. Ahmadinejad wrote to President Bush, the first direct communication between an Iranian head of state and a US president since 1979, asking for talks to focus on "new solutions for getting out of international problems and the current fragile situation of the world."[79]

The US reply came at the end of May 2006 from Condoleezza Rice, who appeared to hold out a hand, saying that America was prepared to talk, until Tehran read the small print which revealed that she had reheated the no-win bargaining position previously used by the US against North Korea in October 2002. Rice set as her deal-breaker a request that Iran suspend all nuclear activities and agree on more intrusive IAEA inspections, to be implemented before anyone even sat down. Ahmadinejad declined and blocked weapons inspectors from a scheduled visit to Natanz in August.[80] When the UN Security Council, which had resolved that Iran had to suspend enrichment by 31 August or face reprisals, put the date of compliance back to October, the US jumped the gun, preferring unilateral action, by passing the Iran Freedom Support Act which threatened economic sanctions against nations found to be aiding Iran's nuclear program.[81] Iran unveiled a second cascade of 164 centrifuges at Natanz.

No carrot, no stick, no talks. Evidence that this US policy was headed nowhere other than disastrous conflagration came when North Korea (which had gone from discussing the rollback of its enrichment program to withdrawing from the Nuclear Non-Proliferation Treaty in a few short months after John Bolton and James Kelly interceded in October 2002) conducted its first nuclear weapons test, in an underground tunnel 240 miles northeast of Pyongyang on 9 October 2006. "It marks a historic event as it greatly pleased the Korean people's army and people that wished to have a powerful self-reliant defense capability," said a spokesman.[82] China called the test "brazen." Japan said it was "unpardonable." In the US, House speaker Dennis Hastert decried the blast as "the desperate act of a criminal regime" although old hands, including Robert Gallucci, saw it as the first significant failure of the new US counter-proliferation policy which continued to stalk Iran.[83]

The psychological operations against Tehran escalated. In November 2006, the *Daily Telegraph* in London alleged that Iran was working on a secret military project, code-named "Zirzamin 27" (where Zirzamin was Farsi for basement and 27 was the number of years since the revolution). It was said to be a program to enrich uranium to weapons grade, the evidence for it being swab samples taken by the IAEA, which had found traces of weaponized uranium on equipment in Iran.[84] However, the IAEA board had already attributed these samples to Pakistan (and possibly China), which had covertly sent contaminated equipment to Iran, as well as drums of highly enriched uranium, as part of Project A/B. The story was clearly mischievous, but more on the same theme would follow it.

Not even the loss of both houses of Congress to the Democrats in the November 2006 mid-term elections and Donald Rumsfeld's resignation as defense secretary on 8 November stopped the brinkmanship. President Bush publicly acknowledged that the Republican defeat was partly a reflection of "displeasure with the lack of progress being made [in Iraq]," but three months later a glimpse of the inner workings of the psychological operations emanating from the Pentagon emerged when Rumsfeld, along with Wolfowitz and Eric Edelman, the under secretary of defense, were accused of having massaged intelligence on Iraq, recruiting after 9/11 a small team of civilians within the Pentagon to undermine CIA findings on the matter and undertake a "fresh, critical look" at links between terror networks and governments.

This group sifted through existing classified material which Bush officials claimed had been overlooked and poorly analyzed by the intelligence community. In reality, the group was charged with feeding intelligence fitting the Vulcan agenda to the commander-in-chief. It focused on Iran, North Korea and Iraq. By the summer of 2002, all efforts were concentrated on connecting Saddam Hussein to al-Qaeda, a thesis that came to fruition in a memo written for Douglas Feith, then under secretary of defense for policy, entitled, "Iraq and al-Qaeda making the case," which became a central plank in the case for regime change in Iraq.[85]

In July 2004, the 9/11 Commission concluded that there had been "no evidence" that contacts between the Iraqi government and al-Qaeda "ever developed into a collaborative operational relationship," a charge that was probed by Senator Carl Levin (Democrat, Michigan), the senior Democrat on the Senate armed services committee. Levin's investigations uncovered Rumsfeld's unofficial intelligence team, which was "inappropriately producing alternative analyzes" and had "exaggerated a connection between Iraq and al-Qaeda while the intelligence community remained consistently dubious."[86] The inspector general was called in to investigate and in February 2007 he would criticize civilian Pentagon officials who "developed, produced and then disseminated alternative intelligence assessments on the Iraq and al-Qaeda relationship which included some conclusions that were inconsistent with the consensus of the intelligence community."[87] In short, Rumsfeld's team had spun the context for war with Iraq. Describing the findings as a "very strong condemnation of the Pentagon," Levin, by then chairman of the Senate committee on the armed services, said: "They made it clear they wanted any kind of possible connections, no matter how skimpy, and they got it."[88]

But in November 2006, the Bush administration was still at it, this time with Iran in the frame.[89] Unsourced stories found their way into US and UK newspapers, including one in the *Daily Telegraph* that claimed: "Iran is seeking to take control of Osama bin Laden's al-Qaeda terror network by encouraging it to promote officials known to be friendly to Tehran."[90] It gave the impression of a hostile takeover, with Tehran moving in to control bin Laden's outfit. The thought that a conservative Shia revivalist movement had hijacked a band of Wahhabi Sunni extremists, and was even raising their new chiefs, would have sounded far-fetched to anyone in the Middle East who could tell the difference between the two branches of Islam and was aware of the 700 years of internecine warfare between them. But it was evidence enough for the American Enterprise Institute (AEI) to join up the dots and, on 19 November 2004, Joshua Muravchik, AEI resident scholar, spoke for those closest to Bush with a paper that began: "We must bomb Iran."[91]

Muravchik was no stranger to the Vulcans. He had sat on the board of the now-defunct Committee for the Liberation of Iraq, was associated with the Washington Institute and the Project for the New American Century, the think tank that had urged Clinton to eliminate Saddam Hussein. Muravchik proclaimed that there was overwhelming evidence of how the Shia were beginning to win over the Sunnis, a necessary prerequisite to Iran taking over al-Qaeda.[92] It could be seen in the *Daily Telegraph*'s allegations that Tehran was grooming terrorists, but also in the recent—and ultimately short-lived— pacts between the Shia Hezbollah in Lebanon and Sunni Palestinians in Gaza. "The only way to forestall these frightening developments is by the use of force. Not by invading Iran, as we did Iraq, but by an air campaign against Tehran's nuclear facilities," Muravchik wrote. He claimed the number of targets identified by the Pentagon was up to 1,500. "If we hit a large fraction of them, in a bombing campaign that might last from a few days to a couple of weeks, we would inflict severe damage." Not to act would be a travesty of history akin to the British cabinet ignoring the warnings of Winston Churchill to crush the Bolshevik revolution of 1917. "Ahmadinejad wants to be the new Lenin. Force is the only thing that can stop him," railed Muravchik.

There were still some in the US committed to a different approach. In December 2006, the bipartisan Iraq Study Group, formed before the midterm elections by the Republican-controlled Congress in order to find a way out of the increasingly bloody melee, reported that with "no foreseeable end" to the war, only increased diplomatic measures with Iran and Syria, combined with US troop withdrawals, could save the day.[93] However, a few weeks later Iraq's Shia government hanged Saddam Hussein, with his executioners filmed taunting him as the noose was tied around his neck, and Bush returned to the issue of force. In a widely anticipated address on 10 January 2007, the president stood in the library of the White House and confessed on national TV to having pursued a flawed strategy in Iraq. But there would be no withdrawal. He had not sent enough troops, and he appealed to the American people to support his decision to send in an additional 21,500.[94]

The "troop surge," as it was described, had been shaped by Frederick Kagan, an AEI scholar and West Point military historian, whose brother, Robert, had been a signatory to the 1998 Clinton letter. Frederick Kagan argued that "victory is still an option" and maintained, "failure in Iraq today will require far greater sacrifices tomorrow in far more desperate circumstances. Committing to victory now will demonstrate America's strength to our friends and enemies around the world."[95] Kagan's argument was so seductive that the president had already adopted it. New US forces were already on their way, with ninety advance troops from the 82nd Airborne Division arriving in Baghdad on the morning of Bush's televised address.[96] A US Navy battle group of seven vessels was also sailing from the Red Sea, as part of a deployment of fifty ships, including two aircraft carriers and several British vessels, which represented the biggest naval build-up since the start of the Iraq war in 2003. Its purpose was shrouded in doublespeak. But it was most closely monitored by Tehran, which had finally been subjected to limited sanctions by the UN Security Council in December 2006. The following March, fifteen British sailors and marines would be seized from the Shatt al-Arab waterway of the Persian Gulf and held in captivity by Tehran for two weeks, accused of spying. The nuclear stand-off continued in January 2007, with Ahmadinejad banning thirty-eight nuclear inspectors from entering the country and announcing that Iran's nuclear fuel cycle would be completed within a matter of weeks—with UF_6 produced in Esfahan and enriched to 4.8 percent by 3,000 centrifuges spinning in Natanz.[97]

Far from lancing Iran's nuclear threat, US counter-proliferation strategy had escalated it, and Ahmadinejad, whose combative foreign policy had previously been criticized, was bolstered.[98] As Tehran hunkered down for possible war, Iranians fell behind their president. In April 2007, speaking at Natanz, Ahmadinejad announced that Iran's scientists had made a dramatic leap forward, achieving uranium enrichment "on an industrial scale" with 3,000 centrifuges now running smoothly at the facility, which Western scientists estimated could generate enough fissile material for Iran to build a nuclear bomb in nine months' time. Ali Ansari, director of the Iranian Institute at the University of St. Andrews, wrote: "While Ahmadinejad has been his own worst enemy, the US hawks are his best friends."[99] At the IAEA, where ElBaradei called for "time out" to allow both the US and Iranian sides to cool down, one European diplomat warned: "If the US attacks, Ahmadinejad will become the new Saddam Hussein of the Arab world, but with more credibility and power."[100]

From inside the State Department there was an increasing sense of anxiety. "The net result of counter-proliferation was that one 'Axis of Evil' power had been goaded into testing a nuclear device and another was edging towards doing the same," a senior analyst said.[101] Even more embarrassing for Bush in February 2007 was the administration's admission that it had abandoned its belligerent approach to Pyongyang—the strategy of "threaten and neglect," put in place in 2001.[102] Forced back to the negotiating table by China, Bush officials had been pressed into dropping most of the sanctions imposed on Pyongyang over the past five years. Han Seung-joo, the former foreign minister of South Korea and close to the talks, said: "[The US] is going back to where it was before. The US has talked tough without having achieved anything."[103]

The drumbeat from Washington was ceaseless, though, and continued to be heard all around the world. Lumping together two foreign policy failures into one giant threat, the *Daily Telegraph* in London reported that North Korea was alleged by unidentified intelligence officials to have offered to help Iran with a nuclear test within the year.[104] Three weeks later, the Bush administration returned to an older theme, once again accusing the Iranian leadership of meddling in Iraq by supplying weapons and know-how which had been used to fatal effect against US and British soldiers.[105]

However, it was too much even for the normally acquiescent General Peter Pace, chairman of the joint chiefs of staff, a flag officer who had become renowned for painting a rosy picture of events in Iraq, but who this time could not agree.[106] He told reporters that he was not ready to conclude that Iran's leadership had been behind the arms supply, leaving President Bush's staff hurriedly to call the general to ask what it was that he did believe.[107] Their conversation was not revealed, but mindful of the midterm elections disaster in which the administration's propensity to fake intelligence to justify war had been attacked, Bush amended his statement, adding that it was possible Ahmadinejad had not been personally involved. Speaking in the Senate about hyped intelligence, Hillary Clinton (Democrat, New York) warned: "We have all learned lessons from the conflict in Iraq, and we have to apply those lessons to any allegations that are being raised about Iran. Because, Mr. President, what we are hearing has too familiar a ring and we must be on guard that we never again make decisions on the basis of intelligence that turns out to be faulty."[108] But nothing would change the administration's resolve, with Bush warning: "If I thought we could achieve success, I would sit down [with the Iranians]. But I don't think we can achieve success right now."[109]

The strategists affiliated to al-Qaeda must have been delighted that the US remained resolute on Iran, as the prospect of war dovetailed well with their long-term plans. The US military has a system for analyzing its shortcomings, a process known as "lessons learned," run by a military body based at Fort Leavenworth, Kansas.[110] Unusually for a terrorist movement forged in the heat of battle, al-Qaeda, too, had become reflective, acknowledging the hammering it had taken when the Taliban had fallen in November 2001 and three-quarters of its cadres had been killed.

Back then, a middle-class, redheaded Syrian, with a black belt in judo and a nose for a political scuffle, was hiding out, writing a defining work, *The Call for Worldwide Islamic Resistance*.[111] Mustafa Setmariam Nasar, who had assumed the nom de guerre of Abu Musab al-Suri, planned to upload his 1,600-page masterwork in Arabic onto the Internet as a call to arms, heralding a new phase in the war that aimed to "bring about the largest number of human and material casualties possible for America and its allies"—a plan that involved jihadis obtaining WMDs.

Al-Suri was guaranteed an audience in the East, since he had once served on al-Qaeda's inner council. His journey was also instructive for readers in the West, as it was typical of that undertaken by many new emirs of the jihad. Having become involved in politics while studying mechanical engineering at the University of Aleppo in Syria in the 1970s, al-Suri had graduated, moved to Jordan and joined the Muslim Brotherhood, before renouncing it, appalled by slack tactics which resulted in the "sacrifice" of thousands of brothers by Syrian security forces. Grieving and contemptuous, al-Suri, a specialist in explosives and guerrilla warfare, had fled, seeking shelter in Spain.[112]

In the early 1980s he married and became a Spanish citizen, before leaving Europe again in 1987, when he headed to Afghanistan and met Osama bin Laden. Unlike others, al-Suri was not mesmerized by the soft-spoken and ascetic mujahid. All he could see was the disorganization in bin Laden's desert camps and the lack of premeditation in his approach. For al-Suri, bin Laden was simply not serious enough, writing: "People come to us with empty heads and they leave with empty heads."[113]

Disaffected, al-Suri moved back to Spain, then to the UK, where he filed news stories to Abu Qatada, a cleric and newspaper editor who would soon be described by the British and US authorities as al-Qaeda's point man in Europe— and would become most infamous for having allegedly given spiritual guidance to Richard Reid, the shoe bomber, and Zacarias Moussaoui, sentenced in 2006 to life imprisonment for planning the 9/11 attacks. In the cold light of day, Abu Qatada was an overweight Palestinian who had travelled little and fought nowhere, and he was captivated by al-Suri. But in 1997 al-Suri took off for Afghanistan, tipped off that the British authorities had correctly connected him with the Paris metro bombings of July 1995, when a gas canister studded with nails had killed seven passengers. He arrived one year after the Taliban had taken Kabul. It was a "golden opportunity," al-Suri wrote. A wanted man in the West, al-Suri would, along with many others, be given protection by a sovereign state bound by ancient tribal rules of hospitality. An entire country forged out of the heat of jihadism would also conceal al-Qaeda's operations.

While hiding there, and always in the vanguard, al-Suri worked at the Al-Ghuraba training camp, near Kabul, where he found a common bond with an Egyptian chemist, Midhat Mursi al-Sayid Umar, who had assumed the nom de guerre of Abu Khabab al-Masri and was al-Qaeda's WMD chief, joining forces with him to improve on the arsenal available to al-Qaeda.[114] Al-Suri was intent on becoming a master of destruction, calamity and catastrophe. He was also by now an avowed Salafist. Taken from the Arabic word *salaf* or "ancient one," this referred to the companions of the Prophet and had come to represent a school of puritanical Muslims who believed in taking their faith back to that time and towards a literal interpretation of ancient texts, stripping away what they saw as the centuries of decadence—which other people argued represented progress.

Al-Suri later claimed that he was responsible for encouraging bin Laden truly to embrace Salafism and into believing that there should be no end to jihad until US troops had been ousted from the Arabian Peninsula's holy soil.[115] However, by 1999 al-Suri and bin Laden had fallen out, for reasons spiritual and corporeal, including the latter's love of publicity. "I think our brother has caught the disease of screens, flashes, fans and applause," al-Suri wrote after one of bin Laden's impromptu broadsides on camera had captured headlines on CNN and al-Jazeera.[116] By the following year, al-Suri was out, leaving al-Masri to run the WMD program, and while in hiding he finished his writing.

From what he had seen in Afghanistan, al-Suri predicted in his manuscript the downfall of al-Qaeda as a standing army, warning that it needed to become an essence, a guiding hand, rather than a cumbersome band of armed desert dwellers ill equipped to defend themselves against Western firepower. Al-Suri wrote: "Al-Qaeda is not an organization. It is not a group. It is a call, a reference, a methodology." By 2002, with the Taliban routed and al-Qaeda fleeing, he had concluded that the new fight had to be carried by a "leaderless resistance," cells that would wear down the enemy, preparing the ground for when al-Qaeda was ready to wage a more ambitious war with WMDs for territory "on open fronts."[117]

Al-Suri pointed to those battlegrounds: Afghanistan—which the remnants of the Taliban were working hard with their Pakistani sponsors to make ungovernable; Central Asia—where the Soviet glue had come unstuck, to be replaced by equally brutal Russian repression which had unleashed Islamic forces eager for freedom of expression; Yemen and Morocco—where authoritarian Western-leaning regimes had long suppressed grass-roots Islamic movements; and especially Iraq—in which he predicted that a new kind of war would be demonstrated following the US invasion. He also warned of the importance as a springboard for al-Qaeda of Pakistan, where, in 2005, he would eventually be captured in a Jaish-e-Mohammed safe house in Quetta, to be rendered by the CIA to another country that the US authorities declined to identify.[118]

The writings of pen-jihadi al-Suri were a trigger. In his absence, others pulled the strands of the new plan together, taking account of the failures he had identified. Only months after al-Suri had uploaded his manifesto in December 2004, another thesis emerged that provided insight into what had already happened, as al-Qaeda saw it, and what might happen yet. This book also purported to come from the molten core of the al-Qaeda movement, drawn from the thinking of its leading cadres. Written by a Jordanian journalist, Fouad Hussein, it was based on prison-cell conversations he had had in 1996 with Abu Musab al-Zarqawi, a jihadi then completely unknown in the West.[119] Nicknamed after al-Zarqa, the Jordanian city fifteen miles east of Amman in which he was born in 1966, al-Zarqawi was already a known troublemaker in Jordan and elsewhere in the region, along with his mentor and godfather, also in the cell, Abu Muhammed al-Maqdisi. Seven years his senior, al-Maqdisi, a "Jordanian Palestinian," had become a stellar firebrand and author, widely revered as the Jean-Paul Marat of the Sunni mujahids.

All three had been incarcerated at Jordan's Suwaqah prison, a forbidding desert jail crammed with 6,000 inmates, marooned sixty miles south of Amman. Journalist Hussein was in for petty political misdemeanors, and al-Zarqawi and al-Maqdisi for plotting the overthrow of the Jordanian kingdom. Al-Maqdisi had caused the entire region to swallow its tongue after publishing *The Evident Sacrileges of the Saudi State*, a brimstone book that called for the excommunication and destruction of the Saudi royal family, a work that has triggered uprisings in Saudi Arabia from the mid-1990s until the present.[120] He had discovered the rough-edged al-Zarqawi, a former gang leader and violent drunk, in 1989 as both men travelled to fight the Soviets over the border in Afghanistan. Al-Zarqawi was trying to redeem himself by going on jihad. Together they fought beside the rabid Gulbuddin Hekmatyar, Pakistan's chosen Afghan mujahid, taking part in the battle for Khost and the final push on Kabul. When the war was over, al-Maqdisi and al-Zarqawi were stuck for a cause. They returned to Jordan still brimming with zeal and determined to take on the monarchy, only to be rounded up by Jordan's secret police, who slung them in jail in 1994, where they languished for two years before ending up in conversation with the journalist Fouad Hussein.

Hussein recalled: "I went to their cell on the first day. Al-Maqdisi and al-Zarqawi were sitting in the center. I greeted them and introduced myself, 'I am a reporter who follows political issues.' " Hussein later wrote that he had been terrified of these fierce jihadis with their long beards and dour expressions. They had no friends in common and he had nothing obvious to offer them. He chose an honest approach and told them: "I am not affiliated with any Islamic group but I am interested in your case, which I have followed in the media." Al-Zarqawi, a self-styled "lion of the jihad," smiled. "He served me a cup of tea that warmed my heart and made me feel safe," wrote Hussein.

Al-Zarqawi needed Hussein. Having been incarcerated for eight months in solitary confinement, he had been tortured so badly that he had lost his toenails. When they met he was about to be thrown back into the punishment pit for being insolent to the guards. But al-Zarqawi, along with followers in other cells, was resisting and the prison was cranking up for an explosive showdown, with bars pulled from windows and beds sharpened into spears and machetes. Hussein mediated and through him an agreement was reached. Al-Zarqawi was returned to the general pond of prison life. Grateful, al-Zarqawi and al-Maqdisi unburdened themselves to the slight Jordanian journalist, and after Fouad Hussein's release these interviews served to unpick the locks inside the al-Qaeda movement, with others previously suspicious of outsiders agreeing to share their thoughts and writings, from which Hussein would draw together a book on the future war. Fouad Hussein's book, coming so soon after al-Suri's prescriptions, provided proof-positive that a community of fighters and radical Islamic thinkers was bartering ideas and attempting to put a structure on what had already taken place, in order to plan for what was about to happen.

Al-Zarqawi and al-Maqdisi were released from prison in 1999.[121] While al-Maqdisi remained in Jordan to militate on behalf of Salafism, al-Zarqawi tried to create mayhem, plotting to blow up the Radisson Hotel in the Jordanian capital, Amman, on millennium eve. Having failed, with some of his foot soldiers rounded up, al-Zarqawi headed for Chechnya, via Pakistan, only to fall foul of corrupt border guards who, claiming he had the wrong travel documents, deported him to Afghanistan, where he temporarily rejoined al-Qaeda. The quarrelsome al-Zarqawi argued that the network had gone soft and, falling out with al-Qaeda, he travelled west, opening a separate training camp in the Afghan city of Herat, ensuring loyalty from his followers and recruits by encouraging them to intermarry so as to become one large, extended family. But in November 2001, with the Northern Alliance, the Western-friendly political umbrella of anti-Taliban forces, pressing, they were forced to abandon their camp.[122] Spotting American intentions in Iraq, in 2002 al-Zarqawi trekked on foot to a country that he believed would further his agenda, certain that the US was about to become mired there. He was not alone in drawing these conclusions, as bin Laden, too, had predicted that the US would be unable to stop itself going into Iraq, with al-Qaeda's task being to "provoke and bait" to ensure that Bush did so, in order that a "bleeding war" could be launched by the terror network against the US forces. It was a strategy learned from the mountains of Afghanistan, where bin Laden and the mujahideen, armed and trained by the CIA and Pakistan's ISI, had entrapped the Soviet Red Army.[123]

Initially a freelancer, travelling and fighting alongside childhood friends and his new family, the emir of his own fringe group known as al-Tawhid wa al-Jihad (Monotheism and Jihad), al-Zarqawi was soon based north of the alluvial plains between the Tigris and Euphrates rivers, on Iraq's arid al-Jazirah plateau. From there, as the US launched its war, he pieced together a network so that when the official battle concluded in May 2003 he was able, within a matter of weeks, to kick off a slew of attacks which grew quickly into brutal outrages that stole headlines away from al-Qaeda and jangled Western and Iraqi nerves. His strategy was simple: divide and rule. First, he blew apart the delicate international component of the postwar coalition, decimating UN head-quarters in Baghdad with a truck bomb that claimed the life of the top UN envoy in Iraq, Sérgio Vieira de Mello. Coalition forces were harried in Karbala, the Italians in al-Nasiriyah, the Americans on the al-Khalidiyah bridge, a US intelligence station at the al-Rashid Hotel, and Polish troops in al-Hillah. Then he began to prey on the sectarian divides in the country. In February 2004, al-Zarqawi also repeatedly and brutally targeted the Shia in Karbala and al-Kazimiyah, massacring hundreds and injuring thousands. In March, he struck in the Shia-dominated port city of Basra, leading to the US placing an $11 million reward on his head—and al-Qaeda issuing an extraordinary com-muniqué denying it had anything to do with the monstrous sectarian murders to which the Iraq war had given birth. But al-Zarqawi was unrepentant. In May 2004, he came to the world's attention when his group al-Tawhid posted a live video clip on the Internet showing the beheading of kidnapped American businessman Nicholas Berg. "We have harvested their heads," al-Zarqawi declared, "and tore up their bodies in several places ... There is a long list of targets. Some chapters were completed but the upcoming chapters will be more violent and far more bitter. God Willing."

Al-Zarqawi's bloodthirsty strategy was revealed in a letter to bin Laden written in 2004. Found on a CD taken from a Pakistani jihadi, Hasan Jahl, arrested by US forces in Iraq, it showed that al-Zarqawi, like al-Suri, instinctively felt that anti-Americanism alone as a motive had failed to grow the movement. Arabs had been agog at 9/11 rather than inspired by it. Al-Qaeda had been too monolithic, its single-issue platform of attacking America having found little long-term support among the commercially astute Arab nations that prayed five times a day but also doffed their caps to the US dollar. Al-Zarqawi urged al-Qaeda to tap into far older and more rancorous prejudices, making the Sunnis believe that the Shia were threatening them, to whip up a maelstrom of sectarianism that reached back to Dark Ages squabbles over the line of the Prophet. "If we succeed in dragging the Shia into the arena of sectarian war," al-Zarqawi wrote to bin Laden, "it will be possible to awaken the inattentive Sunnis as they feel imminent danger." According to Fouad Hussein, Osama bin Laden agreed and in the winter of 2004 the internecine bloodbath in Iraq increased, with al-Zarqawi's men slaughtering thousands of Shia (and some Westerners), filming the worst bits, shaking the al-Qaeda movement to its core.[124]

His men also enacted another of al-Suri's tenets, devolving cadres from the main group in Iraq, which was now bloated with members racing towards the banner of religious vengeance. In ones and twos, they were sent racing west, slipping into Europe unseen—cells, not groups, guided by al-Qaeda but not led by it—with intelligence agencies connecting them to the Madrid railway station bombings of 2004 and to the London tube and bus bombings in July 2005.[125]

However, al-Suri's "plan" would only surface in 2005 when Fouad Hussein at last published in Arabic the results of his years of interviews, which had also succeeded in culling the thoughts of Saif al-Adl. An Egyptian whose real name was Muhammad Ibrahim Makkawi, he was wanted by the FBI since the September 11 attacks and also in connection with the US embassy bombings in Africa in 1998. Al-Adl was yet another authentic voice. A consultant in charge of bin Laden's security, he had served in many terrorist theaters and was at the heart of the hands-on fight. He gave Hussein's work the stamp of authority from the front line (before disappearing in 2005, thought to be somewhere in Iran).

The Hussein book was wide-ranging, difficult, and in places impenetrable, with plenty of it unsourced and some of it unintelligible. Although he stressed that he had gone to extreme lengths to verify most of what he had been told, the nature of the organization and the war it is involved in made it impossible for Hussein to straighten out all of the allegations put to him. However, it became an Arab blockbuster. It spelled out a blueprint that looked ahead twenty years, ending in 2020 with a chilling finale. Here was al-Qaeda's grand plan, a route map to the restoration of the caliphate and a time of all-out war with the West when the jihadis would unfurl what they described as "real terrorism," using nuclear weapons to blast away the world of unbelievers.

The first stage, a phase that had already happened, had been known as the "Awakening." Spanning the years 2000 to 2003, it was a period in which jihadis had planned to "strike at the head of the serpent and encourage it to act chaotically." This manifested itself in the 9/11 attacks, following as they did a ladder of terrorism that had seen US forces, ships and then embassies assaulted in Africa, South Asia and the Middle East. "The first phase was judged by the strategists and masterminds ... as very successful," Hussein wrote. Acts of terror had required reprisals that lured the US back into the Middle East. "The battlefield was opened up and the Americans became a closer and easier target." The network was reportedly happy that its message could now be heard "everywhere." Al-Qaeda had an audience.

The second stage had been called "Opening Eyes." It was concluded at the end of 2006. This phase was intended to broaden the movement against America into an anti-Shia insurgency, as prescribed by al-Zarqawi and eventually sanctioned by bin Laden. It was also an attempt to force the US and Europe to act in such a way that it would be easy to portray the West as essentially anti-Muslim. This, too, had happened, with Shia slaying Sunni and vice versa, and also with the draconian laws enacted in North America and Europe which appeared (alongside heavy-handed police raids and lengthy criminal trials) to discriminate against even well-integrated Muslims.

It manifested itself in countries like Pakistan. Visa restrictions slapped on

Islamic nations made it near impossible for well-heeled Muslims to leave the countries of their birth, as the US and Europe raised the entry bar, requiring ever more justification to let someone in. Instead, Islamic money which had always come to the West flooded back into places like Pakistan, where thousands were now stuck due to the tightened travel restrictions. Pakistan's banks flourished and cities like Karachi witnessed a property boom. A corollary of the visa crunch was born-again Islamism, with Pakistan's middle classes moving closer to the mosque as the West edged away. For the first time, the suited business people of smart Karachi districts like Clifton and Defense Colony began redirecting some of their wealth to religious schools and charities populated by shoeless students and maulvis who they knew belonged to the jihadi movement. Fear and loathing made people in Pakistan from all walks of life choose sides, and even those in the upper echelons were increasingly expressing themselves in terms of Islam and against the West, including the military clique and, most worryingly, those educated scientists who ran Pakistan's nuclear industry.

Hussein's book turned to Israel. The al-Qaeda activists and thinkers had all remarked on the need to engage in a direct confrontation with the Jewish state, provoking Jerusalem into new and costly wars over its borders, such as the one that was triggered on cue by the kidnapping of an Israeli soldier in Lebanon in 2006. Such battles, they wrote, would be lost by a war-weary Israel and would serve also to replenish fragmented Islamic groups, like Hezbollah, which had previously been flagging but whose admirers flocked to it after it had rebuffed the Israel Defense Forces.

This was, according to Hussein, also the period of electronic jihad, in which the Internet would be used to deploy ideas like al-Suri's and Hussein's books, and where the World Wide Web would act as a megaphone for a movement as well as a university to pass on modular lessons in urban warfare, nuclear know-how and a proliferation of religious ideas. This was critically important. Al-Qaeda needed to engage in a war of ideas to counter the repeated US claim that Western values and civilization were under attack by a culture that used bombs and had nothing else to say. Now the uploaded books offered ideas aplenty.

From 2007 and for three years thereafter, Fouad Hussein's sources predicted a third period of "Rising and Standing Up." The struggle was to broaden, with al-Qaeda intent on exploiting every instance where control was lost by powers in the Middle East. Syria was to come under constant attack. The avowedly Sunni state, which for political reasons had stood with Shia Iran, had an Islamic underbelly looking for an opportunity to unseat the dictatorial regime of Bashar al-Assad. Lebanon, already fragmented into pro-Western Sunnis and anti-Western Shias, as well as Druze and Maronites, was to be made to fall to pieces. The Sunni in these countries, and in Jordan too, would be called on to unite behind a common purpose, as they had done in Iraq.

By 2010, and for the three years afterwards, al-Qaeda hoped to move into phase four, having brought about the collapse of "hated Arab governments." In this era, they planned to burn Arab oil, to use gold rather than dollars, harming the global economy, and to launch a sustained period of cyber-terrorism. The US would by then be weak, they calculated, and unable to shoulder responsibility for the current world order. Instead, Washington would retreat into isolationism, impacting on Israel's ability to defend itself. All these events would enable the fifth stage, the declaration of an Islamic state between 2013 and 2016, a period when Western influence would have been so greatly reduced in the Islamic world that resistance to al-Qaeda's ideas would be negligible. There followed phase six: "Total Confrontation." This would be a final struggle, an Armageddon that pitted believers against non-believers, "faith against atheism," and in which weapons nuclear, chemical and biological were to be deployed to bring total domination and a global caliphate. "The truth will now have arrived," Hussein wrote, quoting a verse from the Koran, "and falsehood perished. For falsehood by its nature is bound to perish. We will terrify the enemy and prompt them to retreat rapidly." By 2020 the whole world would belong to the one and a half billion Muslims.

Finally, Hussein identified what all al-Qaeda thinkers believed would be the trigger, the pivot that would ensure the plan would move forward: Iran. Those who had spoken to Fouad Hussein between 1996 and 2002 claimed that an American-led war in Iran over its nuclear program was what they were deliberately working towards. The US would be unable to resist assaulting Iran's nuclear sites, they predicted. "Al-Zarqawi and al-Qaeda have already started to implement this plan, according to information available to us," Hussein wrote in 2005. "The strategy ... is based on intelligence information that confirmed that Iran has succeeded in possessing the components of an atomic bomb. Iran expects that the United States and Israel will deal a powerful and sudden strike to a number of nuclear, industrial and strategic Iranian facilities. Accordingly, Iran is preparing to retaliate by means of using powerful cards in its hand." Such action would include striking against the oil industry, pitching much of the world into economic chaos. The West would ride this out. But Iran would not stop there. Preying on US and British fears of an Iranian conspiracy to fuel the chaos in Iraq, Hussein's subjects claimed that Tehran had trained an undercover army, 30,000 strong and led by two undercover Lebanese jihadis, that would strike around the world against Jewish and American targets. Israel would be targeted, too, by Hamas from Gaza and Hezbollah from the Lebanon. Such an attack would provide succor to the Sunnis and leave Tehran in chaos, opening up the Iranian borders to enable al-Qaeda agents to relocate freely. Syria, too, would be undermined, with al-Qaeda hopeful that the US would strike against it, enabling more of its cadre to move unhindered along Syria's enormous border with Iraq, infiltrating into Lebanon.

The latter stages would have read like a showground tarot card act if it were not for the precision with which the early stages of the plan had been articulated and then played out for real. For the first time, those who remotely controlled the young men and women strapped into ball-bearing girdles and explosive belts, were couching their ideology within a time period, enshrining it in ideas, ascribing to it motives. Unfettered by Western sensibilities, they warned that they were readying to seize far more destructive weapons and reap the whirlwind. In such a clash—potentially one using nuclear weapons—the loyalty of the West's allies would become as important as the ferocity of its enemies.

20

AWAKENING

On his only visit to Pakistan, in March 2006, President Bush had said that Pervez Musharraf "understands the stakes, he understands the responsibility, the need to make sure the strategy is able to defeat the enemy." The best way to vanquish al-Qaeda was to "share good intelligence, to locate them, and then be prepared to bring them to justice. President Musharraf understands that in the long run the way to defeat terrorism is to replace an ideology of hatred with an ideology of hope ... We will win this war together."[1]

However, the ground realities had jeered, burned, shot and blasted their way to the surface in the run-up to this trip. Shortly before Air Force One flew in, David Foy, aged fifty-one, the facilities manager at the US consulate in Karachi, and three others were killed when Foy's car was rammed by another vehicle packed with explosives in the secure zone outside the consulate, one of the best-protected areas of the country's largest and most prosperous city. Scores were injured. As a consequence, the presidential jet flew to Pakistan through the night with no lights so as to reduce its profile in the air, as the US knew only too well that those who were against the visit had access to US-supplied Stinger missiles—rockets that Pakistan's former army chief General Beg and former ISI director General Javid Nasir had declined to help the CIA claw back after the Afghan war.

When the president and Laura Bush disembarked at Islamabad airport on 3 March, there were several helicopters and decoy armored escorts waiting to foil any assassination attempts on the journey to the US embassy compound, which more resembled the Green Zone in Baghdad. Nowadays, to get into the embassy was a marathon process. It began with requesting an appointment from a voice-mail bank, which if granted required the visitor to park up several miles away, walk to the outer perimeter of the diplomatic security zone, strip down to the bare essentials at the checkpoint (shirt, trousers and shoes—no watches, jewelry, wallets or mobile phones), board a secure embassy bus which came and went on an unpublicized timetable and which after the interview would dump passengers miles from anywhere useful. For the duration of his twenty-four-hour visit, Bush never got near to the people of Pakistan. A heavy security blanket enveloped Islamabad, which was patrolled by thousands of riot police and paratroopers while US Black Hawks buzzed the skies which were empty of any commercial traffic. Those citizens who dared venture out in other parts of Pakistan did so to vent their anger, with religious parties augmented by madrasah students setting fire to vehicles and igniting pyres of rubber tires in violent demonstrations which coiled many cities in a veil of choking smoke.

Musharraf spent most of Bush's brief visit firefighting, too. Five days earlier, the US president had made a surprise stop in Kabul to bolster the government of President Hamid Karzai, elected after the Taliban had been routed from Afghanistan. The Taliban might have run from Kabul, but their remnants were still capable of bloody and increasingly audacious attacks in the west and south of the country, murdering those who supported reform as well as coalition troops, Afghan, British and American. President Karzai had used the opportunity to hand Bush a dossier of evidence that purported to show how the Pakistani military and ISI continued to shelter and arm the Taliban and al-Qaeda. There were hundreds of names of activists and warlords said to be living in Pakistan, including the erstwhile Taliban leader, the one-eyed Mullah Omar, who, it was claimed, had recently been seen riding around the Pakistani city of Quetta in a pickup, and of course the elusive bin Laden.[2] Karzai's point had been underscored on 13 January 2006, when US Predator drones firing Hellfire missiles had struck a mud-walled compound in the Pakistani village of Damadola, five miles from the Afghan border, after an intelligence intercept had led Washington to believe that Ayman al-Zawahiri, al-Qaeda's number two, was attending a meeting inside. He was not. However, among the corpses was that of Abu Khabab al-Masri, al-Qaeda's WMD chief.[3]

Musharraf remained bullish. When he met Bush he claimed that 80,000 of his troops were committed to fighting the terrorists hiding out on the border and had all but eradicated them. He derided Karzai's dossier as "ridiculous," concluding that two-thirds of the names were out of date and "a waste of time."[4] He pointed to a timely attack four days earlier (while Bush was en route from Kabul to Islamabad) in which twenty-five foreign militants had been killed by the Pakistan army, although eyewitnesses told it differently, claiming the dead were predominantly children, women and teenage students attending a village school.[5]

However, it was not only Karzai whom Musharraf would have to silence regarding Pakistan's ambivalent relationship to al-Qaeda and the Taliban. After Bush's visit, Eliza Manningham-Buller, the director of MI5, the British security service, made an unusual outing in public to warn that "resilient networks" of terror in Britain and elsewhere in Europe were being "directed by al-Qaeda in Pakistan." The group's capabilities, she told an invited audience in London, "were serious and growing."[6] Bruce Riedel, formerly President Clinton's National Security Council (NSC) director for Near East and South Asian affairs, who also went on to serve in the first Bush administration, agreed. Al-Qaeda's chiefs were hiding out in Pakistan, Riedel said in one of his first interviews outside of government. "Between 2002 and 2004, their focus was on survival and creating a new base of operations in Pakistan, especially around Quetta and Balochistan. By 2005, signs of revival were clear. And in 2006, they stormed back with a vengeance." Using Pakistan as it base, the refreshed al-Qaeda resumed its propaganda offensive "with new audio and videotapes of bin Laden and Ayman al-Zawahiri, as well as new operational activities." From there, they began to reach out to the expatriate population of Pakistanis and Bangladeshis living in Britain and North America, who, it was hoped, would mount terror attacks, "as it was increasingly difficult to bring Arab or South Asian operatives into the West using their own passports." Riedel also warned that, comfortable in its new base, al-Qaeda had moved "very vigorously" to bond with Pakistan's terrorist groups such as the supposedly banned Lashkar-e-Taiba and Jaish-e-Mohammed. "There is no question," Riedel said, "that Pakistan continues to tolerate those who harbor bin Laden and his lieutenants in Pakistan, that is the Taliban, their Afghan fellow travellers, and the Kashmiri terrorist infrastructure that is intimately connected with it"—one that had been assembled by General Pervez Musharraf.[7]

Shortly after Riedel made these comments, the mujahids backed him up. Gulbuddin Hekmatyar, the viciously anti-Western mujahideen leader alongside whom al-Zarqawi and al-Maqdisi had fought to capture Kabul, a man who was the creation of the Pakistani military and ISI, openly bragged that he had led Osama bin Laden and his followers away from US troops, through the Tora Bora mountains and into Pakistan in November 2001, where they continued to live today under the protection of the military and intelligence factions.[8]

Shortly after the Bush visit, the exact nature of the Taliban/al-Qaeda revival became explicitly clear, with a chilling story emerging from a reliable source who had reached the normally impenetrable town of Miramshah in Pakistan's north Waziristan, a chaotic and feudal gateway to Afghanistan which did not welcome outsiders. Zahid Hussain, one of Pakistan's most formidable journalists, found "a scene from hell," writing: "A line of bullet-ridden bodies strung from electric poles ... a severed head with currency notes shoved into the mouth rolling on the ground ... a dead dog thrown on the mutilated bodies in a crowded bazaar. 'This is the fate of criminals and of those who disobey God,' thundered a long-bearded mullah, as he hit one of the bodies with the butt of his rifle."[9]

The area was being openly run by a new militia of black-turbaned clerics who bore arms and styled themselves on the Taliban, with the Pakistani military and civil authorities standing by, even during public executions. Even more senior authorities had blessed the militia, according to the local political agent, Syed Zaheer-ul-Islam, who claimed that he was under strict instructions from Islamabad not to impede the movements of local neo-Talibs, as they had become known. After consolidating their position, the medievalism spread outwards to adjoining towns—Tank, Dera Ismail Khan, Bannu and Kohat—where barbers were banned, wedding bands became unemployed, television sets were burned in huge mounds and cable TV operators were attacked in scenes reminiscent of the dour monasticism that had spread out from Kabul in 1996.

However, the crisis went even deeper than was first thought, reaching right into the heart of Musharraf's army headquarters. The neo-Talibs operating in south Waziristan had in April 2004 signed a tentative peace accord with the Pakistan army, which, despite having overwhelming firepower, claimed to have been unable to suppress them. The following November, Musharraf had agreed to extraordinary measures to appease them. In return for pledging loyalty to Pakistan and an end to sheltering or assisting foreign terrorists, the neo-Talibs were given $540,000 with which to settle debts they claimed to owe al-Qaeda.[10] There was no means of monitoring the deal and no questions asked about why the leaders were indebted. At least one of those who received a handout, local warlord Baitullah Mehsud, vanished underground soon afterwards, before re-emerging in 2006 with a revitalized and better-armed terrorist army.[11]

In February 2005, the Pakistan army had agreed to leave south Waziristan entirely, after a meeting with the neo-Talibs at Sararogha.[12] It made a similar pact with militias controlling the north of the province in September 2006. To force home the deal, the government agreed to halt major ground and air operations, free prisoners, retreat to barracks, compensating the neo-Talibs for their losses and allowing tribesmen to carry small arms. It emerged that in making peace with the militia in Waziristan, Musharraf's generals had gone even further, signing an arm's length deal with Mullah Dadullah, a one-legged Taliban commander who was on the US most-wanted list for leading the insurgency against NATO forces in the southwestern Afghan provinces of Kandahar and Helmand, and whose men were responsible for the deaths of many NATO soldiers.[13] Far from taming the cross-border violence, the secret Waziristan truce was blamed by NATO commanders for contributing to deterioration in the eastern Afghan border provinces of Khost, Paktia and Paktika. With the Pakistan army gone, militants operated with impunity, sending weapons and fighters over the Pakistan border, where they created mayhem in local villages and towns, fatally ambushing yet more NATO troops. The figures were stark, with Taliban attacks rising from 1,600 in 2005 to more than 5,000 in 2006, and suicide operations increasing from twenty-seven to 139 over the same period of time.[14]

The situation grew so bad that local bureaucrats petitioned senior government officials. On 6 March 2007, the governor of Pakistan's lawless Northwest Frontier Province, Lieutenant General Ali Mohammad Jan Aurakzai, was presented with a report that starkly warned: "Inaction on the part of the law-enforcement agencies has led to the government being on the retreat: writ of the government shrinking with every passing day; vacuum being filled by non-state actors; respect for law and state authority gradually diminishing; morale of the law-enforcing agencies and people supportive of the government on the decline; Talibanization, lawlessness and terrorism on the rise."[15]

One Pakistani journalist who regularly toured the region agreed. "The government policy has swung from one extreme to another, from the use of brute military force to what appears to be total capitulation to militants," he wrote.[16] The International Crisis Group, a global think tank that specializes in conflict resolution, also voiced extreme concern: "Despite these deals the militancy continued unabated as did cross-border infiltration into Afghanistan. Military operations have failed to yield 'high-value al-Qaeda targets' and many militants have found sanctuary elsewhere."[17]

But the neo-Talibs and their al-Qaeda sponsors did not rise on their own. US intelligence and senior intelligence sources in India both accused elements of Pakistan's intelligence establishment and army of giving succor to the new movement. A hard-core group had emerged that was alleged to have consorted, coached and sheltered the neo-Taliban et al. They included General Mohammed Aziz, who until October 2004 was Musharraf's chairman of the joint chiefs of staff; General Hamid Gul, the former director general of the ISI, forced out of office by Benazir Bhutto after planning with Osama bin Laden to assassinate her; General Javid Nasir, the former director general of the ISI who blocked CIA attempts to recall Stinger missiles from Afghanistan; General Mahmood Ahmed, another former ISI director who had been linked by the FBI to the World Trade Center bombers; General Zahir-ul-Islam Abbasi, who had plotted a coup against Benazir Bhutto in 1995 and was pardoned by Musharraf in October 2001; and Squadron Leader Khalid Khawaja, a former ISI officer, a man accused of knowingly leading the Jewish-American reporter Daniel Pearl to meet Islamists in Karachi before they decapitated him in February 2002. Khawaja was already in jail on another matter, having instigated a band of female students at the Jamia Hafsa madrasah in central Islamabad, a seminary very closely connected to the Taliban (and to the ISI's headquarters in the capital), to demonstrate in support of Osama bin Laden. On 28 March 2007 the same women students stormed a building they said was a brothel, taking three women and two police officers hostage. The deputy imam of the Lal Masjid, Maulana Abdul Aziz, teacher to the students, supported the actions and went even further, telling his congregation that they should become suicide bombers if the government ever decided to move against them.[18] This was not the tribal areas—this was happening, with no reaction from Musharraf, in the nation's sophisticated capital.

On the Rawalpindi–Islamabad highway, where a monument to Pakistan's founding father, Muhammad Ali Jinnah, depicts his profile and three founding principles in flashing bulbs that spell out "Unity, Faith and Discipline," an unknown hand reordered the message one night to read "Faith, Unity and Discipline." Despite the fact that Musharraf and many of his government ministers passed this spot on a daily basis, nobody bothered to rearrange the words.

Inevitably, Musharraf had to tread carefully in a country of mantraps and sinking sand, where faith and the state had always had a combative relationship. He had to balance his own survival with the need to appease the religious extremists and the demands of his new Western allies. His military was also under attack. On 27 March 2007 masked gunmen on motorbikes hurled grenades at an army vehicle in the Bajaur Agency, part of the Federally Administered Tribal Areas occupying 10,000 square miles in the northwest of Pakistan, killing five, including two ISI officers, one of them an assistant director. On 29 March an unidentified suicide bomber blew himself up at an army training ground ninety miles southeast of Islamabad, killing three soldiers. But however hard it was becoming to govern Pakistan, there was also growing and irrefutable evidence that Musharraf was downgrading his pledges to the West and predicating everything on his own need to prosper. The fact that the Pakistani military was unwilling or incapable of routing al-Qaeda or its proxies raised serious questions as to exactly what the West, and the US in particular, was getting in return for its billions of dollars in aid money. By 2007, Washington was beginning to understand that it had made a Faustian pact in agreeing to cover up the nuclear black-market scandal, with A. Q. Khan being sacrificed to salve the Pakistani military.

As for replacing an ideology of hatred with an ideology of hope, Bush's cure-all for combating terrorism which had been laid out in his historic visit to Islamabad in 2006—something essential if the treatise of al-Suri, al-Zarqawi and al-Maqdisi were to be addressed—Musharraf had done nothing at all. Back in 2002, Pakistan's president had unveiled on state television a blueprint to combat Islamic extremism and terrorism, saying: "No individual, organization or party will be allowed to break the law of the land." He had promised to register all religious schools, regulate their curriculum and prevent them from being used as centers of extremism. But proposed legislation, including the restriction of foreign grants and donations, as well as barring foreign students and teachers without valid visas, stalled for the next three years.

Despite a promise from Musharraf to establish model madrasahs to pave the way ahead, only three such institutions ever opened, enrolling 300 students, as compared with the hundreds of thousands being indoctrinated in unregistered schools, which mushroomed from 6,996 in 2001 to more than 13,000 in 2005.[19] It was not until the 7 July 2005 bombings in London that Musharraf was goaded into trying again, after it was revealed that Shehzad Tanweer, who blew himself up on a Circle Line underground train near Aldgate station, killing seven and injuring scores, had spent four months in a madrasah run by Lashkar-e-Taiba in Lahore. Musharraf ordered every madrasah to register by the end of 2005 or be shut down. However, by 2007 his reform program, according to the International Crisis Group, remained "a shambles" with "banned sectarian and jihadi groups supported by networks of mosques and madrasahs continuing to operate openly."[20] Most madrasahs had declined to sign the register. The change in the madrasah curriculum, too, fell by the wayside, even though 8,000 schools had already been given $255 million to reform. Musharraf pessimistically called for the money back but did not bother to pursue it when none was returned.

If the jihadi seminaries were still open for business, so were the indoctrination centers and training camps established by government-backed militant groups to fight in Afghanistan, then in Kashmir, and more recently as part of the global jihad—the groups that had, according to Riedel and Manningham-Buller, merged with al-Qaeda. All these groups had done was to change their names. In January 2002, Sipah-e-Sahaba, which had acted as patron for Ramzi Yousef, the World Trade Center bomber, in 1993, had finally been banned and its leader, Maulana Azam Tariq, jailed. However, despite facing more than twenty terrorist charges, Tariq contested the October 2002 Pakistani elections from his prison cell. After winning a seat in the National Assembly, and pledging support for Musharraf's government, he was released, despite a number of non-bailable warrants that had been issued against him under anti-terrorism laws. Unsurprisingly, Tariq's organization re-emerged too, as Millat-e-Islamia. Only an assassin's bullet stopped Tariq: he was shot dead by rivals in Islamabad in October 2003. But his armed front, the Millat, continued unfettered.

Jaish-e-Mohammed was banned, too, in January 2002, with its leader, Maulana Azhar Masood, detained under maintenance of public order legislation. Masood had been Musharraf's protégé and previously ran Harkat-ul-Ansar, which had been behind the kidnapping of Western tourists in Kashmir in 1995, at least one of whom was murdered. But as Masood was not charged under Pakistan's stringent anti-terrorism act of 1997 he was soon freed and renamed his movement Khuddam-ul-Islam.

Within months, an entire phalanx of outlaws had been allowed to sidestep the law. Hafiz Muhammad Saeed, leader of Lashkar-e-Taiba (connected to the 7 July bombings in London), renamed his group Jamaat-al-Dawa after he was freed.[21] Saeed and Masood continued openly to call for jihad in Kashmir and the formation of a global caliphate, both of them appearing at an annual congregation in Patoki in the central Punjab in October 2003 to recruit and distribute extremist leaflets, one year after Musharraf had ruled that such activities were illegal.[22] The sleight of hand provoked a rare rebuke from the US, with Nancy Powell, US ambassador to Islamabad, warning Musharraf in November 2003 that the Bush administration had noted how terrorist groups were resurgent under new names. Still nothing was done. The outlawed groups continued to run their madrasahs.

By 2006 there were nine university-style recruitment and training operations running in Karachi, directly linked to Sipah-e-Sahaba Pakistan, Jaish-e-Mohammed, Harkat-ul-Mujahideen and Harkat-ul-Jihadi-Islami. They were churning out cadres and the ramifications were immediately visible. Although no group admitted responsibility for the murder of US diplomat Denis Foy in March 2006, the authorities linked two men charged with the killing to jihadi groups operating out of the city's madrasahs.[23] One month later, on 11 April 2006, in what the International Crisis Group called "one of the worst massacres of its kind in Pakistan's history," forty-seven people were killed and more than a hundred injured when a suicide bomber attacked a religious gathering in Nishtar Park, Karachi, which was celebrating the birth of the Prophet Muhammad. Sipah-e-Sahaba and another jihadi group, Lashkar-e-Jhangvi, were the chief suspects.

Three months later, on 21 July 2006, a suicide bomber killed Allama Hasan Turabi, president of the Pakistan Islami Tehreek, the country's largest Shia political party, who had narrowly escaped a previous assassination attempt on 6 April. Sipah-e-Sahaba and Lashkar-e-Jhangvi were again the prime suspects.[24] On 30 September 2006, a Pakistani suicide bomber killed twelve civilians, this time outside a government building in Kabul, an attack whose participants and planning, according to the International Crisis Group, "was traced back to a madrasah attached to the Masjid-e-Noor, a mosque in Masehra Colony, in north-eastern Karachi." One of those who had planned the attack, and who was due to have launched a second suicide mission himself, claimed that it was all sanctioned by Maulvi Abdul Shakoor Khairpur at the Masjid-e-Noor madrasah, a man accused of being an activist in the banned Harkat-ul-Mujahideen.[25]

The dire earthquake of October 2005 which levelled much of Kashmir, leaving 75,000 dead and more than 3 million people homeless, fuelled the re-emergence of seventeen extremist groups previously banned by Musharraf (and the US and Europe) or placed on Pakistan's terrorist watch list.[26] As the military, through poor organization and leadership, struggled to make it into the mountains with supplies, these groups, with their offices closer to the epicenter of the quake, were quicker off the mark, distributing food, tents and blankets. They also erected banners and billboards, one from the outlawed Al-Badr Al-Mujahidin reading: "Custodian of the blood of 10,000 mujahideen." Scores more fluttered across the refugee camps, in full view of the Pakistan army.[27]

Jamaat-al-Dawa (formerly Lashkar-e-Taiba) opened a field hospital in Muzaffarabad, headed by Dr. Amir Aziz Khan, who had been arrested in October 2002 for his links to al-Qaeda and Osama bin Laden (whom he admitted meeting). Musharraf praised Jamaat-al-Dawa for its swift response and sustained efforts in the first weeks after the earthquake. Jamaat-e-Islami, an Islamic organization whose leaders had provided a safe house for Khalid Sheikh Mohammed, the 9/11 planner, set up a tent school in the devastated town of Battagram under the guise of the Al-Khidmat Foundation and took in hundreds of orphaned children.[28] Khuddam-ul-Islam, aka Jaish-e-Mohammed, appeared with its charity, the Al-Rasheed Trust, in the earthquake zone. Its work was praised by Musharraf, even though the trust, whose founding philosophy called on all members to fight jihad, was on the UN Security Council list of sanctioned organizations with links to al-Qaeda.[29]

Musharraf could see nothing wrong: "Since they are there, certainly we would not like them to stop. Why should we not allow our own people who are going there and assisting ... whether they are jihadis or anybody?"[30] Musharraf's oft-quoted mantra was "one man's terrorist is another man's freedom fighter," and, for him, those committed to the struggle in Kashmir (now inextricably linked to al-Qaeda) would always be freedom fighters. It was a dangerous play on words which abrogated responsibility and ultimately enabled Pakistan's government to play to the Islamist crowd.

Those on the ground in the earthquake-struck areas predicted a feeding frenzy. Tehseenullah Khan, a development worker campaigning for madrasah reform, argued: "I am afraid that the jihadi schools will replace the destroyed education network. They will find a way to take the people and their children into confidence. Many children are now orphans. The earthquake zone is a fertile area for jihadis."[31] Jamaat-al-Dawa announced it had 180 madrasahs which would be taking orphan children from the disaster zone. When some parents discovered that their children were still alive and living at Jamaat-al-Dawa institutions in the Punjab, the organization refused to give them up.[32]

Pakistan was awash with extremists: Taliban, neo-Talibs, al-Qaeda, Sunni irregulars and a hotchpotch of non-aligned, live-to-fight muscle-mullahs who would pack their bags and a Koran to take off at a moment's notice for a battle in the name of Islam anywhere in the world. What most alarmed the masters of "old think" in the West was the prospect of these hordes (acting on al-Suri's prescriptions) gaining access to Pakistan's nuclear complex, whether through the instability of the weapons program, hodgepodge the disaffection of its scientists, or through the political intent of an impoverished and unprincipled government in Islamabad which understood the value in hard cash of KRL.

However, the White House masters of "new think" were so distracted by Iraq, North Korea and especially Iran that no one seemed to recall that Pakistan had got them into trouble in the first place. By 2006 the nuclear scandal had been relegated to an historical footnote. The only stories about A. Q. Khan that filtered out of Pakistan concerned his failing health. But they also hinted at his political rehabilitation, further underlining the total collapse of the Armitage–Musharraf deal. On 24 August 2006, two government officials had visited Khan at home in Hillside Road, Islamabad, before releasing a photograph of a smiling but frail "Father of the Bomb," who, they revealed, had prostate cancer.[33] Mosques all over Saudi Arabia offered prayers for his speedy recovery, while the family discussed with the government where he was to be treated.

On 7 September, Khan was granted a temporary reprieve from house arrest and flown on a government aircraft to Karachi along with his wife, two daughters and personal physician, General Chowhan. Rather than be taken under armed guard straight to Aga Khan University Hospital, Khan visited the home of his sister, Razia Hussein, for tea and cakes, and it was several days before he admitted himself to room 130 in the hospital's private wing. Three days later, surgeons removed his prostate gland. Henny, Dina and Ayesha were at his bedside soon after. Such was the apparent normalcy surrounding him— Khan once again described by everyone as a national hero—that newspapers commented on the insolence of local politicians who declined to stop by to inquire after the great man's health. When Khan was discharged, on 16 September, he was not dispatched straight back to life under house arrest but allowed to return to his sister's home in Karachi to recuperate for several more weeks. Those closest to Khan claimed that President Musharraf was making a concerted effort to woo him, after a series of events had compromised KRL, the nuclear industry and Pakistan's national security.[34]

The first had occurred eleven months earlier, after the earthquake of October 2005 had not only wreaked destruction in Kashmir but in the KRL labs too. No one could be allowed to know. Khan's closest aides claimed an inspection had found that one-third of the centrifuges had been destroyed when their concrete bases had cracked as the rotors were spinning, sending millions of parts flying around the cascade hall. One Khan aide, still working at KRL, recalled: "Back in 1979 when we were experimenting with one of the early P-1s, it shattered mid-rotation, sending shards of glass into the ceilings and walls. In 1983 there had been an earthquake that had forced us to put in bigger and stronger floors. But even they had not withstood the force of this monster quake and its aftershocks. It played havoc. Can you imagine the scene where thousands of centrifuges have blown apart in an instant?"[35] There was mangled wreckage everywhere. More significantly, the feed-and-withdrawal systems had been ruptured, sending clouds of UF_6 and partially enriched uranium into the air-conditioned hall and out through its ducts. The Pakistani government declined to comment. The military too. But those closest to Khan insisted that Kahuta was immediately shut down while teams were sent in to contain the disaster and the political fallout. "No news was allowed out. No one was to talk about it. To this day no one has talked about it," an aide to Khan said. "The trouble was, the only person who would know what to do was A. Q. Khan. But he was indisposed, having been framed by Musharraf, humiliated on TV and then bashed around by the ISI."

All the old hands—including Brigadier Sajawal, who had designed the infrastructure and installed the air conditioning—were still under house arrest. Musharraf's purges at KRL had left no one experienced enough to clear up the mess. "In the end Musharraf was so desperate, he called on Khan personally and appealed to him to get the other scientists behind him and come back to the plant. Khan said, 'I'll do it if you give me a couple of weeks off from house arrest.' Musharraf agreed but, still smarting, Khan prevaricated and then went back on his word. He could not quite bring himself to help the man who had ambushed him. As a punishment, Musharraf stopped Khan's daughter Ayesha from visiting."

In the end, inexperienced engineers in protective suits were sent in. The Khan aide watched them file off the coach. "These guys could not fix anything. There was no one in control of the radioactive disaster. There had been casualties, people suffering with burns and all sorts of injuries, but because of the lack of leadership nothing was done properly. The plant will take a long time to recover. The only reason Musharraf made so little fuss—apart from his obvious embarrassment at having to admit that there had been a nuclear accident—was that Khan had already stockpiled massive reserves of highly enriched uranium and rebuilding the plant could wait."

The next clash had come the following March, when President Bush had visited Pakistan. Officially, Bush had come to discuss US aid for earthquake victims, as well as the Islamic Republic's supposed role in dampening radical Islam. However, he was also in town to reassure his ally about ongoing US negotiations with New Delhi, from where he had just come, discussing with India's leaders a groundbreaking and controversial proposal to allow them to purchase American civil nuclear technology.[36] Given that India was an unlicensed nuclear power, sanctioned after it had tested a nuclear device in 1998, the deal had been criticized by many in the West, who complained that it was being rewarded for breaching international law. Those in favor of the pact argued that it would bring Washington closer to New Delhi, which had been a responsible nuclear power since 1974, rarely accused of proliferating, unlike its neighbor. Bush acknowledged as much when he touched down in Islamabad, saying: "Pakistan and India are different countries with different needs and different histories."

Either way, the US–India deal was an unmitigated disaster for Musharraf, who had thrown his lot in with the US after 9/11. Having spent the previous thirty years being persecuted for buying equipment for its nuclear program, Islamabad had to watch as tactical, commercial and potentially military advantage was handed over to the hated enemy over the border. It also appeared to Musharraf (and to his enemies) that Bush was shopping around for a new ally in South Asia.

Only days before Bush landed, the president of Pakistan had sought out Khan for advice on what he should ask from Bush in order to bargain for equal treatment. The same close Khan aide recalled: "Doctor Sahib told Musharraf, 'I can help you, but I won't. Go and lick Bush's balls.' " The Bush visit came and went, with Pakistan winning no new nuclear concessions. In retribution, Musharraf began a purge at KRL which would see the last vestiges of Khan's influence removed. The Khan aide said: "Javid Mirza, Khan's successor at KRL, was retired on 1 April 2006. He went off to live a listless life in Wah. Mohammed Karim, who replaced him, leapfrogged thirteen more senior officers. Karim was a run-of-the-mill guy and a Musharraf crony who knew little about the job." A hostile takeover, which had begun with Khan's retirement in 2001 and had been consolidated with his house arrest in 2004, was now complete. However, Project A/B was still very much alive.

In January 2006, a fifty-five-page highly classified "early warning" intelligence assessment was produced by Germany's BND security service with the pooled knowledge of British, French and Belgian spies. Seen by board members of the IAEA in Vienna, it consisted of lists of front companies, diplomatic missions, academic organizations, government offices and charitable institutes that were accused of being engaged in illegal nuclear weapons research and procurements on behalf of nation states.[37] It was a circuit board of proliferation, the soldered links and connections of a vast network that spanned the world, from Pyongyang to Beijing, from Sophia to Tehran, servicing countries ranging from Syria, Egypt and Sudan to Iran and North Korea. It was designed as a warning to legitimate European engineering companies and import-export firms of who not to do business with if they wanted to stay out of court. Ignorance would no longer be accepted as a defense for selling dual-use components to countries illegally shopping for a nuclear bomb through front companies that disguised the real end-user.

The report also bore some bad news about Musharraf's Pakistan: confirmation that it was still secretly buying and just as stealthily selling nuclear weapons technology. It reported that, since Khan's confession, "extensive procurement efforts for the Pakistan nuclear sector have been registered." Its authors found that a range of materials and components were still being imported to Pakistan that "clearly exceeds" what Islamabad needed for its domestic nuclear program. One of the report's authors concluded: "They were buying to sell and it could no longer be hived off as rogue scientists doing the deed."[38]

Despite the dispatching of Khan and the forced retirement of his successor, the KRL labs had continued to coordinate the Pakistani sales program and now ran a network of front companies in Europe, the Gulf and Southeast Asia which deployed all the old tricks: disguising end-user certificates by shielding the ultimate destinations from sellers, and lying on customs manifests. A contract that Khan established to source high-grade aluminum tubing to manufacture centrifuge components for Libya was still running. "The procurement efforts for such tubing were not halted after the uncovering of the network," the report noted. Since Khan had been removed, Musharraf's appointees were in the frame and, as worrying, since Gaddafi was out of the loop, having renounced his program in 2003, no one was sure who the new customer for the centrifuge parts was.

The Pakistan–North Korean relationship was also still very much alive, the report stating that "the export of arms equipment is currently noted to be North Korea's most important source of income," with Pakistan among its key clients, alongside Egypt, Iran and Syria. More than thirty front companies and institutions involved in the North Korean arms network had been discovered. But it was not just weapons they were selling. Islamabad had hooked Pyongyang into its old nuclear procurement network in western Europe, buying raw materials and machinery for production lines in North Korea that were churning out cheap centrifuge components. Pakistan was one of the key customers, selling the parts on to other clients. But this was not the only facet of their new relationship.

In the late 1990s, Khan's Sri Lankan protégé, B. S. A. Tahir, had opened a production line for simple centrifuge components in Shah Alam, Malaysia, outsourcing complex engineering contracts to companies in South Africa and

Europe before gathering everything in Dubai, from where shipments were exported to the end-user. Now, after an introduction by Islamabad, Pyongyang had followed Tahir's lead, outsourcing some of its centrifuge component manufacturing work to Chinese state-run engineering firms (six of whom were sanctioned in December 2005 by the US for supplying Iran's military industry).

The old nexus, China–Pakistan–North Korea, had not been broken either. It had simply evolved. According to the report, the three countries traded freely in uranium enrichment components, missile technology and conventional weapons, with the old clients (among them Iran and Saudi Arabia) continuing to be serviced as well as an expanded list of new clients which was believed to include Syria and Egypt.

Most alarming was the finding that hundreds of thousands of components amassed by Khan had vanished since he had been put out of operation. The biggest missing consignment had been shipped to Sudan between 1998 and 2001 and consisted of £320 million of dual-use engineering equipment, much of which had been sourced from German companies, according to invoices recovered in Sudan. The haul had been destined for Libya, and Khan had negotiated with the Sudanese to warehouse the stockpile during his trips to Africa. By 2006, another unknown Pakistani entity had seized control of the equipment and redirected it. No longer in Sudan, it had not gone to Libya. Intelligence sources suggested that it had probably been handled by KRL and ended up in Tehran, marking the Islamabad–Iran trade as live and pursued under Musharraf's watch.

There had been many other reroutings. Two shipping containers, one filled with centrifuge components and a ton of high-strength aluminum, the other containing precision tools and parts for two specialized lathes, had vanished en route to Libya after Gaddafi had renounced his WMD program. Last seen in Turkey and Malaysia, the shipments, the IAEA believed, had been redirected to a new client.[39] Olli Heinonen, a senior weapons inspector investigating the Libyan program, told German prosecutors in the trial of one Khan supplier that he was just as concerned about the location of seven missing sets of rotors for P-2 centrifuges, which had been part of a shipment of nine bound for Libya which had never arrived. They had left Pakistan in early 2000, arriving in Dubai that June.[40] However, only two of the rotor sets had ever reached Tripoli. Tahir, who admitted to Malaysian investigators that he had organized the shipments, claimed they had been destroyed. Heinonen suspected they had ended up with another buyer.[41]

But the clearest indication that the Pakistani military was determined to continue with the procurements beyond Khan's tenure came with a brazen attempt by an Islamabad-based company, used by Pakistan's military, to buy US components to build a nuclear bomb—while Musharraf was negotiating A. Q. Khan's staged demise with Bush in New York.[42] The deal had begun in August 2002, more than a year after Khan's official retirement, when Humayun Khan, a Pakistani businessman who ran Pakland, an Islamabad-based company with significant contracts to supply equipment to the Pakistani military, contacted an Israeli businessman based in South Africa, looking for a deal.

Asher Karni of Top-Cape Technology, a Cape Town firm that imported US electronic goods to South Africa, was asked to procure thirty-six US-manu-factured oscilloscopes for Pakistan, costing $1.3 million. The equipment was most often used for monitoring voltage and frequency, but it could also play a critical part in the nuclear weapons industry, where it was used to measure the effectiveness of a test blast. Pakistan had been caught out trying to import oscilloscopes from the West before and they were controlled items. But, with the order coming from South Africa, a non-nuclear state, to which normal US export controls on dual-use items did not apply, the oscilloscopes were likely to get through.[43]

While Humayun Khan waited for the machines to arrive, in the spring of 2003 he contacted Karni again, asking for a consignment of 200 triggered spark gaps. Small pocket-sized cylinders, they emitted an intense electrical pulse and were used in hospitals to destroy kidney stones. However, they could also be used as detonating devices for nuclear weapons and would have been subjected to export licenses if officially requested by Pakistan. An email from Humayun Khan to Karni on 4 June spelled out the caution required. "Pls do not disclose the end destination," Khan wrote.[44]

On 17 June 2003, while Pervez Musharraf was in London being feted by the establishment and softened up before his visit to the US, where Bush was to have dressed him down over the A. Q. Khan affair, Karni wrote to Humayun Khan in Pakistan, stating that he had been unable to source the spark gaps after a company in France had turned him down for having no export license. Humayun Khan had replied an hour later: "I know it is difficult but that's why we came to know each other ... pls do look around for another source."

On 24 June, Musharraf arrived at Camp David, where Bush failed to make any reference to the A. Q. Khan scandal. Three days later, Karni in South Africa sent an email to Islamabad trumpeting his success in finding somebody willing to sell him spark gaps in the US, at $950 per piece. He was certain he could get them to Pakistan.

On 28 August, DHL shipped two US-manufactured oscilloscopes from Karni's warehouse in Cape Town to Pakistan, via the smugglers' hub of Dubai. Humayun Khan sent an email two weeks later, on 15 September, asking for an estimated time of arrival for the spark gaps. Eight days later, Musharraf was called to President Bush's suite on the thirty-third floor of the Waldorf-Astoria in New York for the long-awaited showdown over A. Q. Khan. The following day Musharraf had claimed ignorance when George Tenet deluged him with evidence of Pakistan's complicity in the nuclear black market. But the purchase of oscilloscopes and spark gaps showed that Pakistan still was very much in the business of building bombs, and four days after the Tenet briefing, Karni in South Africa wrote to his purchaser in Islamabad informing him that the triggered spark gaps were about to leave the US. The first batch of sixty-six arrived in South Africa on 6 October, the same day that Richard Armitage sat down with Musharraf in Islamabad to hammer out the terms of the A. Q. Khan deal. But that did not stop Humayun Khan, who took delivery of the first batch of spark gaps in Pakistan on 21 October 2003.[45]

In the end, the shipment was useless, because US Customs were on to Karni and Humayun Khan after receiving an anonymous tip-off from a source that they nicknamed "South African John." Customs agents had switched the spark gaps for harmless components, keeping an eye on the deal—and keeping it from Musharraf. On New Year's Day 2004, Karni, his wife and teenage daughter were arrested by US Customs agents at Denver international airport as they were about to board a flight. Karni was charged with violating American export laws, prompting a remarkable response from his wife, Shulamit, who contested that her husband thought he was selling Pakistan much-needed medical equipment. "He had only gone ahead with the deals after seeing President Bush with Musharraf on US cable news, announcing: 'We are now friends, and we shall cooperate, especially in the medical field,' " she said.[46]

Initially the US authorities were gung-ho about the Karni–Humayun Khan affair. Justice Department spokesman Channing Phillips told reporters that the investigation was ongoing "in several countries." Peter Lichtenbaum, acting under secretary for industry and security, asked: "Were [the spark gaps] going to the Pakistani military? Were they intended for onward proliferation to an al-Qaeda nuclear weapons program? I mean, it's speculative and we want to find that out." John McKenna, a special agent at the Department of Commerce, was delighted with the outcome: "'South African John' ... has provided information that's been extremely valuable in probably one of the most high-profile cases we've had in recent years in the nuclear field."[47]

But when the case finally came to court in March 2005, investigators complained that the trail had run cold. They were being blocked, and not by Pakistan. Instead, the US State Department had closed down many avenues, turning down their requests to travel to Pakistan to interview Humayun Khan, who if extradited and found guilty could have been jailed for up to thirty-five years—as well as revealing much-needed evidence of the Pakistani military's collusion in the ongoing nuclear trade. A source in the Commerce Department said: "Suddenly the US government was afraid of offending Pakistan, its partner in the war on terror." A federal judge sealed all of the Karni records in September 2005, in a replay of the lengths to which the Reagan administration had gone to save President Zia while he enabled the US to fight the Soviets in Afghanistan. Then, too, court cases had been ambushed, cases sealed, with the accused allowed to plea-bargain themselves out of custody and onto planes back to Pakistan. It was happening all over again—under Presidents Bush and Musharraf.

Pakistan was proliferating with the kind of candor that came from knowing no one was likely to touch it, least of all its partner in the war on terror, the Bush administration. Believing that no one was going to intervene, the military became even more ambitious, revamping an old facility to manufacture banned materials for export to a whole new range of unidentified clients. In the 1980s and 1990s, A. Q. Khan had put the designs and know-how to enrich uranium and build a bomb out there for anyone who had the money to see, and now Pakistan was supplying the raw materials, machines and components to finish off the job.

As a young student, metallurgist Khan had repeatedly written in the 1960s to the People's Steel Mill in Karachi requesting work, only to be rudely rejected. However, he had got his revenge after Benazir Bhutto had handed the factory over to him in 1994, when he promptly sacked all those who had turned him down. Khan had been placed in charge of revamping the mill to manufacture specialist metals that would help at the Kahuta labs—substances like maraging steel which was subject to stringent export controls in Europe and North America. The CIA and British intelligence often used the movement of this highly restricted metal as a key indicator of nuclear proliferators at work, and although there was evidence that Khan had imported equipment and raw materials with which to manufacture maraging steel, the project had never gone into production in his time.

Musharraf had taken over Khan's mill in 1999, almost as soon as he had made himself president, restructuring it and injecting massive new funding, transforming the mill into a European-standard facility with an extraordinary new output. He became the first head of state to visit the plant in more than twenty years when he inaugurated a new study center there in May 2005. Greeting the president, Lieutenant General Abdul Qayyum, the chairman of the mill, had said: "It was through President Musharraf's daring, honest and visionary leadership that we have seized the moment." While Qayyum did not expand further on what that meant, another senior military officer was candid. General K. M. Arif, who had effectively run the nuclear program until his retirement in 1987, and had maintained an influential role in Pakistan's establishment ever since, was a man renowned for caution. But on the nuclear business and the People's Steel Mill he could barely hide his glee. "Now we have a new generation of men and the technology. We have labs and the industry to rival the West," the general said. "Once we skulked around. Now Pakistan is producing high-frequency inverters. They used to come from the UK and now we are selling them ourselves. Maraging steel too—once we struggled but now, finally, we are manufacturing it at the People's Steel Mill and exporting it. It is better than you can get outside."[48]

Pakistan continues to sell nuclear weapons technology (to clients known and unknown) even as Musharraf denies it—which means either that the sales are being carried out with Musharraf's secret blessing, or that he did not know and is no more in control of his country's nuclear program than he is of the bands of jihadis in the tribal belt and Pakistan-administered Kashmir, which have merged with al-Qaeda and with whom he has wrapped up deals.

When politicians in London and Washington describe Musharraf as a key ally in the war on terror, what they really mean is that he is their only Islamic ally in the region.[49] So with the White House and 10 Downing Street unable to countenance an alternative, Musharraf's Pakistan remains at the epicenter of terror, a disingenuous regime with its hands on the nuclear tiller.

It will only be a matter of time before the rising tide of Sunni extremism and the fast-flowing current of nuclear exports find common cause and realize their apocalyptic intent. There are plenty of ideologues, thinkers and Islamic strategists who are working towards precisely that goal, and here is a regime in Islamabad that has no hard and fast rules, no unambiguous goals or laws, and no line that cannot be bent or reshaped. Zbigniew Brzezinski, Jimmy Carter's former national security adviser, who in 1979 was the first to recommend that the US look the other way when it came to Pakistan's nuclear ambitions, warned in March 2007 that if the Bush administration did not back off from its current course in Iraq and Iran, the US faced the prospect of "twenty years in a war [with] ... Iraq, Iran, Afghanistan and probably Pakistan, and that will be the end of American global supremacy."[50]

Robert Gallucci, Bush's former WMD adviser, who tracked Pakistan's nuclear progress from its inception at Multan in 1972, goes even further: "Pakistan is top of the list. It is the number one threat to the world at this moment in time. If it all goes off, a nuclear bomb in a US or European city, I'm sure we will find ourselves looking in Pakistan's direction."[51]

PRINCIPAL CHARACTERS

In the US

Armitage, Richard, deputy assistant secretary of defense for East Asia and Pacific Affairs, 1981–3; assistant secretary of defense for international security policy, 1983–9; special aide to king of Jordan and ambassador to the former Soviet states, 1991–3; deputy secretary of state, 2001–5

Barlow, Richard, intelligence officer, Arms Control and Disarmament Agency (ACDA), 1980–2; intelligence officer, CIA's Office of Scientific and Weapons Research (OSWR), 1985–8; intelligence officer, Office of the Secretary of Defense (OSD), 1989–92

Bolton, John, under secretary of state for arms control and international security, 2001–5; ambassador to the UN, 2005–7

Brzezinski, Zbigniew, national security adviser, 1977–81

Bush, George H. W., vice president, 1981–9; president, 1989–93

Bush, George W., president, 2001–9

Carter, Jimmy, president, 1977–81

Casey, William, director of central intelligence, 1981–7

Cheney, Richard, secretary of defense, 1989–93; vice president, 2001–9

Clinton, Bill, president, 1993–2001

Cranston, Senator Alan (Democrat, California), 1969–93

Gallucci, Robert, analyst at the Arms Control and Disarmament Agency (ACDA), 1974–8; Department of State's Bureau of Intelligence and Research, 1978–9; secretary of state's policy planning staff, 1979–81; director of Bureau of Near Eastern and South Asian Affairs, 1982; director of the Bureau of Politico-Military Affairs, 1983; deputy executive chairman of the United

Nations Special Commission (UNSCOM) for the disarming of Iraq, 1991–2; Office of the Deputy Secretary as senior coordinator responsible for non-proliferation and nuclear safety initiatives in the former Soviet Union, 1992; assistant secretary of state for politico-military affairs, July 1992; chief US negotiator with North Korea, 1994; ambassador at large, Department of State, 1994–6; special envoy on the proliferation of ballistic missiles and weapons of mass destruction, 1998–2001

Gates, Robert, National Security Council staff, 1974–9; CIA's directorate of central intelligence, 1981; deputy director for intelligence, 1982; deputy director of central intelligence, 1986–9; deputy assistant to the president for national security affairs, March–August 1989; assistant to the president and deputy national security adviser, August 1989–November 1991; director of central intelligence, 1991–3; secretary of defense, 2006–

Glenn, Senator John (Democrat, Ohio), 1974–99

Hadley, Stephen, assistant secretary of defense for international security policy, 1989–93; national security adviser, 2005–

Haig, Alexander, secretary of state, 1981–2

Inderfurth, Karl "Rick," assistant secretary of state for South Asian affairs, 1997–2001

Joseph, Robert, under secretary of state for arms control and international security, 2005–

Khalilzad, Zalmay, State Department's policy planning department, 1984–5; special adviser on Afghanistan to under secretary of state Michael Armacost, 1985–9; deputy under secretary for policy planning, Defense Department, 1990–2; special assistant to the president and senior director for Southwest Asia, Near East and North African Affairs, National Security Council, May 2001–December 2001; special envoy for Afghanistan, December 2001–November 2003; US ambassador to Afghanistan, November 2003–June 2005; US ambassador to Iraq, 2005–7

Libby, Lewis "Scooter," policy planning staff, 1981; director, special projects, Bureau of East Asian and Pacific Affairs, 1982–5; principal deputy under secretary (strategy and resources), 1982–5; principal deputy under secretary of defense for policy, 1989; Cheney's chief of staff and national security adviser, 2001–5

Oakley, Robert, deputy assistant secretary of state for East Asia and the Pacific, 1977–9; director of the State Department's Office of Terrorism, September

1984; assistant to the president for Middle East and South Asia on the National Security Council staff, 1 January 1987; US ambassador to Pakistan, August 1988–September 1991

Oehler, Gordon, director of CIA's Center for Weapons Intelligence, Non-Proliferation and Arms Control, 1992–7

Percy, Senator Charles, (Republican, Illinois), 1967–85

Powell, Colin, national security adviser, 1987–9; chairman, joint chiefs of staff, 1989–93; secretary of state, 2001–5

Pressler, Larry, representative (Republican, South Dakota) 1975–9; senator (Republican, South Dakota), 1979–97

Reagan, Ronald, president, 1981–9

Rice, Condoleezza, special assistant to the joint chiefs of staff, 1986–9; director, then senior director, of Soviet and East European Affairs, National Security Council, and special assistant to the president for national security affairs, 1989–91; national security adviser, 2001–5; secretary of state, 2005–

Riedel, Bruce, special assistant to the president and senior director for Near East and South Asian Affairs, National Security Council, 1997–2001

Rumsfeld, Donald, presidential envoy to the Middle East, 1983–4; secretary of defense, 2001–November 2006

Shultz, George, secretary of state, 1982–9

Smith, Gerard, special representative for non-proliferation, 1977–80

Sofaer, Abraham, legal adviser to Department of State, 1985–90

Solarz, Stephen, representative (Democrat, New York) 1975–93

Talbott, Strobe, deputy secretary of state, 1994–2001

Tenet, George, director of central intelligence, 1997–2004

Wolfowitz, Paul, analyst at the Arms Control and Disarmament Agency (ACDA); deputy assistant secretary of defense for regional programs, 1977–9; director of policy planning, 1981–2; assistant secretary of state, 1982–6; under secretary of defense for policy, 1989–93; deputy defense secretary, 2001–5

Wulf, Norman, deputy assistant director for non-proliferation and regional arms control at the Arms Control and Disarmament Agency (ACDA), 1985–99; special representative to the president for nuclear non-proliferation, 1992; deputy assistant secretary of state for non-proliferation 2001–5

In Pakistan

Ahmed, General Mahmood, corps commander, Rawalpindi, until 1999; director general, Inter Services Intelligence (ISI), 1999–2001

Arif, General K. M., chief of staff, 1977–84; vice chief of army staff, 1984–7

Aziz, General Mohammed, chief of general staff, 1999; commander of 4 Corps until 2001; chairman, joint chiefs of staff, 2001–4

Babar, General Naseerullah, interior minister, 1993–6

Beg, General Mirza Aslam, vice chief of army staff, 1987–8; chief of army staff, 1988–91

Bhutto, Benazir, prime minister, 1988–90, 1993–6

Bhutto, Zulfikar Ali, president 1971–3; prime minister, 1973–7

Durrani, General Asad, director general, Inter Services Intelligence (ISI), 1990–1

Gul, General Hamid, director general, Inter Services Intelligence (ISI), 1987–9

Karamat, General Jehangir, director general military intelligence and chief of army staff, 1996–7; chairman, joint chiefs of staff and chief of army staff, 1997–8; ambassador to US, 2004–6

Khan, General Ghulam Ahmed, chief of staff, 1999–2001

Khan, Ghulam Ishaq, secretary general, ministry of defense, 1975–7; finance minister, 1977–85; chairman of senate, 1985–8; president, 1988–93

Khan, Sahabzada Yaqub, ambassador to US, 1974; foreign minister 1982–91, 1996–7

Leghari, Farukh, president 1993–7

Musharraf, General Pervez, director general, military operations, 1993–5; promoted lieutenant general and commander of 1 Corps (Mangla), 1995; chief of army staff, 1998–9; chief executive of Pakistan, 1999–2001; president, 2001–

Nasir, General Javid, director general, Inter Services Intelligence (ISI), 1991–3

Niazi, Kauser, minister for religious and minority affairs and minister of information, 1972–7

Pirzada, Sharifuddin, attorney general, 1977–85; minister for law and parliamentary affairs, 1979–85; honorary roving ambassador, 1995; senior adviser to the chief executive, member of National Security Council, 1999–2000; senior adviser to the chief executive on foreign affairs, law, justice and human rights, 2000–2

Rahman, General Akhtar Abdur, director general, Inter Services Intelligence (ISI), 1980–7; chairman, joint chiefs of staff, 1987–8

Shahi, Agha, foreign secretary, 1973–7; foreign minister, 1977–82

Sharif, Nawaz, prime minister 1990–3, 1997–9

ul-Haq, General Zia, chief of army staff, 1976–1977; chief martial law administrator, chief of army staff, president, 1977–88

Usmani, General Muzzaffar, commander 5 Corps, until 1999; vice chief of army staff, 1999–2001

Yusaf, General Mohammed, chief of general staff, vice chief of army staff, 2001–4

Khan network

Bhatti, I. A., financial comptroller ERL/KRL and paymaster to Khan's foreign agents

Farooq, Mohammed, head of foreign procurements and liaison with foreign agents

Hashmi, Farooq, metallurgist trained at Southampton University; deputy director, KRL

Khan, Abdul Qadeer, chairman, Engineering Research Laboratories (ERL) 1976–81, (renamed as) Dr. A. Q. Khan Research Laboratories (KRL), 1981–2001; under house arrest from January 2004

Mirza, Javid, graduate of Glasgow University; director general, electronics division and air weapons systems at ERL/KRL, 1976–98; deputy chairman, KRL, 1998–2001; chairman KRL, 2001–6

Qazi, Colonel Rashid Ali, head of Khan's production machine shop and liaison with foreign agents

Pakistan's nuclear establishment

Khan, Munir Ahmed, trained at the US Argonne National Laboratory, 1957; worked at the nuclear power and reactors division of the International Atomic Energy Agency (IAEA), Vienna, until 1972; chairman of the Pakistan Atomic Energy Commission (PAEC) 1972–91; died in Vienna, 1999

Mubarakmand, Samar, joined PAEC in 1962, ran its weapons design shop from 1974; director general, National Defense Complex (manufacturing nuclear-capable missiles), 1990s; chairman, National Engineering and Scientific Commission (designing defense systems), 2001

Khan confidants and associates

Butt, Sulfikar Ahmed, procurement chief for A. Q. Khan, based in Pakistan's embassies in Paris and Brussels with the rank of counsellor, early 1980s

Chowhan, Lieutenant General Dr. Riaz, former surgeon general to the Pakistan army and personal physician to A. Q. Khan

Farouq, S. M., B. S. A. Tahir's uncle and former business partner, also a key Khan agent

Khan, Henny (née Donkers), married A. Q. Khan in 1964

Khan, Ikram ul-Haq, head of procurement for Khan, based at the Pakistan embassy in Bonn, until 1982

Malik, Brigadier Sajawal Khan, civil engineer with the army, co-opted to work on building ERL for A. Q. Khan, 1976; Khan's trusted aide thereafter, arrested January 2004

Siddiqui, Abdul, London-based accountant and confidant of A. Q. Khan, accompanying him on his trips to Africa, 1998–2000

Siddiqui, Abu Bakr, son of Abdul, European business partner of B. S. A. Tahir through SMB Europe, arrested October 2001

Tahir, Buhary Seyed Abu (aka B. S. A. Tahir), Khan's Sri Lankan-born protégé, who took over SMB Computers and led proliferation network, arrested November 2003

Ul-Haq, Brigadier Inam, military agent for A. Q. Khan, based in Lahore, connected to many North American and European deals in 1980s

Ur-Rehman, Dr. Shafiq, son of Brigadier Sajawal Khan Malik, doctor at KRL, partner in Tradewall International with Nauman Shah, Khan's son-in-law

European contacts

Cire, Gunes, Turkish-born electrical engineer; worked for Siemens; arrested by

Turkish authorities, accused of supplying Pakistan and its clients; died during interrogation in 2004

Geiges, Daniel, Swiss engineer, Wisser's employee; allegedly built the centrifuges in South Africa at Tradefin Engineering; arrested and facing trial

Griffin, Peter, Welsh-born engineer who supplied machine tools and engineering parts to A. Q. Khan, 1970s–90s; moved to Dubai in 1997; business associate of B. S. A. Tahir's until 2004; denies any illegal activity

Lerch, Gotthard, German engineer; manager at Leybold Heraeus, accused of supplying Khan network and its surrogates in South Africa; on trial in Germany charged with supplying Libya's nuclear program; denies all allegations

Mebus, Heinz, helped build two nuclear-related plants for Pakistan, 1970s; arrested in Amsterdam, 1984, attempting to export equipment for Pakistan's nuclear program

Meyer, Johan, owner of Tradefin, South Africa; seized in connection with the Libyan centrifuge operation, 2004; later released without charge

Migule, Albrecht, convicted by West German court for trading with A. Q. Khan, March 1985; later denied he knew his exports were nuclear-related

Salam, Abdus, British businessman of Pakistani descent; supplier of tools and technical assistance to A. Q. Khan and Griffin's business partner, 1977–82

Slebos, Henk, Dutch Khan supplier; convicted of illegally exporting controlled items to Pakistan, sentenced to twelve months in jail and $120,000 fine, 2005; maintained innocence and appealed

Tinner, Friedrich, arrested by German authorities, October 2004, extradited to Switzerland and charged with producing centrifuge parts in Malaysia and Switzerland for Pakistan and Libya; sons, Urs and Marco, also in custody pending trial on similar charges

Wisser, Gerhard, former Leybold Heraeus representative in South Africa; friend of Lerch; owner of Krisch Engineering; accused of building centrifuge plant for Libya at behest of Pakistan

Jihadis

Al-Masri, Abu Khabab, Egyptian-born chemist; WMD chief for al-Qaeda; killed by US predator drones in Pakistan, 13 January 2006

Al-Suri, Abu Musab, Syrian engineer; WMD specialist; worked with Abu

Khabab al-Masri; trained with Osama bin Laden in Afghanistan in 1980s; arrested in Jaish-e-Mohammed hideout in Pakistan, November 2005

Al-Zarqawi, Abu Musab, Jordanian criminal; trained with Osama bin Laden in Afghanistan; fled, December 2001, via Pakistan; launched al-Qaeda in Mesopotamia, 2003; killed by US forces, June 2006

Azhar, Maulana Masood, leader of banned Pakistan-based terror group Jaish-e-Mohammed; previously of Harkat ul-Ansar; accused of kidnapping Western tourists in Kashmir, 1995

Bin Laden, Osama, Saudi businessman and jihadi; fought Soviets in Afghanistan, 1980s; based in Peshawar, 1989; associate of General Hamid Gul; financier of plot to kill Benazir Bhutto, 1989; moved back to Afghanistan, 1997; founder of al-Qaeda; launched jihad against the US and its allies in 1998; thought to be hiding in Pakistan

Mahmood, Sultan Bashiruddin, KRL scientist for twenty years; met Osama bin Laden, August 2001, to discuss WMD program

Majeed, Chaudiri Abdul, former nuclear scientist; met Osama bin Laden, August 2001, to discuss WMD program

Mohammed, Khalid Sheikh, uncle of Ramzi Yousef; 9/11 planner; caught in Karachi, 11 September 2002

Tariq, Maulana Azam, deputy leader of Sipah-e-Sahaba, banned Sunni extremist group; paid Ramzi Yousef to kill Bhutto in 1993; shot dead in Islamabad, October 2003

Yousef, Ramzi, blew up World Trade Center, 26 February 1993; attempted assassination of Benazir Bhutto, July 1993; seized in Islamabad, February 1995, having lived there under ISI protection for two years

Zubaida, Abu, al-Qaeda's lead planner; seized in Faisalabad, March 2002

LIST OF ABBREVIATIONS AND ACRONYMS

ACDA	Arms Control and Disarmament Agency
AEOI	Atomic Energy Organization of Iran
BCCI	Bank of Credit and Commerce International
BND	Bundesnachrichtendienst, Germany's foreign intelligence agency
BNFL	British Nuclear Fuels Limited
CENTCOM	US Central Command
CIA	Central Intelligence Agency
COAS	Chief of Army Staff
DCI	Director of Central Intelligence
Dem	Democrat
DIA	Defense Intelligence Agency
DESTO	Defense Science & Technology Organization
FBI	Federal Bureau of Investigation
FBIS	Foreign Broadcast Information Service
HEU	Highly Enriched Uranium
IAEA	International Atomic Energy Agency
IC	Intelligence Community
IDF	Israel Defense Forces
IG	Inspector General
IMF	International Monetary Fund
INR	Bureau of Intelligence and Research
ISI	Inter Services Intelligence
ISN	Bureau of International Security and Non-Proliferation

JIC	Joint Intelligence Committee
KANUPP	Karachi Nuclear Power Plant
KRL	Khan Research Laboratories
MI5	British Security Service
MI6	British Secret Intelligence Service
MQM	Muttahida Qaumi Movement
NEA	Bureau of Near Eastern and South Asian Affairs, Department of State
NIE	National Intelligence Estimates
NPT	Nuclear Non-Proliferation Treaty
NSA	National Security Agency
NSC	National Security Council
OSD	Office of the Secretary of Defense
OSWR	Office of Scientific and Weapons Research
PAEC	Pakistan Atomic Energy Commission
POF	Pakistan Ordnance Factories
PINSTECH	Pakistan Institute of Nuclear Science & Technology
PML	Pakistan Muslim League
PPP	Pakistan People's Party
PRC	People's Republic of China
PTV	Pakistan Television
Rep	Republican
SUPARCO	Space and Upper Atmosphere Research Commission
UF_6	Uranium Hexafluoride
UN	United Nations
UNSCOM	United Nations Special Commission
WMD	Weapons of Mass Destruction

NOTES

1: THE ANGRY YOUNG MAN

1 Former information minister Maulana K. Niazi writes of this letter in his Urdu book *Aur Line Kat Gayee* (Lahore, 1987), Chapter 9, "Unknown Facts about the Reprocessing Plant."

2 Moments after the blast, the Foreign Ministry in New Delhi signalled its success with a prearranged telegram that enigmatically read: "The Buddha is smiling."

3 This episode was recounted by Agha Shahi, former foreign secretary of Pakistan, to the authors in an interview in Islamabad, April 2006. See also Dennis Kux, *The United States and Pakistan 1947–2000* (Woodrow Wilson Center Press, Washington, DC, 2001), pp. 211–19.

4 The phrase "most allied ally" comes from the autobiography of Pakistani dictator General Ayub Khan, *Friends Not Masters* (OUP, London, 1967). Pakistan had joined the South-East Asia Treaty Organization (SEATO) in 1954 and the Central Treaty Organization (CENTO) four years later. In 1959 it also signed the Mutual Security Pact with the US. For more details of this early relationship, see also Kux.

5 National Security Archive (NSA) 65/4205, NSA, George Washington University, Washington, DC. Letter from Thomas Hughes (INR) to CIA director W. F. Raborn, 21 July 1965.

6 The Islamic Republic was accused of preferring to attend conferences with the Chinese in April 1963, and in Moscow in April 1965, rather than those sponsored by the US. For more, see Kux.

7 In December 1970, East Pakistan's first general election had seen the East Pakistanis overwhelmingly vote for autonomy, while in West Pakistan, Zulfikar Ali Bhutto, a former foreign minister from the 1960s, won a surprise victory with his Pakistan People's Party (PPP). However, the country's president, General Yahya Khan, failed to honor either result, launching a brutal crackdown in East Pakistan with thousands shot dead in the streets. Islamabad had also launched air strikes into Indian territory in Kashmir.

8 Pakistanis like to say that they had an army before they had a country, and at partition the Islamic Republic received 30 percent of British India's army, 40 percent of its navy and 20 percent of its air force. But all munitions and armaments factories were situated on the Indian side, leaving Pakistan struggling to build a defense

industry. For many years it relied on the generosity of allies like the US. But Pakistan had stopped receiving military assistance in 1965 after President Lyndon Johnson, enraged that the Islamic Republic had deployed US-manufactured Sherman tanks against India in Kashmir, imposed an arms embargo. Even after India had launched its East Pakistan offensive in 1971, the US embargo held, leaving Pakistan incapable of holding off the Indian advance.

9 This quote comes from Zulfikar Ali Bhutto, *If I Am Assassinated* (Classic Books, Lahore, 1994).

10 Author interview, Islamabad, April 2006. For more on the fallout from the Indian test, see Kux.

11 NSA 7613887, Department of State, Memorandum of Conversation, Proposed Cable to Tehran on Pakistani Nuclear Reprocessing, 12 May 1976.

12 Frank Barnaby, *How to Build a Nuclear Bomb* (Granta Publications, London, 2003).

13 Pakistan Atomic Energy Commission chairman Dr. Ishrat Usmani had also helped to negotiate the deal.

14 Maulana Kauser Niazi.

15 Much of the ISI material comes from author interviews with a former ISI officer in Islamabad in April 2006. He wishes to remain anonymous.

16 Barnaby.

17 A. Q. Khan quoted by Niazi.

18 For more detail on the centrifugal process, see Barnaby.

19 The Commercial Nuclear Obreptitious Rotor.

20 Maulana Kauser Niazi.

21 General Ayub Khan, the then ruler of Pakistan, had appointed him.

22 Eisenhower's program came into being as a result of debates at the UN in 1953.

23 Bhutto, *If I Am Assassinated*.

24 Bhutto, *If I Am Assassinated*. Re: training in the US: for developing nations like Pakistan, by far the most significant aspect of Atoms for Peace was the access it gave scientists to the US Department of Energy laboratories at Argonne, Illinois, founded by the University of Chicago in 1946 to conduct atomic research. It constituted the West's most advanced nuclear research facility, with supercomputer technology and a working accelerator where atomic particles were bombarded against each other in order to study fission.

25 Zulfikar Ali Bhutto, *The Myth of Independence* (OUP, Karachi, 1969), p. 153.

26 In November 1973 the nawab would be appointed chief minister of the Punjab.

27 Dr. Samar Mubarakmand, "A Science Odyssey," Khwarzimic Science Society speech, 30 November 1998. Author archives.

28 Steve Weissman and Herbert Krosney, *The Islamic Bomb* (Times Books, New York, 1981), p. 47.

29 He was there from January to May 1957, according to a letter from Argonne National Laboratory, 8 May 1987, quoted in Zahid Malik, *Dr. A. Q. Khan and the Islamic Bomb* (Hurmat Publications, Islamabad, 1992), p. 129.

30 Bashiruddin was named by President George W. Bush as a terrorist in a speech in October 2003, when the US accused him and others of meeting Osama bin Laden to discuss building a nuclear bomb for al-Qaeda.

31 See Chapter 2.

32 Bhutto visited Iran, Saudi Arabia, the United Arab Emirates, Turkey, Syria, Morocco, Egypt, Algeria, Tunisia, Libya and China.

33 This phrase, favored by Bhutto for the Western powers, is referred to in Kux.

34 See Kux for more on this promotional tour.

35 For full details on Pakistan's failed attempt to purchase a reprocessing plant from France, see Weissman and Krosney.

36 Niazi recalled: "The prime minister sent instructions in August 1974 to Dr. Qadeer that without operating a doubt in the mind of anybody, he should take leave in the normal course and come to Pakistan and meet [Bhutto's] military secretary, Brigadier Imtiaz Ahmed."

37 Weissman and Krosney.

38 Author interviews with Dr. Shafiq ur-Rehman, Islamabad, April 2006.

39 There was a commander called General Malik Haji Bahbal, but his ancestry recorded no connection to Khan. Story recounted by Zahid Malik.

40 Malik.

41 Malik.

42 A. Q. Khan remained at home with his elderly parents.

43 Malik.

44 Khan presented the painting to the Senate on 11 November 1995. For a photograph of it, see S. Shabbir Hussain and Mujahid Kamran, *Dr. A. Q. Khan on Science and Education* (Sang-E-Meel Publications, Lahore, 1997).

45 Malik.

46 Badrul Islam, recollections of former classmate at D. J. Sindh College, Malik, p. 48.

47 Malik.

48 This interview originally appeared in *Hurmat* weekly newspaper, 17 May 1986. It is reproduced in Malik.

49 Malik.

50 Slebos was interviewed by Hilversum Nederland-3 TV network for its *Zembla* current affairs program special report, "The Netherlands Atomic Bomb," 7 November 2005.

51 The photograph is reproduced in Malik.

52 See letters of A. Q. Khan, quoted by Sreedhar, *Pakistan's Bomb* (ABC Publishing House, New Delhi, 1986).

53 "Experiments with a Small Cupola Furnace," report, Tech. Univ. Delft, Dept Metallurgy, 1965; "The Development of Aluminum-Lithium Alloys," report, Delft, 1965; "Anisotropy in Cold Rolled Copper," report, Delft, 1966.

54 In 1965 he became involved in a particularly vitriolic exchange with a notable Dutch historian, Professor de Jong, who had presented a documentary series on the Indo–Pakistan wars.

55 Malik and *Hurmat* newspaper.

56 For a full CV, see Sir Syed University of Engineering and Technology, Karachi, Pakistan, 26 March 2001, Convocation, honors degree conferred on A. Q. Khan. Author archive.

57 The trial was suspended while prosecutors attempted to gain testimony from witnesses living outside Germany and appealed to the US intelligence community to assist in providing critical evidence. Lerch had been charged in the 1980s, having admitted to shipping valves, vacuum pumps and a gas purification system to Pakistan through his

employer Leybold Heraeus, although he was not convicted. In 1987 the German authorities once again investigated Lerch's business links to Pakistan, but by then he had moved to Switzerland, which declined to extradite him on the grounds that the statute of limitations had passed. When he was interrogated in 2005 in connection with the Mannheim trial he claimed that he was unable to recall whether he had ever seen Khan again after leaving Leybold Heraeus in 1985. See Juergen Dahlkamp, Georg Mascolo and Holger Stark, "The Network of Death on Trial," *Der Spiegel*, 13 March 2006. See also Steve Coll, "The Atomic Emporium," *New Yorker*, 7 and 14 August 2006; Kenley Butler, Sammy Salama and Leonard S. Spector, "Where Is the Justice?," *Bulletin of the Atomic Scientists*, November–December 2006. Lerch's name has repeatedly come up in evidence prepared for the forthcoming trial in South Africa of Daniel Geiges and Gerhard Wisser at the Pretoria High Court, where they are charged under the Non-Proliferation of Weapons of Mass Destruction Act and the Nuclear Energy Act of activities connected to the A. Q. Khan network. In several instances Lerch's name appeared on documentation connected to the manufacture of a centrifuge cascade ordered by an associate of A. Q. Khan's on behalf of Libya. At the time of writing this trial was pending. See also Coll.

58 Mebus died of natural causes in 1992.

59 Migule would later tell a court in Germany, where he was prosecuted for violating foreign trade laws, that he had "built and delivered to Pakistan a laboratory with test equipment, test devices, which, in my opinion, has nothing to do with nuclear bombs."

60 At the time of writing he was in custody, alongside his sons, Urs and Marco, with the trial pending. See Butler, Salama and Spector.

61 He died after being interrogated by the Turkish authorities in 2004.

62 Brabers was particularly close to Khan and would remain a friend long after Khan returned to Pakistan, becoming one of only a handful of Westerners to see Khan's secret centrifuge project near Islamabad. He was so highly thought of that in the early 1990s, Khan even invited him to become rector of a scientific college, the GIK Institute of Science and Technology in Topi, Northwest Frontier Province.

63 Fysisch Dynamisch Onderzoekslaboratorium.

64 Khan told his colleagues he had received two offers from Australia, one a teaching post and the other with the Australian Atomic Energy Commission. Malik.

65 FDO was a subsidiary of a large Dutch firm, VMF, that manufactured everything from railway engines to desalination plants and actually held the contract with UCN.

66 Binnenlandse Veiligheidsdienst is the full name for the acronym BVD.

67 Details of this screening process were later revealed in the Dutch government report by the inter-ministerial working party responsible for investigating the Khan Affair, October 1979. Quoted in Sreedhar, pp. 58–104.

68 Dutch inter-ministerial inquiry, quoted in Sreedhar, p. 63.

69 Badhoevedorp detail from *Zembla* TV report.

70 Weissman and Krosney, p. 179.

71 Barnaby. Scientists at the University of Virginia had experimented with the extraction of uranium-235 by spinning it in a centrifuge in 1934, but during the war the US had switched to diffusion. In 1942 the Nazis had built a small centrifuge device and enriched small quantities of uranium, and in 1945 the Soviets designed a thin-walled rotor needle centrifuge at a secret lab at Suchumi, near the Black Sea. Later, one of the

Soviet scientists defected to the University of Virginia, but the US still never took enrichment seriously.

72 See Khan's CV, as above.

73 These details came from an inquiry launched by the Dutch government three years after Khan returned to Pakistan with URENCO's blueprints.

74 Dr. Aslam Khan, head of Pakistan's Defense and Science Technology Organisation, and his deputy, Dr. Sibitain Bhokari. Details from Weissman and Krosney.

75 Seeing the Indian test blast, Khan wrote: "The unjustified reaction of the world community [to the Indian test] jolted the Pakistan government. Instead of punishing New Delhi for violating a sacred trust by clandestinely using [its] Canadian-supplied reactor and American heavy water to make a nuclear weapon, attempts were made to pressurize Pakistan into conforming to Western dictates. We were penalized for the mischief done by India ... Pakistan was left high and dry." From *Dr. A. Q. Khan Research Laboratories 1976–2001: 25 Years of Excellence and National Service*, Islamabad, 31 July 2001. Author archive.

76 Details of German attempts to protect data and details of new G-2 and ditching of Dutch centrifuge from article by Sajjad Hyder, former ambassador to The Hague, *The Muslim*, 28 February and 1 March 1984, quoted in Sreedhar, p. 205.

77 Dutch inter-ministerial inquiry, October 1979.

78 The former chief security officer from the Almelo plant would later confirm this version of events on the *Zembla* TV report. He claimed that there had been a cover-up by the Dutch authorities, who were appalled and embarrassed by the security blunders. He first raised the alarm with his superiors when he was asked to witness Khan signing a secrecy pledge concerning the G-2. When the security official questioned his superiors in the BVD about the sagacity of letting the Pakistani scientist see such sensitive material, he was told to back off. "Sometimes we are simply told to do certain things, regardless of whether we like it or not and an order is an order," he said.

79 Chatting with his UCN colleagues in the canteen over lunch he learned more details about the G-2 device. Only several years later, after UCN discovered that its processes had been stolen and a Dutch criminal inquiry was launched, did a colleague recall how he had asked Khan why he was keeping notes "in a foreign script," only to be told by him that he was writing a letter in Urdu to his family in Karachi. Another had seen Khan repeatedly touring the centrifuge plant, notebook in hand, despite the cast-iron rule that no writing or recording material was allowed. Dutch inter-ministerial inquiry and Weissman and Krosney.

80 Dutch inter-ministerial inquiry.

81 NSA A0001, Assessment of Indian Nuclear Test, 5 June 1974, a classified US mission to NATO report.

82 Mubarakmand.

83 A full account of this rivalry can be found (from A. Q. Khan's perspective) in Malik.

84 Niazi.

85 Niazi.

2: OPERATION BUTTER FACTORY

1 Steve Weissman and Herbert Krosney, *The Islamic Bomb* (Times Books, New York, 1981), p. 178.

2 Veerman's recollections come from an interview with William Langewiesche for his article, "The Wrath of Khan," *Atlantic Monthly*, Volume 296, No. 4 (November 2005), pp. 62–85.
3 Langewiesche.
4 Weissman and Krosney, p. 182.
5 Maulana K. Niazi, *Aur Line Kat Gayee* (Pakistan, 1987), Chapter 9, "Unknown Facts about the Reprocessing Plant."
6 Statement of Colonel Qazi Rasihid Ali, Khan's procurement chief, quoted in Zahid Malik, *Dr. A. Q. Khan and the Islamic Bomb* (Hurmat Publications, Islamabad, Pakistan, 1992), p. 69.
7 Niazi.
8 A. Q. Khan interview with *Nawa-i-Waqt*, Islamabad, 10 February 1984.
9 Niazi was with him at the time.
10 Langewiesche.
11 Weissman and Krosney.
12 A. Q. Khan and Henny's recollections of this dispute can be found in Malik.
13 Niazi recalled: "Mr. Bhutto called me to the PM House and said: 'I cannot let this golden opportunity go away. This man [Dr. Qadeer] is very valuable. Find a solution to this problem.' "
14 *Dr. A. Q. Khan Research Laboratories 1976–2001: 25 Years of Excellence and National Service*, Islamabad, 31 July 2001. Author archive.
15 For a full account of Khan's search for a site, see *25 Years of Excellence and National Service* and Malik.
16 Author interview with Dr. Shafiq ur-Rehman, Islamabad, April 2006. Dr. Shafiq became a business partner in Tradewall International with Nauman (Nomi) Shah, Khan's son-in-law, during the 1990s.
17 Sajawal would move in 1983 into A. Q. Khan's former house in F-7, Islamabad, when Khan and his family moved out and built their own home, one block to the north on Hillside Road.
18 Mark Hibbs, "The Unmaking of a Nuclear Smuggler," *Bulletin of the Atomic Scientists*, November–December 2006.
19 When Khan's computer specialist, Dr. G. D. Alam, was observing the first test of a centrifuge two years later the bottom bearing was still causing problems; when the centrifuge unbalanced, the glass case containing the machine exploded so violently that pieces were embedded in the ceiling.
20 *25 Years of Excellence and National Service*.
21 In October 2005 a powerful earthquake destroyed much of the plant, including one third of the centrifuges, which were thrown off balance by the tremors. Interview with Dr. Shafiq. See Chapter 13 for more details.
22 Cited in Malik.
23 *25 Years of Excellence and National Service*.
24 Author interviews with Peter Griffin, France, 2006–7.
25 The man had gone to Hameedia High School in Bhopal with A. Q. Khan, who had tracked him down to London in 1975, looking for help importing engineering equipment to Pakistan. However, the ex-school friend was now retired. He turned down the job and instead offered it to his friend at the Colindale mosque, Salam.
26 Another was SMB Europe, a ramshackle computer store in the innocuous London

suburb of West Ealing which was run by Abu Bakr Siddiqui and in the near future would ship to A. Q. Khan furnaces, a 5-ton gantry crane and sophisticated measuring equipment. Sue Clough, "Exporter Helped in Nuclear Race," *Daily Telegraph*, 9 October 2001.

27 Griffin recalled: "I would take Qazi and others around the country for a month, paying all their travel and hotel bills, introducing them to UK-based engineering firms. The only money they ever spent was at Marks and Spencer, on Oxford Street, buying gifts to take home."

28 Author interview with Peter Griffin.

29 Ibid.

30 Letter of A. Q. Khan:
I urgently need the following for our research program:
1. Etches of pivots:
    (a) Tension—how many volts?
    (b) Electricity—how many amperes?
    (c) How long is etching to be done?
    (d) Solution (electrolytic) HCl or something other is added as an inhibitor.
If it is possible, [I would be] grateful for 3–4 etched pivots.
I shall be very grateful if you could send a few negatives for the pattern. You would be having the negatives of these.
2. Lower shock absorber. Can you provide a complete absorber of CNOR? Please give my greetings to Frencken, and try to get a piece for me ... Frits, these are very urgently required, without which the research would come to a standstill.

31 According to Dutch inter-ministerial inquiry into the Khan Affair, October 1979.

32 Until German customs officers arrested him in the early 1980s and he admitted to having already supplied DM1.3 million worth of equipment to Pakistan, although he would not be convicted of any charges. See Juergen Dahlkamp, Georg Mascolo and Holger Stark, "Network of Death on Trial," *Der Spiegel*, 13 March 2006.

33 Karl Gunther Barth, "How German Scientists Have Helped Pakistan to Build an Atomic Bomb," *Stern*, 2 July 1981.

34 The plant would annually supply 198 tons of UF_6 and 177 tons of UF_4, uranium tetrafluoride.

35 Also there was Mr. Yousi, another member of Khan's scientific team.

36 Barth.

37 Court records, Freiburg Municipal Court, March 1985, Migule was sentenced to eight months in prison and a fine of DM30,000. However, Migule would later tell a court in Germany, where he was prosecuted for violating foreign trade laws, that he had "built and delivered to Pakistan a laboratory with test equipment, test devices, which, in my opinion, has nothing to do with nuclear bombs."

38 Barth.

39 A. Q. Khan interview with German journalist Egmont Koch, quoted in Steve Coll, "The Atomic Emporium," *New Yorker*, 7 and 14 August 2006.

40 The company was called ETI Elektroteknik, in Istanbul, and Slebos took a 15 percent stake in it after it got into financial difficulties. See also Hibbs.

41 Griffin recalled: "I knew Slebos was his big buddy from university. He and A. Q. Khan always wore matching safari suits made by Good Looks, Fabrics and Tailors. But I never completely trusted Slebos."

42 Slebos was interviewed by Hilversum Nederland-3 TV network for its *Zembla* current affairs program special report, "The Netherlands Atomic Bomb," 7 November 2005.

43 Henk Slebos talks about this in great detail in the *Zembla* TV report.

44 *Zembla* TV report.

45 Weissman and Krosney.

46 Ul-Haq moved into the apartment on 11 January 1977.

47 German customs agents, who seized some cigar box-shaped crates containing what had been declared as semi-manufactured spindles for making ballpoint pens, eventually caught Piffl at Stuttgart airport in 1993. The German agents discovered that Piffl's ballpoint pens were actually unfinished machine parts called "preforms," in this case segmented, narrow aluminum tubes, 15 centimeters long, that were destined for Pakistan where they would be finished off as scoops: little tubes inside a centrifuge that would collect and withdraw the separated particles of enriched uranium from inside the spinning rotor. See also Hibbs. Piffl would eventually be convicted in 1998 of having exported centrifuge parts to Pakistan in violation of German export controls and receive a forty-five-month sentence. At the conclusion of his trial Piffl admitted that for several years he had cooperated with the Bundesnachrichtendienst (BND), Germany's foreign intelligence agency, as they tracked A. Q. Khan's procurement network in Germany.

48 See letters of A. Q. Khan, quoted by Sreedhar, *Pakistan's Bomb* (ABC Publishing House, New Delhi, 1986).

49 Details of how these agents worked comes from interviews with Peter Griffin and Dr. Shafiq ur-Rehman and from Weissman and Krosney.

50 Weissman and Krosney, p. 183.

51 Weissman and Krosney, p. 182.

52 Author interview with Dr. Shafiq, Islamabad, April 2006.

53 *25 Years of Excellence and National Service.*

54 For more details on tunnel construction, see Rai Muhammed Saleh Azam, *When Mountains Move: The Story of Chagai* (Islamabad, 1998).

55 Dr. Samar Mubarakmand recalled: "Why were we doing all this so keenly in 1975 and 1976? We were told that whenever you were ready, we would detonate the bomb. So we were all very enthusiastic. We were running day and night." Dr. Samar Mubarakmand, "A Science Odyssey," Khwarzimic Science Society speech, 30 November 1998. Author archive.

56 NSA A0008, Robert Gallucci, State Department, Draft Report on Pakistan and the Non-Proliferation Issue, 22 January 1975, NSA, George Washington University, Washington, DC.

57 This meeting was in February 1976.

58 While Kissinger had fronted the deal, in private he thought the US was crazy to offer it and that Bhutto would be mad to take it up. In a classified transcript from a State Department meeting held on 12 May 1976, Kissinger admitted: "I am frankly getting off the [Iran deal]. I have endorsed it publicly, but in any region you look at, it is a fraud. Pakistan does not want to be in a plant located in Iran and a plant in Pakistan would just be a cover [for a bomb]. We are the only country, which is fanatical and unrealistic enough to do things, which are contrary to our national interests. The Europeans are not so illogical." NSA 7613887, Department of State, Memorandum of Conversation,

Proposed Cable to Tehran on Pakistani Nuclear Reprocessing, 12 May 1976.

59 The Symington amendment, named after Senator Stuart Symington (Democrat, Missouri), was adopted in June 1976. For details on Pakistan's aid package at that time, see Dennis Kux, *The United States and Pakistan 1947–2000* (Woodrow Wilson Center Press, Washington, DC, 2001), p. 218. In 1975 the US agreed to supply $65 million worth of wheat and $78 million in development loans.

60 Niazi.

61 Bhutto told Niazi: "We should take a firm stand on this showpiece in such a way that the USA itself should put pressure on France to cancel the agreement. In this way, the demurrage that Pakistan would have to pay to France would actually be paid by France to Pakistan."

62 The election was called a year early. For more detail, see Kux.

63 The coalition of nine parties was called the Pakistan National Alliance (PNA). For more details on the 1977 election and Jamaat-e-Islami, see Husain Haqqani, *Pakistan; From Mosque to Military* (Carnegie Endowment for International Peace, Washington, DC, 2005).

64 Haqqani, pp. 117–19.

65 Stanley Wolpert, *Zulfikar Ali Bhutto of Pakistan* (Oxford University Press, New York, 1993), pp. 278–9.

66 Author interview with Howard Schaffer, Washington, October 2006.

67 This episode was recounted to the authors by Benazir Bhutto in an interview in Dubai, July 2006. See also Kux.

68 Address to the National Assembly, 28 April 1977.

69 Kux, p. 232.

70 General Khalid Mahmud Arif, *Working with Zia* (Oxford University Press, Karachi, 1995).

71 Kux, p. 229.

72 Niazi.

73 Howard Schaffer, the US political consul, was at this party and recalled: "Bhutto had a practice of sitting in side rooms at receptions like these, and people would be brought in to see him. General Zia was at the party too and my staff said, 'Would you like to see the prime minister?' He said, 'No, I don't think so.' Another aide said to Zia, 'I hope we'll see you later.' " He was referring to a long-standing invitation for the following afternoon that Zia had previously been very keen to fix. But now the general responded: "No, I'll be very busy tomorrow." Author interview.

74 Author interview with General Khalid Mahmud Arif, chief of staff to Zia, (1977–84,) Rawalpindi, April 2006.

75 Zulfikar Ali Bhutto had always planned for Benazir to be his successor, taking her with him to the UN Security Council in 1971 and the Indo–Pakistan talks in Simla in 1972.

76 Arif, *Working with Zia*.

77 These charges were highly contentious and their veracity is hotly debated even today in Pakistan.

78 Haqqani, p. 123.

79 All trial details from Arif, *Working with Zia*, p. 186.

80 Author interviews with Benazir Bhutto, Dubai, July 2006.

81 Zafar Niazi's role was described by Peter Griffin. Griffin inadvertently got caught up

in the slipstream of Bhutto's trial when Khan rang him up in London, asking him to help Niazi escape from Pakistan. Griffin recalled: "Niazi's surgery was round the corner from A. Q. Khan's house. They'd known each other for years. Now Khan told me Niazi had been to see Bhutto in prison. He was being kept in a concrete hole and all his gums had gone rotten. On his way out of the prison, the authorities had told Niazi that he would have to sign a gagging agreement. The government was trying to pretend Bhutto was living in luxury with newspapers and TV. Niazi wouldn't sign. He decided to flee to London. A. Q. Khan asked me to find him a place. I got him a flat at the Barbican [in the City of London]. Every time I got a cable from A. Q. Khan about the 'bird of paradise' I knew it was a code for me to take money round. In the end such was Khan's fondness for Dr. Niazi that he even paid the deposit when Niazi bought the flat." Author interviews, France, 2006–7.

82 "A Decade of Uranium Enrichment at Kahuta," *Dawn* (Karachi), 1 August 1986.

3: INTO THE VALLEY OF DEATH

1 Benazir Bhutto was now being held under house arrest at her family home in Larkana, in Sindh Province. The letters were later seized by General K. M. Arif, Zia's chief of staff, and are quoted in his *Working with Zia* (OUP, Karachi, 1995), pp. 192–4.

2 Zia quotes from Arif, *Working with Zia*. Arif's book ridicules Benazir Bhutto for needing foreign friends, whom he derides as "external crutches" that were "inherently a poor substitute for internal strength."

3 Zahid Malik, *Dr. A. Q. Khan and the Islamic Bomb* (Hurmat Publications, Islamabad, 1992), p. 282.

4 Author interview with Agha Shahi, Islamabad, spring 2006.

5 General Zia ul-Haq's address to the nation was on 5 July 1977. For more, see Hasan-Askarj Rizvi, *The Military and Politics in Pakistan, 1947–86* (Lahore Progressive Publishers, 1986), pp. 289–93.

6 For more on Zia's background and Islamization measures, see Husain Haqqani, *Pakistan: From Mosque to Military* (Carnegie Endowment for International Peace, Washington, DC, 2005); Arif, *Working with Zia*; and K. M. Arif, *Khaki Shadows, 1947–1997* (Oxford University Press, Oxford, 2001).

7 Author interview with K. M. Arif, Rawalpindi, spring 2006.

8 Malik, p. 255.

9 Author interviews with Benazir Bhutto, Dubai, summer 2006.

10 Evidence submitted to Montreal High Court by the Canadian police in the prosecution of A. A. Khan, Salem Elemenyawai and Mohammed Ahmad, arrested 20 August 1980 for trying to smuggle nuclear components to Pakistan. Quoted in Sreedhar, *Pakistan's Bomb, a Documentary Study* (ABC Books, New Delhi, 1986).

11 Ibid.

12 On 7 July 1978, Khan wrote again, thanking Aziz for his letter of 29 June. "I have to go to London on Sunday on a rendezvous," he said, referring to a forthcoming meeting with Griffin and Salam, before revealing that his colleagues were thrilled about the enrichment breakthrough. "Everybody is in high spirits. The hesitation and doubts are finished, now only hard work is needed."

13 The air-conditioning plant and all utilities would be run by Bader ul-Islam.

14 This numbering system was confirmed by Dr. Shafiq ur-Rehman, Brigadier Sajawal's son, author interview, Islamabad, spring 2006.

15 Its address was House No. 12, Street No. 3, F-1. Henk Slebos confirms he used this address to make deliveries in Mark Hibbs, "The Unmaking of a Nuclear Smuggler," *Bulletin of the Atomic Scientists*, November–December 2006. Richard Barlow, a former CIA officer who tracked A. Q. Khan's procurement network, also confirmed that the Pakistanis frequently used the home addresses of Kahuta staff for deliveries and sensitive correspondence. Author interviews with Richard Barlow, Montana, autumn 2006.

16 Details from A. Q. Khan to Aziz Khan, 21 November 1978, quoted in Sreedhar.

17 Author interviews with Peter Griffin, France, 2006–7.

18 Peter Griffin alleged: "Dr. Hashmi, Khan's deputy for years, a metallurgist trained at Southampton University, in England, was imposed on him by the Pakistani government. He was an arch-bureaucrat even though he was supposed to be Khan's heir. Of course this suited Khan fine as Hashmi made Khan look good." Author interviews with Peter Griffin, France, 2006–7.

19 Peter Griffin.

20 Peter Griffin said: "Team sold about twenty inverters but Piffl cheated A. Q. Khan on prices and I was brought in to control the costs and promised that all future orders would come through Weargate Ltd." Author interview.

21 Steve Weissman and Herbert Krosney, *The Islamic Bomb* (Times Books, New York, 1981), p. 187.

22 Tony Benn was interviewed by *Fifth Estate*, the flagship documentary program of the Canadian Broadcasting Corporation in 1979.

23 Peter Griffin said: "The VAT inspectors came to my office in Swansea. They were turning over everything in my office. 'What's this for? What's that for? Don't you realize the Paks are trying to make a bomb?' One of them turned round and said, 'We'd like you to tell us everything you know and we can offer you a lot of money.' I said, 'What's a lot of money?' They replied, '£50,000.' I said, 'I won't break my confidences for any amount of money. Piss off.'" Author interview.

24 It was his first public appearance since March and newspapers reported that he was "haggard and pale."

25 Arif, *Working with Zia*.

26 Khan wrote: "Everybody is working like mad. The first eight are working fine, after that we started the four together ... they worked alright, then we distributed the sweets." Letters quoted in Sreedhar.

27 Khan was determined to sit it out, saying: "Unless this work is completed, I am not going to budge from here." Referring to a new home he was building on Hillside Road, Khan continued: "It is coming into shape. Hoping it will finish in three months. Honey is very anxious to go there and so are the daughters."

28 Hibbs.

29 Malik, p. 207.

30 Hibbs. In the end the Dutch government prepared two reports on the outcome of its investigations into what became known as the "Khan Affair," only one of which was unclassified and delivered to the Dutch parliament. See Sreedhar for more extracts of this report. The political backlash forced the Dutch government to reinvestigate, in the form of a commission of inquiry. It concluded weakly that "engineer Dr. Khan has

been able to assist Pakistan in acquiring ultra-centrifuge know-how."

31 William Langewiesche, "The Wrath of Khan," *Atlantic Monthly*, Volume 296, No. 4 (November 2005), pp. 62–85.

32 Hibbs.

33 For details of the Begin letter, see Weissman and Krosney.

34 This episode is recounted in Malik.

35 Arif recalled: "I accompanied General Zia to Karachi. We discussed the burial arrangements and the security measures." From *Working with Zia*.

36 Benazir Bhutto, *Daughter of the East* (Hamish Hamilton, London, 1989). Also author interviews with Benazir Bhutto, Dubai, summer 2006.

37 Arif, *Working with Zia*.

38 Author interview with Giresh Saxena, New Delhi, spring 2006. In the mid-1980s, Giresh Saxena was chief of RAW and was officially known as Secretary R. Later he became a security adviser to consecutive prime ministers, including Rajiv Gandhi. In the 1990s he twice held the position of governor of Jammu and Kashmir, at the height of the insurgency.

39 Zulfikar Ali Bhutto, *If I Am Assassinated* (Classic Books, Lahore, 1994).

40 Bhutto.

41 Author interview with Agha Shahi, Islamabad, spring 2006.

42 For details of Chinese personnel visits in and out of Pakistan see NSA 4205/A, National Security Archive, George Washington University, Washington, DC.

43 "We all got up and clapped," said Shahi. "Then my ally the Tanzanian ambassador, Salim Ahmed Salim, led a conga dance through the meeting. Bush was angry, he got up to the rostrum and said it was a 'day of infamy.' "

44 The US suspected as much. See NSA E11, Secretary's Talking Points: US–China Relations, Department of State, June 1981.

45 The Chinese used diffusion rather than centrifuges at their Lanxhou nuclear fuel complex in Gansu and at another facility at Heping, in Sichuan.

46 A classified intelligence report to Congress reported: "Throughout the era of Mao Zedong, the PRC generally remained aloof from the international community on nuclear matters ... China argued that the spread of nuclear weapons to additional countries would diminish the power of the United States and the Soviet Union, and rejected the view that an increase in the number of nuclear-weapons states would enhance the risk of nuclear war. China also postulated that the introduction of nuclear weapons to nations of the Third World could increase the opportunity for revolutionary change." See NSA N6J, 18 September 1977.

47 Author interview with K. M. Arif, Rawalpindi, spring 2006.

48 General Zia firmed up Zulfikar Bhutto's secret deal when Chinese vice premier Geng Biao visited Islamabad in June 1978 and offered to build Pakistan a reprocessing plant and reactor to replace the French contract, which had finally collapsed in February 1979. Author interview.

49 The Symington amendment was invoked on 6 April 1979.

50 For more on early US–Pakistan discussions on Afghanistan, see Steve Coll, *Ghost Wars* (Penguin Press, New York, 2004); Kux; and Robert M. Gates, *From the Shadows* (Simon & Schuster, New York, 1996).

51 The shah was forced to flee in January 1979 and Khomeini returned in February after nineteen years in exile in France.

52 For more on Pakistan–Iran relations see Husain Haqqani, *Pakistan: From Mosque to Military* (Carnegie Endowment for International Peace, Washington, DC, 2005), and Vali Nasr, *The Shia Revival* (W. W. Norton & Company, New York, 2006).

53 Gates, pp. 128–31.

54 Author interviews with Robert Gallucci, Washington, 2006.

55 Report of the Dutch Inter-Ministerial Working Party, October 1979, Chapter 7, section 7.5.

56 NSA E8, Pakistan Nuclear Issue: Briefing of IAEA Director General Eklund, Office of Secretary of State to Jane Coon, Bureau of Near Eastern and South Asian Affairs, 9 July 1979.

57 It also was used for firing pins in automatic weapons, high-wearing parts in conveyor belts, fencing blades, and hypodermic syringes.

58 NSA E8.

59 "Ambassador Smith noted that he felt we still had some time, as he doubted the Pakistanis would be able to explode a device for two or three years ... Eklund said there was not so much time, as the more work the Pakistanis did, the harder it would be to stop them." Quoted from NSA E8.

60 Peter Nieswand, "Pakistan plays nuclear 'bluff,' " *Observer*, 5 July 1979.

61 Three days later, Chris Sherwell, a journalist with the *Financial Times*, was beaten up by ISI agents and held for three hours at an undisclosed location after repeatedly riding past what he thought was A. Q. Khan's Islamabad house.

62 Letter written on 25 July 1979, quoted in Sreedhar.

63 Letter to *Der Spiegel*, 1979.

64 NSA, Transcript of General Advisory Committee on Arms Control and Disarmament, 14 September 1979, pp. 309–477.

65 11 August 1979.

66 One of them, "Mr. Akhtar," had called up Aziz in a panic. Aziz wrote: "I told him he should not worry, he will get 20 years of free boarding and lodging (if character is good he would be out in 14). There is nothing to be scared about. I am looking for the bright side," he said, adding that all the Canadian authorities could pin on him was "some technical suggestions about normal motors and electrical wires."

67 Author interview with Agha Shahi, Islamabad, spring 2006.

68 On 4 November 1979.

69 Mark Bowden, *Guests of the Ayatollah* (Atlantic Books, London, 2006), pp. 8–15.

70 Gates, pp. 118–23.

71 Author interview with Agha Shahi.

72 Zbigniew Brzezinski, Memorandum for the President, Reflections on Soviet Intervention in Afghanistan, 26 December 1979, released by Cold War International. History Project, Woodrow Wilson Center, Washington, DC.

73 *Observer*, 21 July 1980.

4: PEANUTS

1 Terence Smith, "Carter Embargos Technologies for Soviets and Curtails Fishing and Grain," *New York Times*, 5 January 1980.

2 23 January 1980 was the date of the State of the Union address.

3 This eyes-only memo was from Stansfield Turner to Jimmy Carter, 16 January 1980.

See also Robert Gates, *From the Shadows* (Simon & Schuster, New York, 1996), p. 147.

4 NSA P800001 80000002, released 14 February 1991, Department of State Briefing Memorandum to the Secretary from Bureau of Near Eastern and South Asian Affairs, Harold Saunders, NSC Discussion of Support for Pakistan, 1 January 1980, National Security Archive, George Washington University, Washington, DC.

5 For more, see Dennis Kux, *The United States and Pakistan 1947–2000* (Woodrow Wilson Center Press, Washington, DC, 2001).

6 The special session was on 9 January 1980.

7 Details of hardware from NSA P800001 80000002.

8 Japan was an exception to the NATO deal on F-16s, something that further antagonized Pakistan.

9 Zia speaking to journalists on 18 January 1980.

10 Author interview with K. M. Arif, Islamabad, spring 2006.

11 This meeting and these quotes were recounted by K. M. Arif.

12 "I think Zia was impressed. The atmosphere at lunch was good though this may have just been good manners. We go back in at 5 p.m. and may then get some reactions," Hummel wrote. NSA P870097–0636, incoming telegram from Arthur Hummel, Islamabad, Talks with the Pakistanis, to Department of State.

13 As recounted by K. M. Arif.

14 See Kux for more on this fund-raising tour.

15 Kux.

16 For more details on the desert crash, see Mark Bowden, *Guests of the Ayatollah* (Atlantic Books, London, 2006).

17 Arif, *Working with Zia*, p. 337.

18 The *Panorama* program was broadcast on 16 June 1980.

19 Zahid Malik, *Dr. A. Q. Khan and the Islamic Bomb* (Hurmat Publications, Islamabad, 1992), p. 277.

20 For more on Zia's presentations to the OIC and the UN, and the meeting with Carter, see Kux and Arif, *Working with Zia*.

21 Nixon said: "I do not know the details of your nuclear effort. But if you have weapons capability, personally I won't mind if you get over with it." See Arif, *Working with Zia*, pp. 337–8.

22 See Kux, p. 256.

23 Author interview with Howard Schaffer, Washington, DC, autumn 2006.

24 Gates, *From the Shadows*.

25 Ibid.

26 Ibid.

27 Robert Gates wrote: "In a city where symbols of power are well known and count for much, [this] relegation to the basement spoke volumes about the downgrading for the NSC."

28 Author interviews with Richard Barlow, Montana, autumn 2006.

29 Dr. Geoff Kemp, who served as special assistant to the president for national security affairs and as senior director for Near East and South Asian affairs, recalled: "It was Hummel's idea but it wasn't rocket science. The answer came back from the White House, 'Yes.' The Soviet Invasion [of Kabul] was a clear and present danger and we should do whatever we can to get the Soviets out. And we would do it with the

[financial] help of our authoritarian Arab friends [in Saudi Arabia] too. We would give and the Saudis would give. By us giving, Pakistan would also keep its hands off the bomb." Author interview, Washington, spring 2006.

30 NSA P800087, Peter D. Constable, Bureau of Near Eastern and South Asian Affairs to Secretary of State, Assistance for Pakistan, 22 May 1980.

31 *Nuclear Fuel* carried an early story on the policy shift on 2 February 1981.

32 Usmani had been sacked by Bhutto after ridiculing claims made by his colleagues at the Multan conference in 1972 that a plutonium bomb could be built in just three years.

33 Rob Laufer, "Pakistan's Nuclear Patriarch Faults Homeland's Nuclear Policies," *Nucleonics Week*, 8 January 1981, p. 4.

34 NSA 01863, Peter Constable, Bureau of Near Eastern and South Asian Affairs, to the Secretary of State, Security Assistance for Pakistan, 16 February 1981.

35 Author interview, Agha Shahi, Islamabad, spring 2006.

36 Weiss had taught at Brown University and the University of Maryland. Eventually he became Glenn's staff director on the governmental affairs committee.

37 Author interview, Len Weiss, Virginia, spring 2006.

38 Pressure intensified when Representative Jonathan B. Bingham (Democrat, Bronx), chairman of the international economic policy and trade subcommittee, warned on 3 March that Pakistan's nuclear program, rather than the Soviet threat, presented the "clear and present danger to the US and indeed Western security interests in the Persian Gulf and South Asia." Judith Miller, "Cranston Sees Iraq as Nuclear Power by '82," *New York Times*, 18 March 1981.

39 Solarz went on to chair the House foreign affairs subcommittee on Asian and Pacific affairs. Author interview, Stephen Solarz, Washington, DC, spring 2006.

40 The plan, Percy was advised, was for an immediate grant to Pakistan of $100 million for the next financial year. See NSA 01889, 13 May 1981.

41 Ibid.

42 This assessment was written by P. D. Constable, Bureau of Near Eastern and South Asian Affairs, Department of State, to the National Security Adviser, 1 December 1980. See NSA 01854 and 01858.

43 The Office of Management and Budget was run by David Stockman, the former Republican representative for Michigan. See NSA 01879.

44 Alexander Haig testified to the Senate on 19 March 1981 and James Buckley testified to the House the same day.

45 Author interview, Agha Shahi, Rawalpindi, spring 2006.

46 Author interview with K. M. Arif, Islamabad, spring 2006.

47 Kux, p. 257.

48 Agha Shahi's last job in Washington before leaving for Islamabad was to brief the press about the surface details of their meetings: "I believe we have moved forward in developing a Pak–US friendship on a durable basis. The previous Carter admin offer did not carry for us credibility in a US–Pak relationship commensurate with what we considered to be the magnitude of the threat."

5: THE TIES THAT BIND

1 Dr. Shafiq ur-Rehman, author interview, Islamabad, spring 2006.

2 *Dr. A. Q. Khan Research Laboratories 1976–2001, 25 Years of Excellence and National Service*, Islamabad, 31 July 2001. Author archive.
3 Author interviews with a former close aide to Khan, Islamabad, 2006.
4 Steve Coll, *Ghost Wars* (Penguin Press, New York, 2004), p. 59.
5 Coll reproduces these quotes; also memoirs of K. M. Arif, and Mohammed Youssaf, and Mark Adkin, *The Bear Trap* (Jang Publishers, 1992).
6 UN General Assembly, 2 June 1981, document A/36/298: The Situation in the Middle East.
7 Cable to Tel Aviv from NEA, Pakistan Nuclear Program, box PARM-Non-proliferation, NSA, George Washington University, Washington, DC.
8 See CV and pamphlet, *Dr. Abdul Qadeer Khan*, prepared by Sir Syed University of Engineering and Technology, Karachi, 26 March 2001, having awarded Khan an honorary doctorate. Author archive.
9 Author interview with Moshe Ya'alon, Washington, DC, spring 2006.
10 The classified memo was later recovered by the NSA, document 7195, April 1979. It is quoted in full in George Perkovich, *India's Nuclear Bomb* (University of California Press, Berkeley, 1999), p. 532.
11 A report about the Ras Koh tunnels construction was given to the Indian cabinet by K. Santhanam, RAW's deputy director.
12 Lieutenant General Krishnaswami Sundarji was at that time commandant of the College of Combat, and he edited the *Combat Papers* containing articles from a number of Indian scholars, in which the war-gaming manual appeared.
13 Israel had an intelligence-sharing arrangement with the US and had unlimited access to US overheads, although not in real time. After this attack, the rules changed to allow Israel access to these overheads only for defensive purposes. For more on this bombing, see Steve Weissman and Herbert Krosney, *The Islamic Bomb* (Times Books, New York, 1981).
14 For more on the bombings, see Weissman and Krosney, pp. 296–301. Also Juergen Dahlkamp, Georg Mascolo and Holger Stark, "Network of Death on Trial," *Der Spiegel*, 13 March 2006.
15 Walti said: "When the company was cited to the Swiss government we discovered that the Americans had such good records of what we were doing that if we ever lost our own files we could always go and ask them to use theirs." Weissman and Krosney.
16 Weissman and Krosney, and author interviews with senior intelligence sources, Israel, June 2006.
17 Weissman and Krosney.
18 The company director had been put in touch with S. A. Butt, Pakistan's nuclear procurement agent in Paris, and had sold to him lead shielding and remote-controlled equipment to maneuver radioactive substances. The company director received three more threatening calls. Another was made to the local Reuters office. "It was an attempt to put psychological pressure on us but it didn't affect delivery to Pakistan. We kept on with the orders," a spokesman for the company recalled. Weissman and Krosney.
19 Weissman and Krosney.
20 Author interviews with Peter Griffin, France, 2006–7.
21 The president's news conference, 16 June 1981, The Public Papers of President Ronald W. Reagan, Ronald Reagan Presidential Library, University of Texas, <www.reagan.utexas.edu>.

22 25 June 1981, Senate Government Affairs Committee. For a good chronology of statements by Buckley and other Reagan officials, see <http://www.globalsecurity.org/wmd/world/pakistan/nuke-statements.htm>.

23 Material placed into the record by Senator Glenn, 20 September 1995, p. S13962 and ff.

24 The president made an annual statement to Congress on nuclear non-proliferation under the terms of the Non-Proliferation Act of 1978 in which he was required to identify potential nuclear proliferators and state the aims and intentions of the US government with regard to its non-proliferation policy. In his 1981 statement Reagan said: "Military assistance by the United States and the establishment of a new security relationship with Pakistan should help to counteract its possible motivations towards acquiring nuclear weapons." The president would repeat these words on 11 March 1982, telling Congress that his administration believed in "continuity in United States policy to prevent the spread of nuclear explosives" and that he would "continue our efforts to strengthen the non-proliferation regime." Reagan said he "looked forward to working closely with Congress toward these shared objectives." Author interview with Len Weiss, Virginia, spring 2006.

25 K. M. Arif and Agha Shahi both recall being told that Reagan would ignore the nuclear program if cooperation on the Afghan war continued. Agha Shahi made similar allegations from meetings he attended with Buckley or that others attended and told him about. The sum of them was that nuclear issues were now at the bottom of the agenda for the Reagan White House.

26 This meeting was on 14 September 1981. Author interview with K. M. Arif, Rawalpindi, spring 2006.

27 Author interview with Agha Shahi, Islamabad, spring 2006.

28 The case was heard in Quebec and the goods had been bought in the US and Canada. See "On the Trail of the A-Bomb Makers," *Christian Science Monitor*, 1 December 1981.

29 Rick Atkinson, "Use in Arms Feared: Nuclear Parts Sought by Pakistanis," *Washington Post*, 21 July 1984.

30 It continued to operate, and was only shut down in 2004 when Henk Slebos, Khan's Dutch associate, was charged with breaking export laws in Holland. Slebos was charged in May 2004 with having illegally exported an array of dual-use goods to Pakistan. He went on trial in November 2005 and was convicted on 16 December 2005, receiving a one-year prison sentence, which was reduced to four months, and fined Euros 197,500. For more, see Mark Hibbs, "The Unmaking of a Nuclear Smuggler," *Bulletin of the Atomic Scientists*, November–December 2006.

31 The interview with President Zia ul-Haq was published in Turkish *Hurriyet*, 25 November 1981.

32 Leslie Maitland, "US Studying Foiled Bid to Export a Key Reactor Metal to Pakistan," *New York Times*, 20 November 1981.

33 28 June 1981, cable to US embassy in Ankara, quoted by AP and published in the *New York Times*, "Turkey Warned by U.S. on Goods for Pakistanis," on that day.

34 Its location was kept secret but was thought to be somewhere near Fatehjung, a town in rolling countryside northwest of Islamabad. For more, see Rai Muhammad Saleh Azam, *When Mountains Move: The Story of Chagai* (Islamabad, 1998).

35 Among the members of this team were Hafeez Quereshi, former head of the

Radiation and Isotope Applications Division at the Pakistan Institute of Nuclear Science and Technology (PINSTECH), Dr. Riazzuddin, PAEC, Dr. Zaman Sheikh, Defense, Science and Technology Organization.

36 Confirmed by Dr. Shafiq, author interview, Islamabad, spring 2006. See also Azam.

37 Toasts of President Reagan and President Mohammad Zia ul-Haq of Pakistan, 7 December 1982, Public Papers of President Ronald W. Reagan.

38 He said this during an appearance at the US National Press Club on 8 December 1982.

39 General Zia's *Meet the Press* appearance was on 12 December 1982.

40 For transcripts of all Reagan's speeches see Public Papers of President Ronald W. Reagan.

41 Walters's trip was later reported by Simon Henderson, "Anxious US Could Probe Zia over N-Plans," *Financial Times*, 8 December 1982, and Kim Rogal, "Worries About the Bomb," *Newsweek*, 20 December 1982.

42 Author interviews with Robert Gallucci, Washington, DC, 2006.

43 Author interview with former senior State Department official, Virginia, spring 2006.

44 Author interview with K. M. Arif, Rawalpindi, spring 2006.

45 This was Reagan's annual requirement under the terms of the Non-Proliferation Act of 1978. See Public Papers of President Ronald W. Reagan.

46 NSA F0007, Robert Gallucci, The Pakistani Nuclear Program, Department of State Intelligence Report, 23 June 1983.

47 Gallucci's report began with an overview of Pakistan's nuclear fuel cycle. He confirmed that Pakistan had constructed a plant to "concentrate uranium ore" and that another to produce UF_6 was "already in operation." Gallucci went on to detail the work being done at Kahuta, and the technology being assembled there based on the stolen URENCO designs. He warned of the increasing confidence of Khan's procurement network which was active and "disguising their activities by providing false end-use statements."

48 NSA document 02057, Robert Gallucci, The Pakistani Nuclear Program, Department of State Intelligence Report, 23 June 1983.

49 The model was later shown to Benazir Bhutto, and she spoke of having seen it, during interviews with the authors in Dubai in 2006.

50 Wisconsin Project. <http://www.wisconsinproject.org/pubs/reports/1991/bombs-beijing.html>.

51 Author interviews in Washington and Jerusalem in 2006.

52 Author interview with Dr. Shafiq ur-Rehman, Islamabad, spring 2006.

53 For a detailed description of how a nuclear bomb works, see Frank Barnaby, *How to Build a Nuclear Bomb* (Granta Books, London, 2003).

54 David K. Willis cites this draft of Reagan's annual classified report to Congress on non-proliferation in a report for the *Christian Science Monitor*, 25 February 1983.

55 Author interview with Dr. Shafiq ur-Rehman, Islamabad, spring 2006.

56 Quote taken from Reagan's annual classified report to Congress on non-proliferation, March 1983. See Public Papers of President Ronald W. Reagan.

57 The supercomputers were supplied by SMB International, the Dubai-based company of Khan's supplier S. M. Farouq. Mubarakmand is quoted in Azam.

58 This classified account of the cold test is quoted in Azam.

59 Author interview with K. M. Arif, Islamabad, spring 2006.

60 They reached their verdict on 31 October 1983. For more details of Khan's conviction and appeal, see the account of his Pakistani lawyer, S. M. Zafar, in his Urdu book, *Mere Mash'hoor Muqaddame*. Extracts in English can be found in an article, "The Trial of a Nation," 1 December 2005, on the website <www.chowk.com>.

61 Author interview with Dr. Shafiq ur-Rehman, Islamabad, spring 2006.

62 Some of the Khan–Napley correspondence and an account of this episode is reproduced by Zahid Malik, *Dr. A. Q. Khan and the Islamic Bomb* (Hurmat Publications, Islamabad, 1992).

63 Author interviews with Khan family friends, Islamabad, spring 2006.

64 Haroon Ahmed is the founder of the Pakistan Psychiatric Society and chairman of the Pakistan Association of Mental Health, having trained at the Royal Maudsley Hospital, in London, in the 1960s. Author interview with Haroon Ahmed, Karachi, spring 2006.

6: A FIGMENT OF THE ZIONIST MIND

1 For details on what the US knew of China's aid to Pakistan, see NSA 02057, Robert Gallucci, The Pakistani Nuclear Program, Department of State Intelligence Report, 23 June 1983, NSA, George Washington University, Washington, DC. Gallucci also recalled the reluctance within the White House to action any of this intelligence: "We had intel of every conceivable nature using most of our agencies and facilities. We expected a response from President [Reagan]. But the mantra that Reagan was the president most committed to non-proliferation was, to be frank, a fairy tale." Author interview.

2 NSA 920488, Box 11159, China–Pakistan, January 1984, Paul Wolfowitz, Bureau of East Asian and Pacific Affairs, Department of State, to Kenneth Dam, Deputy Secretary, The Secretary's Meeting with Premier Zhao—Nuclear Cooperation, 10 January 1984.

3 Author interviews in Virginia with a former senior official and non-proliferation specialist at the State Department in the spring and winter of 2006. This same official revealed that Reagan's envoy, General Vernon Walters, told him how he was ordered in October 1982 to tell Zia to "keep the nuclear program off our radar" rather than shut it down.

4 Shultz made this trip in February 1982.

5 Author interview with former senior official in the Arms Control and Disarmament Agency, Virginia, spring 2006.

6 The negotiations had begun in July 1983 and the Agreement for Cooperation in the Peaceful Uses of Nuclear Energy was eventually signed on 23 July 1985. See also <www.ostiweb.osti.gov/up/docs/IAEM docs/pdf/493.pdf> for wording.

7 During an official visit to Pakistan in 1969, President Nixon had asked Yahya Khan, then Pakistan's president, to broker an opening with China. This request led to two years of secret diplomacy between Washington, Islamabad and Beijing, and culminated in Henry Kissinger's historic visit to China in July 1971. The following February, President Nixon visited China himself. For more on this crucial role played by Pakistan in brokering the Sino–US rapprochement, see Dennis Kux, *The United States and Pakistan 1947–2000* (Woodrow Wilson Center Press, Washington, DC, 2001), pp. 182–93.

8 Author interview with a former senior official in the Arms Control and Disarmament Agency, Virginia, spring 2006.

9 Author interview with Dr. Shafiq ur-Rehman, Islamabad, spring 2006.

10 See Chapter 7 for a fuller explanation of the financial investigations and their findings.

11 This interview appeared in *Qaumi Digest* on 16 January 1984. The fact that Khan redrafted his own questions is referred to by Zahid Malik, *Dr. A. Q. Khan and the Islamic Bomb* (Hurmat Publications, Islamabad, 1992). Khan's habit of setting his own questions was also confirmed by Husain Haqqani, a former journalist with *The Muslim* newspaper and later an adviser to three prime ministers, who knew Khan. Author interview with Husain Haqqani, Washington, spring 2006.

12 *Nawa-i-Waqt* on 9 February 1984.

13 *Daily Jang* on 10 February 1984.

14 Hinton reported this back to the State Department. Author interviews with Robert Gallucci, Washington, 2006.

15 In an interview with the authors in Islamabad in the spring of 2006, Sharifuddin Pirzada confirmed that he helped create the legal framework for Zia ul-Haq staying in power.

16 For more on Zia's mandate, see Husain Haqqani, *Pakistan: From Mosque to Military* (Carnegie Endowment for International Peace, Washington, 2005).

17 Sharifuddin Pirzada also holds the rank of a federal minister, advising the leadership on subjects as diverse as foreign affairs and human rights.

18 The quote is from a letter written by Chaudhary Aitzaz Ahsan, one of Pakistan's leading supreme court advocates and a former vice president of the Human Rights Commission of Pakistan, to the president of the Supreme Court Bar Association. *Daily Times* report "Aitzaz Refuses to Join Constitutional Reforms Body," 23 December 2005.

19 Author interview with Sharifuddin Pirzada, Islamabad, spring 2006.

20 Indian prime minister Indira Gandhi had ordered her chief of air staff to draw up plans for such an operation. For details on the planning and US intervention in the raid, see below.

21 Zia's statement was issued on 13 February 1984.

22 Author interview with K. Subrahmanyam, New Delhi, spring 2006.

23 Bharat Karnad, *Nuclear Weapons and Indian Security: The Realist Foundations of Strategy* (Macmillan, New Delhi, 2002), pp. 346–7.

24 During this shopping trip, the Israelis had proposed a trade. If New Delhi gave Jerusalem technical data on the MiG-23 combat aircraft supplied to India by the Soviet Union, the Israelis would pass to India classified manuals it had obtained from the US that would enable New Delhi to jam the radar frequencies used by the new F-16 fighters that had recently arrived in Islamabad from Fort Worth, Texas. The electronic warfare equipment bought from Israel arrived at the Indian air force's Jamnagar base in Gujarat in March 1983. See Karnad, p. 346.

25 An interview with Raja Ramanna, director of India's Bhabha Atomic Research Center, appeared in "India Is Pursuing Uranium Enrichment Technology," *Nuclear Fuel*, 28 February 1983, pp 3–4.

26 They met during an IAEA session in the autumn of 1983.

27 Author interviews in New Delhi in the winter and summer of 2006. For another account, see George Perkovich, *India's Nuclear Bomb: The Impact on Global*

Proliferation (University of California Press, Berkeley, 1999), p. 241.

28 Confidential State Department memo, from US Consul, Lahore, to Secretary of State, Washington, DC, Pakistan's Nuclear Scientist Says more Nuclear Centers Possible, 24 December 1984. See also NSA 02164.

29 The "rain fire" phrase was recalled by K. Subrahmanyam. For more on India's response, see Karnad. The US State Department also pointed to the obvious subtext in a classified cable: "Khan's comments seem meant to serve as a message that a preemptory attack on Pakistan's nuclear center would not stop their nuclear program." See also the above Confidential State Department memo, Pakistan's Nuclear Scientist Says More Nuclear Centers Possible.

30 "Lahore Civic Reception in Honor of Chinese President," Xinhua General Overseas News Service, 7 March 1984. "Pakistan Has No Atomic Bomb, Says Pakistani Foreign Office Spokesman," Xinhua General Overseas News Service, 28 March 1984. Author interviews with senior Israeli intelligence sources in the winter of 2006 drew out the claim that Israeli intelligence, too, had learned that China had agreed to test Pakistan's nuclear device.

31 A raft of stories in the *Financial Times* and *Observer* created ripples on Capitol Hill, especially Tony Walker and Alain Cass, "Peking N-technology Talks Likely for Shultz," *Financial Times*, 1 February 1983, and also, a little later, Simon Henderson, "U.S. Warns Pakistan on Enriching Uranium," *Financial Times*, 7 December 1984. See also 27 March reports in the *Financial Times* which related how India, too, suspected that China was collaborating with Pakistan on its nuclear program and Pakistan's response, "Pakistan Denies A-bomb Allegation," 9 April 1984.

32 Author interview with Len Weiss, Virginia, spring 2006.

33 George Crile, *Charlie Wilson's War* (Grove Press, New York, 2003), p. 278.

34 Dale Nelson, "Committee Overrides Administration Objections," Associated Press, 28 March 1984.

35 "The Senate Foreign Relations Committee has Reversed a Decision to Block," *Nucleonics Week*, 12 April 1984, p. 8.

36 The letter was sent on 29 May 1984.

37 Quoted in Kux, p. 272.

38 Author interview with K. M. Arif, Islamabad, spring 2006.

39 See Russell D. Renka, Speeches and Other Media Uses by Ronald Reagan, 40th President of the United States: <www.cstl-cla.semo.edu/Renka/Modern_Presidents/reagan_speeches>.

40 "Cranston Says Pakistan Can Make A-Bomb," *New York Times*, 21 June 1984.

41 Ibid.

42 Ibid.

43 Leslie H. Gelb, "Pakistan Tie Imperils US–China Nuclear Pact," *New York Times*, 22 June 1984.

44 From Secretary of State to US Ambassador, Islamabad, Cranston Nuclear Speech, June 1984, guidance prepared by NEA. See also NSA documents on Pakistan for a running account of Cranston's demands on Pakistan and China.

45 Author interviews with Robert Gallucci, Washington, 2006. This view was echoed in multiple interviews over the same period with former senior State Department analysts and officials, who all remarked that US authority was being undermined by its duplicity over Pakistan.

46 In 1984 the Soviet Union got that point precisely. The US embassy in Moscow highlighted two lengthy articles from the state newspaper, *Pravda*. Debating the effectiveness of the global non-proliferation regime, the articles argued that while for twenty years the number of nuclear nations had been fixed by purposeful legislation, US political and military support for a number of nations that were near-nuclear states, including Pakistan and Israel, threatened to jeopardize this outcome. See Confidential Briefing from the US Embassy, Moscow, to the Department of State and the US Ambassador to the IAEA in Vienna, March 1984, and Soviet Press Critical of US Non-Proliferation Policy, NSA 02122, 23 March 1984. In the latter, an analyst warned: "The articles imply that US aid to these nations—such as the sale of F-16s to Pakistan—encourages their nuclear ambitions ... We are going to have a difficult time in the up and coming Non-Proliferation Treaty talks ... We can also expect to hear more about the non-proliferation implications of US policies towards Israel and Pakistan."

47 FBI surveillance had begun on 20 October 1983.

48 Mohamedy contacted the company on 23 March 1984 to pay a bill of $3,187. See Rick Atkinson, "Use in Arms Feared; Nuclear Parts Sought by Pakistanis," *Washington Post*, 21 July 1984.

49 An investigator close to the inquiry said: "They called a Houston freight forwarder, AEI, and asked the company to pick up a package for export to Pakistan." See Atkinson.

50 "Pakistanis Accused of Moving Nuke Parts," United Press International, 17 July 1984.

51 The statement read: "Pakistan does not deny that it has an R&D program on uranium enrichment at Kahuta. But it is of a modest scale and is designed entirely for ... meeting Pakistan's future power generation requirements ... Pakistan has no team for designing nuclear weapons ... For its non-existent nuclear weapons program Pakistan has neither sought nor received assistance from China."

52 8 August 1984. <http://www.reagan.utexas.edu/archives/speeches/1984/80884b.htm>.

53 A senior Indian air force officer later disclosed the Jaguars were hidden in the woods adjacent to the airfield at Ambala as part of a passive air defense drill. See Perkovich, p. 258.

54 The CIA briefed the Senate select committee on intelligence on 13 September 1984.

55 Classified telegrams seen by the authors in Jerusalem, 2006, copies of which were verified by former US State Department officials in Washington in the summer of 2006.

56 Author interview with K. M. Arif, Rawalpindi, spring 2006.

57 On 15 September 1984 Congress approved a bill to aid Pakistan with another $630 million for 1985. George Shultz said: "We have full faith in President Zia's assurance that Pakistan will not make the bomb." John Glenn responded: "We cannot sacrifice the great idea of non-proliferation on the altar of Afghanistan." See Glenn material placed on congressional record on 20 September 1995, p. S13962 and ff.

58 The letter was dated 12 September 1984. See David Ignatius, "US Pressuring Pakistan to Abandon Controversial Nuclear-Arms Program," *Wall Street Journal*, 25 October 1984.

59 See Arnold Raphel to Secretary of State, Your Meeting with Pakistan Foreign Minister: Additional Talking Points, NSA 02149, 27 September 1984. Reagan's letter and the subsequent hand-holding of the Pakistanis is referred to also in NSA 02150 and 02152.

60 Arnold Raphel to Secretary Shultz, NSA E10.

61 The story of this letter was told to the authors by General Arif. Author interview with K. M. Arif, Rawalpindi, spring 2006.

62 This letter was written to Zahid Malik, then the editor of the Pakistan *Observer*, in August 1999. It was later reproduced in *Dr. A. Q. Khan Research Laboratories 1976–2001, 25 Years of Excellence and National Service*, Islamabad, 31 July 2001. Author archive.

63 The delegation visited Pakistan in December 1984 and consisted of senators John Glenn, Sam Nunn, Bennett Johnston and James Sasser and several staffers.

64 Author interview with Sharifuddin Pirzada, Islamabad, spring 2006.

65 Author interview with Len Weiss, Virginia, spring 2006.

66 Sam Nunn served as a senator from 1972–96 and was chairman of the Senate armed services committee and the permanent subcommittee on investigations.

67 See Steve Coll, *Ghost Wars* (Penguin Press, New York, 2004).

68 Author interview with Len Weiss, Virginia, spring 2006.

69 Atkinson; "Pakistanis Accused of Moving Nuke Parts."

70 John J. Fialka, "Nuclear Club: Set to Explode?—Nuclear Spread: How Pakistan Secured US Devices in Canada to Make Atomic Arms—Despite Proliferation Barriers, Nation Will Soon Have Ability to Produce Bombs—Jitters in India and the West," *Wall Street Journal*, 26 November 1984.

71 Ibid.

72 Author interview with Len Weiss, Virginia, spring 2006.

73 Author telephone interviews with Peter Galbraith, 2006.

74 Ibid.

75 The Senate foreign relations committee adopted this amendment for debate on 28 March 1984.

76 It was written by Hans Binnendijk, Republican deputy staff director, Senate foreign relations committee.

77 It was passed by the Senate foreign relations committee on 3 April 1984.

78 12 February 1985, Public Papers of President Ronald W. Reagan, Ronald Reagan Presidential Library, University of Texas <www.reagan.utexas.edu>.

79 This episode is referred to by William E. Burrows and Robert Windrem, *Critical Mass* (Simon & Schuster, New York, 1994). Steve Bryen, however, declined on several occasions to be interviewed for this book, but the allegation was confirmed by several others in the CIA including Richard Barlow, the CIA's foremost expert on Pakistan's nuclear program, who worked as the Defense Department's first non-proliferation intelligence officer at the Pentagon from 1989–90.

80 For more details of Khan's conviction and appeal, see the account of his Pakistani lawyer, S. M. Zafar in his Urdu book, *Mere Mash'hoor Muqaddame*. Extracts in English can be found in an article, "The Trial of a Nation," 1 December 2005, on the website <www.chowk.com>.

81 Ibid.

82 Lubbers was interviewed by Hilversum Nederland-3 TV Network for its *Zembla* current affairs program special report, "The Netherlands Atomic Bomb," 7 November 2005.

83 The allegations were also made by Robert Gallucci, author interviews, Washington, 2006. Norman Wulf served as deputy assistant director for non-proliferation and

regional arms control at ACDA from 1985–99 and then as the special representative of the president for nuclear non-proliferation until his retirement in late 2002. He also served as deputy assistant secretary of state at the Non-Proliferation Bureau in 2001 and 2002. Author interview with Norm Wulf, Virginia, spring 2006.

84 Author interview with Norm Wulf, Virginia, spring 2006.

85 Ibid.

86 Slebos was fined DM30,000.

87 *Zembla* TV report.

88 According to Peter Griffin, who visited Cire in Istanbul, his company still bore the Siemens logo on its buildings, which misrepresented the legitimacy of Cire's operation.

89 Migule received an eight-month suspended sentence and was fined DM30,000.

90 There were twenty-six centrifuge components added that year. See Milton Benjamin, "More Curbs Sought on A-Materials; Nations Widening List of Exports Subject to Controls," *Washington Post*, 3 January 1983.

91 The review was in June 1983. On 1 December representatives from Britain, Canada, the US, Japan, Italy, France and West Germany met to discuss the lists and finally proscribed certain countries from buying nuclear weapons technology—including Pakistan, although it had by then cold-tested its nuclear device and was preparing for a hot test.

92 Author interviews with Richard Barlow, Montana, USA, autumn 2006.

93 Reagan made this statement on 25 November 1985 as part of the Pressler amendment in the form of a letter to Congress.

94 Author interview with Howard Schaffer, Washington, autumn 2006.

95 The US State Department monitored the Lizrose episode and the involvement of German companies. Some of their findings were reported in a classified memo of 17 July 1986, Pakistan Getting Atomic Bomb through Back Door. The State Department, in other memos, made it clear that they had relied for information, initially, on the journalism of a German writer, Egmond Koch, who broadcast on the topic in 1986 for West German Broadcasting in a film entitled *Wanted ... Bomb Business*. He also wrote for *Stern* on the same subject, in the same year.

96 The British caller would later defend his actions by claiming he had ordered the steel only as a favor to his friend.

97 The approximate value was £1.4 million.

98 See also Egmond Koch, "FRG Firm Said to Export Uranium Enrichment Plant Design to Pakistan," *Stern*, 29 April 1987.

99 Peter Griffin—who claimed he had nothing to do with the Lizrose maraging trade—recalled meeting Qazi for lunch in Paris and being introduced to a Lizrose executive. The same executive welcomed many of Khan's European agents to his house in the smart Regent's Park area of central London. Author interviews with Peter Griffin, France, 2006–2007.

100 Interviews with authors in Berlin, 2006, by former intelligence officers working on non-proliferation. See also Koch, "FRG Firm Said to Export Uranium Enrichment Plant Design to Pakistan," *Stern*.

101 Ibid.

102 Approximately valued at £2 million. See Steve Weissman and Herbert Krosney, *The Islamic Bomb* (Times Books, New York, 1981) and Koch in *Stern*, "FRG

Firm Said to Export Uranium Enrichment Plant Design to Pakistan."

103 The order included steel containers, autoclaves, special pipes and a desublimator. See Koch as above and unclassified memo from US embassy in Bonn to secretary of state, March 1989, which reflected back on all of the cases and their histories.

104 Elder worked for MWB's parent company. See above for more details.

105 Ibid.

106 Ibid.

107 Ibid.

108 Interviews by the authors in the summer of 2006 in Berlin and Jerusalem with intelligence analysts who worked on Pakistan and non-proliferation.

109 Approximately £11.4 million.

110 Interviews by the authors in the summer of 2006 in Berlin and Jerusalem with intelligence analysts who worked on Pakistan and non-proliferation.

111 Murphy testimony to Senate subcommittee, 18 March 1987. See Foreign Operations, Export Financing and Related Programs Appropriations Act, 1996 (Senate— September 20, 1995), material placed into the record by Senator Glenn, *Congressional Record*, 20 September 1995, p. S13962.

112 Ibid.

7: A BOMB FOR THE UMMAH

1 In multiple interviews with British diplomats then stationed in Islamabad and with senior German and Israeli intelligence analysts in the winter and summer of 2006, conducted in Berlin, Jerusalem and London, they described how a kind of running total was kept on Pakistan's spending by the West's intelligence community. The CIA and European intelligence got hold of suppliers' manifests and even faxes from Pakistan in which the orders were made. They intercepted phone calls and had sources within the nuclear industry, too. Using these multiple means, a calculation was reached of the value of Pakistan's nuclear imports. From this, the intelligence community extrapolated, working out what ancillary equipment Pakistan needed to run its systems, to give a running total. The rake-off figures were similarly totted up, using human sources and electronic interception. Often, and in later years when the role of German companies in supplying Khan became more obvious, a combination of public and private sources (and often investigative journalism in *Stern, Der Spiegel* and British and American newspapers) was relied on to analyze spending. See, for example, a range of memos from US embassies or consuls in West Germany to the State Department, NSA, 02613, 02614, 02620, 02621, 02623, 02625, 02626, NSA, George Washington University, Washington, DC.

2 Author interview with Mirza Aslam Beg, Islamabad, spring 2006. Beg said he had made the review when he ascended to the top military job in Pakistan, becoming chief of the army staff in 1988 after the death of President Zia in a plane crash.

3 <http://www.imf.org/external/country/PAK/index.htm?pn=8>.

4 Ghulam Ishaq Khan's firm hand over KRL finances was confirmed to the authors by K. M. Arif, Mirza Aslam Beg, Sharifuddin Pirzada and former ISI directors General Asad Durrani and General Hamid Gul.

5 A senior State Department official, who served at this time in non-proliferation, as

well as former analysts in non-proliferation at the CIA and the Pentagon, all raised worries about the raiding of US cash. There were attempts, they claimed, to get this issue "out into the open," but Casey at the CIA beat them down. "There was no sympathy with our viewpoint in the White House," said the State Department source. "But they had a fairly explicit idea of what they were losing in cash."

6 Author interview with K. M. Arif, Rawalpindi, spring 2006.

7 For 1985, the CIA and Saudis put in $600 million, with Congress topping up with another $300 million. Arif's figures were strenuously contested in author interviews with US and European intelligence sources, London, Washington and Jerusalem, 2006.

8 The inquiry began in 1982, according to British and German government analysts in the non-proliferation field, who talked to the authors in the summer of 2006.

9 The US attempted to monitor the movement of weapons purchases and aid, using devious and often covert electronic means, including trackers. However, two senior ISI sources, interviewed by the authors in Islamabad and Rawalpindi in the winter of 2006, claimed the agency was wise to this maneuver and removed the tags, which were sent forward while the shipments went elsewhere. Norman Wulf, who would rise to become one of the most senior non-proliferation officials within the State Department, also commented on how Robert Gates and others claimed to be "pissed off" at having had to watch Pakistan "ripping off funding."

10 This method of funding was confirmed to the authors by General Mohammed Youssaf, former ISI head of the Afghan war, interview, Taxila, spring 2006. For more details on the funding of the Afghan war, see Steve Coll, *Ghost Wars* (Penguin Press, New York, 2004) and Dennis Kux, *The United States and Pakistan 1947–2000* (Woodrow Wilson Center Press, Washington, DC, 2001).

11 Interview with British non-proliferation analyst in spring 2006 in London, who worked with CIA and European counterparts on the KRL build-up.

12 Author interview with Dr. Shafiq ur-Rehman, Islamabad, spring 2006. In the 1980s and 1990s Shafiq entertained many of Khan's European suppliers in Dubai and spoke of seeing suitcases filled with cash passing through. In interviews with the authors in France, 2006–7, Griffin recalled: "I saw the worst of Dubai myself when people like Dr. Hashmi and Mohammed Farooq would be sitting in Tahir's office with bundles of money. One time at Tahir's apartment Dr. Hashmi waved a bundle of dollar notes in my son's face and said, 'Your father is stupid. If he were clever he'd be making real money like this.' My son, who was only about twenty at the time, replied that they were looting their country, something his father would never do." See also The BCCI Affair, A Report to the Committee on Foreign Relations, United States Senate, by Senator John Kerry and Senator Hank Brown, December 1992, 102nd Congress 2nd session, Senate print 102–40.

13 The audit was begun in 1988 and concluded in 1991 after the bank collapsed. See The BCCI Affair: report John Kerry and Hank Brown. The CIA also suspected this money was destined for Khan, having spent several years tracking payments between BCCI's London branches and the Pakistan High Commission. Author interviews with Richard Barlow and other CIA analysts, USA, 2006.

14 Millions of dollars from Pakistan government accounts held at BCCI were funnelled through the BCCI Foundation in the 1980s, according to former employees. Author interviews Karachi, Islamabad and London, 2006. See also The BCCI Affair: report by John Kerry and Hank Brown.

15 The BCCI Affair report by John Kerry and Hank Brown.

16 This quote was recalled by Abdur Sakhia, a former senior BCCI official, interviewed on 7 October 1991 for the The BCCI Affair report by John Kerry and Hank Brown.

17 The transfer was made on 26 May 1985. See The BCCI Affair report by John Kerry and Hank Brown.

18 Ibid. Chinoy was interviewed by the Senate foreign relations committee and had served with the bank in the late 1970s and early 1980s.

19 Author interview, London, 2006.

20 This conversation between Norm Wulf and Gates in 1990 was recounted by Norm Wulf in an interview with the authors in Virginia, spring 2006.

21 Author interview with Stephen Solarz, Washington, spring 2006.

22 Author interview with Mohammed Youssaf, Taxila, spring 2006.

23 Robert Gates, *From the Shadows* (Simon & Schuster, New York, 1996).

24 This was the figure by 1987. Author interview with Mohammed Youssaf. See also Coll.

25 The audit was confirmed to the authors by K. M. Arif and former ISI director General Hamid Gul.

26 The Stingers were introduced in 1986, at a time when Soviet helicopters were massacring the Afghan mujahideen. For more, see Coll.

27 Peter Griffin, author interviews, France, 2006–7.

28 The official inquiry was led by Lieutenant General Imran Khan, a corps commander.

29 Author interview with General Hamid Gul, Rawalpindi, spring 2006.

30 Author interviews with Hamid Gul and K. M. Arif, spring 2006, Rawalpindi. This figure was also referred to in Kux, p. 290.

31 Author interview with Agha Shahi, Islamabad, spring 2006.

32 Gates, p. 428. By November 1987 the CIA had learned of this timetable after George Shultz revealed that Soviet foreign minister Edvard Shevardnadze had told him as much earlier in the year.

33 Background briefings from three officers who served Zia, Islamabad and Rawalpindi, 2006. The discussions were also confirmed by Agha Shahi, Pakistan's former foreign minister, who was consulted by Zia, particularly in connection with discussions about Iran, where Shahi had considerable experience dealing with the ayatollah's regime. Author interview, Islamabad, spring 2006.

34 *Haaretz*, 9 September 1985. General Mati Peled, *Worldwide Report*, 9 January 1986, pp. 61–3.

35 Author interview.

36 Across the border in India the view was the same. The strategist and intelligence chief K. Subrahmanyam said: "They converted the NPT into one licensing unlimited nuclear proliferation by the five nuclear weapons powers, with a total ban on acquisition of weapons by all other nations. It was a hegemonic imposition of a discriminatory treaty dividing the world into five privileged ones and the rest." Author interview, New Delhi, spring 2006.

37 For more on the complexities of the Pakistan–Iran relationship and the conflict between General Zia and Ayatollah Khomeini, see Husain Haqqani, *Pakistan: From Mosque to Military* (Carnegie Endowment for International Peace, Washington, 2005).

38 For more on the bonds between the two nations, see Vali Nasr, *The Shia Revival* (W. W. Norton & Company, New York, 2006).

39 For more on Iran's role in the Afghan war, see Coll. For more on Pakistan's relationship with Iran over Afghanistan, see Nasr. That Zia was prepared to engage with the Iranians at this time was confirmed to the authors by K. M. Arif, Zia's chief of staff, who represented his president many times on official visits to Tehran.

40 Author interview with Dr. Shafiq ur-Rehman, Islamabad, spring 2006.

41 "German Concern Ends A-Contract," *New York Times*, 1 August 1 1979; *Facts on File World News Digest*, 3 August 1979, p. 586.

42 "Discovery of Uranium," BBC Summary of World Broadcasts, 21 December 1981.

43 *Nuclear Engineering International*, December 1984. China had assisted in its construction and was also thought to have supplied Iran with a research reactor and a small calutron, a device conceived by the Manhattan Project to separate the isotopes of uranium using a mass spectrometer rather than a centrifuge. *Economist*, 14 March 1992, p. 46.

44 Bushehr was bombed on 24 March 1984. See Anthony H. Cordesman, "Iran and Nuclear Weapons: A Working Draft," Center for Strategic and International Studies, 7 February 2000. There were other attacks, too, on 12 February 1985, 4 March 1985, 5 March 1985, 12 July 1986, 17 November 1987, 19 November 1987 and 19 July 1988. For information on the German leak, see April 1984 edition of *Jane's Defense Weekly* and also Dominique Leglu, *Liberation*, 29 April 1984.

45 Ibid.

46 The ore was mined in the Saghand region of Yazd province.

47 For details on the pact, see Alon Pinkas, "Thinking the Unthinkable About Iran," *Jerusalem Post*, 23 April 1992.

48 Also there was Seyyed Mohammad Haj Saeed, head of the directorate of research for the AEOI. Ayatollahi is currently the director of the National Organization for Civil Registration and Haj Saeed is a member of the AEOI.

49 This meeting and A. Q. Khan's collaboration with Eslami was reported to the US State Department by Alireza Jafarzadeh, National Council for the Resistance for Iran. Author interviews with Jafarzadeh, Washington, 2006.

50 This meeting was discussed with the authors by Agha Shahi, who said that Zia consulted him about the proposed nuclear trade. Author interview, Islamabad, spring 2006.

51 Ann Maclachlan, "Iran Seeking Way to Finish Bushehr Plant but Bonn Denies Exports," *Nucleonics Week*, 30 October 1986, pp. 4–5.

52 Kenneth R. Timmerman, Weapons of Mass Destruction: The Cases of Iran, Syria and Libya (Los Angeles, Simon Wiesenthal Center, 1992) quoted by the Nuclear Threat Initiative <http://www.nti.org/e_research/profiles/Iran/1825_1826.html>.

53 Mark Hibbs, "Agencies Trace Some Iraqi Urenco Know-How to Pakistan Re-Export," *Nucleonics Week*, 28 November 1991, p. 1.

8: THE PINEAPPLE UPSIDE-DOWN CAKE

1 The stories of Khan's vasectomy and affair were confirmed to the authors by Khan family friends. Author interviews, London and Islamabad, 2006.

2 Author interviews with Peter Griffin, France, 2006–7.

3 Today it is called Baniyas Square.

4 Author interviews with Peter Griffin, France, 2006–7.

5 Ibid.

6 Ibid.

7 Ibid. Also author interview with Dr. Shafiq ur-Rehman, Islamabad, spring 2006.

8 Dr. Shafiq recalled: "We shared the same car and were roommates in that appalling flat owned by *chacha* Farouq. You know it started very gently and small. I thought we were going to get on fine." Author interview, Islamabad, spring 2006.

9 Griffin recalled: "Khan was not an ostentatious man. He disliked eating out. Everyone would crowd into his apartment for a Pakistani-style meal, all using their fingers and lots of fruit. After twenty minutes all the food would be gone and some would go out shopping, others would go to sleep, while Khan did the business." Author interview.

10 This meeting was confirmed by close business associates of those who attended and by Dr. Shafiq ur-Rehman, whose father was there. Also see IAEA, Implementation of the NPT Safeguards Agreement in the Islamic Republic of Iran, Report by the Director General, GOV/2006/15, para. 11 <www.iaea.org>.

11 Implementation of the NPT Safeguards Agreement.

12 Ibid.

13 This estimate was made by the IAEA. Ibid.

14 Ibid. Khan's and Zia's low opinion of Iran's technical expertise was confirmed by Dr. Shafiq ur-Rehman in an author interview, Islamabad, spring 2006.

15 Author interview with Haroon Ahmed, Karachi, spring 2006.

16 Author interviews with Peter Griffin, France, 2006–7.

17 The judge had become famous for castigating the Pakistan army after the 1971 East Pakistan debacle, recommending the trials of the military chiefs and politicians. For a complete list of Khan's awards, medals and citations, see CV and pamphlet, *Dr. Abdul Qadeer Khan*, prepared by Sir Syed University of Engineering and Technology, Karachi, 26 March 2001, having awarded Khan an honorary doctorate. Author archive.

18 See the GIK Institute website, <http://www.giki.edu.pk/us/genesis.htm>.

19 Zahid Malik worked for *Hurmat* and describes the genesis of his long relationship with A. Q. Khan in his book, *Dr. A. Q. Khan and the Islamic Bomb* (Hurmat Publications, Islamabad, 1992).

20 The article was published in *Hurmat*, March 2–14, and included in a 1985 memorandum from the American consul in Karachi to the secretary of state. See also NSA 02223, NSA, George Washington University, Washington, DC.

21 This killing had actually occurred in 1980, but Khan brought it up with Zahid Malik specifically during this visit to Kahuta. For more on the killing, see Steve Weissman and Herbert Krosney, *The Islamic Bomb* (Times Books, New York, 1981).

22 A version of this story was researched by Terence Henry, "The Covert Option, Can Sabotage and Assassination Stop Iran from Going Nuclear?," *The Atlantic*, December 2005.

23 Peter Griffin recalled that Chowhan's most notable feature was a deep scar that ran the length of his palm, an injury sustained when he was a young officer in Kashmir, had found a frozen yak in a crevasse and attempted to butcher it. Chowhan's knife had slipped, gouging a deep cut into his hand.

24 NSA 02226, Rajiv Gandhi Asserts That the US Should Do More to Prevent Pakistan from Completing Nuclear Weapons Development, cable, 5 June 1985.

25 NSA 02228, Press Guidance for the Rajiv Gandhi Visit (June 1985), from the US

Department of State, Bureau of Near Eastern and South Asian Affairs, 5 June 1985.

26 The trip was planned for 25 September 1985.

27 NSA 02254, US Department of State Press Guidance, from the US Department of State, Bureau of Near Eastern and South Asian Affairs, 14 September 1985.

28 The certification was done under the terms of the Pressler amendment and was announced on 25 November 1985. It was supplementary to the president's requirement to make an annual statement on non-proliferation, in February of each year, regarding countries that posed a threat.

29 This aid package was announced on 17 July 1986.

30 See NSA 02318.

31 The certification was done under the terms of the Pressler amendment.

32 Author interview with Stephen Cohen, Washington, DC, spring 2006.

33 Abramowitz was also director of the State Department's Bureau of Intelligence and Research (INR). In an interview with the authors in Washington in the autumn of 2006, he said he recalled no palace coup but just a rumbling of suspicion about administration policy, which, it was feared, had been blinded by Afghan needs.

34 Author interview with Norm Wulf, Virginia, spring 2006.

35 Author interview with K. Subrahmanyam, New Delhi, spring 2006.

36 According to his then vice chief of army staff, General K. M. Arif. Author interview, Rawalpindi, spring 2006.

37 This story was told to the authors by Kuldip Nayar, Husain Haqqani, Dr. Shafiq ur-Rehman and K. M. Arif.

38 This phone call took place on 28 January 1987. Mushahid Hussain was getting married and had sent an invitation to Nayar, which had prompted him to call.

39 Author interview with Kuldip Nayar, New Delhi, spring 2006.

40 Ibid.

41 2 March 1987. See Public Papers of President Ronald W. Reagan, Ronald Reagan Presidential Library:
<http://www.reagan.utexas.edu/archives/speeches/1987/030287c.htm>.

42 In February 1987, General Zia travelled to India under the pretence of watching a cricket match and held talks with the Indian leadership to defuse the crisis. These talks were followed by additional talks in Islamabad between 27 February and 2 March at which both sides agreed to a phased troop withdrawal to peacetime positions. See <http://www.globalsecurity.org/military/world/war/brass-tacks.htm>.

43 *New York Times*, 2 March 1987.

44 Press interviews, 3 March 1987.

45 "Minister States 'No Desire' to Have Atomic Bomb," Karachi Overseas Service, 5 March 1987. See also Nuclear Threat Initiative (NTI) Nuclear and Missile Database, 2 April 1987 <http://www.nti.org/db/nuclear>.

46 Zia spoke to *Time* on 23 March 1987 and to *Defense Week* on 6 April 1987.

47 These allegations and the story concerning Pamela Bordes were first published in *Hurmat* newspaper in Islamabad and later by Malik.

48 The story concerning Mohammed Farooq was told by Dr. Shafiq ur-Rehman, author interview, Islamabad, spring 2006.

9: THE WINKING GENERAL

1 Oehler had joined the agency in 1972 and graduated from the National War College in 1981.

2 He became national intelligence officer in 1989.

3 The Apex system was introduced by Admiral Stansfield Turner, the CIA director under President Carter.

4 For more on the intelligence system, see Bob Woodward, *Veil: The Secret Wars of the CIA 1981–1987* (Simon & Schuster, London, 1987).

5 Author interviews with Richard Barlow, Montana, USA, autumn 2006.

6 Michael R. Gordon, "Pakistani Seized by US in a Plot on A-Arms Alloy," *New York Times*, 15 July 1987.

7 Configured in 1985 following the case of the Lahori smuggler Nazir Ahmed Vaid, the amendment signed by Representative Stephen Solarz provided for a cut-off to any country that attempted to export controlled items with nuclear applications from the US. "US Pressing Pakistan on Export Plot," *New York Times*, 16 July 1987.

8 That contact happened on 5 November 1986. See also Hedrick Smith, "Inside Pakistan's Continuing Quest for Nuclear Weapons," *New York Times Magazine*, 9 March 1988.

9 "2 Charged in Plan on Pakistani Arms," *New York Times*, 29 July 1987.

10 Author interviews with Richard Barlow.

11 For more details on the uses of beryllium in nuclear devices, see Frank Barnaby, *How to Build a Nuclear Bomb* (Granta Books, London, 2003).

12 Author interviews with Richard Barlow.

13 Author interviews with Len Weiss and other staffers who recalled how the White House rallied as the bad news on Pakistan mounted.

14 Amy Kurland was the assistant district attorney. See Gordon.

15 Author interview with Richard Barlow. See also Bryan Brumley, "Senator Seeks Sanctions Against Pakistan," Associated Press, 21 July 1987.

16 David Warren was the head of US Customs and delivered a testimony before Congress at Armacost's request. See Brumley.

17 Gordon.

18 Ibid.

19 Pell said: "With alarming regularity, Pakistan has violated its commitments not to manufacture nuclear weapons and not to enrich uranium. After each previous Pakistani nuclear outrage the administration has offered excuses and argued that a hard-line approach would be counter-productive." Brumley.

20 Michael Armacost arrived in Islamabad on 5 August 1987. See also NSA 02254.

21 The allegation that the State Department attempted to make this case look like private profiteering comes from Richard Barlow. The allegation was supported by Stephen Solarz, Senator John Glenn, and by Len Weiss, author interview, Virginia, spring 2006.

22 For more on the arrest warrant, see "Pakistan Reports a Nuclear Inquiry," *New York Times*, 22 July 1987. For Pakistan statements, see Elaine Sciolino, *New York Times*, 2 August 1987; "Prime Minister Affirms 'Peaceful' Nuclear Program," Karachi Domestic Service, 24 August 1987, and "Noorani Reiterates Stand on Atomic Program," Karachi Domestic Service, 28 August 1987.

23 In fact, these briefings were held prior to Armacost's flight. The two hearings were scheduled before the House foreign affairs committee on 22 July 1987, one open, one closed.

24 According to Richard Barlow the official authority should have come from the acting director of central intelligence, who at that time was Robert Gates, but it was possible that "Einsel might have just filled the vacuum" and pushed himself forward. Author interviews, Richard Barlow, 2006–7.

25 Author interviews with Richard Barlow.

26 Charles Burke was the CIA's chief of the Nuclear Energy Division.

27 Steven Aoki was a specialist in non-proliferation. At the time of the Solarz hearing he held positions in the bureaus of Politico-Military Affairs and Near Eastern and South Asian Affairs at the State Department, specializing in non-proliferation, counter-terrorism and regional security.

28 The CIA used a specific hierarchy, with an Office at its summit, beneath which was a Division, and beneath that was a Branch.

29 For more on Iran–Contra, see Woodward, *Veil*. The CIA had been barred from funding the overthrow of the government in Nicaragua by the Boland amendment, named after Edward Boland (Democrat, Massachusetts), chairman of the House intelligence committee, who backed the amendment to the Intelligence Authorization Act on 8 December 1982.

30 This was Barlow's view.

31 Ultimately these would be watered down and George H. W. Bush, when he became president, would issue pardons. For more, see Woodward, *Veil*.

32 Author interviews with Peter Griffin, France, 2006–7.

33 Author telephone interview with Inam ul-Haq, Lahore, spring 2006.

34 Author interviews with Richard Barlow.

35 Even today most of these cases remain classified, although Barlow stands by his claim that there were scores.

36 Peck was overheard by a senior colleague from the State Department who was sitting in the hallway and related the story to the authors in an interview in Washington in the autumn of 2006.

37 Author interviews with Robert Gallucci, Washington, 2006.

38 Barlow took with him some impressive references. Norman Terrell, an assistant director at ACDA, who went on to work on policy for NASA's Washington bureau, found Barlow performed "his duties with a degree of competence and dedication that is normally expected of more experienced and senior officers." Dean F. Rust, then an ACDA deputy division chief, who would become acting deputy director of the State Department's Non-Proliferation Bureau, wrote that Barlow was so able and trustworthy that he was allowed access to the "most sensitive intelligence available to the US government in the area of non-proliferation," even though he was a junior.

39 Barlow's excessively honest streak would be used against him during subsequent investigations into his professional conduct by the Department of Defense.

40 "US Indicts 3 in the Export of Equipment to Pakistan," *New York Times*, 18 July 1987.

41 The Californian couple, Rona and Arnold Mandel, from Grass Valley, always protested their innocence. The focus of the legal dispute was whether prosecutors must turn over to defense lawyers classified documents showing why the equipment

NOTES

was subject to export controls in the first place. The defense wanted to be able to question the equipment's effect on national security. In August 1988, US district judge Lawrence Karlton ruled that the government must produce records pertaining to its administrative decision to place the items on the Department of Commerce's commodity control list. But a three-judge panel of the US 9th circuit Court of Appeals, in San Francisco, overturned Karlton's ruling on 14 September 1990: "Whereas a court is well suited to determine whether a prior deportation or classification hearing was fairly and properly conducted, it is ill suited to determine whether a particular oscilloscope has an impact on war and peace." In September 1991 a federal judge sentenced both to prison terms. See also Steve Coll, "Banking System Aided Pakistani Nuclear Plan; No Special BCCI Role in Arms Scheme," *Washington Post*, 11 August 1991.

42 McGoldrick was the director of the State Department's Office of Non-Proliferation.
43 Author interviews with Richard Barlow. See also Seymour Hersh, "On the Nuclear Edge," *New Yorker*, 29 March 1993.
44 Author interviews with Richard Barlow.
45 Letter quoted to the authors by Richard Barlow.
46 This document is in Richard Barlow's archive but remains classified so cannot be quoted directly by the authors.
47 This comes from Barlow's subsequent report to Gordon Oehler and Charles Burke. Barlow archive, classified document.
48 According to Richard Barlow.
49 As told to the authors by Richard Barlow, who retains a large archive of declassified documents obtained by Barlow himself and his lawyers during his work with the inspector general for State and as a result of the legal process to gain Barlow restitutions.
50 The form of the certification was a letter from Reagan to speaker Jim Wright (Democrat, Texas): "The administration has fulfilled its legal obligation to keep the appropriate committees of Congress fully and currently informed of activities in Pakistan which are significant from the proliferation standpoint." Based on the statutory standard, one that had been created in 1985 to shelter the Islamic Republic while it did service for the US, Reagan wrote: "I have concluded that Pakistan does not possess a nuclear explosive device." 17 December 1987.
51 "Businessman Convicted in Pakistan Nuclear Plot," *New York Times*, 18 December 1987. Pervez was ultimately cleared on appeal.
52 <http://www.reagan.utexas.edu/archives/speeches/1988/011588d.htm>.
53 Certificates held by Richard Barlow.
54 Clarke was referring to investigations run by the Department of State.
55 Brubaker worked at the Department of Defense Office for Non-Proliferation Policy.
56 This statement was required annually under the terms of the Non-Proliferation Act 1978 and was separate from and supplementary to the President's requirement to certify annually that Pakistan had no bomb under the terms of the Pressler amendment.
57 <http://www.reagan.utexas.edu/archives/speeches/1988/032588f.htm>.
58 Robert Oakley, who was then the NSC's senior director for the Middle East and South Asia, recalled this message being given to Reagan by the NSC. Author interview, Washington, spring 2006.

59 Author interview with Robert Oakley.

60 Dennis Kux, *The United States and Pakistan 1947–2000* (Woodrow Wilson Center Press, Washington, 2001), pp. 286–8.

61 George Shultz, *Turmoil and Triumph: My Years as Secretary of State* (Charles Scribner & Sons, New York, 1993).

62 Author interview with Robert Oakley.

63 The Geneva accords to end the war in Afghanistan were signed in Geneva on 14 April 1988 by Eduard Shevardnadze, George Shultz, Zain Noorani and Afghan envoy Abdul Wakil, and marked a milestone in the winding down of the Cold War. For more, see Kux, pp. 289–91.

64 Leonard S. Spector, *Nuclear Ambitions: The Spread of Nuclear Weapons, 1989–90* (Boulder, Colorado, Westview, 1990), p. 100.

65 Sahabzada Yaqub Khan had resigned from office in the autumn of 1987 after falling out with Mohammad Junejo, Pakistan's prime minister, who was in conflict with Zia. After Zia dismissed Junejo on 29 May 1988, Yaqub Khan was reinstated as foreign minister.

66 Author interview with Robert Oakley.

67 Ibid.

68 This regional pact was described to the authors by Mirza Aslam Beg and Hamid Gul in interviews in Islamabad and Rawalpindi, spring 2006.

69 Author interview with Mirza Aslam Beg, Rawalpindi, spring 2006.

70 Suspicions about a Pakistan–Iran pact were first aired in the press in June 1988. See *Al-Watan* newspaper, Kuwait, 13 June 1988, and *Kayhan International*, Tehran, 14 June 1988.

71 According to Dr. Shafiq ur-Rehman and Haroon Ahmed, author interviews, Islamabad and Karachi, 2006–7.

72 For more, see Rai Muhammad Saleh Azam, *When Mountains Move: The Story of Chagai* (Islamabad, 1998).

73 25 May 1988 was first firing of the Hatf. According to the CIA, the former had a range of about 60 km and the latter 300 km. See Lionel Barber, "Pakistan Tests 'Nuclear' Missile," *Financial Times*, 25 May 1988.

74 This deal with Saudi Arabia was tracked from the US by Robert Gallucci at the State Department, Norm Wulf at ACDA and Richard Barlow at the CIA. Agha Shahi, too, in author interviews, commented on the Saudi intentions and goals and backed up the thesis concerning their desire for a finished product rather than a process.

10: GANGSTERS IN BANGLES

1 Author interview with K. M. Arif, Rawalpindi, spring 2006.

2 Zia's reasons for getting on the plane come from an author interview with Mirza Aslam Beg, Zia's vice chief of army staff, Rawalpindi, spring 2006. Also, for more on Zia's character, see Husain Haqqani, *Pakistan: From Mosque to Military* (Carnegie Endowment for International Peace, Washington, 2005) and K. M. Arif, *Working with Zia* (Oxford University Press, Karachi, 1995).

3 Durrani was then the commander of 1 Armoured Division in Multan. Author interview with K. M. Arif.

4 There was no truth in the rumor that the Americans were also unexpected

passengers. Although there was a US embassy plane running a shuttle service between Rawalpindi and Bahawalpur on that day, it was fully loaded with demonstrators from General Dynamics, which manufactured the M1 Abrams. Looking back over the manifests, General Arif established that as early as 13 August 1988, Major General Durrani had rostered Raphel and Wassom to fly back on Pak 1 with Zia. If this was sabotage, then the deaths of the high-flying diplomat Raphel and his attaché were part of the plan or collateral damage.

5 The Pakistan investigation claimed to have found traces of phosphorus, chlorine, potassium, antimony and pentaerythritol tetranitrate. See also Barbara Crossette, "Who Killed Zia," *World Policy Journal*, Vol. XXII, No. 3 (2005).

6 The mangoes and tanks were gifts for those who had attended the Bahawalpur display and were the only things not to have been searched before being loaded. Robert Oakley, then at the National Security Council and very soon to be drafted in as US ambassador to Islamabad, said in an interview with the authors that an independent US inquiry had found no evidence of foul play. Author interview, Washington, spring 2006.

7 See Haqqani, and Dennis Kux, *The United States and Pakistan 1947–2000* (Woodrow Wilson Center Press, Washington, 2001).

8 The Afghan intelligence bureau was known as Khad. For more on their infiltrations see Steve Coll, *Ghost Wars* (Penguin Press, New York, 2004). The KGB and Khad had used VX gas before and the final report into the crash would reveal small amounts of VX explosive used in a controlled charge—like the one needed to blow open a gas canister. See Christopher Andrew and Vasili Mitrokhin, *The Mitrokhin Archive II: The KGB and the World* (Allen Lane, London, 2005).

9 Author interview with Moshe Ya'alon, former head of Israel's military intelligence and until 2005 chief of staff to the Israel Defense Forces, Washington, spring 2006.

10 While Hekmatyar's men were frenzied in their attacks against the army of occupation, they were equally murderous with Afghanis in opposing parties, giving rise to the joke doing the rounds in Washington that Hekmatyar had a better strike rate than the Soviet 40th Army. For more, see Coll.

11 For more on Hekmatyar's relationships with Zia, the ISI and jihadis, see Coll.

12 See Andrew and Mitrokhin, *Mitrokhin Archive II*. One of the missiles was unsuccessfully fired at Zia's personal jet as it came in to land in Islamabad in January 1982. A second was launched on 7 February 1982, missing the same jet as it came in to Lahore with the president on board.

13 Author interview with Sharifuddin Pirzada, Islamabad, spring 2006.

14 Also aboard was Major General Jehangir Karamat, director general of military operations, and Brigadier General Ejaz Amjad.

15 Author interview with Mirza Aslam Beg, Rawalpindi, spring 2006.

16 General Beg's first call was to Lieutenant General Hamid Gul, who had taken over as chief of the ISI the previous year.

17 Born in 1915 to a family without patronage or influence, Ghulam Ishaq Khan grew up in the village of Ismail Khel in the district of Bannu, marooned in Pakistan's remote and insular Northwest Frontier Province, a small community famous for little apart from its sticky dates and nutty *halwa*. He had clawed his way up in a manner that was fabled, his rise supposedly demonstrating that in the Islamic Republic of Who You Know, it also mattered what you know. An ascetic,

modest Pashtun, he developed a reputation for severity and integrity. A religious man, by inclination a conservative, Ishaq Khan saw his duty as ensuring the stability of Pakistan and had a close circle of powerful friends who thought likewise.

18 The mosque was named after Faisal bin Abdul Aziz, the king of Saudi Arabia, who had donated more than $100 million for its construction, which began in the early 1970s.

19 Zia had suspended democracy several times, most recently by invoking the 8th amendment to the 1973 constitution on 29 May 1988, when he dismissed prime minister Junejo and the National Assembly on grounds of corruption and failing to maintain law and order. For more, see Kux, pp. 290–2.

20 The court ruled on 27 September 1988 on the legitimacy of the late president's dismissal of prime minister Junejo and the National Assembly and found that "the grounds given for the dissolution are so vague, general or non-existent that the orders are not sustainable in law."

21 Author interview with Hamid Gul, Rawalpindi, spring 2006.

22 Gul also said: "Right from the day the Jews were allowed to come back they wanted a state and they got a state. But the birth of that state was based on terrorism. The US would ultimately have to support this terrorism while trying to explain to its Muslim allies how it was critical to fight other kinds of terror. Churchill once said, is it not ironic that the Christ and the Antichrist were born in the same place?" Author interview.

23 Author interview with Hamid Gul. Aslam Beg, too, in an author interview, claimed that the nuclear program was to be accelerated so as to become truly effective and deployable.

24 Author interview with Mirza Aslam Beg, Rawalpindi, spring 2006.

25 Haqqani, p. 201. The story was originally told by General Sher Ali Khan, a soldier and diplomat who became minister for information for the dictator/president Yahya Khan in the 1960s.

26 IJI stood for Islami Jamhoori Ittehad, or Islamic Democratic Alliance.

27 In an interview with the authors, Robert Oakley said that US officials had been warned away after the CIA had attempted unsuccessfully to investigate the crash site.

28 Previously Powell had been senior military assistant to the defense secretary. This meeting was related to the authors by Robert Oakley in an interview in Washington, spring 2006.

29 Author interview with Robert Oakley, Washington, spring 2006.

30 Teresita Schaffer assumed this position in 1989.

31 Author interviews with Benazir Bhutto, Dubai, 2006.

32 Story as told to the authors by Peter Galbraith, telephone interviews, 2006, and Benazir Bhutto, Dubai, 2006.

33 For more on Benazir Bhutto's rise to power, see Benazir Bhutto, *Daughter of the East* (Hamish Hamilton, London, 1989), and Haqqani.

34 Author interview with Benazir Bhutto.

35 Bhutto, *Daughter of the East*.

36 Author interview with Husain Haqqani, Washington, spring 2006. See also Haqqani, *Pakistan: From Mosque to Military*.

37 These views were repeated to the authors in interviews with Hamid Gul and Mirza Aslam Beg, Rawalpindi, spring 2006. See also Haqqani.
38 Author interview with Husain Haqqani, Washington, spring 2006. Among those roped in were the leaders of Jamaat-e-Islami, an Islamic party credible among the middle classes and in universities. It took part in the vilification of Bhutto after being threatened with financial and political ruin by Hamid Gul.
39 Author interview with Husain Haqqani. See also Haqqani, ibid.
40 Haqqani, p. 207.
41 Author interview with General Beg, Rawalpindi, 2006.
42 The cable was sent in October 1988 from the American embassy in Islamabad to the Secretary of State in Washington. See also NSA 02607, George Washington University, Washington, DC. Also author interview with Robert Oakley, Washington, spring 2006.
43 Cable from the American embassy in Islamabad to the secretary of state, November 1988. See also NSA 02609. Oakley also reported: "Anti-PPP parties are eager for issues to use against Benazir, so we can expect these parties to keep picking up the nuclear issue, this in turn would force the PPP to take a tougher approach to the nuclear issue in order not to seem weak."
44 Author interviews with Benazir Bhutto, Dubai, 2006.
45 Author interview with Robert Oakley.
46 In his letter Bush did confirm that Pakistan had violated nuclear export controls and that "material, equipment or technology covered by that provision was to be used by Pakistan in the manufacture of a nuclear explosive device." For a good rundown on Pressler and presidential certifications, see also <http://www.fas.org/news/pakistan/1992/920731.htm>.
47 Author interviews with Norm Wulf, Virginia, spring 2006, Richard Barlow, Montana, autumn 2006, and Robert Gallucci, Washington, 2006.
48 Author interview with Sharifuddin Pirzada, Islamabad, spring 2006.
49 Author interviews with Benazir Bhutto, Dubai, 2006.
50 Ibid.
51 Author interview with Sharifuddin Pirzada, Islamabad, spring 2006.
52 Ibid.
53 Author interview with Robert Oakley, Washington, spring 2006.
54 Author interviews with Benazir Bhutto, Dubai, 2006.
55 These figures came from an author interview with Benazir Bhutto. For more details of Pakistan's economy, see G. T. Kurian, *The New Book of World Rankings* (New York, 1991).
56 For more on Musharraf's role in this conflict, see Pervez Musharraf, *In the Line of Fire* (Free Press, New York, 2006).
57 Author interview with Mirza Aslam Beg, Rawalpindi, spring 2006.
58 This episode concerning *The Satanic Verses* is described in Haqqani.
59 Author interview with Mirza Aslam Beg, Rawalpindi, spring 2006. Beg added that there was another sensitive matter on the agenda. "They wanted to discuss the Pakistan missile program. The US had also learned that we were developing a nuclear-capable missile that could strike deep into India. I played it down. The administration did not believe me."
60 Ibid.

61 Author interviews with Benazir Bhutto, Dubai, 2006.
62 Ghulam Ishaq Khan cited article 177 of Pakistan's constitution which gave the president authority over these appointments.
63 Author interview with Husain Haqqani, Washington, spring 2006.
64 Bhutto recalled: "I told Gul that the whole notion of strategic depth was wrong. I said we should get on with making a negotiated peace in Afghanistan. We didn't need a colony. We should get the Afghans to agree to the Durand Line [which historically demarcated the 1,500-mile border between the two countries]. Gul dismissed me. I said to him, 'Your policy is not strategic depth, it's strategic threat.' What these spies and generals wanted was a swath of theocracies: Turkey, Iran, Pakistan and Afghanistan. Gul disagreed. He said that through Afghanistan we gained access into Central Asia. He said the Durand Line would become a wedge between us and them. He wanted Islamists in power in Kabul, indebted to Pakistan and hostile to our enemies. He warned me to drop the idea." Author interviews, Dubai, 2006.
65 Author interviews with Benazir Bhutto, Dubai, 2006, Husain Haqqani, Washington, spring 2006, and Qazi Hussain Ahmed, emir of Jamaat-e-Islami, Islamabad, spring 2006.
66 Qazi Hussain Ahmed confirmed that Osama bin laden visited the Jamaat-e-Islami headquarters in Mansehra to strike the deal and soon afterwards Ahmed met bin Laden at Jamaat-e-Islami offices in Peshawar and Lahore. "Bin Laden was prepared to pay anything for buying this deal. We declined the request," Ahmed said. Author interview.

11: A GUEST OF THE REVOLUTIONARY GUARD

1 Gnehm served as deputy assistant secretary of defense for the Near East and South Asia.
2 <http://www.whitehouse.gov/nsc/hadleybio.html>.
3 Author interview with Richard Barlow, Montana, USA, 2006.
4 Author interview with Robert Oakley, Washington, spring 2006.
5 Gnehm invited Barlow to brief two policy coordination committee meetings, the main forum for flagging up crises.
6 For more on the work of the DIA, see Bob Woodward, *Veil: The Secret Wars of the CIA 1981–1987* (Simon & Schuster, London, 1987).
7 <http://www.globalsecurity.org/military/world/pakistan/f-16.htm>.
8 The value of the contract and General Dynamics' reliance on it comes from Richard Barlow.
9 Author interview with Richard Barlow.
10 Gnehm became deputy assistant secretary of state in the Bureau of Near Eastern and South Asian Affairs, later becoming the US ambassador to Kuwait.
11 Author interview with Richard Barlow.
12 Gerald Brubaker had asked Barlow to contact the staffers for the House foreign affairs committee.
13 Lionel Barber, "Pakistan Tests 'Nuclear' Missile," *Financial Times*, 25 May 1988.
14 Classified memo from joint staff and DIA, Washington, DC, to DIA CURINTEL or Current Intelligence, Washington, DC, February 1989; see also NSA 02617, George Washington University, Washington, DC.

15 <http://www.wisconsinproject.org/countries/pakistan/hatf.html>.

16 Author interview with Mirza Aslam Beg, Rawalpindi, spring 2006.

17 February 1989. Beg increasingly placed into the public domain stories about Pakistan's hardware development. These bits of news, always put into the Urdu press, were followed closely by the US embassy in Islamabad, which filed bulletins to the DIA in Washington, DC. See, for an example and as relates to SAM missiles, NSA 02615.

18 Peter Griffin, author interviews, France, 2006–7.

19 Sura Al Qamar, verses 44–6, in which Hazrat Zubair, a companion of the Prophet, killed his enemy using a striking lance during the battles of Badr.

20 This was confirmed by Benazir Bhutto and Robert Oakley, author interviews.

21 The telegram was from Oakley, at the US embassy in Islamabad, to the secretary of defense in Washington, and also to the DIA in Washington, in February 1989. See also NSA 02616. See also: <http://www.wisconsinproject.org/countries/pakistan/hatf.html>.

22 The account of this failed initiative came from an interview with Benazir Bhutto.

23 Ibid.

24 Hamid Gul was sacked on 31 May 1989. Author interview with Benazir Bhutto.

25 Benazir Bhutto also established a committee to review how the intelligence agencies in Pakistan functioned. The former Air Chief Marshal Zulfiqar Ali Khan undertook the ISI inquiry. After Bhutto appointed General Kallue, General Beg made him persona non grata, snubbing him if ever they met, preventing him from attending the corps commanders' conferences. Beg also temporarily transferred all of ISI's responsibility for the proxy war in Kashmir to the Pakistan army intelligence directorate, working under the chief of the general staff.

26 The bombing campaign lasted from January 1989 to July 1990.

27 Leading business organizations brought in kidnap experts from the US and Italy after more than eighty businessmen had to pay ransoms over six months in 1990. For more on these efforts to destabilize Bhutto, see Husain Haqqani, *Pakistan: From Mosque to Military* (Carnegie Endowment for International Peace, Washington, DC, 2005).

28 The army accused the prime minister of failing to act when the PPP's student wing became involved in tit-for-tat clashes with the Muttahida Qaumi Movement (MQM), a militarized party that represented the interests of Muslims who had emigrated from India. When Bhutto finally asked for assistance from the army, it requested the power to set up military courts in the heartland of her constituency at Larkana, in Sindh Province, something that would have sidestepped the democratic process.

   Instead, on 27 May 1990, the provincial government in Sindh launched its own crackdown, imposing curfews wherever the MQM had a stronghold, with the police given shoot-on-sight orders. Crowds of MQM supporters spilled from the Hyderabad Fort holding prayer books above their heads. However, with the PPP claiming there were snipers in their midst, an allegation never verified, the police fired on the crowd, killing twenty-one women and children. Scores more died in the riots that followed. It was the trigger that the military needed and the Pakistan army imposed military rule in Sindh, forcing its way into the crisis to restore peace and further weakening Bhutto.

29 Author interview with Benazir Bhutto.

30 See Haqqani, p. 217.

31 The exercise was conducted from 14 November to 23 December 1989. For details from the vantage point of Pakistani defense experts, see <http://www.pakdef.info/pids/paf/highmark2.html>.

32 Author interview with Mirza Aslam Beg, Rawalpindi, spring 2006.

33 The BND information was also repeated by *Der Spiegel* on 24 July 1989.

34 The hearing was on 2 August 1989.
<http://www.fas.org/news/pakistan/1992/920731.htm>.

35 The hearing was on 2 August 1989.
<http://www.fas.org/news/pakistan/1992/920731.htm>.

36 Ibid.

37 Deposition made by Richard Barlow. Barlow recalled: "On 4 August 1989, slightly more than a month after I had been promoted, my acting supervisor, Gerald Brubaker (now deceased) suddenly handed me a termination notice with no warning whatsoever. When I challenged his authority to do this, he declared that 'Steve Hadley has approved this' (my firing). I doubt he would have fabricated this since he knew me well enough to know that I would look into this. In fact, I tried to see Hadley repeatedly almost immediately. I spoke with Hadley's military assistant, Colonel Sellars, and have him on tape (from my answering machine) confirming my firing in Hadley's name. Brubaker immediately called the DIA office where some of the relevant intelligence was stored and removed my access to it, and told them I was headed to the Congress to blow the whistle." Author interview.

38 As above. The military assistant was Colonel Sellars. A formerly secret memo from Stephen O'Toole, chief of the security division, Department of Defense, records the allegations made against Barlow, including claims that he was receiving treatment "by psychiatrists and psychologists."

39 These allegations were made by Richard Barlow and supported by documents obtained under the Freedom of Information Act, including Brubaker's fabricated "memo of conversation" written on 11 August which described an imaginary conversation in which Barlow had supposedly walked into his office and expressed his "intention" to go Congressman Stephen Solarz (a member then of the House permanent select committee on intelligence), via House foreign affairs committee staffers Robert Hathaway and Arch Roberts (the people whom Brubaker had ordered Barlow to contact), to "straighten them out" about a classified CIA briefing on Pakistan's clandestine nuclear procurement activities. The Brubaker memo also falsely stated that Barlow had learned of this CIA briefing secondhand. The nearest Barlow had got to Congress was the transcript of the committee hearing in which Hughes and Schaffer had said that Pakistan's F-16s would not be nuclear-capable. All allegations in this Brubaker memo were dismissed by investigations chief Stephen O'Toole at the Pentagon in a memo written by him to Barlow's lawyers, which was classified but that has been seen by the authors.

40 The allegations made by Brubaker were again dismissed by the investigations chief at the Defense Department, as above, who found: "No information was developed in the investigation to support the contention that Mr. Barlow would fail to protect classified information. There is a considerable amount of detail in the investigative report which refutes the allegations made against him." Brubaker's claims were also cited by the inspector general for the State Department, Sherman Funk, who also found that all of the reasons given for revoking Barlow's clearances were spurious. Sherman

Funk to Derek J. Vander Schaaf, Joint Investigation by the DoD, DoS, and CIA Inspectors General Pertaining to a Former DoD Employee, 17 September 1993. Author archive.

41 The chain of command for the decision to dismiss Barlow was revealed after he won partial disclosure under the Freedom of Information Act. This information, when combined with the documents that surfaced as Barlow prepared a court case against his former employers, enabled him to draw a "wiring diagram" of who was involved in his case. Scooter Libby (principal deputy under secretary—policy), Stephen Hadley (assistant secretary), James Hinds (deputy assistant secretary), Victor Rostow (principal director) and Gerald Brubaker (acting office director) all featured.

42 As head of administration for the Pentagon it fell to Hampton to process the request from Brubaker for Barlow to be sacked. Correspondence from Hampton to Barlow confirms that this was the case, but Hampton was not part of the attempt to smear Barlow. He was simply doing his job. Author archive.

43 In 1995, Redd founded the US Fifth Fleet and in 2005 he would be picked by President Bush to head up his new National Counterterrorism Center. In his dealings with Barlow, he wrote a confidential memo to Leon Kniaz, director of personnel and security, Washington Headquarters Service (WHS), in which he declined to portray the Barlow affair as a "performance-related issue," when that charge had been found to be untrue, and declined to support O'Toole's recommendation that Barlow be re-employed.

44 Deposition by Barlow to O'Toole 1989/1990.

45 WHS route slip, from Leon Kniaz to David O. Cooke [director of WHS], re Richard Barlow, 14 May 1990. Author archive.

46 Mervyn Hampton's role was confirmed in the disclosure required for Barlow's court case. Barlow said: "He told me that Wolfowitz had approved all the actions, but once again he could not tell me what I was accused of, since it was 'classified.' I recall he did not like the classification of the charges against me and the denial of due process and I believe he was the one who eventually forced the release of some of the Brubaker–Rostow memos to me months later."

47 The comment, Barlow alleges, was made by Victor Rostow, then Brubaker's boss at OSD.

48 The discovery was made under Freedom of Information Act applications that led to a partial release of documents, and also during the court case taken by Barlow for reinstatement and compensation in which files emerged showing that the standing intelligence assessment was not the one written by Barlow but one that was materially incorrect.

49 The new assessment was by MacMurray and misrepresented the "known knowns," according to Barlow. MacMurray denied this.

50 The admission came during the court case taken by Barlow, elicited by his lawyers.

51 <http://www.pakdef.info/pids/paf/highmark2.html>.

52 Anger that was heightened by Kashmir's ruling National Conference (NC) party, already accused of corruption, forming an alliance with India's Congress Party, a union that appeared to demolish any ideas Kashmiris had of winning autonomy. The Muslim United Front (MUF) formed in opposition, recruiting activists who campaigned for an independent Kashmir, immediately attracting overwhelming support and making victory in the Kashmir state elections of 1987 likely. However,

following allegations of a massively rigged poll, victory swung to the unpopular NC, and after the results were announced the Indian security forces rounded up hundreds of MUF leaders and activists. Cells were brimming with Kashmiris and the bodies of assassinated activists were found in the back lanes and gutters as hit squads cracked down on dissent. Kashmiri armed factions rose up and rallied support for a statewide boycott of the national parliamentary elections that were held in November 1989. After a militant group abducted the daughter of India's home minister, Mufti Mohammad Sayeed, in December 1989, the government capitulated and released five detainees, bolstering the power of the militants.

53 Author interviews with Benazir Bhutto, Dubai, 2006.

54 This trip took place in late January 1990.

55 Author interview with Robert Oakley, Washington, spring 2006.

56 Douglas Frantz, "Pakistan's Role in Scientist's Nuclear Trafficking Debated— Islamabad's Awareness of a Black Market Led by the Father of Its Atomic Bomb Is Still Uncertain," *Los Angeles Times*, 16 May 2005. See also: <http://cisac.stanford .edu/news/cisac_experts_suggest_pakistan_probably_knew_of_scientists_nuclear_ trafficking_20050523/>.

57 Seymour Hersh, "On the Nuclear Edge," *New Yorker*, 29 March 1993.

58 The allegation was made by two former senior establishment figures in Pakistan, one diplomatic and the other military, in author interviews in 2006. Beg denied this categorically.

59 Author interview with Mirza Aslam Beg, Rawalpindi, spring 2006.

60 William Clark made these comments in 1994 when the Washington-based Stimpson Center held a conference to analyze the May 1990 military confrontation between Pakistan and India. *Conflict Prevention and Confidence Building Measure in South Asia: the 1990 Crisis*, Occasional Paper number 17, April 1994.

61 Stephen P. Cohen, P. R. Chari and Pervaiz Iqbal Cheema, *Perception, Politics and Security in South Asia: The Compound Crisis of 1990* (Routledge, London, 2003).

62 Stimpson Center, as above.

63 Oakley also sensed the rise in Islamic zealotry throughout Pakistan, a feeling that even Bhutto, not wanting to be outflanked, contributed to by visiting Muzaffarabad, the capital of Pakistan-administered Kashmir, and declaring the struggle in Kashmir a "holy jihad."

64 The defense attaché argued at the Stimpson Center conference that the same maneuver was required to practice dropping a 2,000-lb conventional weapon.

65 Hersh.

66 Sharma was promoted in 1988. This quote was referred to in the Stimpson Center conference.

67 Quoted in *Dr. A. Q. Khan Research Laboratories 1976–2001, 25 Years of Excellence and National Service*, Islamabad, 31 July 2001. Author archive.

68 Author interview with Benazir Bhutto.

69 Author interview with Mirza Aslam Beg.

70 Author interview with Benazir Bhutto.

71 Author interview with Robert Oakley.

72 The final report, which was classified, was signed off by Stephen O'Toole, chief of the security division, who recommended that Barlow's clearances be returned to him.

73 Author interview with Richard Barlow.

12: PROJECT A/B

1 Gerard Smith had help brief members of the Atomic Energy Commission on President Eisenhower's Atoms for Peace proposal in 1953. The following year he had transferred to the Department of State and became a special assistant for atomic energy to secretary of state John Foster Dulles. In 1957, Smith was promoted to assistant secretary of state for policy planning and became director of the policy planning staff. Under Nixon, Smith was appointed director of the Arms Control and Disarmament Agency and led the US delegation in the Strategic Arms Limitation Talks (SALT) with the Soviet Union, which triggered the Anti-Ballistic Missile Treaty of 1972. Smith was also a special adviser to Carter.

2 Smith's article was carried in *Foreign Affairs*, the magazine of the Council on Foreign Relations, "A Blind Eye to Nuclear Proliferation," Vol. 68, No. 3 (1989). The article was co-authored by Helena Cobban.

3 Smith argued that by 1984 the US and European intelligence community had known that Pakistan had designed, built and cold-tested a nuclear implosion device. "Nevertheless Reagan continued to certify that Pakistan did not possess a nuclear device," Smith wrote. Not only did Reagan claim there was no bomb, he rewarded Pakistan. In 1987, "at the urging of Secretary of State George Shultz," Congress approved the waiving of Symington for another two and a half years and released a further $480 million in aid. In proposing the flow of aid to Pakistan, Shultz had steam-rollered Kenneth Adelman, the director of ACDA, who had specifically warned against pandering to Pakistan, given the state of its nuclear program.

4 Stuart Auerbach, "Pakistan Tried to Buy Nuclear Aids; Attempts to Purchase Furnaces Detailed," *Washington Post*, 10 October 1990.

   According to one study carried out by the Wisconsin Project on Nuclear Arms Control on dual-use components manufactured in the US, from 1988 until 1990, 80 percent of Pakistan technical orders submitted for licensing had been sanctioned for shipping to Islamabad, with 16 percent returned without action, and only 4 percent rejected outright. The Khan network had penetrated and exploited the chaos. See also <http://www.wisconsinproject.org/>.

5 Author interview with Robert Oakley, Washington, spring 2006. The Pakistanis were also warned of another serious piece of interfering. US intelligence sources claimed that they had become aware that Pakistan was now receiving considerable funding for its nuclear program from Saudi Arabia in return for which a nuclear pact had been signed. If the Saudis were ever subjected to a nuclear attack, then Pakistan pledged to respond in kind.

6 Pakistan had already made a $200 million down payment for these planes and would spend years trying to get a refund, which was finally delivered in 1998 in the form of a credit to the debt Pakistan owed the World Bank. For more, see <www.fas.org/news/pakistan/1998/04/980423-pak.htm>.

7 There were contacts between the US military and the Pakistani military, particularly during the Gulf War, as the Pentagon believed that Pakistan could become useful in the Gulf region, especially Pakistan's ports at Karachi and Gwadar.

8 Author interview with Norm Wulf, Virginia, spring 2006.

9 Dennis Kux, *The United States and Pakistan 1947–2000* (Woodrow Wilson Center Press, Washington, 2001), pp. 309–11.

10 Author interviews with Husain Haqqani, Washington, spring 2006.

11 In an interview with the authors Durrani denied any knowledge of Khan's activities in Germany in the early 1980s, Rawalpindi, spring 2006.

12 The allegations were revealed in 1994 when Air Marshal Asghar Khan filed a human rights action in the supreme court (HRC 19/96) against General Beg, General Asad Durrani, the former ISI chief, and Younis Habib, relating to the disbursement of public money and its misuse for political purposes, which is still pending hearing by the court. The matter was first raised in public in 1994 by General Naseerullah Babar, Benazir Bhutto's interior minister during her second term, who warned in the National Assembly that a slush fund had been used by the ISI to win the 1990 election. The slush fund had allegedly been placed in a business account operated by Major General Qazi in the name of "Survey Section 202." More than $1.8 million was paid out by Qazi to an electoral cell coordinated by President Ghulam Ishaq Khan.

13 Author interview with Mark Siegel, Washington, spring 2006.

14 Ambassador Abida Hussein. See Kux, pp. 315–16.

15 The legal authority was finally withdrawn on 1 January 1992. For more, see Steve Coll, *Ghost Wars* (Penguin Press, New York, 2004).

16 For more, see Kux and Coll.

17 Peter Tomsen, US envoy to the Afghan resistance, 1989–92, quoted by Coll, p. 239.

18 Without US assistance, or even a phased withdrawal of American aid, new sources of cash for living, fighting and political trading were found indigenously. Poppy fields began to flourish across Helmand province to the south and by 1992 so did the opiate refineries that sprang up all along Afghanistan's border with Pakistan, sending tons of heroin, triple the amount produced in the Golden Triangle, via Karachi and across Central Asia towards Europe and North America. With it, steered by the ISI, which had severed virtually all links with its former CIA collaborators, came the forces of fundamentalism.

19 This article, "Pakistan's Nuclear Material and Equipment for Sale," was reproduced in an Urdu book by Shahid Nazir Ahmed, *Dr. A. Q. Khan* (Islamabad, 2001).

20 The fact that Khan's outward proliferation for cash was accelerated at this point comes from multiple sources, including author interviews with Dr. Shafiq ur-Rehman, K. M. Arif, Mirza Aslam Beg and Asad Durrani, although all deny any direct involvement.

21 Javid Nasir was put forward by Brigadier Imtiaz Billa, an agent in the ISI who had General Beg's ear and was closely linked to Gulbuddin Hekmatyar. Billa was a figurehead for the zealous wing of the ISI.

22 Javid Nasir's North Korean trip and the Stinger deal were confirmed to the authors in interviews with former ISI agents and former army chiefs in Pakistan in 2006.

23 The US Security Council vote was on 29 November 1990.

24 This offer was confirmed to the authors by a former senior KRL employee in an interview in Islamabad in 2006.

25 Details of this offer come from a former senior KRL employee in an interview with the authors in Islamabad in 2006. They were confirmed in an author telephone interview with Gary Dillon of the IAEA Iraq inspection team, UK, autumn 2006.

26 Gary Dillon.

27 Author interview with Nawaz Sharif, London, summer 2006.

28 Author interviews with Husain Haqqani, Washington, spring 2006.

29 Related to the authors by Chaudhary Nisar Ali Khan, Sharif's minister for petroleum

and natural resources, in an interview in Rawalpindi, spring 2006. See also the story by Zahid Hussain, "Nuked," *Newsline*, Karachi, January 2004.

30 Author interview with Nawaz Sharif.

31 Nisar's brother was Lieutenant General Iftikhar Ali Khan, who would be called up as defense minister when Pervez Musharraf took power in 1999.

32 Author interview with Chaudhary Nisar Ali Khan.

33 Author interview with Nawaz Sharif.

34 This allegation was made to the authors in interviews with Nawaz Sharif and Shahbaz Sharif, London, summer 2006, and confirmed by Chaudhary Nisar Ali Khan, author interview, Rawalpindi, spring 2006.

35 "An Iranian Nuclear Chronology 1987–1982," *Middle East Defense News*, 8 June 1992.

36 See Yossef Bodansky, *Pakistan's Nuclear Brinkmanship* (Freeman Center for Strategic Studies, Houston, Texas, 1996).

37 See interview with Professor Husayn al-Shahristani in *Al-Sharq Al-Awsat* newspaper, London, 15 April 2001.

38 Shahristani later repeated these claims. See Ghalib Darwis in *Al-Majallah*, London, 28 January 1996.

39 Mujahedine-Khalq, also known as the National Council for Resistance in Iran (NCRI). Author interviews with Alireza Jafarzadeh, NCRI, Washington, 2006.

40 Amir Taheri, *Die Welt*, 22 January 1992.

41 The agent was Dr. Mahdi Chamran, who worked with the Iranian general command headquarters. See also Alon Pinkas, "Thinking the Unthinkable About Iran," *Jerusalem Post*, 23 April 1992.

42 Roger Fallgot and Jan Mather, "Iran Has N-Bomb," *The European*, 30 April–3 May 1992.

43 Leonard Spector, "Islamic Bomb West's Long-Term Nightmare," *Washington Times*, 19 January 1994.

44 The timing was confirmed to the authors by a former senior KRL employee in an interview in Islamabad in 2006.

45 Author interviews with Marvin Peterson, Washington, autumn 2006.

46 Marvin Peterson was working for the US mission to international organizations in Vienna (UNVIE).

47 Marvin Peterson would later be suspended from his job at the IAEA after an allegation was made by persons unknown that he was a security risk and had leaked classified information to "unauthorized individuals." The FBI launched an inquiry, reporting back only on 23 March 1999. Obtained under the Freedom of Information Act, this inquiry report concluded that there was no basis for the allegations, apart from an element of malice. Peterson had ardently believed in non-proliferation and had argued as much, while he felt that there were officials working alongside him who had a more flexible definition of non-proliferation in mind. He in particular had complained that Iran had made serious overtures for peace in 1995, which were disregarded without any due thought. Author interviews with Peterson and also his case file, released by the FBI.

48 These figures come from an author interview with Nawaz Sharif and are confirmed by IMF appraisals from that year.

49 Nawaz Sharif recounted his maneuverings in an interview with the authors in London, summer 2006.

50 General Asif Nawaz was Beg's replacement as chief of army staff.

51 Author interview with Hamid Gul, Rawalpindi, spring 2006.

52 Author interviews with Husain Haqqani, Washington, spring 2006.

53 The interview was published on 7 February 1992.

54 Quoted in *Dr. A. Q. Khan Research Laboratories 1976–2001, 25 Years of Excellence and National Service*, Islamabad, 31 July 2001. Author archive.

55 Reports on his sentence were carried by AP on 29 September 1992.

56 "Pakistani General Gets Lenient Sentence in Nuclear Materials Case," 29 September 1992, Agence France-Presse.

57 For more on this period, Gul and Beg, see Husain Haqqani, *Pakistan: From Mosque to Military* (Carnegie Endowment for International Peace, Washington, 2005).

58 Yousef's records were in Kuwait because he had been born there.

59 Simon Reeve, *The New Jackals, Ramzi Yousef, Osama bin Laden and the Future of Terrorism* (André Deutsch, London, 1999). Also author interview with Dan Coleman, formerly of Special Agency Squad I-49, the FBI's Osama bin Laden unit. In 1997 Coleman was assigned to Alec Station (the CIA's bin Laden Unit). Author interview, New York, autumn 2006.

60 Ibid.

61 Author interview with Nawaz Sharif, London, summer 2006.

62 For more on Hekmatyar's rule of terror, see Coll, and Haqqani.

63 Hekmatyar was eventually forced out of the Kabul area in February 1995. See also <http://www.hrw.org/reports/2001/afghan2/Afghan0701-01.htm#P325_88217>.

64 For more on Sharif's self-obsession, see Haqqani, and Strobe Talbott, *Engaging India* (Brookings Institution Press, Washington, 2004).

65 See Kux, pp. 324–6.

66 Moeen Qureshi, who had served as a vice president of the World Bank, was installed as caretaker prime minister.

67 Author interview with Agha Shahi, Islamabad, spring 2006.

68 Christopher, who had served as deputy secretary of state under Jimmy Carter, was nominated by Clinton as secretary of state and made the unfortunate comparison at his Senate confirmation hearing on 16 January 1993. See Kux, p. 321.

69 Kux, p. 316.

70 The jets were still being stored in the US Air Force base near Tucson, Arizona.

71 Pendley was deputy assistant secretary for East Asia and Pacific affairs. A transcript of the hearing was forwarded to Barlow by his lawyers, a copy of which the authors obtained, too.

72 Its engineers lacked computing and electronics competence, Pendley claimed, reiterating what Arthur Hughes had told Representative Stephen Solarz in 1989. The rear admiral's testimony was signed off by Les Aspin, Clinton's new secretary of defense.

73 Author interview with Norm Wulf, Virginia, spring 2006.

74 Author interviews with Richard Barlow, Montana, 2006.

75 Quote taken from a letter written on 9 October 1991, by Susan J. Crawford, IG Defense, to David I. Boren (Democrat, Oklahoma), Senate select committee on intelligence.

76 The IG reported on 30 August 1991 on "personnel actions" taken against Barlow, namely his sacking in August 1989. In a memo to the head of the Washington

Headquarters Service, the IG, Susan J. Crawford, concluded that Barlow's case had been handled "prudently" and that the Defense Department had been right to suspend Barlow's clearances in the light of his "weakness."

77 Letter sent on 16 June 1993 from Judith Miller, general counsel of the Department of Defense, to Senator Strom Thurmond (Republican, South Carolina), chairman of the armed services committee.

78 The initial findings were presented on 24 December 1991.

79 This quote came from Robert Hathaway, a senior staffer on the foreign affairs committee in the House of Representatives, who worked mostly for Stephen Solarz and was an acknowledged expert on Pakistan.

80 Letter from Sherman Funk to Derek J. Vander Schaaf, the deputy IG for the Department of Defense, 17 September 1993.

81 The Defense Department insisted that Barlow had "failed to read assigned intelligence compartments," having become obsessed by Pakistan. Funk concluded that Barlow had been "sandbagged" by Gerald Brubaker, his superior, who had deliberately not told him what to do in order that he would seem to fail. The OSD claimed that Barlow had "failed to complete assignments." But Funk found that Barlow's supervisor rated him: "exceeds fully successful." Barlow was, according to his bosses, "a bright, aggressive and intelligent action officer," who was promoted soon afterwards. Taken from a letter from Sherman Funk to Derek J. Vander Schaaf, deputy IG for the Department of Defense, 17 September 1993. Author archive.

82 Ibid.

83 Ibid.

84 These conclusions were drawn again by Funk in a letter to Donald Deline, general counsel, Senate committee on armed services, on 15 August 1995. Author archive.

85 Letter from Sherman Funk written on 9 November 1993 to the deputy IG for the Department of Defense, Derek J. Vander Schaaf. Author archive.

86 Ibid.

87 Funk wrote to Senator Jeff Bingman (Democrat, New Mexico) on 13 December 1993. Author archive.

88 Author interview with Haroon Ahmed, Karachi, spring 2006.

89 Durrani was responsible for Khan's security while he was head of the ISI from 1990 to 1991.

90 Author interview with Asad Durrani, Rawalpindi, spring 2006.

91 Author interviews with Peter Griffin, France, 2006–7.

92 Author interviews with Pervez Hoodbhoy, Islamabad, spring 2006.

93 A. Q. Khan joined the university's board in 1996.

13: CHESTNUTS AND STEAMED FISH

1 Author interviews with Benazir Bhutto, Dubai, 2006. See also Simon Reeve, *The New Jackals, Ramzi Yousef, Osama bin Laden and the Future of Terrorism* (André Deutsch, London, 1999).

2 Benazir Bhutto was Shia, and her mother, Nusrat Bhutto, was of Kurdish descent.

3 Maria Ressa, *Seeds of Terror* (Free Press, New York, 2003).

4 Reeve.

5 The assassination attempt was on 26 July 1993.

6 Author interviews with Benazir Bhutto.

7 Pervez Musharraf, *In the Line of Fire* (Free Press, New York, 2006).

8 Some accounts place the deaths at higher than 700. The claim made that Musharraf orchestrated the SSP move to Gilgit was by two of his contemporaries who spoke to the authors in the spring of 2006. The same claim was made in an author interview with Hamid Gul in the same month. B. Raman also made the claim in a paper for the South Asian Analyst Group. See <http://www.saag.org/papers5/paper484.html>.

9 For details, see Husain Haqqani, *Pakistan: From Mosque to Military* (Carnegie Endowment for International Peace, Washington, 2005), and International Crisis Group reports: *Pakistan: Madrasas, Extremism and the Military*, Asia Report Number 36, 29 July 2002; *Pakistan: The Mullahs and the Military*, Asia Report Number 49, 20 March 2003; *Unfulfilled Promises: Pakistan's Failure to Tackle Extremism*, Asia Report Number 73, 16 January 2004; *The State of Sectarianism in Pakistan*, Asia Report Number 95, 18 April 2005; and *Pakistan's Tribal Areas: Appeasing the Militants*, Asia Report Number 125, 11 December 2006.

10 This incident, when Musharraf asked for unfettered military power for the Pakistan army, was related to the authors in an interview with Benazir Bhutto.

11 General Musharraf mentioned to Bhutto extreme sectarian groups like Lashkar-e-Taiba and Harkat-ul-Ansar.

12 For more on bin Laden's involvement with jihadi groups in Pakistan, see B. Raman's writing at the South Asian Analyst Group, <http://www.saag.org/papers/paper5.html> and also *The Herald* in Pakistan.

13 See the South Asia Terrorist Portal, <http://www.satp.org/satporgtp/countries/india/states/jandk/terrorist_outfits/lashkar_e _toiba.htm>.

14 Harkat-ul-Ansar was formed when Harkat-ul-Mujahideen and Harkat-ul-Jehad-al-Islami merged in 1993. Musharraf's role in contacting, encouraging and merging jihadi groups such as HuA was described in detail to the authors by CIA sources in the US, ISI sources (former and serving) in Pakistan, sources with Mossad in Israel, and intelligence sources in the UK. For more, see US State Department, Patterns of Global Terrorism, South Asia Overview, Washington, 2000, <http://www.state.gov/ s/ct/rls/crt/2000/2432.htm>. Also see remarks on this report by Colin Powell, secretary of state, Washington, 30 April 2001, <http://www.state.gov/secretary/ former/powell/remarks/2001/2557.htm>. Also see Husain Haqqani, "Selective War Against Terror," *Indian Express*, 20 June 2005, and Haqqani, *Pakistan: From Mosque to Military*. Also see International Crisis Group reports, as above, note 9.

15 Author interviews with Indian civil servants and intelligence sources, including B. Raman and K. Subrahmanyam, in spring 2006.

16 Author interviews with K. Subrahmanyam and Naresh Chandra, former cabinet secretary (1990), India's ambassador to Washington (1996–2001), and intelligence adviser to several Indian prime ministers (2001 to present), New Delhi, spring 2006. Also author interviews with Husain Haqqani, Washington, spring 2006.

17 The first approaches to coach and sponsor the Taliban were made in 1994 by Musharraf and General Naseerullah Babar, interior minister (1993–6). Author interviews with Benazir Bhutto, Dubai, 2006, and General Naseerullah Babar, Peshawar, spring 2006. See also Haqqani, *Pakistan: From Mosque to Military*, and

Ahmed Rashid, *Taliban* (Yale University Press, New Haven, 2000).

18 Author interview with General Naseerullah Babar.

19 Author interviews with Benazir Bhutto.

20 See "North Korea Strengthens Ties with Syria, Iran and Pakistan—Foreign Minister Makes Official Tours," *North Korea News*, No. 645, 24 August 1992, pp. 5–6; "Foreign Minister Kim Yong-nam Visits Syria, Iran and Pakistan," *North Korea News*, No. 641, 10 August 1992, p. 5; "Kim Yong-nam Leaves for Syria, Iran, Pakistan," North Korean Central News Agency, 27 July 1992. All cited and translated in Federal Broadcast Information Service (FBIS) document FBIS-EAS-92-145, 28 July 1992, p. 15. See also Lally Weymouth, "In Israel, a New View of Syria," *Washington Post*, 6 July 1992.

21 See "Missiles-Context-Iran," *United Press International*, 1 August 1985, and Jack Anderson and Dale Van Atta, "North Korea Aids Iran's War of Terror," *Washington Post*, 3 February 1986.

22 The test flights began on 29–30 May 1993 with an apparently successful launch 270 miles into the Sea of Japan. This flight test of the No-dong 1 was almost certainly at high altitude with warhead separation being demonstrated. See Joseph Bermudez and Greg Gerardi, "An Analysis of North Korean Ballistic Missile Testing," *Jane's Intelligence Review*, April 1995, pp 184–91. Author interview with Dr. Shafiq ur-Rehman, Islamabad, spring 2006.

23 Author interviews with Husain Haqqani.

24 See also the Nuclear Threat Initiative for a decent chronology on the development of the North Korean program and what was known as the Soviet IRT-2000 research reactor, <http://www.nti. org/e_research/profiles/NK/Missile/45_515.html>.

25 According to Robert Gallucci, who negotiated with Pyongyang on the US side in 1994, this was the most likely explanation for North Korea's retreat from international nuclear cooperation around this time, although it was never testified to by the leadership, which has always maintained it has no substantial weapons program. Author interviews, Robert Gallucci, Washington, 2006.

26 This agreement was signed on 20 July 1977. See also Joseph S. Bermudez, "North Korea's Nuclear Program," *Jane's Intelligence Review*, September 1991, and also the Nuclear Threat Initiative, <http://www.nti.org/e_research/profiles/NK/Nuclear/46.html>.

27 The claims were made by the South Korean government. See <http://www.nti.org/e_research/profiles/NK/Nuclear/46.html>.

28 The agreement was called the South–North Joint Declaration on the Denuclearization of the Korean Peninsula. See <http://www.armscontrol.org/factsheets/dprkchron.asp>.

29 It was signed on 30 January 1992 and the Supreme People's Assembly ratified the agreement on 9 April 1992.

30 BBC Summary of World Broadcasts, broadcast on 31 December 1993, entitled "Benazir Bhutto Arrives in Pyongyang, Meets Kim Il-sung," source: Pyongyang, in English, 10.46 GMT, 29 December 1993.

31 Author interviews with Benazir Bhutto.

32 Sitting beside Bhutto at the banquet was her foreign minister, Sardar Aseff Ahmad Ali, and her defense minister, Aftab Shaban Mirani. They had helped draft the script.

33 BBC Summary of World Broadcasts, 31 December 1993, "Kim Il-sung, Benazir Bhutto Deliver Banquet Speeches."

34 North Korean Central News Agency, in English, 15.04 GMT, 29 December 1993.

35 Author interviews with Benazir Bhutto.

36 Author interviews with Husain Haqqani.

37 Author interviews with Benazir Bhutto.

38 According to *Jane's Defense Weekly*, 15 October 1994, this pact officially concerned only missiles and guidance systems. See also *Wall Street Journal*, 14 September 1994.

39 Author interview with Dr. Shafiq ur-Rehman, Islamabad, spring 2006.

40 "Foreign Ministry Group Leaves for Iran, Pakistan," North Korean Central News Agency, 31 March 1994. For translated version, see FBIS-EAS-94-063, 1 April 1994, p. 13.

41 "Science Delegation Leaves for Pakistan 26 Sep," North Korean Central News Agency, 26 September 1994. For translated version, see FBIS-EAS-94-187, 26 September 1994.

42 "Military Delegation Leaves for Pakistan," Pyongyang Korean Central Television Network, 19 November 1995, see FBIS-EAS-95-223; "Choe Kwang-Led Delegation Arrives in Pakistan," Pyongyang Korean Central Broadcasting Network, 20 November 1995, see FBIS-EAS-95-224; "Choe Kwang Delegation Meets Pakistani President," Pyongyang Korean Central Broadcasting Network, 22 November 1995, see FBIS-EAS-95-226; "Delegation Visiting Pakistan Attends Banquet," Pyongyang Korean Central Broadcasting Network, 24 November 1995, see FBIS-EAS-95-227.

43 Several KRL sources and Khan aides confirmed the marshal's visit to KRL.

44 Department of State, "Imposition of Missile Proliferation Sanctions Against Entities in North Korea and Pakistan," *Federal Register*, Vol. 63, No. 85, 4 May 1998.

45 Author interviews with Dr. Shafiq ur-Rehman.

46 John Childs recounted his experiences at the University of Hartford's World Affairs Council in Connecticut at a talk on 11 October 1995.

47 The conclusions were drawn by the US State Department as the kidnap group's principal demands were for the release of five members of Harkat-ul-Ansar, including Masood Azhar, Sajjad Afgani and Nassrullah Langaryar. Later, according to RAW sources interviewed by the authors in New Delhi, in 2005 and 2006, it was thought that Amjad Farooqi, a former SSP activist who had gone on to join HuA, was responsible for the kidnappings.

48 Hans Ostro's body was discovered on 13 August 1995. See John F. Burns, "Terror in Paradise Keeps Tourists from Kashmir," *New York Times*, 21 August 1995.

49 The group claimed to be called Al-Faran, the name of a mountain in Saudi Arabia. The group was unheard of in Kashmir.

50 Author interviews with Benazir Bhutto.

51 Haqqani, *Pakistan: From Mosque to Military*.

52 For more details on this period of Osama bin Laden's life, see Ahmed Rashid, *Taliban* (Yale University Press, New Haven, 2000); Reeve; Lawrence Wright, *The Looming Tower* (Allen Lane, London, 2006); and Peter L. Bergen, *The Osama bin Laden I Know* (Free Press, New York, 2006).

53 Reeve.

54 Author interviews with Benazir Bhutto.

55 "Habib Wife Shot Dead in Clifton on Tuesday," *Dawn*, Karachi, 12 September 1995.

56 Maulana Masood Azhar would become the chief of Jaish-e-Mohammad, which would be accused of having carried out the attack on the Indian parliament on 13

December 2001. The exit control order was issued on 15 April 1995.

57 Major General Ali Quli Khan Khattak, then the director general of military intelligence, was the first to unearth the plot.

58 Interviews with Benazir Bhutto, and also see South Asia Analysis Group papers 1010, 1081, 146, and Dagestan Focus on Pakistan's Tablighi Jamaat, at <www.saag.org>. See also November 1995 issue of *The Herald* news magazine, Karachi.

59 Although the prime minister thwarted this coup, another plot consumed her when her brother Murtaza was shot dead in Karachi in an unexplained encounter with the police on 20 September 1996. Pakistan's intelligence agencies spread a rumor, still pungent today, that the prime minister's husband, Asif Ali Zadari, had arranged Murtaza's assassination, having been accused by him of corruption. For more on Murtaza's murder, see Haqqani, *Pakistan: From Mosque to Military*.

60 The US Treasury was forced to modify the $100 bill in 1996.

61 Author interviews with Benazir Bhutto.

62 In 1984, Zia had deliberately created fissures in Karachi, the traditional heartland of the Bhutto dynasty, by sponsoring the birth of a political movement for Sunnis called the Muhajir Qaumi Movement, or MQM, representing muhajirs or "migrant" Muslims who had come to Pakistan from India. The MQM grew so large and cantankerous that it also turned against its creators, leading the ISI to create a split, establishing another MQM in 1992. This one was known as MQM "H," standing for the Urdu word "Haqqiqi" which means "real," and it rounded on its rival, MQM "A," standing for Altaf Hussain, the original party's leader, who went into exile in the UK in 1992. Both branches fought the PPP and in 1997 the MQM "H" renamed itself the Muttahida Qaumi Movement, a party not just for mujahirs but for all people. Altaf Hussain remains in exile in London.

63 This figure is derived from a report published by the IMF on 20 October 1997 analyzing Pakistan for the years 1996 and 1997. <www.imf.org>.

64 Author interviews with Dr. Shafiq ur-Rehman, Islamabad, spring 2006.

65 Bhutto visited Tehran in December 1993 and again in November 1995 when she met with Rafsanjani on 7 November. The two sides officially discussed gas pipeline projects and the construction of new land routes. "Bhutto Tries to Reassure Iran," *Middle East Economic Digest*, 17 November 1995.

66 David Frost interview with Benazir Bhutto, prime minister of Pakistan, Public Broadcast System (PBS), New York, 18 November 1994.

67 Author interview with Moshe Ya'alon, Washington, spring 2006.

68 See Report by the Director General, "Implementation of the NPT Safeguards Agreement in the Islamic Republic of Iran," GOV/2005/67, IAEA, Vienna, 2 September 2005, paragraph 20, and Report by the Director General, "Implementation of the NPT Safeguards Agreement in the Islamic Republic of Iran," GOV/2004/83, IAEA, Vienna, 15 November 2004, paragraphs 42–8.

69 Gaurav Kampani, *Proliferation Unbound: Nuclear Tales from Pakistan* (Center for Non-Proliferation Studies, 23 February 2004).

70 Author interview with Moshe Ya'alon.

71 In an interview with the authors Benazir Bhutto disputed this allegation, saying as far as she was concerned it was always a cash deal and the money was paid.

72 In addition to promising to sign the NPT, China signed the Missile Technology Control Regime (MTCR), a multinational agreement to restrict missile sales.

73 Oehler began contributing regularly to national intelligence assessments and the president's daily brief.
74 See also Wayne M. Morrison, *China's Proliferation of Weapons of Mass Destruction* (Congressional Research Service Economics Division, Washington, 15 July 1998).
75 In the early 1980s, China had given Pakistan a tested nuclear weapon design and enough highly enriched uranium to fuel it.
76 Sanctions were imposed after Washington determined that China had violated the terms of the MTCR a second time.
77 The *International Herald Tribune* reported on 23 June 1995 that the CIA had found China had delivered "in the last three months" missile parts to Pakistan that could be used in M-11s. According to a *Washington Post* report on 25 August 1996, the US intelligence community had agreed in a national intelligence estimate that China was providing plant for making missiles that would violate MTCR guidelines.
78 Robert Einhorn, Clinton's assistant secretary of state for non-proliferation, recalled: "We didn't have smoking-gun proof of the M-11 deal." Author interview, Washington, DC, autumn 2006.
79 See *Washington Times*, 5 February 1996, and *New York Times*, 12 May 1996. CIA director John Deutch reportedly said at the White House meeting that Chinese officials had approved the sale of magnets.
80 Interview with senior non-proliferation official in the State Department, Washington, DC, spring 2006.
81 Oehler submitted this report in September 1996.
82 Seth Carus, "Iran as a Military Threat," National Defense University Strategic Forum, Number 113, May 1997.
83 China Task Force Investigation, Senate hearing, 16 July 1998, p. S8281. At the same hearing, John Kyl, a Republican senator on the House intelligence committee, rebuked the president for "giving Chinese firms a green light to sell missile technology to Iran and Pakistan."
84 Speaking at a hearing in June 1998.
85 Interview with senior non-proliferation official in the State Department, Washington, DC, spring 2006.
86 The boat was the *Chon Sung* and it was boarded on 12 March 1996.
87 Author interviews with senior Foreign Office and CIA sources, London and Washington, 2006. For more on the official response to A. Q. Khan's activities around this time, see Rt Hon. Lord Butler of Brockwell, *Review of Intelligence on Weapons of Mass Destruction*, Report of a Committee of Privy Counsellors, 14 July 2004 (The Stationery Office, London, 2004). pp. 17–26.
88 Author interviews with Wajid Shamsul Hasan, London, 2006–7. He got the call in July 1996.
89 Shown to the authors by Brigadier Sajawal's family in Islamabad, 2006.
90 Julian West, *Sunday Telegraph*, 1 November 1998.
91 By November 1997, Iran, too, had pinged back on to the intelligence screens, with the German BND warning the US that Pakistan had established a network of dummy export companies on behalf of Tehran which were being used to purchase weapons. See also testimony of Dr. Gary Milhollin, director, Wisconsin Project on Nuclear Arms Control, Washington, to *Iran and Proliferation: Is the US Doing Enough?* and *The Arming of Iran: Who Is Responsible?* Hearings before the Subcommittee on Near

Eastern and South Asian Affairs of the Committee on Foreign Relations United States Senate, 17 April and 6 May 1997 (US Government Printing Office, 40–187 CC, Washington, 1998).

92 China Task Force Investigation, Senate hearing, 16 July 1998, p. S8281. See also testimony of Milhollin to *Iran and Proliferation: Is the US Doing Enough?* and *The Arming of Iran: Who Is Responsible?*

93 John Deutch, "The Threat of Nuclear Diversion," Testimony for the Record before the Permanent Subcommittee on Investigations of the Senate Committee on Government Affairs, 20 March 1996.

94 This was reported on 9 April 1996.

95 Karamat made this statement on 4 July 1996. It is quoted in *Dr. A. Q. Khan Research Laboratories 1976–2001, 25 Years of Excellence and National Service,* Islamabad, 31 July 2001. Author archive.

96 Bin Laden drove openly through Pakistan army checkpoints en route to Afghanistan. His arrival was carried in *Asharq Al-Awsat,* a pan-Arab newspaper published in London on 6 May 1996.

97 They were joined by Harkat-ul-Jehad-al-Islami known as "HuJI," the Movement for an Islamic Holy War, formed in 1980 to fight the Soviets in Afghanistan, which had gone on to wage war in Kashmir and now claimed Kabul alongside the Taliban.

98 The flight was IC 814. Azhar was released in a hostage swap on 31 December 1999 and formed JEM in Karachi on 31 January 2000 before relocating to Afghanistan.

14: A NEW CLEAR VISION

1 Sharif won the election on 4 February 1997.

2 Author interview with Karl Inderfurth, Washington, autumn 2006.

3 Dennis Kux, *The United States and Pakistan 1947–2000* (Woodrow Wilson Center Press, Washington, 2001), p. 340.

4 Senator Hank Brown (Republican, Colorado), chairman of a subcommittee of the Senate foreign relations committee. Despite vocal opposition from John Glenn and others, who were terrified by Pakistan's growing instability and the possible impact of the sales on its nuclear program, the amendment slipped through on 21 September 1995, by one vote.

5 See B. Raman, "A. Q. Khan, Sudan, Iran and al-Qaeda," *International Terrorism Monitor:* Paper No. 21, South Asia Analysis Group, 28 January 2006, <http://www.saag.org/%5Cpapers17%5Cpaper1690.html>. See also Abdul Mah'bood Siddiqui (Hurmat Publications, Islamabad, 2001).

6 Author interviews with Peter Griffin, France, 2006–7. He said he stopped doing business with B. S. A. Tahir in February 2004.

7 In October 2001, Abu Bakr Siddiqui was convicted for exporting nuclear-related items to KRL and trying to evade export restrictions. Among the items cited was a 5-ton gantry crane, a 12-ton furnace and measuring machines. SMB Europe was dissolved in April 2001, before the court case. Sue Clough, "Exporter Helped in Nuclear Race," *Daily Telegraph,* 9 October 2001.

8 Author interviews with Peter Griffin, France, 2006–7.

9 Ibid.

10 Ibid.

11 Khan's expansion plans around 1998 were confirmed by Dr. Shafiq ur-Rehman, whose father accompanied Khan on all trips, author interviews, Islamabad, spring 2006.

12 Griffin also recalled that Khan owned a restaurant in Islamabad called the Great Wall. Author interview with Peter Griffin.

13 The Ghauri was test-fired on 6 April 1998.

14 See Center for Defense Information, <http://www.cdi.org/issues/nukef&f/database/innukes.html>.

15 Naeem Ahmad Salik, "Missile Issues in South Asia," *Non-Proliferation Review*, summer 2002, p. 52.

16 Strobe Talbott, *Engaging India* (Brookings Institution Press, Washington, 2004).

17 Karl Inderfurth told the authors that shortly before he was sent to Islamabad to try to stop Pakistan from following India's lead, colleagues described his job as "mission impossible."

18 This comment is recalled by Talbott.

19 Ibid.

20 Ibid.

21 Author interview with Karl Inderfurth.

22 Talbott.

23 Author interview with Nawaz Sharif, London, summer 2006.

24 This quote was recalled by Karl Inderfurth.

25 Peter Bergen, *The Osama Bin Laden I Know* (Free Press, New York, 2006), p. 341.

26 Al-Qaeda and a coalition of Islamist groups known as the International Islamic Front for Jihad against Jews and Crusaders declared war on the US in January 1998 in a statement written by Ayman al-Zawahiri. It was published on 23 February 1998, in London, in the newspaper *Al-Quds al-Arabi*.

27 Richard A. Clarke, *Against All Enemies* (Free Press, London, 2004).

28 For more on this meeting, see Rai Muhammad Saleh Azam, *When Mountains Move: The Story of Chagai* (Islamabad, 1998).

29 Ibid.

30 Dr. Samar Mubarakmand, "A Science Odyssey," Khwarzimic Science Society speech, 30 November 1998.

31 Azam.

32 Ibid.

33 Ibid.

34 Author interview with Nawaz Sharif, London, summer 2006.

35 Mubarakmand.

36 See Talbott, and Bruce Riedel, *American Diplomacy and the 1999 Kargil Summit at Blair House* (Center for the Advanced Study of India, Policy Paper Series, University of Pennsylvania, 2002).

37 Azam.

38 Mubarakmand.

39 Azam, and Mubarakmand.

40 For more details on how a nuclear bomb works, see Frank Barnaby, *How to Build a Nuclear Bomb* (Granta Books, London, 2003).

41 Mubarakmand.

42 Talbott.

NOTES

43 Ibid., and author interview with Nawaz Sharif.

44 "Interview with Abdul Qadeer Khan," *The News*, Islamabad, 30 May 1998.

45 The letter was dated 30 June 1998 and is quoted in *Dr. A. Q. Khan Research Laboratories 1976–2001, 25 Years of Excellence and National Service*, Islamabad, 31 July 2001. Author archive.

46 The award ceremony was held on 14 August 1998 and accompanying speeches are quoted at length in *Dr. A. Q. Khan Research Laboratories 1976–2001, 25 Years of Excellence and National Service*. Author archive.

47 This letter was written on 16 August 1999 and is quoted in *Dr. A. Q. Khan Research Laboratories 1976–2001, 25 Years of Excellence and National Service*. Author archive.

48 This article was shown to the authors by Karl Inderfurth, Washington, autumn 2006.

49 Author interview with senior US official based at the US embassy in Islamabad in 1998.

50 The defectors were Colonel Ju-Hwai Choi and diplomat Young Hwan-Ko. Choi revealed that while he was military attaché at the North Korean embassy in Czechoslovakia, he had been frequently ordered to "obtain technology and equipment" for his country's nuclear reactors.

51 *Jane's Missiles and Rockets*, Vol. 2, No. 5 (May 1998), and Yossef Bodansky, *Pakistan's Nuclear Brinkmanship* (Freeman Center for Strategic Studies, Houston, Texas, 1996).

52 The first test of the Taepodong 1 was on 31 August 1998. See <http://www.fas.org/nuke/guide/dprk/missile/td-1.htm>.

53 Sharon A. Squassoni, *Weapons of Mass Destruction: Trade between North Korea and Pakistan* (Congressional Research Service, Washington, 11 March 2004).

54 Dana Priest, "US Labs at Odds on Whether Pakistani Blast Used Plutonium," *Washington Post*, 17 January 1999, and David E. Sanger and William J. Broad, "Pakistan May Have Aided North Korea A-Test," *New York Times*, 27 February 2004.

55 As told to the authors in multiple interviews both on the Pakistan side and with intelligence analysts in the US working on the Khan trail in 1998 and 1999.

56 Author interviews with Robert Einhorn, Washington, 2006.

57 North Korea signed the Agreed Framework with the United States government in Geneva on 21 October 1994. For the full wording, see <http://www.armscontrol.org/documents/af.asp>. For more background to this agreement, see Squassoni.

58 See Nuclear Threat Initiative, North Korea Missile Chronology, <www.nti.org/e_research/profiles/NK/Missile/65_689.html–111k>.

59 Author interviews with Robert Gallucci, Washington, 2006. Sometimes the visits were high profile: in December 1997, General Jehangir Karamat, Pakistan's army chief, travelled openly to Pyongyang as part of a senior military delegation, although he subsequently claimed that this trip was connected only to missile purchases.

60 This comment was related to the authors by Robert Einhorn and is confirmed by General Feroz Khan in an interview with Gordon Corera. See Gordon Corera, *Shopping for Bombs* (Hurst & Company, London, 2006).

61 CIA unclassified white paper to Congress, November 2002. See Squassoni.

62 Ibid. The plant was at Kusong, thirty miles west of Yongbyon-kun.

63 The concentration facility was at the Namch'on Joint Chemical Industry Company,

thirty miles north of the demilitarized zone. See Joseph S. Bermudez, Jr, "Exposing North Korea's Secret Nuclear Infrastructure," *Jane's Intelligence Review*, 1 July 1999.

64 Larry A. Niksch, *North Korea's Nuclear Weapons Program* (Congressional Research Service, Washington, 25 March 2005).

65 Since 1989, IAEA inspectors had monitored reports that troops from North Korea's elite 3rd/27th Engineer Bureau were excavating 400,000 square meters of mountainside between Kumch'ang-ni and a neighboring town.

66 Bermudez.

67 Evidence had emerged in January 1998 that the North Koreans were constructing a nuclear-related facility at Ha'gap which "included thirty completed buildings and five more under construction ... four tunnels linking a hill with eleven support and service buildings." The debriefing of an unidentified defector in 1999 was said to have elicited information that there was a secret uranium processing site beneath the hill. See Bermudez, and a report in *Sankei Shimbun*, Tokyo, September 2000.

68 Squassoni.

69 General Feroz Khan. See Corera.

70 The Pakistan army's decision to move Khan on from Dubai was confirmed by Dr. Shafiq ur-Rehman in an interview with the authors in Islamabad, spring 2006. Dr. Shafiq said that Khan did nothing without the authority of the generals, who tracked his every move through the ISI.

71 Author interviews with Peter Griffin, France, 2006–7.

72 According to Dr. Shafiq ur-Rehman, author interview.

73 According to Siddiqui.

74 Author telephone interview with Joseph Wilson, Washington, autumn 2006.

75 The allegation that Khan co-owned the al-Shifa plant was made to the authors by K. Subrahmanyam, former chairman of India's joint intelligence committee, author interview, New Delhi, spring 2006. Also author interview with officials from Mossad, Tel Aviv, spring 2006.

76 For more on the FBI investigation into the US embassy bombings, see Lawrence Wright.

77 US intelligence was told by sources in Sudan and Pakistan that Osama bin Laden had paid for the construction of the Hendrina Khan Hotel on the understanding that A. Q. Khan would supervise mining interests left behind in Sudan by bin Laden when he returned to Afghanistan in 1996. See also Raman.

78 USA vs Usama bin Laden, testimony of Jamal al-Fadl, 7 and 20 February 2001.

15: THE WINDOW OF VULNERABILITY

1 The bombings had come just six months after a coalition of Islamist groups issued a fatwa against America in January 1998. It was published in London newspaper *Al-Quds al-Arabi*, 23 February 1998, and just weeks later Osama bin Laden had issued his own warning to the US in his television interview with *ABC News*.

2 For more on this summit, see Dennis Kux, *The United States and Pakistan 1947–2000* (Woodrow Wilson Center Press, Washington, 2001), p. 351. Also see Strobe Talbott, *Engaging India* (Brookings Institution Press, Washington, 2004). For more on the bombings of al-Qaeda's bases in Khost, Afghanistan, see Simon Reeve, *The New Jackals, Ramzi Yousef, Osama bin Laden and the Future of Terrorism* (André

Deutsch, London, 1999) and Lawrence Wright, *The Looming Tower* (Allen Lane, London, 2006).

3 For more on America's response and the IMF reaction, see Kux.

4 Reports of this visit appeared in *Khabrain*, Pakistan's second-largest-selling Urdu newspaper.

5 "Pakistan Offers UAE Nuclear Training but Not Atomic Bombs," *Jasarat*, 26 May 1999.

6 Author interviews with Husain Haqqani, Washington, spring 2006.

7 For more on the Indian perspective, see The Kargil Review Committee Report, *From Surprise to Reckoning* (Sage Publications, New Delhi, 1999).

8 Pervez Musharraf, *In the Line of Fire* (Free Press, New York, 2006).

9 Author interview with Nawaz Sharif, London, summer 2006.

10 Bruce Riedel, *American Diplomacy and the 1999 Kargil Summit at Blair House* (Center for the Advanced Study of India, Policy Paper Series, University of Pennsylvania, 2002).

11 Interview with Karl Inderfurth, Washington, autumn 2006. See also Riedel.

12 Blair House is the presidential guest house.

13 Riedel.

14 Ibid.

15 Author interview with Karl Inderfurth.

16 Author interviews with Shahbaz Sharif, London, summer 2006.

17 Musharraf, pp. 101–10.

18 Ibid.

19 Ibid.

20 Author interview with Nawaz Sharif.

21 Author interview with Sharifuddin Pirzada, Islamabad, spring 2006.

22 Gulzar became 10 Corps commander (Rawalpindi), Aziz stayed on in his previous position as chief of general staff, and Usmani became 5 Corps commander (Karachi).

23 Author interview with Sharifuddin Pirzada.

24 Author interview with Karl Inderfurth.

25 This quote was recalled by Karl Inderfurth to the authors.

26 Wright, p. 265.

27 Author interview with Karl Inderfurth.

28 Author interviews with Robert Gallucci, Washington, 2006.

29 Author interview with Daniel Coleman, FBI investigator seconded to Alec Station in 1996, New York, autumn 2006. For more on the genesis of Alec Station, see Wright.

30 Peter L. Bergen, *The Osama bin Laden I Know* (Free Press, New York, 2006), p. 339.

31 Author interview with Daniel Coleman.

32 Ibid. The letter is quoted in full in Bergen, p. 345.

33 For discussions in the US about the unsuitability of the trip, see Talbott.

34 Newt Gingrich was the Republican speaker of the House. This story was told to the authors by Karl Inderfurth.

35 Talbott, p. 191.

36 Author interview with Karl Inderfurth.

37 Ibid. See also Richard P. Cronin, K. Alan Kronstadt, Sharon A. Squassoni, *Pakistan's Nuclear Proliferation Activities and the Recommendations of the 9/11 Commission*

(Congressional Research Service, Washington, 25 January 2005).

38 Hassan Abbas, *Pakistan's Drift into Extremism* (M. E. Sharpe, New York, 2004), p. 190.

39 For more on the thinking behind these measures, see interview with General Feroz Khan in Gordon Corera, *Shopping for Bombs* (Hurst & Company, London, 2006).

40 Author interviews with Husain Haqqani.

41 General Feroz Khan later explained why Khan had continued to proliferate after this order had been issued by suggesting he had been impossible to rein in, and that he did not have the authority to stop him. Corera.

42 Author interview with Dr. Shafiq ur-Rehman, Islamabad, spring 2006. Dr. Shafiq said that when Khan heard stories that he was being investigated by the ISI, he laughed.

43 Corera, p. 147.

44 This quote was related to the authors by Dr. Shafiq ur-Rehman, whose father was responsible for monitoring all C-130 transport aircraft delivering items to and from KRL.

45 The advertisements were placed in *The News* and *Dawn*. Author archive.

46 This article, headlined "Pakistan's Nuclear Material and Equipment for Sale," was reprinted in an Urdu book by Shahid Nazir Ahmed, *Dr. A. Q. Khan* (Islamabad, 2001). Author archive.

47 In an interview with the authors, Robert Einhorn explained that the US had been negotiating with Pakistan to improve export controls on nuclear-related items from Pakistan for some time, but that the last thing Washington had envisaged was a promotional offer. Author interviews, Washington, 2006.

48 This report was dated June 2000 and is quoted in Cronin, Kronstadt and Squassoni, p. 14.

49 Author interviews with Robert Einhorn. He recalled first raising the issue of Libya with Pakistan in the summer of 2000.

50 This missile was the Shaheen II, developed by Samar Mubarakmand at PAEC.

51 Luke Harding and Rory McCarthy, "Nuclear Rivals to Test Fire Missiles," *Guardian*, 27 September 2000.

52 IDEAS 2000 was held in Karachi from 14–17 November 2000 and is featured in *Dr. A. Q. Khan Research Laboratories 1976–2001, 25 Years of Excellence and National Service*, Islamabad, 31 July 2001. Author archive.

53 Alan Coke was interviewed by Alan Urry for the radio documentary *Dirty Wars, File on Four*, BBC Radio 4, 17 August 2004.

54 The *New York Times* coined the phrase. For more on the emergence of the Vulcans and their individual backgrounds, see Jim Mann, *Rise of the Vulcans* (Penguin Books, New York, 2004).

55 During the hearing Paul Wolfowitz insisted that most of the events in 1989 concerning Richard Barlow's F-16 report being withdrawn, his dismissal and the subsequent investigation, had taken place before he became under secretary of defense and that he had been unaware of Barlow's case entirely until he was contacted eighteen months before the nomination hearing to supply an affidavit to Barlow's lawyers. Hearing of the Senate Armed Services Committee, Nomination of Paul Wolfowitz to be Deputy Secretary of Defense, 27 February 2001.

56 <www.telegraph.co.uk/news/main.jhtml?xml=/news/2000/08/04/wus04.xml>.

57 Wulf made several inspection trips to North Korea after it had signed the Agreed

Framework with the US government in 1994. Author interview with Norm Wulf, Virginia, spring 2006.

58 Mann.

59 The treaty was signed in Helsinki in May 1972.

60 John Cassidy, "The Next Crusade," *New Yorker*, 9 April 2007.

61 Mann.

62 For the full letter, see <http://www.newamericancentury.org/iraqclintonletter.htm>.

63 <http://www.newamericancentury.org/defjull698.htm>.

64 Richard A. Clarke, *Against All Enemies* (Free Press, London, 2004).

65 Ibid.

66 Author interviews with Robert Einhorn.

67 A similar territorial stand-off between government agencies would lead to the intelligence disasters that foreshadowed 9/11, where the CIA was pushing for action while the FBI held back.

68 Clarke.

69 Barton Gellman and Dafna Linzer, "Unprecedented Peril Forces Tough Calls," *Washington Post*, 26 October 2004.

70 The attack was on 12 October 2000.

71 Clarke.

72 Israeli intelligence had reported that in 1998 bin Laden had paid more than $2 million to a middleman in Kazakhstan who promised to deliver a stolen warhead—but the delivery, for reasons unknown, never took place. A British freelance cameraman who had been living in Kabul since 1980 intercepted another offer to sell old Soviet nuclear materials, including 150 g of highly enriched uranium, by a group based in the northern Afghan city of Mazar-e-Sharif. Some group members had become sick after handling the material, which turned out to be radioactive waste, probably from a hospital X-ray machine. See the story of Peter Jouvenal, as told to Bergen, p. 345.

73 Richard A. Falkenrath, *Combating Proliferation of WMDs*, May 2002.

74 Clarke.

75 B. Raman, "Looming Jihadi Anarchy in Pakistan," International Terrorism Monitor, Paper No. 212, 30 March 2007; see South Asia Analysis Group, <www.saag.org>.

76 Amy Waldman and David Rhode interview with President Musharraf, *New York Times*, 15 February 2004.

77 Zahid Malik, *Dr. A. Q. Khan and the Islamic Bomb* (Hurmat Publications, Islamabad, 1992).

78 Author interviews with Ghulam Hasnain, Islamabad, 2006.

79 In an interview published in *The Muslim* on 11 March 2001.

80 The missile concerned was the Haider, a project actually under the wings of Dr. Samar Mubarakmand at PAEC, and was still very much in development.

81 Musharraf.

82 The text was later carried by all newspapers in Pakistan.

83 *Dr. A. Q. Khan Research Laboratories 1976–2001, 25 Years of Excellence and National Service*. Author archive.

84 This happened shortly before the Agra summit of 14–16 July 2001, a landmark meeting between Musharraf and Indian prime minister Atal Bihari Vajpayee to discuss nuclear diplomacy. Before it, Musharraf had called in Sharifuddin Pirzada, who recalled: "He

told me that the president of India was supposed to meet him off the plane in New Delhi. But Indian protocol said he could not meet a general. 'What should I do?' he asked." Pirzada had a solution. "Make yourself president too, I said. He did immediately." Author interview with Sharifuddin Pirzada, Islamabad, spring 2006.

85 Dr. Shafiq ur-Rehman, author interview, Islamabad, spring 2006.

86 Author interviews with former ISI officer, Islamabad, spring 2006.

87 Stephen Fidler and Edward Luce, "US Fears North Korea Could Gain Nuclear Capability through Pakistan," *Financial Times*, 1 June 2001.

88 Ibid.

89 Mann, p. 293.

90 Author interview with senior ISI officer, Islamabad, spring 2006.

91 The biographical information on Sultan Bashiruddin Mahmood and Chaudiri Abdul Majeed was obtained in author interviews with several nuclear scientists in Pakistan who wish to remain anonymous. Also author interviews with Pervez Hoodbhoy, Islamabad, spring 2006.

92 *Doomsday and Life after Death—The Ultimate Fate of the Universe as Seen through the Holy Quran* was published in 1987. *Cosmology and Human Destiny* was published in 1998.

93 See David Albright and Holly Higgins, "A Bomb for the Ummah," *Bulletin of the Atomic Scientists*, March–April 2003.

94 Ibid. See also Robert Sam Anson, "The Journalist and The Terrorist," *Vanity Fair*, 1 August 2002.

95 This was according to Mahmood's son, who spoke to local journalists in Islamabad.

96 See Albright and Higgins. See also Clarke.

97 Clarke.

98 Musharraf, pp. 199–200.

99 Associated Press, 22 August 2002.

100 Mann, p. 306.

101 Armitage asked Pakistan's US ambassador Maleeha Lodhi to come along with him. The description of this meeting comes from multiple sources, including Musharraf, and Bob Woodward, *Bush at War* (Simon & Schuster, New York, 2003).

102 Woodward, *Bush at War*.

103 Musharraf.

104 Ibid, p. 201.

105 Ibid.

106 The description of this meeting comes from Sharifuddin Pirzada, author interview, Islamabad, spring 2006, and from a high-ranking Pakistan army officer who does not wish to be named.

107 Author interview with Sharifuddin Pirzada.

16: MUSH AND BUSH

1 Bush was questioned in 2000 while campaigning for the presidency. Questioner: Can you name the general who is in charge of Pakistan? Bush: Wait, wait, is this fifty questions? Questioner: No, it's four questions of four leaders in four hot spots. Bush: The new Pakistani general, he's just been elected—not elected, this guy just took over office. It appears this guy is going to bring stability to the country, and I think that's

good news for the subcontinent. Questioner: Can you name him? Bush: General. I can't name the general. <http://thinkprogress.org/2006/03/03/bush-on-pakistan/>.

2 He would make the remark in a press conference with Musharraf and Mohammed Karzai in Washington on 28 September 2006.

3 This was how the match would come to be described in Pakistan after 9/11. See *The Herald* and *Newsline*.

4 These pictures were taken by Karen Davies, a British photographer based in Islamabad, and would be used over and over again in the Western press.

5 See K. Alan Kronstadt, *Pakistan–US Relations* (Congressional Research Service, Washington, 27 April 2005).

6 This amendment would be carried out by Sharifuddin Pirzada, who discussed it with the author in an interview, Islamabad, spring 2006.

7 Washington's opinion mattered, as in Pakistan the forces calling for democracy traditionally relied on the US to back their campaigns, such as the election of Benazir Bhutto in 1988.

8 This quote comes from the American Civil Liberties Union (ACLU). For more on the impact of the Patriot Act, see the ACLU website, <http://www.aclu.org/safefree/resources/17343res20031114.html>.

9 The press conference in which Fleischer said this was in October 2002. See Glenn Kessler, "Pakistan's N. Korea Deals Stir Scrutiny—Aid to Nuclear Arms Bid May Be Recent," *Washington Post*, 13 November 2002.

10 Colin Powell discussed military action against Afghanistan in an interview on *Meet the Press*, NBC, 23 September 2001.

11 For more on the Iraqi National Congress intelligence, see Public Broadcasting Service, *Paths to Power*, <http://www.pbs.org/wgbh/pages/frontline/shows/pentagon/paths/bush2.html>.

12 For more on the lobbying for war in Iraq by Wolfowitz and Libby, see Jim Mann, *Rise of the Vulcans* (Penguin Books, New York, 2004).

13 For more analysis, see Vali Nasr, *The Shia Revival* (W. W. Norton & Company, New York, 2006).

14 General Ahmed was demoted to corps commander on 7 October 2001.

15 Ahmed Rashid, *Daily Telegraph*, 12 October 2001.

16 Usmani went on 7 October. The view that Musharraf was simply consolidating power came from author interviews with, among others, Sharifuddin Pirzada, Islamabad, spring 2006.

17 For more on the backgrounds and connections between these officers, see B. Raman, "Pakistan: The Mullahs' Blue-Eyed General," South Asia Analysis Group, Paper 146, 9 September 2000, <www.saag.org/papers2/paper146.html>.

18 Aziz was retained as chief of general staff, a position that enabled him to travel around the country overseeing the Pakistan army's jihad operations. The protest was led by Qazi Hussain Ahmed, the leader of Jamaat-e-Islami.

19 B. Raman, "Pakistan: The Mullahs' Blue-Eyed General."

20 Aziz held the position of chairman of the joint chiefs of staff from 7 October 2001 to October 2004.

21 Raman, "Pakistan: The Mullahs' Blue-Eyed General."

22 "Pakistan Confirms ISI Chief Replaced," *Times of India*, 9 October 2001, <http://timesofindia.indiatimes.com/articleshow/1454746255.cms>.

23 Musharraf's democratic-leaning personal adviser and chief of staff, General Ghulam Ahmed Khan, died in a car crash on 24 August 2001: <http://www.presidentof pakistan.gov.pk/PRPressReleaseDetail.aspx?nPRPressReleaseId=379&nYear=2006& nMonth=9>. Also author interviews with Sharifuddin Pirzada, spring 2006, Islamabad.

24 Graham Allison, *Nuclear Terrorism* (Owl Books, Henry Holt Company, New York, 2004).

25 Richard Clarke had warned of this prospect months in advance and the intelligence on such a plan had been recovered from Ramzi Yousef's computer, seized in the Philippines in 1993. See Richard A. Clarke, *Against All Enemies* (Free Press, London, 2004), and Simon Reeve, *The New Jackals, Ramzi Yousef, Osama bin Laden and the Future of Terrorism* (André Deutsch, London, 1999).

26 See Allison, and Clarke.

27 Azim Mahmood spoke to Pakistani reporters in Islamabad. His interview was later carried by the *Guardian* in London on 1 November 2001.

28 The two senior military officers in UTN were Brigadier Mohammad Hanif, who was the foundation's finance director, and Commodore Arshad Ali Chaudhary, vice president of the foundation. See David Albright and Holly Higgins, "A Bomb for the Ummah," *Bulletin of the Atomic Scientists*, March–April 2003.

29 David Sanger, James Risen and Douglas Frantz, "Nuclear Experts in Pakistan May Have Links to Al Qaeda," *New York Times*, 9 December 2001.

30 Ibid.

31 See Albright and Higgins. For more on Gul's activities after he was dismissed from the ISI by Benazir Bhutto, see B. Raman, "Looming Jihadi Anarchy in Pakistan," International Terrorism Monitor, Paper No. 212, 30 March 2007.

32 Mike Boettcher, "Live from Afghanistan—Was Al Qaeda Working on a Superbomb?" CNN, 24 January 2002.

33 This quote is from Donald Rumsfeld and is cited in Allison, p. 25.

34 Boettcher.

35 *Washington Post*, 12 December 2001.

36 US State Department, "Bush Blocks Assets to Two More Terrorist Groups," 20 December 2001, <http://usinfo.state.gov/is/Archive_Index/Bush_Blocks_Assets_of_Two_More_Terrorist_Groups.html>.

37 *Mercury News*, 28 October 2001.

38 Another article quoted a Pakistani military spokesman as saying that it was "inconceivable that a nuclear scientist would travel to Afghanistan without getting clearance from Pakistani officials." Daniel Pearl and Steve Levine, "Pakistan Has Ties to Group It Vowed to Curb: Military State's Elite Is Linked to Activities of Nuclear Scientist," *Wall Street Journal*, 24 December 2001. Another Pakistani official told a Washington-based reporter that he had received instructions in the mid-1990s that in all contacts with American officials he should deny that Pakistan was developing nuclear weapons. "It's just one of those things you can't be absolutely straightforward about," he said. John Burns, *New York Times*, 1 November 2001.

39 Hekmatyar would reveal that he led bin Laden and his men to freedom across the Tora Bora mountains of Afghanistan and into Pakistan in an interview with Geo TV, Islamabad, 11 January 2007, <http://news.bbc.co.uk/2/hi/south_asia/6252975.stm>.

40 Boettcher.
41 Ibid.
42 CNN news report from Afghanistan, 1 November 2001; CNN news report from Afghanistan, 24 January 2002; *Washington Post*, 22 November 2001; *New York Times*, 18 March 2002.
43 Some documents showed a far less sophisticated approach, including a one-page typed document in English that simplistically discussed hydrogen bombs, comparing the chemical structure of plutonium to fictitious elements Saturium, Jupiternium, and Marrissum. Someone had gone through the text and written in the margin in Arabic: "This is bullshit."
44 The speech was on 12 September 2002. See <www.whitehouse.gov/news/releases/2002/09/20020912-1.htm>.
45 The interview was in April 2002. See: <http://www.jihadwatch.org/archives/015710.php>.
46 Middle East Media Research Institute, Special Dispatch Series 388, 12 June 2002.
47 The US government said that Zubaida named José Padilla, an American citizen of Puerto Rican origin, as being involved in a scouting mission for an al-Qaeda operation to attack the United States with a dirty bomb designed by Abu Khabab al-Masri. Padilla was subsequently arrested at Chicago O'Hare airport getting off a flight from Pakistan in May 2002 and accused of travelling to Afghanistan for training in 1998 where he allegedly met Abu Zubaida, who sent him to an al-Qaeda training camp near Lahore. However, when Padilla was finally charged in November 2005, there was no mention of the dirty bomb allegation, only that he was accused of aiding terrorists and conspiracy to murder US nationals overseas.
48 Mann.
49 In March 1983, while lobbying for support for the Star Wars program, a prohibitively expensive space-based system to defend the nation from attack by ballistic missiles, Reagan had denounced the Soviet Union as an "evil empire" in a speech to the National Association of Evangelicals.
50 Rumsfeld was then sitting on the congressional missile commission.
51 The 1992 defense planning guidance recommended the US adopt pre-emptive force and lone superpower status, and the Defense Department team also took advice from independent experts Albert Wohlstetter and Richard Perle. See Mann.
52 For full text of the speech, see: <www.whitehouse.gov/news/releases/2002/06/20020601-3.html>.
53 Rt Hon. Lord Butler of Brockwell, *Review of Intelligence on Weapons of Mass Destruction*, Report of a Committee of Privy Counsellors (Stationery Office, London, 14 July 2004).
54 Author interviews with Peter Griffin, France, 2006–7.
55 Ibid.
56 Director of the Special Branch, Polis Diraja Malaysia (Royal Malaysian Police), "Report by Inspector General of Police in Relation to Investigation of Alleged Production of Components for Libya's Uranium Enrichment Program," Bukit Aman, Malaysia, 20 February 2004. Also interviews with intelligence and Foreign Office sources, London, 2006.
57 Badawi became deputy prime minister in 1999 and prime minister in 2003.
58 Tahir joined Kaspadu as a non-executive director and investor. Leslie Lopez, "How

the Pakistani Nuclear Ring Managed to Skirt Export Laws," *Wall Street Journal*, 17 February 2004.

59 The Swiss company was called Vacuum Apparat Technik. For more on this company's relationship to A. Q. Khan, see Steve Weissman and Herbert Krosney, *The Islamic Bomb* (Times Books, New York, 1981).

60 *Report by Inspector General of Police in Relation to Investigation of Alleged Production of Components for Libya's Uranium Enrichment Program*; Kenley Butler, Sammy Salama and Leonard S. Spector, "Where Is the Justice?" *Bulletin of the Atomic Scientists*, November–December 2006; Juergen Dahlkamp, Georg Mascolo, Holger Stark, "Network of Death on Trial," *Der Spiegel*, 13 March 2006; Steve Coll, "The Atomic Emporium," *New Yorker*, 7 and 14 August 2006.

61 Peter Griffin recalled: "Siddiqui had already been warned by British Customs that he would need export licenses for many of the things going to Pakistan. They'd warn you that something you were about to export was on a list. When I was doing it, I would heed their advice and I wouldn't get prosecuted. I wrote an assessment on Siddiqui's likelihood of being convicted for his lawyer. I said that Siddiqui would be prosecuted. He was." Author interview.

62 For more on the preparations for war in Iraq, see James Risen, *State of War* (Free Press, New York, 2006); Bob Woodward, *Plan of Attack* (Simon & Schuster, New York, 2004); Michael R. Gordon and Bernard E. Trainor, *Cobra II* (Knopf, New York, 2006); and Thomas E. Ricks, *Fiasco* (Penguin Group (USA), New York, 2006).

63 For a transcript of this speech, see <www.whitehouse.gov/news/releases/2002/04/20020406-3.html>.

64 Robert Gallucci as far back as 1996 had coined this phrase, and it was also being bandied about by CIA and ACDA analysts. Author interviews with Robert Gallucci, Washington, 2006.

65 Tony Blair interview, *Today*, BBC Radio 4, 5 May 2005.

66 Ibid.

67 Memo from Matthew Rycroft to David Manning, 23 July 2002. Reproduced by Michael Smith, "Blair Planned Iraq War from Start," *Sunday Times*, 1 May 2005.

68 Butler, *Review of Intelligence on Weapons of Mass Destruction*.

69 Author interviews with Alireza Jafarzadeh, Washington, 2006.

70 News reports from Associated Press, Deutsche Press Association, United Press International, Washington, 14 August 2002.

71 Jafarzadeh's revelations had a more immediate impact in Tehran, where the Khatami regime angrily denounced the "wave of extensive propaganda" emanating from Washington, while the Revolutionary Guard Corps announced that it had launched military exercises to defend the nation against a US-led attack.

72 <http://www.iran-interlink.org/files/info/Jafarzadeh%20bio.htm>.

73 Having studied at the universities of Michigan and Texas after leaving Iran shortly before the 1979 revolution, Jafarzadeh was granted permanent right to work in the US.

74 Author interviews with Alireza Jafarzadeh.

75 Two of the scientists to be trained were identified as Saeed, or Sayyid, Reza and Hadi Ranbshahr or Rambashahr. See report in *Al-Watan*, Kuwait, 13 June 1988.

76 Author interview with Moshe Ya'alon, Washington, spring 2006.

77 This allegation was made to the authors by Moshe Ya'alon. Jafarzadeh bitterly denied it was true.

78 The images were taken on 16 September 2002.

79 Paul Brannan and David Albright, "ISIS Imagery Briefing: New Activities at the Esfahan and Natanz Nuclear Sites in Iran," Institute for Science and International Security (ISIS), 14 April 2006.

80 David Albright and Corey Hinderstein, "The Iranian Gas Centrifuge Uranium Enrichment Plant at Natanz: Drawing from Commercial Satellite Images," ISIS, 14 March 2003.

81 Seymour Hersh, "The Cold Test," *New Yorker*, 27 January 2003. The quote comes from the CIA national intelligence estimate, June 2002.

82 Warren P. Strobel, "Career Weapons Experts Booted by Bush Team," *Philadelphia Inquirer*, 8 February 2006. See also Glenn Kessler, "Administration Critics Chafe at State Department Shuffle," *Washington Post*, 21 February 2006.

83 Author interview with Norm Wulf, Virginia, spring 2006.

84 Ibid.

85 In an interview with *Der Spiegel* on 21 February 2005, ElBaradei said: "It becomes unpleasant when you apparently cannot even have a private phone conversation with your wife or your daughter."

86 Hersh.

87 Ibid.

88 Bob Woodward, *Bush at War* (Simon & Schuster, New York, 2003).

89 Bolton made his remarks while part of the State Department's delegation to six-party talks on the North Korean nuclear program in August 2003. See Soo-Jeong Lee, "North Korea Bans Bolton from Talks," Associated Press, 4 August 2003.

90 Hersh.

91 Larry A. Niksch, *North Korea's Nuclear Weapons Program* (Congressional Research Service, 17 March 2003).

92 *Nightline*, ABC and *Face the Nation*, CBS, 20 October 2002.

93 This episode was described to the authors by Norm Wulf.

94 Pyongyang ejected the two IAEA officials staying at the nuclear power plant's guest house and also announced it would resume construction of two large reactors that had been frozen in 1994, charging the Bush administration with planning a "pre-emptive nuclear attack." This episode was described to the authors by Norm Wulf. See also Niksch.

95 Author interviews with Robert Gallucci, Washington, 2006.

96 David E. Sanger, "Pakistan, North Korea Set Up Nuclear Swap," *New York Times*, 24 November 2002.

97 Powell made his comments on 25 November 2002, <http://www.state.gov/secretary/former/powell/remarks/2002/15494.htm>.

98 See Dennis Kux, *The United States and Pakistan 1947–2000* (Woodrow Wilson Center Press, Washington, 2001).

99 Author interviews with Richard Barlow, Montana, 2006.

100 The error was that it was required first to pass the bill through a subcommittee of the Senate judiciary committee.

101 The rules of the committee allowed a bill to be dropped if one senator objected to it.

102 It was referred by the Senate judiciary committee, which voted on 8 October 1998.

103 Author interview with Robert Gallucci.

104 28 January 2003, <www.whitehouse.gov/news/releases/2003/01/20030128-19.html>.

105 The Iraq–Niger uranium connection had been highlighted first in a British government white paper advocating war against Iraq in September 2002.

106 Dana Priest and Dana Milbank, "President Defends Allegations on Iraq," *Washington Post*, 15 July 2003.

107 28 January 2003, <www.whitehouse.gov/news/releases/2003/01/20030128-19.html>.

108 See Gary Milhollin, *Licensing Mass Destruction, US Exports to Iraq, 1985–1990* (Wisconsin Project on Nuclear Arms Control, June 1991).

109 Khatami's speech was on 9 February 2003. See Paul Kerr, "Iran Mining Uranium, Greatly Expanding Nuclear Facilities," *Arms Control Today*, March 2003.

110 Gareth Porter, "Neocons Block 2003 Nuclear Talks with Iran," Inter Press Service, 29 March 2006, <http://www.antiwar.com/orig/porter.php?articleid=8778>.

111 The visit was conducted on 21 February 2003. Author interviews with Alireza Jafarzadeh.

112 IAEA Board of Governors, "Implementation of the NPT Safeguard Agreement in the Islamic Republic of Iran," IAEA, GOV/2003/75, 10 November 2003.

113 Paul Kerr, "IAEA 'Taken Aback' by Speed of Iran's Nuclear Program," *Arms Control Today*, April 2003. The centrifuges were twice as efficient as those produced by URENCO, with a throughput as high as 12 to 14 SWU per year.

114 Gordon Corera, *Shopping for Bombs* (Hurst & Company, London, 2006).

115 For a copy of this cable, see <http://www.judicialwatch.org/archive/2006/statedocqadhafi.pdf>.

116 Interview from *File on Four*, "Libya and the Nuclear Walmart," BBC Radio 4, September 2004. However, a senior Pentagon official, who was briefed by MI6 about the negotiations, said: "It became more urgent for [Gaddafi] to get off the bad list when he saw the fate of the Taliban regime and the Saddam Hussein regime."

117 Interview from *File on Four*, "Libya and the Nuclear Walmart."

118 Author interviews with Wajid Shamsul Hasan, London, 2006–7.

119 Corera.

120 Author interviews with intelligence and Foreign Office sources in London and CIA sources in the US. Also author interviews with Robert Gallucci, Washington, 2006.

121 A crucial issue, according to those involved in the affair, was Muammar Gaddafi's demand that if Libya abandoned its WMD program, the US in turn would drop its goal of regime change, a compromise that the hard-line Bolton would never willingly accept. Author interviews with intelligence and Foreign Office sources in London and CIA sources in the US.

122 Author interviews with intelligence and Foreign Office sources in London and CIA sources in the US.

123 On 24 March 2003, the USA imposed two-year sanctions against KRL and the Changgwang Sinyong Corporation, which would debar them from any trade or technological exchanges with the US.

124 Author interviews with Peter Griffin, France 2006–7. Griffin recalled that he was in Islamabad from 27 March to 4 April 2003.

125 Two months after Griffin was in Pakistan he flew to Dubai to sign papers with a new sponsor for his Dubai-based import-export company, Gulf Technical Industries. Al Abbar had pulled out, concerned that the company was attracting an unwarranted

amount of attention from intelligence services in the Gulf and Europe.

126 Author interviews with Anna Griffin, France, 2006–7.

127 Author interviews with Peter Griffin.

128 The fact that the CIA and State Department were very selective with what intelligence they passed to the IAEA was confirmed to the authors by Marvin Peterson, who worked as science attaché to the US mission in Vienna in the mid-1990s. Author interviews, Washington, autumn 2006.

129 *Implementation of the NPT Safeguards Agreement in the Islamic Republic of Iran*, IAEA, Gov/2003/75, 10 November 2003.

130 Interview with Flynt Leverett, then the National Security Council's senior director for Middle East affairs. Gareth Porter, "Neocons Block 2003 Nuclear Talks with Iran," Inter Press Service, 29 March 2006, <http://www.antiwar.com/orig/porter.php?articleid=8778>.

131 Ibid.

132 Ibid.

133 Ibid. See also ABC News, 30 May 2003, for reports on the Pentagon position.

17: MISSION ACCOMPLISHED

1 The terms of this informal agreement were spelled out to the authors during interviews in London with British politicians and civil servants privy to the deal, and in the US with a former State Department official who worked in non-proliferation and was familiar with A. Q. Khan during this period, conducted in 2006 and 2007.

2 Ibid.

3 The official end of combat was declared on 1 May 2003.

4 In several interviews with the authors in spring and summer 2006, officials then in the State Department and CIA characterized these comments by Musharraf as "cringe-worthy," knowing as they did that the Pakistan military was proliferating.

5 Author interviews in London with British politicians and civil servants privy to the deal, and in the US with a former State Department official who worked in non-proliferation and was familiar with A. Q. Khan during this period.

6 Author interview with White House official, Washington, spring 2006.

7 This scene was later described in Pervez Musharraf, *In the Line of Fire* (Free Press, New York, 2006).

8 Author interviews in 2006 with close former aides to Musharraf in Islamabad and Rawalpindi, officers and civil servants.

9 He made these claims in his book, *In the Line of Fire*.

10 Ibid. Musharraf added that the allegations had not come as a complete surprise, as "in my gut, I was getting more and more suspicious of him."

11 Khan's inner circle maintained in interviews with the authors in 2006 in Islamabad and Rawalpindi that a leak had sprung from within their group. They tracked it down and reduced the number of suspicious parties to a small circle of European agents working on the Libyan program for Pakistan. See below for their conclusions.

12 CENTCOM is US Central Command, whose jurisdiction is the Middle East, East Africa and Central Asia.

13 The road is officially now known as Khayaban-e-Iqbal.

14 Author interview with Humayun Gauhar, Islamabad, spring 2006.
15 Author interviews with two Pakistani civil servants and one politician who attended a briefing on Khan, conducted by the authors in Islamabad in spring 2006.
16 He was also president of the Atomic Energy Organization of Iran. See also IAEA report GOV/2003/75, 10 November 2003.
17 See "Iran Provides Nuclear Declaration to the IAEA," IAEA Media Advisory 2003/2310, 23 October 2003.
18 David Albright and Corey Hinderstein, "The Centrifuge Connection," *Bulletin of the Atomic Scientists*, March–April 2004.
19 Author interviews with IAEA officials familiar with the Iranian negotiations, spring 2006.
20 Document shown to IAEA at meeting on 12 January 2005. See also IAEA report GOV/2005/67, 2 September 2005.
21 See IAEA report GOV/2003/75.
22 The UF_6 had arrived in 1991, although Iran initially would not confirm from where the drums had come. The source of the UF_6 was, however, confirmed by Pakistani sources close to A. Q. Khan, who said it had been a military prerequisite to offer UF_6 to any state clients, as this ensured they could get their programs running quicker and see the value of the Pakistani technology. It made no sense to sell the technology alone. Author interviews with A. Q. Khan aides and senior military officers, Islamabad, spring 2006.
23 The first test cascade was installed by the autumn of 2003.
24 While IAEA inspectors were briefed by Iranian scientists about further elements of the previously clandestine program, representatives of the supreme council met with the foreign ministers of Germany, France and Britain to sign the IAEA's Additional Protocol, suspending enrichment and reprocessing activities in exchange for technology.
25 Interviews by the authors with IAEA officials in Vienna who were close to the Iranian talks, summer 2006.
26 Ibid. The second secret plant idea was being constantly pushed at the IAEA and other international forums by John Bolton and other Bush officials.
27 On 2 December 2003, on CNN, Bolton argued: "The United States believes that the long-standing, massive and covert Iranian effort to acquire sensitive nuclear capabilities makes sense only as part of a nuclear weapons program." One month earlier, John Bolton had said it was "impossible to believe" the IAEA report on Iran and that it underscored the US stance that "the massive and covert Iranian efforts to acquire sensitive nuclear capabilities make sense only as part of a nuclear weapons." See Carol Giacomo, "US Seeking Consensus Approach with Allies on Iran," Reuters, 12 November 2003.
28 Burns was assistant secretary of the Bureau of Near Eastern Affairs at the State Department.
29 Author interviews with IAEA and British officials closely connected to the Libyan operation conducted in the UK in the winter of 2006 and spring of 2007.
30 IAEA Board of Governors Implementation of the NPT Safeguards Agreement of the Socialist People's Libyan Arab Jamahiriya, IAEA, GOV/2004/12, 20 February 2004.
31 A copy of the complete report by the Malaysian police into B. S. A. Tahir was given to the authors and is referenced throughout this chapter. See also published report

Director of the Special Branch, Polis Diraja Malaysia (Royal Malaysian Police), *Report by Inspector General of Police in Relation to Investigation of Alleged Production of Components for Libya's Uranium Enrichment Program* (Bukit Aman, Malaysia, 20 February 2004).

32 Tinner had erased all technical drawings and taken with him all of his blueprints, the hard disk of the company's computer and his personnel file. "This gave the impression that Urs Tinner did not wish to leave any trace of his presence there," the police reported. Polis Diraja Malaysia (Royal Malaysian Police), *Report by Inspector General of Police.*

33 The Malaysian special branch gave an account of the debriefing, although they were selective about exactly what Tahir had said, preferring to characterize his reactions and "mood." Author interviews with Malaysian investigators, February 2006.

34 This meeting, referred to by Tahir in his interrogation in Malaysia, was also confirmed by two Khan confidants in Pakistan.

35 Parts of this story are contained in the Malaysian special branch report and others were confirmed by Dr. Shafiq ur-Rehman, son of Brigadier Sajawal, who was also involved in the negotiations. Author interviews, Islamabad, spring 2006.

36 A member of the Khan inner circle, close to Tahir, gave insights into the Libyan deal during interviews in March and April 2006, in Islamabad and Europe.

37 Author interviews with intelligence and Foreign Office officials, London, 2006.

38 See also Juergen Dahlkamp, Georg Mascolo and Holger Stark, "Network of Death on Trial," *Der Spiegel*, 13 March 2006.

39 Polis Diraja Malaysia (Royal Malaysian Police), *Report by Inspector General of Police.*

40 See a good account of this in Dahlkamp, Mascolo and Stark. This slip-up showed that whoever had tipped off the MI6–CIA team had only been aware of that part of the shipment connected to Shah Alam. It was later alleged that the source was Urs Tinner, who had allegedly been recruited by the CIA shortly before the end of his Malaysian mission.

41 Polis Diraja Malaysia (Royal Malaysian Police), *Report by Inspector General of Police.*

42 Author interview with Dr. Shafiq ur-Rehman.

43 Peter Griffin would contest this vehemently and claim that the number just referred to a page in an innocuous order book, one that related to a prospective deal with the Libyan oil industry. He was told by Tahir that the workshop was to have been located in the UAE and had nothing to do with the fledgling Libyan nuclear program.

44 Author interviews with Peter Griffin, France, 2006–7.

45 They were looking for a lathe turning machine, small lathes, large and small milling machines, grinding machines, drilling machines.

46 Author interviews with Peter Griffin.

47 In fact, Griffin maintained a relationship with B. S. A. Tahir until 20 February 2004: "I was still connected with him, up until that date, chasing various outstanding cash he owed to GTI." In early 2004, GTI collapsed after adverse publicity led to the sponsor pulling out and the bank closing its accounts.

48 Saeed Buhary is still imprisoned in Dubai at the time of publication.

49 Cire died during or shortly after interrogation in Turkey on 9 August 2004, according to his family and friends in Turkey and Europe.

50 Author interview with Dr. Shafiq ur-Rehman.

18: THEY HAVE FED US TO THE DOGS

1 Here and elsewhere in the chapter are recollections from an official who worked on the team trying to lock down the Libyan program, interviewed by the authors in London and Vienna, in the winter of 2006.

2 Ibid.

3 At the time of writing Lerch's trial in Germany had been suspended, pending attempts by prosecutors to obtain testimony from foreign witnesses, and his lawyers were arguing to reduce his bail from 5 million euros.

4 A claim that was backed up by senior IAEA investigator Olli Heinonen in Vienna, who traced documents for a consignment of two P-1 rotors and seven rotors for an advanced type of centrifuge that had been flown from Islamabad to Dubai aboard a PIA jet in early to mid-2000.

5 This report was seen by the authors. See also Ian Traynor and Ian Cobain, "Clandestine Nuclear Deals Traced to Sudan," *Guardian*, 5 January 2006.

6 See Juergen Dahlkamp, Georg Mascolo and Holger Stark, "Network of Death on Trial," *Der Spiegel*, 13 March 2006, and Steve Coll, "The Atomic Emporium," *New Yorker*, 7 and 14 August 2006.

7 This is according to South African prosecutors, who have indicted Wisser for fraud and violations of the country's nuclear-control laws, while naming Lerch as a participant in the conspiracy.

8 A recollection from someone who worked on the team trying to lock down the Libyan program, interviewed by the authors in London and Vienna, winter 2006.

9 Author interviews with Peter Griffin, France, 2006–7. The lathe arrived in South Africa in November 2001.

10 See Dahlkamp, Mascolo and Stark, "Network of Death on Trial," and Coll.

11 Geiges made these allegations to South African prosecutors.

12 See Juergen Dahlkamp, Georg Mascolo and Holger Stark, "The First Accomplices Head to Trial," *Der Spiegel*, 14 March 2005.

13 Lerch later testified that he was in Johannesburg at this time. For his part, Geiges said that he remembered two visits by Lerch, one in early 2001 and another in late February 2002, during which time the two men discussed technical problems for several hours. See Dahlkamp, Mascolo and Stark, "Network of Death on Trial."

14 Coll.

15 These allegations were made in the South African indictment.

16 Gotthard Lerch was arrested by Swiss police in 2004, extradited to Germany in 2005, and arraigned in 2006.

17 Lerch's trial began in Mannheim in March 2006. In a statement he gave to prosecutors that was read out in court, he also confirmed that he had been to Iran twice. Lerch claimed his travels had nothing to do with uranium enrichment. According to court documents, he told German investigators that he was just a businessman who wanted to slow down as he approached retirement. The trial ended in July 2006 on procedural grounds. See Ian Traynor, "First Trial over Libya's Nuclear Bomb Plans Collapses," *Guardian*, 27 July 2006. See also Coll, and Gordon Corera, *Shopping for Bombs* (Hurst & Company, London, 2006), pp. 116–17.

18 Dr. Shafiq reflected on the Libyan deals: "The program was a non-starter," he said. "Whatever they got over the years, uranium from Russia, equipment from Europe and

expertise from Pakistan, was kept lying in warehouses. The Libyans did not have the resources to put any of it together; they just shifted it around to keep it from the IAEA. These guys were all nincompoops. You could give Gaddafi everything on God's earth and he would still not be able to put it together. Gaddafi had come nowhere near to realizing his dream of a centrifuge factory at Janzour. An IAEA inventory of the rusting equipment which was conducted in January 2004 found it stacked up in warehouses in its original shipping crates, and showed that the equipment was not sufficient to turn out the most sensitive P-2 components, such as the maraging steel rotors. One of the less than ideal machine tools recovered was a Spanish-made flow-forming lathe, presumably the second one that Tahir had got from Peter Griffin.

19 Douglas Frantz, "Vital Nuclear Parts Missing," *Los Angeles Times*, 25 April 2005.

20 Saddam Hussein was found on 13 December 2003.

21 Sir William Ehrman has since been appointed as ambassador to China.

22 Author interviews with US and British officials closely associated with the Libyan deal in London and Washington, 2006 and 2007.

23 See <http://news.bbc.co.uk/1/hi/uk_politics/3336073.stm>.

24 See the prime minister's website for a full text, in the speeches from 2003 section, or <http://www.pm.gov.uk/output/Page5077.asp>.

25 Dahlkamp, Mascolo and Stark, "Network of Death on Trial." Fred Kaplan, "Bush's foreign fantasy, the president thinks the world is safer than it was three years ago. Which world is he living in?" 16 July 2004, <www.Slate.com/id/2103989/>.

26 Later, these documents were recovered by South African detectives and became crucial evidence in several trials connected to the Libya deal.

27 Sam Sole, "State Bid For Secret Nuke Trial," *Mail and Guardian*, South Africa, 31 March 2007. Meyer was arrested by South African authorities in 2004 and charged with importing and exporting a lathe without permits and possessing and producing certain components for a centrifuge enrichment plant without necessary government authorization, but he was released six days later and all charges dropped, prompting immediate speculation that he had cut a deal with the authorities in connection with the ongoing prosecution of Wisser and Geiges. See also press release from the Department of Foreign Affairs, Republic of South Africa, South African Council for the Non-Proliferation of WMD, 7 September 2004: <www.dfa.gov.za/docs/2004/weap0906.htm>, and Dafna Linzer and Craig Timberg, "S. African's Arrest Seen as Key to Nuclear Black Market," *Washington Post*, 4 September 2004, and also Tiziana Cauli, "Charges Dropped against South African Accused of Trafficking in Nuclear Equipment," Associated Press, 8 September 2004.

28 Urs Tinner was arrested in Germany in October 2004 and was extradited to Switzerland, where he has been in custody awaiting trial since September 2005. His father is also in custody awaiting trial in the same case. Marco Tinner is in custody in Switzerland in the same case and is under investigation in Turkey and Malaysia. See Kenley Butler, Sammy Salama and Leonard S. Spector, "Where Is the Justice?" *Bulletin of the Atomic Scientists*, November–December 2006.

29 For more on the phone-tap saga, see for example, Dafna Linzer, "IAEA Leader's Phone Tapped, US Pores over Transcripts to Try to Oust Nuclear Chief," *Washington Post*, 12 December 2004.

30 February 2004. See <http://news.bbc.co.uk/1/hi/uk_politics/3488642.stm>.

31 Bolton turned the screw further on the IAEA, arguing that according to the agency's

necessarily tight operating conditions, ElBaradei (an Egyptian), Heinonen (a Finn), as well as many more leading IAEA officials, were not cleared to look at a Libyan warhead design since they were not citizens of a declared nuclear weapons state. To Bolton it seemed only sensible that those who could do this job properly (i.e., citizens of the US, UK, France, Russia or China) should replace ElBaradei and his team.

32 His speech at the Oak Ridge National Laboratory was on 12 July 2004.

33 Hasan Akhtar, "Inquiry Hints at Personal Greed: Action if Scientists Found Culpable: FO," *Dawn*, Islamabad, 23 December 2003.

34 <http:7/news.bbc.co.uk/2/hi/south_asia/5399158.stm>.

35 For more on Musharraf's childhood in Karachi, where he describes himself as a "street-fighter," see Pervez Musharraf, *In the Line of Fire* (Free Press, New York, 2006).

36 This chapter relies on a number of interviews with some of Khan's inner circle, made in Islamabad and Rawalpindi in the winter and spring of 2006.

37 The interview was published in Pakistan's *Daily Times*, 22 December 2003. The minister also talked to Associated Press on the same day.

38 Author interviews with IAEA sources in Vienna and London in 2006 and 2007. Also see board reports from 2005 and 2006, which reflect back on the Iran debriefing. See also *Implementation of the NPT Safeguards Agreement in the Islamic Republic of Iran*, 18 December 2004, or <http://www.iaea.org/Publications/Documents/Board/2004/gov2004-60.pdf> and others from that period.

39 IAEA Report, GOV/2005/67, 2 September 2005, p. 5.

40 Coll.

41 IAEA Report, GOV/2005/67, 2 September 2005.

42 David Kay resigned on 23 January 2004 and appeared before the Senate armed forces committee on 28 January 2004.

43 See *In the Line of Fire*, p. 293.

44 Legal actions for all families of the arrested scientists were combined and referred to in a file handed over to the supreme court of Pakistan, CP No. 726 of 2004, Dr. Mohammed Shafiq ur-Rehman vs Inter Services Intelligence (ISI) and others, 21 January 2004.

45 The round-ups were described to the authors by the KRL Kids, and by others close to their families, in Islamabad and Rawalpindi in 2006.

46 See "Qadeer's Aide Among Three Detained," *Daily Times*, 19 January 2004.

47 Ibid.

48 Report of the Respondent No. 1, Lahore High Court, Rawalpindi Bench, WP No. 185 of 2004. This was issued on 16 February 2004.

49 This section and what occurs below is largely taken from the notes taken by the KRL Kids and their families during this period, copies of which were given to the authors in the spring and winter of 2006.

50 The attorney general, siding with the families, hit back, issuing a counter-order preventing the government from handing any of the detained men over to foreign investigators or allowing them to be removed from the country.

51 These notes gathered by the families were shown to the authors.

52 The official investigation would be completed by Lieutenant General Khalid Kidwai, Musharraf's director of the Strategic Plans Division.

53 The notes written by Khan were seen by the authors in the spring and winter 2006, during interviews with Khan's inner circle in Islamabad and Rawalpindi.

54 For a transcript of this interview, see <www.cnn.com/2004/WORLD/asiapcf/01/23/musharraf.transcript.cnna/index.html>.

55 A version of this interview was later carried by Reuters: "Musharraf Admits Nuclear Leaks," 23 January 2004.

56 Even still, the government appeared unable to speak with one voice, with Sheikh Rashid Ahmed, the information minister, denying on 28 January 2004 that Khan was under any form of detention—the announcement making it official news only percolating out to the local press on 31 January.

57 According to Kidwai's briefing, Khan had told government investigators that his motives had not been financial but a gesture of support to other Muslim countries.

58 According to Musharraf's account, the president told Khan he would look favorably upon a mercy petition if Khan agreed to take full responsibility for his activities. Musharraf, *In the Line of Fire*. But in truth, Musharraf's primary concern was that whatever was said publicly would ensure he and his government were let off the hook. Every stage of the day's choreographed events was relayed back to US intelligence agents in the US embassy compound in Islamabad.

59 For a full version, see the *Guardian* of 5 February 2004, or <http://www.guardian.co.uk/pakistan/Story/0,2763,1141630,00.html>.

60 See M. Ziauddin, "Dr. A. Q. Khan Pardoned. Other Scientists" Fate Hangs in the Balance. Beg, Karamat Cleared: Musharraf," *Dawn*, Karachi, 5 February 2004.

61 *In the Line of Fire*, p. 294.

62 Musharraf, who took over as director general of military operations in 1993, denied allegations that he had been fully aware of the nuclear dimension to Benazir Bhutto's trip to North Korea in December 1993. Musharraf also absolved former army chiefs General Beg and General Jehangir Karamat of any wrongdoing and said: "The National Command Authority was finally established in February 2000 and since then the program has been fully secured."

63 The entire press briefing can be found online at <http://www.state.gov/r/pa/prs/dpb/2004/28983.htm>. It was given by Richard Boucher, the assistant secretary for public affairs at the State Department, on 5 February 2004. Since 2006, Boucher has been assistant secretary of state for South and Central Asian affairs.

64 See Corera, p. 215.

65 Powell said he would be asking Musharraf to ensure "there is a full understanding of what the A. Q. Khan network has done over the years so there are no remnants of it left and there is no possibility of further proliferating activities coming out of that network." He did so in a late-night telephone call to Islamabad two days later.

66 White House press release, "President Announces New Measures to Counter the Threat of WMD," Remarks by the President on Weapons of Mass Destruction Proliferation, Fort Lesley J. McNair—National Defense University, Washington, 11 February 2004.

67 Confirmation of Washington's close role in the Pakistani investigation eventually came with the news on 12 February that CIA director George Tenet had flown into Islamabad for a secret debriefing at Army House. Later it was revealed that a twenty-four-member US delegation led by Tenet had arrived at Chaklala airbase at around

7 p.m. on the Wednesday and left the country on the Thursday afternoon.

68 ElBaradei told reporters that the Khan case "raises more questions than it answers" and that cracking the case of the Pakistani scientist represented only "the tip of an iceberg" in the wider global nuclear black market. "We need to know who supplied what, when, to whom," ElBaradei stressed. "Dr. Khan was not working alone." In an op-ed published in the *New York Times* on 13 February, ElBaradei underlined the need for urgent action to toughen the world's non-proliferation regime in order to stop the spread of nuclear weapons, and called for the strengthening of export controls and the acceleration of movement towards nuclear disarmament.

69 But taking a line similar to the US, Annan chose not to criticize President Musharraf's decision, saying: "Obviously it is a very difficult situation that [Musharraf] has to deal with—he is dealing with a national hero."
See <http://jang.com.pk/thenews/feb2004-daily/07-02-2004/main/main1.htm>.

70 Author interviews with close civilian aides of Musharraf in Islamabad in spring 2006.

71 See Dina's comments in <http://news.bbc.co.uk/2/hi/south_asia/5399158.stm>.

72 Ibid.

19: NEW THINK

1 Author interviews with Dr. Shafiq ur-Rehman, Islamabad, spring 2006.

2 Author interviews with Peter Griffin, France, 2006–7.

3 The clampdown began in 2005, but the situation tightened in 2006 and 2007.

4 Author interview with Sharifuddin Pirzada, Islamabad, spring 2006.

5 Author interview with Humayun Gauhar, Islamabad, spring 2006.

6 Author interviews with Benazir Bhutto, Dubai, 2006.

7 According to papers that Dr. Ahmed filed with the Sindh high court on 10 December 2002, "the armed men accompanying defendant No. 1 and his associates confronted the [hospital] security guards, pushed them aside and adopted positions in a somewhat dramatic battle order. One of the two colonels forcibly herded the entire staff into a room and proclaimed the change of administration." Dr. Ahmed recalled: "When I called Khan for an explanation, he screamed down the phone: 'Jinnah created Pakistan and I saved it.'" In early 2003 Dr. Ahmed won an injunction from the Sindh high court to eject Khan's men from the hospital. A. Q. Khan filed a counter-suit, which began, "The plaintiff is a national hero. He is singularly responsible for facilitating the requisition of nuclear technology for Pakistan, developing the enrichment of uranium plant at Kahuta, and an atomic bomb for the country. He has also been the recipient of many awards, including the national awards of Nishan-i-Imtiaz and Hilal-i-Imtiaz." Dr. Ahmed papers and author interview.

8 Author interview with Haroon Ahmed, Karachi, spring 2006.

9 See the statement from 4 February 2004 given by Khalid Kidwai at the briefing of the Strategic Plans Division in which the two dead Bhutto confidants were named. The names were mentioned again in briefings with the international press on 8 and 9 February 2004, leading to publications like this, by Mubashir Zaidi, <http://www.latimes.com/technology/la- fgkhan10feb10,1,3344559.story?coll=la-headlines-technology>. The same names were reheated and briefed again in 2006.

10 A senior State Department non-proliferation specialist familiar with the Khan Affair described his thoughts on the Armitage trip to Pakistan in October in which the so-

called deal was struck. No one at the State Department was in any doubt that it was a quid pro quo. Author interviews, Washington, 2006.

11 Author interviews with Robert Einhorn, Washington, 2006.

12 The announcement was made on 2 May 2006.

13 The releases happened quietly in the summer of 2006.

14 The announcement was made on 2 May 2006. See also: <http://news.bbc.co.uk/1/hi/world/south_asia/4965566.stm>.

15 Author interviews with Robert Gallucci, Washington, 2006.

16 Author interview with Norm Wulf, Virginia, spring 2006.

17 Rust, who retired in 2005, spoke out in an article for *Arms Control Today*, entitled "Reorganization Run Amok: State Department's WMD Effort Weakened," June 2006.

18 Powell resigned on 15 November 2004 and was replaced by Rice the following day. The IG report that introduced the ISN was signed off in December 2004.

19 The comments were made at the Global Structures Convocation hosted by the World Federalist Association (now Citizens for Global Solutions). See also Roland Watson, "Bush Deploys Hawk as New UN Envoy," *The Times*, 3 August 2005.

20 Appointment confirmed 1 June 2005.

21 National Institute of Public Policy report authored by William Schneider, Jr., January 2001. In addition to Joseph, other contributors to this report included Stephen Hadley, Bush's national security adviser, and Stephen Cambone, under secretary of defense for intelligence.

22 Joseph's role in this inclusion was revealed to Congress by Alan Foley, the CIA's top expert on WMDs.

23 Joseph served there from 1992–2001.

24 The proliferation security initiative involves eleven countries—Australia, France, Germany, Italy, Japan, the Netherlands, Poland, Portugal, Spain, the United Kingdom and the United States. See <http://www.state.gov/r/pa/prs/ps/2003/27365.htm>.

25 State Department Reorganising to Match Today's Priorities, 29 July 2005. See also <http://london.usembassy.gov/forpo769.html>.

26 As defined by the president's national security strategy.

27 The ISN opened for business on 13 September 2005 with no formal management structure and no employees.

28 Fleitz had served in WINPAC, the CIA's Weapons Intelligence Non-Proliferation and Arms Control Center.

29 Frederick H. Fleitz, *Peacekeeping Fiascos of the 1990s: Causes, Solutions, and U.S. Interests* (Praeger, Westport, CT, 2002).

30 These included the principal deputy assistant secretaries of the three bureaus, Frank Record, Andrew Semmel and Christopher Ford, as well as ambassador Jackie Sanders, who resided in Geneva and served as the president's special representative for non-proliferation.

31 The "New Think" vs "Old Think" paradigm is Rust's.

32 See Warren P. Strobel, "State Department Sees Exodus of Weapons Experts," *Philadelphia Inquirer*, 8 February 2006.

33 Ibid.

34 See Glenn Kessler, "Administration Critics Chafe at State Dept. Shuffle; Merger Has Brought Appointees into Conflict with Longtime Workers, Who Say They Are Sidelined," *Washington Post*, 21 February 2006. See also Warren P. Strobel, "Career

Weapons Experts Booted by Bush Team," *Philadelphia Inquirer*, 8 February 2006.

35 Interview with the authors, Washington, spring 2006.
36 Ibid.
37 There were a variety of outlets for Bush allies to make their claims, including Committee on the Present Danger, an advocacy group that includes many neoconservatives and whose aim has been to militate against the danger of Islamic extremism. In 2004 the CPD, and former Reagan speechwriter Mark Palmer, called for regime change in Iran. "They want to free themselves from Khamenei's oppression and they want Iran to join the community of prosperous, peaceful democracies," his report said, advocating a "forceful strategy to engage with the Iranian people to remove the threat and establish the strong relationship which is in both nations' and the region's interests." Palmer also published *Breaking the Real Axis of Evil: How to Oust the World's Last Dictators by 2025* (Rowman & Littlefield Publishers, 2003).
38 See the commendable Vali Nasr, *The Shia Revival* (W. W. Norton & Company, New York, 2006).
39 For a view of Iranian expediency vis-à-vis Afghanistan and the Iran-Contra affair, see George Crile, *Charlie Wilson's War* (Grove Press, New York, 2003), and also Bob Woodward, *Veil: The Secret Wars of the CIA 1981–1987* (Simon & Schuster, London, 1987).
40 Gary Sick, quoted by former CIA agent Ray Close in a letter to the authors, and also by Jonathan Steele, *Guardian*, 2 February 2007.
41 "Iran Secretly Acquiring Super-Strong Steel for Nuclear Bomb—Exile," Iran Focus, 28 July 2005. See also "Iran After Obtaining Maraging Steel to Build Nuclear Bomb Casing," National Council of Resistance of Iran, 28 July 2005.
42 Author interview with Moshe Ya'alon, the former head of the Israel Defense Forces and military intelligence, Washington, spring 2006.
43 Author interviews with Mossad officials, Tel Aviv, Israel, 2006.
44 William J. Broad and David E. Sanger, "Relying on Computer, US Seeks to Prove Iran's Nuclear Aims," *New York Times*, 13 November 2005.
45 He studied and then lectured at the university's Institute of Science and Technology.
46 Zarqawi's group was known in Arabic as Tanzim al-Qaeda wa'l-Jihad fi Balad al-Rafidayn.
47 As Vali Nasr, of the US Naval Postgraduate School, argued: "Those who voted for Ahmadinejad came from humble religious backgrounds. Regardless of what they felt about politics, they were deeply attached to the core values and piety of Shi'ism, which in turn is tightly bound up with the shrine cities of Iraq, and they were offended by the tenor and ferocity of the sectarian violence [there]."
48 Those familiar with Ahmadinejad and his supporters placed his unpleasant but canny rhetoric in the context of a Shia revival. Vali Nasr described the president as attempting to reach out to the Sunnis and Wahhabis with a rhetorical handshake in order that they might notice a little less how, in Iraq and elsewhere, the Shia, repressed for so many decades, were up on their feet and extending their influence.
49 Seymour Hersh, "The Iran Plans," *New Yorker*, 17 April 2006, and online at <http://www.newyorker.com/archive/2006/04/17/060417fa_fact>.
50 Chalabi rose to the office of deputy prime minister until May 2006, when he fell from grace, accused by the US of passing on intelligence to Iran, and criticized

heavily in Washington and Europe for having supplied (via the Iraqi National Congress) much of the misleading intelligence against Saddam Hussein prior to the invasion.

51 See Connie Bruck, "Exiles: How Iran's Expatriates Are Gaming the Nuclear Threat," *New Yorker*, March 2006.

52 Ibid.

53 This conclusion was reached by Christopher de Bellaigue, "Bush, Iran and the Bomb," *New York Review of Books*, 24 February 2005.

54 Laura Rozen, "Just What Is the Bush Administration up to Regarding Iran?" American Prospect, 12 January 2007, online at <http://www.prospect.org/web/page .ww?section=root&name=ViewWeb&articleId=12378>.

55 S. 3870, "A bill to hold the current regime in Iran accountable for its human rights record and to support a transition to democracy in Iran." The bill has been read twice and referred to the committee on foreign relations. It "authorizes the president to provide financial and political assistance to eligible foreign and domestic individuals, organizations, and entities that support human rights and the promotion of democracy in Iran and that are opposed to the non-democratic government of Iran."

56 Hersh, "The Iran Plans."

57 Seymour Hersh quoted: "a government consultant with close ties to the civilian leadership in the Pentagon said that Bush was 'absolutely convinced that Iran is going to get the bomb' if it is not stopped. He said that the president believes that he must do 'what no Democrat or Republican, if elected in the future, would have the courage to do,' and 'that saving Iran is going to be his legacy.' "

58 *Washington Post*, 14 August 2005.

59 Joel Brinkley, "Saudi Minister Warns US," *New York Times*, 23 September 2005.

60 Seymour Hersh wrote about this operation. They were predominantly Kurds, Baluchis and Azeris.

61 Covert actions require a finding or directive from the president, but if this order can be avoided then the operation becomes untraceable and unaccountable.

62 The meetings were said to have taken place in the spring of 2006, according to two senators, one a committee chairman, interviewed by the authors in the summer of 2006. See also Seymour Hersh's piece on Iran (as above).

63 This allegation was made by senior Pentagon officials interviewed by the authors in the winter of 2006, but broken first as a story by Seymour Hersh who included it in his April 2006 *New Yorker* piece. The practice runs were said to have begun in August 2005.

64 Los Alamos Study Group, "B61-11 Concerns and Background," <http://www.brook .edu/FP/PROJECTS/NUCWCOST/lasg.htm#endback17>. For the US anti-Libyan plans for the nuclear bunker-buster, see: Art Pine, "A-Bomb Against Libya Target Suggested," *Los Angeles Times*, 24 April 1996.

65 See Hersh "The Iran Plans."

66 Ibid. The Defense Science Board is chaired by William Schneider, Jr., who also sat on the National Institute of Public Policy panel in 2001 and along with Robert Joseph recommended the use of tactical nuclear weapons as an essential part of the US arsenal.

67 See Transcript of Director General's Remarks at Conclusion of IAEA Board Meeting, 8 March 2006 at <http://www.iaea.org/NewsCenter/Transcripts/2006/

transcr08032006.html>. See also Christopher de Bellaigue, "Iran and the Bomb," *New York Review of Books*, 27 April 2006.

68 Speech given in Cleveland, Ohio, quoted by Seymour Hersh, "The Iran Plans."

69 Failed States Index published by *Foreign Policy Magazine*, Iraq being fourth in autumn 2006. Online it can be seen at: <http://www.foreignpolicy.com/story/cms.php?storyid=3420&page=1>.

70 Iran broke the seals on 4 January 2006 and began injecting on 13 February 2006. When Iran was referred, Ahmadinejad continued to challenge the West, describing his enemies as "idiots," the UN vote as "funny," claiming: "We do not need you at all. Issue as many resolutions as you like and make yourselves happy."

71 Hersh, "The Iran Plans."

72 de Bellaigue, "Iran and the Bomb."

73 Hersh, "The Iran Plans."

74 Iran was reported on 4 February 2006.

75 He was said to have been killed on 15 Januray 2007.

76 David Shelby, "State's Burns Rejects Direct US Iran Talks," US State Department, 16 March 2006.

77 See Jonathan Steele, *Guardian*, comment section, 2 February 2007.

78 The speech was on 11 April 2006. See "Ahmadinejad, Aqazadeh Announce Iranian Success in Uranium Enrichment," Tehran Vision of the Islamic Republic of Iran Network in Persian, 11 April 2006, FBIS document IAP20060411011076. See also Nazila Fathi, David E. Sanger and William J. Broad, "Iran Says It Is Making Nuclear Fuel, Defying UN," *New York Times*, 12 April 2006.

79 "Ahmadinejad Sends Letter to Bush," BBC, 8 May 2006.

80 Iran responded by blocking weapons inspectors from going to Natanz on 21 August 2006.

81 In the autumn of 2006, Bank Saderat, Iran's largest commercial bank, was sanctioned by the US which accused it of directing funds to Hezbollah and other "terrorist organizations." In 2007, the state-controlled Bank Sepah, and its wholly owned British subsidiary, would also be targeted, accused by Washington of being "the financial linchpin of Iran's missile procurement network." The bank was also accused of having links to a North Korean missile technology exporter. Action was taken in January 2007. See Simon Tisdall, *Guardian*, 13 February 2007.

82 The announcement was made by the Central News Agency, Pyongyang, 9 October 2006. For an online account, see <http: //www.pbs.org/newshour/extra/features/july-dec06/northkorea_10-09.html>.

83 The US did its best to undermine its significance, intelligence officials announcing that air samples gathered from the test site pointed to the size of the blast as being less than 1 kiloton, with the bomb itself "undeliverable." Author interviews with Robert Gallucci, Washington, 2006.

84 The Press Complaints Commission (PCC) launched an investigation following the submission of a report alleging a catalogue of inaccurate and misleading stories about Iran run by the *Daily Telegraph* and mostly written by Con Coughlin. The report, put together by Campaign Iran, alleged that Coughlin, who had highlighted the erroneous story about Iraq's forty-five-minute WMD capacity, was behind sixteen other articles containing allegations against Iran published over a twelve-month period, virtually all

of which have been disproven. The PCC was asked to examine whether the stories were in breach of clause 1 of their code of practice, requiring accuracy. Coughlin, the PCC was told, was also the journalist who, in 2003, unearthed "the link" between the 9/11 hijacker Mohammed Atta and Iraq.

85 The memo was written on 25 July 2002. See also David S. Cloud and Mark Mazzetti, "Pre-war Intelligence Unit at Pentagon Is Criticized," *New York Times*, 9 February 2007.

86 Report of an Inquiry into the Alternative Analysis of the Issue of an Iraq–al Qaeda Relationship by Senator Carl Levin (D-MI) Ranking Member, Senate Armed Services Committee, 21 October 2004. Levin reported as much on 21 October 2004.

87 The inspector general's report states that Feith's office "developed, produced, and then disseminated alternative intelligence assessments on the Iraq and al-Qaeda relationship, which included some conclusions that were inconsistent with the consensus of the intelligence community, to senior decision-makers." The report also noted that Feith's briefing to the White House in 2002 "undercuts the intelligence community" and "did draw conclusions that were not fully supported by the available intelligence." See also Walter Pincus and R. Jeffrey Smith, "Official's Key Report on Iraq Is Faulted, 'Dubious' Intelligence Fuelled Push for War," *Washington Post*, 9 February 2007.

88 Levin became chairman of the Senate committee on the armed services when the Democrats took control of the Senate, having served as ranking member on the committee since 1997. Levin previously chaired the committee when the Democrats were the majority party in the Senate, 3–20 January 2001 and 6 June 2001–6 January 2003. See also Cloud and Mazzetti.

89 <http://news.bbc.co.uk/2/hi/americas/6130740.stm>.

90 Con Coughlin, *Daily Telegraph*, 15 November 2006, or <http://www.telegraph .co.uk/news/main.jhtml?xml=/news/2006/11/14/wiran 214.xml>.

91 Muravchik's comments were published in the *Los Angeles Times* on 19 November, headlined "Bomb Iran." For all his writings, see the AEI website <www.aei.org>.

92 The Iranian group was formed in 2002.

93 Also known as the Baker–Hamilton Commission, which reported on 6 December, it was formed in March 2006 as the security situation in Iraq worsened. In reaction, Frank Wolf (Republican, Virginia) proposed finding experts to provide "fresh eyes" to resolve the conflict. A ten-person panel, with five Republicans and five Democrats, was selected, headed by former secretary of state James A. Baker, and former congressman Lee Hamilton (Democrat, Indiana), who also co-chaired the 9/11 Commission. The United States Institute of Peace (USIP), a government-funded think tank, oversaw the research. See also <http://www.cfr.org/publication/12010/>.

94 Michael Abramowitz and Robin Wright, "Bush to Add 21,500 Troops in an Effort to Stabilize Iraq," *Washington Post*, 11 January 2007.

95 Frederick W. Kagan, "Choosing Victory, A Plan for Success in Iraq," AEI Iraq Planning Group.

96 See ABC report online at <http://abcnews.go.com/WNT/IraqCoverage/story?id=2785532>.

97 Iran banned thirty-eight inspectors on 22 January 2007. Sanctions were imposed 23 December 2006.

98 Before the naval build-up, Ahmadinejad was said by officials in Tehran close to the clerics to have been strongly criticized by Iran's supreme leader, Ayatollah Khamenei, and Iran's former president, Rafsanjani. See Robert Tait, "Tehran Power Struggle Intensifies," *Guardian*, 24 January 2007.

99 Ali Ansari, "Only the US Hawks Can Save the Iranian President Now," *Guardian*, comment section, 30 January 2007.

100 Hersh, "The Iran Plans."

101 Author interview with senior State Department analyst who was a specialist in disarmament, Washington, spring 2006.

102 The US policy of "threaten and neglect" towards North Korea was declared an "abject failure" by a roster of luminaries, including Professor Graham Allison, director of Harvard's Belfer Center for Science and International Affairs. See his interview online at <http://www.cfr.org/publication/10933/>.

103 jonathan Watts, "Washington Poised for a Climbdown as North Korea Nuclear Talks Near Deal," *Guardian*, 9 February 2007.

104 Con Coughlin, "North Korea Helping Iran with Nuclear Testing," *Daily Telegraph*, 26 January 2007.

105 Officials briefed journalists in Baghdad using a 200-page classified document that highlighted the use of sophisticated shaped charges capable of penetrating the armor of US tanks. Further evidence came with the seizure by US forces in Iraq of six Iranians, including a member of the al-Quds Brigade, an elite section of the Revolutionary Guard.

106 See Thomas E. Ricks, *Fiasco, The American Military Adventure in Iraq* (Allen Lane, New York, 2006). Ricks gives an interesting account of General Pace's attitude to the war and his briefings on it.

107 See Al Pessin, "Top American General Disputes US Military Claim on Iran," Voice of America, 12 February 2007. Listen to the report online at: <http://voanews.com/english/archive/2007-02/2007-02-12-voa20.cfm?CFID=58067229&CFTOKEN=76504018>.

108 Hillary Clinton made her comments on 14 February 2007. See Seymour Hersh, "The Redirection," *New Yorker*, 5 March 2007.

109 Ewen MacAskill, "Bush Retreats on Claim That Leaders in Tehran Are Arming Insurgents," *Guardian*, 15 February 2007.

110 It is known as the Center for Lessons Learned or CALL. For a good explanation of the process, see Ricks.

111 The treatise's Arabic title is *Da'wat al-Muqawama al-Islamiyya al-'Alamiyya.*

112 Al-Suri had joined the Syrian jihadist movement al-Tali'a al-Muqatila, or "The Fighting Vanguard," and deepened his military expertise at the hands of refugee Syrian military officers in Jordan, and Egyptian and Iraqi instructors in Baghdad and Cairo. Specializing in explosives engineering and urban guerrilla warfare, he had trained recruits in the military camps of the Muslim Brotherhood in Jordan and Baghdad. See also Stephen Ulph's piece, "Setmariam Nasar: Background on al-Qaeda's Arrested Strategist," in the Jamestown Foundation's *Terrorism Focus*, vol. 3, issue 12 (28 March 2006) or online at: <http://www.jamestown.org/terrorism/news/article.php?articleid=2369941>.

113 By "us" he meant those running the camps in Afghanistan, broadly al-Qaeda, and more specifically the jihadi instructors.

114 Al-Masri trained the shoe bomber Richard Reid and Zacarias Moussaoui.

115 This version of al-Suri's life story comes from Fouad Hussein's book, *Al Qaeda—Second Generation*. It was serialized in three parts; see Fu'ad Husayn, "Al-Zarqawi: the Second Generation of Al-Qa'ida," *Al-Quds Al-'Arabi*, London, 8 June 2005.

116 Ibid.

117 See al-Suri's own writings but also Hussein's book, which details letters written by al-Suri from this time and later.

118 Lisa Myers, Jim Popkin and Robert Windrem, "Key al-Qaeda Figure Reportedly Captured," *NBC News*, 3 November 2005.

119 Zarqawi's real name was Ahmad Fadil al-Khalayilah. Fouad Hussein's book would emerge serialized in 2005 by *Al-Quds Al-'Arabi*; see above.

120 Al-Maqdisi's second book, *Al-Kawafir al-Jaliyyah fi Kufr al-Dawlah al-Sa'udiyyah (The Evident Sacrileges of the Saudi State)* excommunicated the Saudi royal family, and those behind the bombings in Al-Khubar and Riyadh in the mid-1990s admitted to having been influenced by it.

121 This was part of a general amnesty issued by King Abdallah II on the occasion of his succession to throne of his father King Husayn.

122 The Northern Alliance was the name used in the West, while in Afghanistan the coalition was known as the United Islamic Front for the Salvation of Afghanistan, formed with US guidance in 1996.

123 Bruce Riedel, Clinton's former National Security Council director for Middle East and Asian issues, talked about bin Laden's goals in Iraq in January 2007, at a lunch co-organized by the Brookings Institution and the Saban Center for Middle East Policy.

124 A flurry of communiqués from al-Qaeda operatives around this time, as well as writings that appeared on bulletin boards sympathetic to al-Qaeda, showed that a debate had been triggered on the bloodbath started by al-Zarqawi. It would lead to a thesis, *The Management of Savagery*, being uploaded on to the Internet in Arabic by Abu Bakr Naji, and translated in 2006 by Will McCants, a fellow at the Combating Terrorism Center at West Point and director of its Salafi Ideology Project, with the support of the John M. Olin Institute for Strategic Studies at Harvard University. Savagery (or Brutality as some translate it) in this case refers to the period after the collapse of the US "empire," a key stage in the al-Qaeda game plan.

125 Amer al-Azizi, an al-Zarqawi ally, remains a suspect in the Madrid bombings. The UK bombings derived strategically from this change of emphasis, carried out by a sleeper cell of unknowns ("clean skins" as they are known), who, having been radicalized, then operated completely at their own pace and with their own resources.

20: AWAKENING

1 See the BBC report on the visit at:
<http://news.bbc.co.uk/2/hi/south_asia/4772134.stm>.

2 Author interview with Karzai's officials before the Bush visit.

3 Christina Lamb, "Airstrike Misses Al-Qaeda Chief, 'Wrong Information' Blamed for Pakistan Deaths," *Sunday Times*, 15 January 2006.

4 On 6 March 2006 Musharraf told ABC that the Karzai list was a "waste of time" and told CNN on the same day: "Two-thirds of it is months old, and it is outdated, and there is nothing. The location that they are talking of Mullah Omar is nonsense. There's nobody there. I am totally disappointed with their intelligence, and I feel there is a very, very deliberate attempt to malign Pakistan by some agents, and President Karzai is totally oblivious of what is happening in his own country." See <http://www.cnn.com/2006/WORLD/asiapcf/03/05/musharraf/index.html>.

5 "Pakistan Reports Killing 25 Foreign Militants near Afghan Border," *New York Times*, 2 March 2006.

6 See the BBC account of her speech at <http://news.bbc.co.uk/2/hi/uk_news/6134516 .stm>.

7 Bruce Riedel was President Clinton's National Security Council senior director for Near East and South Asian affairs (1997–2001) and served as President Bush's National Security Council senior director for Near East and North African affairs (2001–2). He then became an adviser to the UN secretary general, Kofi Annan. Riedel's quotes are from January 2007 and come from an event sponsored by the Brookings Institution and the Saban Center for Middle East Policy.

8 See the BBC report about the Geo TV interview with Hekmatyar: <http://news.bbc.co .uk/2/hi/south_asia/6252975.stm>.

9 Zahid Hussain, "Terror in Miramshah," *Newsline*, April 2006, online at <http://www.newsline.com.pk/NewsApr2006/cover1apr2006.htm>.

10 International Crisis Group (ICG), "Pakistan's Tribal Areas, Appeasing the Militants," Asia Report No. 125, 11 December 2006, online at <http://www.crisisgroup.org/ home/index.cfm?id=4568&1=1>.

11 Author interviews with army leaders and politicians in Islamabad, Peshawar and Quetta, spring and summer of 2006.

12 Amir Mir, "War and Peace in Waziristan," *Asia Times*, 4 March 2005. Online at <http://www.atimes.com/atimes/South_Asia/GEO4DfO3.html>.

13 Author interviews with senior army officers and civil servants in Quetta and Peshawar, spring and summer 2006.

14 The figures were revealed by Bruce Riedel in January 2007.

15 What purported to be extracts were published in *Dawn* newspaper, Karachi, 29 March 2007.

16 Ismail Khan writing in *Dawn*, 6 September 2006.

17 "Pakistan's Tribal Areas, Appeasing the Militants," ICG Asia Report No. 125, 11 December 2006.

18 See the BBC story online at <http://news.bbc.co.uk/2/hi/south_asia/6532825.stm>.

19 Figures from the Madrasah Union, 2005, and also quoted in "Pakistan: Madrasas, Extremism and the Military," ICG Asia Report No. 36, 29 July 2002. See also "Pakistan: The Mullahs and the Military," ICG Asia Report No. 49, 20 March 2003. See also, "Unfulfilled Promises: Pakistan's Failure to Tackle Extremism," ICG Asia Report No. 73, 16 January 2004.

20 See "Pakistan: Karachi's Madrasas and Violent Extremism," Asia Report No. 130, 29 March 2007. See online at <http://www. crisisgroup.org/home/index.cfm?id=4742&1 =1>.

21 For details of charges made against the LeT, see <http://www.satp.org/satporgtp/ countries/india/states/jandk/terrorist_ outfits/lashkar_e_toiba_1t.htm>.

22 "Pakistan: Political Impact of the Earthquake," ICG Asia Briefing No. 46, 15 March 2006.

23 "Three More Prosecution Witnesses Examined: U.S. Diplomat Killing Case," *Dawn*, 14 December 2006, and also "Two Witnesses Examined in Diplomat Case," *Dawn*, 27 January 2007. Both stories also quoted in the excellent "Pakistan: Karachi's Madrasas and Violent Extremism."

24 "Allama Turabi Escapes Unhurt in Bomb Blast," *The News*, 7 April 2006. See also "Police Arrest 3 in Turabi Case," *The News*, 26 July 2006, and Behroz Khan and Munawar Afridi, "Turabi's Alleged Killer Dies in a Mysterious Blast," *The News*, 10 September 2006. See also <http://www.crisisgroup.org/home/index.cfm?id=4742&1=1>.

25 Carlotta Gall, "Pakistan Link Seen in Rise in Afghan Suicide Attacks," *New York Times*, 14 November 2006. See also <http://www.crisisgroup.org/home/index.cfm?id=4742&1=1>.

26 The earthquake occurred on 8 October 2005.

27 "Pakistan: Political Impact of the Earthquake," ICG Asia Briefing No. 46, 15 March 2006.

28 Ibid.

29 It was the first group to reach Balakot, the worst-hit area.

30 Interview with Musharraf in the *Financial Times*, 26 October 2005.

31 Interview conducted by the ICG, Islamabad, December 2005.

32 Ibid.

33 Chaudhary Shujaat Hussain and Mohammad Ali Durrani paid the call on A. Q. Khan.

34 Author interviews with some of those in Khan's inner circle, Islamabad and Rawalpindi, spring 2006.

35 Author interviews with two senior KRL officials who were still employed at the plant at the time of the earthquake. The story was also confirmed by Dr. Shafiq ur-Rehman, interviewed in Islamabad in the spring of 2006.

36 The nuclear pact had tentatively been agreed upon in July 2005, when Manmohan Singh, the Indian prime minister, visited Washington and signed a nuclear accord.

37 Ian Traynor and Ian Cobain, "Intelligence Report Claims Nuclear Market Thriving," *Guardian*, 4 January 2006.

38 Author interview with BND official, Berlin, autumn 2006.

39 Douglas Frantz, "Vital Nuclear Parts Missing," *Los Angeles Times*, 25 April 2005.

40 Ibid.

41 Ibid.

42 A good investigation into the case, called "The Guru," was researched by FRONTLINE/World and the Center for Investigative Reporting in association with *Mother Jones* magazine. See <http://www.pbs.org/frontlineworld/stories/nuclear/>.

43 Ibid. and also *US vs Humayun Khan*, US District Court for the District of Columbia, Grand Jury Indictment, 31 October 2003.

44 *US vs Humayun Khan*.

45 Ibid.

46 At the time of writing the trial was still pending.

47 All these quotes come from "The Guru."

48 Author interview, K. M. Arif, Rawalpindi, spring 2006.

49 India, of course, although formerly known as Hindustan, is one of the most populous Muslim communities in the world, and the nuclear deal with New Delhi might, in part, be an attempt by Washington to win closer ties with such a strong Islamic constituency, a move to overcome the historic skepticism that India has felt towards the US.

50 Brzezinski was interviewed on *The Daily Show* by Jon Stewart on 15 March 2007. For the full interview, see <http://www.crooksandliars.com/2007/03/15/zbigniew-brzezinski-on-the-daily-show/>.

51 Author interviews Robert Gallucci, Washington, 2006.

BIBLIOGRAPHY

Abbas, Hassan, *Pakistan's Drift into Extremism*, M. E. Sharpe, New York, 2004.

Akhund, Iqbal, *Trial and Error*, OUP, Karachi, 2000.

Akhund, Iqbal, *Memoirs of a Bystander: A Life in Diplomacy*, OUP, Karachi, 1997.

Al-Zawahiri, Ayman, *Knights Under the Prophet's Banner*, as reproduced by Asharq al-Awsat, Riyadh, 2 December 2001.

Allison, Graham, *Nuclear Terrorism*, Owl Books, Henry Holt Company, New York, 2004.

Anderson, John Lee, *The Lion's Grave: Dispatches from Afghanistan*, Grove Press, New York, 2002.

Andrew, Christopher, and Mitrokhin, Vasili, *The Mitrokhin Archive II: The KGB and the World*, Allen Lane, London, 2005.

Arif, K. M., *Khaki Shadows, 1947–1997*, Oxford University Press, Oxford, 2004.

Arif, K. M., *Working with Zia*, Oxford University Press, Karachi, 1995.

Baer, Robert, *See No Evil: The True Story of a Ground Soldier in the CIA's War on Terrorism*, Crown, New York, 2002.

Barnaby, Frank, *How to Build a Nuclear Bomb*, Granta Books, London, 2003.

Bearden, Milt, and Risen, James, *The Main Enemy: The Inside Story of the CIA's Final Showdown with the KGB*, Random House, New York, 2003.

Bergen, Peter, *Holy War, Inc: Inside the Secret World of Osama bin Laden*, Free Press, New York, 2001.

Bergen, Peter L., *The Osama bin Laden I Know*, Free Press, New York, 2006.

Bhaskar, Commodore Uday, *The May 1990 Nuclear "Crisis:" An Indian Perspective*, IDSA, Studies in Conflict and Terrorism, New Delhi, 1997.

Bhutto, Benazir, *Daughter of the East*, Hamish Hamilton, London, 1989.

Bhutto, Zulfikar Ali, *If I Am Assassinated*, Classic Books, Lahore, 1994.

Bhutto, Zulfikar Ali, *The Myth of Independence*, Oxford University Press, Karachi, 1969.

Bodansky, Yossef, *Pakistan's Nuclear Brinkmanship*, Freeman Center for Strategic Studies, Houston, Texas, 1996.

Bowden, Mark, *Guests of the Ayatollah*, Grove/Atlantic, New York, 2006.

Brzezinski, Zbigniew, *Power and Principle: Memoirs of the National Security Advisor, 1977–1981*, Farrar, Straus, Giroux, New York, 1983.

Brzezinski, Zbigniew, *Second Chance*, Basic Books, New York, 2007.

Burke, Jason, *Al-Qaeda: Casting a Shadow of Terror*, IB Taurus, London, 2003.

Burrows, William E., and Windrem, Robert, *Critical Mass: The Dangerous Race for Superweapons in a Fragmenting World*, Simon & Schuster, New York, 1994.

Butler of Brockwell, Rt Hon. Lord, *Review of Intelligence on Weapons of Mass Destruction*, Report of a Committee of Privy Counsellors, Stationery Office, London, 14 July 2004.

Cheema, Parvaiz, *Pakistan's Quest for Nuclear Technology*, Australia National University, Canberra, 1980.

Choudhury, Golam, *Pakistan, Transition from Military to Civilian Rule*, Scorpion, Essex, 1988.

Clarke, Richard A., *Against All Enemies*, Free Press, London, 2004.

Cohen, Stephen P., Chari, P. R., and Cheema, Pervaiz Iqbal, *Perception, Politics and Security in South Asia: The Compound Crisis of 1990*, Routledge, London, 2003.

Cohen, Stephen P., *The Pakistan Army*, University of California Press, Berkeley, 1984.

Coll, Steve, *Ghost Wars: The Secret History of the CIA, Afghanistan, and Bin Laden, from the Soviet Invasion to September 10, 2001*, Penguin Press, New York, 2004.

Cordovez, Diego, and Harrison, Selig, *Out of Afghanistan*, Oxford University Press, New York, 1995.

Corera, Gordon, *Shopping for Bombs*, Hurst & Company, London, 2006.

Crile, George, *Charlie Wilson's War*, Grove Press, New York, 2003.

Crile, George, *My Enemy's Enemy*, Atlantic Books, London, 2003.

Crossette, Barbara, "Who Killed Zia?," *World Policy Journal*, Fall 2005.

DeYoung, Karen, *Soldier: The Life of Colin Powell*, Knopf, New York, October 2006.

Downing, General Wayne A., and Meese, Colonel Michael J., *Harmony and Disharmony, Exploiting al-Qa'ida's Organizational Vulnerabilities*, Combating Terrorism Center, Department of Social Sciences, United States Military Academy, West Point, 14 February 2006.

Durrani, Asad, *An Un-historic Verdict*, Mir Shakeel-ur-Rehman, Lahore, 2001

Durrani, Mahmud Ali, *India and Pakistan: The Cost of Conflict, the Benefits of Peace*, John Hopkins University Foreign Policy Institute, Baltimore, 2000.

Dr. A. Q. Khan Research Laboratories 1976–2001, 25 Years of Excellence and National Service, Islamabad, 31 July 2001. Author archive.

Ferguson, Charles D., Potter, William, Sands, Amy, and Spector, Leonard S., *The Four Faces of Nuclear Terrorism*, Routledge, New York, 2005.

Fleitz, Frederick H., *Peacekeeping Fiascos of the 1990s: Causes, Solutions, and U.S. Interests*, Praeger, Westport, Connecticut, 2002.

Gates, Robert, *From the Shadows: The Ultimate Insider's Story of Five Presidents and How They Won the Cold War*, Simon & Schuster, New York, 1996.

Gheissari, Ali, and Nasr, Vali, *Democracy in Iran, History and the Quest for Liberty*, OUP, Oxford 2006.

Gordon, Michael R., and Trainor, Bernard E., *Cobra II*, Knopf, New York, 2006.

Grau, Lester W., and Gress, Michael, *The Soviet Afghan War: How a Superpower Fought and Lost*, University Press of Kansas, 2002.

Griffin, Michael, *Reaping the Whirlwind: The Taliban Movement in Afghanistan*, Pluto, London, 2001.

Haqqani, Husain, *Pakistan: From Mosque to Military*, Carnegie Endowment for International Peace, Washington, DC, 2005.

Hersh, Seymour, *Chain of Command*, HarperCollins, New York, 2004.

Hiro, Dilip, *The Longest War: The Iran–Iraq Military Conflict*, Grafton, London, 1990.

Hussein, Fouad, "Al-Zarqawi: The Second Generation of al-Qaeda," *Al-Quds Al-'Arabi*, 8 June 2005.

Hussain, S. Shabbir, and Kamran, Mujahid, *Dr. A. Q. Khan on Education and Science*, Sang-e-Meel, Lahore, 1997.

Inderfurth, Karl F., and Johnson, Loch K., *Fateful Decisions: Inside the National Security Council*, OUP, 2004.

Jain, Rashmi, *The United States and Pakistan, 1947–2006*, Radiant, New Delhi, 2007.

Jan, Tarik, *Pakistan's Security and the Nuclear Option*, Institute of Policy Studies, Islamabad, 1995.

Kahana, Ephraim, *Historical Dictionary of Israeli Intelligence*, Historical Dictionaries of Intelligence and Counterintelligence, No. 3, Scarecrow Press, Lanham, Maryland, 2006.

Kargil Review Committee Report, *From Surprise to Reckoning*, Sage Publications, New Delhi, 1999.

Karnad, Bharat, *Nuclear Weapons and Indian Security: The Realist Foundations of Strategy*, Macmillan, New Delhi, 2002.

Khan, Mohammad Ayub, *Friends Not Masters*, OUP, London, 1967.

Kurian, G. T., *The New Book of World Rankings*, New York, 1991.

Kux, Dennis, *The United States and Pakistan 1947–2000*, Woodrow Wilson Center Press, Washington, 2001.

Lamb, Christina, *Waiting for Allah: Pakistan's Struggle for Democracy*, Penguin, London, 1992.

Litwak, Robert S., *Rogue States and U.S. Foreign Policy: Containment after the Cold War*, Woodrow Wilson Center Press, 2000.

Malik, Zahid, *Dr. A. Q. Khan and the Islamic Bomb*, Hurmat Publications, Islamabad, 1992.

Mann, Jim, *Rise of the Vulcans*, Penguin Books, New York, 2004.

Martin, Bradley K., *Under the Loving Care of the Fatherly Leader*, Thomas Dunne Books, New York, 2004.

McCants, William, Brachman, Jarret, and Felter, Joseph, *Militant Ideology Atlas Research Compendium*, Combating Terrorism Center, West Point, New York, 2006.

Menon, Raja, *A Nuclear Strategy for India*, Sage, New Delhi, 2000.

Mishra, Pankaj, *Temptations of the West: How to Be Modern in India, Pakistan and Beyond*, Picador, London, 2006.

Mubarakmand, Dr. Samar, *A Science Odyssey*, Khwarzimic Science Society, Islamabad, November 1998. Author archive.

Musharraf, Pervez, *In the Line of Fire*, Free Press, New York, 2006.

Naji, Abu Bakr, *The Management of Savagery: The Most Critical Stage through which the Umma Will Pass*, translated by William McCants, funded by the John M. Olin Institute for Strategic Studies at Harvard University, 23 May 2006.

Nasr, Vali, *The Shia Revival*, W. W. Norton & Company, New York, 2006.

Niazi, Maulana Kauser, *Aur Line Kat Gayee*, Lahore, 1987.

Palit, D. K., and Namboodiri, P. K. S., *Pakistan's Islamic Bomb*, Vikas Publishing, New Delhi, 1979.

Palmer, Mark, *Breaking the Real Axis of Evil: How to Oust the World's Last Dictators by 2025*, Rowman & Littlefield Publishers, Lanham, Maryland, 2003.

Perkovich, George, *India's Nuclear Bomb: The Impact on Global Proliferation*, University of California Press, Berkeley, 1999.

Rai Muhammad Saleh Azam, *When Mountains Move: The Story of Chagai*, Islamabad, 1998.

Raman, B., *Intelligence, Past, Present and Future*, Lancer, New Delhi, 2002.

Rashid, Ahmed, *Taliban*, Yale University Press, New Haven, 2000.

Reeve, Simon, *The New Jackals, Ramzi Yousef, Osama bin Laden and the Future of Terrorism*, André Deutsch, London, 1999.

Ressa, Maria, *Seeds of Terror*, Free Press, New York, 2003.

Ricks, Thomas E., *Fiasco, The American Military Adventure in Iraq*, Penguin Group (USA), New York, 2006.

Risen, James, *State of War*, Free Press, New York, 2006.

Rizvi, Hasan-Askarj, *The Military and Politics in Pakistan, 1947–86*, Lahore Progressive Publishers, 1986.

Scheuer, Michael, *Imperial Hubris*, Potomac, Virginia, 2004.

Scheuer, Michael, *Through Our Enemy's Eyes*, Potomac, Virginia, 2003.

Schroen, Gary C., *First In: An Insider's Account of How the CIA Spearheaded the War on Terror in Afghanistan*, Ballantine Books, New York, 2005.

Shahi, Agha, *Pakistan's Security and Foreign Policy*, Progressive Printers, Lahore, 1988.

Shultz, George, *Turmoil and Triumph: My Years as Secretary of State*, Charles Scribner & Sons, New York, 1993.

Singh, Jasjit, *Nuclear India*, Knowledge World, New Delhi, 1998.

Spector, Leonard S., *The Undeclared Bomb*, Ballinger, 1988.

Sreedhar, *Pakistan's Bomb, a Documentary Study*, ABC Books, New Delhi, 1986.

Subrahmanyam, K., and Sinha, P. B., *Nuclear Pakistan: An Atomic Threat to South Asia*, Vision Books, New Delhi, 1980.

Subrahmanyam, K., *Nuclear Myths and Realities*, ABC, New Delhi, 1981.

Talbott, Strobe, *Engaging India*, Brookings Institution Press, Washington, 2004.

Tellis, Ashley J., *India's Emerging Nuclear Posture*, OUP, New Delhi, 2001.

Weissman, Steve, and Krosney, Herbert, *The Islamic Bomb*, Times Books, New York, 1981.

Wolpert, Stanley, *Zulfikar Ali Bhutto of Pakistan*, Oxford University Press, New York, 1993.

Woodward, Bob, *Bush at War*, Simon & Schuster, New York, 2003.

Woodward, Bob, *Plan of Attack*, Simon & Schuster, New York, 2004.

Woodward, Bob, *State of Denial*, Simon & Schuster, New York, 2006.

Woodward, Bob, *Veil: The Secret Wars of the CIA 1981–1987*, Simon & Schuster, London, 1987.

Wright, Lawrence, *The Looming Tower*, Allen Lane, London, 2006.

Youssaf, Mohammed, and Adkin, Mark, *The Bear Trap*, Jang Publishers, Lahore, 1992.

INDEX